D0615326

Managing Currency Crises in Emerging Markets

**A National Bureau
of Economic Research
Conference Report**

mgen
mr914

Managing Currency Crises in Emerging Markets

Edited by **Michael P. Dooley and Jeffrey A. Frankel**

Université d'Ottawa
BIBLIOTHEQUES
Université d'Ottawa
University of Ottawa
LIBRARIES
University of Ottawa

The University of Chicago Press

Chicago and London

b 29325626

MICHAEL P. DOOLEY is a research associate of the National Bureau of Economic Research and a managing editor of the *International Journal of Finance and Economics.* Professor Dooley joined the faculty at the University of California, Santa Cruz, in 1992 following more than twenty years' service at the Board of Governors of the Federal Reserve System and the International Monetary Fund. JEFFREY A. FRANKEL is the James W. Harpel Professor of Capital Formation and Growth at the Kennedy School of Government and director of the International Finance and Macroeconomics program at the National Bureau of Economic Research.

To Rudiger Dornbusch, from whom we have learned so much.

The University of Chicago Press, Chicago 60637
The University of Chicago Press, Ltd., London
© 2003 by the National Bureau of Economic Research
All rights reserved. Published 2003
Printed in the United States of America
11 10 09 08 07 06 05 04 03   1 2 3 4 5
ISBN: 0-226-15540-4 (cloth)

Chapter 8, "An Evaluation of Proposals to Reform the International Financial Architecture" by Morris Goldstein © 2001, Institute for International Economics.
Comment by Edwin M. Truman on chapter 11, "IMF and World Bank Structural Adjustment Programs and Poverty" by William Easterly © 2001, Institute for International Economics.

Library of Congress Cataloging-in-Publication Data

Managing currency crises in emerging markets / edited by Michael P. Dooley and Jeffrey A. Frankel
     p.   cm. — (A National Bureau of Economic Research conference report)
     Proceedings of a conference held in Monterey, Calif., in March 2001.
     Includes bibliographical references and index.
     ISBN 0-226-15540-4 (cloth : alk. paper)
     1. Currency question—Developing countries—Congresses.
     2. Foreign exchange rates—Developing countries—Congresses.
     3. Financial crises—Developing countries—Congresses.   I. Dooley, Michael P.   II. Frankel, Jeffrey A.   III. Series.
     HG1496 .M36 2003
     332.4'91724—dc21

2002018126

HG
1496
M36
2003

⊗ The paper used in this publication meets the minimum requirements of the American National Standard for Information Sciences—Permanence of Paper for Printed Library Materials, ANSI Z39.48-1992.

National Bureau of Economic Research

Officers

Carl F. Christ, *chairman*
Michael H. Moskow, *vice-chairman*
Martin Feldstein, *president and chief executive officer*
Susan Colligan, *vice president for administration and budget and corporate secretary*

Robert Mednick, *treasurer*
Kelly Horak, *controller and assistant corporate secretary*
Gerardine Johnson, *assistant corporate secretary*

Directors at Large

Peter C. Aldrich
Elizabeth E. Bailey
John H. Biggs
Andrew Brimmer
Carl F. Christ
John S. Clarkeson
Don R. Conlan
George C. Eads

Martin Feldstein
Stephen Friedman
Judith M. Gueron
George Hatsopoulos
Karen N. Horn
Judy C. Lewent
John Lipsky
Michael H. Moskow

Alicia H. Munnell
Rudolph A. Oswald
Robert T. Parry
Peter G. Peterson
Richard N. Rosett
Kathleen P. Utgoff
Marina v. N. Whitman
Martin B. Zimmerman

Directors by University Appointment

George Akerlof, *California, Berkeley*
Jagdish Bhagwati, *Columbia*
William C. Brainard, *Yale*
Glen G. Cain, *Wisconsin*
Franklin Fisher, *Massachusetts Institute of Technology*
Saul H. Hymans, *Michigan*
Marjorie B. McElroy, *Duke*

Joel Mokyr, *Northwestern*
Michael J. Brennan, *California, Los Angeles*
Andrew Postlewaite, *Pennsylvania*
Nathan Rosenberg, *Stanford*
Michael Rothschild, *Princeton*
Craig Swan, *Minnesota*
David B. Yoffie, *Harvard*
Arnold Zellner, *Chicago*

Directors by Appointment of Other Organizations

Mark Drabenstott, *American Agricultural Economics Association*
Gail D. Fosler, *The Conference Board*
A. Ronald Gallant, *American Statistical Association*
Robert S. Hamada, *American Finance Association*
Robert Mednick, *American Institute of Certified Public Accountants*
Angelo Melino, *Canadian Economics Association*

Richard D. Rippe, *National Association for Business Economics*
John J. Siegfried, *American Economic Association*
David A. Smith, *American Federation of Labor and Congress of Industrial Organizations*
Josh S. Weston, *Committee for Economic Development*
Gavin Wright, *Economic History Association*

Directors Emeriti

Thomas D. Flynn
Lawrence R. Klein

Franklin A. Lindsay
Paul W. McCracken

Bert Seidman
Eli Shapiro

Since this volume is a record of conference proceedings, it has been exempted from the rules governing critical review of manuscripts by the Board of Directors of the National Bureau (resolution adopted 8 June 1948, as revised 21 November 1949 and 20 April 1968).

Contents

Acknowledgments

This volume consists of papers that were presented at a National Bureau of Economic Research Conference, held in Monterey, California, in March 2001, together with comments and discussion. A preconference held in Cambridge in July 2000 kept everyone on track. The main purpose of the conference was to bring together a group of academics, officials in the multilateral organizations, and public- and private-sector economists to discuss issues related to the management of financial crises in the emerging-market countries.

A companion conference was held two months earlier to discuss what can be done to avoid or minimize crises in emerging-market countries in the first place. The corresponding volume is *Preventing Currency Crises in Emerging Markets*, edited by Sebastian Edwards and Jeffrey A. Frankel. These two conferences were part of a larger NBER project on exchange rate crises in emerging markets, directed by Frankel together with Martin Feldstein. The editors would like to thank the Ford Foundation for support and Feldstein for originating the entire project.

Michael P. Dooley is a research associate of the National Bureau of Economic Research and a managing editor of *International Journal of Finance and Economics*. Professor Dooley joined the faculty at the University of California, Santa Cruz in 1992 following more than twenty years' service at the Board of Governors of the Federal Reserve System and the International Monetary Fund. Jeffrey A. Frankel is the James W. Harpel Professor of Capital Formation and Growth at the Kennedy School of Government and director of the International Finance and Macroeconomics program of the National Bureau of Economic Research.

Introduction

Michael P. Dooley and Jeffrey A. Frankel

The management of financial crises in emerging markets is a high-stakes and contentious problem for public policy. Policy interventions must be implemented quickly and under the worst possible economic circumstances. After the dust settles it is difficult to construct a convincing counterfactual in order to evaluate alternative policies.

An example, addressed directly by the first two chapters in this volume, is the debate over the proper use of interest rates to limit exchange rate depreciation in the midst of a crisis. Senior officials of the International Monetary Fund (IMF) and the World Bank have taken different sides in this debate, even though these institutions have not been well known for allowing internal debate to spill into the public press in the past. This public controversy underscores the importance of the issues involved and the depth of the uncertainty within the economics profession concerning the nature of good policy in this area. These problems are not solving themselves. As the papers in this volume were being written, further crises were brewing in Turkey, Argentina, and perhaps elsewhere, and the hot debate about the role of the official sector has intensified.

The papers collected in this volume were presented at a conference in March 2001. The main purpose was to bring together a group of academics, officials in the multilateral organizations, and public- and private-sector

Michael P. Dooley is a research associate of the National Bureau of Economic Research and a managing editor of *International Journal of Finance and Economics.* Professor Dooley joined the faculty at the University of California, Santa Cruz in 1992 following more than twenty years' service at the Board of Governors of the Federal Reserve System and the International Monetary Fund. Jeffrey A. Frankel is the James W. Harpel Professor of Capital Formation and Growth at the Kennedy School of Government and director of the International Finance and Macroeconomics program of the National Bureau of Economic Research.

economists to discuss issues related to the management of financial crisis in the emerging market countries. (A companion conference produced the volume *Preventing Currency Crises in Emerging Markets,* edited by Sebastian Edwards and Jeffrey Frankel.) In commissioning a series of original papers, the editors and Martin Feldstein, the originator of the National Bureau of Economic Research's project on Exchange Rate Crises in Emerging Markets, called on economists who have contributed to the academic literature and, in many cases, have participated in the policy process.

The volume is divided into three parts, which can be viewed almost chronologically, as three phases counting forward from the moment that a country is hit by a crisis: first, the initial attempt to defend the currency; second, the IMF rescue program; and, third, the impact of the crisis and rescue program on the real economy. The first three chapters focus on the immediate defense of the regime under attack. The important issue here is whether unnecessary damage to economies can be avoided by the right response in the first few hours and days of a financial crisis. The next five chapters examine the adjustment programs that follow crises. It is now clear that crises have long-lasting negative effects on economic growth. Adjustment programs supported by financial assistance are designed to shorten the recovery phase and minimize the probability of further difficulties. Finally, the third group of four papers provides empirical evaluation of adjustment programs. Do they accomplish what they are designed to accomplish? Do they impose disproportionate costs on the poorest members of society?

It would be nice to believe that these difficult questions are resolved in the pages that follow. That goal is surely unrealistic. However, we hope that scholars and policy makers will find the work presented useful in thinking about how to reduce the frequency and costs of financial crises in the years to come.

The Defense

In "Interest Rates and Exchange Rates in the Korean, Philippine, and Thai Exchange Rate Crises," Dongchul Cho and Kenneth D. West consider the relationship between exchange rates and interest rates immediately after the onset of a crisis. They propose a two-equation model for exchange rates and interest rates: a monetary policy reaction function, with the interest rate as the instrument, and an interest parity equation. The important identifying assumption is that the currency risk premium depends on the level of interest rates. The effects of interest rates on exchange rates are ambiguous because increases in interest rates can increase a risk premium. Cho and West estimate a special case of the model using weekly data from 1997 and 1998 for Korea, the Philippines, and Thailand. Their results suggest that increases in interest rates following crises led to exchange rate appreciation in Korea and the Philippines but to depreciation in Thailand. Confidence intervals around point estimates are very large, however, and they cannot rule out the possibility that the sign of the actual effect is the opposite of the one estimated.

Alan Drazen's chapter, "Interest Rate Defense Against Speculative Attack as a Signal: A Primer," also deals with an interest rate defense against a speculative attack. He argues that high interest rates per se are unlikely to deter speculators when a discreet devaluation is likely. However, an interest rate defense might nevertheless succeed if high interest rates are a signal of the government's willingness or ability to defend the exchange rate. Drazen explores a class of models in which an interest rate defense alters the speculators' views of the type of government they face. In other words, this model allows for building credibility. The interest rate increase allows the government to distinguish itself from other governments that would not defend. This model presumes that the only available strategy for supporting a peg is an interest rate defense; if, instead, central banks can also run down or borrow reserves, the high interest rate defense may signal low reserves and hence encourage speculation. Drazen argues that empirical work supports both possibilities.

In "Does It Pay to Defend Against a Speculative Attack?" Barry Eichengreen and Andrew K. Rose compare the behavior of failed and successful defenses of currency pegs. They show that the costs of unsuccessfully defending against an attack are large. They are equivalent to approximately one year of economic growth: 3 percentage points of GNP in the year immediately following a crisis and roughly half that amount in the succeeding year. These losses are only evident for short periods. This finding helps to account for a number of observations about the behavior of open economies and their policy makers. Authorities have good reasons for defending currency pegs. International organizations tend to provide generous financial assistance to countries seeking to defend their currencies against attack. Finally, it appears that the V-shaped pattern of recovery from the Asian crisis is quite general—it is the prototypical response of output to a successful attack. These results are robust to the following sensitivity checks: (a) how tranquil versus crisis periods are defined; (b) inclusion of capital control variables; (c) addition of financial variables, or external sustainability variables (like foreign exchange reserves to debt, etc.); (d) exclusion of high inflation countries; and (e) exclusion of OECD countries.

The Program

In "The International Lender of Last Resort: How Large is Large Enough?" Olivier Jeanne and Charles Wyplosz explore the idea that an international lender of last resort would be a useful addition to the international financial architecture. Could an international lender of last resort

(ILOLR) function effectively as a fund with limited and predetermined resources? If so, how much resources would it need? Using a model of an emerging economy that is vulnerable to international liquidity crises, the authors find that the required size of the ILOLR depends on how its resources are used by the domestic authorities. If the ILOLR resources are used to finance foreign exchange intervention by the domestic central bank, the bad equilibrium is not removed, even by an arbitrarily large LOLR. If, in contrast, the LOLR backs a guarantee of the foreign currency liabilities of domestic banks, its resources do not need to be larger than the liquidity gap in the domestic banking sector.

In "Rescue Packages and Output Losses Following Crises," Michael P. Dooley and Sujata Verma take on several issues. The first is analyzing the role of the IMF in a game theoretic context. The key assumption is that creditors cannot distinguish between nonpayment for liquidity reasons (liquidity defaults) and strategic defaults. In this environment, it may be optimal for creditors to precommit to imposing losses on the debtors by deliberately making the contracts difficult to renegotiate (this entails "excess sanctions" from a first best perspective). In this framework the IMF can have a role by facilitating negotiations so that the proceeds from the assets can still be shared following default. The IMF can also serve a welfare-improving role if it possesses more information than the creditor does about the state of nature facing the debtor.

A second major issue that is explored is why there are large output losses postcrisis. Most first-generation models of currency crises do not predict output losses. Second-generation (multiple-equilibrium) models might predict large output losses; and, in most such models, adding liquidity (increasing the size of the rescue packages) will reduce the output losses associated with crises. The explanation forwarded is an extension of Dooley's "insurance model." Capital inflows are "insured" by governments. The extent of the inflow is a function of the amount of insurance available—reserves, liquid assets of the government, credit lines from other governments and international institutions. Hence, in this framework, a crisis is the exchange of assets between the government and private investors. It is differentiated from a default by the fact that, in an uncertain world, guesses about the extent of insurance may be too high. In this case the country must default, and real resources will have to be transferred. A corollary of this is that the default durations will be linked to the size of the rescue packages. The authors provide some empirical evidence suggesting that output losses (a proxy for default durations) are indeed correlated with ex post rescue packages.

In "Financial Restructuring in Banking and Corporate-Sector Crises: What Policies to Pursue?" Stijn Claessens, Daniela Klingebiel, and Luc Laeven examine a micro dataset for 700 companies in nine crisis countries with the objective of identifying what policies are important in minimizing the costs of the crises. They find that liquidity support early in the crisis and the use of a government-run asset management corporation (AMC) can mitigate the severity of a financial crisis. On the other hand, government guarantees of the banking system's financial liabilities do not appear to be helpful. Finally, the extent and quality of the legal framework are critical factors in determining whether the financial system's recovery from a financial shock is sustained and durable.

In "On the Fiscal Implications of Twin Crises," A. Craig Burnside, Martin Eichenbaum, and Sergio Rebelo explore the implications of different strategies for financing the fiscal costs of twin crises for rates of inflation and currency depreciation. They use a first-generation-type model of speculative attacks that has four key features: (a) the crisis is triggered by prospective deficits; (b) there exists outstanding nonindexed government debt issued prior to the crises; (c) a portion of the government's liabilities is not indexed to inflation; and (d) there are nontradable goods and costs of distributing tradable goods, so that purchasing power parity does not hold. The model can account for the high rates of devaluation and moderate rates of inflation often observed in the wake of currency crises. Their analysis suggests that the Mexican government is likely to pay for the bulk of the fiscal costs of its crisis through seigniorage revenues. In contrast, the Korean government is likely to rely more on a combination of implicit and explicit fiscal reforms.

In "An Evaluation of Proposals to Reform the International Financial Architecture," Morris Goldstein provides an assessment of some of the leading reform proposals. He uses lending policies and practices of the IMF as an organizing device for discussing selected issues in the reform debate, namely, interest rate increases and reduction of IMF loan maturity, the size of IMF packages, and issues of conditionality. The paper emphasizes the importance of currency mismatches and argues that most of the antidotes for currency mismatching problems proposed so far appear to be either too costly or too drastic. Instead of such antidotes, the paper favors a combination of managed floating and active development of hedging mechanisms. Furthermore, it suggests that every request for an IMF program should contain data on existing currency mismatching by the banking and corporate sectors, analysis of the sustainability of these mismatches, and explicit conditions for reducing the mismatch.

The Impact

In "Recovery and Sustainability in East Asia," Yung Chul Park and Jong-Wha Lee analyze macroeconomic adjustment following the crisis in East Asia from a broad international perspective. The stylized pattern that emerges from the previous 160 currency crisis episodes shows a V-type adjustment of real gross domestic product (GDP) growth in the years prior to and following a crisis. The adjustment shows a much sharper V-type adjustment in the crisis episodes with an IMF program, compared to those without. Cross-country regressions show that depreciation of real exchange rate, expansionary macroeconomic policies, and favorable global environments are critical for the speedy postcrisis recovery. In this sense, the East Asian process of adjustment is not much different from the previous currency crisis episodes.

However, the degree of initial contraction and following recovery has been far greater in East Asia than what the cross-country evidence predicts. This paper attributes the sharper adjustment pattern in East Asia to the severe liquidity crisis that was triggered by investors' panic and then amplified by the weak corporate and bank balance sheets. They find no evidence for a direct impact of currency crises on long-run growth.

In "A Cure Worse Than The Disease? Currency Crises and the Output Costs of IMF-Supported Stabilization Programs," Michael M. Hutchison concludes that participation in an IMF program is associated with a 0.75 percentage point reduction in GDP growth. He notes, however, that the growth slowdown usually *precedes* participation in an IMF program, suggesting that the relationship might not be causal. On the one hand, participation in an IMF-supported program following a balance-of-payments or currency crisis does not appear to mitigate the output loss associated with such events. On the other hand, Malaysia—the one crisis country in the East Asian episode that did not have an IMF program—suffered more than those countries with programs. Countries participating in IMF programs significantly reduce domestic credit growth, while no effect is found on budget policy. Applying this model to the collapse of output in East Asia following the 1997 crisis, the author finds that the unexpected (forecast error) collapse of output in Malaysia—where an IMF program was not followed—was somewhat larger on average than in those countries adopting IMF programs (Indonesia, Korea, the Philippines, and Thailand).

In "IMF and World Bank Structural Adjustment Programs and Poverty," William Easterly argues that structural adjustment, as measured by the number of adjustment loans from the IMF and World Bank, reduces the sensitivity of poverty reduction to the rate of growth. Growth does reduce poverty, but he finds no evidence for a direct effect of structural adjustment on the average rate of growth. Instead, the poor benefit less from output expansion in countries with many adjustment loans than in countries with few. By the same token, the poor suffer less from an output contraction in countries with many adjustment loans than in countries with few adjustment loans. Why would this be? One hypothesis is that adjustment lending is countercyclical in ways that smooth consumption for the poor. There is evidence that some policy variables under adjustment lending are countercyclical, but there is no evidence that the cyclical component of those policy variables affects poverty. He speculates that the poor may be ill placed to take advantage of new opportunities created by structural adjustment reforms, just as they may suffer less from the loss of old opportunities in sectors that were artificially protected prior to reforms.

In "Impacts of the Indonesian Economic Crisis: Price Changes and the Poor," James Levinsohn, Steven Berry, and Jed Friedman provide early estimates of the impact of the July 1997 Indonesian economic crisis on Indonesia's poor. They find that price increases have affected the cost of living of poor households disproportionally. Just how hard the poor have been hit, however, depends on where the household lives, on whether the household is in an urban or rural area, and on just how the cost of living is computed. What is clear is that the notion that the very poor are so poor as to be insulated from international shocks is simply wrong. Rather, in the Indonesian case, the poor appear the most vulnerable.

I

The Defense

1

Interest Rates and Exchange Rates in the Korean, Philippine, and Thai Exchange Rate Crises

Dongchul Cho and Kenneth D. West

1.1 Introduction

A standard policy prescription in exchange rate crises is to tighten monetary policy, at least until the exchange rate has stabilized. Indeed, in the East Asian countries whose currencies collapsed in 1997, interest rates were raised, usually quite dramatically. For example, short-term rates rose from 12 to 30 percent in the space of a month in December 1997 in South Korea. The successful recovery from the crisis may seem to vindicate this policy.

However, that is not clear. High interest rates weaken the financial position of debtors, perhaps inducing bankruptcies in firms that are debt constrained only because of informational imperfections. The countries might have recovered, perhaps with less transitional difficulty, had an alternative, less restrictive, policy been followed. This has been argued forcefully by, for example, Furman and Stiglitz (1998) and Radelet and Sachs (1998).

There is mixed empirical evidence on the relationship between interest and exchange rates, even for developed countries (Eichenbaum and Evans 1995; Grilli and Roubini 1996). For countries that have undergone currency crises, Goldfajn and Gupta (1999) found that, on average, dramatic increases in interest rates have been associated with currency appreciations. However, there was no clear association for a subsample of countries that have undergone a banking crisis along with a currency crisis. This subsample includes the East Asian countries.

Dongchul Cho is a research fellow at the Korea Development Institute. Kenneth D. West is professor of economics at the University of Wisconsin and a research associate of the National Bureau of Economic Research.

The authors thank Akito Matsumoto, Mukunda Sharma, and Sungchul Hong for research assistance, and Robert Dekle, Gabriel Di Bella, and conference participants for helpful comments. West thanks the National Science Foundation for financial support.

Papers that focus on the 1997 currency crises in East Asia also produce mixed results. Representative results from papers using weekly or daily data are as follows. Goldfajn and Baig (1998) decided that the evidence is mixed but on balance favor the view that higher interest rates were associated with appreciations in Indonesia, Korea, Malaysia, the Philippines, and Thailand. Cho and West (2000) concluded that interest rate increases led to exchange rate appreciation in Korea during the crisis. Dekle, Hsiao, and Wang (2001) found sharp evidence that interest rate changes are reduced-form predictors of subsequent exchange rate appreciations in Korea, Malaysia, and Thailand, though with long and variable lags. Finally, Gould and Kamin (2000) were unable to find a reliable relationship between interest rates and exchange rates in the five countries.

This paper conducts an empirical study of the relationship between exchange rates and interest rates during the 1997–98 exchange rate crises in Korea, the Philippines, and Thailand. Our central question is: in these economies, did exogenous monetary-policy-induced increases in the interest rate cause exchange rate depreciation or appreciation? Our central contribution is to propose a model that identifies a monetary policy rule, in a framework general enough to allow either answer to our central question. Our starting point is the observation that the sign of the correlation between exchange and interest rates—used in many previous studies to decide whether an increase in interest rates causes an exchange rate appreciation— will be sufficient to answer our question only if monetary policy shocks are the dominant source of movements in exchange and interest rates. Since shocks to perceived exchange rate risk are also arguably an important source of variability during an exchange rate crisis, one must specify a model that allows one to distinguish the effects of the two types of shocks.

We do so with a model that has two equations and is linear. One equation is interest parity, with a time-varying risk premium. Importantly, we allow the risk premium to depend on the level of the interest rate. The second equation is a monetary policy rule, with the interest rate as the instrument. The two variables in the model are the exchange rate and domestic interest rate. These two variables are driven by two exogenous shocks, a monetary policy shock and a shock to the component of the exchange rate risk premium not dependent on the level of the interest rate. The model has two key parameters. One parameter (a) indexes how strongly the monetary authority leans against incipient exchange rate movements. The other parameter (d) indexes the sensitivity of exchange rate risk premiums to the level of interest rates.

Whether interest rates should be increased or decreased to stabilize a depreciating exchange rate depends on how sensitive risk premiums are to interest rates. Interest rates should be increased unless risk premiums are strongly increasing with the level of the interest rate. This is the orthodox policy. Interest rates should be lowered if risk premiums are strongly positively related to the interest rate. This is the view of Furman and Stiglitz (1998). Our model precisely defines "strongly positive" as meaning that the parameter d referenced in the previous paragraph is greater than 1.

According to our model, the sign of the correlation between exchange and interest rates suffices to reveal whether exogenous increases in interest rates led to exchange rate appreciation only if shocks to monetary policy dominate the movement of exchange and interest rates. Suppose instead that shocks to the exchange rate risk premium are the primary source of movements in exchange and interest rates. Then in our model, the correlation between the two variables may be positive even if, in the absence of risk premium shocks, increases in interest rates would have stabilized a depreciating exchange rate (i.e., $d < 1$). (We measure exchange rates so that a larger value means depreciation. Thus, a positive correlation means that high interest rates are associated with a depreciated exchange rate.) The correlation between the two may be negative even if interest rate increases would have destabilized exchange rates (i.e., $d > 1$) in the absence of risk premium shocks.

Using a special case of our model, we find that exchange rate risk premiums in Korea were inversely related to the level of interest rates. In the Philippines, risk premiums were increasing in interest rates, though modestly so. In both these countries, stabilization required raising interest rates. In Thailand, on the other hand, risk premiums were strongly increasing, in the precise sense that the parameter referenced in the preceding paragraph was estimated to be greater than 1. Accordingly, ceteris paribus, an exogenous increase in the interest rate led to exchange rate appreciation in Korea and the Philippines, and exchange rate depreciation in Thailand.

Unfortunately, confidence intervals for model parameters are huge. They do not rule out the possibility that interest rate increases led to depreciation in Korea and the Philippines, to appreciation in Thailand. To a certain extent this seems to follow unavoidably from the fact that our sample sizes are small, as is suggested by the similarly weak evidence found in most of the papers cited above. A second reason our results are tentative is that for tractability and ease of interpretation we base our inference particularly simple assumptions about the behavior of unobservable shocks. These assumptions are roughly consistent with the data, but alternative, more complex models no doubt would fit better. Moreover, we use an inefficient estimation technique. A final reason our results are tentative is that we do not allow for the possibility of destabilizing monetary policy, that is, a period during which a monetary authority moved interest rates in a destabilizing direction, perhaps before adopting a policy that ultimately led to exchange rate stabilization. We leave all such tasks to future research.

We also leave to future research the larger, and more important, issue about what constitutes good policy in an exchange rate crisis. High interest rates may be bad policy even if they stabilize exchange rates, and may be good policy even if they do not. We believe that our paper contributes to our understanding the larger issue, since any policy analysis must take a stand on the interest rate–exchange rate relationship. In our own work, brief discussions of policy during the Korean crisis may be found in Cho and Hong (2000) and Cho and West (1999).

Section 1.2 describes our model, section 1.3 our data, and section 1.4 our results. Section 1.5 concludes. An appendix contains some technical details.

1.2 Model

Our simple linear model has three equations and two observable variables. The three equations are interest parity, a relationship between exchange rate risk and interest rates, and an interest rate reaction function (monetary policy rule). The two variables are the domestic interest rate and the exchange rate.

We write interest parity as

$$
(1) \qquad i_t = i_t^* + E_t s_{t+1} - s_t + d_t.
$$

In equation (1), i_t and i_t^* are (net) domestic (i.e., Asian) and foreign nominal interest rates; s_t is $100 \times \log$ of the nominal spot exchange rate, with higher values indicating depreciation; E_t denotes expectations; d_t is a risk premium. If $d_t \equiv 0$, equation (1) is uncovered interest parity. The variable d_t, which may be serially correlated, captures default risk as well as the familiar premium due to risk aversion.

It presumably is safe to view i_t^* as substantially unaffected by domestic (Asian) monetary policy. The same cannot be assumed for $E_t s_{t+1}$, s_t, and d_t, all of which are determined simultaneously with i_t. However, for the moment we follow some previous literature (e.g., Furman and Stiglitz 1998) and perform comparative statics using equation (1) alone. Evidently, if i_t is increased, but $E_t s_{t+1}$ and d_t are unchanged, then s_t must fall (appreciate): the orthodox relationship. If, as well, increases in interest rates today cause confidence that the exchange rate will stay strong (i.e., that s_{t+1} will be lower than it would have been in the absence of an interest rate hike), then s_t must fall even farther for equation (1) to hold.

However, this channel will be offset insofar as increases in i_t are associated with increases in d_t. Such a rise may come about because higher interest rates are associated with higher default rates, or because higher interest rates raise risk premiums. This, in turn, may lead to expectations of depreciation (increase) in s_{t+1}. Furman and Stiglitz (1998) argue on this basis that equation (1) alone does not tell us even whether increases in i_t will be associated with increases or decreases in s_t, let alone the magnitude of the change.

We agree with this argument. Our aim is to specify a model that allows for the possibility of either a positive or negative response of s_t to an exogenous monetary-policy-induced increase in i_t, and then to estimate the model to quantify the sign and size of the effect. To that end, we supplement the interest parity condition in equation (1) with two additional equations. The first is a simple monetary policy rule. We assume that the nominal interest rate is the instrument of monetary policy. During a period of exchange rate crisis, the focus of monetary policy arguably is on stabilizing the exchange rate. We therefore assume

(2) $$i_t = a(E_{t-1}s_t - \bar{s}_t) + \tilde{u}_{mt}.$$

In equation (2), a is a parameter, and $\bar{s}_t$ is the target exchange rate. Conventional interpretation of International Monetary Fund (IMF) policy is that the IMF argues for $a > 0$. This means that the monetary authority leans against expected exchange rate depreciations. Of course, $a < 0$ means that the monetary authority lowers the interest rate in anticipation of depreciation. For simplicity, we impound the target level into the unobservable disturbance $\tilde{u}_{mt}$. Upon defining $u_{mt} = \tilde{u}_{mt} - a\bar{s}_t$, equation (2) becomes

(2') $$i_t = aE_{t-1}s_t + u_{mt}.$$

The variable u_{mt}, which may be serially correlated, captures not only changes in the target level of the exchange rate, but all other variables that affect monetary policy. Ultimately it would be of interest to model u_{mt}'s dependence on observable variables such as i_t^* and the level of foreign reserves; once again, we suppose that in the crisis period it is reasonable to focus on the exchange rate as the dominant determinant of interest rate policy. The "exogenous monetary policy induced increase in i_t," referenced in the previous paragraph is captured by a surprise increase in u_{mt}.

Note the dating of expectations: period t expectations appear in equation (1), period $t - 1$ expectations in equation (2'). This reflects the view that asset market participants, whom we presume to be setting exchange rates, react more quickly than does the monetary authority to news about exchange rate risk premiums (i.e., to shocks to the variable that we call u_{dt}, below). Capturing this view by using $t - 1$ expectations in the monetary rule is most appealing when data frequency is high. Accordingly, we assume daily decision making, and allow for the effects of time aggregation when we estimate our model using weekly data. Of course, we do not literally believe that in setting the interest rate each day the monetary authority is ignorant of intraday developments. Rather, we take this as a tractable approximation.

The final equation is one that relates the risk premium d_t to the interest rate i_t.

(3) $$d_t = di_t + \tilde{u}_{dt}$$

Equation (3) is an equilibrium relationship between risk premiums and interest rates. In the conventional view, $d < 0$, in which case higher interest rates are associated with lower risk, or perhaps $d = 0$, in which case there is no link between interest rates and risk. The $d < 0$ interpretation seems consistent with Fischer (1998, 4), who argues that temporarily raising interest rates restores confidence. In an alternative view, such as that of Furman and Stiglitz (1998), $d \gg 0$, and higher interest rates are associated with higher risk. We suppose that d is structural, in the sense that one can think of d as remaining fixed while one varies the monetary policy reaction parameter a. Obviously this cannot hold for arbitrarily wide variation in a, but perhaps is a tolerable assumption for empirically plausible variation in a.

The variable $\tilde{u}_{dt}$ captures all other factors that determine the risk premium. Ultimately it would be of interest to partially proxy $\tilde{u}_{dt}$ with observable variables. Candidate variables include the level of reserves and debt denominated in foreign currency (see Cho and West 2000) for the role such variables played in Korea). However, because such data are not available at high frequencies, for simplicity we treat $\tilde{u}_{dt}$ as unobservable and exogenous.

To simplify notation, and for consistency with our empirical work, we impound i_t^* in the unobservable disturbance to interest parity, defining $u_{dt} = i_t^* + \tilde{u}_{dt}$. We then combine equations (3) and (1) to obtain

(4) $$(1 - d)i_t = E_t s_{t+1} - s_t + u_{dt}.$$

Equations (2′) and (4) are a two-equation system for the two variables i_t and s_t. Upon substituting equation (2′) into equation (4) and rearranging, we obtain

(5) $$s_t + a(1 - d)E_{t-1}s_t = E_t s_{t+1} + u_{dt} - (1 - d)u_{mt}.$$

Equation (5) is a first-order stochastic difference equation in s_t. To solve it, we assume homogeneous and model-consistent expectations. That is, we assume that private-sector and government expectations are consistent with one another, in that the variables used in forming E_{t-1} in equations (2) and (2′) are the period $t - 1$ values of the period t variables used in forming E_t in equations (1) and (4). Moreover, these expectations are consistent with the time series properties of u_{dt} and u_{mt}. To make these assumptions operational, we assume as well that E_t denotes expectations conditional on current and lagged values of u_{dt} and u_{mt} (equivalently, current and lagged values of s_t and i_t).

Define $b = [1 + a(1 - d)]^{-1}$. We make the stability assumption $0 < b < 1$ and the "no bubbles" assumption $\lim_{j \to \infty} b^j E_{t-1}s_{t+j} = 0$. The stability assumption requires

(6) $$a < 0, d > 1 \quad \text{or} \quad a > 0, d < 1.$$

The algebraic condition in equation (6) captures the following commonsense stability condition. Suppose risk premiums are so sensitive to interest rates that $d > 1$. Stability then requires that the monetary authority lower interest rates ($a < 0$) in response to anticipated depreciations. For if it instead raised interest rates, we would have the following neverending spiral: A positive shock to the risk premium causes exchange rates to depreciate, which with $a > 0$ causes the monetary authority to raise interest rates, which with $d > 1$ causes a further depreciation and a further raising of interest rates. . . . Similarly, if $d < 1$, stability requires increasing interest rates in the face of anticipated depreciation. Note that one can have a stable system when $a > 0$ even if $d > 0$, as long as $d < 1$: In our model, a policy of leaning against exchange rate depreciations ($a > 0$) is stable even if increases in interest rates are associated with increased risk ($d > 0$), as long as the increase in risk is not too large ($d < 1$).

To solve the model, project both sides of equation (5) onto period $t - 1$ information, and then solve recursively forward. The result is

$$(7) \qquad E_{t-1}s_t = b \sum_{j=0}^{\infty} \{b^j E_{t-1}[u_{dt+j} - (1 - d)u_{mt+j}]\}.$$

For given processes of u_{dt} and u_{mt}, we can solve for $E_{t-1}s_t$ using equation (7). Putting this solution into equation (2′) yields i_t, which in turn may be used in equation (4) to solve for s_t.

The data we use are to a certain extent consistent with a random walk for both u_{mt} and u_{dt}, say,

$$(8) \qquad u_{mt} = u_{mt-1} + e_{mt}, \quad u_{dt} = u_{dt-1} + e_{dt}.$$

Such shocks make for quick, one-period movements from one steady state to another in response to a shock. They are special in other ways as well, as noted below. Under the assumption that e_{mt} and e_{dt} are uncorrelated with one another, figures 1.1–1.4 plot responses of i_t and s_t to 1 percent increases in e_{mt} and e_{dt}, for each of four parameter sets: $a = 0.2, d = -9; a = 0.7, d = -9; a = 0.7, d = 0.6; a = -0.5, d = 1.2$.

Figure 1.1 plots the response of i_t to a 1 percent increase in e_{mt}. Only one line is plotted because for all four parameter sets, response is identical. As is obvious from equation (2′), the impact response is a 1 percent increase. The interest rate then returns to initial value. That is, a *permanent* increase in u_{mt} leads to a *transitory* change in i_t. Evidently, from equation (2′), in steady state s_t must fall by $1/a$ (i.e., rise by $-1/a$ when $a < 0$). This is depicted in figure 1.2. Consider first the case in which $a > 0$. Then an exogenous in-

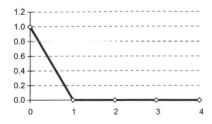

Fig. 1.1   **Response of i_t to a 1 percent shock to e_{mt}**

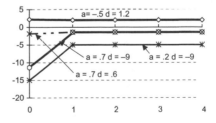

Fig. 1.2   **Response of s_t to a 1 percent shock to e_{mt}**

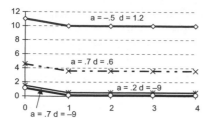
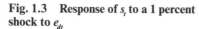

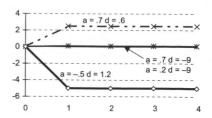

Fig. 1.3   Response of s_t to a 1 percent shock to e_{dt}

Fig. 1.4   Response of i_t to a 1 percent shock to e_{dt}

crease in the interest rate causes an exchange rate appreciation: with $a > 0$, exogenous increases in interest rates stabilize a depreciating exchange rate. In the three specifications with $a > 0$, the impact elasticity ranges from about -2 to -15. For given d, the impact effect is smaller for $a = 0.7$ than for $a = 0.2$: larger a means a harsher monetary policy response and greater exchange rate stability. On the other hand, when $a < 0$, an exogenous increase in the interest rate causes the exchange rate to depreciate.

These long responses are of course consistent with long-run neutrality of monetary policy. An increase in e_{mt} means a commitment to raise the interest rate for any given expected level of exchange rates, now and forever. Because the level of the exchange rate adjusts in the long run, there is no long-run effect on the *rate* of exchange rate depreciation, and therefore no long-run effect on the *level* of the interest rate.

Figure 1.3 depicts the response of s_t to a 1 percent increase in the risk premium. In all specifications, the exchange rate increases in both the short and the long run. The impact effect is greater than the long-run effect because according to equation (2') it takes a period before interest rates respond to the increased risk. For given d, the response is less for larger a; for given a, the response is greater for larger d.

Figure 1.4 plots the response of i_t to a 1 percent increase in the risk premium. By assumption, there is no contemporaneous response. When $a > 0$, the interest rate is increased; when $a < 0$, it is decreased. When a is larger in absolute value, there is a larger increase. In accordance with equation (4), the long-run response of i_t is $1/(1 - d)$, and thus it is governed only by d but not a; in the simple random-walk specification, the long run is achieved in one period and so the responses for $(a = 0.2)/(d = -9)$ and $(a = 0.7)/(d = -9)$ are identical.

Some implications of the above are worth noting. First, upon comparing the figures, we see that when $a > 0$, risk premium shocks cause interest and exchange rates to move in the same direction, while monetary shocks cause them to move in opposite directions. For $a < 0$, risk premium shocks cause interest and exchange rates to move in the opposite direction, while monetary shocks cause them to move in the same direction. This result holds not only for random-walk shocks but also for arbitrary stationary AR(1) shocks.

The implication is that the sign of the correlation between interest and exchange rates is not sufficient to tell us that interest rate hikes stabilized a depreciating currency. A negative correlation may result when $a < 0$ because the data are dominated by risk premium shocks. A positive correlation may result when $a > 0$ because the data are dominated by risk premium shocks.

Second, suppose one takes a as a choice parameter for a monetary authority that aims to stabilize a rapidly depreciating exchange rate. If exchange rate risk does not rapidly increase with the level of interest rates ($d < 1$), then the monetary authority should raise interest rates (set $a > 0$) when further depreciation is expected. However, if exchange rate risk does rapidly increase with the level of interest rates ($d > 1$), then the monetary authority should lower interest rates (set $a < 0$) when further depreciation is expected. In either case, stabilization smoothes exchange rates.

A third point is that with random-walk shocks—an assumption we maintain in our empirical work—this stabilization of exchange rates will induce a negative first-order autocorrelation in Δs_t. That is, smoothing in the face of random-walk shocks causes exchange rates to exhibit some mean reversion relative to a random-walk benchmark. (Our model is capable of generating positive autocorrelation in Δs_t, but only if the shocks exhibit dynamics beyond that of a random walk.)

Finally, with random-walk shocks, one can read the sign of $1 - d$, and hence whether d is above or below the critical value of 1, directly from the sign of the correlation between Δi_t and Δs_{t-1}. When d is less than 1, this correlation is positive; when d is greater than 1, this correlation is negative: If stabilization involves increasing (decreasing) interest rates in response to incipient exchange rate depreciations, then, naturally, Δi_t will be positively (negatively) correlated with Δs_{t-1}. Again, this simple result applies because we assume random-walk shocks and need not hold for richer shock processes.

1.3   Data and Estimation Technique

We obtained daily data for Korea, the Philippines, and Thailand, either directly from Bloomberg or indirectly from others who reported Bloomberg as the ultimate source. The mnemonics for exchange rates are KRW (Korea), PHP (the Philippines), and THB (Thailand). The mnemonics for interest rates are KWCRIT (Korea), PPCALL (the Philippines: Philippine Peso Interbank Call Rate), and BITBCALL (Thailand: Thai STD Chartered Bank Call Rate). Because many days were missing, we constructed weekly data by sampling Wednesday of each week. If Wednesday was not available we used Thursday; if Thursday was not available we used Tuesday. Interest rates are expressed at annual rates; exchange rates are versus the U.S. dollar.

We start our samples so that we are two weeks into what arguably can be considered the postcrisis exchange rate targeting regime. Two weeks allows both the current and lagged value of interest and exchange rate differences to fall inside the new regime. For Thailand and the Philippines, this means a start date of Wednesday, 23 July 1997. (As noted above, our weekly data are for Wednesday.) For Korea, the date is Wednesday, 17 December 1997. We ended our samples one year later (sample size of 53 weeks), since the simple monetary rule (eq. [2]) probably did not well describe policy once the countries had stabilized. We also tried 27-week samples, with little change in results. Figures 1.5–1.7 plot our data, in levels. The dashed lines delimit our one-year samples.

Formal unit root tests failed to reject the null of a unit root. Hence, we examine interest and (log) exchange rates in first differences. We failed to find cointegration between i_t and s_t. (Using similar weekly data, Gould and Kamin 2000 and Dekle, Hsiao, and Wang 2001 also failed to find cointegration.) Hence, in our regression work (mentioned briefly below) we estimated a vector autoregression (VAR) in Δi_t and Δs_t without including an error correction term. We note in passing that the lack of cointegration meant that we could not turn to estimation of a cointegrating vector to identify the monetary policy parameter a.

To identify a and d, we assume that u_{mt} and u_{dt} follow random walks. In this case, our model implies a vector MA(1) process for $(\Delta i_t, \Delta s_t)'$, which, as explained in the next section, is more or less consistent with our data. We allow the innovations in u_{mt} and u_{dt} to be contemporaneously correlated. Such a correlation might result, for example, if the level of foreign reserves importantly affected both monetary policy and exchange rate risk. Because we allow this correlation, it will not be meaningful to decompose the variation of exchange or interest rates into monetary and risk components. (We do not, however, model or exploit cross-country correlations in u_{dt} or u_{mt}, deferring to future work the attractive possibility of using information in such correlations.) We allow for decisions to be made daily rather than weekly. That is, we assume that the model described in section 1.2 generates the data with a time period corresponding to one day. However, we sample the data only once every five observations.

We use five moments to compute the five parameters a and d and the three elements of the variance-covariance matrix of $(e_{mt}, e_{dt})'$. The moments we used included three chosen because they were estimated relatively precisely: var (Δi_t), var (Δs_t) and corr $(\Delta i_t, \Delta s_t)$. The final two moments used, corr $(\Delta i_t, \Delta s_{t-1})$ and corr $(\Delta s_t, \Delta s_{t-1})$, were largely chosen for clarity and convenience. As explained at the end of section 1.2 above, our model has simple and direct implications for the signs of these correlations. As a technical matter, with this choice of moments, the parameters could be solved for analytically, although the equations are nonlinear.

An appendix gives details on how we mapped moments into parameters.

Fig. 1.5   Overnight interest rate and won/dollar exchange rate, Korea

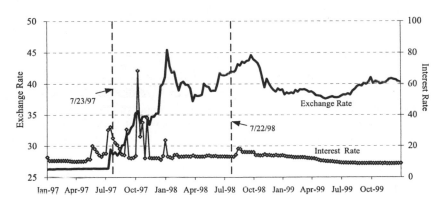

Fig. 1.6   Overnight interest rate and peso/dollar exchange rate, the Philippines

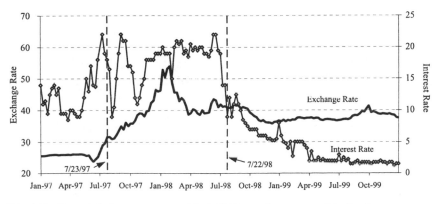

Fig. 1.7   Overnight interest rate and baht/dollar exchange rate, Thailand

Two points about the mapping are worth noting here. The first is that since the five equations are nonlinear, in principle they can yield no reasonable solutions. For example, for a given set of moments, the implied value of the variance of e_{dt} might be negative. The second is that our algorithm solves for a from a root to a quadratic. If the estimated first-order autocorrelation of Δs_t is between -0.5 and 0, this quadratic is guaranteed to have two real roots, one implying a positive value of a, the other a negative value. We chose the root consistent with stability: the root implying a positive value of $\hat{a}$ if $\hat{d} < 1$, a negative value if $\hat{d} < 1$. (The solution algorithm is in part recursive, with d estimated prior to a.) We made this choice because an unstable solution implies explosive data, at least if the unstable policy is expected to be maintained indefinitely; this is inconsistent with our use of sample moments.

We report 90 percent confidence intervals. These are "percentile method" intervals, constructed by a nonparametric bootstrap using block resampling with nonoverlapping blocks. Details are in the appendix.

1.4   Empirical Results

Table 1.1 has variances and auto- and cross-correlations for lags 0, 1, and 2, with the bootstrap confidence intervals in parentheses. A skim of the table reveals that virtually all the auto- and cross-correlations are insignificantly different from zero at the 10 percent level. The only exceptions are the correlations between Δs_t and Δi_{t-1} in the shorter sample in Korea, between Δi_t and Δi_{t-1} in the longer sample in the Philippines, and between Δi_t and Δs_t in both samples in Thailand. (We did not report confidence intervals for $\text{var}[\Delta i_t]$ and $\text{var}[\Delta s_t]$ in table 1.1; all point estimates of these variances were significant at the 90 percent level—indeed, at any significance level—by construction.)

The insignificance of the point estimates at lag 2 is consistent with a vector MA(1) process for $(\Delta i_t, \Delta s_t)'$, because population auto- and cross-correlations will all be zero for lags 2 and higher for such a process. This is the main sense in which a random walk for u_{mt} and u_{dt} implies a process more or less consistent with the data. As well, the estimates of the first-order autocorrelation of Δs_t is negative in all samples, though barely so for the Philippines and Thailand in the one-year samples (point estimates = -0.07 and -0.02); as noted in section 1.2 above, a negative autocorrelation is implied by our model if shocks are random walks.

On the other hand, the insignificance of the point estimates at lag 1, and of the contemporaneous correlation between Δi_t and Δs_t in Korea and the Philippines, is bad news for our MA(1) model, and, in our view, for any empirical study of these data. Because the data are noisy, estimates of model parameters—which of course will be drawn from moments such as those reported in table 1.1—will likely be imprecise. That, perhaps, is an inevitable

Correlations

Sample	Change Rate[a]	Variance	Δi_t	Δi_{t-1}	Δi_{t-2}	Δs_t	Δs_{t-1}	Δs_{t-2}
			A. Korea					
12/17/97–12/16/98	Δi_t	2?06	1.00	0.15 (−0.06,0.28)	−0.28 (−0.41,0.17)	0.54 (−0.01,0.69)	0.12 (−0.05,0.27)	−0.17 (−0.24,0.20)
	Δs_t	20?49	0.54 (−0.01,0.69)	**−0.22** (−0.30,−0.05)	0.00 (−0.56,0.12)	1.00	−0.39 (−0.45,0.27)	0.21 (−0.15,0.27)
12/17/97–06/17/98	Δi_t	?.83	1.00	0.14 (−0.16,0.17)	−0.33 (−0.53,0.04)	0.57 (−0.14,0.76)	0.11 (−0.10,0.27)	−0.18 (−0.24,0.38)
	Δs_t	3?.04	0.57 (−0.14,0.76)	**−0.24** (−0.35,−0.06)	0.01 (−0.68,0.14)	1.00	−0.45 (−0.54,0.35)	0.24 (−0.22,0.33)
			B. The Philippines					
07/23/97–07/22/98	Δi_t	14?.91	1.00	**−0.59** (−0.75,−0.11)	0.30 (−0.18,0.42)	0.20 (−0.11,0.37)	0.05 (−0.08,0.27)	0.10 (−0.14,0.33)
	Δs_t	1?.62	0.20 (−0.11,0.37)	−0.25 (−0.49,0.20)	0.17 (−0.15,0.33)	1.00	−0.07 (−0.11,0.16)	0.01 (−0.15,0.11)
07/23/97–01/21/98	Δi_t	2?3.87	1.00	**−0.61** (−0.76,−0.14)	0.31 (−0.21,0.44)	0.24 (−0.12,0.47)	0.06 (−0.15,0.33)	0.14 (−0.19,0.35)
	Δs_t	5.17	0.24 (−0.12,0.47)	−0.28 (−0.64,0.25)	0.22 (−0.22,0.42)	1.00	−0.18 (−0.24,0.25)	−0.05 (−0.27,0.10)
			C. Thailand					
07/23/97–07/22/98	Δi_t	5.22	1.00	0.11 (−0.30,0.24)	0.10 (−0.22,0.37)	**0.32** (0.20,0.49)	−0.20 (−0.45,0.08)	−0.00 (−0.19,0.20)
	Δs_t	16.74	**0.32** (0.20,0.49)	0.01 (−0.10,0.23)	0.01 (−0.14,0.17)	1.00	−0.02 (−0.18,0.20)	0.09 (−0.27,0.16)
07/23/97–01/21/98	Δi_t	5.93	1.00	0.31 (−0.30,0.31)	−0.02 (−0.35,0.19)	**0.36** (0.14,0.56)	−0.13 (−0.60,0.02)	−0.14 (−0.46,0.26)
	Δs_t	14.58	**0.36** (0.14,0.56)	−0.08 (−0.29,0.30)	0.12 (−0.15,0.23)	1.00	−0.47 (−0.49,0.22)	0.11 (−0.33,0.28)

Notes: 90 percent confidence intervals from bootstrap, in parentheses. Point estimates in bold are significant at the 90 percent level.

[a] Δi_t is the weekly change in the overnight interest rate, expressed at annual rates; Δs_t the weekly percentage change in the exchange rate versus the U.S. dollar. Higher values of s_t indicate depreciation.

consequence of our decision to focus on a sample small enough that it a priori seemed likely to have a more or less stable interest rate rule.

We note in passing that when a second-order VAR in $(\Delta i_t, \Delta s_t)$ is estimated for one-year samples, F-tests (not reported in the table) yield slightly sharper results. Specifically, the null of no predictability is rejected for lagged interest rates in the Δi_t equation in the Philippines and for lagged exchange rate changes in both the Δi_t and the Δs_t equations in Korea but not otherwise. This suggests the importance of allowing for richer dynamics in the shocks, an extension suggested as well by the fact that the absolute value of the Philippine estimate of corr $(\Delta i_t, \Delta i_{t-1})$ is greater than 0.5, a magnitude inconsistent with Δi_t following an MA(1) process. We leave that as a task for future research.

Using the algorithm described in the appendix and the previous section, we estimated a and d from some moments reported in table 1.1. (The algorithm also automatically produces estimates of the variance-covariance matrix of $(e_{mt}, e_{dt})'$, which we do not discuss because these are not of economic interest.) Columns (3) and (4) in table 1.2 present these estimates, again with 90 percent confidence intervals from a bootstrap given in parentheses. The algebraic values of the estimates of d are lowest for Korea and highest for Thailand, with

(9) $\hat{d}$ for Korea $< 0 < \hat{d}$ for Philippines $< 1 < \hat{d}$ for Thailand.

Table 1.2   **Parameter Estimates**

| | | | | % Response of s_t to a 1% Shock to u_{mt} | |
	Sample (1)	a (2)	d (3)	Impact (4)	Long-Run (5)
Korea	12/17/97–12/16/98	0.25	−8.87	−13.9	−4.1
		(−0.05,0.35)	(−27.7,14.2)	(−43.9,36.3)	(−15.2,12.1)
	12/17/97–06/17/98	0.36	−11.27	−15.0	−2.8
		(−0.12,0.37)	(−27.7,39.4)	(−46.8,61.7)	(−20.6,17.0)
The Philippines	07/23/97–07/22/98	0.76	0.57	−1.8	−1.3
		(−1.77,5.76)	(−0.72,2.43)	(−8.6,7.1)	(−6.9,5.9)
	07/23/97–01/21/98	1.12	0.31	−1.6	−0.9
		(−2.70,9.04)	(−0.92,3.25)	(−6.7,7.5)	(−3.8,4.9)
Thailand	07/23/97–07/22/98	−0.54	1.16	2.0	1.8
		(−1.07,0.19)	(−2.25,7.74)	(−12.4,21.8)	(−9.0,15.1)
	07/23/97–01/21/98	−0.96	6.59	6.6	1.0
		(−1.33,0.11)	(−3.7,14.5)	(−13.8,23.4)	(−8.9,10.4)

Notes: a is a monetary policy reaction parameter defined in equation (2); d measures the sensitivity of exchange rate risk premia to the interest rate, as defined in equations (1) and (3). 90 percent confidence intervals, from bootstrap, in parentheses. The elasticities in columns (5) and (6) are the response to a surprise, permanent 1 percent increase in u_{mt}.

The implication is that in equilibrium, increases in interest rates were associated with decreases in exchange rate risk in Korea. The association between interest rates and exchange rate risk was positive in the Philippines, but sufficiently small that if monetary policy is to be stabilizing, interest rates must be increased in response to expected exchange rate depreciations ($a > 0$). The association is also positive in Thailand, with the estimated value of d greater than 1. Hence if monetary policy is to be stabilizing in Thailand, interest rates must be decreased in response to expected exchange rate depreciations ($a < 0$). As explained above, the signs of $\hat{a}$ follow from the signs of the estimates of the correlation between Δi_t and Δs_{t-1}; negative in Thailand, positive in Korea and the Philippines.

As we feared, the confidence intervals on the estimates of a and d are large; indeed, they are staggeringly large. Using a two-tailed test, one can reject the null that $a = 0$ in Korea in the one-year sample at the 16 percent level (not reported in the table); all other parameters are even more imprecisely estimated.

Let us abstract from the confidence intervals and focus on the point estimates. We do not know of estimates from other studies that can be used to gauge directly the plausibility of the estimate of d. This ranking does conflict with Barsuto and Ghosh (2000), who concluded that real interest rate hikes increased the exchange rate risk premium in Korea, decreased it in Thailand. (Barsuto and Ghosh did not study the Philippines.) On the other hand, it is our sense that the ranking in equation (9) accords with the view that fundamentals were best in Korea, worst in Thailand. Moreover, the bottom-line conclusion—that interest rate increases caused depreciation in Thailand, appreciation in Korea and the Philippines—is consistent with Goldfajn and Baig (1998, table 3, full sample estimates) and with Di Bella's (2000) findings for Thailand (Di Bella does not consider other Asian countries).

For all practical purposes, impulse responses to orthogonal movements in e_{mt} and e_{dt} are given in figures 1.1–1.4. For Korea, see the lines for $a = 0.2$, $d = -9$; for the Philippines, see $a = 0.7$, $d = 0.6$; for Thailand, see $a = 0.5$, $d = 1.2$. The exact responses of s_t to a 1 percent positive value of e_{mt} are given in columns (5) and (6) of table 1.2. Once again, the confidence intervals are very large, as is inevitable since these elasticities are simple transformations of the estimates of a and d.

Now, Thailand's agreements with the IMF called for Thailand to maintain interest rates in indicative ranges that were high relative to precrisis levels (e.g., 12–17 percent in the August 1997 agreement [IMF 1997a, annex B], 15–20 percent in the December 1997 agreement [IMF 1997b, annex B]. Some agreements also suggested raising interest rates when the exchange rate is under pressure (IMF 1997b, 1998). How can this be reconciled with our Thai estimates ($\hat{a} < 0$, $\hat{d} > 1$), which indicate that the stabilization was accomplished by lowering interest rates in the face of incipient deprecia-tion? One interpretation is that IMF increases appear in our data as occa-sional and very visible large positive values of u_{mt}; most of the day-to-day systematic component of policy implicitly lowered interest rates in the face of incipient exchange rate depreciation, despite the agreement to raise in-terest rates when the exchange rate was pressured. On this interpretation, the appreciation would have occurred sooner absent the early increases in interest rates. A second interpretation is that policy *did* raise interest rates in the face of depreciation, both in the form of one-time increases early in the sample, and systematically throughout the sample. However, sampling error caused the estimate of d to be greater than 1 and thus the estimate of a to be negative. (We refer to $\hat{d}$ rather than $\hat{a}$ because $\hat{a}$ is solved from a quadratic with one negative and one positive root, and we choose the root consistent with stability: the root that yields $\hat{a} < 0$ when $\hat{d} > 1$, the root that yields $\hat{a} > 0$ when $\hat{d} < 1$. See section 1.3 and the appendix.)

We do not have any direct evidence on either of these interpretations. We hoped that some indirect evidence might be found by rolling the samples forward, recomputing the estimates of a and d. Table 1.3 presents results of such an exercise, for one-year samples, and for all three countries. We dropped the initial observation as we added a final observation, keeping the sample at $T = 53$ weeks. In Korea and Thailand, we stopped the process when the estimated first-order autocorrelation of Δs_t turned positive. That date does not occur until January 1998 for the Philippines, and so to con-serve space we stopped at September 1997.

The estimates for the Philippines and Thailand move little—surprisingly

Table 1.3   **Rolling Sample Estimates of a and d**

	Korea			The Philippines			Thailand	
Start	$\hat{a}$	$\hat{d}$	Start	$\hat{a}$	$\hat{d}$	Start	$\hat{a}$	$\hat{d}$
12/17/97	0.24	−8.99	07/23/97	0.74	0.57	07/23/97	−0.53	1.16
12/24/97	0.48	−3.37	07/30/97	0.68	0.54	07/30/97	−0.54	1.12
12/31/97	0.41	−1.82	08/06/98	0.68	0.55	08/06/98	−0.54	1.13
01/07/98	0.29	−2.28	08/13/98	0.63	0.55	08/13/98	−0.52	1.14
01/14/98	0.31	−1.93	08/20/98	0.66	0.51	08/20/98	−0.49	1.21
01/21/98	0.35	−1.27	08/27/98	0.70	0.53	08/27/98	−0.53	1.29
01/28/98	0.35	−0.36	09/03/98	0.73	0.55	09/03/98	−0.58	1.39
02/06/98	n.a.	n.a.	09/10/98	1.41	0.75	09/10/98	−0.56	1.31
02/13/98	n.a.	n.a.	09/17/98	1.41	0.75	09/17/98	−0.59	1.14
02/20/98	n.a.	n.a.	09/24/98	1.41	0.73	09/24/98	n.a.	n.a.

Notes: The estimates of a and d are computed from 53-week samples with the indicated starting date. For each country, the estimate in the first line repeats the figures in table 1.2. The algorithm used to map data to parameters cannot be used when the estimate of the first-order autocorrelation of Δs_t is positive. The n.a. entries flag samples in which the estimate of this autocorrelation is positive.

little, in light of the huge confidence intervals in the previous table. In the Philippines, the estimate of d ranges from about 0.5 to 0.7; in Thailand, the range is about 1.1 to 1.4. Moreover, the estimate of a does not fall, which one might expect if Thailand systematically raised interest rates in response to incipient exchange rate depreciation in the early but not the later parts of the sample. Thus this exercise is not particularly helpful in interpreting the results for Thailand.

One estimate that *is* quite sensitive to the sample is that for d, for Korea. The estimated value rises rapidly, from -8.99 to -0.36. A possible rationalization of this pattern is that as a country stabilizes, exchange rate risk becomes insensitive to the level of the interest rate. Perhaps $d = 0$ in developed countries, or at least in countries without credit rationing (see Furman and Stiglitz 1998). Clearly, however, this is a speculative interpretation, and the large confidence intervals in table 1.2 make it reasonable to attribute the wide variation to sampling error in estimation of d.

1.5   Conclusions

We have formulated and estimated a model that allows for interest rate shocks to either appreciate or depreciate exchange rates. Using weekly data, we have estimated a special case of the model using data from Korea, the Philippines, and Thailand. We have found that an exogenous increase in interest rates caused exchange rate appreciation in Korea and the Philippines, depreciation in Thailand. The estimates are, however, quite noisy.

One set of priorities for future work is to use higher frequency data, allow for richer shock processes, and use more efficient estimation techniques. A second is to allow for the possibility that for some period of time, monetary policy was destabilizing, with a switch in the sign of the interest rate reaction function necessary for stabilization. A third is to bring additional variables, such as the level of foreign reserves, into the model. A final, and broad, aim of our future work is to use our knowledge of the relationship between interest rates and exchange rates to analyze the macroeconomic effects of monetary policy in countries undergoing currency crises.

Appendix

Mapping from Moments to Model Parameters

Let u_{dt} and u_{mt} follow random walks

(A1) $$u_{dt} = u_{dt-1} + e_{dt}, \quad u_{mt} = u_{mt-1} + e_{mt},$$

where e_{dt} and e_{mt} are vector white noise. Then the solution of the model is

(A2) $i_t = (1 - d)^{-1}u_{dt-1} + e_{mt}$,

$s_t = -(a^{-1} + 1 - d)u_{mt} + (1 - d)u_{mt-1} + [1 + (1 - d)^{-1}a^{-1}]u_{dt} - u_{dt-1}$.

Define $\tilde{u}_{dt} = (1-d)^{-1}u_{dt}$, $\tilde{e}_{dt} = (1-d)^{-1}e_{dt}$, $\delta = 1-d$, $\alpha = a^{-1}$. Rewrite equation (A2) as

(A3) $i_t = \tilde{u}_{dt-1} + e_{mt}$, $s_t = (\alpha + \delta)(\tilde{u}_{dt} - u_{mt}) - \delta(\tilde{u}_{dt-1} - u_{mt-1})$.

Suppose we sample data every n periods ($n = 5$ in the computations in the text). Then

(A4a) $i_t - i_{t-n} = \tilde{e}_{dt-1} + \tilde{e}_{dt-2} + \ldots + \tilde{e}_{dt-n} + e_{mt} - e_{mt-n}$.

(A4b) $s_t - s_{t-n} = (\alpha + \delta)(\tilde{e}_{dt} - e_{mt}) + \alpha(\tilde{e}_{dt-1} - e_{mt-1})$

$+ \ldots + \alpha(\tilde{e}_{dt-n+1} - e_{mt-n+1}) - \delta(\tilde{e}_{dt-n} - e_{mt-n})$.

Define $\Delta^n i_t = i_t - i_{t-n}$, $\Delta^n s_t = s_t - s_{t-n}$, $\tilde{\sigma}_{md} = \text{cov}(e_{mt}, \tilde{e}_{dt})$, $\tilde{\sigma}_d^2 = \text{var}(\tilde{e}_{dt})$, $\sigma_m^2 = \text{var}(e_{mt})$. Then

(A5) $\text{var}(\Delta^n i) = n\tilde{\sigma}_d^2 + 2\sigma_m^2 - 2\tilde{\sigma}_{md}$,

(A6) $\text{var}(\Delta^n s) = (n\alpha^2 + 2\alpha\delta + 2\delta^2)(\tilde{\sigma}_d^2 + \sigma_m^2 - 2\tilde{\sigma}_{md})$,

(A7) $\text{cov}(\Delta^n i, \Delta^n s) = [(n - 1)\alpha - \delta]\tilde{\sigma}_d^2 - (\alpha + 2\delta)\sigma_m^2$

$- [(n - 1)\alpha - \alpha - 3\delta]\tilde{\sigma}_{md}$,

(A8) $\text{cov}(\Delta^n s, \Delta^n s_{-n}) = -\delta(\alpha + \delta)(\tilde{\sigma}_d^2 + \sigma_m^2 - 2\tilde{\sigma}_{md})$,

(A9) $\text{cov}(\Delta^n i, \Delta^n s_{-n}) = (\alpha + \delta)(\tilde{\sigma}_d^2 + \sigma_m^2 - 2\tilde{\sigma}_{md})$.

Equations (A5) to (A9) were used to solve for $\tilde{\sigma}_d^2$, σ_m^2, $\tilde{\sigma}_{md}$, α, and δ. From these, a and d can be computed. When $\text{cov}(\Delta^n s, \Delta^n s_{-n}) < 0$, a quadratic that is used to solve for α is guaranteed to have one negative and one positive root. We chose the root consistent with stable monetary policy: the negative root when the estimate of d was greater than 1, the positive root otherwise.

Description of Bootstrap Technique

The bootstrap confidence intervals in table 1.2 were based on 5,000 replications of the following procedure. Each replication was based on an artificial sample constructed by sampling, with replacement, nonoverlapping blocks of size 6, from the actual data. For the larger sample ($T = 53$ weeks), we sampled the blocks from a sample of 54 weeks. We used 54 rather than 53 weeks so that the sample contained an integral multiple of blocks; the 54 weeks consisted of the 53 used in the estimation plus an additional week at the end of the sample (e.g., 12/17/97–12/23/98 for Korea). In the smaller sample ($T = 27$ weeks), we sampled the blocks from a sample of 30 weeks, adding three weeks to the data used in estimates reported in the table (e.g., 12/17/97–07/08/98 for Korea).

For each of the 5,000 samples, we applied the procedure used to obtain the point estimates, to samples of size 53 or 27. We sorted the results from lowest to highest. For the autocorrelations in table 1.1, the confidence intervals were obtained by dropping the lowest and highest 5 percent of the results (i.e., the 500 lowest and 500 highest). For the point estimates in table 1.2, we first dropped all results in which (1) the point estimate of the first-order autocorrelation of Δs_t was positive or less than –0.5, or (2) the point estimate of var (e_{dt}) or var (e_{mt}) was negative. The confidence intervals were then obtained by dropping the lowest and highest 5 percent of the remaining results. The number of observations that remained after dropping those with inadmissable point estimates were as follows: Korea, 3,318 ($T = 53$) and 2,746 ($T = 27$); the Philippines, 1,977 ($T = 53$) and 2,728 ($T = 27$); Thailand, 1, 661 ($T = 53$) and 2,285 ($T = 27$). The relative paucity of remaining observations in the Philippines and Thailand for $T = 53$ results from a relatively large number of bootstrap samples in which the point estimate of the first-order autocorrelation of Δs_t was positive.

References

Basurto, Gabriela, and Atish Ghosh. 2000. The interest rate–exchange rate nexus in currency crises. IMF Working Paper no. WP/00/19. Washington, D.C.: International Monetary Fund, February.

Cho, Dongchul, and Kiseok Hong. 2002. Currency crisis of Korea: Internal weakness or external independence? In *Regional and global capital flows: Macroeconomic causes and consequences,* ed. Takatoshi Ito and Anne O. Krueger, 337–73. Chicago: University of Chicago Press.

Cho, Dongchul, and Kenneth D. West. 2000. The effect of monetary policy in exchange rate stabilization in post-crisis Korea. In *The Korean crisis: Before and after,* ed. I. Shin, 255–86. Seoul: Korea Development Institute.

Dekle, Robert, Cheng Hsiao, and Siyan Wang. 2001. Interest rate stabilization of exchange rates and contagion in the Asian crisis countries. In *Financial crises in emerging markets,* ed. Reuven Glick, Ramon Moreno, and Mark Maury Spiegel, 347–83. Cambridge, England: Cambridge University Press.

Di Bella, Gabriel. 2000. Exchange rate stabilization in Mexico and Thailand: Was the tight monetary policy effective? University of Wisconsin, Department of Economics. Unpublished Manuscript.

Eichenbaum, Martin, and Charles L. Evans. 1995. Some empirical evidence on the effects of shocks to monetary policy on exchange rates. *Quarterly Journal of Economics* 110 (4): 975–1009.

Fischer, Stanley. 1998. The Asian crisis: A view from the IMF. Address at the Midwinter Conference of the Bankers' Association for Foreign Trade. 22 January,

Washington, D.C. Available at [www.imf.org/external/np/speeches/1998/012298. htm].

Furman, Jason, and Joseph E. Stiglitz. 1998. Economic crises: Evidence and insights from East Asia. *Brookings Papers on Economic Activity,* Issue no. 2:1–135. Washington, D.C.: Brookings Institution.

Goldfajn, Ilan, and Taimur Baig. 1998. Monetary policy in the aftermath of currency crises: The case of Asia. IMF Working Paper no. WP/98/170. Washington, D.C.: International Monetary Fund.

Goldfajn, Ilan, and Poonam Gupta. 1999. Does monetary policy stabilize the exchange rate following a currency crisis? IMF Working Paper no. WP/99/42. Washington, D.C.: International Monetary Fund.

Gould, David M., and Steven B. Kamin. 2000. The impact of monetary policy on exchange rates during financial crises. International Financial Discussion Paper no. 669. Washington, D.C.: Board of Governors of the Federal Reserve System.

Grilli, Vittorio, and Nouriel Roubini. 1996. Liquidity models in open economies: Theory and empirical evidence. *European Economic Review* 40 (3–5): 847–59.

International Monetary Fund. 1997a. Thailand letter of intent, 14 August 1997. Available at [http://www.imf.org/external/np/loi/081497.htm].

———. 1997b. Thailand letter of intent, 25 November 1997. Available at [http:// www.imf.org/external/np/loi/112597.htm].

———. 1998. Thailand letter of intent and memorandum on economic policies, 24 February 1998. Available at [http://www.imf.org/external/np/loi/022498.htm].

Radelet, Steven, and Jeffrey D. Sachs. 1998. The East Asian financial crisis: Diagnosis, remedies, prospects. *Brookings Papers on Economic Activity,* Issue no. 1:1–74. Washington, D.C.: Brookings Institution.

Comment   Robert Dekle

During the recent East Asian currency crisis, the relationship between exchange rates and interest rates became a topic of intense controversy. The traditional view stresses that tight monetary policies are necessary to support the exchange rate: higher interest rates raise the returns that an investor obtains from investing in the country, reduce capital flight, and discourage speculation. However, recently some prominent economists (Radelet and Sachs 1998; Furman and Stiglitz 1998) have argued a revisionist view that a rise in interest rates depreciates the exchange rate.

The revisionist view is that under the unique conditions of a financial panic, tight monetary policies and high interest rates would result in capital outflows and exchange rate depreciation. That is, high interest rates cause a financial implosion and raise default probabilities, causing capital to flow out and weakening the currency. High rates can compromise the net worth of many firms, and the bankruptcy of these firms can have adverse effects on the net worth of the firms' creditors, especially that of domestic

Robert Dekle is associate professor of economics at the University of Southern California.

banks. In turn, as these banks fail and cut lending, credit can become constrained, further raising bankruptcies and causing capital to flee.

Recently, there has been much empirical work examining the interest rate–exchange rate nexus in emerging-market countries during crisis. This work can be divided into those using high-frequency (daily or weekly) time series data and those using cross-country or panel data. As to the work using time series data, the results have generally been mixed. Goldfajn and Baig (1998) and Dekle, Hsiao, and Wang (1999) find sharp evidence that interest rates appreciate exchange rates, whereas Gould and Kamin (2000) are unable to find a reliable relationship between interest rates and exchange rates. As to the work using cross-country or panel data, the results are again mixed. Goldfajn and Gupta (1999) find that high interest rates appreciate the exchange rate, but only in countries with strong banking sectors. Furman and Stiglitz (1998) find that if the sample is restricted to low-inflation countries—which include East Asia—high interest rates lead to exchange rate depreciations.

The paper by Kenneth West and Dongchul Cho is a significant advance over the earlier work that uses time series data. The earlier work was nonstructural and simply ran vector autoregressions (VARs) of nominal exchange rates on nominal short-term interest rates. The work tried to infer causality by testing whether changes in interest rates temporally preceded (led) changes in exchange rates. The results from these VARs were fragile and depended critically on sample frequency (daily or weekly), sample period (starting and ending dates), and lag length. Moreover, given that both exchange rates and interest rates are endogenous, forward-looking variables, it was difficult to infer causality from simple leads and lags.

West and Cho's paper significantly improves upon the earlier time series work. The authors develop and estimate an explicit structural model of the interest rate–exchange rate nexus. The West and Cho model contains three equations. In addition to the usual uncovered interest rate parity equation (their equation [1]), the model contains a monetary policy equation, in which monetary authorities react to expected exchange rate depreciations (equation [2]), and an equation relating the exchange rate risk premium to the interest rate (equation [3]). Given explicit assumptions about expectations formation (model consistent, rational expectations), the timing of monetary policy, and the nature of shocks, the parameters of the model can be identified. The estimation of these equations allows for an explicit test of the revisionist view: whether the risk premium increases in response to a rise in interest rates, and if so, whether the response is strongly positive enough to warrant a depreciation of the exchange rate.

West and Cho estimate their model on weekly data for Korea, the Philippines, and Thailand. In Korea, exchange rate risk premiums are found to be negatively related to interest rates, thus supporting the traditional view of the relationship between interest rates and exchange rates. In the Philippines, risk premiums are positively related to interest rates, but not strongly positive enough to warrant the reversal of the traditional view. In Thailand, risk premiums are strongly positively related to interest rates, thus supporting the revisionist view. West and Cho vary their sample starting dates, and although their parameter estimates are somewhat unstable, their conclusions, based on their point estimates, are generally robust.

Some international economists may be surprised by West and Cho's success in finding a relationship between exchange and interest rates, especially in emerging markets during crises. After all, it is well known that, in general, there is no stable empirical short-run relationship between exchange and interest rates, even in industrial countries, in tranquil times (Frankel and Rose 1995). Nominal exchange rates move as if they are a random walk. On closer examination, however, West and Cho's results appear consistent with the earlier findings. In particular, West and Cho admit that their standard error bands are very wide; for example, the sensitivity of Korea's risk premium to the interest rate is –8.87, with a 90 percent confidence interval of –27.7 to 14.2. Varying the sample period results in a different sensitivity, implying some parameter instability, just as in earlier findings. Moreover, given the large standard error bands, should the West and Cho model be used to predict exchange rates, the predictive performance (root mean squared error) of their model would probably be inferior to that of a simple random walk.

I have two minor quibbles with the underlying assumptions of West and Cho's model. First, the solution to West and Cho's model imposes rational expectations. Thus, agents are assumed to know not only the model, but the parameters and the shock processes of the model as well. Although this may be a reasonable assumption for industrialized economies in tranquil times, for emerging markets in crisis, the rational expectations assumption may be too strong. For most East Asian countries, the crisis was an unexpected, one-off event. The residents in these countries had no experience with crisis regimes. Thus it is unlikely that the residents would know or be able to estimate the parameters of the model.

Second, in West and Cho's monetary policy reaction function, equation (2), the monetary authorities' interest rate rule is assumed to depend solely on the expected depreciation rate. As the authors acknowledge, during the Asian crisis the monetary authorities also cared about additional variables, such as the levels of economic activity and foreign exchange reserves. For example, during the crisis period in Korea, the authorities were carefully observing daily bankruptcies in the Seoul area, as a measure of economic activity, and the level of foreign exchange reserves. Figure 1C.1 shows that during the crisis period, the authorities' monetary control variable, the overnight call rate, was positively correlated with daily bankruptcies and negatively correlated with reserves.

Strong assumptions, however, are necessary in any useful model. To un-

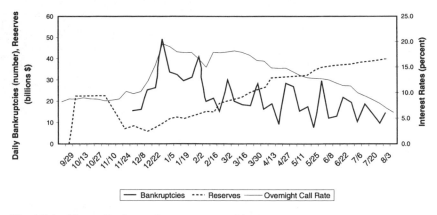

Fig. 1C.1   Korea: Bankruptcies, reserves, and interest rates

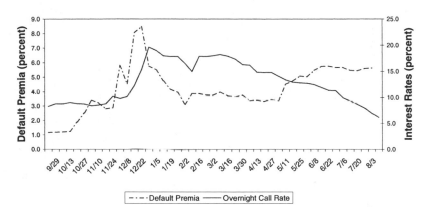

Fig. 1C.2   Korea: Default premia and interest rates

derscore the usefulness of the West and Cho model in understanding the interest rate–exchange rate nexus during the Asian crisis, examine figure 1C.2. The figure shows the correlation between the Korean overnight call rate and the default premiums on Korean sovereign bonds. From the figure it is difficult to draw any firm conclusions about the relationship between interest rates and the default premiums. The default premiums are positively correlated with the interest rate, thus tending to support the revisionist view. However, the default premiums temporally lead the interest rate, rather than lagging, which casts doubt on whether the interest rate is causing changes in the default premiums. West and Cho's model shows that if monetary authorities are, as it were, leaning against the wind in expected exchange rate depreciations, the interest rate rises, and the exchange rate appreciates with a lag in response to a risk premium shock (their figures 1.3 and 1.4). Interest rates and exchange rates are positively correlated, and this correlation is a result of monetary authorities' actively raising the interest rate. Thus, if observed default premiums on Korean bonds are contemporaneously correlated with risk premium shocks, the pattern observed in figure 1C.2 is certainly consistent with the traditional view of the interest rate–exchange rate nexus.

In sum, the West and Cho paper is very useful in understanding the interest rate–exchange rate nexus during the East Asian crisis. It should become the standard reference on this topic.

References

Dekle, R., C. Hsiao, and S. Wang. 1999. Interest rate stabilization of exchange rates and contagion in the Asian crisis countries. University of Southern California. Unpublished Manuscript.

Frankel, J., and A. Rose. 1995. Empirical research on nominal exchange rates. In *Handbook of international economics,* Vol. 3, ed. G. Grossman and K. Rogoff, 1689–721. Amsterdam: North-Holland.

Furman, J., and J. Stiglitz. 1998. Economic crisis: Evidence and insights from East Asia. *Brookings Papers on Economic Activity,* Issue no. 2:1–135. Washington, D.C.: Brookings Institution.

Goldfajn, I., and T. Baig. 1998. Monetary policy in the aftermath of currency crisis: The case of Asia. IMF Working Paper no. WP/98/170. Washington, D.C.: International Monetary Fund.

Goldfajn, I., and P. Gupta. 1999. Does monetary policy stabilize the exchange rate following a currency crisis? IMF Working Paper no. WP/99/42. Washington, D.C.: International Monetary Fund, March.

Gould, D. M., and S. Kamin. 2000. The impact of monetary policy on exchange rates during financial crisis. International Finance Discussion Paper no. 699. Washington, D.C.: Board of Governors of the Federal Reserve System.

Radelet, S., and J. Sachs. 1998. The East Asian financial crisis: Diagnosis, remedies, prospects. *Brookings Papers on Economic Activity,* Issue no. 1:1–74. Washington, D.C.: Brookings Institution.

Discussion Summary

Jeffrey Shafer suggested that specific histories and observations are often helpful in terms of understanding economic relationships. He added that an interest rate increase often stabilizes the exchange rate, whereas a subsequent premature lowering of the interest rate will destroy credibility.

Yung Chul Park made reference to figure 1.5 of the paper and noted that Korean interest rates and exchange rates were stabilized around February 1998. He argued that debt restructuring was the cause of the observed stabilization.

Martin Feldstein remarked that the real question is not just whether the interest rate can stabilize the currency but whether it makes sense to let the interest rate increase when we consider the adverse effects on the economy.

Andrew K. Rose remarked that he was generally suspicious of case-study approaches, although he agreed with the conclusion of the paper, that interest rate defense does seem to work.

Martin Feldstein pointed to Sweden and Turkey as examples of regions where interest rate defense didn't work. *Allan Drazen* concurred and emphasized the issue of sample selection bias.

Robert P. Flood suggested that the authors take account of differences in fundamentals.

Michael M. Hutchison remarked that the argument for or against interest rate defense depends on the state of the financial sector and the debt positions of the country. He added that the type of debt structure matters as well.

Edwin M. Truman made a reference to Turkey's failed interest rate defense and remarked that the political implications of an interest rate defense should not be overlooked. Shafer added that Turkey's unwillingness to supply reserves to banks that were being squeezed in the interbank market for the financial sector caused the failure.

Andrew Berg pointed to the difference between the defense of a peg and a crisis in a free float. He added that the degree of capital mobility is essential in thinking about the interest rate defense.

Peter B. Kenen remarked that the timing of the introduction of the IMF programs differed across countries under attack. He concurred with Truman and asked whether the exchange rate depreciation or the interest rate increase will hurt the economy the most.

Kenneth D. West agreed with Shafer and Park that there is useful country-specific information. He agreed with Feldstein that the fundamental question is what constitutes good monetary policy; the Cho and West paper considers an important element of the answer to this question. He emphasized that the Cho and West paper allows for interest rate hikes to be associated with either exchange rate appreciations or depreciations. In response to Rose, he pointed out that the Cho and West paper provides for the possibility that variation in exchange rate risk premiums dominates exchange rate movements, thus allowing a stronger result than the work that Rose cited on the interest rate defense during crises. He agreed with the comments of several participants that in future work it would be useful to study countries with failed stabilization programs.

Interest Rate Defense against Speculative Attack as a Signal
A Primer

Allan Drazen

2.1 Introduction

In the light of recent currency crises, two key policy questions are how to defend a currency against attack and what the effects of different avenues of defense are. A commonly used defense is to raise short-term interest rates sharply to deter speculation. Interest rate defense has had both successes and failures, some quite spectacular. For example, Hong Kong raised overnight rates to several hundred percent and successfully defended its currency in October 1997 against speculative attack. On the other hand, Sweden similarly raised its interest rate by several hundred percent in its currency defense in September 1992, but the success was short-lived. These are but two examples. In many countries, raising very short-term rates to very high levels to defend the exchange rate appeared to have little effect in deterring speculation, whereas in others, moderate increases in the interest rate have seemed to dampen speculative pressures. In short, a first look at episodes leaves the question of the effectiveness of an interest rate defense very much open.

More formal empirical models are far from resolving this question. On the basis of a sample of over 300 successful and failed attacks, Kraay (1999) argues that high interest rates are neither a necessary nor a sufficient condition for preventing a devaluation. Hubrich (2000), in a large-sample study similar to Kraay's, does identify significant effects of monetary policy during

Allan Drazen is professor of economics at Tel-Aviv University and the University of Maryland and a research associate of the National Bureau of Economic Research.

The empirical work surveyed here is either from Stefan Hubrich's thesis or done jointly with him. The author owes him a large debt of gratitude for countless conversations on these issues. Financial support from the Yael Chair in Comparative Economics, Tel-Aviv University is also gratefully acknowledged.

currency crises. He finds that raising the nominal discount rate may *increase* the probability of a successful speculative attack, but that the result is conventional when the monetary policy stance is identified through domestic credit. He also examines how these results are affected by country characteristics, finding, for example, that countries with low prior reserves are more likely to choose an interest rate defense than countries with high reserves.

The lack of empirical consensus is mirrored by a relatively small number of theoretical papers on the interest rate defense. In spite of the importance of the question, the role of interest rates is deterring a speculative attack is only beginning to receive attention.[1] Textbook models indicate that with imperfect capital mobility high domestic currency interest rates are a tool to attract foreign capital and strengthen the domestic currency. From a more micro perspective, high interest rates deter speculation by increasing the cost of speculation. More precisely, when speculators borrow domestic currency to speculate against a fixed exchange rate (they short the domestic currency), high short-term interest rates make such borrowing very costly.

However, in assessing how high interest rates can deter speculation, this argument runs into a simple arithmetic problem. If the horizon over which a devaluation is expected is extremely short, interest rates must be raised to extraordinarily high levels to deter speculation when there is even a small expected devaluation. For example, even if foreign currency assets bore no interest, an expected overnight devaluation of 0.5 percent would require an annual interest rate of over 500 percent $[(1.005^{365} - 1) \times 100 = 517]$ to make speculation unprofitable. (See, e.g., the discussion in Furman and Stiglitz 1998, 75–76.)

This reasoning has been used to call into question how effective high interest rates can be in deterring an attack, suggesting, for example, why the Swedish defense failed. It suggests that sharply raising interest rates will have only marginal beneficial effects at best. Although the arithmetic problem suggests why spectacular defenses may have only limited effects, this reasoning leaves other questions unanswered. First, why, as seems sometimes to be the case, might an interest rate defense lead to even greater spectacular pressures against the currency? That is, why would there be *perverse* feedback from raising interest rates to speculative pressures? Second, even in the absence of perverse feedback effects, the arithmetic problem raises the question of why they ever work. How can an effectively minor change in the cost of speculation have such significant, and one might say *disproportional*, effects? There is another sort of disproportionality as well, namely that short-lived increases in interest rates sometimes appear to have much longer-term effects. Something other than a simple cost-of-borrowing effect must be present.

---

1. Formal models of an interest rate defense include Lall (1997), Drazen (2001), Lahiri and Végh (2000), Drazen (2000), and Flood and Jeanne (2000).

One possibility, which has been the focus of my research in this area, is that both disproportional and perverse effects reflect the *information* that raising interest rates provides to market participants. Specifically, high interest rates may signal the commitment of policy makers to defend the currency. (Anecdotal evidence suggests that this was the message the Swedish Riksbank wanted to send.) If so, the direct cost implications of high interest rates for speculators are irrelevant relative to the signal they provide. The signal may be what makes interest rate defense successful.

By the same token, *increases* in speculative pressure in the wake of an interest rate defense may also reflect a signaling effect. Raising interest rates instead of letting reserves decumulate in order to defend the currency may signal weak fundamentals, such as low reserves. It may also be read as a sign of government panic by speculators. Such information would only encourage further speculation.

Our central argument is that a major effect of high interest rates is to signal the government's willingness or ability to defend the exchange rate. That is, there are unobserved characteristics of the government that affect the probability that a defense will be mounted or continued, with policy choices being correlated with these characteristics. Hence, given imperfect information about these government characteristics, speculators use observed policy choices to make inferences about them and hence form (that is, update) the probability they assign to a devaluation. Signaling is presented not as an esoteric theoretical point, but as what I hope will be seen as a very sensible view of what governments are doing.

The purpose of this paper is to summarize some of this research, concentrating on the underlying theory, but with some discussion of the empirical work supporting the argument that the effects of high interest rates are in part due to their signal content. The paper is meant as an introduction to the basic approach that I have used in a number of papers, rather than as a paper meant to break new ground. That is, it is meant as a simple user's guide, as it were, to interest rate defense as a signal. Thus, the stress is on simple models meant to get the basic points across. The plan of the paper is as follows. In section 2.2, I discuss interest rate defense as a signal of commitment to defending the exchange rate. In section 2.3, I introduce an alternative way of defending and consider the information an interest rate defense conveys about the ability of a government to defend. A key result is that raising interest rates may send a negative signal, suggesting why there can be perverse effects. Section 2.4 presents some empirical evidence on the signaling hypothesis. Section 2.5 contains conclusions.

2.2   A Basic Model of Signaling Commitment

I begin with a model of signaling commitment to keeping the exchange rate fixed by raising short-term interest rates. I want to keep the model extremely simple in order to highlight how this signaling of commitment might work, that is, how raising interest rates allows a government that is committed to defending the exchange rate to separate itself in the eyes of investors from one that is not. The model presented is a variant of the model in Drazen (2001).

2.2.1   Basic Structure and Assumptions

Consider a finite-horizon discrete time model of defending the exchange rate or abandoning it. The timing of actions within a period is as follows. At the beginning of each period t a stochastic shock η_t is observed by both government and speculators. This shock may be to reserves, to the economy, and so on; the key point is that it affects the cost of maintaining the fixed exchange rate, as modeled below. Speculators then choose how much to speculate against the currency, given η_t, the interest rate i_t, and the probability p_t they assign to a devaluation (of known size) at the end of the period. Specifically, speculators borrow domestic currency from the government at an interest rate i_t to be repaid at the end of the period and use it to buy foreign currency reserves.

Maintaining the fixed exchange rate at t requires that reserves remain above some critical level. This determines a minimum interest rate i_t^H that must be maintained if the government is to defend the fixed parity, where i_t^H will depend on both p_t and η_t. On the basis of η_t and i_t^H, the government then decides in each period whether to defend the fixed exchange rate (denoted by choice of policy F) by holding the interest rate at i_t^H, or not to defend the parity and devalue (a policy N), consistent with a lower interest rate, which we will call i_t^o.

A number of features allow this dynamic signaling model to be kept simple without sacrificing the robustness of the basic insights. First, I consider an irreversible decision to abandon the fixed parity (in a way that will be made clear later). The important assumption is that not defending has a discrete cost. Considering, for example, a return to a fixed rate at some point in the future makes the model too complicated, whereas my goal is to illustrate the analytics of interest rate defense as a signal as simply as possible. What is central to a signaling approach is that demonstrating commitment to not abandoning the fixed rate is costly, where this cost is unobserved. Second, I concentrate on the decision of whether to raise interest rates, rather than how much to raise them (that is, on the optimal path of interest rates and reserves in defense of a fixed rate). This is reflected in the modeling assumption of a reserve target and a minimum interest rate increase consistent with maintaining the fixed rate. I discuss later some implications of raising interest rates to even higher levels to signal even greater "toughness."

Third, for simplicity of exposition, I do not explicitly model the decision of speculators. (See Drazen 2000 for an explicit model.) For an interest rate defense to be possible, there must be some deviation from interest rate parity. Simple uncovered interest parity cannot hold if the central bank is to have the ability to raise the interest rate in order to increase the net cost of speculation. Different models of interest rate defense use different arguments in this respect. In Drazen (2001), I assumed that speculators face an upward-sloping borrowing schedule when they borrow to finance their speculation. Hence, the speculators' decision implies a well-defined demand curve for borrowing at each point as a function of the interest cost of borrowing and expectations about a devaluation over the immediate future. Combined with the previous assumption about a level of reserves consistent with not abandoning the fixed exchange rate, this implies that at any point in time there is some interest rate that chokes off speculation in the very short term. These assumptions allow me to focus on the government's decision problem in a signaling context, on the role of uncertainty about the government's commitment to fixed rates in driving these decisions, and on exogenous shocks in determining the dynamics of interest rate defense.

2.2.2   The Government's Choice Problem

We now consider the workings of the model in more detail. A standard model of interest rate defense has two actors: speculators, who choose relative demands for currency given short-term interest rates and their beliefs about the likelihood of a devaluation in the near term; and the government (or central bank), which must choose whether and how to defend the currency in the face of speculative pressure.

Speculators' behavior may be summarized by the decision of how large a position to take, given the probability they assign to the fixed exchange rate's collapsing over the immediate horizon (call it p_t) and the interest cost of speculation (summarized as i_t). Speculator behavior implies, as indicated, that demand for reserves is a function of i_t, of the probability p_t, and of η_t, the variable summarizing the state of the economy, where η_t has a cumulative distribution $N(\eta_t)$, which we assume is unchanging over time. (We return to this assumption later.) As indicated above, this determines an interest rate consistent with defending the exchange rate in each period denoted i_i^H. Given i_i^H, we can then concentrate on the government's choice problem in period t, subject to the constraint that speculators' beliefs are rational given the government's behavior. This will be addressed later.

At time 0, the government announces a commitment to a fixed exchange rate, and at each subsequent date $t = 1, \ldots, T$, the government chooses either to maintain the fixed parity (policy F) or to devalue (policy N). In choosing whether or not to defend in a given period, the government minimizes a loss function, reflecting the costs it assigns to abandoning the exchange rate and the costs of defending. If the government is to maintain the fixed parity in period t, it must raise the interest rate to the level i_i^H. This implies a cost of high interest rates to the economy, denoted $\ell(i_i^H, \eta_t)$, where this cost reflects the now-standard arguments on the costs of high interest rates: the negative impact on economic activity; the effect of high interest rates on the corporate and financial sectors, with a risk of destabilizing a fragile banking system; the negative impact on mortgage interest rates, especially when these rates are directly indexed to money market rates and defense of the exchange rate requires holding market rates high for significant periods; and the impact of interest rates on increasing the government budget deficit. We assume that increases in η represent a worsening of the economy, so that an increase in η_t implies that $\ell(\cdot, \eta_t)$ rises for any value of i_t.

If the government chooses not to maintain the fixed parity, interest rates can be kept lower, at a level i_t^o. For simplicity it is assumed that $\ell(i_t^o, \cdot) = 0$, which is simply a normalization. However, abandoning the commitment to the fixed exchange rate has a cost x in the period of a devaluation and thereafter. This represents both the social loss the government assigns to abandoning the fixed rate (that is, the value to the economy that the government had put on maintaining fixed rates) and the cost it assigns to having reneged on its commitment to a fixed exchange rate.[2] It is assumed that a fixed exchange rate has no other costs per se, that is, costs associated with fixed rates themselves, rather than with the defense of fixed rates. (Alternatively, we could think of $\ell(\cdot,\cdot)$ as including such costs.) It is assumed that x is *not* observed by speculators, where governments can differ in their x, that is, in the cost they assign to abandoning the fixed exchange rate. A government that is more committed to defending the fixed rate is thus modeled as having a higher value of x. Whereas the policy maker knows his type, speculators know only the distribution of possible types x, as summarized by an initial distribution $G(x)$, initially defined over $[\underline{x}, \overline{x}]$, where $\underline{x} > 0$ is the lowest possible type at the beginning of period one. This distribution will be updated over time as a function of observed actions in a way that will be made explicit below.

The decision of a government of whether or not to defend in any period t can then be represented as comparing the cost of abandoning the exchange rate to the cost of defending it. Given our assumptions on the irreversibility of the decision to abandon, so that x must be paid every period thereafter, the cost of abandoning the exchange rate at t can be represented as

$$(1a) \qquad\qquad x + \beta x + \beta^2 x + \ldots + \beta^{T-t}$$

The immediate cost of defending at t is the loss $\ell(i_t^H, \eta_t)$. Defending today gives the option of either defending or abandoning the exchange rate next period, depending on which has a lower cost. Defending next period, in turn, allows the option of defending or not the following period, and so on.

---

2. Models of abandoning fixed exchange rates typically do not model the value of fixed rates per se, so this simple approach is consistent with the literature.

Hence, the cost of defending today may be represented as (see the appendix)

(1b)
$$\ell(i_t^H, \eta_t) + \beta E_t \min [x + \beta x + \beta^2 x + \ldots + \beta^{T-t-1},$$
$$\ell(i_{t+1}^H, \eta_{t+1}) + \beta E_{t+1}\min(\cdots)],$$

where E_t is the expectations operator and $\ell(i_{t+1}^H, \eta_{t+1}) \equiv \ell_{t+1}$ is a random variable as of t (due to the randomness of η_{t+1} and ℓ_{t+1} as of t), as are all values of $\ell(\cdot,\cdot)$ dated $t + 2$ and higher, with a distribution $F_{t+1}(\ell_{t+1})$ that is induced by the distribution of η_{t+1}. (In other words, the future cost of defending is uncertain because of uncertainty about the future state of the economy.) In period T the cost of defending is simply $\ell(i_T^H, \eta_T)$, which is compared to x. Equating equations (1a) and (1b) and assuming that a government that is indifferent defends, one can show that the condition in period t for defending the exchange rate is

(2)
$$x \geq \ell(i_t^H, \eta_t) - \beta O_{t+1},$$

where O_{t+1} is defined by the recursive relation

(3a)
$$O_{t+1} = \int_{\ell_{t+1}=0}^{\ell_{t+1}=x+\beta O_{t+1}} (x + \beta O_{t+1} - \ell_{t+1}) \, dF_{t+1}(\ell_{t+1})$$

and the terminal condition

(3b)
$$O_T = \int_{\ell_T=0}^{\ell_T=x} (x - \ell_T) dF_T(\ell_T).$$

(See the appendix) In equation (2), O_{t+1} can be interpreted as the option value of choosing to defend in period t.

Note that equation (2) with equality determines a cutoff type, x_t^*, who is just indifferent between defending and not defending (conditional on having previously defended), given speculative pressures and η_t. Note that an increase in η, by raising the cost $\ell(i_t^H, \eta_t)$ of defending, will raise the cutoff value x_t^*. This observation will be important later. A government's problem of whether to defend is easily represented. A government of type x will defend the exchange rate in period t as long as $x \geq x_t^*$. All types that satisfy this condition will defend; all types that do not and have previously defended will abandon the defense in period t.

2.2.3   The Evolution of Beliefs over Time and the Nature of Equilibrium

Using the above results, we can now consider the signal inherent in high interest rates. To do this, we must first consider how information about the government's commitment evolves over time. That is, how does information about the government's possible type x evolve as a function of past observed policy? The key to answering this question is to note first that if a government chose to defend the exchange rate at t, it is known that its type is greater than or equal to x_t^*. Hence, observing a defense at time t implies that as of the beginning of time $t + 1$, the lowest possible type is x_t^*; that is, $\underline{x}_{t+1} = x_t^*$. Hence, the set of possible types as of the beginning of time $t + 1$ is $[x_t^*, \overline{x}]$. Second, note that if the realization of η_t is sufficiently low, all possible types at t will defend; that is, $x_t^* < \underline{x}_t$, so that $\underline{x}_{t+1} = \underline{x}_t$.

We can summarize this discussion in terms of the type of equilibrium that prevails at t and the evolution of beliefs about government type that it implies. If fixed rates had been maintained until t, then if $x_t^* \le \underline{x}_t$ (that is, if η_t is sufficiently low), an equilibrium with no probability of devaluation prevails, that is, a pooling equilibrium. In this case, policy observed in t gives no new information about type and $\underline{x}_{t+1} = \underline{x}_t$. If, instead, $x_t^* > \underline{x}_t$, then a separating equilibrium prevails: types in the range $[\underline{x}_t, x_t^*)$ devalue; types in the range $[x_t^*, \overline{x}]$ maintain fixed rates. Observing a defense provides new information about possible types that is used to update beliefs. That is, observing a defense at t when $x_t^* > \underline{x}_t$, speculators truncate the set of possible types for $t + 1$, so that $\underline{x}_{t+1} = x_t^* > \underline{x}_t$. Formally, based on the policy action observed in t, speculators update the distribution of possible types and form a new distribution $G(x \mid \underline{x}_{t+1})$ from the initial distribution $G(x)$, defined by

(4)
$$G(x \mid \underline{x}_{t+1}) = \frac{G(x) - G(\underline{x}_{t+1})}{1 - G(\underline{x}_{t+1})},$$

where $\underline{x}_{t+1}$ is defined as above. Updating of possible types provides information on the possible course of future policies that is the essence of the signaling argument.

On the basis of the evolution of $\underline{x}_t$, we can derive rational beliefs of speculators consistent with optimal government behavior. This closes the model, because government behavior in each period was based on speculative demand derived from p_t, the probability that speculators assigned to a devaluation. That is, we equate p_t to the probability of a devaluation based on optimal government behavior, where this probability reflects beliefs over possible government types. Given that speculators observe η_t before forming their expectation of p_t, the probability of a devaluation in the current period, conditional on no previous devaluation's having been observed, is simply the probability that x lies in the interval $[\underline{x}_t, x_t^*)$ conditional on the cumulative distribution $G(x \mid \underline{x}_t)$ as defined by equation (4). This is simply $G(x_t^* \mid \underline{x}_t)$.

2.2.4   High Interest Rates as a Signal

The signal content of high interest rates follows from the nature of a separating equilibrium as described above. When there is a nonzero probability that a government would not defend (which is necessary for speculators to launch an attack), a defense leads to a discrete upward revision in x_t. This implies a discrete upward revision in the probability of a future defense under any circumstances in which this probability was less than 1. (That is, for any realization of η_t such that $x_t^* > \underline{x}_t$, an increase in $\underline{x}_t$ raises the probability of a defense.) An especially clear example is that a defense under a given set of circumstances today (that is, for a specific realization of η_t) implies that the exchange rate will be defended in the future under the same circumstances.[3] (Remember that the distribution of η_t was assumed to be unchanging over time.) This example gives a clear illustration of a disproportionality effect, because the effect in choking off future speculation under identical circumstances is independent of the size of the interest rate increase needed to defend the exchange rate today.

Put another way, this formulation makes it possible to formalize the notion that it may be optimal to hang tough to send a signal, as it were. A government with a relatively high value of x will find it optimal to defend a fixed exchange rate in circumstances in which weaker (that is, lower x) governments would not in order to separate itself. By "hanging tough" in difficult circumstances today, a government can induce speculators to raise their expectation of the government's x. This will be especially true when a high value of η_t is seen as transitory.

This model could be extended in several ways. Economic circumstances could be deteriorating over time, as in the basic first-generation model, so that the cost of defense is becoming progressively higher. (Formally, this could be represented by the distribution of η_t's changing over time so that high realizations of η are becoming more likely.) Known deterioration would generally imply that there is a lower benefit from defending today. This case is studied in greater detail in Drazen (2001). This effect would be strengthened if deterioration is endogenous to tough defense, for example, when a defense weakens the reserve or the fiscal position of a country, thus making it more vulnerable to future attack. This general sort of argument was explored in a different context in Drazen and Masson (1994); we return to it in section 2.3.3, in the context of signals of the ability to defend the exchange rate.

The discussion in the previous two paragraphs should shed light on the question of whether it is sensible to incur costs today to build a reputation, in the sense of increasing speculators' rational expectation of type. It depends on the government's beliefs about the evolution of η_t. If the government believes that the current (speculation-inducing) state is transitory, then incurring high costs today to build a reputation is sensible. On the other hand, if the high values of η_t are believed to have a strong permanent

---

3. Technically speaking, the finite horizon makes this statement inexact, as the same realization of η at a later date implies a different choice problem. It will be strictly correct for an infinite horizon and approximately correct if T is sufficiently far in the future. Conceptually, the point being made should be clear.

component, then hanging tough to build a reputation not only makes little sense, but also implies a futile waste of costly resources. The latter scenario seems to describe the situation of many countries that vainly attempt to maintain a fixed parity, as in the case of the United Kingdom in the early 1990s.

Another extension is to consider the possibility of raising the interest rate even higher than what is necessary to deter current speculation (what we called i_t^H). One might argue that such action is the essence of sending a signal about commitment to defending the fixed exchange rate. I postponed discussion of this issue until now, because I think that the framework that has been set out and the discussion in the previous paragraphs make it easier to understand what is involved. Consider raising the interest rate to a level $i_t^{HH} > i_t^H$, that is, strictly above what is necessary to defend the exchange rate. The higher interest rate implies a higher economic cost $\ell(i_t^{HH}, \cdot)$, so that the associated cutoff level would be $x_t^{**} > x_t^*$. Hence, a tougher reputation could be obtained (in the sense of a lower value of $G(x_t^{**} \mid \underline{x}_t)$) at the cost of a larger current economic loss from the interest rate policy used to defend the exchange rate. Allowing a choice of the level of the interest rate used to defend the exchange rate could then be analyzed in a signaling model in terms of considering this tradeoff in an intertemporal context. I do not pursue the details here.

2.3 Signaling Ability to Defend the Exchange Rate

The foregoing model does not allow for interest rate defense to send a *negative* signal. That is, there is no possibility that raising interest rates in the face of a speculative attack not only may fail to reduce speculative pressures over time, but may actually serve to increase them. Both specific episodes and the findings of Kraay (1999) suggest that this is a real possibility. Because there was only one way to defend the exchange rate in the model, defense signals commitment and thus has a positive effect. Hence, one may ask what signal might be sent by use of interest rate defense when it is used in place of another defense option. This is exactly the question posed in Drazen (2000), in which it is shown that, depending on what government characteristics are unobserved, an interest defense may send a negative or mixed signal. In this section we explore this possibility more fully.

In the previous section we concentrated on signaling commitment to defend the exchange rate, with speculation being fueled by the belief that a government is not willing to bear too-high costs of defending the exchange rate. Speculation against a currency may also reflect the belief that the government lacks the ability or the resources to defend the exchange rate. The most basic argument here is that a government lacks the reserves to defend the exchange rate, where neither the central bank's reserve position nor its commitment to fixed rates is fully observed by speculators,[4] and governments may differ in both of these dimensions, that is, in their type.

2.3.1   Interest Rate versus Borrowing Defense

The starting point is that, in reality, a central bank has a number of actions available to it in meeting a speculative attack. It may intervene in either the forward or the spot market; if it intervenes in the spot market, intervention may be financed either with its own reserves or with borrowed reserves; it may restrict domestic credit to speculators or raise the interest rate at which they borrow; or it may put controls on credit to specific borrowers or on other foreign exchange operations (such as foreign exchange swaps). Except for the strategy of imposing credit controls, active defense strategies come down to either letting interest rates increase to reduce speculative demand, or using its reserves to meet demand (or some combination of these). This strategy often entails borrowing reserves to meet large outflows, hence the term *borrowing defense*.

The key point is that when both a borrowing and an interest rate defense are possible, these strategies have *different* costs, depending on whether there is a devaluation. If the fixed rate is successfully defended, then the reserve outflow associated with the attack will be reversed, so that borrowing can be easily paid back. The cost is the interest cost of borrowing, although this may not be large, especially if borrowing is from other central banks under existing short-term financing facilities. However, if there is a devaluation, then closing the short position in foreign currency can be quite costly. It is this that leads central banks to limit their short positions and that constitutes the principal direct cost of a borrowing defense. Hence, the cost of a borrowing defense may be less than that of an interest rate defense if defense is successful, but greater if it is unsuccessful.

Denoting by ℓ^H, ℓ^{ZS}, and ℓ^{ZU} an interest rate defense (with or without devaluation), a successful borrowing defense, and an unsuccessful borrowing defense, we may represent relative costs by the ranking

$$(5) \qquad\qquad \ell^{ZU}(\cdot) > \ell^{H}(\cdot) > \ell^{ZS}(\cdot).$$

The key assumption is that $\ell^{ZU} > \ell^H$; that is, an unsuccessful borrowing defense is seen by the government as more costly than an interest rate defense. In other words, a borrowing defense is preferred if it is successful but not if it is unsuccessful. The source of this distinction is the significant capital loss on its short foreign currency position that a central bank will suffer if it borrows massively and then devalues.

---

4. The idea is that published statistics on foreign exchange reserves do not give a fully accurate picture of reserves available to defend the exchange rate.

2.3.2   A Basic Model: Setup

The role of these assumptions can be seen in a model that is a variant of the one presented in section 2.2. A full treatment may be found in Drazen (2000). A key change is that there must be a possibility that the government mounts a defense that subsequently fails. Abandoning the fixed exchange rate may reflect not only a policy decision even when reserves are sufficient to continue, but also the realization of an adverse reserve shock. For simplicity of exposition, we represent this as a probability $q(R_t)$, where R_t are reserves of the central bank at the beginning of the period, and where $q' < 0$. As indicated above, it is assumed that speculators do not observe the government's reserve position as of the beginning of the period, as well as not observing their x.

In this extended model, the sequencing of actions is as follows. At the beginning of each period, speculators choose how much to speculate against the currency, on the basis of previously and currently observed variables, the distribution of unobserved variables, the probability they assign to a devaluation at the end of the period on the basis of those distributions, and the interest cost of speculation. The central bank then chooses whether to defend the fixed exchange rate and, if so, whether to do so via borrowing or raising interest rates. (If it chooses not to defend, it devalues at the beginning of the period.) After the central bank has chosen a defense, there is a shock to reserves that may force a devaluation, as represented in the previous paragraph. Hence, the model allows both devaluation as a policy choice, consistent with second-generation models of currency crisis, and devaluation as unavoidable, due, for example, to running out of reserves, as in first-generation models of currency collapse. At the end of the period, speculators exchange their foreign currency for domestic currency and pay off their borrowing. In the case of no devaluation, speculators update the probability of a devaluation in the following period.

2.3.3   Signaling Ability to Defend

One may then ask how a government will behave when both its x and its R are not observed. A key result in Drazen (2000) is that a government that chooses an interest rate defense is one with a high x but a low R, that is, with a strong commitment to fixed rates to defend, but with a relatively weak reserve position. The result and the intuition behind it may be illustrated by period T. With a probability q of a devaluation and using the fact that the loss from an interest rate defense is the same whether or not there is a devaluation, the expected loss from an interest defense is

$$(6) \qquad q(x + \ell^H) + (1 - q)\ell^H = qx + \ell^H,$$

and the expected loss from a borrowing defense that implies the same level of reserves is

(7)
$$q(x + \ell^{ZU}) + (1 - q)\ell^{ZS}.$$

Equating equations (9) and (10), we obtain a critical value of the devaluation probability, which we will call $q_T^*(\cdot)$, such that the government is indifferent between the two policies. This in turn implies a critical level of reserves, R_T^*, namely

(8)
$$R_T^* = q^{-1}[q_T^*(\cdot)].$$

For $R_T \geq R_T^*$, equation (5) implies that the expected loss from an interest rate defense in equation (6) exceeds the expected loss from a borrowing defense in equation (7), so that a borrowing defense is chosen, whereas for $R_T < R_T^*$, the ranking of the expected loss from the two policies is reversed, so that the interest rate defense is chosen.

Drazen (2000) shows (in the context of a two-period example that could be extended) that the government's decision in an earlier period is similarly characterized once the signal inherent in type of defense is taken into account; that is, a government with reserves below a critical level will choose an interest rate defense (if it chooses to defend), whereas one with a higher level of reserves will choose a borrowing defense. The intuition of these results is straightforward. Suppose that the fixed rate must be abandoned if the reserve position is too low and that the reserve position is also affected by exogenous reserve shocks, as discussed above. Then a central bank with a low level of reserves would have a greater incentive to hold onto its reserves than one with a high level of reserves and, hence, would be more likely to use an interest rate defense than a reserve defense to try to maintain the fixed rate. (Of course, in a separating equilibrium, low reserve governments find it optimal to choose the interest rate defense in spite of the negative signal it sends, due to the risks of either letting reserves run down or borrowing reserves.) Hence, raising interest rates would signal low reserves and thus may only encourage further speculation.[5] To employ our earlier terminology, if the raising of interest rates is taken as a signal of low reserves, there may be a "perverse feedback" effect.

Conditional on the type of defense chosen, we can then ask the question of whether a defense is undertaken. This is the question addressed in section 2.2. Combining those results with the results here, one may argue that observing an interest rate defense indicates that $R_T < R_T^*$ and that $x \geq x_t^*$. Hence, an interest rate defense is a mixed signal, as it indicates a high degree of commitment to the fixed rate but a low level of R, that is, weak fundamentals.

An alternative story is one in which high interest rates signal strong fundamentals. Suppose that rather than reserves, the key fundamental that is not fully observed is the government's fiscal position. To see why this can be

---

5. In common parlance, a high interest rate defense might signal that the government is panicking due to a weak reserve position.

a positive signal when the fiscal position is unobserved, consider first the case in which it is observed. High interest rates weaken the government's fiscal position, so that a tough defense today may actually lower the credibility of the fixed rate tomorrow due to the deterioration in the fiscal position it implies. (This is the effect stressed by Drazen and Masson 1994.) This is true both for weak fiscal fundamentals and for other structural weaknesses. It also suggests one reason that an interest rate defense is not mounted, as in the case of the United Kingdom in September 1992.

If the fiscal position is unobserved, then the willingness to raise the interest rate may signal a strong fiscal position, because the negative impact of high rates may be stronger the weaker is the fiscal position. That is, the worse the fiscal position, the less willing the government will be to raise interest rates to defend the currency (and the more fragile is the fixed exchange rate if the government's fiscal position is important to its health). Hence, if, for example, the level of government debt is not fully observed, raising interest rates in defense of the currency is a signal of fiscal health and may have a positive effect in deterring speculation beyond what the increase in the arithmetic cost of borrowing would imply.

To close the model, one calculates the probability that the fixed exchange rate collapses in a period, where this includes the possibility that the government chooses not to defend and that the fixed rate collapses due to an exogenous shock, and where this depends on the distribution of the unobserved fundamental. For example, in the case of unobserved reserves and commitment, the probability that speculators assign to collapse would be of the form

$$(9) \quad p_t = \int_{R_t} \{G[x_t^*(R_t) \, | \, j_{t-1}] + 1 - G[x_t^*(R_t) \, | \, j_{t-1}]\Omega(R_t)\} d\Psi(R_t \, | \, j_{t-1})$$

where $\Omega(R_t)$ is the probability of a shock forcing devaluation conditional on R_t, $G[x_t^*(R_t) \, | \, j_{t-1}]$ is the cumulative distribution of commitment types conditional on policy previously observed, denoted j_{t-1}, and $\Psi(R_t \, | \, j_{t-1})$ is the cumulative distribution of reserves conditional on the policy previously observed. Lower reserves make a devaluation more likely both because a given x type is less likely to defend and because, having chosen to defend, he is more likely to be forced to devalue due to an exogenous shock.

2.4   Testing the Signaling Approach

In this section, we quickly review some evidence on whether the signaling approach is relevant, based on Hubrich (2000) and Drazen and Hubrich (2002).

2.4.1   Country Characteristics

Hubrich (2000) considers whether the effectiveness of restrictive monetary policy during an attack actually differs according to certain characteristics, such as debt or prior reserves, and finds evidence that this is the case in a large cross-country sample of speculative attacks on fixed exchange rates. Attacks are identified as large observations of an index aggregating reserve losses and exchange rate devaluations. The policy variables considered are domestic credit (the net domestic assets on the central bank's balance sheet) and the nominal discount rate. The stance of policy is determined as the policy during the attack relative to a prior average, where of course a contractionary policy refers to contractions in domestic credit or increases in the discount rate. The sample is then split into a high and a low subsample according to a certain characteristic, and the policy rule has been obtained separately for each subsample. Comparing the policy rule between the two subsamples, Hubrich examines whether the policy pursued during an attack is related to country characteristics in a way that, if the characteristic were unobserved, could signal crucial information. He finds that contractionary policies are more likely for countries characterized by low reserves or low public debt. The former is fully consistent with the perverse signaling effect previously discussed, whereby governments with low prior reserves are more likely to use an interest rate defense than a reserve-based defense. The latter finding is in line with the positive signaling argument presented for the case of unobserved fiscal fundamentals, whereby a country with high public debt is averse to an interest rate defense because of the impact on its fiscal position.

However, note that these findings are a rather weak test for the signaling hypothesis. If we found these characteristics did not matter (or mattered in the wrong direction), such a finding *would* have constituted strong evidence against signaling. However, finding that the policy rule does differ in the required manner is only the first step *toward* a signaling mechanism. In addition, signaling requires that these characteristics are not observed by investors, which is much more difficult to establish and was not pursued in Hubrich (2000).

2.4.2   The Term Structure of Exchange Rate Expectations

Because the signaling framework outlined above is based on policy providing information about exchange rate fundamentals otherwise unobserved, a natural direct test consists of relating exchange rate expectations to that policy. Signaling models suggest that "temporary" policies have permanent effects, in the sense that the signaling effect of high interest rates may outlast the high interest rate policy itself. This can be examined by looking at the term structure of exchange rate expectations: does interest rate policy affect exchange rate expectations similarly at all horizons, or does it only have an impact on short-term expectations? The more the effect is spread out across the entire term structure, the more it would seem that something fundamental is being signaled. Drazen and Hubrich (2002) present evidence using a set of survey data for exchange rate forecasts of different horizons to study the effect of interest rates on exchange rate expectations during the 1992–93 ERM crisis and in Brazil during the various crises between 1994 and 1998.

As far as signaling, there were several key findings. First, although there was generally little or no clear statistically significant effect of raising interest rates on next month's expected exchange rate, this result masks significant effects on different components of the expected exchange rate and at different horizons. There was some evidence of a positive (i.e., appreciating the exchange rate) short-term effect, coupled with a negative longer-term effect, at horizons of twelve months or longer. An increase in overnight interest rates often induces an increase in the n month ahead rate relative to the k month ahead rate ($n > k$), thus implying an appreciation of next month's exchange rate, but also an increase in risk premiums and the exchange rate forecast a year ahead, implying a depreciation.

Second, the effects of changes in overnight interest rates that are observed are clearly nonlinear, often significantly so, and these effects may be either concave or convex. This is in contrast to the simple "arithmetic" argument for the effect of raising interest rates, but it is consistent with the signaling explanation (as well as some other explanations). The effects are mostly smaller in absolute value the larger the total interest rate increase is. This suggests that much of the information effect is already triggered by comparatively small interest rate defenses and that resorting to very high interest rates adds little information.

To summarize, the typical picture is that short-term effects are negative (representing improved expectations) for the very short term, and then they gradually increase as the term becomes longer, ending up in positive territory for the forecasts twelve months out or more (representing a deterioration of long-term expectations). Drazen and Hubrich (2002) suggested that this may reflect two signaling effects at work. First, there is a short-term effect, in that high interest rates today signal high interest rates (or strong commitment) for a couple of months to come. This effect is skewed toward the short term and dominates the short-term results, but it dies out in the medium to long term. The other effect is a negative signaling effect, in which high interest rates signal bad news about the overall fundamentals of the peg, deteriorating expectations at all horizons alike. This negative effect is outweighed by the policy signal in the short term, but it comes through dominantly in the medium to long term as the policy signal dies out. This picture is consistent with the mixed signal of an interest rate defense discussed at the end of section 2.3.

Drazen and Hubrich find that that these results are remarkably consistent across the countries in their sample, including Brazil. This suggests that signaling effects are surprisingly similar among fixed exchange rate regimes, even when the countries behind them are fairly different.

A final note of caution. Some of these findings are also consistent with alternative hypotheses, such as the "revisionist" argument of Furman and Stiglitz (1998) that the effect of high interest rates on the banking sector leads to an increase in default risk. They are also in part consistent with first-generation models of interest rate defense (see Flood and Jeanne 2000 or Lahiri and Végh 2000) in which an interest rate defense may bring the crisis forward because of its impact on the very macroeconomic fundamentals (specifically, debt) underlying the peg.

2.5   Conclusions

In this paper I have set out some basic results on the signaling effect of high interest rates. As was indicated in the introduction, the goal was neither to present a comprehensive or extremely technical exposition, nor to concentrate on new results. The aim was to present a fairly simple presentation of the main concepts and results, with the hope of making the ideas clear for a wider audience. My further aim was to try to convince readers of the usefulness of this approach in explaining the empirical findings about the effectiveness of interest rate defense. To this end, I also reviewed some econometric evidence consistent with the signaling approach. Although the tests are open to alternative explanations, they provide significant evidence toward the importance of signaling.

Appendix

We here derive the condition in equation (2) for an interest rate defense and the associated definition for O_t. In period T, the condition for a defense is obviously

$$(A1) \qquad\qquad x \geq \ell(i_T^H, \eta_T).$$

As of period $T-1$, the central bank may devalue (at a present discounted cost of $x + \beta x$) or may defend, in which case it faces a cost of $\ell(i_{T-1}^H, \eta_{T-1}) \equiv \ell_{T-1}$ and then chooses optimally in period T according to equation (A1). Thus, the condition for a defense in period $T-1$ is

$$(A2) \qquad\qquad x + \beta x \geq \ell(i_{T-1}^H, \eta_{T-1}) + \beta E_{T-1} \min(x, \ell_T),$$

where ℓ_T is a random variable as of time $T-1$. The "min" operator implies that

$$(A3) \quad E_{T-1}\min(x, \ell_T) = \int_{\ell_T=0}^{\ell_T=x} \ell_T dF(\ell_T) + \int_{\ell_T=x}^{\ell_T=\infty} x dF(\ell_T) = x - \int_{\ell_T=0}^{\ell_T=x} (x - \ell_t) dF(\ell_t),$$

so that equation (A2) becomes

$$(A4) \qquad x \geq \ell_{T-1} - \beta \int_{\ell_T=0}^{\ell_T=x} (x - \ell_T)dF(\ell_T),$$

with the second term on the right-hand side defining O_T. Similarly, in period $T-2$, we may write the condition for a defense as

$$(A5) \quad x + \beta x + \beta^2 x$$

$$\geq \ell(i^H_{T-2}, \eta_{T-2}) + \beta E_{T-2} \min\{x + \beta x, \ell_{T-1} + \beta E_{T-1}\min[x, \ell_T]\},$$

where ℓ_T and ℓ_{T-1} are random variables as of time $T-2$. Working from the inside bracket outward, one obtains

$$(A6) \qquad x \geq \ell_{T-2} - \beta \int_{\ell_{T-1}=0}^{\ell_{T-1}=x+\beta O_T} (x - \ell_{T-1})dF(\ell_{T-1}),$$

with the second term on the right-hand side defining O_{T-1}. In this manner one can easily derive that the condition for a defense in period t is as given in equation (2).

References

Drazen, A. 2000. Interest rate and borrowing defense against speculative attack. *Carnegie-Rochester Conference Series on Public Policy* 53:303–48.
———. 2001. Interpreting exchange rate defense against speculative attack. University of Maryland. Working Paper.
Drazen, A., and S. Hubrich. 2002. Assessing the effectiveness of interest rate defense: Interest rates as a signal. University of Maryland, Department of Economics. Working Paper.
Drazen, A., and P. Masson. 1994. Credibility of policies versus credibility of policymakers. *Quarterly Journal of Economics* 109:735–54.
Flood, R., and O. Jeanne. 2000. An interest rate defense of a fixed exchange rate? IMF Working Paper no. WP/00/159. Washington, D.C.: International Monetary Fund, October.
Furman, J., and J. Stiglitz. 1998. Economic crisis: Evidence and insights from East Asia. *Brookings Papers on Economic Activity,* Issue no. 2:1–114.
Hubrich, S. 2000. What role does interest rate defense play during speculative currency attacks? Some large-sample evidence. University of Maryland, Department of Economics. Working Paper.
Kraay, A. 1999. Do high interest rates defend currencies during speculative attacks? Working Paper. Washington, D.C.: World Bank.
Lahiri, A., and C. Végh. 2000. Delaying the inevitable: Optimal interest rate policy and BOP crises. University of California, Los Angeles, Department of Economics. Working Paper.
Lall, S. 1997. Speculative attacks, forward market intervention, and the classic bear squeeze. IMF Working Paper no. WP/97/164. Washington, D.C.: International Monetary Fund.

Comment   Robert P. Flood

The last time I commented on Allan Drazen's work on the interest rate defense of a fixed exchange rate was at the Spring International Finance and Macroeconomics meeting in Cambridge two years ago. I now think I got the interest rate defense issue almost half right at those meetings.

My discussion then was connected to Drazen's work at three points. First, both Drazen's work and my discussion took off from some kind of policy-exploitable wedge in the uncovered interest parity (UIP) relation. Without such a wedge, interest rate policy has no real-interest rate implications and is either a nonstarter—end of story—or it is really a nominal aggregates defense.

Second, in all of the work, beliefs about future policy actions determine, in part, market reactions to current policy moves. That's pretty standard. Drazen's emphasis has been on the rational formation of beliefs by private agents concerning some relevant information known only to the policy maker that cannot be revealed directly to the public in a completely convincing way.

Third, the two strands of work are "connected in the breach" in terms of fiscal policy. In, for example, Flood and Jeanne (2000; hereafter FJ), the real primary fiscal deficit/surplus is assumed invariant to the interest rate defense. This, plus perfect capital mobility, is the source of FJ's results. In Drazen's work, in contrast, feedback from the fiscal deficit is not modeled. I am fairly sure the only way he could be ignoring fiscal implications is if it is assumed implicitly that the primary deficit/surplus adjusts to pay the cost of the interest defense.

In my discussion today I want to do two things while keeping my eye on one other thing: First, as I said above, my previous discussion was almost half right. In later work (FJ), Olivier Jeanne and I got it completely half right. I would like to show the direction that I now think is more than half right. Second, I'll talk a little toward the end about adding aspects of signaling about future policy moves in this setup. Third, while I do the above, I will be clear about this fiscal deficit/surplus.

Here is a quick recap of the FJ-type results. FJ is a *shadow-rate* model (i.e., hypothetical flex rate with reserves exhausted). The FJ "money stuff" is suppressed presently.[1]

$$i_t = i^* + E_t e_{t+1} - e_t + \theta\left(\frac{N_t}{P_t}\right) \quad \text{portfolio balance}$$

Robert P. Flood is a senior economist at the International Monetary Fund.

1. At the end of this comment I discuss some of the (not very important) shortcuts, for example, "money stuff," that I use for presentation purposes.

$$\left(\frac{N_{t+1} - N_t}{N_t}\right) = i_t + \left(\frac{P_t d}{N_t}\right) \quad \text{nominal deficit}$$

$$\ln(P) = e \qquad\qquad \text{PPP}$$

where N is nominal debt, P is the price level, d is the real deficit/surplus, $(g - t)$ *minus real seigniorage*, for simplicity. In FJ, after an attack, the real side of the model is fixed and $N/P = PV(d)$, where PV represents the present value operator.

These are the results:

1. Raising i before a potential speculative attack always depreciates the shadow currency and thereby brings the attack closer in time.

2. Raising i after a speculative attack can appreciate the shadow value of the currency before the attack (strengthen the currency) if the economy is on the upward-sloping part of seignorage "Laffer Curve;" that is, raising i post-collapse will increase d through seigniorage.

Although I'm sure FJ is logically correct, I'm just as sure that the seigniorage Laffer curve really can't be what's going on here. If the above is half right, which I think it is, what is (somewhat) more than half right? Let's make the following changes:

$$i^s_t = i^{*s} + E_t e_{t+1} - e_t + \theta\left(\frac{N_t}{P_t}\right)$$

represents portfolio balance (watch for little s's). I am now using the portfolio balance condition for short-term debt, denoted s. Disaggregate government debt payments by term to maturity into

$$\frac{N_{t+1} - N_t}{N_t} = i^s_t \lambda + i^l_{t-1}(1 - \lambda) + \left(\frac{P_t d}{N_t}\right).$$

This is the nominal deficit again, but with debt shares. The short-term debt share is λ, with $0 \le \lambda \le 1$. Watch d. Remember too that i^l_{t-1} is contractual from last period.

Finally, make price (P) predetermined[2]

$$\ln(P_t) = E_{t-1} e_t \quad \text{sticky prices.}$$

The way I want to pay for the interest rate increase here is with N during period t and then for Pd to increase permanently next period by *just enough to service the new debt*. The budget was balanced before the interest rate defense, and it returns to balance in the period after the defense. This is needed just to keep the math simple. (Drazen must be doing something like this in the background, or else his fixed rate would explode. More on this later.)

---

2. This is the model of Flood and Engel (1985), with an as yet unspecified yield curve.

To see how the model works, let $\lambda = 1$, and suppose it is announced and believed that i_t^s is to be increased by, say, 10 percentage points (e.g., 0.10 to 0.20) for one period (one year) and then returned to its previous level and the budget rebalanced. Then, with N_t and P_t predetermined, N_{t+1} will increase by 10 percent as will other nominal variables. Since $e_t + 1$ will rise by the full 0.10, the current level of e_t need not move. The defense is ineffective—worse, actually, in terms of next period.

Now suppose $0 < \lambda < 1$: not all debt is short-term. Holding i_{t-1}^l fixed by contract at $t-1$, N increases now by the proportion $\lambda*0.10$, and other nominal variables increase in the same proportion. Since i_t^s rose by the full 0.10, however, e_t must fall by $(1-\lambda)*0.10$.

The implication is simple, plausible, and pretty obvious: low short-term (ST) debt makes it possible to "stick it to" long-term (LT) debt owners in an effective surprise *temporary* defense. Basically, the unwary LT debt owners are being taxed with a capital loss that is passed on to money and ST debt owners.

That a temporary short-term interest rate increase can strengthen the (shadow) currency when prices are sticky is an "interest rate policy update" of the famous Dornbusch overshooting result. Recall Dornbusch's finding that a (surprise) once-and-for-all monetary increase results in a more than proportionate short-term currency depreciation. Presently, a (surprise) short-term interest rate increase results in an equal increase in expected currency depreciation and *future* nominal debt expansion. Positioning for the required expected depreciation may require an initial currency appreciation (the flip side of overshooting).

The following are some things to work on:

1. There is a long-term bond price that I have left out for simplicity. A term-structure theory will price new LT bonds. (Second-period LTs are priced at $[\{1 + i_{t-1}^l\}/\{1 + i_t^s\}]$, but first-period LT pricing needs a bit of modeling. For now I'm assuming 100 percent ST financing on the margin.)

2. There seems to be a government versus LT bond holder game that must be lowering the price of LT bonds and influencing deficit financing. This may be making countries move more toward ST debt financing, particularly in turbulent times.

3. The way we got the math to work out is if the private sector believes with probability 1 that the interest rate increase is temporary, one period. If it lasts longer (say it dies away at the rate ρ where $0 < \rho < 1$), then $E_t e_{t+1}$ will rise by more than $\lambda*0.10$, so e_t need not fall.

Somehow the government must convince the private sector about temporariness with reference to i^s and about the debt-service cleanup with future Pd. This is exactly the problem Drazen is addressing, but in a slightly different setting. He uses i^s to convey *both* the promise of an interest check to bond holders and information about likely future actions.

Models of the Krugman, Flood, and Garber (KFG) type were based on agents who use unlimited data to infer correctly average future policy actions—the standard rational expectations methodology of the 1970s and 1980s. The innovation of many more recent models is an apparent "taste change" by both policy makers and researchers. Agents in the newer models have more realistic data endowments and therefore cannot possibly determine perfectly average future government actions.

Complete models that have both signaling and (say) KFG fundamentals will have reduced-form coefficients on fundamentals with a KFG part and a signaling part. Model-constrained estimation will allocate the importance of the parts.

Finally, there are two more areas that warrant further work:

1. Although the interest rate defense may have worked this period, there is nothing we have done to indicate it did not set in motion events that will spell the fixed rate's demise next period.

2. When Drazen discusses his and Hubrich's key empirical findings he invokes a second signaling effect, which makes all this appear remarkably similar to the standard fundamentals story.

These are some places where I have cheated (a little):

1. The complete (in levels) UIP "wedge" is $\theta[(N - M)/P]$. I've left out the M/P term. It complicates things but does not change the argument fundamentally.

2. $d = g - t + i(M/P)$

3. In the disaggregated part, I've said that the wedge in ST UIP depends on real ratio aggregate debt N/P, where N is total debt.

References

Flood, Robert P., and C. Engle. 1985. Exchange rate dynamics, sticky prices, and the current account. *Journal of Money, Credit and Banking* 17 (3): 312–27.

Flood, Robert P., and Olivier Jeanne. 2000. An interest rate defense of a fixed exchange rate? IMF Working Paper no. WP/00/159. Washington, D.C.: International Monetary Fund, October.

Discussion Summary

Michael P. Dooley remarked that if a successful interest rate defense depends on whether the incurred losses are imposed on the private sector, it is crucial whether the government is truly separated from the private sector.

Andrew Berg noted that Hong Kong conducted an interest rate defense without a large change in debt position.

Vince Reinhart remarked that a successful defense has implications for the term structure of interest rates and asked about the consequences of the endogeneity of interest rate defenses. He pointed to the question of whether the costs of a defense are hurting the government or the society as a whole and noted that in the discussant's model the costs are inflicted on the holders of consols.

Robert P. Flood remarked that the interest rate defense is factored into the long-run prices of debt.

John McHale made reference to the early stages of the Asian crisis and pointed to the importance of transparency.

Olivier Jeanne remarked that the presented model would benefit from the addition of two-sided imperfect information.

Allan Drazen acknowledged that two-sided imperfect information is desirable, but it also substantially complicates the model. He remarked that the economic costs of giving in to a speculative attack are not the only costs incurred; there is also the cost of losing face to be considered. Regarding the issue of whether the private sector or the government picks up the tab, he argued that a government will have an incentive for setting up an interest rate defense and inflicting the costs of borrowing on others, provided that there is time to readjust the fiscal position after the attack.

Does It Pay to Defend against a Speculative Attack?

Barry Eichengreen and Andrew K. Rose

3.1 Introduction

This paper adds an observation to the stock of empirical regularities in the literature on speculative attacks. Comparing the behavior of successful attacks on pegged exchange rates with successful defenses (instances when a speculative attack occurred but did not precipitate a significant change in the prevailing rate), we show that there are costs of failing to successfully defend against the attack. These are equivalent to approximately a year of economic growth, or 3 percentage points of gross national product (GNP). However, the output losses that follow successful attacks are only evident for short periods; the difference between successful attacks and successful defenses is significant for just one year.

This finding helps to account for a number of observations about the behavior of open economies and their policy makers.

Barry Eichengreen is the George C. Pardee and Helen N. Pardee Professor of Economics and Political Science at the University of California at Berkeley, a research associate at the National Bureau of Economic Research, and a research fellow at the Centre for Economic Policy Research. Andrew K. Rose is the B. T. Rocca Jr. Professor of Economic Analysis and Policy in the Haas School of Business at the University of California, Berkeley, a research associate at the NBER, and a research fellow at the Centre for Economic Policy Research.

The authors thank Carlos Arteta and Galina Hale for research assistance; the National Science Foundation, the Ford Foundation, and the World Society Foundation for financial support; Cam Harvey, Aart Kraay, David Leblang, and Gian Maria Milesi-Ferretti for help with data; and Allan Drazen, Kenneth Kletzer, Richard Portes, and conference participants for comments. The analysis was begun while Rose visited the Reserve Bank of New Zealand and Victoria University in Wellington; he thanks those institutions for hospitality and support. The STATA data set used to generate the results is available at [http://haas.berkeley.edu/~arose].

- Readiness to mount a defense. We regularly observe governments and central banks undertaking difficult policy adjustments (sharp hikes in interest rates, large fiscal cuts) in order to defend their currencies, despite objections that these policies may precipitate a recession. Our finding explains this behavior: the output costs of the alternative—failure to defend the currency—can be even higher.
- International Monetary Fund (IMF) exchange rate advice and conditionality. Although the IMF has repeatedly urged its members to abandon soft pegs in favor of greater exchange rate flexibility, it has also extended generous financial assistance to countries seeking to defend their currencies against attack.[1] Again, our finding helps to explain this behavior: exiting a peg in a crisis tends to result in costly output losses, something that the IMF as well as the national authorities wish to avoid.
- The V-shaped recovery from the Asian crisis. A number of observers have commented on the "V-shaped" recovery of the Asian countries from their 1997–98 crisis (sharp falls in output were followed by equally sharp recoveries after an interval of one to two years). We show that, rather than reflecting unique characteristics of Asia's crisis or its economies, as is sometimes suggested, this pattern is quite general.[2] It is the typical response of output to a successful attack.

The question is whether this post-crisis behavior of output is a *consequence* of the success of the attack or simply a reflection of the *causes* of that outcome. Is it the resolve to mount a successful defense that determines the subsequent behavior of output, or is it the behavior of output (and associated variables) that determines the success or failure of the attack? To put the same point another way, is it the decision of how to respond to the speculative attack that shapes the subsequent performance of the economy, or do countries that are unable to defend their currencies have other problems that both render them unable to beat back the speculators and contribute to the severity of their post-crisis recessions?

The benefit of the doubt should be given to the view that it is differences in the pre-crisis characteristics of economies that explain both differences

---

1. In the words of the managing director, "Experience has shown that heavily managed or pegged exchange rate regimes can be tested suddenly by exchange markets, and that it can be very costly either to defend them or to exit under disorderly circumstances. On balance, we have a responsibility to advise our members that while such regimes can succeed, the requirements for a country to maintain a pegged or heavily managed exchange rate are daunting—especially when the country is strongly engaged with international capital markets" (Koehler 2001, 3–4).

2. Thus, authors like Sachs and Stiglitz have pointed to the quick rebound of output in countries like Korea as evidence that their crises reflected problems of investor panic rather than flawed fundamentals like those that underlie currency crises in many other emerging markets. Insofar as our results suggest that there was nothing special about the nature of the postcrisis behavior of output, such inferences become more difficult to draw.

in their abilities to rebuff a speculative attack and differences in the post-attack behavior of output. Imagine, for example, that growth is weakening and unemployment is rising. The authorities will then be less ready to employ higher interest rates to defend the currency. Knowing this, speculators will have more incentive to attack and a greater likelihood of success (Jeanne 1997). To the extent that output movements are persistent, post-crisis macroeconomic performance will be disappointing. However, it is not the success or failure of the attack that determines the behavior of output; rather, it is the behavior of output that determines the success or failure of the attack. To put the point another way, it is a third variable (the pre-crisis state of the economy) that determines the response of both policy makers and the economy to the crisis.[3]

Given this presumption, it is striking that we are unable to detect differences in the pre-crisis state of the economy that can explain the very different post-crisis performance in cases where speculative attacks succeed and cases where they fail.

- The behavior of output appears to be no different prior to successful attacks and prior to successful defenses.
- The behavior of other economic and financial variables appears to be no different prior to successful attacks and prior to successful defenses.
- The behavior of a variety of political variables appears to be no different prior to successful attacks and prior to successful defenses.
- Econometric techniques designed to account for unobservable differences in countries mounting successful and unsuccessful defenses do not weaken the finding of significant differences in the subsequent behavior of output.
- The addition of country credit ratings as a way of capturing otherwise unquantifiable economic and financial vulnerabilities changes none of our findings.
- Our key results survive a battery of additional sensitivity analyses.

Although the facts are clear, their implications are less so. Our preferred interpretation is as follows. Failure to successfully defend a currency against attack is a shock to confidence. Involuntary abandonment of the exchange rate regime that previously served as the nominal anchor for policy raises doubts in the minds of the markets about the prospects for stability. We thus observe a loss of policy discipline following a successful attack: the growth of the money base accelerates, and inflation rises (relative to cases

---

3. One can imagine a variety of other plausible arguments working in the same direction. For example, a heavy load of short-term foreign currency–denominated debt could both make governments less willing to raise interest rates to defend the currency (since higher interest rates will raise debt-servicing costs) and make the post-crisis economic performance weaker (since devaluation will make life more difficult for firms whose debts are denominated in foreign currency but whose revenues are domestic currency denominated).

in which the speculative attack is successfully rebuffed). Risk premia rise, depressing consumption and investment. Only countries that succeed in establishing a clear and credible alternative monetary anchor succeed in avoiding these costs. Examples that spring to mind include the United Kingdom and Sweden, which embraced inflation targeting, first implicitly and then formally, following their 1992 crises; Italy's continued commitment to European monetary unification following its ejection from the exchange rate mechanism (ERM); and Brazil's resort to inflation targeting following involuntary abandonment of its exchange rate peg in early 1998.

We establish these points in our paper, which is organized as follows. Section 3.2 describes the data and their characteristics. Section 3.3 then subjects them to multivariate analysis. Section 3.4 reports the results of a series of sensitivity analyses. Section 3.5, in concluding, returns to the broader implications of our findings.

To avoid confusion, we should reiterate what we do and do not set out to establish in this paper. Our concern is to compare post-crisis economic performance in cases in which the speculative attack succeeds and those in which it fails. It is to show that there is little evidence of differences in the pre-crisis structure and performance of the economies falling into these two categories that can help to account for the apparent different post-crisis outcomes. Our concern is *not* whether there are differences between countries that do and do not experience speculative attacks. The latter is a separate question. It is the subject of a different literature (much of which purports to identify leading indicators of currency crises). It is not our topic here.

3.2 Data

The macroeconomic and financial data used in this paper were extracted from the 2000 *World Development Indicators* CD-ROM produced by the World Bank.[4] They are annual and cover the period 1960–98. We consider essentially all middle- and high-income countries with average populations

---

4. The macroeconomic and financial variables we utilize include real GDP, private consumption, the consolidated government budget deficit (as a percent of GDP), the official bilateral dollar exchange rate, gross international reserves, the ratio of reserves to imports, the current account balance (as a percent of GDP), exports and imports of goods and services, total debt service (as a percent of GNP), deposit and lending rates (in percent), the interest rate spread (defined as the lending rate minus LIBOR), the consumer price index inflation rate, M1 and M2, credit to the private sector (as a percent of GDP), banking sector credit to the private sector (as a percent of GDP), and the market capitalization of listed companies (as a percent of GDP). The data set was checked and corrected for outliers and transcription errors. In addition, we use series on capital controls from the IMF's annual report on *Exchange Arrangements and Exchange Restrictions,* country credit ratings from *Institutional Investor,* and political variables kindly provided by David Leblang.

of at least one million (eighty-nine in number, of which fifty-seven experience at least one crisis during the sample period).[5]

Our country sample is chosen to align closely with that used in Kraay (1998), enabling us to use that author's crisis dates.[6] Kraay defines a successful attack as the first observation following a year of stable exchange rates when the rate of currency depreciation exceeds 10 percent.[7] Failed attacks are defined as episodes when nongold reserves decline by at least 20 percent after a year in which neither a successful nor a failed attack occurred.[8]

We begin with simple comparisons of economic and financial variables before and after successful attacks and successful defenses. In both cases, the average behavior of the variable in question is compared to the average behavior of the same variable for noncrisis periods—that is, tranquil peri-

---

5. The exact list of countries is (in order of World Bank country code): Albania; United Arab Emirates; Argentina; Australia; Austria; Belgium; Bulgaria; Bolivia; Brazil; Brunei; Botswana; Canada; Switzerland; Colombia; Costa Rica; Cuba; Cyprus; Czech Republic; Germany; Denmark; Dominican Republic; Ecuador; Egypt; Spain; Finland; France; Gabon; United Kingdom; Greece; Guatemala; Hong Kong; Hungary; Indonesia; Ireland; Iran Islamic Rep.; Iraq; Israel; Italy; Jamaica; Jordan; Japan; Korea; Kuwait; Lebanon; Libya; Morocco; Mexico; Macedonia FYR; Mauritius; Malaysia; Namibia; the Netherlands; Norway; New Zealand; Oman; Peru; the Philippines; Papua New Guinea; Poland; Korea Dem. Rep.; Portugal; Paraguay; Singapore; Slovak Republic; Sweden; Syrian Arab Republic; Thailand; Trinidad and Tobago; Tunisia; Turkey; Uruguay; United States; Venezuela; Yugoslavia FR (Serbia/Montenegro); and South Africa. Kraay does not actually list his countries, but we have followed his description as closely as possible.

6. Among other things, this frees us of the objection that we have selected successful and unsuccessful attacks as a function of the subsequent behavior of output (especially since the purpose of Kraay's paper—to analyze the efficacy of the interest rate defense—is independent of our research).

7. Kraay writes: "I first identify all episodes in which the one-month depreciation rate (i.e., the increase in the nominal exchange rate) exceeds 10%, which is roughly two standard deviations above the mean depreciation rate for the entire sample. In order for these large depreciations to be meaningfully considered successful speculative attacks, it is necessary that the exchange rate be relatively fixed prior to the depreciation itself. Accordingly, for each observation I construct the average over the previous twelve months of the absolute value of percentage changes in the nominal exchange rate. I then eliminate all large depreciation episodes for which this average exceeded 2.5%, or about one half of one standard deviation from the mean for the entire sample. I define these events as successful speculative attacks. Finally, in order to avoid 'double-counting' prolonged crises in which the nominal exchange rate depreciates sharply for several months, I further eliminate successful attacks that were preceded by successful attacks in any of the prior twelve months."

8. Again, to quote Kraay: "To identify unsuccessful speculative attacks, I first consider all episodes in which the monthly decline in non-gold reserves exceeds 20%, which is about two standard deviations above the mean decline in reserves for the entire sample. In order to restrict attention to large reserve losses incurred defending relatively fixed exchange rates, I eliminate all those episodes for which the same moving average of absolute values of changes in the nominal exchange rate as before was greater than 2.5%. Next, to eliminate large reserve losses accompanying successful attacks, I exclude all episodes in which the change in the nominal exchange rate in the same month or any of the three following months was greater than 10%. I define these episodes as failed speculative attacks and, as before, I eliminate all failed attacks that are preceded by a failed attack in any of the twelve previous months."

ods in which neither successful attacks nor successful defenses occur—and surrounded by a 2–standard deviation band.

Figures 3.1 and 3.2 portray the variables of interest from three years prior to three years after the event. Figure 3.1 considers domestic variables, figure 3.2 external variables, for our 92 successful attacks and 184 failed attacks. Adding a three-year exclusion window to ensure that we do not double-count crisis observations (note that this is the same exclusion window that we use in the formal statistical analysis that follows) does not change the results.

Consider first the two top-left-hand panels of figure 3.1, which display GNP growth around the time of successful attacks and successful defenses. They show that growth rate averages about 3 percent in the three years preceding both successful attacks and successful defenses. This is quite close to the average in noncrisis periods (as denoted by the horizontal line). Growth then falls sharply, to barely zero, in the year of a successful attack and the year following, before recovering to pre-attack levels. In contrast, there is little change in growth rates either before or after successful defenses.

We can reject at the 99 percent confidence level that the post-crisis behavior of output is the same in countries that succumb to attacks and those that mount successful defenses. Here, then, the first key result of this paper makes its appearance.

The other panels hint at what may be driving these differences in post-crisis performance. Narrow money (M1) growth and inflation rise in the wake of successful attacks but not in the wake of successful defenses, suggesting a loss of monetary discipline when defense of the currency is abandoned.[9] Consumption and investment growth both fall, despite the decline in real interest rates that accompanies the acceleration in inflation, further suggesting a loss in confidence.[10] Interest rate spreads (defined as the lending rate minus London Interbank Offered Rate [LIBOR]) rise following successful attacks, again suggesting declining confidence and rising risk perceptions.

However, there are no comparable differences in the behavior of any of these variables in the three years preceding the event. Growth is no different in the run-up to successful attacks and successful defenses. Inflation and money growth are no different. Budget deficits are no different. It is not obvious, in other words, that differences in the precrisis development of these macroeconomic variables explain the different outcome of the speculative attack.[11]

9. The difference in M1 growth between successful and unsuccessful defenders just misses statistical significance at the 95 percent confidence level. The difference in inflation does not approach significance at conventional confidence levels.

10. The difference in post-crisis real interest rates between successful and unsuccessful defenders is statistically significant at the 95 percent confidence level, but the difference in post-crisis consumption growth is not. (The same is true of investment.)

11. Formal statistical tests show that none of these variables behaves significantly differently at anything approaching standard (95 percent) confidence levels in the year preceding the event.

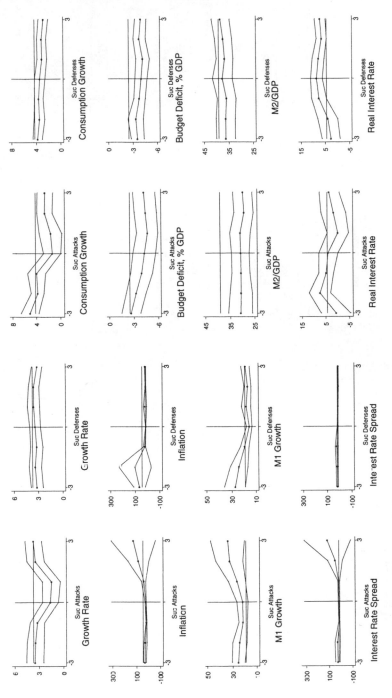

Fig. 3.1   Movements three years before and after crises

Notes: Mean plus 2–standard deviation band; all figures are percentages. 92 successful attacks and 184 defenses. Tranquil averages marked. Data from eighty-nine countries, 1960–98. Scales and date vary.

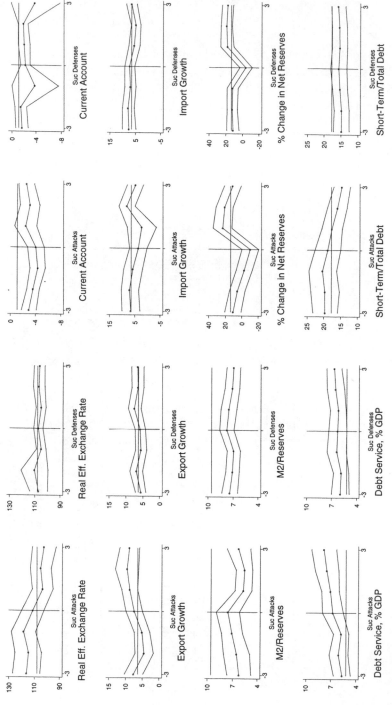

Fig. 3.2 Movements three years before and after crises

Notes: Mean plus 2–standard deviation band; all figures are percentages. 92 successful attacks and 184 defenses. Tranquil averages marked. Data from eighty-nine countries, 1960–98. Scales and data vary.

Figure 3.2 provides analogous evidence for external variables. Countries that experience a crisis display somewhat more real exchange rate appreciation, larger current account deficits, and higher ratios of debt service to GNP (compared to countries that do not) prior to the event. This consistent with mainstream models of the determinants of speculative attacks.[12] However, to repeat, our concern in this paper is not whether there are differences between countries that do and do not experience crises, but whether there are differences in the pre-crisis behavior of these variables between countries that mount successful and unsuccessful defenses. While there is some sign that countries that are unable to defend against speculative attacks tend to have more short-term debt in their total debt loan and to have experienced more real effective exchange rate appreciation in the run-up to the crisis (compared to the successful defenders), in no case is the behavior of these variables significantly different from in tranquil periods (as indicated by the 2–standard deviation bands), and in no case is the behavior of these variables significantly different between successful attacks and successful defenses in the year preceding the crisis.[13] There are no differences between successful attacks and successful defenses in the size of the current account deficit in the year immediately preceding the crisis, and there are no discernible differences in the consequent debt service burdens.[14] We cannot reject (at anything approaching conventional confidence levels) the null that these external variables behave the same in the successful attack and successful defense cases in the year immediately preceding the crisis.

Following the crisis, the real effective exchange rate depreciates in countries that abandon defense of their currencies, relative to both the no-crisis cases and the successful defenders. Export growth accelerates and current accounts strengthen, consistent with the aforementioned collapse of consumption. These patterns are consistent with the very different post-crisis behavior of GNP growth in countries that mount successful and unsuccessful defenses against speculative attacks.[15]

Tables 3.1 through 3.3 take a different look at this same question. We now ask not whether there are significant differences in the behavior of these variables before successful attacks and successful defenses (which was the question that occupied us before), but whether there is evidence that a given value of these variables has a different impact on the likelihood of successful attacks and successful defenses. Table 3.1 is most directly comparable to

12. For completeness, we note that the differences between the crisis and noncrisis countries are statistically significant at conventional confidence levels for the current account but not for the other two variables.

13. Formally, we are unable to reject the null that their values are the same in successful attacks and successful defenses at the 95 percent confidence level.

14. The statement in the preceding footnote again applies.

15. However, the evolution of none of these three variables differs significantly (that is, at the 95 percent confidence level) in the post-crisis period between successful and unsuccessful defenders.

Table 3.1 **Univariate Multinomial Logit Results**

	Year Before		Year After	
	Successful Attacks	Successful Defenses	Successful Attacks	Successful Defenses
GDP growth	−0.02	−0.00	−0.06	0.01
	(0.02)	(0.02)	(0.02)	(0.02)
Consumption growth	0.00	−0.01	−0.06	−0.02
	(0.02)	(0.02)	(0.02)	(0.02)
Budget (% GDP)	−0.05	−0.03	−0.08	−0.06
	(0.03)	(0.03)	(0.03)	(0.03)
M1 growth	0.001	−0.00	0.004	−0.01
	(0.004)	(0.010)	(0.003)	(0.010)
M2 growth	−0.001	−0.002	0.000	−0.01
	(0.002)	(0.002)	(0.001)	(0.010)
Interest rate spread	−0.000	−0.002	0.000	−0.003
	(0.002)	(0.003)	(0.002)	(0.005)
Real interest rate	0.01	−0.00	−0.01	0.02
	(0.01)	(0.01)	(0.01)	(0.01)
Current account (% GDP)	−0.04	−0.04	−0.02	−0.01
	(0.02)	(0.02)	(0.02)	(0.02)
Export growth	−0.01	−0.01	0.02	0.01
	(0.01)	(0.01)	(0.01)	(0.01)
Import growth	−0.00	0.00	−0.02	−0.00
	(0.01)	(0.01)	(0.01)	(0.01)
M2/GDP	−0.01	0.002	−0.01	0.002
	(0.010)	(0.005)	(0.010)	(0.005)
M3/GDP	−0.01	0.005	−0.01	0.001
	(0.010)	(0.004)	(0.010)	(0.005)
CPI inflation	−0.001	−0.001	−0.0001	−0.01
	(0.0010)	(0.0020)	(0.0005)	(0.0100)
GDP inflation	−0.001	−0.002	−0.002	−0.01
	(0.0020)	(0.0020)	(0.0005)	(0.0100)
M2/reserves	−0.01	−0.02	−0.03	−0.02
	(0.01)	(0.01)	(0.02)	(0.01)
Net international reserves	−0.008	−0.000	0.005	0.005
(% change)	(0.002)	(0.003)	(0.002)	(0.002)
Real effective exchange rate	0.005	−0.003	−0.004	−0.004
	(0.003)	(0.006)	(0.007)	(0.005)
$ Exchange rate (% change)	−0.000	−0.002	0.008	−0.004
	(0.004)	(0.004)	(0.002)	(0.004)
Short-term/total debt	0.01	−0.01	0.00	−0.03
	(0.01)	(0.01)	(0.01)	(0.01)
Debt service (% GDP)	0.01	0.02	0.08	0.03
	(0.03)	(0.04)	(0.03)	(0.04)

Notes: Multinomial logit regression coefficients (z-statistics). Default cell is tranquility. Each row tabulates coefficients from two separate logits (before and after crises). Three-year exclusion window (82 successful, 85 failed attacks). Intercepts not reported. Entries in bold indicate that the coefficients differ between successful and failed attacks at the 90% confidence level.

Table 3.2   **Multivariate Multinomial Logit Results: Year Before Crises**

	Successful Attacks	Successful Defenses	Successful Attacks	Successful Defenses	Successful Attacks	Successful Defenses
GDP growth	−0.04	−0.00	−0.07	−0.05	−0.15	−0.07
	(0.04)	(0.04)	(0.04)	(0.05)	(0.05)	(0.05)
Inflation	−0.004	−0.004				
	(0.003)	(0.003)				
Budget deficit	−0.08	−0.08				
	(0.04)	(0.04)				
Current account	−0.03	0.02				
	(0.04)	(0.03)				
M2/GDP	−0.03	−0.02				
	(0.01)	(0.01)				
Interest spread			−0.003	−0.001		
			(0.005)	(0.004)		
Short-term/ total debt			0.05	0.03		
			(0.02)	(0.03)		
Debt service			−0.03	−0.05		
			(0.04)	(0.06)		
Real effective exchange rate					0.01	−0.00
					(0.01)	(0.01)
M2/reserves					−0.07	−0.03
					(0.03)	(0.02)
N		460		269		335
Pseudo-R^2		0.05		0.04		0.06
Equality test (P-value)		0.67		0.97		0.29

Notes: Multinomial logit estimation: z-statistics in parentheses. Default cell is tranquility. Intercepts not reported. Three-year exclusion window (82 successful, 85 failed attacks).

figures 3.1 and 3.2, in that we consider the variables one at a time (in simple bivariate regressions). The first two columns confirm that there are few significant differences in the impact of these variables between the default state (tranquility) and the crisis state in the year preceding the event. The conclusion holds for both successful attacks and successful defenses. Similarly, there are few significant differences in their impact between successful attacks and successful defenses in the immediately preceding period. In particular, differences are evident only in the effect of financial depth, for which we do not have an explanation, and in the effect of changes in international reserves, which is inevitable, given the way we define successful attacks and successful defenses. Recall that successful attacks are cases in which reserve losses have a large effect—in the present context, a large coefficient—on the probability of an exchange rate change, whereas successful defenses are cases in which reserve losses—in the present context, evidence of an attack—do not have an analogous effect. Thus, it must be the case that we obtain different coefficients on the net change in reserves prior to successful

Table 3.3   Multivariate Multinomial Logit Results: Year After Crises

	Successful Attacks	Successful Defenses	Successful Attacks	Successful Defenses	Successful Attacks	Successful Defenses
GDP growth	-0.15	-0.03	-0.14	0.06	-0.16	-0.02
	(0.03)	(0.04)	(0.04)	(0.05)	(0.04)	(0.05)
Inflation	-0.001	-0.020				
	(0.001)	(0.010)				
Budget deficit	-0.10	-0.11				
	(0.03)	(0.04)				
Current account	0.04	-0.01				
	(0.03)	(0.03)				
M2/GDP	-0.03	-0.01				
	(0.01)	(0.01)				
Interest spread			-0.002	-0.002		
			(0.004)	(0.007)		
Short-term/			0.060	0.001		
total debt			(0.02)	(0.03)		
Debt service			0.06	-0.02		
			(0.04)	(0.05)		
Real effective					-0.01	-0.00
exchange rate					(0.01)	(0.01)
M2/reserves					-0.10	-0.03
					(0.05)	(0.02)
N	486		282		353	
Pseudo-R^2	0.11		0.08		0.07	
Equality test exchange rate	0.01		0.01		0.07	

Notes: Multinomial Logit Estimation: z-statistics in parentheses. Default cell is tranquility. Intercepts not reported. Three-year exclusion window (82 successful, 85 failed attacks).

attacks and successful defenses. (Note that we are discussing here the effect of reserve losses on the outcome, not the size of those reserve losses. In fact, reserves are actually smaller and fall faster prior to successful defenses, which cuts against the argument that successful attacks are those that are somehow more intense.)

On the other hand, a number of significant differences are evident in the year following the crisis, most notably in the behavior of gross domestic product (GDP) growth, as we emphasize throughout the paper, but also in money growth, import growth, the real interest rate, and the ratio of saving accounts (M2) to GNP.

In sum, we find that failure to successfully defend the currency against attack has real costs in terms of GNP. That post-crisis decline in growth is not obviously attributable to precrisis characteristics of the economy (compared to countries that successfully defend the currency against attack). The proximate source of that decline in growth in turn is the fall decline in consumption and rise in the risk premium, suggesting a deterioration in confidence. Although the real exchange rate, export growth, and the current account buffer these negative effects, they do so incompletely. The acceleration of M1 growth and inflation suggests that it is loss of the monetary anchor and of monetary discipline that lies behind the deterioration in confidence and precipitates the output losses.

3.3 Multivariate Analysis

The preceding comparisons are univariate. We now turn to multivariate analysis, drawing models from the literature on the determinants of currency crises.

Again, we first ask whether there is any evidence that economic and financial variables have different impacts on the likelihood of a successful attack and a successful defense, now considering a variety of such variables simultaneously. We then ask whether the pre- and post-crisis behavior of output and other variables differs significantly depending on the success or failure of the attack, now controlling for other characteristics of the economy. The null is that the evolution and effects of the variables of interest are statistically distinguishable from one another before (after) successful attacks and successful defenses.

Tables 3.2 and 3.3 summarize the results of estimating a series of multinomial logit models by maximum likelihood. Table 3.2 contains estimates for three different specifications, using data for the year *preceding* the crisis. Table 3.3 reports the same three specifications, but using data for the year *following* the crisis. We report the coefficients and their associated z-statistics (the latter in absolute value terms).[16] Tranquility (i.e., observations that are not within three years of an attack) is the default cell; the coefficients therefore capture the differential impact of a variable on the probability of a successful attack or a successful defense, compared to the tranquil default state.

The bottom of the table provides various diagnostics and hypothesis tests. The most important of these is the p-value for the test statistic that the coefficients are identical for the successful attacks and the successful defenses. A high number is consistent with the hypothesis, whereas a low one rejects it.

The default specification is at the left of the table: it includes growth, inflation, measures of monetary and fiscal policy, the interest rate, and the current account.[17] The fit (as measured by the R^2) is predictably unimpres-

16. All slopes are multiplied by 100. Constants are included in the regressions but not recorded.

17. This specification is not the result of extensive pretesting; rather, we simply adopt the specification used to analyze the correlates of crises in Eichengreen and Rose (2000b). However, to establish robustness, we also display the results of estimating two additional specifications.

Table 3.4   Costs of a Successful Attack (Dependent variable is growth of GDP)

	(1)	(2)	(3)	(4)	Without High Inflation Obs (5)	One-Year Window (6)
Lagged successful	−3.19	−1.22	−3.76	−3.20	−3.06	−2.80
attack	(0.82)	(0.59)	(1.19)	(0.83)	(0.88)	(0.72)
Lagged successful	−0.61	−0.09	−0.98	0.64	−0.81	0.11
defense	(0.64)	(0.56)	(0.92)	(0.66)	(0.69)	(0.57)
Lagged growth	0.36	1.91	0.39	0.35	0.36	0.36
	(0.05)	(0.24)	(0.07)	(0.04)	(0.05)	(0.05)
Lagged inflation	0.01		0.01	0.01	0.01	0.01
	(0.01)		(0.01)	(0.01)	(0.01)	(0.01)
Lagged budget	−0.02		−0.01	−0.01	−0.03	−0.02
deficit	(0.04)		(0.04)	(0.04)	(0.05)	(0.04)
Lagged money	−0.01		0.01	0.01	−0.01	−0.01
growth	(0.01)		(0.01)	(0.01)	(0.01)	(0.01)
Lagged current			−0.05			
account def.			(0.07)			
Lagged interest			−0.01			
rate spread			(0.01)			
Capital controls				−0.41		
				(0.29)		
R^2	0.17	0.20	0.22	0.17	0.17	0.16
N	1,003	2,501	580	983	903	1,003

Note: Constant terms estimated but not reported. Standard errors in parentheses.

sive, consistent with the generally poor performance of leading-indicator models.[18] However, what matters is that there continue to be few significant differences between successful attacks and successful defenses before the event, but a variety of significant differences thereafter. An alternative specification (in the middle two columns) uses a trio of financial variables as controls: the interest rate spread, the share of short-term debt in the external debt burden, and the ratio of debt service to GDP. Still another specification (in the last two columns) substitutes two measures of external vulnerability: reserve adequacy (the M2-reserve ratio) and the real effective exchange rate. The results for output are the same regardless of the choice of controls.

Table 3.4 quantifies the cost of a successful speculative attack. It reports the results of regressing the growth rate of real GDP on one-year lags of dummy variables for successful attacks and successful defenses, along with a variety of controls. If speculative attacks, whether successful or unsuccessful, have no effect on growth rates after a year, then the coefficients on both dummy variables should be zero. However, given what we have seen so

18. This is something we have emphasized elsewhere; see Eichengreen and Rose (2001a).

far, we expect the coefficient on the lag of a successful attack to be negative, large, and significantly different from zero. We expect the coefficient on successful defenses to be less important and to differ significantly from the coefficient on successful attacks.

Table 3.4 shows six variants of this output equation, estimated on a variety of controls and samples. Regardless of sample and specification, we find that both hypotheses are supported. The coefficients indicate a significant negative effect on output in the case of successful attacks but not in the case of successful defenses. In each case, the coefficients on successful attacks and successful defenses differ from one another at conventional confidence level. The results suggest that the cost of a successful attack (relative to a successful defense) is 2–3 percentage points of GDP.

3.4   Sensitivity Analysis

In this section we report additional sensitivity analysis in order to establish the robustness of our findings. We first consider a variety of perturbations of the basic methodology, and we then implement a variety of further corrections for observable and unobservable heterogeneity.

3.4.1   Perturbations of the Methodology

In perturbing the basic methodology, we started with our default specification, which includes inflation, the budget and current account balances (relative to GDP, multiplied by 100), and the ratio of M2 to GDP. We then made the following changes. We

- substituted a one-year exclusion window for the three-year window;
- added the IMF dummy for the presence or absence of capital controls;
- added the trio of financial controls (the interest rate spread, the share of short-term debt in the external debt burden, and the ratio of debt service to GDP) to the benchmark specification (rather than substituting them, as in table 3.4);
- added controls for external vulnerability (reserve adequacy and the real effective exchange rate) to the benchmark specification (rather than substituting them, as in table 3.4);
- dropped the high-inflation countries (defined as countries with inflation in excess of 100 percent per annum);
- added a measure of (lagged) banking crises, to test whether countries with financial-sector problems were both less able to mount a successful defense and more likely to suffer large output losses subsequently;
- added lags of currency crises to test whether countries that suffered from chronic exchange-rate problems were both less able to defend (reflecting, inter alia, less credibility) and more likely to suffer severe recessions when attacked;

Table 3.5   *P*-Values for Test of Equality of Slopes for Successful Attacks and
                   Successful Defenses

	Year Before Crises	Year After Crises
One-year windowing	0.73	0.00
With IMF capital controls measure added	0.53	0.00
Benchmark + financial	0.89	0.01
Benchmark + external	0.84	0.05
Without high inflation observations	0.32	0.01
With banking crises	0.49	0.07
With lagged currency crises	0.64	0.00
Without OECD observations	0.73	0.02
With per capita income interactions added	0.45	0.02
With country credit rating added	0.45	0.00

Notes: A low *P*-value number indicates rejection of the hypothesis that the slopes for successful and failed attacks are identical. Default multinomial logit specification, with five macro regressors.

- dropped Organization for Economic Cooperation and Development (OECD) countries;
- added interaction terms between successful attacks and successful defenses on the one hand and per capita income on the other as a way of testing whether the output effects of successful defenses are smaller in high-income countries.

Many of these perturbations yield interesting and plausible results. For example, countries that suffered currency crises in previous periods are more likely to suffer currency crises in the current period. However, critically, none of these changes significantly weakens either of our key results. Table 3.5 reports the relevant *p*-values (where a low number indicates that we can reject the null that output growth is the same for successful and unsuccessful attacks). It will be evident that none of these perturbations modifies the finding that successful attacks and successful defenses are essentially indistinguishable prior to the event. Similarly, the evidence of a more severe post-crisis recession in countries that fail to rebuff the attack remains robust. Interestingly, there is only weak evidence that the output effects of successful attacks are smaller in high-income countries (the interaction term between successful attacks and per capita income has the expected sign—indicating smaller effects in high-income countries—but it is insignificant at standard confidence levels).

3.4.2   Other Sources of Heterogeneity

A potential objection to our results is that countries that fail to defend themselves against speculative attacks differ in ways that are not easily captured by standard macroeconomic and financial aggregates. These unobservable characteristics could both make it more difficult for their governments to defend the currency against attack and lead to disappointingly weak economic performance in the subsequent period. For example, the Asian crisis trained the spotlight on the importance of bank regulation for economic and financial stability. In this case, the argument would be that a hidden problem of nonperforming loans that does not show up in the statistics both makes it more difficult for a government to fend off a speculative attack (it is reluctant to raise interest rates and hold them at higher levels for fear of further aggravating the problems of an already weak banking system) and makes for a deeper recession following the collapse of the currency (because the banking system is in fact weaker than in countries that succeed in mounting a successful defense). It is not the success or failure of the defense per se that produces the different macroeconomic outcome subsequently, in other words, but an omitted third variable (some other characteristic of the country that is difficult to observe by the econometrician) that is responsible for both the success of the attack and the depth of the post-crisis recession.

These difficult-to-observe characteristics of countries are what the rating agencies are in business to detect. We therefore added to our specification the country credit ratings published in *Institutional Investor* magazine.[19] We use annual averages of semiannual ratings, which range from 0 at the bottom to 100 at the top.

Adding credit ratings changes little (again, see table 3.5). Although the raw credit ratings are somewhat higher for countries that succeed in defending their currencies against attack (not surprisingly), the difference is not significant once we control for observable macroeconomic and financial characteristics. Rating-agency intelligence does not suggest, in other words, that countries that succeed and fail to defend their currencies against attack differ significantly before the event in otherwise unobservable ways. Our first result—that countries that succeed and fail to defend themselves against a speculative attack are basically indistinguishable ex ante—survives this extension. So does our second result: countries that are unable to defend themselves against the speculative attack continue to do significantly worse in the post-attack period even after we control for the difficult-to-quantify characteristics captured by their pre-attack credit ratings.[20]

It could be that in focusing on macroeconomic and financial variables we have neglected important political determinants of both the ability of gov-

19. A regression of these credit ratings on country characteristics (on annual data for the 1990s) yields an R-squared of 0.46 (Eichengreen and Mody 2000). Thus, readily quantified economic and financial conditions explain less than half of the variation in this measure, suggesting that it may add value.

20. Following their crises, countries unable to mount successful defenses of course do worse both in terms of output and credit ratings. This reflects the tendency for ratings to follow actual performance.

ernments to defend their currencies against attack and the severity of the postattack recession. Where the government lacks public support and is unable to credibly commit to policy reform, statements of readiness to, inter alia, raise interest rates to defend the currency will not be taken at face value. High interest rates may be seen as a sign of desperation rather than as a commitment to defend. If such a government is then forced to abandon its exchange rate commitment, doubts about its commitment to the pursuit of sound and stable alternative policies may lead to an unusually severe post-crisis recession. This is the story told of Indonesia following its 1997 crisis, for example. Again, the implication is that a third variable—in this case, political weakness—explains both the failure of the defense and the poor performance of the economy following the crisis; there is no direct connection between the success or failure of the defense and what comes after.

We therefore considered a series of political variables: whether the electoral system was proportional or majoritarian, whether the crisis occurred in a year immediately before or after an election, whether government was divided or the same party controlled all houses of the congress or parliament, whether the government was left or right wing, and whether the political system was presidential or parliamentary.[21] One finds in the literature on the political economy of exchange rate policy (e.g., Garrett 1998; Leblang 1999; Leblang and Bernhard 2000) arguments for the reasons each of these variables should affect the ability to make credible commitments to defend the rate.

Their introduction changed nothing. There are no statistically significant differences in these political variables either before or after the event.[22] Adding them reveals no statistically significant differences before successful attacks and successful defenses in the behavior of the major macroeconomic and financial variables. Moreover, their addition does nothing to weaken our finding of large differences in the post-crisis evolution of output as a function of whether defense of the currency was successful.

Some readers will worry that our benchmark specification, even augmented by country credit ratings and political variables, still does not capture ways in which countries that were unable to defend their currencies and subsequently suffered post-crisis recessions differ from other countries.[23] We therefore applied an econometric treatment for unobserved heterogeneity. We estimated a first-stage probit designed to explain why some countries succeeded in defending their currencies while others did not, constructed the Inverse Mills Ratio from the residuals of this equation, and added that ratio as an additional explanatory variable to our benchmark regression ex-

21. We thank David Leblang for kindly providing these data.
22. This is true whether we consider them individually in bivariate comparisons, or as a group in multivariate analysis.
23. The criticism to which the rating agencies have been subjected for failing to predict recent crises provides some grounds for this suspicion.

Table 3.6   Determinants of GDP Growth with "Heckit" Correction

Output growth lagged	0.36	0.36
	(0.05)	(0.05)
Successful attack lagged	–3.2	–3.2
	(0.79)	(0.80)
Successful defense lagged	–0.6	–0.6
	(0.5)	(0.5)
Inflation lagged		0.000
		(0.001)
Budget lagged (% GDP)		–0.01
		(0.05)
M1 growth lagged		0.001
		(0.007)
Observations	889	885
P-value: coefficients = 0	0.00	0.00
ρ (s.e.)	0.27	0.30
	(0.12)	(0.13)

Notes: OLS coefficients (corrected for selection) with robust standard errors. Selection equation includes inflation, M2/GDP, budget deficit (% GDP), and current account (% GDP).

plaining postattack economic performance. We modeled the success or failure of the defense as a function of inflation, the government deficit-GDP ratio, and the M2-GDP ratio. We used two variants to explain GDP growth. As in table 3.4, our default specification controls for the effects of lagged growth, inflation, the government deficit-GDP ratio, and the growth rate of M1. The alternative specification controls for lagged output growth alone.

Our key finding survives this extension unscathed. As shown in table 3.6, adding the Inverse Mills Ratio to the regression for post-crisis economic performance does not alter the central finding that countries that successfully defend themselves against attacks grow faster in the post-crisis period.

3.5   Implications

Summarizing, we find that countries that are unable to defend their currencies against attack experience significant post-crisis output losses compared to countries that mount a successful defense. Those output losses are significant; we consistently obtain estimates on the order of 3 percent of GNP. However plausible the assumption, we detect no evidence that countries that fail to sustain a successful defense and suffer post-crisis output losses enter their crises with greater economic, financial, and political weaknesses than do countries that succeed in repelling the speculative attack and avoiding post-crisis output losses. We do find plausible and significant differences between pre-crisis conditions in countries that do and those that do not experience speculative attacks, but, to repeat, this is not the subject of our paper.

The output losses that follow failed defenses generally reflect a collapse of consumption, along with some fall in investment. That this takes place despite a decline in real interest rates clearly signals a negative shock to confidence, as does the post-crisis rise in risk premiums in countries that involuntarily abandon their fixed rates. The rise in money growth and inflation in countries that fail to mount a successful defense is a strong hint of where the shock to confidence is originating: namely, it reflects the decline in monetary discipline that follows the loss of the nominal anchor provided by the previously prevailing exchange rate regime.

These results reinforce the findings of previous studies of exits from pegged exchange rates like Eichengreen et al. (1998). These authors analyze twenty-nine exits by developing countries from single-currency pegs or basket pegs to managed exchange rates or independent floats. They find that growth is significantly lower in the year of the exit than in two control groups of countries: those that continued to peg without exiting, and all other developing countries in the World Bank database. Our results are more refined in that the sample of exits is larger, we limit the control group to other countries that also experienced speculative attacks but did not exit, and we control for a variety of economic, financial, and political characteristics of the countries experiencing crises. However, the central conclusion of that previous study continues to hold: exiting involuntarily in response to a crisis is painful and tends to result in significant output losses. It is better for countries seeking to move to greater exchange rate flexibility to do so voluntarily when the currency is strong rather than as the result of an attack.

This previous study speculated that loss of the nominal anchor—that is, of the exchange rate peg that provided the focal point for the country's monetary policy operating strategy—resulted in a loss of policy discipline and of confidence that compounded the crisis. Our paper provides evidence in support of this conjecture.

A final fact that emerges from our study is that defenses, like attacks, are heterogeneous.[24] This is evident in the relatively large 2–standard deviation bands that surround the macroeconomic and financial variables in figures 3.1 and 3.2. The negative output effects of failed defenses may average 3 or 4 percentage points of growth, but they vary widely. Some recent cases— Brazil in 1998 springs to mind—are notable for having held these costs to lower levels. The popular explanation for their success is that they were quick to put in place an alternative monetary policy operating strategy: Brazil, for example, replaced its currency peg with an explicit inflation-targeting framework. There was no loss of monetary discipline, and the acceleration of inflation was minimal. The risk premium fell rather than ris-

---

24. The heterogeneity of currency crises—that is to say, speculative attacks—was a theme of Eichengreen, Rose, and Wyplosz (1995).

ing, and consumption did not collapse. There can be no clearer example of what the authorities should do to minimize the costs of a failed defense.

We see the broader policy implications as follows. There are two types of monetary-cum-exchange rate arrangements that are compatible with a world of high capital mobility. One is a very hard exchange rate peg that the authorities commit to defending unconditionally if attacked. The other is a clear and credible monetary policy operating strategy not oriented around the level of the exchange rate, such as a full-fledged inflation-targeting framework. A very hard peg, supported by a credible commitment to defend it, can prevent costly speculative attacks that collapse the currency, whereas the installation of a clear and credible alternative monetary policy strategy such as inflation targeting, in the event that the decision is taken to abandon the exchange rate anchor, can help to minimize the disturbance to confidence. Soft pegs, with no provision for an alternative monetary anchor, are the worst of all worlds.

References

Eichengreen, Barry, and Paul Masson, with Hugh Bredenkamp, Barry Johnston, Javier Hamann, Esteban Jadresic, and Inci Otker. 1998. *Exit strategies: Policy options for countries seeking greater exchange rate flexibility.* IMF Occasional Paper no. 168. Washington, D.C.: International Monetary Fund.

Eichengreen, Barry, and Ashoka Mody. 2000. What explains the changing spreads on emerging-market debt: Fundamentals or market sentiment? In *Capital flows and emerging economies,* ed. Sebastian Edwards, 107–36. Chicago: University of Chicago Press.

Eichengreen, Barry, and Andrew Rose. 2000a. The empirics of currency and banking crises. *Austrian Economic Review* 4 1:395–402.

———. 2000b. Staying afloat when the wind shifts: External factors and emerging market banking crises. In *Money: Capital mobility and trade, essays in honor of Robert Mundell,* ed. Guillermo Calvo, Rudi Dornbusch and Maurice Obstfeld, 171–206. Cambridge: MIT Press.

Eichengreen, Barry, Andrew Rose, and Charles Wyplosz. 1995. Exchange market mayhem: The antecedents and aftermath of speculative attacks. *Economic Policy* 21:249–312.

Garrett, Geoffrey. 1998. *Partisan politics in the global economy.* Cambridge: Cambridge University Press.

Jeanne, Olivier. 1997. Are currency crises self-fulfilling? A test. *Journal of International Economics* 43:263–86.

Koehler, Horst. 2001. New challenges for exchange rate policy. Remarks at the Asia-Europe (ASEM) Meeting of Finance Ministers. 13 January, Kobe, Japan. Available at [http://www.mof.go.jp/english/asem/aseme03a1.htm].

Kraay, Aart. 1998. Do high interest rates defend currencies against speculative attacks? The World Bank. Unpublished Manuscript.

Leblang, David. 1999. Domestic political institutions and exchange rate commitments in the developing world. *International Studies Quarterly* 43:599–620.

Leblang, David A., and William Bernhard. 2000. The politics of speculative attacks in industrial democracies. *International Organization* 54:291–324.

Comment   Richard Portes

This paper provides convincing evidence of the output costs of failing to defend a currency peg. This is powerful and important, and the empirical work is careful and thorough. But, the interpretation and some of the specific results raise a number of questions.

There are several puzzling results. First, the authors find that no variables characterizing the precrisis state of an economy affect the probability that a speculative attack against its currency will succeed. As they acknowledge, this appears to go against several papers that claim to have identified leading indicators of crises. I myself do not find this particularly surprising. I have been consistently skeptical about the early-warning systems, because they use little theory (or many theories, without discrimination) on lots of numbers and often come close to data mining. Still, it might be helpful if the authors could give us their considered view of why their regressions refuse to reveal any information about when and why attacks succeed rather than fail. That might be difficult, however, since here too there is no underlying model. That weakens their interpretation of the main result, as I shall suggest.

There are other puzzles. No variables characterizing the precrisis state of an economy explain differences in postcrisis performance as between cases of successful attacks and successful defenses. In particular, the magnitude of output loss consequent upon a successful attack seems independent of the precrisis state. This is certainly counterintuitive and indeed goes against the authors' priors, as they tell us.

The role of the real exchange rate in these results is at best confusing, at worst quite surprising. There seems to be no identifiable difference in the behavior of the real exchange rate in the postcrisis period between economies that succumb to a successful attack, going off their currency peg, and those that defend the peg successfully. If the reader too finds this anomalous, see note 15, the "Year After" section of table 3.1, and table 3.3. I cannot believe there is any problem with the data the authors use, but if a successful attack should have any consequences at all relative to successful defense within a year, the expected outcome is real exchange rate depreciation. Again, we are due some attempt at explanation here.

Richard Portes is professor of economics at London Business School and a research associate of the National Bureau of Economic Research.

The last of my puzzles relates to the central result itself. The International Monetary Fund (IMF) tells a country to tighten both monetary and fiscal policy in order to prop up its currency, and we have regularly witnessed sacrifices to this end—most recently and tragically in Argentina. It is therefore no less than astonishing that a successful defense against speculative attack appears to have no output cost. I doubt that even the strongest proponents of the "franc fort" in the early 1990s would argue that the successful defense of the French franc in the exchange rate mechanism in autumn 1992 was costless. (It is not an out to say that the attacks were ultimately successful in July 1993.) There are many similar examples.

Regarding the output loss due to a failed defense, my prior would have been that the effect would be less strong in more advanced economies with more robust economic institutions. The authors claim to have dealt with this issue (raised at the conference) with the interaction term involving per capita income, in order to assess whether the output effects of successful attacks are smaller in high-income countries. They do indeed find evidence that this is so, but the coefficient is not significant. Still, that is not dealing directly with the conjecture, which suggests simply running the regressions separately for Organization for Economic Cooperation and Development (OECD) and non-OECD countries. I would be very surprised if the output effect were not significantly smaller in the former.

Why should a country try hard to defend against a speculative attack? I doubt that it is simply that they know the Eichengreen-Rose result and are desperately trying to avoid the short-run output cost of a failed defense. Many countries have seen maintaining a currency peg as a long-run issue. The peg may be their last shot at a consistent monetary policy strategy; it may deeply implicate the credibility of policy makers; it may be a key element in a trade or political system that the country takes very seriously; it may be simply that the policy makers are afraid of floating and its implications.

This relates to the authors' interpretation of their key result. They argue that a successful attack shocks the confidence of markets in the prospects for economic stability. "We thus observe a loss of policy discipline." This is a non sequitur, however: that markets become skeptical might in fact induce sensible policy makers to maintain discipline in order to change market perceptions. In any case, if they do lose discipline, we might see an acceleration of money growth, as the authors suggest. This is reminiscent of the second-generation crisis models, which the authors know well but leave out of the story. But, they also suggest that we should see a rise in risk premia: this is unrelated to policy discipline, but it would indeed follow from their original story about market confidence. They should decide which interpretation they prefer, or explicitly maintain both (although, as I suggested, they may be contradictory).

Wherever they do end up, their empirical work provides no evidence to support either interpretation. Table 3.1 shows no effects of a successful attack on risk premiums, nor on inflation. Moreover, although a standard test shows that the coefficients on money growth do differ between cases of successful attack and successful defense, if you look at the estimated coefficients and z-statistics, it is hard to take this very seriously. The story or stories simply do not come out of the data.

Discussion Summary

Allan Drazen noted that the paper does not make a clear distinction between a successful (and unsuccessful) defense and a successful (and unsuccessful) attack. Either a failed defense or a decision not to attempt a defense might result in a successful attack.

Martin Eichenbaum remarked that it seems from the data that it is a random decision whether to defend, which, to him, seemed improbable.

Andrew K. Rose responded that he is looking into attempted defenses only: following Kraay, these are ones in which reserves decreased by a certain percent. *Andrew Berg* noted that in this case a country's decision to pay back a large loan to the IMF is identified as a successful defense even though there was no attack.

Peter B. Kenen noted that there does not seem to be any difference in interest rate spreads between the two subsets, so it seems there are interest rate defenders in both subsets.

Joshua Aizenman questioned whether it is possible to test directly for the output cost as a result of the loss of the nominal anchor, suggesting that it may be possible by controlling for the duration of the peg and history of previous crises.

Kenneth Kletzer made a reference to previous research that was unable to find leading indicators of crises. Having said that, he noted that in table 3.1 there is a difference in net international reserves prior to the crisis. He suggested that might help explain the paper's findings.

Michael M. Hutchison remarked that devaluing the currency would likely have dynamic long-run effects that are not captured in this model. He suggested extending the sample period in order to capture these reversal effects.

Edwin M. Truman, following others, noted that the Kraay variable of currency crises is problematic, as there are a lot of reasons that reserves can go down. He also noted that it seems likely that either governments that are in a very strong position or ones that are weak choose to attempt a defense. This asymmetry, he suggested, should be accounted for in the model. Third, he asked what the policy implications of the paper's findings are. That depends, he stated, on the exact nature of the crisis in question.

Martin Feldstein inquired whether the output costs of a defense that the authors find are permanent and, if so, how that can be, since the exogenous effect is of a demand shock.

Vincent Reinhart commented that the output loss could be due to a loss of confidence or to a rejection of the present regime. It might even be caused by the change in regime following the crisis, so it will be beneficial to examine those ex post changes and control for them.

Michael P. Dooley questioned whether the big crises, such as the Mexico 1994 or Asia 1997 crises, are not fundamentally different from the many other small crises in the authors' data set.

Rose responded first to Portes's concern that the paper does not differentiate between OECD and non-OECD countries by noting that it was one of the sensitivity checks in table 3.5. In response to Hutchison, he noted that they did run some long-run regressions covering three years but found significant results were for the first year only. He added that they used other crisis definitions besides Kraay's, but that did not make much difference. He also stated that it seems the status of the banking industry is accounted for by the inclusion of market perceptions in the regressions. He also doubted whether the data would allow differentiation between permanent and temporary effects. *Barry Eichengreen* responded that he and Andrew Rose planned to follow through on a number of these suggestions, but he was skeptical that doing so would change the central results. He noted that there had been much general discussion of the policy implications of the findings. His take on these implications was that only very hard pegs and relatively free floats are workable in a world of high capital mobility. A hard peg will be workable if the commitment to defend it is fully credible, whereas floating will be feasible provided that the authorities articulate a clear and coherent monetary policy operating strategy such as inflation targeting. Intermediate exchange rate regimes, on the other hand, are a recipe for disaster.

II

The Program

4

The International Lender of Last Resort
How Large Is Large Enough?

Olivier Jeanne and Charles Wyplosz

4.1 Introduction

The Asian crises have triggered a debate on how new rules and institutions could increase the resilience of the international monetary system. Among many proposals, it has been suggested that an international lender of last resort would be a useful addition. One idea, a distant reminder of Keynes's proposal in Bretton Woods, is to set up an international central bank that would issue a global currency (Garten 1998). Other ideas start from the observation that crisis lending by the international community has already evolved toward de facto lending in last resort since the Mexican bailout—a trend that, some argue, should be developed and institutionalized (Fischer 1999). A report to the U.S. Congress recently advocated the transformation of the International Monetary Fund (IMF) into a "quasi-lender of last resort" lending at penalty rates and against good marketable collateral (International Financial Institution Advisory Commission [IFIAC] 2000). Others have argued that the international lending-in-last-resort function should be un-

Olivier Jeanne is a researcher at the International Monetary Fund. Charles Wyplosz is professor of international economics at the Graduate Institute of International Studies.

For helpful comments on the previous versions, the authors thank participants in the NBER conference, and especially our discussant, Olivier Blanchard. The authors also thank Philippe Bacchetta, Patrick Bolton, Peter Clark, Daniel Cohen, Giovanni Dell'Ariccia, Enrica Detragiache, Piti Disyatat, Stanley Fischer, Gerhard Illing, Peter Isard, Christian Mulder, John Pattison, Pascal Rousseau, Alexander Swoboda, and participants at seminars at the Graduate Institute of International Studies, Humboldt University, the International Monetary Fund, the fifth annual meeting of the Latin American and Caribbean Economic Association, and the National Bank of Switzerland for helpful comments and discussions. This paper reflects the views of its authors, which are not necessarily those of the IMF.

dertaken by the Bank of International Settlements (BIS; Fratianni and Pattison 2001).

The idea that an international lender of last resort (LOLR) could and should become the linchpin of the global financial architecture has been criticized on different grounds. It has been noted, first, that an international LOLR might worsen the moral hazard problem, which, some argue, is one of the main causes of fragility of the international financial system (Calomiris 1998). Another argument is that although a true international lender of last resort might be desirable in theory, it has no chance of being instituted in practice because the institutional changes involved go well beyond what the international community is ready to accept (Eichengreen 1999). Some further claim that an international LOLR cannot function effectively unless it can issue an indefinite amount of its own currency (Capie 1998), and others argue that the LOLR would need an amount of hard currencies that, although finite, is unrealistically large (Eichengreen 1999; Rogoff 1999).

The debate suggests that the notion of an international LOLR is not well understood, or at least is subject to different interpretations. Questions range from the nature of crises to the arrangements required for the LOLR to operate.[1] This paper proposes a formal framework that may help shed light on several of these issues.

The question with which this paper is primarily concerned is that of the *size* of the international LOLR. Does the international LOLR have to be a global central bank, or could it function effectively as a fund with limited and predetermined resources? In the second case, how large should the fund be? To answer these questions, we build a model of an emerging economy that is vulnerable to international liquidity crises. An international LOLR can in principle cope with these crises by providing hard currency to cash-strapped countries. We scrutinize the size of LOLR interventions that are required to that effect.

This paper focuses on the effectiveness of an international LOLR in dealing with twin (banking and currency) crisis.[2] The need for an international LOLR stems, in our model, from a currency mismatch in the balance sheet of the emerging economy's banking sector. The domestic banking sector does not hold enough foreign currency assets to cover its short-term foreign

---

1. This lack of consensus reflects, to some extent, the state of the literature on the lending-in-last-resort doctrine. Indeed, the dominant genre in this literature seems to be the exegesis—the spirit and letter of Bagehot's *Lombard Street* being invoked to promote various interpretations of the "classical" doctrine. The more formal (model-based) literature, which is generally based on variants of the Diamond-Dybvig model, fails to capture many insights of its less formal counterpart. Naturally, the transposition of these debates to the international context makes things more difficult. See Freixas and Rochet (1997, chap. 7) or Bordo (1990) for reviews of the main debates on lending in last resort.

2. The role of the international LOLR in connection with *sovereign* liquidity crises is discussed by Sachs (1995), Jeanne (2000b), and Kumar, Masson, and Miller (2000).

currency liabilities.[3] It is vulnerable, as a result, to panics in which short-term creditors withdraw their credit lines and depositors run on domestic banks. As in some recent models of twin crises, these panics can be self-fulfilling because of the two-way feedbacks between the depreciation of the currency and the deterioration of banks' balance sheets (Burnside, Eichenbaum, and Rebelo 1999; Schneider and Tornell 2000).

The question, then, is how large the international LOLR should be to remove the bad equilibrium. We find that the required size of the international LOLR crucially depends on how its resources are used. We compare two approaches, which correspond to the distinction—originally made by Goodfriend and King (1988) in a domestic context—between "lending-in-last-resort as an input in monetary policy" and "lending-in-last-resort as an input in banking policy." In the former approach, the international LOLR injects its resources into the financial market, directly or through the domestic monetary authorities. In the second approach, the resources of the international LOLR are used to back domestic banking safety nets, such as discount-window lending policy by the central bank or a government guarantee of banks' foreign currency liabilities. The two approaches have the following implications for the size of the international LOLR.

- If the resources of the international LOLR are injected into the market, lending in last resort has to be carried out by the issuer of the international currency (the U.S. Federal Reserve). The panic equilibrium is not removed by a limited fund, even a very large one.
- The lending-in-last-resort function can be effectively carried out by a limited fund if its resources are used to back domestic banking safety nets. Then the international LOLR resources do not need to be larger than the *liquidity gap* in the domestic banking sector, that is, the difference between the domestic banking sector's short-term foreign currency liabilities and its foreign currency liquid assets.

Clearly, the second approach seems more practical than the first one. We argue, however, that it raises knotty agency problems that seem difficult to address under the current international financial architecture. In the second approach, the international LOLR would have to be an "International Banking Fund" closely integrated with the domestic systems of financial safety nets and supervision in emerging economies. It would have to assume a significant role in supervising domestic banking sectors. We do not see such an evolution as likely, at least in the foreseeable future. Nations remain jealous of their prerogatives in the regulation and supervision of their banking sectors, and there seems to be little political appetite for a globally inte-

---

3. If the assets and liabilities of domestic banks were denominated in the domestic currency, the domestic authorities would not need any external assistance to lend in last resort (Chang and Velasco 2000; Goodhart and Huang, 2000). There would be no need for an *international* lender of last resort.

grated system with the IMF, the BIS, or any new institution at its center (Eichengreen 1999; Giannini 2002).

As a by-product, our model yields interesting insights on monetary policy and exchange rate regimes in emerging economies. In particular, we find that the country's vulnerability to twin crises is the same under a flexible exchange rate regime as under a fixed peg. The reason is that the scope offered by exchange rate flexibility is largely illusory in a twin crisis. A floating exchange rate regime allows the domestic monetary authorities to set lower interest rates, but the associated exchange rate depreciation is no less destabilizing for the domestic financial sector—when there is a currency mismatch—than high interest rates.[4] Indeed, if our analysis has any implications for exchange rate regimes, it is to suggest the optimality of very hard pegs, or dollarization. In our model, a credible commitment not to devalue the currency removes the bad equilibrium at no cost to the international community.

The paper is structured as follows. Section 4.2 presents some evidence on the Asian crises to motivate the model. Section 4.3 presents the model. Section 4.4 examines the role of domestic monetary policy, and section 4.5 that of an international lender of last resort. Section 4.6 concludes.

4.2   The Asian Twin Crises: Some Stylized Facts

Although the concomitance of banking and currency crises is not an original feature of the Asian 1997 crisis,[5] it appeared as a very salient one for market participants at the time. Market analysts generally viewed the banking crises as the primary determinant of the currency instability and conditioned their exchange rate forecasts on the prospects of a recovery in the banking sector (see, e.g., the *Financial Time Currency Forecaster* 1997–98). This section presents a few stylized facts on the banking and currency crises in the four countries most affected by banking instability: Indonesia, Korea, Malaysia, and Thailand. Our main purpose is to motivate the assumptions of the model presented in the following section.

4.2.1   Maturity and Currency Mismatches

The four crisis-hit countries received an exceptionally high level of capital inflows in the period leading up to the crisis. A significant fraction of these inflows took the form of short-term credit in foreign currency. Meanwhile, current account deficits were draining the foreign exchange reserves, leading to the buildup of a large and increasing gap between short-term external debt and the foreign exchange reserves at the central bank (fig. 4.1). On the eve of the crisis, only Malaysia had enough reserves to cover its

---

4. A similar point is made by Bacchetta (2000) and Aghion, Bacchetta, and Banerjee (2000). See also Céspedes, Chang, and Velasco (2000); Christiano, Gust, and Roldos (2000); and Gertler, Gilchrist, and Natalucci (2000) for recent models of monetary policy with a balance sheet channel for the exchange rate.

5. Kaminsky and Reinhart (1999) count nineteen twin crises prior to 1995.

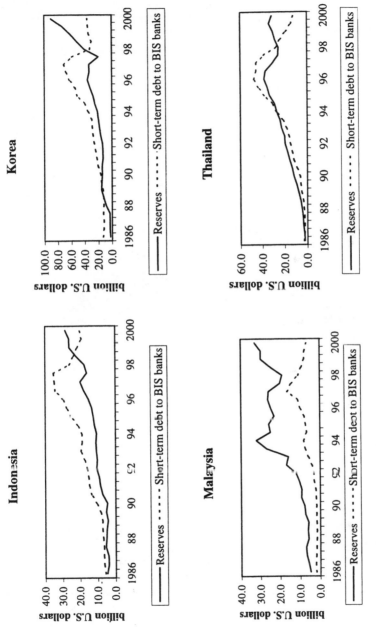

Fig. 4.1   Reserves and short-term debt

Table 4.1   **The Asian Twin Crises**

	Indonesia	Korea	Malaysia	Thailand
Foreign exchange reserves (end of 1996)	7.8	6.4	26.0	20.5
Short-term debt to BIS-reporting banks (end of 1996)	15.0	12.0	11.2	25.1
Foreign liabilities of domestic banks (end of 1996)	5.6	8.7	11.2	27.1
Peak-to-trough decline in reserves	5.3 (6/97–2/98)	3.4 (7/97–12/97)	16.5 (3/97–1/98)	7.3 (1/97–8/97)
Decline in domestic banks' foreign liabilities	−0.8 (6/97–2/98)	3.2 (7/97–12/97)	4.1 (3/97–1/98)	2.4 (1/97–8/97)
Liquidity support to financial institutions (6/97–6/99)	31.9	6.9	13.8	22.5
IMF-supported packages (disbursement)	8.8	6.0	—	7.9
Bank closures (percentage points of total banking assets)	18.0	15.0	0.0	13.0
Memorandum items				
Total bank assets (1996)	90.0	300.0	300.0	190.0
1996 GDP (US$ billions)	227.4	520.2	100.7	181.9

Note: The variables are expressed in percentage points of 1996 GDP, except when specified otherwise.

short-term debt to BIS-reporting banks. The international liquidity gap was especially large in Indonesia, where it exceeded 7 percent of gross domestic product (GDP) at the end of 1996 (table 4.1). A significant fraction of this buildup in short-term external debt reflected borrowing by domestic banks. The foreign liabilities of domestic banks increased markedly in all countries, most dramatically in Thailand, where they were approaching one third of GDP on the eve of the crisis (table 4.1).

Most of the external borrowing by banks and corporates was denominated in foreign currency, and the resulting currency risk was largely unhedged. Data limitations make it very difficult to assess the extent to which the currency risk was assumed directly by banks or passed along to their borrowers. Although bank regulation typically disallows currency mismatches, one of the lessons from the recent crises is that they do occur and can be sizable. Even when the banks themselves avoid currency mismatches, firms that are their customers may carry such a risk on their own books. If many large firms fail simultaneously, so will their banks, especially as maturity transformation is a key function of the banking system.

4.2.2   The Bust

The crisis was accompanied by sharp depreciations of the exchange rate in all countries, a phenomenon that was more pronounced and persistent in

Indonesia than elsewhere (fig. 4.2). Indonesia was also exceptional in the level at which it raised its interest rate, a difference that reflected more the burst of inflation that followed the depreciation than an aggressive defense of the currency (fig. 4.3). By contrast, the interest rates in Malaysia seem to have been somewhat insulated from exchange rate developments by capital controls.

Simultaneously, the banking problems that had started to surface before the crisis took a sudden turn for the worse under the joint pressure of high interest rates, a depreciated currency, and a general loss of confidence. The currency depreciation had an adverse effect on the solvency of banks and firms because of the currency mismatches in their balance sheets. A large-scale run by domestic depositors was observed in Indonesia, where, by mid-December 1997, 154 banks representing half of the total assets of the system had faced a significant erosion of their deposit base (Lindgren et al. 1999). The other countries had to cope with a similar pressure coming from short-term creditors, especially foreign banks in Korea.

Although the withdrawal of foreign credit lines certainly exercised a drain on the foreign exchange reserves, it does not seem to have been in general the primary cause of capital outflows. Table 4.1 reports peak-to-trough

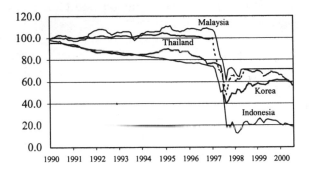

Fig. 4.2   Exchange rates (1990–2000)

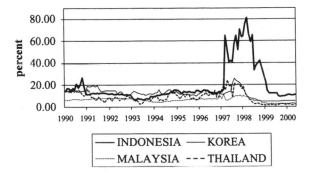

Fig. 4.3   Money market interest rates

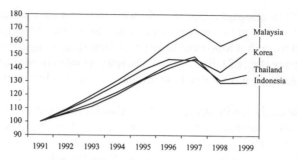

Fig. 4.4   Real GDP (1991 = 100)

changes in foreign exchange reserves, as well as the change in the foreign liabilities of domestic banks at the time of the crisis. With the exception of Korea, the drop in reserves was driven much more by speculative capital outflows than by the repayment of banks' foreign debt. On average (excluding Korea), the fall in reserves was six times as large as the decline in banks' foreign liabilities. In other words, out of each dollar flowing out of these economies, less than fourteen cents were used to repay the foreign liabilities of domestic banks. The rest was capital flight caused by domestic and foreign residents' shifting their portfolio toward foreign assets and by speculation against the domestic currency.

The four countries suffered large falls in output (see fig. 4.4) and there is evidence that the banking problems contributed to the slumps. The importance of banks in financial intermediation had increased markedly in the period leading up to the crisis.[6] As the crisis developed, the most insolvent banks were closed, and the others saw their ability to lend curtailed by the withdrawal of short-term credit lines. Banking problems were associated with a severe decline in real credit (Lindgren et al. 1999). Although it is delicate, as always, to disentangle the respective contributions of demand and supply in the credit crunch, some studies have found evidence that it was in part supply driven (Ghosh and Ghosh 1999; Ding, Domaç, and Ferri 1998).

4.2.3   Policy Responses

Countries responded to the crisis on several fronts. We briefly review the emergency measures in macro and banking policies, leaving aside the more structural policies that were also initiated at the time of the crisis.

The first and most immediate decision in a currency crisis is the choice between increasing the interest rate in order to defend the currency and letting the exchange rate go. Our four countries did both to various extents, in

6. Total commercial bank and near-bank assets grew from between 50 and 100 percent of GDP in 1992 to between 150 and 200 percent of GDP at the end of 1996 (see table 4.1). As a comparison, deposit money banks held assets equal to 80 percent of GDP in the United States.

part as the reflection of a dilemma in which the monetary authorities were caught. On the one hand, there were limits to which the interest rate could be raised, given the fragile state of the banking and corporate sectors. On the other hand, letting the currency depreciate also had adverse effects because of the currency mismatch in the balance sheets of banks and firms.

The limited scope offered by monetary policy led the authorities to rely on policies that were more directly targeted at banks. In all four countries central banks provided liquidity to financial institutions under various emergency lending and LOLR facilities. The amounts were especially large in Indonesia and Thailand, where they exceeded 20 percent of GDP (table 4.1). This liquidity support was provided in domestic currency except in Korea, where it was primarily in U.S. dollars. To the extent that its impact on the monetary base was sterilized, however, the liquidity support provoked the same reserves losses irrespective of the currency in which it was provided.[7]

The provision of emergency liquidity was enhanced by various forms of government guarantees of banks' liabilities. None of the four countries had a formal insurance scheme on bank deposits at the beginning of the crisis, so the guarantees had to be introduced under the pressure of events. As the severity of the crisis became apparent and the introduction of more limited guarantees failed to restore confidence, the four countries ended up providing blanket guarantees for all depositors and most creditors (Lindgren et al. 1999). The guarantees did not always succeed in stemming capital outflows, however, possibly because of uncertainty about the government's ability to honor them. In Korea, for example, the guarantee on foreign debt was not sufficient to convince short-term foreign creditors to roll over their credit lines. This was followed by an effort to coordinate creditors and was resolved by voluntary debt restructuring. In all four countries, the guarantees were announced to be temporary and meant to maintain public confidence during the period of restructuring.

These policies were backed by large rescue packages arranged under the auspices of the IMF, with the notable exception of Malaysia. Interestingly, the size of these packages was of the same order of magnitude as—and in fact slightly larger than—the liquidity gap before the crisis (table 4.1). Malaysia instead chose to introduce drastic capital controls.

4.3   Model

One feature of twin crises that the Asian experience illustrates very well is the mutually self-reinforcing nature of banking and currency fragilities. As Kaminsky and Reinhart (1999) put it, "Financial-sector problems

---

7. Sterilization was largely effective in Korea and Thailand, but not in Indonesia and Malaysia.

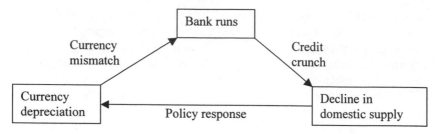

Fig. 4.5   The vicious spiral

undermine the currency. Devaluations, in turn, aggravate the existing banking-sector problems and create new ones. These adverse feedback mechanisms . . . can be amplified, as we have seen in several of the recent Asian crises, by banks' inadequate hedging of foreign-exchange risk."

We present a model (fig. 4.5) in which these negative feedback effects are linked together in the following vicious spiral: The currency depreciation triggers bank runs because of a currency mismatch in the balance sheets of domestic banks. Banking problems in turn depress domestic supply by inducing a credit crunch. Finally, the decline in domestic supply weakens the currency, as the domestic authorities attempt to boost output by a depreciation. This closes the circle.

In our model this vicious circle goes beyond making twin crises simply persistent or difficult to manage: it makes them self-fulfilling. We would like to emphasize, however, that we do not view this paper as a contribution to the debate on whether twin crises are self-fulfilling in the real world. The purpose of this paper is *not* to convince the reader that they were, in Asia or elsewhere. It is to study the *feasibility* of an international LOLR. It makes sense to look at this question in the context of a model with self-fulfilling bank runs, which is the problem that a LOLR is supposed to solve in theory.

4.3.1   The Linkage from the Currency Depreciation to Bank Runs

We consider a two-period model of an open emerging economy ($t = 1, 2$). The agents are the domestic private banks, their depositors, and the domestic central bank. For the sake of brevity and *couleur locale* we call the domestic and foreign currencies *peso* and *dollar* respectively. We denote by S_t the price of one peso in terms of dollars at time t. An increase in S_t thus corresponds to an appreciation of the peso.

The peso/dollar exchange rate satisfies uncovered interest parity (UIP):

$$(1) \qquad S_1 = \frac{1 + i}{1 + i^*} S_2^e,$$

where S_2^e is the expected exchange rate, and i and i^* are respectively the peso and dollar riskless interest rates in period 1.

Domestic banks have deposits and income streams denominated in dollars and pesos. The currency composition of banks' assets and liabilities is inherited from an earlier time, in which some banks found it optimal to borrow or lend in dollars or for some reason could not borrow in pesos.[8] It does not seriously weaken our analysis to take the structure of banks' balance sheets as given, because we focus here on the policy measures at the time of the crisis, after the currency and maturity mismatches have built up.[9] We denote by $D(j)$ and $D^*(j)$ the quantities of peso and dollar deposits at bank j, and by $R_t(j)$ and $R_t^*(j)$ its peso-denominated and dollar-denominated income streams in period t.

Deposits are repayable on demand, and demand is served sequentially, as in Diamond and Dybvig's (1983) model of bank runs. Each bank has a continuum of atomistic depositors who decide at $t = 1$ whether or not to withdraw their deposits. The withdrawing depositors are randomly allocated in a queue that determines the order in which they are served. The bank repays depositors by selling its assets for pesos or dollars in the market. If the bank does not have enough assets to repay all the withdrawing depositors in period 1, the depositors at the end of the queue, and those who have not joined the queue, receive nothing. In the opposite case, the assets that remain in the possession of the bank at the end of period 1 are sold in period 2 to repay the remaining depositors—those who have not withdrawn in period 1. Deposits are interest bearing and yield the riskless interest rate corresponding to their currency of denomination. The holder of one dollar (peso) of deposit at time 1 is entitled to withdraw $1 + i^*$ $(1 + i)$ dollars (pesos) at time 2.

We assume that bank assets are liquid in the sense that they can be sold costlessly on a perfectly competitive market at their present discounted value. This assumption is important insofar as it rules out bank runs à la Diamond and Dybvig, which are caused by the illiquidity of bank assets.[10] Bank j is solvent if, and only if, the present value of its income streams exceeds the value of its deposits, that is:

$$(2) \qquad D^*(j) + S_1 D(j) \leq R_1^*(j) + \frac{R_2^*(j)}{1 + i^*} + S_1 \left[R_1(j) + \frac{R_2(j)}{1 + i} \right]$$

8. Chang and Velasco (2000) and Goldfajn and Valdes (1999) endogenize the maturity mismatch in open-economy versions of the Diamond-Dybvig model of bank runs. Burnside, Eichenbaum, and Rebelo (1999) and Schneider and Tornell (2000) endogenize the currency mismatch as the result of a government guarantee on foreign currency liabilities, whereas in Caballero and Krishnamurthy (2000) it is the result of domestic financial underdevelopment.

9. Of course it would be essential to endogenize the currency mismatch if we wanted to understand how policy measures can prevent its emergence ex ante (Jeanne, 2000c).

10. In theory, the benefit of banking intermediation should be linked to the illiquidity of bank assets. Assuming that bank assets are sold at a discount relative to their present value would not change the thrust of our results, and it is interesting to see that in fact we do not need this assumption. The role played by the illiquidity assumption in the bank run literature is played here by a state-conditional depreciation of the domestic currency.

If this solvency condition is satisfied, the bank can repay all its depositors irrespective of the date at which they withdraw, and depositors have no (strict) incentives to withdraw early. If this condition is not satisfied, then all depositors run on the bank at period 1. Some depositors will have to take a loss, and each depositor minimizes the likelihood of being one of them by withdrawing his deposits early. Note that, by contrast with the Diamond-Dybvig model, the equilibrium is unique at the level of an individual bank. For a given balance sheet structure, the occurrence of a run is determined by interest and exchange rates, variables that are exogenous to the actions of the bank's depositors (the bank being very small).

In order to simplify the exposition we shall consider an extreme case of currency and maturity mismatch: all the deposits are denominated in dollars, and banks receive only one income stream, which is denominated in pesos and arrives in period 2. In terms of the variables of our model, this corresponds to the case in which R_1^*, R_2^*, R_1 and D are equal to zero. The assumption that R_1^* and R_2^* are equal to zero does not restrict the generality of the analysis, and it is made simply to alleviate the algebra. The case in which R_1 and D are different from zero is analyzed in the appendix. It has interesting implications for domestic monetary policy, which we choose not to discuss here because they are not essential to the core of our argument.

Using the interest parity condition in equation (1) to substitute S_1 and i out of the solvency condition in equation (2), we find that bank j is solvent if and only if

$$(3) \qquad D^*(j) \le \frac{S_2^e}{1 + i^*} R_2(j)$$

In order to avoid the discontinuity associated with the use of integers, we assume that the set of banks is isomorphic to a continuum of mass 1 and that the banks' characteristics are continuously distributed. As equation (3) makes clear, the set of solvent banks shrinks if the expected peso exchange rate depreciates (S_2^e goes down). Consequently, the number of bank runs in period 1, n, is a continuous and decreasing function of the expected exchange rate:

$$(4) \qquad n = N(S_2^e), \quad N' < 0$$

An expected depreciation of the peso reduces the value of bank assets relative to their liabilities, drawing a larger number of banks into insolvency.

4.3.2   The Reverse Linkage

The linkage from bank runs to exchange rate expectations is in the spirit of the escape clause or second-generation approach to currency crises (Jeanne 2000a). It involves the endogenous policy response of the domestic authorities to the disruption in real activity induced by the bank runs.

We assume that period-2 output is given by a standard Phillips curve augmented by a term reflecting the real disruption induced by runs on domestic banks in period 1. The law of one price applies, so that the Phillips curve can be written in terms of the exchange rate:

$$(5) \qquad Y_2 = \overline{Y} - \alpha(S_2 - S_2^e) - f(n), \quad f(0) = 0, \quad f' > 0,$$

$\overline{Y}$ is the natural level of output, and n is the number of banks that are subject to runs in period 1. Bank runs reduce output by inducing a credit crunch: the banks that are subject to runs are no longer able to provide loans to borrowers with no easy access to other forms of finance.[11] Function $f(\cdot)$ characterizes how the output loss in period 2 depends on the number of bank runs in period 1. The output loss is increasing with the number of runs, presumably in a nonlinear way: for example, one could assume that a small number of bank runs has no effect on output but that widespread runs (the truly systemic banking crises) entail large output losses.

The domestic government minimizes the quadratic loss $L_2 = (Y_2 - \overline{Y})^2 + \beta(S_2 - \overline{S})^2$. As in the classical Barro-Gordon setting, the exchange rate term captures an aversion to changes in the domestic price level (which are equivalent to changes in the exchange rate under the law of one price). We assume that the domestic government behaves in a discretionary way; that is, it minimizes its loss function in period 2, taking period 1 expectations as given. Using equation (5) to substitute out Y_2 in L_2, and minimizing over S_2, one finds that the period-2 exchange rate is a function of the number of bank runs and of the expected exchange rate:

$$(6) \qquad S_2 = \frac{1}{\alpha^2 + \beta} [\beta \overline{S} + \alpha^2 S_2^e - \alpha f(n)]$$

The expected exchange rate in period 2 is decreasing with the number of bank runs in period 1, as the authorities attempt to mitigate the effect of the credit crunch on domestic output with a depreciation of the domestic currency.

4.3.3   Multiple Equilibria

We look at rational expectations Nash equilibria, in which each depositor decides whether or not to withdraw in period 1, taking the actions of the other depositors as given. Under rational expectations, the expected exchange rate and its realized level must coincide, because there is no uncertainty in the model. Replacing S_2^e with S_2 in equations (4) and (6), we find

---

11. Disyatat (2000) presents a model of an open economy in which a depreciation tends to stimulate output because of a short-run Phillips curve but reduces the domestic banks' ability to lend. The credit crunch in his model comes from a reduction in banks' net worth, not from runs.

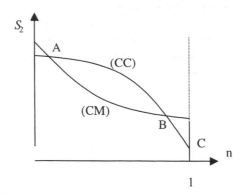

Fig. 4.6   Twin-crisis equilibria

that the number of bank runs and the second-period exchange rate are linked by two relationships:

$$n = N(S_2), \quad (CM)$$

$$S_2 = \overline{S} - \frac{\alpha}{\beta}f(n), \quad (CC)$$

The currency mismatch (CM) relationship characterizes the linkage from the exchange rate to the number of bank runs. Its shape is determined by the currency mismatch in banks' balance sheets: in the absence of mismatch, the number of bank runs would not depend on the exchange rate. The credit crunch (CC) relationship characterizes the linkage from bank runs to the exchange rate. This link arises because the domestic authorities depreciate the currency in response to a credit crunch.

Figure 4.6 shows the CC and CM curves with the number of bank runs on the x-axis and the exchange rate on the y-axis. Both curves are downward-sloping, so that the model generically gives rise to multiple equilibria. In the case represented in figure 4.6 there are two stable equilibria, corresponding to points A and C. In the good equilibrium (point A) the currency is strong and only the "truly insolvent" banks are subject to runs. In the bad equilibrium (point C) the currency is expected to depreciate markedly, and all the banks are subject to runs. The equilibrium corresponding to point B is unstable.[12]

Note that, although bank runs may be self-fulfilling in this model, they never hit an "illiquid but solvent" bank. There is a perfect coincidence, in equilibrium, between runs and insolvency. In the bad equilibrium, the banks that are subject to runs are made insolvent by the pressure on the exchange rate. Some of these banks are "truly" or "virtually" solvent, in the sense that they would be solvent in the good equilibrium. However, it is im-

---

12. At point B, the bank runs caused by a slight fall in the expected exchange rate tend to depreciate the exchange rate even further, pushing the economy to point C.

portant to keep in mind that "true" solvency, understood in this sense, is an out-of-equilibrium concept.

4.3.4   How Panics Depend on the Fundamentals

The model makes several predictions about the conditions under which twin crises occur. First, there must be a significant currency mismatch in the balance sheets of domestic banks: the equilibrium is uniquely determined if banks' assets and liabilities are denominated in the same currency and, by continuity, if the two are sufficiently close. Second, the weight of the exchange rate (or price) objective in the authorities' loss function must be sufficiently small. If this weight, β, is large, the bad equilibrium disappears because bank runs are no longer expected to significantly depreciate the currency.[13] Finally, self-fulfilling twin crises are more likely when the foreign interest rate, i^*, is high, because this increases the number of insolvent banks, other things being equal.[14]

It is not difficult to complicate the model slightly so as to make the multiplicity of equilibria contingent on other economic variables. For example, we could introduce a persistence effect in the Phillips curve, replacing equation (5) with

$$(7) \qquad Y_2 = \overline{Y} + \rho(Y_1 - \overline{Y}) - \alpha(S_2 - S_2^e) - f(n)$$

The second-period output now depends on its first-period level. Consequently, the second-period exchange rate will also depend on the first-period output Y_1, and twin crises can occur only if Y_1 is not too high. These results are broadly consistent with Kaminsky and Reinhart's (1999) observation that twin crises are preceded by recessions or below-normal economic growth and tend to occur when U.S. interest rates are high. The contingency of the multiplicity on output is not essential for our discussion, however, and we use the simpler model.

Whether the economy lands on one or the other of the equilibria may depend on a sunspot variable, which may or not be correlated with the underlying fundamentals. As one of us has argued elsewhere, the sunspot should not be interpreted literally, but rather as a "black box" for the little-understood phenomena involved in the selection of the equilibrium in the real world (Jeanne 2000a).[15] We do not lose much from using this black box

---

13. In the limit case in which β is infinite, the CC curve in figure 4.6 is horizontal, so that there is one unique equilibrium.

14. Raising i^* increases the number of insolvent banks for a given exchange rate and shifts the CM locus to the right. Thus, this could shift the economy from a state in which the CM is everywhere below CC—so that there is one unique equilibrium with no bank run—to a state in which the CM and CC curves have multiple intersections.

15. Morris and Shin (1998) present a possible theory for the selection of the equilibrium. Their approach requires the number of equilibria to depend on the value of some exogenous hidden fundamental about which market participants receive private signals. It could be applied to our model by assuming, for example, that market participants do not know the true value of the domestic government's aversion to inflation, β.

in this paper, because we look at policy measures that aim at removing the multiplicity of equilibria, not measures that aim at favoring the selection of the good equilibrium.

4.4   The Limits of Monetary Policy

This section presents the implications of the model for domestic monetary policy. We show that domestic monetary policy does not offer the right tools for dealing with twin crises. This point, which is of independent interest, is also important to justify the intervention of an international LOLR. If the domestic authorities could deal with twin crises by using monetary policy, there would be no need for an international LOLR. In addition, the model has interesting implications for exchange rate regimes, which we briefly discuss in section 4.4.2.

4.4.1   The Irrelevance of Interest Rates

The most immediate question that policy makers have to solve in the heat of crises is macroeconomic: what to do with the interest rate? The debates spurred by the IMF's policy recommendations in the Asian crisis have seen the opposition between two views: the view that the interest rate should be raised, at least for a while, in order to defend the currency, and the view that it should be kept at a low level to spare the domestic economy. The advocates of the latter view have pointed out that a policy of high interest rate may be self-destructive to the extent that it aggravates the real problems in the economy, in particular in the banking sector (Furman and Stiglitz 1998). The opposite side has emphasized that letting the currency depreciate is not a viable alternative when there is a currency mismatch in the balance sheet of banks or firms. Our model is consistent with at least one part of each view: monetary policy simply does not offer the right tools to deal with twin crises.

In our model, low or high interest rates are equally ineffective against twin crises. In order to establish this point, it is sufficient to recall that the domestic interest rate, i, was not in the list of variables that determine the set of equilibria. Hence, if the economy is vulnerable to a self-fulfilling twin crisis, there is nothing that the domestic authorities can do about it by manipulating the domestic interest rate.

One may dig out the economic intuition behind this result by going back to the condition for bank solvency, equation (3). The solvency of banks is determined by one variable: the time-1 dollar price of time-2 pesos, $S_2^e/(1 + i^*)$. Under UIP, his price can be decomposed as the product of two terms, the time-1 peso price of a time-2 peso, and the time-1 exchange rate:

$$P* = \frac{1}{1 + i} \cdot \frac{(1 + i)S_2^e}{1 + i^*}$$

The first term is decreasing with i, while the second term is increasing with i. Increasing i, thus, has two opposite effects, which capture the two sides of the debate mentioned above. On the one hand, raising i undermines banks' solvency by depressing the peso price of long-term peso assets. On the other hand, this enhances banks' solvency by appreciating the domestic currency. The first effect arises because of the maturity mismatch in the balance sheet of banks, and the second effect because of the currency mismatch. On balance, the two effects cancel each other out, so that the level of the interest rate is irrelevant.

The two effects *exactly* cancel each other out because of the particular assumptions we have made on the currency and maturity structure of banks' balance sheets—that bank deposits are denominated in dollars, and that their receipts are given in period-2 pesos. The robustness of our results to more general assumptions is explored in the appendix. We show there that the solvency of banks is no longer independent of the level of the interest rate, so that a policy of high interest rates may or not dominate a policy of low interest rates. A policy of high interest rates tends to become more desirable when the maturity mismatch between the peso-denominated assets and liabilities of banks is less pronounced.

This extension, however, does not invalidate our main conclusion. If the weight of price stability in domestic objectives is too low and the currency mismatch is severe, self-fulfilling twin crises may exist, and if they do, monetary policy is powerless in preventing them. This is because the scope of monetary policy in preserving banks' solvency, although no longer completely empty, remains limited and contingent on exchange rate expectations.

4.4.2   Implications for Exchange Rate Regimes

The recent major twin crises were all associated with fixed but adjustable currency pegs, whence the natural conclusion that in order to be viable, exchange rate regimes have to be either more flexible or more fixed. The exchange rate alternative, for emerging economies, is increasingly defined as a choice between corner solutions—between exchange rate flexibility and very hard pegs (Eichengreen 1999; Rubin 1999).

In the debate between the extremes, a classical argument in favor of flexibility is that it gives monetary policy more scope to respond to shocks, especially in times of crisis. However, the apparent margin of maneuver offered by a flexible exchange rate is largely illusory in our model.[16] The reason is that the threat is not a currency crisis (a run on the central bank's foreign exchange reserves) but a bank crisis (a run on dollar deposits in banks). The occurrence of bank runs is determined by the dollar price of future pesos. Whether a given change in this price is achieved by changing the inter-

---

16. It is completely illusory under the assumption that D and R_1 are equal to zero. It is not completely illusory, but remains limited, in the more general case (see appendix).

est rate or the exchange rate is irrelevant for financial stability. Although it is true that a floating regime allows the monetary authorities to set a lower interest rate in the face of speculative pressure, the resulting depreciation hurts domestic banks no less than high interest rates.

Indeed, if the model has an implication for exchange rate regimes, it is rather to suggest the optimality of very hard pegs, or dollarization. If the defense of the fixed peg is delegated to a conservative central banker putting a very high weight β on exchange rate stability, the bad equilibrium disappears. If, more generally, the domestic authorities find a way to make a credible commitment to exchange rate stability, the vicious spiral that underpins twin crises is broken, because bank runs no longer feed devaluation expectations. Dollarization can be interpreted as the limit case in which β is infinite, so that there is no exchange rate uncertainty. Twin crises obviously cannot arise in countries that have dollarized, because then there is no currency mismatch in the balance sheets of banks: both banks' assets and liabilities are denominated in dollars.

This might lead us to conclude in favor of very hard pegs over exchange rate flexibility. However, this conclusion should be qualified by two important caveats. First, the currency mismatch that is taken as exogenous in the model could in fact be endogenous to the exchange rate regime. It is often argued that regimes with fixed but adjustable exchanges are conducive to currency mismatches because domestic borrowers tend to underestimate the risk of a devaluation (Lindgren et al. 1999). The model does not capture one possible benefit of exchange rate flexibility—in fact, the only possible benefit, under our assumptions—which is that it prevents the emergence of currency mismatches.

The second caveat is that although hard pegs or dollarization remove the twin crises resulting from currency mismatches in the banking sector—the crises that we focus on in this paper—they do not remove banking panics à la Diamond and Dybvig, which result instead from the illiquidity of bank assets. If bank runs à la Diamond and Dybvig are possible, a group of countries linked by a system of hard pegs or a common currency may still need an international lending-of-last-resort arrangement. This is why the reluctance of the U.S. Federal Reserve to assume the role of LOLR abroad may be viewed as a valid argument against dollarization in Latin American countries. This is also why the euro area may need an international LOLR.[17]

4.5 The International Lender of Last Resort

Our model seems to provide an ideal setting for the intervention of an international LOLR. Domestic banks are vulnerable to self-fulfilling runs be-

---

17. See Prati and Schinasi (2000) for a discussion on lending-in-last-resort arrangements in the euro area.

tional liquidity. Perhaps the bad
ational LOLR standing ready to
to the country in the event of a

ext of the model, with some new
gate level of dollar deposits in the
reign exchange reserves at the do-
endowment of the international
romise to augment the domestic
o L^*, in which case the domestic
dity is limited to $X^* + L^*$ in a cri-
could use its resources directly,
uthorities. The question, in both
e the bad equilibrium.
e international LOLR to remove
e good one. In the good equilib-
ones—are subject to runs (see fig-
s a bailout, not a lending-in-last-
anks has costs in terms of moral
t explicitly modeled in our frame-
As a matter of definition, it is not
ent institutions.

in a domestic context, that the
rket by open market operations.[19]
ould involve the same operations
as *monetary policy* in normal times, although possibly to a much larger scale. According to this view, lending-in-last-resort policies in which the authorities attempt to bypass the market and target liquidity directly at selected institutions—for example, by lending to them at the discount window—is a vestige of a time when financial markets did not have the depth and efficiency that they have achieved today.

This view is based on the premise that market forces will allocate the liquidity better than the authorities. Market participants have more information than the authorities on the situations of individual banks and are not subject to the temptation of bailing out insolvent banks under political

18. The lending-in-last-resort arrangement could involve a pool of private banks. However, there are reasons (outside of the model) that the provision of liquidity by public institutions may be more effective. In particular, it may be difficult for private banks to commit not to hedge their risk by market operations that drain international liquidity from the country in the event of a crisis. A comparison between the various possible types of lending-in-last-resort arrangement is outside the scope of this paper.

19. The origin of this view is sometimes traced back to Thornton ([1802] 1978) and Humphrey (1975)—see Fischer (2000).

pressure. Market forces, thus, will ensure that the liquidity is allocated to the "truly solvent" banks. Goodfriend and King call this policy "lending-in-last resort as an input into monetary policy," as opposed to "lending-in-last resort as an input into banking policy."

What should the international LOLRs do, according to this approach? In the closed-economy context, considered by Goodfriend and King, the LOLR injects liquidity into the market by open market operations, that is, by buying bonds in exchange of domestic money. The open-economy analog is an injection of international liquidity, that is, in our model, dollars. The international LOLR provides international liquidity to the market by buying peso-denominated bonds in exchange of dollars, that is, by a sterilized foreign exchange intervention. If markets are perfectly integrated internationally, it does not matter whether the foreign exchange intervention is realized by the international LOLR or by the domestic central bank, or in which point of the globe the intervention is implemented.

In our model, this approach is completely ineffective in removing the bad equilibrium. Because of UIP, sterilized foreign exchange interventions have no impact on the interest rate, the exchange rate, or the depositors' actions. In particular, every billion dollars that is injected in the market by the domestic central bank simply goes out of the country in capital outflows. Domestic foreign exchange interventions, in other words, are immediately sucked out of the country in capital outflows instead of going to the agents that need foreign liquidity the most, the domestic banks that are subject to runs.

Our model suggests that if lending in last resort is an input into monetary policy, then it should be carried out by the center's monetary authorities (in the present case in which foreign assets are dollar denominated, the U.S. Federal Reserve). There are at least two ways in which this statement can be understood. First, as we already saw, lowering the foreign interest rate, i^*, may remove the bad equilibrium. Second, the Federal Reserve could successfully peg the dollar price of future pesos at the good equilibrium level, P_A^*. If the dollar price of peso bonds is equal to P_A^*, the number of bank runs is equal to its good equilibrium level, n_A, so that the set of equilibria is reduced to the good equilibrium.

In our model, the dollar price of future pesos cannot be pegged at a level that is inconsistent with UIP. In order to peg this price, the international LOLR would have to inject dollars in the market until the point when market participants can no longer increase their short positions in peso (because of credit constraints or for other reasons) so that UIP ceases to apply. This would require an immense liquidity injection at the global scale, which can be implemented, in practice, only by the issuer of the center currency. Making international lending in last resort an input in monetary policy thus vindicates Capie's (1998) claim that the international LOLR must be the issuer of the international currency: a global central bank, or the U.S. Federal Reserve if the international currency is the dollar.

These results stem, in part, from our assumption that financial markets are perfectly integrated internationally. If financial markets were segmented, international liquidity might have a better chance to reach domestic banks if it were injected in the domestic financial market. Uncovered interest parity also plays a role. In the presence of portfolio effects, the domestic currency could in principle be strengthened by sterilized foreign exchange interventions.

Market segmentation is to some extent a policy variable: the domestic authorities can enhance the segmentation of financial markets by introducing capital controls. Although the analysis of capital controls is outside the scope of this paper, it would be interesting to study whether, and how, capital controls can remove self-fulfilling twin crises in our model. Although capital controls may prevent depositors from taking their dollar deposits out of the country, they will not prevent them from running on the domestic banks that they view as insolvent. The solvency of banks in turn results from the expected exchange rate. Hence, capital controls can remove twin crises only to the extent that this gives the authorities more scope in influencing exchange rate expectations. This could be the case, for example, if the controls introduce a wedge in the interest parity condition.

Let us conclude this section with a metaphor—a hydraulic one, as is often the case in monetary economics. Imagine a small harbor in Brittany: the tide is low and boats are resting on the bottom of the sea, inside the harbor. Lending in last resort by injecting liquidity into the market is like trying to lift the boats by pouring water into the ocean. To be successful, this approach requires an immense reserve of water (an ability to melt the North Pole, say). Imagine now that the harbor is separated from the ocean by a wall and a door. Once the door is closed (capital controls are introduced), one obviously needs to pour much less liquidity inside the harbor to lift the boats.

4.5.2   An "International Banking Fund"

We now consider some arrangements in which the international LOLR can operate as a limited fund. The main difference from the previous section is that the resources of the international LOLR are channeled to the banks on a case-by-case basis instead of being simply "thrown at the market," in Goodfriend and King's terminology, the international LOLR provides an input into banking policy instead of monetary policy. We consider two arrangements. In the first one, the resources of the international LOLR are used to finance discount-window lending by the domestic central bank. In the second one, the international LOLR backs limited guarantees on dollar deposits at domestic banks.

In the discount-window lending policy, the domestic banks that are subject to runs queue at the discount window of the domestic central bank.[20] The latter selects the "truly solvent" banks and lends them all the dollars they need to repay their depositors. The remaining banks receive nothing and collapse. It is important to keep in mind that the solvency of banks is contingent on the equilibrium and that we define "true" solvency with reference to the good equilibrium. In other terms, in the bad equilibrium the authorities assess the solvency of banks as if the economy were in the good equilibrium. In a banking panic, "true" solvency is an out-of-equilibrium attribute, not an observable, objective reality.

That banks' solvency should be assessed with reference to hypothetical market conditions is consistent with some interpretations of the classical doctrine of lending in last resort. This is, for example, the way Fischer (1999) interprets Bagehot's rule that the LOLR should lend "on any collateral that is marketable *in the ordinary course of business when there is no panic.*" The requirement that lending should be made on the basis of the value of collateral *in normal times* can be interpreted as taking the good equilibrium as the benchmark to assess the solvency of banks. In terms of our model, the authorities must assess the value of banks' collateral on the basis of the price that prevails in the good equilibrium, P_A^*. In the bad equilibrium, P_A^* is a shadow price that is larger than the observed market price, P_C^*.

It is easy to see that this arrangement reduces the set of equilibria to the good equilibrium. The international LOLR's intervention breaks the vicious circle depicted in figure 4.5 by preventing bank runs from resulting in an excessive depreciation of the exchange rate. It ensures that the solvent banks remain in operation and that their balance sheets do not shrink in response to runs. For these banks, the only effect of the run is a substitution of creditors: private depositors are replaced by the central bank. As a result, there is no credit crunch in the "truly solvent" part of the banking sector, and the pressure on the exchange rate is reduced accordingly.

The argument can be presented more formally—in terms of the equations of the model—as follows. Let n_A denote the number of insolvent banks in the good equilibrium. With discount-window lending, runs on the (truly) solvent banks no longer contribute to the credit crunch, so that in the Phillips curve of equation (5) variable n must be replaced by $\min(n, n_A)$, the number of insolvent banks that are subject to runs. The equation for the linkage from bank runs to the exchange rate then becomes

$$S_2 = \overline{S} - \frac{\alpha}{\beta} f[\min(n, n_A)] \quad (CC')$$

20. This is the way lending in last resort is modeled in Chang and Velasco (2000) and Goldfajn and Valdés (1999).

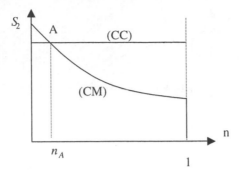

Fig. 4.7   Discount-window lending

In figure 4.6 the locus (CC) becomes horizontal to the right of point A, implying that the set of equilibria is reduced to the good equilibrium (see figure 4.7).

The case in which the international LOLR backs a domestic guarantee on the dollar deposits can be analyzed along similar lines, although there is an interesting difference in the economic mechanism involved. The government announces that it guarantees deposits at (truly) solvent banks (again, true solvency is assessed with reference to the good equilibrium). This breaks the vicious circle depicted in figure 4.5 by suppressing the linkage from the currency depreciation to bank runs. The depositors, once insured, no longer have (strict) incentives to run against the (truly) solvent banks. The expectation of a depreciation is no longer self-fulfilling because it does not provoke a banking collapse.

In terms of the equations of the model, the guarantee affects the relationship between the expected exchange rate and the number of bank runs, equation (4). Developments in the foreign exchange market no longer affect the (truly) solvent banks, so that equation (4) is replaced by $n = \min[n_A, N(S_2^e)]$. The equation for locus (CM) becomes

$$n = \min[n_A, N(S_2)] \quad (CM')$$

In figure 4.6 the locus (CM) becomes vertical in point A, so that again the good equilibrium is the only one (see fig. 4.8). In order for these arrangements to be operational, the resources of the international LOLR do not need to be larger than the liquidity gap in the domestic banking sector, D^* $- X^*$. Indeed, its resources could even be smaller, because the liabilities of the truly insolvent banks do not have to be covered in the event of a crisis. This does not seem unrealistically large. As documented in section 4.2, the IMF-supported rescue packages were of the same order of magnitude as the liquidity gap in the Asian countries that were most affected by the crisis.

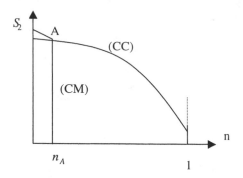

Fig. 4.8   Guarantee on dollar deposits

In sum, we find that an international LOLR backing domestic safety nets needs much less resources than an international LOLR injecting liquidity in the market. It can operate as a limited "International Banking Fund" and would not necessarily need to be considerably larger than existing international financial institutions. This conclusion, however, ignores one important aspect of the problem, to which we now turn: agency problems between the international LOLR and the domestic authorities.

4.5.3   International Agency Problems

One question that we have not addressed so far is the articulation between the international LOLR and the domestic authorities. To what extent should the international LOLR rely on the domestic authorities to funnel the liquidity toward domestic banks? So far, this question has not come up because we implicitly assumed that the international LOLR and the domestic authorities shared the same objectives. However, the involvement of two different authorities in the international lending-in-last-resort arrangement might give rise to agency problems (Tirole 2001). We discuss in this section how agency problems might arise in our framework, as well as the measures to mitigate them.

An agency problem would arise if the domestic authorities thought that the cost of bailing out the truly insolvent banks could somehow be transferred to the international community. The domestic authorities would then be tempted to use the lending-in-last-resort resources in order to bail out the domestic banks that are insolvent in the good equilibrium, at the expense of the foreign taxpayers. As argued by Jeanne and Zettelmeyer (2001), an agency problem could arise even if the fiscal cost of the bailout is borne by the domestic taxpayer. In this case, the problem is that the domestic authorities use the bridge loans from the international community to be overly generous with the domestic special interests that benefit from the bailout, at the expense of the *domestic* taxpayers.

Agency problems could arise at several levels. First, the international

LOLR might be unable to ensure that its resources were not misused by the domestic authorities (to bail out insolvent banks). Second, even if the international LOLR had full control of the way its resources were used—which would be the case, for example, if it lent directly to domestic banks—it might not have all the information that is required to use these resources appropriately. Ideally, the international LOLR should be able to assess the "true" solvency of banks in a crisis. This is informationally very demanding: it requires a precise knowledge of the various feedbacks between the banking system, the productive sector, and the foreign exchange market, as well as the structure of banks' balance sheets.[21] In a world where banking supervisory policies are determined at the national level, most of the relevant knowledge is the private information of the domestic authorities, and they would have little incentive to reveal it truthfully to the international LOLR.

There are different ways to deal with this agency problem, but they all seem to require a significant involvement of the international LOLR in banking supervision and safety nets. The international LOLR would have to be associated with the lending-in-last-resort decisions at the time of the crisis and should be able to form an independent judgment on the true solvency of banks in a banking crisis. This supposes some access to the information of the banking supervisors and some assurance that this information is reliable. Consequently, the international LOLR would probably have to take an active role in monitoring domestic banking systems or cooperate closely with an international agency in charge of international supervision.[22]

How realistic is this involvement of the international LOLR in the supervision of domestic banking sectors? In spite of efforts to promote international standards, the operation of financial safety nets and financial oversight policies remains—and will remain for the foreseeable future—squarely within the bounds of national sovereignty (Eichengreen 1999). Nations remain jealous of their prerogatives in the regulation and supervision of their banking sectors, and there seems to be little political appetite for a globally integrated system with the IMF, the BIS, or any new institution at its center. The domestic resistance to the integration of banking supervision in the euro area—which is so closely integrated in other respects—gives an idea of the difficulties that would arise at the global level. Ultimately, it is not clear that a globally integrated system of banking supervision is more realistic than a global central bank.

21. As we saw in the previous section, banks' solvency must be assessed on the basis of an appropriate shadow price for the collateral. Computing the shadow price is challenging. In general, there is no reason to presume that the appropriate shadow price is close to the precrisis level. In a world where crises are associated with the arrival of news about the fundamentals, the appropriate shadow price should be revised in light of the new information revealed by (or causing) the crisis.

22. The IMF has recently enhanced its monitoring of domestic banking and financial systems with, for example, the development of its Financial Sector Assessment Programs (FSAP); see IMF (2001).

4.6   Concluding Comments

The main result of this paper should be to instill a solid degree of skepticism regarding the feasibility of an international LOLR without sweeping institutional reforms. If the international LOLR uses its resources as an input into monetary policy, the model presented here vindicates those who claim that it must stand ready to provide virtually unbounded amounts of currency. Central banks satisfy this condition, not any existing international financial institution. The alternative is an "International Banking Fund" that is directly involved in the supervision of the domestic banking systems that it might be called upon to rescue—an institutional arrangement that would also require significant reforms in the international financial architecture.

An interesting by-product of the paper is an interpretation of the tradeoff that central banks often face at the time of currency crises. A vigorous interest rate defense weakens the banking system. If banks are fragile, central banks risk triggering a bank run and may end up with both a currency crash and a bank collapse. On the other hand, letting the currency go is not a solution either, because this also weakens the banking system by decreasing the dollar value of its assets. This dilemma explains part of the debate that has arisen after the Asian crisis between those who favored a vigorous interest rate defense and those who called for a sharp decline in interest rates.

The model presented has a number of microeconomic loose ends. The special role of banks in financial intermediation, which is invoked to justify the credit crunch term in the Phillips curve, is not explicitly modeled. The balance sheet effects, which are so important in triggering bank runs in period 1, are neglected in period 2. Fixing these loose ends will probably lower the insight-to-algebra ratio, a price that seems to us worth paying now that we have taken a panoramic shot of the range of policy issues on which the model sheds light.

The model also glosses over several important moral hazard issues. This includes the role of a fixed exchange rate as an implicit guarantee on foreign borrowing and the effect of a LOLR on risk taking. Finally, it should be noted that if regulation prohibiting open currency position by banks is effective, none of our results obtain. Then, however, we would need to take into account the fact that firms rarely face such a regulation. If the corporate sector becomes insolvent, as banks do in our model, and precipitates bank failures, most of our results stand. However, there are interesting differences in the effectiveness of financial safety nets, which would be interesting to explore further. It is not so clear that the provision of liquidity to the banking sector, or government guarantees on banks' liabilities, would remove the bad equilibrium if the currency mismatch is in the corporate sector.

Appendix A
Data Sources

Foreign exchange reserves: *International Financial Statistics,* line 1d.

Short-term debt to Bank of International Settlements (BIS) reporting banks: BIS.

Foreign liabilities of deposit money banks: *International Financial Statistics,* line 26 c.

Liquidity support to financial institutions: author's computations based on Lindgren et al. (1999, table 3).

IMF-supported packages (disbursements): author's computations based on different sources; this variable includes the loans by the IMF, other multilaterals, and governments; it reflects the actual disbursements, which were lower than the initial commitments.

Bank closures: Lindgren et al. (1999, table 7).

Total assets owned by banks: Lindgren et al. (1999, box 3).

GDP (US$billions): International Financial Statistics, line 99b (Gross Domestic Product, national currency) divided by line rf (exchange rate).

Appendix B

This appendix solves for the equilibria in the general case in which banks have peso- and dollar-denominated deposits and income streams. The quantities of peso and dollar deposits at bank j are denoted by $D(j)$ and $D^*(j)$. Bank j's peso-denominated and dollar-denominated income streams in period t are denoted by $R_t(j)$ and $R_t^*(j)$.

Using UIP in equation (1) to substitute S_1 out of equation (2), the condition for bank j's solvency becomes

$$(A1) \quad D^*(j) - \left[R_1^*(j) + \frac{R_2^*(j)}{1 + i^*} \right]$$

$$< \frac{S_2^e}{1 + i^*} \{ [R_1(j) - D(j)](1 + i) + R_2(j) \}$$

The impact of the interest level on bank j's solvency depends on the sign of $R_1(j) - D(j)$, which reflects the maturity mismatch between assets and liabilities denominated in domestic currency. If $R_1(j) - D(j) < 0$, that is, if the bank has more short-term debt than liquid assets in domestic currency, then raising the interest rate undermines the bank's solvency. On the other hand, if $R_1(j) - D(j) > 0$, raising the interest rate enhances the bank's solvency.

In aggregate, raising the interest rate increases (reduces) the number of insolvent banks if $R_1(j) - D(j) < 0$ $[R_1(j) - D(j) > 0]$ for all banks. If the sign of $R_1(j) - D(j)$ differs across banks, then the impact of the interest rate on the number of insolvent banks is ambiguous. We denote by $I(S_2^e)$ the interest level that minimizes the number of insolvent banks when the expected exchange rate is S_2^e, and by $N(S_2^e)$ the corresponding number of insolvent banks.

How does the minimum number of insolvent banks, $N(S_2^e)$, vary with the expected exchange rate? This question is easy to answer if we assume that all the banks are short in dollars, that is, if the left-hand side of equation (A1) is positive. Then the set of solvent banks shrinks for *any* level of the interest rate when S_2^e decreases, implying that the minimum number of insolvent banks, $N(S_2^e)$, is a decreasing function of S_2^e.

We define the rules of the game between the domestic central bank and the depositors as follows. First, the central bank announces how it will adjust the interest rate to the economic conditions, that is, its policy reaction function $i(S_2^e)$. Then depositors play the same Nash game as before, taking the central bank policy reaction function as given. Depositors still maximize their expected consumption, and the central bank minimizes its expected loss L_2^e.

Because the central bank's expected loss is increasing in the number of bank runs, it optimally announces the policy rule that minimizes the number of runs, $I(S_2^e)$. Given this policy rule, the equilibrium number of runs is a decreasing function of the expected exchange rate, like before:

$$n = N(S_2^e), \quad N' < 0.$$

This equation is the same as equation (4) in the text, and the characterization of the equilibria remains the same.

References

Aghion, Philippe, Philippe Bacchetta, and Abhijit Banerjee. 2000. Currency crises and monetary policy in an economy with credit constraints. Harvard University, Department of Economics. Mimeograph.

Bacchetta, Philippe. 2000. Monetary policy with foreign currency debt. Bank of Switzerland, Study Center Gerzensee. Mimeograph.

Bordo, Michael. 1990. The lender of last resort: Alternative views and historical experience. *Federal Reserve Bank of Richmond Economic Review* 76 (1): 18–29.

Burnside, Craig, Martin Eichenbaum, and Sergio Rebelo. 1999. Hedging and financial fragility in fixed exchange rate regimes. Northwestern University, Kellogg Graduate School of Management. Mimeograph.

Caballero, Ricardo J., and Arvind Krishnamurthy. 2000. Dollarization of liabilities: Underinsurance and domestic financial underdevelopment. Massachusetts Institute of Technology, Department of Economics. Mimeograph.

Calomiris, Charles W. 1998. The IMF's imprudent role as lender of last resort. *Cato Journal* 17:275–95.

Capie, Forrest. 1998. Can there be an international lender-of-last-resort? *International Finance* 1:311–25.

Céspedes, L. F., Roberto Chang, and Andrés Velasco. 2000. Balance sheets and exchange rates. NBER Working Paper no. 7840. Cambridge, Mass.: National Bureau of Economic Research.

Chang, Roberto, and Andres Velasco. 2000. Liquidity crises in emerging markets: Theory and policy. In *NBER macroeconomics annual 1999,* ed. Ben S. Bernanke and Julio Rotemberg, 11–58. Cambridge: MIT Press.

Christiano, Lawrence J., Christopher Gust, and Jorge Roldos. 2000. Monetary policy in a financial crisis. Washington, D.C.: International Monetary Fund. Mimeograph.

Diamond, Douglas, and P. Dybvig. 1983. Bank runs, deposit insurance, and liquidity. *Journal of Political Economy* 91:401–19.

Ding, Wei, Ilker Domaç, and Giovanni Ferri. 1998. Is there a credit crunch in East Asia? World Bank Policy Research Working Paper no. 1959. Washington, D.C.: World Bank.

Disyatat, Piti. 2000. Currency crises and the real economy: The role of banks. Princeton University, Department of Economics. Mimeograph.

Eichengreen, Barry. 1999. *Toward a new financial architecture.* Washington, D.C.: Institute for International Economics.

Fischer, Stanley. 1999. On the need for an international lender of last resort. *Journal of Economic Perspectives* 13:85–104.

———. 2000. *On the need for an international lender of last resort.* Essays in International Economics, no. 220. Princeton, N.J.: Princeton University Press.

Fratianni, Michele, and John Pattison. 2001. International lender of last resort: A concept in search of a meaning. Indiana University, Kelley School of Business. Mimeograph.

Freixas, Xavier, and Jean-Charles Rochet. 1997. *Microeconomics of banking.* Cambridge: MIT Press.

Furman, Jason, and Joseph Stiglitz. 1998. Economic crises: Evidence and insights from East Asia. *Brookings Papers on Economic Activity,* Issue no. 2:1–114. Washington, D.C.: Brookings Institution.

Garten, Jeffrey. 1998. In this economic chaos, a global central bank can help. *International Herald Tribune,* 25 September.

Gertler, Mark, Simon Gilchrist, and Fabio M. Natalucci. 2000. External constraints on monetary policy and the financial accelerator. New York University, Department of Economics. Mimeograph.

Ghosh, Swati R., and Atish R. Ghosh. 1999. East Asia in the aftermath: Was there a crunch? IMF Working Paper no. WP/99/54. Washington, D.C.: International Monetary Fund.

Giannini, Curzio. 2002. Pitfalls in international crisis lending. In *Financial crises, contagion, and the lender of last resort: A reader,* ed. Charles Goodhart and Gerhard Illing, 511–46. Oxford, England: Oxford University Press.

Goldfajn, Ilan, and Rodrigo Valdes. 1999. Liquidity crises and the international financial architecture. Pontificia Universidade Catolica do Rio de Janeiro. Department of Economics. Mimeograph.

Goodfriend, Marvin, and Robert King. 1988. Financial deregulation, monetary policy, and central banking. In *Restructuring banking and financial services in America,* ed. W. Haraf and R. M. Kushmeider, 216–53. Lanham, Maryland: American Enterprise Institute and UPA.

Goodhart, Charles, and Haizhou Huang. 2000. A simple model of an international lender of last resort. IMF Working Paper no. WP/00/75. Washington, D.C.: International Monetary Fund.

Humphrey, Thomas. 1975. The classical concept of the lender of last resort. *Federal Reserve Bank of Richmond Economic Review* 61:2–9.

International Financial Institution Advisory Commission (IFIAC). 2000. *Report of the International Financial Institution Advisory Commission,* Allan H. Meltzer, chairman, (Meltzer report). Washington, D.C.: U.S. Congress.

International Monetary Fund (IMF). 2001. *Report of the managing director to the International Monetary and Financial Committee on the IMF in the process of change.* Available at [http://www.imf.org/external/np/omd/2001/report.htm].

Jeanne, Olivier. 2000a. Currency crises: A perspective on recent theoretical developments. Special Papers in International Economics no. 20. Princeton University, Department of Economics.

———. 2000b. Debt maturity and the global financial architecture. Center for Economic Policy Research Discussion Paper no. 2520. London: Center for Economic Policy Research.

———. 2000c. Foreign currency debt and the global financial architecture. *European Economic Review* 44:719–27.

Jeanne, Olivier, and Jeromin Zettelmeyer. 2001. International bail-outs, moral hazard, and conditionality. *Economic Policy* 33 (October): 407–32.

Kaminsky, Graciela, and Carmen Reinhart. 1999. The twin crises: The causes of banking and balance-of-payments problems. *American Economic Review* 89:473–500.

Kumar, Mohan, Paul Masson, and Marcus Miller. 2000. Global financial crises: Institutions and incentives. IMF Working Paper no. WP/00/105. Washington, D.C.: International Monetary Fund.

Lindgren, Carl-Johan, Tomas J. T. Baliño, Charles Enoch, Anne-Marie Gulde, Marc Quintyn, and Leslie Teo. 1999. Financial sector crisis and restructuring: Lessons from Asia. IMF Occasional Paper no. 188. Washington, D.C.: International Monetary Fund.

Morris, Stephen, and Hyun Song Shin. 1998. Unique equilibrium in a model of self-fulfilling currency attacks. *American Economic Review* 88:587–97.

Prati, Alessandro, and Gary Schinasi. 2000. Will the European Central Bank be the lender of last resort in EMU? In *The euro: A challenge and opportunity for financial markets,* ed. M. Artis, A. Weber, and E. Hennessy, 227–56. New York: Routledge.

Rogoff, Kenneth. 1999. International institutions for reducing global financial instability. *Journal of Economic Perspectives* 13:21–42.

Rubin, Robert E. 1999. Testimony on global financial architecture before the House Committee on Banking and Financial Institutions. 20 May. Available at [http://www.ustreas.gov/press/releases/pr3161.htm].

Sachs, Jeffrey. 1995. Do we need an international lender of last resort? Frank D. Graham lecture, Princeton University. 20 April.

Schneider, Martin, and Aaron Tornell. 2000. Balance sheet effects, bailout guarantees, and financial crises. NBER Working Paper no. 8060. Cambridge, Mass.: National Bureau of Economic Research.

Thornton, Henry. [1802] 1978. *An enquiry into the nature and effects of the paper credit of Great Britain.* Reprint, Fairfield: Augustus M. Kelley.

Tirole, Jean. 2001. Liquidity provision and the international financial system. *Bank of Italy Paolo Baffi lectures on money and finance.* Rome: Edizioni dell'Elefante.

Comment   Olivier Blanchard

This is an extremely nice paper. It has two parts, a model of multiple equilibria based on maturity/currency mismatch, and a discussion of the role for a lender of last resort in the context of such multiple equilibria. It has two important propositions, the first about the (near) irrelevance of monetary policy in the context of banking and currency crises, the second about the need for directed intervention by the international lender of last resort. Let me discuss each one in turn.

The Maturity/Currency Mismatch Model

The basic model presented by Jeanne and Wyplosz (JW hereafter) is beautifully simple. It is based on two relations. The first relies on the maturity/currency mismatch of bank liabilities and assets, and it implies a positive relation between expected depreciation and bank failures. The second relies on the response of policy to bank failures, and it implies a positive relation between bank failures and expected depreciation. Two positive relations open the scope for multiple equilibria, including one with high expected depreciation and high bank failures. This is precisely what the model generates.

I shall focus in what follows on the first of these two relations. First, however, let me say a few words about the second relation. JW derive it from a desire by the government, in the face of lower equilibrium output due to bank failures, to boost demand through inflation and, by implication, depreciation. This does the trick, but one can think of other channels. More likely (equally likely?) is a story in which bank failures and a sharp recession lead to a loss of fiscal control, the expectation of higher money growth, higher inflation, and larger depreciation.

Let me turn now to the first of the two relations and the effects of interest rates and the exchange rate on balance sheets.

JW focus in the text on a special case, in which banks have only short-term dollar liabilities and long-term peso (domestic currency) assets. They are right to do so, as the results in this case are indeed striking. However, something is, I think, learned from the more general case (which they work out in the appendix, except for the presence of long-term liabilities).

Take a bank with both peso and dollar short- and long-term liabilities (D_1, D_1^*, D_2, D_2^*), and assets (R_1, R_1^*, R_2, R_2^*), and consequently with this balance sheet:

Olivier Blanchard is the Class of 1941 Professor and chairman of the Department of Economics at the Massachusetts Institute of Technology and a research associate of the National Bureau of Economic Research.

	Assets	Liabilities
	$R_1,\ R_2$	$D_1,\ D_2$
	$R_1^*,\ R_2^*$	$D_1^*,\ D_2^*$

Asterisks denotes dollar assets or liabilities; 1 and 2 refer to the short and the long term respectively. Let, as in the paper, S_1 and S_2^e be the current and the future expected exchange rate, expressed in dollars per peso. Then the net worth of the bank in dollars is given by

$$NW^* = \text{(Terms in dollars)} + \frac{S_1}{1+i}(R_2 - D_2) + S_1(R_1 - D_1)$$

The second term is the value of long-term peso assets minus liabilities, discounted at the domestic interest rate, and expressed in dollars using the current exchange rate. The third term is the value of short-term peso assets minus liabilities, again expressed in dollars using the current exchange rate.

Recall that the interest parity condition is given by

$$\frac{S_1}{1+i} = \frac{S_2^e}{1+i^*}$$

Replacing in the previous equation implies

$$NW^* = \text{(Terms in dollars)} + \frac{S_2^e}{1+i^*}(R_2 - D_2) + S_1(R_1 - D_1)$$

In the model presented in the text, R_1, D_1, and D_2 are all equal to zero. This has two implications:

- Because D_2 is equal to zero, the second term is an increasing function of the expected exchange rate. An expected depreciation decreases the net worth of banks.
- Because both R_1 and D_1 are equal to zero, the last term is equal to zero. Because the second term depends neither on the current exchange rate nor on the current domestic interest rate, then, given S_2^e, the interest rate–exchange rate mix does not affect the net worth of banks.

This last result is perhaps the most striking result of the JW paper. This derivation makes clear, however, that it depends on the last term's being zero, in other words, a zero short-run position in net domestic assets. If the condition is not satisfied, then monetary policy can improve the net worth of banks through manipulation of the exchange rate; whether it does this through a depreciation or an appreciation depends on the sign of the net position.

What should we expect the sign of $(R_1 - D_1)$ to be in practice? The answer is far from clear. On the one hand, currency mismatch leads to a small value of D_1 (peso liabilities). On the other hand, maturity mismatch leads to a small value of R_1 (short-term peso claims).

This gives some perspective to the result emphasized by JW: it is indeed special, but there is no obvious bias relative to the general case.

There are other dimensions in which the JW model is special and could be misleading (JW are not guilty, as the model is just fine for the issues they focus on). Let me mention a few, more as potential extensions than as criticisms.

First, the model focuses exclusively on the banks' balance sheets. Thus, within the logic of the model, one simple way of avoiding crises is for banks to balance their dollar liabilities with dollar claims, therefore eliminating the currency mismatch from their balance sheet and removing the possibility of multiple equilibria.

Although correct in the model, this conclusion is likely to be wrong in fact: It ignores the fact that the ultimate borrowers are domestic firms, which, for the most part, get their revenues in pesos, not in dollars. Denominating bank claims in dollars merely transfers the burden from banks to firms. After a depreciation, some firms may not be able to pay back their dollar liabilities, leading in turn to bank failures.

One should not conclude from this that the denomination of bank claims is irrelevant. Firms may have deeper pockets than banks after a depreciation, so that denominating bank claims in dollars rather than pesos may actually reduce overall firms' and banks' failures. However, the argument clearly implies that the outcome is likely to depend not only on the banks' but also on the firms' net worth distribution.

Second, one can actually push the logic of the argument one more step: firms get their revenues from producing and selling goods. Their peso revenues, and therefore their ability to repay in the future, are likely to vary with the future price level. This in turn raises the issue of whether, when we look at the effect of a decrease in S_2^e, we are looking at a nominal or at a real expected depreciation.

To see why this matters, suppose that banks' claims on firms are stated not in pesos but in terms of domestic goods, or, equivalently, that what happens to the economy depends on the consolidated net worth of banks and firms. Let R_2 now denote revenues in terms of domestic goods and let P_2^e denote the expected future price level. In this case, the present value in dollars of future claims on domestic firms is given by

$$S_1 \frac{P_2^e R_2}{1+i} = \frac{S_2^e P_2^e}{1+i^*} R_2,$$

where the equality follows from interest parity. Now assume that purchasing power parity holds in the long term, so the expected depreciation reflects higher inflation. In the notation of the JW model: $S_2^e P_2^e = $ constant. This in turn implies

$$\frac{S_2^e P_2^e}{1 + i^*} R_2 = \frac{R_2}{1 + i^*}$$

The expression is independent of the future expected depreciation, again breaking the link between expected depreciation and bank failures. Put in slightly paradoxical terms: rather than making things worse, the maturity mismatch helps here. Because the claims are long term, and because, in the long term, purchasing power parity holds, their value in dollars is independent of short-term fluctuations in the exchange rate.

Third, to focus on net worth effects, JW rightly choose to ignore issues of liquidity. Implicitly, they assume that firms can either liquidate projects for the present value of the revenues or that they have enough collateral that they can find some other lender if banks call back the loans. Neither assumption is terribly appealing, and it is interesting to think about what happens when issues of liquidity are reintroduced in the model.

Assume that, if banks call back their long-term peso claims, they get less than the present value of these claims. Assume further that the larger the proportion of claims called back, the higher the discount. This opens the door to two sources of multiple equilibria: first, the multiple equilibria that are the focus of the JW paper, each associated with a different value of S_2^e; and, second, for a given S_2^e, equilibria with and without runs on the banks. In standard fashion, a run on banks forces them to call back loans, decreasing their net worth, triggering failures, and justifying the run in the first place. Note that the lower S_2^e, the lower the net worth of banks in the good equilibrium, the more likely are multiple equilibria.

There is a potentially interesting twist here (this is speculative, but speculating is the privilege of the discussant), namely, the interaction between the two sources of multiple equilibria. For example, in the high S_2^e equilibrium, S_2^e may be high enough to rule out multiple bank run equilibria. However, in the low equilibrium, the weakened net worth position of banks may open the scope for the second type of multiple equilibria, those based on illiquidity.

Directed Lending by the Lender of Last Resort

The mismatch model allows for a precise discussion of the potential role for a lender of last resort, and I find the point emphasized by JW—namely, that such international lending should be directed and used to alleviate directly the currency/maturity mismatch for banks—very convincing and very important. Let me elaborate on two issues here.

I am less worried about moral hazard problems than the authors appear to be. I believe that lending by the international lender of last resort should be to the government, not to the banks themselves, and I do not see why the international lender has to involve itself in the details of domestic bank supervision.

In another paper, Jeanne and Zettelmeyer (2001) have shown that such loans are typically repaid, so the cost is borne within the country, not by international taxpayers. If the government is benevolent (i.e., it cares primarily about domestic taxpayers), then it will indeed want to use the funds for directed lending to banks, or to honor guarantees on dollar-denominated debt. Separating potentially solvent from insolvent banks will entail the usual amount of guesswork and mistakes. However, it is not clear why and how international lending to the government makes this worse.

If the government is not benevolent, but is instead captured by the banks or some of the debtor firms, then it will indeed misbehave. However, it will typically do so whether or not it can borrow from the international lender. It is not clear why, conditional on the government's having to repay the funds lent by the international lender, access to such funds will lead to a worse outcome.

I am more worried, however, about the generality of the directed-lending result.

Consider another example of multiple equilibria, which also opens the case for a potential intervention by a lender of last resort. Forget banks. Take a European Monetary System-type crisis, in which the currency is pegged. An attack on the currency, which requires high interest rates, leads to a recession and forces a devaluation, which in turn justifies the attack. In this case, it is not clear to which institutions, if any, the funds should be directed. For the reasons given in the paper, this makes intervention by a lender of last resort much more difficult and thus, other things being equal, less appealing.

This, in turn, raises at least two issues: first, whether the nature of actual crises is sufficiently identifiable that, in practice, the international lender can assess whether directed lending will work—justifying intervention—or not, in which case it may not want to lend; second, whether the nonmismatch multiple equilibria we can think of all rely, as is the case above, on the defense of a fixed exchange rate. (All those I could think of did). If the answer is yes, then, under floating rates, the mismatch example that is the focus of the paper may be the typical case, in which case directed lending, and intervention by the international lender, can indeed be the solution.

Reference

Jeanne, Olivier, and Jeromin Zettelmeyer. 2001. International bailouts, moral hazard, and conditionality. *Economic Policy* 33 (October): 407–32.

Discussion Summary

Martin Feldstein inquired why, if the IMF has to go in and be a supervisor at the local level, it cannot lend directly to the government.

Morris Goldstein inquired whether the risk is even bigger when there are both bank and corporate mismatches. He also noted that the model's results are invariant to the exchange rate regime only if the regime in place is not relevant to the balance sheet mismatch. Supposedly, a floating regime can deter the creation of this mismatch in the first place.

Jeffrey Shafer questioned the "interest rates don't matter" conclusion. He mentioned the Mexico crisis as a case in which the interest rate played a key role when policy tightened and the money supply was restricted.

Robert P. Flood questioned whether UIP couldn't hold in this model.

Peter B. Kenen stated that, even with a floating exchange rate regime, government debt is still a major problem. Thus, not only bank debt matters. Olivier Jeanne's model, he noted, corresponds to the Meltzer commission's view of the world. However, because the IMF lends money to the government and not the banks that are experiencing a mismatch crisis, there is a principal-agent problem involved. Then, an international supervisor of national supervisors is needed.

Stijn Claessens inquired whether the model implied that the lender-of-last-resort (LOLR) function is only relevant for twin crises, and asked if the model implies that an LOLR is not helpful in a classical balance-of-payments crisis.

Andrew Berg pointed to portfolio balanced effects and their consequences for stabilization programs when capital is mobile. He also questioned the relevance of the model to the Mexican crisis, as investors were fleeing all banks, not only some subset with weaker fundamentals.

Michael P. Dooley inquired whether a LOLR could function if it does not have the power to nationalize the banking industry.

Barry Eichengreen asked whether the banks would not be able to borrow abroad when hit by a liquidity crisis, given the assumptions of the model, and whether this left any need for a LOLR.

Olivier Jeanne's response focused first on the applicability of the model to the LOLR function. He noted that whether the mismatch is in the banking or corporate sector (or both) is not a problem as long as by lending to banks the LOLR solves the problem. He then, in response to Eichengreen's comment, noted that in the bad equilibrium banks are really insolvent and cannot borrow abroad—provided they had a currency mismatch in the first place. He also remarked that it is not easily seen why domestic governments cannot supply the LOLR function. An international LOLR faces a moral hazard problem in its relationship with the domestic authorities. It may need, as a result, to supervise the domestic supervisors—which is possible, in practice, only if it does some supervising of banks directly. He concluded by noting that the result that "the interest rate does not matter in a crisis" corresponds to an interesting but special case of the model. In general the interest rate matters. It could matter, furthermore, for reasons that are not in the model. For example, in a signaling framework (such as Drazen's), the government could raise the interest rate in order to signal its type.

Rescue Packages and Output Losses Following Crises

Michael P. Dooley and Sujata Verma

5.1 Introduction

Beginning with the financial crisis in Mexico in 1992, rescue packages consisting of loan commitments from industrial countries and international organizations have become an important ingredient in crisis management. Rescue packages are designed to limit the damage that follows financial crises by reassuring private investors, stopping runs, and limiting contagion to other countries. The motivation for rescue packages is the belief that the real costs of crises can be reduced by quick and decisive action. Although there are plausible theoretical models of crises that suggest this is an effective policy reaction,[1] there are, in our view, equally plausible models that suggest such intervention is effective only under very stringent conditions.

The intuition behind doubts about the effectiveness of rescue packages is the possibility that output losses are built into international credit arrangements in order to preclude strategic default by debtor governments (Dooley 2000a). In our view, the mechanism that generates the loss in output is the inability of residents of the debtor to engage in domestic financial in-

Michael P. Dooley is a research associate of the National Bureau of Economic Research and a managing editor of the *International Journal of Finance and Economics*. Professor Dooley joined the faculty at the University of California, Santa Cruz in 1992 following more than twenty years' service at the Board of Governors of the Federal Reserve System and the International Monetary Fund. Sujata Verma is professor of economics at Santa Clara University.

The authors thank Andrew Powell for helpful comments and Ilan Neuberger for research assistance. All opinions expressed are those of the authors and not of the National Bureau of Economics Research.

1. Among many others, see Sachs (1995); Miller and Zhang (1998); Bhattacharya and Miller (1999); Chari and Kehoe (1999); Fischer (1999); Giannini (1999); Rogoff (1999); Chui, Ghai, and Haldane (2000); Gavin and Powell (2000); and Ghai, Hayes, and Shin (2001).

termediation while foreign debt is renegotiated. Moreover, international credits are *designed* so that creditors will find it difficult to coordinate debt restructuring following default.[2] The important implication is that coordination problems among creditors are the *feature* of the international monetary system that makes international lending possible.[3]

In a first best world, creditors would be happy to "switch off" the coordination problem if it was clear that default was unavoidable and independent of the debtor's behavior. Following a "bad luck" default, a long recession in the debtor country is clearly not in creditors' collective interest. However, we cannot imagine a contractual mechanism that would accomplish this that does not also eliminate the credibility of creditors' threats to impose the penalty following a strategic default. Following strategic default, a long recession in the debtor country is also not in creditors' interests. If creditors could switch off the coordination problem they would be left, following strategic default, with the threat of shooting themselves in the foot. The unhappy result is that creditors need to commit to punish even though the punishment benefits no one.

Can official lending mitigate this market failure? In the next section we show that this depends on the official sector's ability to act predictably and to commit not to rescue following strategic default. Although it is quite easy to set out a regime for official intervention that moves us toward a first best equilibrium, we have serious doubts that official lenders can, in practice, establish such a regime.

In the final section we evaluate rescue packages in the context of an explicit model of crises. We argue that the insurance model developed in Dooley (2000b) is an attractive vehicle for the analysis because it provides an explanation for surges in capital inflows followed by sudden stops. The model also provides a useful distinction between *crisis* and *default*. A *crisis* in this model is an anticipated asset exchange that generates a transfer from the official sector to the private sector. A *default* is a transfer that is smaller than expected.

As in all first-generation crisis models, a perfect-foresight assumption implies that default would never be observed because the crisis occurs at the point when the official sector's assets are just exhausted. Clearly there is no need to restructure remaining debt.

Uncertainty about the size of the insurance pool (bad luck) or the debtor's willingness to draw on and exhaust the pool (strategy) introduces the possibility of default. Default occurs when the expected value of the transfer exceeds the realized value at the time of crisis. In this event, some creditors that expect to be rescued are not, and debt must be renegotiated.

2. For an excellent analysis of the legal constraints on debt restructuring see Buchhiet and Lee (2001).
3. Diamond and Rajan (2000) use a similar argument to explain the role of short-term debt in sovereign crises.

The intriguing implication is that bad luck includes not only events such as crop failures that reduce the debtor country's ability to pay but also political events that affect the debtor country's access to, or willingness to draw upon, official rescue packages. Larger rescue packages almost certainly imply larger forecast errors for rescue packages and, in turn, larger average output losses following crises. Moreover, because output losses are related to forecast errors, losses should be unrelated to fundamentals prior to the crisis. Predictable crises generate unpredictable costs.

5.2.1   Sovereign Debt Models, Output Loss, and Third-Party Intervention

Bolten and Scharfstein (1996) develop a model of bargaining between the debtors and the creditors in the context of domestic credit markets. They distinguish between two kinds of defaults: liquidity defaults, in which the debtor is unable to pay, and strategic defaults, in which the borrower is able but unwilling to pay. Unless there is some penalty for default, like seizure of the borrower's assets, the lenders will not lend, fearing strategic defaults. The distortion in this model is the inability to condition penalties for nonpayment on the reason for nonpayment. Bad luck defaults are observable but not verifiable.

In a trivial sense, all sovereign defaults are strategic, because, unlike a corporate debtor, countries are always solvent. However, we assume that a sovereign's power to tax is limited, so a solvent country can have an insolvent government. In this environment, bad luck and strategic defaults are possible. Moreover, creditors' fear of cheating on the part of the sovereign determines the design of contracts.

The domestic credit markets differ from the international credit markets in that the lenders cannot seize the assets of the sovereign debtor. However, by making contracts costly to renegotiate, lenders can discourage strategic default.

Consider a three-period model with the periods being denoted by 0, 1, and 2. For simplicity, it is assumed that the (risk-neutral) debtor's wealth is zero (the results hold true even if positive initial wealth is assumed) and it needs to borrow amount K to finance an investment project. The returns on the investment are uncertain in period 0 but are realized in period 1. In the first period, investment gives a return of x in a good state and a return of 0 in the bad state. The respective probability of the two states' occurring is given by θ and $(1 - \theta)$. After the return is realized, the debtor has to choose between repaying the debt and defaulting. In the bad state, the debtor will be forced to default (liquidity default), because the initial wealth is assumed to be zero. In the good state, the debtor may pay out zero (strategic default) or repay the amount specified in the contract denoted by R_x.

The return in period 2 depends on what happens in the first period. The return in period 2 is y if the debtor continues with the project after paying back the debt. As soon as the debtor declares default, negotiations between the creditors and the debtor begin. We assume that structure of the debt determines the expected outcome of this negotiation. A rigid debt structure means that negotiations fail with a high probability, β. A flexible debt structure means that negotiation succeeds with a high probability and the debtor agrees to pay to the creditor αy. For simplicity it is assumed that $\alpha = 1/2$.[4]

5.2.2   Design of Contracts

An optimal debt contract is defined as one that balances two effects—deterring strategic defaults while at the same time minimizing the costs associated with liquidity defaults. A complete contract specifies payments contingent on all possible states of the world. We first outline such a contract. It is assumed that both borrower and lender have complete information about the state of the world, so the lender can distinguish between liquidity and strategic defaults. The contract is specified as follows:

Debtor has to pay R_x $(R_x < x)$ when the return is x in period 1; otherwise, there is renegotiation. These renegotiations are successful with probability $(1 - \beta)$ and result in the creditor's allowing a partial rollover of debt into the second period. When the return is 0 in period 1, the probability of a successful renegotiation is given by $1 - \beta_0$.

In period 1, the state of the world is determined. With probability θ, good state occurs and the project return is x. With possibility $1 - \theta$, bad state occurs and 0 return is realized. The debtor moves next by deciding whether to repay or to default. In the case of a bad return, liquidity default is certain (because we have assumed zero initial wealth). In the case of a good return, the debtor may repay R_x out of the return x or may default and repay nothing, keeping the entire return for itself.

Next, there is renegotiation. If it is successful, both parties agree to share the third-period output. If it is unsuccessful, third-period output is zero. The probability that renegotiation will fail can differ for the strategic default branch of the game and the liquidity default branch if there is full information.

Given this contract, the debtors' expected payoff is given by

(1) $$\theta(x + y - R_x) + (1 - \theta)(1 - \beta_0)\frac{y}{2}$$

The lenders' expected profits must be nonnegative (assume the market interest rate is zero):

(2) $$\theta R_x + (1 - \theta)(1 - \beta_0)\frac{y}{2} - K \geq 0$$

---

4. Endogenizing α does not significantly alter the results of the model. The important issue is how the second-period output sharing will be enforced rather than the relative shares of the debtor and creditors.

The payments must satisfy an incentive constraint to rule out strategic defaults:

(3) $$\beta\frac{y}{2} \geq R_x.$$

The optimal contract maximizes equation (1) subject to equations (2) and (3). The results can be summarized as follows:

(4) $$\beta_0 = 0 \quad \text{or} \quad 1 - \beta_0 = 1$$

It can be shown that optimal value of β_0 is zero. This implies that renegotiation is always successful in the bad state of nature.

The debtor's expected payoff could be written as

(5) $$\theta(x + y) - K$$

This represents the first best solution in terms of net present value of the project.

5.2.3 Incomplete Contracts

Because of incomplete information, lenders may not be able to distinguish between a strategic default and a liquidity default.

The contract may be specified as

Debtor has to pay R_x in period 1; otherwise, there is renegotiation. These renegotiations are successful with probability $(1 - \beta)$ and result in the creditors' allowing a partial rollover of debt into the second period. Alternatively, the renegotiations fail with probability β, and third-period output is reduced to zero.

Given this contract, the debtor's expected payoff is given by

(1b) $$\theta(x + y + R_x) + (1 - \theta)(1 - \beta)\frac{y}{2}$$

The lenders' expected profits should be nonnegative:

(2b) $$\theta R_x + (1 - \theta)(1 - \beta)\frac{y}{2} - K \geq 0$$

The payments must satisfy an incentive constraint to rule out strategic defaults:

(3b) $$x + y - R_x \geq x + (1 - \beta)\frac{y}{2}$$

The optimal debt contract maximizes equation (1b) subject to equations (2b) and (3b):

The results may be summarized as follows: Value of optimum β is given by

(4b)
$$\beta = \frac{K - \dfrac{y}{2}}{\theta y - \dfrac{y}{2}},$$

which will be a feasible solution as long as $\beta \le 1$.

The debtor's expected payoff could be written as

(5b)
$$\theta x + y - K - (1 - \theta)\beta y$$

The first three terms represent the net present value of the project, and the last term is the expected efficiency loss due to sanctions arising due to contractual incompleteness.

As pointed out by Bolten and Scharfstein (1996), from equation (5b) it can be seen that an arbitrary probability of a failed renegotiation, β, is preferable over designing a contract for which renegotiation always fails. The higher the probability of success of renegotiation, the lower are the expected efficiency losses.

Can rescue packages ensure a first best equilibrium? This is the question we explore in the next section.

5.2.4 A Model of Bargaining with Three Players: Debtors, Creditors, and the International Monetary Fund

In terms of the model outlined above, in the presence of informational asymmetries, there will be a bias of the debtor to default strategically. The lenders may still lend if they can design a contract that imposes an incentive constraint on the debtor's behavior so that the debtor would not prefer to default strategically. Any such contract will have a bias toward unnecessary losses. As pointed out by Diamond (1993), the reason for this is that the lenders ignore the part of the future return of a project that accrues only to the debtor. This results in efficiency losses. Third-party intervention can be welfare improving if it can help facilitate renegotiations regarding the sharing of the third-period output while at the same time allowing the debtor to reap these returns.

The debtor is assumed to have no initial wealth and borrows K for investment. The return in period 1 is x with a probability θ and 0 with probability $(1 - \theta)$. The debtor decides whether it will repay the creditor or default. In a bad state there is a liquidity default. If there is repayment, the debtor earns a return of y in the second period. If there is default, the borrower and lender may approach the IMF for resolution, which succeeds with probability π. It is assumed that the International Monetary Fund (IMF) also cannot distinguish between strategic and liquidity defaults.[5] When the

---

5. Ghai, Hayes, and Shin (2001) assume that the IMF has a signal (not necessarily correct) about the nature of default, but not the lender.

debtor is a sovereign nation, there are political problems in obtaining the correct information about the returns. The creditor as well as the IMF faces this problem of verification of returns. The IMF imposes a successful restructuring by buying the debt for $y/2$ and allows the debtor to retain $y/2$. Thus it has enforced a fair distribution of third-period output. If the IMF does not intervene, or if its intervention is unsuccessful, with the probability $1 - \pi$, then the renegotiation, as usual, fails with probability β.

Given this contract, the debtor's expected payoff is given by

$$\text{(1c)} \qquad \theta(x + y - R_x) + (1 - \theta)\left[\pi\frac{y}{2} + (1 - \pi)(1 - \beta)\frac{y}{2}\right]$$

The lenders' expected profits should be nonnegative:

$$\text{(2c)} \qquad \theta R_x + (1 - \theta)\left[\pi\frac{y}{2} + (1 - \pi)(1 - \beta)\frac{y}{2}\right] - K \geq 0$$

The payments must satisfy an incentive constraint to rule out strategic defaults:

$$\text{(3c)} \qquad x + y - R_x \geq x + \pi\frac{y}{2} + (1 - \pi)\left[(1 - \beta)\frac{y}{2}\right]$$

The optimal contract maximizes equation (1c) subject to equations (2c) and (3c).

It can be shown that the optimum value of π is

$$\text{(4c)} \qquad \pi = \frac{\theta\beta y + (1 - \beta)\frac{y}{2} - K}{\theta\beta y - \beta\frac{y}{2}},$$

which will be a feasible solution as long as $\pi \leq 1$.

The debtor's expected payoff is

$$\text{(5c)} \qquad \theta(x + y) - K - (1 - \theta)(y\beta) + (1 - \theta)\beta\pi y$$

The first three terms represent the net present value of the project. The fourth term is the expected efficiency loss due to contractual incompleteness. The intervention of the IMF can reduce the inefficiencies only if β was not set at its optimal level.

If the IMF has information about the state of nature superior to that of the creditor, rescue packages are always welfare improving. It is easy to demonstrate in terms of the first model that if the IMF could distinguish between strategic and liquidity defaults then the first best solution could be easily reached. The incentive to default strategically would be reduced if the true nature of the debtor were revealed. There would be no sanctions in the bad state and the output loss would be eliminated.

5.3.1   Output Losses and Rescue Packages

We start our analysis of output losses with our understanding of the conventional wisdom. In a series of important papers, Calvo (1998) and Calvo and Reinhart (2000) have argued that recent crises have generated relatively large output losses for two reasons. First, they argue that for emerging markets the magnitude of capital flow reversals has increased over time. Sudden stops of capital inflows require sudden improvements in the current account balance. They argue persuasively that it is difficult to imagine how such a dramatic change in real transfers can be accomplished without a short-run decline in output. These effects are more severe if the country faces quantitative restrictions on borrowing following the crisis. Moreover, they argue that emerging markets have become more vulnerable to reversals of capital flows and associated changes in relative prices (nominal exchange rate depreciation), because of dollarization of liabilities.

Calvo and Reinhardt, and many others, argue that financial crises in the 1990s are best understood in the context of second-generation models of crises that focus on multiple equilibria. Such models suggest that crises are triggered by shifts in private expectations that are unpredictable. It follows that an unanticipated shock to financial markets can have economically important real effects. In this section we develop quite a different model of crises.

In the context of multiple equilibria models, it is quite sensible to evaluate government intervention as a way to reduce or eliminate the coordination failures among creditors that generate unnecessary output losses. For example, using an open economy version of a Diamond-Dybvig bank run model, Chui, Ghai, and Haldane (2000) provide a framework for evaluating crisis avoidance policies. In particular, increasing liquidity (including rescue packages) relative to debt reduces the probability of both fundamentals and belief-driven crises and significantly improves welfare.

The insurance model presented in Dooley (2000b) suggests that the timing of crises and the scale of capital inflows leading up to a crisis are the anticipated outcome of private investors' incentives to exploit a pool of government insurance. The insurance model defines the crisis as a reversal of private capital flows, what Calvo and Reinhart call a sudden stop. However, the reversal is not triggered by a change in expectations. Observed crises are anticipated asset exchanges designed to exploit government insurance.

The insurance/sovereign risk framework has two potential advantages over second-generation models in accounting for output losses. In any consistent accounting framework, the impact effect on output of a crisis is related to the size of the swing in private capital inflows and the associated swing in the current account balance. However, although alternative models that we are aware of take the initial vulnerability of the country as exogenous, the insurance model suggests that the increase in the scale of capital inflows and anticipated reversals is related to growth in the availability of insurance. Even if residents of the emerging market know that a crisis is likely in the future, they will be willing to borrow at rates that are subsidized by the expected insurance. Moreover, they will be tempted to consume now, when real interest rates are low, so that part of the capital inflow supports a current account deficit.

It follows that capital inflows generated by insurance will distort real consumption and production decisions before the crisis and that these distortions will have to be reversed following the crisis. In this regard, our explanation for the initial output loss is identical to that suggested by Calvo and Reinhart. However, it also follows that the initial output losses following crises have grown as bailout packages have grown.

The insurance/sovereign risk analysis offers an explanation for the very different patterns and intensities of output losses that have followed crises. The initial downturns in economic activity following recent crises in Asia have been quite similar. However, the cumulative loss in output has been, and is projected to be, much larger in Indonesia than in Korea. Moreover, the duration and cumulative size of output losses following the 1982 debt crisis were much larger than those of recent crises in Asia.

In our model the duration of recession depends on whether or not the anticipated *crisis* was also an unanticipated *default*. An insurance crisis is simply an asset exchange between the government and private investors. A default occurs when the government is unwilling or unable to provide the expected insurance payments. Because the IMF and creditor governments are important sources of insurance, forecast errors for their intervention at the time of crisis are crucial in determining whether default occurs and, in turn, the real effects of the crisis.

Thus, liquidity and rescue packages are important, a result consistent with a variety of econometric work. However, the empirical measure of default is the difference between the expected and realized demand for and supply of insurance at the time of the crisis. Because this is a forecast error, it is unpredictable and is likely to have unpredictable real effects.

5.3.2   The Initial Decline in Output

The loss in output following default reflects several factors. Clearly the model suggests that, following any crisis, private capital inflows will fall to zero, and, if the debtor country was using capital inflows to finance net imports, there will have to be an immediate and probably costly real transfer to nonresidents. Because the government will often decide to devalue in order to help facilitate the needed real transfer, several other channels for contraction of output will also come into play. If the government does not devalue, the same transfer must be made, but now it will have to be accomplished by changes in domestic incomes and prices (Cespédes, Chang, and Velasco 2000). Table 5.1 shows a simple regression of the loss in output

Table 5.1   OLS Regression for Initial Severity of Crisis

Variable	Coefficient
Constant	−7.12***
	(−2.92)
1980s crises dummy	1.13
	(0.50)
Reversal of current account	−52.55**
	(2.69)
N	20
Adjusted R^2	0.19
F-test for combined significance (probability)	0.07

Note: Dependent variable: output cost for the first year following crisis (difference from potential output). Numbers in parentheses are standard deviations.
***Significant at the 1 percent level.
**Significant at the 5 percent level.

in the year following the crisis and the swing in the current account in the year before the crisis and the year following the crisis. The results provide a solid baseline in that the real adjustment in the external balance generates a severe initial downturn in economic activity. From here we can evaluate the additional effects that might be associated with financial variables and default.

5.3.3   Output and Default

To test the idea that output losses are related to default we must first measure the gap between expected and realized values for the insurance pool and for claims on that pool at points in time at which crises have been observed. We have quite a small set of observations of crises that might be useful in evaluating these conjectures. Unlike other empirical work on crises, ours has a single variable, a quite clear measure of when a crisis occurs, and a less clear measure of how long it lasts. The onset of a crisis is the point in time at which private investors begin to exchange claims on residents of the debtor country for international assets. The exchange, however, might stretch over several years as liabilities mature.

The primary source of uncertainty concerning the stock of insured assets, that is, the demand for insurance, is that the government will determine which assets are to be protected at the time of the exchange. This will, in turn, reflect the ability of different classes of creditors to disrupt output in the event of default. Because the government will determine relative places in line, information from one crisis is of limited help in anticipating the outcome in the next crisis. The model suggests that ex ante rates of return should be systematically related to the expected seniority for exchange.

Different types of external liabilities have had clearly different returns preceding crises, and this makes our story plausible. If crises are antici-

Table 5.2   **OLS Regression for Demand for Insurance**

Variable	Coefficient
Constant	−894.50
	(−0.12)
1980s crises dummy	3,605.46
	(0.44)
Bond stocks outstanding at time of crisis	2.07*
	(2.15)
Equity	0.95
	(−1.50)
Foreign direct investment	0.09
	(0.23)
Private loans	0.11
	(0.27)
Short-term debt	−0.17
	(−0.37)
N	19
Adjusted R^2	0.75
F-test for combined significance (probability)	0.00

Note: Dependent variable: rescue package following crisis.
*Significant at the 10 percent level.

pated, the anticipated stock of insurance at the time of crisis should be related to the stock *and structure* of private claims on the country at the time
of crisis. To test this idea we regress the stock of insurance observed at the
beginning of nineteen crises against the stock and composition of external
debt outstanding at that time. The results, reported in table 5.2, provide
some support for the model. Each category of external debt can be interpreted as a demand for insurance. As anticipated, portfolio investment
seems to be insured relative to equity and direct investment. However, the
negative relationship between short-term claims and the demand for insurance is clearly inconsistent with the model.

5.3.4   Supply of Insurance

The anticipated stock of insurance, however, is quite difficult to measure
directly. Although the stocks of international reserves seem to be a predictable source of insurance, investors can never be sure that the government will exchange all these assets. The usual assumption that the government will exhaust its reserves is not consistent with the data. Moreover,
published reserve stocks have often turned out to be much larger than net
reserves because of forward exchange and other derivative commitments
undertaken before the crisis.

Another important source of uncertainty about the stock of insurance is
that, in many cases, a quantitatively important share of the anticipated insurance pool comes from new loans by creditor governments and interna-

tional organizations. At the time of crisis it is likely that a rescue package is assembled that consists of loans from several sources. It follows that investors must evaluate the expected net increase in credit from all official sources for several years into the future. Put another way, they must guess whether the debtor government will be willing and able to borrow from the IMF and other official lenders to pay them off when their claims mature.

For crises after 1990, we assume that announced rescue packages are an unbiased estimate of the resources investors expect to receive from the government. A problem with this interpretation is that rescue packages are seldom followed by official credits of similar magnitude. This has led many observers to doubt the importance of insurance for creditor behavior. Our view is that announced rescue packages are important because they oblige the official sector to lend if alternative adjustment measures do not provide the funds needed to liquidate private debt as it matures. In practice, the single largest alternative source of funds has been the current account surplus that has followed most crises. Thus, we view the package as creditor governments' commitment to underwrite an adjustment effort.

The 1982 crises present a more difficult conceptual problem. Rescue packages announced in 1982 were limited to bridge loans that were very small and very short-term. Dooley (1995) argues that commercial banks expected their own governments to bail them out and that the bailout eventually came, but much more slowly than expected. If we consider the whole crisis period from 1982 to 1989 we see that official credits were eventually quite substantial. One hypothesis is that in 1982 private investors had the amount of the bailout right but were surprised by the very slow disbursement. Our working hypothesis is that the expected package in 1982 was equal to the present value of the official capital flows actually observed through 1989. It follows that at the time of the crises in the early 1980s it was likely that investors were surprised by the announcement that the present value of the rescue package was almost nil. As time passed and governments provided loans to debtor countries, the initial default was reversed.

Investors must guess about the ability and willingness of the government to use its assets and lines of credit at the time of crisis. Table 5.3 reports the results of a regression of measured insurance pools previously discussed against easily observed characteristics of the debtor country. By using the whole sample we are assuming investors used information they did not have, but with only twenty-six observations, alternative approaches are not feasible. The results reported in table 5.3 suggest that the gross domestic product (GDP) of the debtor country is by far the dominant determinant of the size of rescue packages.

5.3.5 Measuring the Forecast Error

The model suggests that a crisis observation occurs when the expected demand for insurance is just equal to the expected supply. It follows that we can

Table 5.3   **OLS Regression for Supply of Insurance**

Variable	Coefficient
Constant	15,879.69*
	(1.90)
1980s crises dummy	−14,662.71
	(−1.94)
GDP at year of crisis	0.07***
	(2.69)
Foreign exchange reserves ($t − 1$)	−0.02
	(−0.50)
Openness (ratio of imports and exports to GDP)	−67.03
	(−0.48)
N	26
Adjusted R^2	0.73
F-test for combined significance (probability)	0.00

Note: Dependent variable: rescue package following crisis (RESCUE2).
***Significant at the 1 percent level.
*Significant at the 10 percent level.

examine the forecast error associated with the demand and supply for insurance for each crisis. Suppose we observe a crisis at time t_0. Our theory suggests that at t_0 the expected demand for reserves was equal to the expected supply. However, because both demand and supply are estimated with error, it is quite possible that our estimates of demand and supply will not be equal when crises are observed. There are many potential sources for such errors. If the demand curve was correct, an insurance pool less than the estimated demand would imply a positive default. If the supply curve was correct, an insurance pool greater than estimated supply would imply no default. Because we do not know which relationship is more likely to be correct, we take the sum of the supply and demand error as our measure of default.

Our model suggests that, other things being equal, the *default* generated by the shortfall of insurance will interfere with financial intermediation as long as the default persists. We should expect to see a larger initial decline in output and a relatively slow recovery following a crisis that involves default relative to a crisis in which insurance is equal to or greater than its expected value.

The regression in table 5.4 is the same as in table 5.1 except that the insurance forecast error is added. As discussed above, the swing in the current account is the most important determinant of the initial decline in output. However, the forecast error for insurance is also positively correlated with the output loss. The regression coefficient is small relative to its standard error, but, given the difficulty in measuring the demand for and supply of insurance, it may not be surprising that this relationship is not precisely estimated.

Table 5.4   OLS Regression for Initial Severity of Crisis

Variable	Coefficient
Constant	−6.79**
	(−2.62)
1980s crises dummy	0.87
	(0.32)
Reversal of current account	−56.91**
	(−2.28)
Forecast error	1.33
	(0.42)
N	16
Adjusted R^2	0.16
F-test for combined significance (probability)	0.18

Note: Dependent variable: output cost for first year following crisis. Numbers in parentheses are t-statistics.
**Significant at the 5 percent level.

Table 5.5   OLS Regression for Prolonged Cost of Crisis

Variable	Coefficient
Constant	0.78
	(1.37)
1980s crises dummy	0.25
	(0.49)
Forecast error	0.36
	(0.72)
Reversal of current account	0.25
	(0.06)
N	12
Adjusted R^2	0.07
F-test for combined significance (probability)	0.88

Note: Dependent variable: output cost for four years following crisis. Numbers in parentheses are t-statistics.

Table 5.5 reports the results for a regression of cumulative output losses against the swing in the current account and the forecast errors for insurance. The swing in the current account loses much of its explanatory power, a result consistent with the idea that for a given transfer quick adjustment probably shortens the duration of the output loss. In contrast, the insurance forecast error is little changed: it remains positive but small relative to its standard error.

5.4   Concluding Remarks

Financial crises have important real costs, and identifying policies that could reduce these costs is a priority. In this paper we argue that predictions for the effects of third-party interventions are quite sensitive to models of sovereign debt. In particular, if concern about strategic default is central to the design of international debt contracts, and we cannot imagine that it is not, intervention by the official sector in negotiations between sovereign debtors and their private creditors is problematic. Our analysis suggests that anticipated and unconditional lending at the time of crisis is rational to avoid the costs of default that are built into contracts. However, the expectation that insurance will be provided subsidizes capital inflows that precede crises and, in turn, intensifies the current account reversals and output losses that follow. Moreover, uncertainty about the size and distribution of insurance can generate unpredictable defaults that intensify and prolong losses in output.

Appendix

LHS

- Output cost for first year—difference from potential output measured as the average over the 5 preceding years (source: *International Financial Statistics* [IFS]).
- Rescue package—data for 1982 debt-crisis countries is cumulative flows (Net Flows/Official Creditors) for 1982–90 from the World Bank's *World Debt Tables* 1989–90. Other data from Dooley (2000).
- Output cost for four years following crisis—cumulative output loss over the four years following the crisis as a fraction of the precrisis year's output (source: IFS).

RHS

- Bond stocks outstanding—gross portfolio bonds (source: DRS).
- Equity—estimate of stock of portfolio equity (source: Lane and Milesi-Ferretti)
- Foreign direct investment (FDI)—estimate of stock of inward direct investment (cumulative flow adjusted for relative price variations; source: Lane and Milesi-Ferretti).
- Forecast error—the demand error minus the supply error in the rescue package estimation equations.
- Foreign exchange reserves—at precrisis year (source: IFS).
- GDP—at year of crisis (source: IFS).
- Openness—sum imports and exports over GDP (source: IFS).
- Private loans—stock (source: World Economic Organization).
- Reversal of current account—change in the current account from the precrisis year to the year following the crisis (source: IFS).
- Short-term debt—stock (source: DRS).

Country Cases

1982: Argentina, Bolivia, Brazil, Chile, Costa Rica, Dominican Republic,
    Ecuador, Jamaica, Mexico, Peru, Uruguay, Venezuela
1994: Mexico
1997: Indonesia, Korea, Malaysia, the Philippines, Thailand
1998: Argentina, Brazil, Turkey

References

Bartolini, Leonardo, and Dixit, Avinash. 1991. Market valuation of illiquid debt and
    implications for conflicts among creditors. *IMF Staff Papers* 38 (4): 828–849.
Bhattacharya, Amar, and Marcus Miller. 1999. Coping with crises: Is there a silver
    bullet? In *The Asian financial crisis: Causes, contagion, and consequences,* ed.
    Pierre-Richard Agénor, Marcus Miller, and David Vines. New York: Cambridge:
    Cambridge University Press.
Bolten, Patrick, and David Scharfstein. 1996. Optimal debt structure and the num-
    ber of creditors. *Journal of Political Economy* 104 (1): 1–25.
Buchheit, Lee C., and Mitu Gulati, G. 2000. Exit consents in sovereign bond ex-
    changes. *UCLA Law Review* 48 (1): 59–84.
Bulow, Jeremy, and Rogoff, Kenneth. 1989. A constant recontracting model of sov-
    ereign debt. *Journal of Political Economy* 97 (February): 155–178.
Calvo, Guillermo A. 1998. Capital flows and capital-market crises: The simple eco-
    nomics of sudden stops. *Journal of Applied Economics* 1 (1): 35–37.
Calvo, Guillermo A., and Carmen Reinhart. 2000. When capital flows come to a
    sudden stop: Consequences and policy options. In *Reforming the international
    monetary system* ed. P. Kenen, M. Mussa and A. Swoboda, 175–201. Washington,
    D.C.: Brookings Institution.
Cespedes, Luis Felipe, Roberto Chang, and Andres Velasco. 2000. Balance sheets
    and exchange rate policies. NBER Working Paper no. W7840. Cambridge, Mass.:
    National Bureau of Economic Research, August.
Chari, V. V., and Patrick Kehoe. 1999. Asking the right questions about the IMF.
    The Region 13:2–26. Minneapolis, Minn.: Federal Reserve Bank of Minne-
    apolis.
Chui, Michael, Prasanna Ghai, and Andrew Haldane. 2000. Sovereign liquidity
    crises: Analytics and implications for public policy. Bank of England Working Pa-
    per no. 121. London: Bank of England, September.
Diamond, Douglas W. (1989) Reputation acquisition in debt markets. *Journal of Po-
    litical Economy* 97:828–841.
———. 1993. Seniority and maturity of debts. *Journal of Financial Economies* 33:
    341–68.
Diamond, Douglas W., and Raghuram G. Rajan. 2000. Banks, short term debt, and
    financial crises: Theory, policy implications, and applications. NBER Working
    Paper no. W7764. Cambridge, Mass.: National Bureau of Economic Research,
    June.
Dooley, Michael P. 1995. A retrospective on the debt crisis. In *Exchange rate policy
    and interdependence,* ed. Peter Kenan, Princeton, N.J.: Princeton University Press.
———. 2000a. Can output losses following international financial crises be

avoided? NBER Working Paper no. 7531. Cambridge, Mass.: National Bureau of Economic Research, February.

———. 2000b. A model of crises in emerging markets. *The Economic Journal* 110 (460): 256–72.

Fischer, Stanley. 1999. On the need for an international lender of last resort. *Journal of Economic Perspectives* 13 (4): 85–104.

Gavin, Michael, and Andrew Powell. 2000. Should international lender of last resort (LOLR) lending be privatized? Universidad Torcuato Di Tella. Mimeo.

Ghai, Prasanna, Simon Hayes, and Hyun Song Shin. 2001. Crisis costs and debtor discipline: The efficacy of public policy in sovereign debt crisis. Bank of England Working Paper no. 136. London: Bank of England, May.

Giannini, Corzio. 1999. Enemy of none but a friend to all? An international perspective on the lender of last resort function. IMF Working Paper no. WP/99/10. Washington, D.C.: International Monetary Fund, October.

Miller, Marcus and Lei Zhang. 2000. Sovereign liquidity crises: The strategic case for a payments standstill. *Economic Journal* 110:335–62.

Rogoff, Kenneth. 1999. International institutions for reducing global financial instability. *Journal of Economic Perspectives* 13 (4): 21–42.

Sachs, Jeffrey. 1995. Do we need an international lender of last resort? Frank Graham Lecture, Princeton University. 20 April.

Verma, Sujata. 2000. The architecture of international capital markets: Theory and evidence. Ph.D. diss., University of California, Santa Cruz.

Comment   Andrew Powell

Michael P. Dooley and Sujata Verma have written a truly fascinating paper (henceforth referred to as DV), which contains many interesting ideas and which is a valuable contribution to the spawning literature on "private-sector involvement" and the role of the private sector, governments, and the multilaterals in crises. In fact, there are really two papers. First, there is a theoretical part that outlines a role for a third party (the International Monetary Fund [IMF]) in a model with the possibility of both liquidity and strategic default. Second, there is an empirical part that attempts to test the "insurance view" of crises following Dooley (2000) and earlier papers by Calvo, Krugman, and McKinnon and Pill, among others.

The theoretical part of the paper develops a specific model of sovereign debt in which there is an information asymmetry in that if the debtor defaults the lender does not know if the default was for liquidity (ability to pay) or "strategic" (willingness to pay) reasons. The approach is taken from Bolton and Sharfstein (1999), hereafter BS. The BS approach has the tremendous advantages of simplicity and tractability, and DV achieve interesting results very quickly. However, in the application of the BS model

Andrew Powell is professor of economics at the Universidad Torcuato Di Tella in Buenos Aires, Argentina.

to the case of sovereign debt, there do appear to be a couple of issues worth discussing.

In BS, lenders can liquidate a defaulting corporate, and there is some probability of obtaining the residual value of the firm's assets (let us refer to this probability as β). Dooley and Verma suggest that in the case of default lenders can sanction borrowers, and the residual value of the firm's assets is analogous to the market value of restructured debt. In the text, DV refer to the BS probability (β) as the restructured value of the debt (β in the latter's model). In the equations, however, they appear to use β as a probability. Perhaps they have in mind that β is the probability that debt is restructured in some way after a failed negotiation, and S is then the utility of that outcome, including whatever was the market level of restructured debt. With this interpretation, the $(1 - \beta)$–type terms in the equations make more sense. (These comments refer to an earlier draft, and the authors have taken up this suggestion.)

Another issue is that if borrowers are to avoid sanctions then there is some negotiation procedure, and they simply share half of the project's output with lenders ($\alpha = 1/2$), and sanctions are lifted. However, surely α is also endogenous. Suppose the failed negotiations imply a 20 percent write-down of the debt. Why would borrowers share a penny more of output than absolutely necessary to make lenders better off, given that alternative? In other words, it looks like α should be specifically linked to the write-down value of the debt. (The authors claim in footnote two that endogenizing α does not significantly alter the results. However, equation 4 shows clearly the optimum β, and hence the expected efficiency loss of equation 5b depends on α.)

These comments raise a more general issue as to whether the BS approach is really applicable in the international debt markets. The Incentive Compatibility constraint is designed to rule out "strategic defaults," but in an important sense all sovereign defaults are strategic. One view might be that default occurs when the present value of future output, net of debt repayments with a high debt level (and possibly higher interest rates), is less than that with a lower debt level achieved through a debt reduction and net of the short-run costs of that reduction due to trade or financing disruptions. A second approach can take place when revenues have fallen so much that it becomes politically more costly to continue to service the debt than to seek some type of renegotiation. These, then, are examples of strategic defaults, although they may occur when the ability to pay has also been reduced substantially.

Let me now turn to the role of the IMF. Dooley and Verma focus on one potential and hitherto ignored role of the IMF in the literature, namely, as an enforcer of contracts. In essence, in the event of default, the IMF says with probability π that the second-period output should be shared fifty-fifty. In terms of the model, this adds some extra probability to the default state's being resolved more efficiently and hence reduces the inefficiency due to contractual incompleteness. It is interesting that there is an optimal value of π, or, in other words, it appears to be optimal for the IMF to intervene unpredictably. In a further addition to the model, the authors claim that in a world where contracts are supported by reputation contracts and not "gunboat" diplomacy, then the role of the IMF as the enforcer of contracts may be redundant.

I have one doubt regarding the basic result, which, in fact, stems from Dooley (2000)! Making the ex post resolution more efficient and in particular less costly for the borrower will surely reduce the amount of debt that can be supported in this model. In the model, rearranging the incentive constraint (eq. [3]) shows that Rx must be less than something to do with the returns of the project and the inefficiencies due to contractual incompleteness. In the model it appears that K, y, and R are all exogenous, but if R is set such that the IC is just met, $K = R$, and $y(K)$, then it looks to me that there may be a trade-off for borrowers. On the one hand, the introduction of the IMF reduces the inefficiencies of the contractual incompleteness, but on the other hand it reduces the amount of debt and hence the potential project returns. (The authors have now taken up this suggestion and find that the credit ceiling depends on IMF intervention in an interesting way as illustrated in equation 6c.)

The IMF obviously plays multiple roles, and a second role, hinted at in the paper, is that of addressing the information asymmetry directly—in other words, considering the IMF not as a contract enforcer but as an auditor. This is the focus of a recent paper by Gay, Hayes, and Shin (2000). In this paper, there is a very similar trade-off to that just described, which is their reference to the IMF as "whistle blower" versus the IMF as "fireman." In their setup, the IMF is generally bad for lenders, because the fireman reduces the ex post cost of resolution and hence reduces the stock of debt that can be supported in equilibrium—following Dooley (2000)—and this unambiguously reduces lenders' welfare. However, for borrowers the IMF may be a net benefit, because improving the information available to lenders reduces the inefficiency of the information asymmetry, and this can outweigh the costs of the lower level of debt.

Gay, Hayes, and Shin (2000) also consider an IMF that acts unpredictably (in a manner they refer to as "case-by-case"), but in their setup they conclude that this will make lenders better off and may make borrowers worse off relative to the regime in which the IMF follows a specific policy rule. It is in effect an intermediate model between a no-IMF model and the full-IMF model. This contrasts with the DV result in which having an unpredictable IMF as enforcer may actually be the optimal policy. Of course, the IMF is doing different things in the two cases, so perhaps this is not too surprising.

The IMF clearly has other roles, too, apart from that of enforcer or auditor. Specifically, the IMF also provides money or promises of money. This role can protect borrowers against coordination problems between lenders. If the IMF offers standby arrangements, then this may prevent costly self-fulfilling-type runs. This is the approach taken by Gavin and Powell (1999). However, the price for such liquidity protection may be moral hazard, thus allowing borrowers or lenders to take greater risks, actually making more fundamental-type runs more likely. Gavin and Powell argue that private sector standbys (contingent facilities) might also provide countries with the same type of liquidity protection and that, if these are correctly priced (i.e., with no information problems), then these may even serve to reduce moral hazard.

To sum up this first part of the paper, DV provide an application of BS to the sovereign debt market and show that within that context the IMF may have an interesting role to play. Although some aspects of the model appear to sit uneasily with the sovereign nature of these markets, the result is intuitive and would probably carry over to other models of strategic default.

Let me now turn briefly to the second part of the paper. Curiously the theoretical model behind the second part of the paper does not appear to be fully consistent with that in the first part of the paper. In the first part of the paper, a crisis occurs when, with a specific probability, there is a bad outcome and debt cannot be renegotiated. In the second part of the paper, a crisis occurs when the demand for insurance just meets the supply. The source of this uncertainty is then different; it is related to how much the insurance is available.

Entering into this second framework, table 5.2 regresses the size of rescue packages on a set of variables. It is not clear how the variables are specified (everything in US$?), and the only variable that is significant is bond stocks outstanding at the time of the crisis. However, bonds outstanding might have as much to do with supply as it has to do with demand (if debt finance has been used to build up reserves, or if multilaterals care more about big countries due to contagion effects, etc.). It might be better to have the dependent variable specified as a percentage of something (gross domestic product [GDP]?) and the other variables expressed either as share variables (e.g., bonds, total liabilities, etc.) or perhaps even as growth variables. Table 5.3 has the same dependent variable, and the only variable that is significant is the GDP at the time of the crisis. Because I would suggest scaling the rescue variable by GDP, this might make this variable insignificant anyway!

However, if it remained significant, this might be interpreted as a kind of too-big-to-fail result. As the text considers issues related to the supply of government guarantees, perhaps some indicators of such things should be included, for example (a) type of deposit insurance in place, (b) the extent of public banks, (c) historical experience in allowing banks or other companies to fail, (d) bankruptcy procedures, and so on.

The results of tables 5.4 and 5.5 appear more interesting. The forecast error of the amount of insurance is proxied by the sum of the supply and demand error from the previous regressions. This raises issues about whether coefficients may be biased and also about units. It would be better to have this error expressed as a percentage and not in US$.

To conclude, this is an interesting paper. It is really a story of two quite different and not necessarily consistent parts. I suspect that the authors could extend both, thus making a fascinating research program.

References

Dooley, Michael P. 2000. Can output losses following international financial crises be avoided? NBER Working Paper no. 7531. Cambridge, Mass.: National Bureau of Economic Research, February.

Gavin, Michael, and Andrew Powell. 1999. Should international lender of last resort lending be privitized? Universidad Torcuato Di Tella. Mimeo.

Gay, P., S. Hayes, and H. Song Shin. 2001. Crisis costs and debtor discipline: The efficiency of public policy in sovereign debt crises. Mimeo. London School of Economics.

Discussion Summary

Robert P. Flood inquired why governments end up in this insurance business. Shouldn't the IMF prevent them from providing insurance? He also noted that Michael Dooley's crisis theory is unique—different from the first- and second-generation crisis models, because in those there is no transfer.

Morris Goldstein noted that the IMF is able to affect negotiations between creditors and debtors: an example of that is the "lending into arrears" policy. He also remarked that the former Compensatory Financing Facility (CFF) lending window in the IMF discredits the notion that the IMF cannot differentiate between liquidity (bad luck) and strategic default.

John McHale asked why, in this theory, real output costs are inevitable, and what the channels are through which this loss comes about.

Martin Feldstein asked whether there were any examples of commercial banks' using denial of trade credits as a punishment tool.

Andrew Berg noted that an important class of creditors is the Paris club and that the IMF does monitor Paris club discussions between debtors and creditors.

Edwin M. Truman suggested that Peru in the 1980s is the closest case to strategic default. He also noted that there were gainers from the precrisis period—for example, through overvalued exchange rate—and these should be accounted for in this output loss accounting.

Vincent Reinhart suggested that if the story is accurate then maybe the IMF should have no access to capital.

Barry Eichengreen inquired whether the theory is consistent with previous statements by Dooley that the IMF should not condition its lending on observable characteristics.

Peter Kenen suggested that "strategic default" is a loaded term and may be used here inaccurately. He also noted that the devaluation and the rapid loss of reserves might be channels for output loss in developing countries.

Martin Eichenbaum then noted that the size of the domestic insurance pool and the definition of strategic default are tied together, and it is unclear how to differentiate between them. In response, Feldstein noted that in the Asian crisis, a lot of the international debt was private, and therefore, at least theoretically, it could be a crisis of insolvency—even though the Asian governments ended up taking over these bad debts.

Michael P. Dooley responded that, in practice, governments cannot roll over debts using their future tax receipts as collateral, because the high interest rates they are facing at the time of the crisis will make the present value of those future taxes very small.

In response to Flood's question, Dooley noted that, historically, governments did go into insurance when there were some big institutional changes with unanticipated consequences. Liberalization, for example, meant that looting was possible, as long as there was no effective supervision. In Korea, the government did not understand how much it needed to regulate, for instance. He also stated that although the IMF can affect the balance of power in negotiations, it can only do good if it has superior information on the nature of crisis. What, uncomfortably, comes out of this theory, Dooley further suggested, is that the IMF should not get involved at all if it cannot monitor domestic financial markets. He added that governments of developing countries could not credibly commit to not bailing out once a crisis hits.

He concluded that the investors cheat the government, which gets money from the IMF to pay those investors. The workers, in turn, pay for these loans. Thus, during crises, there is a real transfer from workers (taxpayers) to investors and financial institutions.

Financial Restructuring in Banking and Corporate-Sector Crises
What Policies to Pursue?

Stijn Claessens, Daniela Klingebiel, and Luc Laeven

6.1 Introduction

Whether as a cause or an effect, a systemic banking and corporate crisis is often part of a currency crisis.[1] Resolving a banking and corporate crisis involves many policy choices ranging from the macroeconomic (including monetary and fiscal policy) to the microeconomic (including capital adequacy rules and corporate governance requirements), with reforms varying in depth. These choices involve trade-offs, including the amount of government resources needed to resolve the crisis, the speed of recovery, and the recovery's sustainability. Despite considerable analysis, these trade-offs are not well known—an oversight that occasionally leads to conflicting policy advice and larger-than-necessary economic costs. Even less is known about the political economy factors that make governments choose certain policies.

This paper reviews knowledge about the trade-offs involved in policies related to systemic financial and corporate restructuring. It finds that a consistent framework for bank and corporate restructuring is the key factor for success—and one that is often missing. Consistency is needed in many areas and involves, among other elements, ensuring that there are sufficient

Stijn Claessens is professor of international finance at the University of Amsterdam. Daniela Klingebiel is a senior financial economist and Luc Laeven is a financial economist in the Financial Sector Policy and Strategy Group of the World Bank.

The opinions expressed do not necessarily reflect those of the World Bank. The authors would like to thank Peter Kenen, Jeffrey Frankel, and other participants at the conference for very helpful comments. They thank Ying Lin for help with the data.

1. In this chapter *systemic* is used to refer to a crisis that is large relative to a national economy, not necessarily one that is large relative to the global economy or that has other global spillovers.

resources for absorbing losses and that private agents face appropriate sticks and carrots for restructuring. Moreover, sustainable restructuring requires deep structural reforms, which often require addressing political economy factors up front.

The paper complements the literature review with some new empirical analysis using data for 687 corporations from eight crisis countries. It investigates the quantitative importance of some specific government policies: liquidity support to financial institutions, the guaranteeing of the liabilities of the financial system during the early phase of the crisis, and the establishment of a public asset management company during the restructuring phase. It finds that a package of these measures can facilitate quicker recovery by the corporate sector from a crisis and assist in the sustainability of the recovery. The particular policies come with large fiscal costs, however, leading to trade-offs in terms of an equitable distribution of the benefits and cost of the government intervention and, possibly, in terms of the ultimate growth impact.

The paper proceeds as follows. Section 6.2 presents an overview of the general characteristics of banking system and corporate-sector crises. Section 6.3 reviews the literature on banking and corporate-sector crises. Section 6.4 provides empirical evidence on the effects of crisis resolution policies using firm-level data from a set of crisis countries. Section 6.5 concludes.

6.2   Characteristics of Banking and Corporate Crises

A systemic banking and corporate crisis is a situation in which an economy faces large-scale financial and corporate distress within a short period.[2] Recent examples include the crisis in Nordic countries in the early 1990s, in Mexico in 1994–95, in East Asian countries after 1997, and in transition economies in the 1990s (although for transition economies, financial distress and structural problems had been longer-term phenomena). Banking and corporate crises appear to have become more common since the early 1980s: Caprio and Klingebiel (2002) identify ninety-three countries that experienced a systemic financial crisis during the 1980s or 1990s (figure 6.1). It also appears that crises became deeper in the 1990s relative to earlier periods (Bordo et al. 2001).

In a systemic crisis, partly as a result of a general economic slowdown and large shocks to foreign exchange and interest rates, corporate and financial sectors experience a large number of defaults and difficulties in repaying contracts on time. As a result, nonperforming loans increase sharply. This

---

2. We do not try to identify the exact causes of systemic distress or determine whether currency crises are caused by systemic financial distress in banks and corporations or vice versa. For such analysis, see Edwards and Frankel (forthcoming).

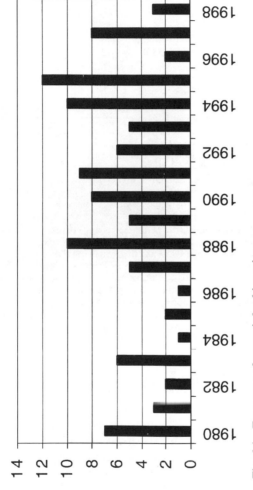

Fig. 6.1   Frequency of systemic banking crises

Source: Caprio and Klingebiel (2002); authors' calculations.

Notes: The frequency on the vertical axis indicates the number of countries that had a crisis starting in the year on the horizontal axis (total sample of crisis countries is ninety-three).

Table 6.1   Patterns of Systemic Banking Crises

	Crisis Year	Fiscal Cost (% of GDP)	Peak NPL (% of Loans)	Real GDP Growth (%)	Change in Exchange Rate (%)	Peak in Real Interest Rates (%)	Decline in Real Asset Prices (%)
Finland	1992	11.0	13	−4.6	−5.5	14.3	−34.6
Indonesia	1998	50.0	65–75	−15.4	−57.5	3.3	−78.5
Korea	1998	37.0	30–40	−10.6	−28.8	21.6	−45.9
Malaysia	1998	16.4	25–35	−12.7	−13.9	5.3	−79.9
Mexico	1995	19.3	30	−6.2	−39.8	24.7	−53.3
The Philippines	1998	0.5	20	−0.8	−13.0	6.3	−67.2
Sweden	1992	4.0	18	−3.3	+1.0	79.2	−6.8
Thailand	1998	32.8	33	−5.4	−13.7	17.2	−77.4

Sources: "Crisis year" (the peak crisis year) is from Caprio and Klingebiel (2002). The "fiscal cost (% of GDP)" variable is from Honohan and Klingebiel (2002). The "peak NPL (nonperforming loans; % of total loans)" variable is from Caprio and Klingebiel (2002) in the case of Indonesia, Korea, the Philippines, and Thailand; from Lindgren, Garcia, and Saal (1996) in the case of Finland and Sweden; and from Krueger and Tornell (1999) in the case of Mexico. Gross domestic product (GDP) data are from the International Monetary Fund's *International Financial Statistics* (IFS). The exchange rate, interest rate, and inflation data are from IFS. We use the Datastream global market indexes for Finland, Mexico, and Sweden, and the IFS global market indexes for the other countries.

Notes: The "real GDP growth" variable equals the percentage change in real fourth-quarter GDP in the crisis year compared to real fourth-quarter GDP one year before the crisis year. Consumer Price Index (CPI) inflation is used to get the real growth in GDP, and the growth in GDP is in terms of local currency. The inflation rate equals the percentage change in the CPI during the crisis year. The "change in exchange rate" equals the percentage change of the exchange rate versus the U.S. dollar during the first quarter of the crisis year. An increase in the exchange rate indicates an appreciation. The "peak in real interest rates" equals the peak in the real money market rate during crisis year. For the Philippines, the real discount rate is reported instead of the money market rate, due to data unavailability. The "decline in real asset prices" variable is the largest drop on a monthly basis in the stock market index during the crisis year compared to the level of the stock market index in January of the year before the crisis year. The return is in local currency and corrected for inflation.

situation is often accompanied by depressed asset prices (such as equity and real estate prices) on the heels of run-ups before the crisis, sharp increases in real interest rates, and a slowdown or reversal in capital flows (table 6.1). In countries with longer-term financial distress and other large-scale structural problems—such as several transition economies—a systemic crisis may not be accompanied by such changes in asset prices and capital flows, partly because run-ups in prices and capital flows may not have occurred.

Developments in crisis countries highlight the complicated coordination problems that arise between corporations, between the corporate and financial sectors, between the government and the rest of the economy, and with respect to domestic and foreign investors. In a systemic crisis, the fate of an individual corporation and the best course of action for its owners and managers will depend on the actions of many other corporations and financial institutions as well as on the general economic outlook. The financial and corporate sectors, always closely intertwined, both need restructuring in a systemic crisis, and the actions taken affect their liquidity and solvency. The government must set the rules of the game and be a prominent actor in restructuring. Moreover, investors, domestic and foreign, will await the actions of owners, the government, labor, and others—often implying a shortage of foreign and domestic capital when it is most needed.

A crisis and its coordination problems are typically aggravated by institutional weaknesses, many of which likely caused the crisis in the first place. Bankruptcy and restructuring frameworks are often deficient. Disclosure and accounting rules may be weak for financial institutions and corporations. Equity and creditor rights may be poorly defined, and the judiciary is often inefficient. There is usually also a shortage of qualified managers in the corporate and financial sectors, as well as a lack of qualified domestic restructuring and insolvency specialists, partly because there may be no history of corporate and financial-sector restructuring. The government itself may face credibility problems because it may have been partly to blame for the crisis, and in general it faces many time consistency problems—such as how to avoid large bailouts while also restarting the economy.

These complicated coordination problems suggest that systemic crises are difficult to resolve. Many observers have tried to develop best practices for resolving such crises. We next review that literature.

6.3   Literature on Banking and Corporate Crises

Governments have used many approaches to try to resolve systemic bank and corporate distress. Resolving systemic financial distress is not easy, and opinions differ widely on what constitutes best practice. Many different and seemingly contradictory policy recommendations have been made to limit the fiscal costs of crises and speed recovery. Empirical research supporting particular views remains limited, and most research is limited to individual cases.

Sheng (1996) made the first attempt to distill lessons from several banking crises. Caprio and Klingebiel (1996) expanded on those lessons using additional crises. The main lesson from both efforts is that managing a financial crisis is much different in industrial countries from in emerging markets because emerging markets have weaker institutions, crises are often larger, and other initial circumstances differ. As a result, best practices from industrial countries do not easily transfer to developing countries. Another key lesson is that there are many trade-offs between various policies.

In reviewing the literature on financial restructuring, especially in emerging markets, it is useful to differentiate between three phases of systemic restructuring. During the first phase, which can be called the containment phase, the financial crisis is still unfolding. During this phase governments tend to implement policies aimed at restoring public confidence to minimize the repercussions on the real sector of the loss of confidence by depositors and other investors in the financial system. The second phase involves the actual financial, and to a lesser extent operational, restructuring of financial institutions and corporations. The third phase involves structural reforms, including changes in laws and regulations, privatization of any nationalized financial institutions and corporations, and so on. Here we discuss the containment phase, the restructuring of financial institutions, and the restructuring of corporations.

6.3.1 Containment Phase

Policy-makers often fail to respond effectively to evidence of an impending banking crisis, hoping that banks and corporations will grow out of their problems.[3] However, intervening early with a comprehensive and credible plan can avoid a systemic crisis, minimize adverse effects, and limit overall losses (Sheng 1996). Early intervention appears to be especially important in stopping the flow of financing to loss-making financial institutions and corporations and in limiting moral hazard in financial institutions and corporations gambling for survival.

Experience also suggests that intervention and closing of weak financial institutions need to be properly managed. Uncertainty among depositors needs to be limited; otherwise, the government may have to try to resolve a loss of confidence with an unlimited guarantee on the liabilities of banks and other financial institutions. However, in practice, ad hoc closures are more the norm and often add to uncertainty, triggering a systemic crisis. For example, in late 1997 the closing of sixteen banks in Indonesia triggered a depositor run because depositors were aware that some politically connected banks known to be insolvent were kept open (Lindgren et al. 2000). Similarly, the suspension of finance companies in Thailand increased uncertainty among depositors as well as borrowers.

Reviewing several cases, Baer and Klingebiel (1995) suggest that, to avoid uncertainty among depositors and limit their incentives to run, policy makers need to deal simultaneously with all insolvent and marginally solvent institutions. Intermittent regulatory intervention makes depositors more nervous and undermines regulatory credibility, especially if regulators had previously argued that the institutions involved were solvent.[4] Moreover, in emerging markets regulations are often weak, supervision is limited, and

---

3. There are many political economy reasons that policy makers may not wish to act—thereby giving rise to a crisis—but we do not discuss them here (see Haggard 2001).

4. Baer and Klingebiel also point out that a comprehensive approach places less demand on supervisory resources. Under a piecemeal approach, insolvent and marginally solvent institutions would continue to exist while other insolvent institutions were being closed or restructured. Marginally solvent institutions would be subject to moral hazard and fraud while being unable and unwilling to raise additional capital. Especially in an environment with weak supervision, comprehensive approaches are thus more necessary.

data on financial solvency are poor, so intervention tools need to be fairly simple.

For example, a rehabilitation program for undercapitalized financial institutions—which involves institutions' indicating how they plan to meet capital adequacy requirements in the future—requires careful government oversight and good financial statements. However, such features are often missing in developing countries. Instead of relying on rehabilitation that requires good oversight and data, regulators could apply a 100 percent (marginal) reserve requirement on deposit inflows and other new liabilities, limiting weak banks' ability to reallocate resources in a detrimental way.

There are two schools of thought on whether to use liquidity support and unlimited guarantees during the containment phase.[5] Some argue that crisis conditions make it almost impossible to distinguish between solvent and insolvent institutions, leaving the authorities with little choice but to extend liquidity support. Moreover, it is argued that an unlimited guarantee preserves the payments system and helps stabilize institutions' financial claims while restructuring is being organized and carried out (Lindgren et al. 2000).

Others argue that open-ended liquidity support provides more time for insolvent institutions to gamble (unsuccessfully) on resurrection, facilitates continued financing of loss-making borrowers, and allows owners and managers to engage in looting. Supporters of this view also argue that a government guarantee on financial institutions' liabilities reduces large creditors' incentives to monitor financial institutions, allowing bank managers and shareholders to continue gambling on their insolvent banks and increasing fiscal costs. They further point out that extensive guarantees limit government maneuverability in allocating losses, often with the end result that the government incurs most of the cost of the systemic crisis (Sheng 1996).

In practice, there is a trade-off between restoring confidence and containing fiscal costs. Evidence on these trade-offs comes from Honohan and Klingebiel (2002), who show that much of the variation in the fiscal cost of forty crises in industrial and developing economies in 1980–97 can be explained by government approaches to resolving liquidity crises. The authors find that governments that provided open-ended liquidity support and blanket deposit guarantees incurred much higher costs in resolving financial crises. They also find that these costs are higher in countries with weak institutions.

Most important, Honohan and Klingebiel find no obvious trade-off between fiscal costs and subsequent economic growth (or overall output

---

5. A third school argues that the granting of government guarantees is the outcome of political economy circumstances and so is often a foregone conclusion. See Dooley and Verma (chap. 5 in this volume).

losses). Countries that used policies such as liquidity support, blanket guarantees, and particularly costly forbearance did not recover faster. Rather, liquidity support appears to make recovery from a crisis longer and output losses larger—a finding confirmed by Bordo et al. (2001). Thus it appears that the two most important policies during the containment phase are to limit liquidity support and not to extend guarantees. Where institutions are weak, governments may need to use simple methods in dealing with weak banks and a loss of confidence to avoid higher fiscal contingencies and costs.

6.3.2   Restructuring Financial Institutions

Once financial markets have been stabilized, the second phase involves restructuring weak financial institutions and corporations. Restructuring is complex because policy-makers need to take into account many issues. Financial restructuring will depend on the speed at which macroeconomic stability can be achieved because that determines the viability of corporations, banks, and other financial institutions, and more generally the reduction in overall uncertainty. However, macroeconomic stability often requires progress on financial and corporate restructuring, so it cannot be viewed independently of the restructuring process (see Burnside, Eichenbaum, and Rebelo, chap. 7 in this volume; Park and Lee, chap. 9 in this volume).

Restructuring refers to several related processes: recognizing and allocating financial losses, restructuring the financial claims of financial institutions and corporations, and operational restructuring of financial institutions and corporations. Recognition involves the allocation of losses and associated redistribution of wealth and control. Losses—that is, differences between the market value of assets and the nominal value of liabilities held by financial institutions and corporations—can be allocated to shareholders (through dilution), to depositors and creditors (by reducing the present value of their claims), to employees (through reduced wages) and suppliers, and to the government or the public (through higher taxes, lower spending, or inflation). Here we discuss the restructuring of financial institutions; the next section discusses the restructuring of corporations.

To minimize moral hazard and strengthen financial discipline, governments can allocate losses not only to shareholders but also to creditors and large depositors who should have been monitoring the banks. Often, however, governments assume all losses through their guarantees. There are exceptions to the model of governments' guaranteeing all liabilities in an effort to restore confidence. Baer and Klingebiel (1995) show that in some crises—notably in the United States (1933), Japan (1946), Argentina (1980–82), and Estonia (1992)—governments have imposed losses on depositors with little or no adverse macroeconomic consequences or flight to currency. In these cases, economic recovery was rapid, and financial intermediation, including household deposits, was soon restored. Thus, allocating losses to creditors or depositors will not necessarily lead to runs on banks or end in contraction of aggregate money, credit, and output. In a related vein, Caprio and Klingebiel's (1996) review of country cases indicates that financial discipline is further strengthened when bank management—often part of the problem—is changed and banks are operationally restructured.

Besides loss allocation, financial and corporate restructuring crucially depends on the incentives under which banks and corporations operate. Successful corporate debt workouts require proper incentives for banks and borrowers to come to the negotiating table (Dado and Klingebiel 2002). The incentive framework for banks includes accounting, classification, and provisioning rules: that is, financial institutions need to be asked to realistically mark their assets to market. The framework also includes laws and prudential regulations. Regulators should ensure that undercapitalized financial institutions are properly disciplined and closed. The insolvency system should enable financial institutions to enforce their claims on corporations, allow for speedy financial restructuring of viable corporations, and provide for the efficient liquidation of enterprises that cannot be rehabilitated. Proper incentives also mean limited ownership links between banks and corporations (because otherwise the same party could end up being both debtor and creditor).

Adequately capitalized financial institutions are a key component of a proper incentive framework, because financial institutions need to have sufficient loss absorption capacity to engage in sustainable corporate restructuring. In a systemic crisis, capital will often have to come from the government through recapitalization. However, general experience—supported by recent events in East Asia—suggests that recapitalization of financial institutions needs to be structured and managed to limit moral hazard. In their analysis of forty bank crises, Honohan and Klingebiel (2002) find that repeated, incomplete recapitalizations tend to increase the fiscal costs of resolving a crisis. One possible explanation is that marginally capitalized banks tend to engage in cosmetic corporate restructuring—such as maturity extensions or interest rate reductions on loans to nonviable corporations—rather than writing off debts.

Besides adequate capitalization, preferably by private shareholders, banks' incentives to undertake corporate restructuring can be strengthened by linking government financing to the restructuring. For example, a capital support scheme in which additional fiscal resources are linked to corporate restructuring through loss sharing arrangements can induce banks to conduct deeper restructuring. Regardless, especially in weak institutional settings, limits on the actions of marginally capitalized banks will typically be necessary.

In principle, governments should only capitalize or strengthen the capital base of financial institutions with charter and franchise value. However, apart from political economy problems, it is often difficult for governments to distinguish good banks from bad. Risk-sharing mechanisms with the private sector, such as cofinancing arrangements with government equity infusion (in the form of preferred shares) when the private sector provides capital, can help identify better banks. This setup still requires decent institutions to avoid misuse. Especially in a weak institutional environment with limited private capital, governments may want to rely more on hard budget constraints on weak banks (such as a 100 percent marginal reserve requirement on new deposits) to prevent a large leakage of fiscal resources, including those that occur through excessive guarantees on financial institutions' liabilities. Additionally, good banks may need to be actively coerced to receive support, because they may resist government interference. Without some support, however, good banks may not be able to provide financial intermediation to corporations, thus aggravating the crisis.

6.3.3   Restructuring Corporations

Providing the Right Incentives

The nature of a systemic crisis, as well as the already close links between the solvency and performance of the corporate and financial sectors in normal times, makes it clear that bank restructuring needs to be complemented by corporate restructuring. To start corporate restructuring, corporations should quickly be triaged into operationally viable and not financially distressed corporations, operationally viable but financially distressed corporations, and financially and operationally unviable corporations. In a normal restructuring of an individual case of financial distress, private agents will make these decisions and start the operational and financial restructuring.[6] However, in a systemic crisis case-by-case restructuring will be difficult because the incentives under which agents operate are likely not to be conducive, private capital is typically limited, and coordination problems are large.[7]

Nevertheless, the starting point is providing proper incentives for private agents to allow and encourage market-based, sustainable corporate restructuring. Given that the crisis was likely to have been partly induced by weaknesses in the environment in which the corporate sector operated, the first step for government will have to be creating an enabling environment. Depending on country circumstances, this can imply undertaking corpo-

---

6. Financial restructuring for corporations can take many forms: reschedulings (extensions of maturities), lower interest rates, debt-for-equity swaps, debt forgiveness, indexing interest payments to earnings, and so on. Operational restructuring, an ongoing process, includes improvements in efficiency and management, reductions in staff and wages, asset sales (such as a reduction in subsidiaries), enhanced marketing efforts, and the like, with the expectation of increased profitability and cash flow.

7. For other papers on systemic corporate restructuring, including specific case studies, see Claessens, Djankov, and Mody (2001).

rate governance reforms, improving bankruptcy and other restructuring frameworks, making the judicial system more efficient, liberalizing entry by foreign investors, changing the competitive framework for the real sector, or introducing other supportive structural measures. In general, the political economy of reform suggests that a crisis can often be a time to get difficult structural reforms accepted or at least initiated (Haggard 2001).

Most crisis countries do reform the incentives for restructuring (see Claessens, Djankov, and Klingebiel 2001; Dado and Klingebiel 2002; Stone 2000a,b; and World Bank 2000 for different groups of crisis countries), although the strengths and depth of the reforms differ. For example, Indonesia adopted a new bankruptcy system to replace its pre–World War II Dutch code in August 1998, twelve months after its crisis started. Similarly, Thailand's senate approved the Act for the Establishment of and Procedure for Bankruptcy Court, intended to increase the efficiency of judicial procedures in bankruptcy cases, in February 1999, nineteen months after its crisis began. Despite the act's adoption, however, bankruptcies in Thailand remained few in number and fraught with difficulties (Foley 2000).

Beyond fixing the environment, it can be necessary to provide extra incentives for private agents to engage in (quick) corporate restructuring. These incentives can involve tax, accounting, and other measures. Banks, for example, may be given more tax relief for provisioning or restructuring loans. Corporations may be given more favorable accounting relief for recognizing foreign exchange losses. In the wake of its crisis, the Republic of Korea adopted more favorable tax rules for corporate restructuring, although they ended up being misused through cosmetic rather than real restructuring. Some countries have offered guarantees on exchange rate behavior, such as Indonesia's INDRA scheme and Mexico's FICORCA scheme (see Stone 2000a). The efficiency of such measures should be evaluated from various perspectives, taking into account their benefits for restructuring and public finance as well as their possible redistributive effects. However, although such measures may speed recovery, they often do not contribute to fundamental reforms. In any case, the general opinion is that such measures should be temporary (that is, equipped with sunset clauses).

Improving the Framework for Restructuring

Even when adequate for normal times, a revamped bankruptcy and restructuring framework might not be sufficient during a systemic crisis, given the coordination problems and weaknesses in other aspects of the institutional framework. Thus, governments have created special frameworks for corporate restructuring, such as the "London rules,"[8] first used in Mex-

---

8. The London rules are principles for corporate reorganization first proposed in the United Kingdom in the early 1990s. Because the rules were not designed for systemic corporate distress, countries have tightened them in various ways.

ico and then in several East Asian countries (Indonesia, Korea, Malaysia, Thailand). The London rules involve an out-of-court accord, under regular contract or commercial law, that all or most creditor institutions are coerced to sign. With such an accord, agreements reached among most creditors can often be enforced on other creditors without formal judicial procedures.

Arbitration with specific deadlines—and penalties for failing to meet the deadlines—can also be part of the accord, avoiding a formal judicial process to resolve disputes.[9] The degree of such enhancements to the London rules has varied among countries. In East Asia the frameworks in Korea, Malaysia, and Thailand were the most conducive to out-of-court restructuring, whereas the framework in Indonesia was the least conducive (Claessens, Djankov, and Klingebiel 2001). These differences appear partly to explain the variations in the speed of restructuring in these four countries.

The most far-reaching proposal for enhancing the restructuring framework is "super-bankruptcy" (or "super Chapter 11"), a temporary tool that allows corporate management to stay in place and forces debt-to-equity conversions (Stiglitz 2001). This tool can preserve firms' value as going concerns by preventing too many liquidations and keeping in place existing managers, who arguably most often know best how to run the firms. An important issue is when to call for a super Chapter 11—that is, when is a crisis systemic, and who has the authority to call for such a suspension of payments? Political economy factors should be taken into account, because some debtors could gain disproportionately from a suspension of payments. To date no country has taken this approach.[10]

Even with a better enabling environment, agents will likely be unable to triage corporations quickly and proceed with restructuring. The resulting debt overhang or deadlock in claims can be especially risky when institutions are weak, and it can greatly increase the final costs to the public sector of resolving the crisis. Weak banks may continue to lend to corporations that are "too big to fail," partly as a way of gambling for resurrection, and so delay sustainable corporate restructuring. Owners of defunct enterprises may strip assets, leaving only shells of liabilities for creditors. Even financially viable corporations may stop paying promptly if faced with an insolvent banking system.

---

9. Out-of-court negotiations and bankruptcy or other legal resolution techniques are not the only ways of dealing with financial distress. Economists have been proposing alternative procedures for some time, centering on versions of an asset sale or cash auction. Cash auctions are easy to administer and do not rely on the judicial system (Hart et al. 1997). Although attractive from a theoretical perspective, these proposals have not had recent followers except Mexico in 1998.

10. Although bankruptcy laws differ considerably even among industrial countries, there has been a general move from more creditor-friendly regimes that are liquidation-oriented to more debtor-friendly regimes that are more restructuring-oriented (Westbrook 2001).

In such cases it may be necessary in the short run to use hard budget constraints to limit the flow of resources to weak corporations from weak financial institutions or other sources. To increase credit to corporations that can actually repay and limit lending to weak corporations it may also be necessary to have temporary across-the-board mechanisms for certain types of borrowers (such as small and medium-sized enterprises) or certain activities (such as trade financing). The need for such blunter tools will increase with a country's institutional weakness. Indonesia's market-based approach to corporate restructuring, for example, seems to have had little impact and probably only led to further asset stripping.

Choosing a Lead Agent

As a next step, it is often necessary for governments to more directly support corporate restructuring. As with support for the financial system, it is essential to restructure strong and viable corporations, not weak ones. All too often, however, unviable corporations (such as those considered too big too fail) receive support instead of deserving, operationally viable corporations. This was the case with Korea's large *chaebol* and with Indonesia and Thailand's large family-controlled conglomerates. These firms ended up receiving disproportionately large financing during the first phase of the crisis, while smaller firms lacked even working capital (Domaç and Ferri 1999). Thus, it is crucial to choose a lead agent that ensures proper analysis of corporations' prospects as well as durable operational and financial restructurings.

The main choice for the lead agent in restructuring is between the government and the private sector. Many approaches are possible. A centralized asset management corporation will put the government in charge. Recapitalization of private banks will put the banks in charge. Under other models, investors and corporations can become the lead agent, with the government sharing the risks. Banks can work out nonperforming loans, for example, but with some stop-loss arrangements with the government. Alternatively, nonperforming loans can be transferred to a number of corporate restructuring vehicles that, although state-owned, can be privately run by asset managers with incentive stakes.

Most important is that the lead agent have the necessary capacity to absorb losses as well as the institutional capacity, incentives, and external enforcement mechanisms to effect restructuring. Undercapitalized banks, for example, will not be very effective restructuring agents; and without a working bankruptcy regime, private agents will not be able to force recalcitrant debtors to the negotiating table—as in Indonesia and in Thailand, where the restructuring of Thai Petrochemical Industry took three years.

Countries often choose a mix of these approaches when dealing with a systemic crisis. In 1995 Mexico tried both an asset management corporation and a more decentralized approach. The four East Asian crisis countries (Indonesia, Korea, Malaysia, Thailand) all eventually used asset management corporations, all used out-of-court systems for corporate restructuring, and most used, after some initial period, fiscal stimulus and monetary policy to foster economic growth. In addition, all enhanced, to varying degrees, their basic frameworks for private-sector operations, including bankruptcy and corporate governance frameworks, liberalization of foreign entry in the financial and corporate sectors, and so on. However, success has varied with the intensity of these measures (Claessens, Djankov, and Klingebiel 2001).

Empirical evidence on these mechanisms is limited but tends to favor the decentralized model. A study of seven centralized approaches using asset management companies found that most of the corporations did not achieve their stated objectives with corporate restructuring (Klingebiel 2001). The study distinguishes corporate restructuring asset management companies from bank rehabilitation asset management companies. Two of the three corporate restructuring companies did not achieve their narrow goal of expediting restructuring. Only Sweden's asset management company successfully managed its portfolio, acting in some instances as the lead agent in restructuring.

Rapid asset disposition vehicles fared somewhat better, with two of four—in Spain and the United States—achieving their objectives. These successes suggest that asset management corporations can be effective, but only for narrowly defined purposes of resolving insolvent and unviable financial institutions and selling their assets. However, even achieving these objectives requires many ingredients: a type of asset that is easily liquefied (such as real estate), mostly professional management, political independence, a skilled human resource base, appropriate funding, adequate bankruptcy and foreclosure laws, good information and management systems, and transparent operations and processes.

The findings by Klingebiel (2001) on asset management companies are corroborated by a review of three East Asian countries (Dado 2000). The centralized asset management companies in Indonesia and Korea did not appear likely to achieve their narrow goal of expediting bank or corporate restructuring, whereas Malaysia's was relatively successful, aided by that country's strong bankruptcy system. Success has also varied when a mix of approaches is tried. In Mexico neither the asset management company nor the enhanced restructuring framework was effective, possibly because fundamental reforms were lacking (Mexico's bankruptcy regime, for example, was not revamped until four years after its crisis). Export-led growth appears to have led Mexico's recovery after 1995 (although growth did not resolve banking problems; see Krueger and Tornell 1999).

Dado and Klingebiel (2002) analyze decentralized restructuring in seven countries: Argentina, Chile, Hungary, Japan, Norway, Poland, and Thailand. They find that the success of this approach depended on the quality of the institutional framework, including accounting and legal rules, and on initial conditions, including the capital positions of banks and ownership links. In Norway the government built on favorable initial conditions to attain a solid overall framework for the decentralized approach. The biggest improvements to the overall framework was made in Chile, with favorable results. Poland and Hungary ranked behind Chile, although Poland improved its framework much faster than did Hungary. Thailand made little progress on strengthening its framework. In Japan, despite many reforms to the overall framework, efforts remained blocked by large ownership links. Argentina relied solely on public debt relief programs and did not change its overall framework for restructuring.

Changing Ownership Structures

Just as a crisis can offer a window for structural reform, it can provide an opportunity to reform a country's ownership structures. As a direct party to the restructuring process, the state often becomes the owner of defunct financial institutions and corporations. This development severely complicates the resolution of the crisis, because the government may not have the right incentives or capacity to effect the needed operational and financial restructuring. At the same time, large ownership by the state of the financial and corporate sectors provides an opportunity to change ownership structures as part of restructuring. This move can have several benefits.

First, the changes can correct ownership structures that contributed to the crisis and so help prevent future crises. To the extent, for example, that ownership concentrated in the hands of a few families contributed to the crisis—as was argued by some for East Asia—the government can try to widen ownership structures.

Second, the government can try to obtain political support for restructuring by reallocating ownership.[11] One option is to reprivatize financial institutions or corporations in a way that redistributes ownership among the general public or employees of the restructured institution. Another option is to use some of the state ownership to endow unfunded pension obligations from a pay-as-you-go system. In this way, the government can create ownership structures that, over time, will reinforce its reforms.

Third, changing ownership structures can introduce third parties who have better incentives and skills in restructuring individual corporations and determining financial relief. One option is to transfer nonperforming loans to a fund jointly owned by private and public shareholders, but with the private stake having lower seniority. Private shareholders in the fund would then have the right incentives when deciding on the financial viabil-

---

11. Regardless of the changes in ownership and the relationships between debtors and creditors, the government may want to create a special social safety net for laid-off workers to help sustain political support for restructuring over time. See Levinsohn, Berry, and Friedman (chap. 12 in this volume) for the case of Indonesia.

ity of a corporation, but without having full formal ownership of the assets. Public resources would be provided only when all parties—creditor banks, other creditors, new private investors, the government, and the private shareholders in the fund—had reached agreement with the corporation.

Pursuing Supportive Macroeconomic Policies

Another common theme in the literature is that corporate restructuring should occur in the context of supportive macroeconomic policies. The right macroeconomic policies (fiscal and monetary) can speed the recovery of overall activity and corporate output. The appropriate fiscal stance has been extensively reviewed, especially in the context of the East Asian crisis. A review by the International Monetary Fund suggests that East Asian countries' fiscal stance was too tight initially (Lane et al. 1999). The appropriate monetary stance has been more controversial and is still being debated (see Cho and West, chap. 1 in this volume; Drazen, chap. 2 in this volume), but mainly in terms of defending the exchange rate.

An important related aspect is the effect on the corporate sector through a possible credit crunch. Microeconomic-based empirical literature suggests evidence of a credit crunch early in the East Asian crisis (Claessens, Djankov, and Xu 2000; Colaco, Hallward-Driemeier, and Dwor-Frecaut 2000; Dollar and Hallward-Driemeier 2000). The crunch was likely the result of tighter capital adequacy requirements and the monetary policies being pursued. More generally, it has been found that although tighter capital adequacy rules have minimal effects on aggregate credit provision, borrowers from weak banks are affected by tighter regulation and supervision (Bank for International Settlements 1999). Given the unbalanced financial systems in East Asia—where banks dominate and little alternative financing was available, and many banks were fragile even before the crisis (Claessens and Glaessner 1997)—it is likely that, at least initially, banking weaknesses and tighter regulation and supervision led to a credit crunch for East Asian corporations (Domaç and Ferri 1999). Following this initial crunch, corporations may have ended up with a debt overhang, with a consequent need for financial restructuring.

6.4   Additional Empirical Evidence on the Effects of Crisis Resolution Policies

In this section, we shed more light on the costs and benefits of alternative crisis resolution policies. Specifically, we empirically investigate how policies affect the performance and financial structures of individual corporations. We focus on the corporate sector for several reasons. First, the final purpose of resolution policies, even if directed toward the financial sector only, is a revitalization of the real sector and overall economic growth. Using corporate-sector indicators can thus provide a better measure of the final outcome. Second, the effects of policies can be more precisely measured by focusing on the corporate sector rather than the financial sector. The performance of banks, for example, will be highly affected by government financial actions, such as recapitalization, and therefore may not provide a good indication of the real outcomes achieved. Third, measuring the impact of resolution policies on a micro rather than a macro level (for example, by gross domestic product) allows us to better differentiate across policies. We can control, for example, for country characteristics, such as different corporate-sector structures, when studying policies commonly adopted.

We collect company-specific data for a sample of crisis countries around the period of crisis in each respective country. Our sample selection proceeded as follows. We collected company data from WorldScope for all emerging markets and developed countries that were classified by Caprio and Klingebiel (2002) as having had a systemic financial crisis. We had to exclude all crises prior to 1989 because WorldScope does not have sufficient data before 1989. We also had to exclude countries for which the crisis period is difficult to time, either because of multiple crises (such as in Argentina) or because the crisis stretches over a long period of time without clear peaks or ends (as in Japan). This left us with seventeen countries with a systemic crisis. We had to further exclude some countries for which we did not have a significant number of corporations with available data. This set of excluded countries includes nine transition countries (Bulgaria, the Czech Republic, Estonia, Hungary, Latvia, Lithuania, Poland, and Slovenia) and Venezuela. For Venezuela, for example, we only had nine corporations for the whole sample period.

Given the data availability, we are left with eight crisis countries, namely Finland, Indonesia, South Korea, Malaysia, Mexico, the Philippines, Sweden, and Thailand. For each country, we distinguish three periods. The crisis year is the year of the peak of the crisis as identified by Caprio and Klingebiel (2002). The precrisis year is defined as the average of the three years before the peak of the crisis and the postcrisis year as one year after the peak of the crisis. Table 6.2 reports the sample of crisis countries and their respective crisis years.

In total, we have company-specific data from WorldScope for 687 firms. The data could suffer from a bias if many sampled firms entered bankruptcy during the crisis years. For most countries, however, the set of firms is quite similar between pre- and postcrisis periods. In fact, the data set includes more firms during the crisis year than during the precrisis year.[12] This suggests that the data set does not suffer from a large survivorship or other re-

---

12. We have data on 990 firms for the precrisis years, 1,183 firms for the crisis years, and 889 firms for the postcrisis years. In the regressions we use a balanced panel of 687 firms.

Table 6.2   Sample Crisis Countries and Crisis Years

	Precrisis	Peak of Crisis	Postcrisis
Finland	1989	1992	1993
Indonesia	1995	1998	1999
South Korea	1995	1998	1999
Malaysia	1995	1998	1999
Mexico	1992	1995	1996
The Philippines	1995	1998	1999
Sweden	1989	1992	1993
Thailand	1995	1998	1999

Source: Caprio and Klingebiel (2002); authors' definitions.

porting bias. The notable exception is the Republic of Korea, for which the number of firms reporting in the postcrisis period is significantly less than those in the precrisis and crisis periods. The main reason is that at the date of data collection many Korean firms had not yet reported their financial statements for 1999.[13]

In estimating the impact of resolution policies on the performance of the corporate sectors, we distinguish between the depth of the crisis, the recovery after the crisis, and the sustainability of the recovery. As a measure for the depth of the crisis, we use the difference in a corporation's operating income, defined as earnings before interest and taxes with depreciation added, as a ratio of sales, that is, the ratio of earnings before interest and taxes with depreciation added (EBITDA) to sales, between the precrisis and crisis periods. Similarly, our measure for the degree of recovery of corporate performance is the difference in EBITDA-sales between the postcrisis and crisis periods. Our measure for the sustainability of the recovery is the difference in EBITDA-sales between the postcrisis and precrisis periods.

Table 6.3 reports summary statistics of the company-specific data for EBITDA-sales, interest coverage, leverage, debt composition (share of short-term) and share of payables (trade) relative to total assets—the main variables used in the empirical analysis—across all countries. It is worth noting that the interest coverage figure (measured as operating income to interest payments) reflects both firm profitability and debt structure. We find that, measured by EBITDA-sales, firms performed the worst during the crisis year. Firms had a worse interest coverage during the crisis year than before and were more leveraged at the peak of the crisis than before the crisis. Firms generally reduced the share of short-term debt over the crisis period, whereas the share of trade debt was mostly unaffected by the crisis.

13. This reporting discrepancy may still result into a sample selection bias if, for example, late reporting is more common among unprofitable firms than among profitable firms. This would lead us to overestimate the recovery and the effects of any policies adopted on the speed of recovery.

Table 6.3   Descriptive Statistics (means, with medians in brackets)

	EBITDA/Sales			Interest Coverage			Debt to Assets			Short-Term Debt/Total Debt			Payables/Total Assets			N
	Precrisis	Crisis	Postcrisis	Precrisis	Crisis	Postcrisis	Precrisis	Crisis	Postcrisis	Precrisis	Crisis	Postcrisis	Precrisis	Crisis	Postcrisis	
All	0.216 [0.168]	0.120 [0.133]	0.167 [0.144]	8.333 [3.125]	2.499 [1.299]	4.863 [1.739]	0.314 [0.312]	0.427 [0.390]	0.424 [0.356]	0.536 [0.513]	0.547 [0.520]	0.504 [0.431]	0.087 [0.070]	0.080 [0.059]	0.084 [0.059]	687
Finland	0.129 [0.107]	0.136 [0.122]	0.157 [0.131]	2.272 [1.587]	1.697 [1.266]	3.184 [1.724]	0.370 [0.357]	0.432 [0.412]	0.409 [0.398]	0.253 [0.207]	0.259 [0.242]	0.281 [0.237]	0.092 [0.070]	0.086 [0.055]	0.092 [0.059]	67
Indonesia	0.256 [0.226]	0.089 [0.153]	0.292 [0.274]	9.813 [3.448]	2.942 [0.645]	9.785 [2.500]	0.323 [0.329]	0.595 [0.609]	0.503 [0.493]	0.652 [0.746]	0.710 [0.969]	0.552 [0.422]	0.097 [0.057]	0.079 [0.046]	0.076 [0.038]	54
Korea	0.162 [0.140]	−0.029 [0.119]	0.170 [0.141]	2.235 [1.515]	−0.274 [1.053]	2.125 [1.852]	0.481 [0.453]	0.566 [0.450]	0.668 [0.390]	0.505 [0.495]	0.569 [0.590]	0.463 [0.414]	0.110 [0.100]	0.092 [0.083]	0.110 [0.066]	50
Malaysia	0.226 [0.181]	0.008 [0.130]	0.122 [0.146]	16.848 [6.567]	4.061 [1.333]	5.187 [1.120]	0.212 [0.192]	0.386 [0.299]	0.390 [0.299]	0.667 [0.762]	0.630 [0.624]	0.647 [0.676]	0.075 [0.051]	0.066 [0.041]	0.067 [0.045]	180
Mexico	0.258 [0.207]	0.241 [0.225]	0.307 [0.272]	10.215 [3.280]	2.665 [1.835]	4.411 [3.125]	0.258 [0.287]	0.338 [0.319]	0.330 [0.303]	0.403 [0.336]	0.431 [0.362]	0.338 [0.252]	0.081 [0.050]	0.071 [0.050]	0.079 [0.059]	49
The Philippines	0.337 [0.271]	0.186 [0.175]	0.215 [0.175]	7.661 [4.348]	−1.908 [0.799]	2.681 [1.282]	0.258 [0.272]	0.319 [0.296]	0.320 [0.335]	0.567 [0.495]	0.505 [0.466]	0.451 [0.321]	0.104 [0.090]	0.102 [0.074]	0.098 [0.072]	46
Sweden	0.144 [0.112]	0.109 [0.088]	0.162 [0.119]	3.621 [2.778]	0.448 [1.118]	3.832 [2.000]	0.299 [0.280]	0.323 [0.346]	0.307 [0.310]	0.380 [0.299]	0.346 [0.309]	0.318 [0.246]	0.099 [0.093]	0.087 [0.078]	0.099 [0.086]	94
Thailand	0.247 [0.200]	0.255 [0.200]	0.130 [0.130]	6.304 [3.226]	4.222 [2.222]	5.840 [0.952]	0.406 [0.411]	0.504 [0.532]	0.507 [0.509]	0.619 [0.651]	0.689 [0.777]	0.635 [0.693]	0.078 [0.059]	0.080 [0.053]	0.084 [0.059]	147

Source: WorldScope.

We also find that, although both the performance and capital structure of firms improved after the peak of the crisis, firms did not reach precrisis performance levels and financing structures within two years after the peak of the crisis.

These general trends are also reflected in figures 6.2 and 6.3, which plot, respectively, the EBITDA-sales and interest coverage ratios for the three periods. The earnings and interest coverage distributions shift to the left between the precrisis and the crisis periods and then recover somewhat, but not to the distribution before the crisis. When performance and sustainability are measured using other measures, similar results obtain. For example, the median operating return on assets falls from 5.5 percent in the precrisis period to 1.4 percent during the crisis period and then recovers to 2.8 percent in the postcrisis period. The median ratio of the market to book value of equity moves from 1.8 before the crisis period to 0.7 during the crisis period, to recover to only 1.03 in the postcrisis period.

Table 6.3 also reports the summary statistics for individual countries for the same set of variables. The patterns for each country are generally the same as for the overall medians. Some exceptions are Finland, Indonesia, Mexico, and Sweden, where postcrisis corporate-sector performance is on average better than precrisis performance. In these countries, some corporations may have benefited from the depreciation of the exchange rate, which would explain the better performance. This is not the case for the other countries: in Thailand, for example, postcrisis performance is actually the worst of all three periods. Korea and Malaysia correspond to the pattern for the whole sample, with the recovery performance above the crisis level but below the precrisis level. In terms of interest coverage, the picture is more uniform across the countries: some deterioration during the crisis, generally followed by an improvement. The exceptions are Malaysia and Thailand, where the average interest coverage ratios decline throughout.

Apart from industry and other corporation-specific factors, such as corporations' initial financial structures, differences in the policies adopted may explain some of the differences. Our literature review, and in particular Honohan and Klingebiel (2002), motivates the specific policy measures we investigate. Honohan and Klingebiel identified for a large sample of countries those policy measures that could be systematically linked to the fiscal costs of resolving a systemic crisis. The three specific policy variables we use from their analysis are (a) whether the central bank has provided liquidity support to financial institutions during the crisis; (b) whether the government has guaranteed bank liabilities; and (c) whether the government has established a publicly owned, centralized asset management company. As noted in section 6.3, Honohan and Klingebiel show that these three measures particularly increased the overall fiscal costs of resolving a crisis, controlling for a number of country-specific factors. Because we investigate

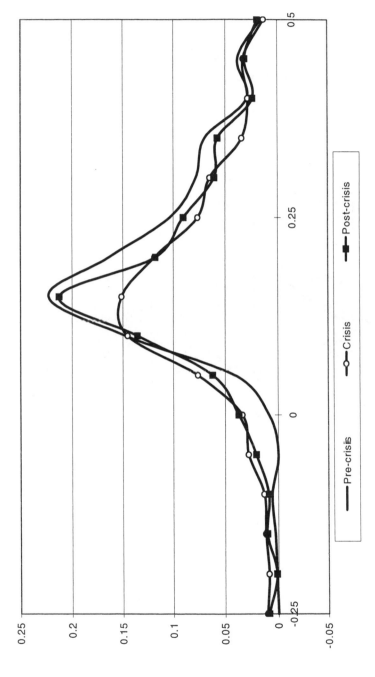

Fig. 6.2   EBITDA-sales across periods (fraction of firms)

Source: WorldScope.

Notes: The sample includes firms from eight countries: Finland, Indonesia, South Korea, Malaysia, Mexico, the Philippines, Sweden, and Thailand. The figure presents the distribution of EBITDA-sales averaged across all firms in the eight countries. The figure is smoothed.

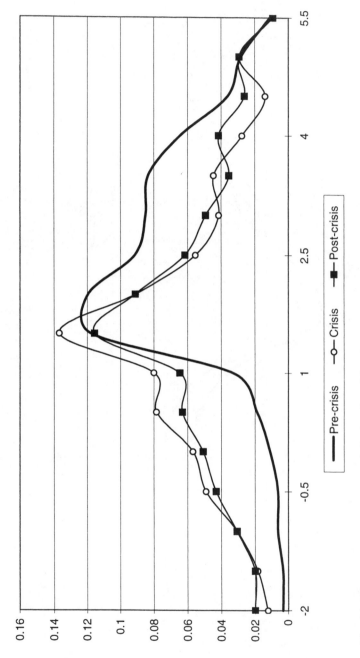

Fig. 6.3 Interest coverage across periods (fraction of firms)

Source: WorldScope.

Notes: The sample includes eight countries: Finland, Indonesia, South Korea, Malaysia, Mexico, the Philippines, Sweden, and Thailand. The figure presents the fraction of firms with specific interest rate coverage across all firms in the eight countries. The figure is smoothed.

Table 6.4   **Resolution Policies across Sampled Countries**

	Yes	No
Guarantee	Finland, Indonesia, Korea, Malaysia, Mexico, Sweden, Thailand (7)	The Philippines (1)
Liquidity support	Finland, Indonesia, Korea, Mexico, Thailand[a] (5)	Malaysia, the Philippines, Sweden (3)
Public AMC	Indonesia, Korea, Malaysia, Mexico (4)	Finland, the Philippines, Sweden, Thailand (4)

Source: Honohan and Klingebiel (2002).

[a]Liquidity support is provided to nonbank financial institutions only, not to deposit and money banks as well.

whether these policies resulted in improved performance and financial sustainability of the corporate sector, we can shed some light on whether a trade-off might exist for certain policies between fiscal costs and corporate-sector outcomes.

Table 6.4 presents the policy measures taken in the sampled countries. There are many similarities in policies across countries. Almost all countries' governments, for example, guaranteed the liabilities of the financial sector during the crisis, and only the Philippines did not. About half of the countries had extensive liquidity support to the financial sector, and, similarly, about half did establish a public asset management corporation. The Philippines is the only country that did not undertake any of the three resolution measures. The correlation between the implementation of these policy measures is substantial,[14] suggesting that they tend to be implemented as a package.

Given the limited number of countries in our sample and the fact that the policy measures are correlated, it is difficult to assess the impact of the implementation of each of the three policy variables in isolation, and regression results from using individual policy dummies could be unreliable. We therefore create a composite policy index in our empirical work. This policy index, called "Policy," is simply defined as the sum of the number of resolution measures taken to restore financial stability in the country. The three resolution measures considered include the provision of guarantees, liquidity support, and the setup of a public asset management company. The Policy variable thus ranges from zero to three. Table 6.5 shows the value for the Policy variable for the eight crisis countries.

As company-specific control variables, we use each corporation's initial leverage ratio (measured as total debt-asset ratio), initial debt composition

14. The simple correlation between "liquidity support" and "guarantees" is 49 percent, between "liquidity support" and "public AMC [asset management corporation]" 47 percent, and between "guarantees" and "public AMC" 49 percent.

Table 6.5   Policy Index across Crisis Countries

	Policy Index
Finland	2
Indonesia	3
South Korea	3
Malaysia	2
Mexico	3
The Philippines	0
Sweden	1
Thailand	3

Source: Honohan and Klingebiel (2002); authors' calculations from table 6.4.

Notes: The policy index is defined as the sum of the number of resolution measures taken to restore financial stability in the country. The three resolution measures considered include the provision of guarantees, liquidity, support, and the setup of a public asset management company.

(measured as ratio of short-term debt to total debt), size (measured as the natural logarithm of sales), and use of trade debt (measured as ratio of payables to assets). To control for any sectoral differences across firms, we use industry dummies (based upon two-digit Standard Industrial Classification codes) in the regressions.

Using these variables, we aim to answer the following questions. What are the effects of the announcement of these policies during the containment phase on firm performance and sustainability? Does the implementation of the set of resolution measures during the resolution phase of a crisis affect the speed of firm recovery? In addition to the resolution policies themselves, we also want to assess how certain firm-specific factors influence both the speed and the sustainability of the recovery of the corporate sector.

We use the following specific model to explain the depth of the crisis, as measured by the deterioration of firm profitability, the EBITDA-sales ratio (equation [1]).

$$(1) \qquad \frac{EBITDA}{Sales}(\text{precrisis}) - \frac{EBITDA}{Sales}(\text{crisis}) =$$

$$f\frac{EBITDA}{Sales}(\text{precrisis}), (\text{Policy index, initial firm-specific variables}$$

[precrisis], industry dummies).

We use first differences, rather than percentage changes, because the EBITDA-sales ratio can take on nonpositive values. Given that the model is specified in first differences, and because we also control already for many firm specifics, we can ignore any fixed firm effects. With the Policy index variable being our main focus, we also ignore any other changes in the macro environment. We therefore assume that, conditional on a crisis taking place, the effect of the implementation of the crisis resolution measures dominates all other changes in country-specific effects. Although we include industry dummies in all regressions, these are not reported. In terms of firm specifics, we expect that larger firms and firms with sounder debt structures suffer less from a crisis. We further expect that trade debt may act as an important substitute for bank financing during a crisis. Given that the number of observations per country differ, we estimate equation (1) using both ordinary least squares (OLS) and weighted least squares (WLS) with weights related to the number of observations. All results are presented in table 6.6.

High firm profitability at the onset of the crisis is found to be strongly correlated with the depth of the crisis. Our interpretation is that the profitabil-

Table 6.6   **Depth of Crisis: EBITDA/Sales**

Variable	OLS (1)	WLS (2)
Constant	0.112	0.224
	(0.183)	(0.199)
EBITDA/sales precrisis	0.522**	0.531***
	(0.244)	(0.120)
Sales	−0.018*	−0.024**
	(0.042)	(0.010)
Payables	0.504**	0.492**
	(0.255)	(0.208)
Leverage	0.079	0.147
	(0.089)	(0.097)
Short-term debt	0.228***	0.171***
	(0.053)	(0.059)
Policy	0.010	0.007
	(0.109)	(0.015)
Adjusted R^2	0.117	0.133
Durbin-Watson stat	1.99	2.06
N	603	603

Notes: Dependent variable is the difference between the EBITDA-sales ratio in the precrisis year and the EBITDA-sales ratio in the crisis year. "Precrisis EBITDA-sales precrisis" is the ratio of EBITDA to sales in the precrisis year. "Policy" is an index of policy measures directed toward restoring financial stability. It is the sum of three dummy variables. The first dummy variable takes value 1 if the government has issued an unlimited guarantee on bank liabilities, and zero otherwise. The second dummy variable takes value 1 if the government has provided open-ended liquidity support to financial institutions, and zero otherwise. The third dummy variable takes value 1 if the government has established a publicly owned, centrally managed asset management company, and zero otherwise. "Sales" is the natural logarithm of net sales in thousands of U.S. dollars in the precrisis year. "Payables" is the ratio of payables to total assets in the precrisis year. "Leverage" is the ratio of total debt to assets in the precrisis year. "Short-term debt" is the ratio of short-term tot total debt in the precrisis year. We include industry dummies, but these are not reported. We report heteroskedasticity-corrected standard errors between brackets. Equation (1) is estimated using ordinary least squares. Equation (2) is estimated using weighted least squares with weights related to the number of country observations.

***Significant at the 1 percent level.

**Significant at the 5 percent level.

*Significant at the 10 percent level.

ity of these firms rose to abnormally high levels until the onset of the crisis, possibly as a result of a credit boom preceding the crisis, and shortly thereafter experienced a sharp decline during the credit crunch. Larger firms are found to be less affected by the crisis than smaller firms. This may be because larger firms were more diversified and could absorb the shocks better. It could also be that banks renewed credit more easily for larger firms and stopped rolling over credits for small and not-well-connected firms. We also find a sharper decline in corporate profitability for firms with larger shares of short-term debt, suggesting that such firms were affected by the increases in interest rates that occurred during the crisis period and were more exposed to the risks of banks' not renewing credit lines. Furthermore, the regression results show that firms that depended more on trade debt were more affected. This suggests that firms themselves were also less willing to offer each other trade credit during a financial crisis. This could be because of a decreased ability of many debtors to repay the credit or, more generally, because of uncertainty on the financial health of firms. The findings on short-term and trade debt together suggest that firms that had healthier financing structures—lower debt-equity leverage and more long-term debt—managed the crisis better.

We do not find that the crisis resolution measures had any impact on reducing the drop in profitability in our sample of countries, as the coefficient on Policy is insignificant. One interpretation is that this set of crisis resolution measures is not sufficient or does not consist of the right type of measures to stop the downfall in corporate profits. Another interpretation is that these measures can only be implemented past the peak of a crisis, making them ineffective to limit the decline. Either interpretation sheds doubt on the common policy advice to adopt these measures quickly.

We use the same type of regression model to explain the (relative) recovery of the profitability of firms (equation [2]).

$$(2) \quad \frac{EBITDA}{Sales}(postcrisis) - \frac{EBITDA}{Sales}(crisis) = f \frac{EBITDA}{Sales}(precrisis)$$

$$- \frac{EBITDA}{Sales}(crisis), (\text{Policy index, initial firm-specific variables (precrisis)},$$

industry dummies).

We again use first differences because the EBITDA-sales ratio can take on nonpositive values. Compared to equation (1), the main difference in the regression setup is that we use the drop in firm profitability (the dependent variable in equation [1]) rather than the initial level of firm profitability as independent variable. This way we control for the possibility that profitability recovers more for firms that are hit more during the initial stage of the crisis. We estimate equation (2) again using both OLS and WLS, with the results presented in table 6.7.

Table 6.7   **Recovery from a Crisis: EBITDA/Sales**

Variable	OLS (1)	WLS (2)
Constant	−0.394**	−0.293**
	(0.157)	(0.141)
EBITA/sales drop	0.772***	0.738***
	(0.138)	(0.062)
Sales	0.025*	0.016**
	(0.014)	(0.008)
Payables	0.544***	0.154
	(0.171)	(0.151)
Leverage	0.044	0.054
	(0.095)	(0.064)
Short-term debt	0.050	0.035
	(0.058)	(0.038)
Policy	0.036***	0.041***
	(0.012)	(0.011)
Adjusted R^2	0.459	0.541
Durbin-Watson stat	2.06	2.20
N	592	592

Notes: Dependent variable is the difference between the EBITDA-sales ratio in the postcrisis year and the EBITDA-sales ratio in the crisis year. "EBITDA/sales drop" is the difference between the EBITDA-sales ratio in the precrisis year and the EBITDA-sales ratio in the crisis year. "Policy" is an index of policy measures directed toward restoring financial stability. It is the sum of three dummy variables. The first dummy variable takes value 1 if the government has issued an unlimited guarantee on bank liabilities, and zero otherwise. The second dummy variable takes value 1 if the government has provided open-ended liquidity support to financial institutions, and zero otherwise. The third dummy variable takes value 1 if the government has established a publicly owned, centrally managed asset management company, and zero otherwise. "Sales" is the natural logarithm of net sales in thousands of U.S. dollars in the precrisis year. "Payables" is the ratio of payables to total assets in the precrisis year. "Leverage" is the ratio of total debt to assets in the precrisis year. "Short-term debt" is the ratio of short-term to total debt in the precrisis year. We include industry dummies, but these are not reported. We report heteroskedasticity-corrected standard errors between brackets. Equation (1) is estimated using ordinary least squares. Equation (2) is estimated using weighted least squares with weights related to the number of country observations.
***Significant at the 1 percent level.
**Significant at the 5 percent level.
*Significant at the 10 percent level.

We find that the recovery of firm profitability is strongly correlated with the decline in firm profitability during the initial stage of the crisis, suggesting a large mean reversion in firm profitability around the crisis period. However, firm profitability does not recover completely to its precrisis level, which suggests that it may take more than one year to recover from a crisis or that there is a permanent loss. The sharp recovery is in line with the results of Eichengreen and Rose (chap. 3 in this volume), Dooley and Verma (chap. 5 in this volume), and Park and Lee (chap. 9 in this volume) that the V-shaped recovery is the norm in currency crises. We also find that the recovery of larger firms is slightly better than those of smaller firms, suggesting that larger firms may be in a better position to absorb shocks because they are more diversified or because larger firms are politically better connected than smaller firms.

The other firm-specific variables are generally not statistically significant, possibly because we already included firm-specific decline in profitability in the regression, which has strong explanatory power. Surprisingly, however, firms' financing structures do not appear to affect recovery. This may reflect some offsetting effects. On one hand, more risky financing structures should make it more difficult for firms to obtain financing to resume their operations. On the other hand, there can be incentive effects from tighter financing situations. It has been found, for example, for a sample of U.S. firms that perform poorly for a year that higher predistress leverage increases the probability of operational restructuring, thus accelerating recovery (Ofek 1993).

Interestingly, we find that the policy index is strongly correlated with the recovery in firm profitability. This suggests that the implementation of measures directed toward restoring the financial health of banks, such as removing nonperforming loans from banks' balance sheets, have a positive spillover effect toward firms by increasing banks' ability to resume lending to more viable firms, thus accelerating the recovery of firms. The quantitative importance of the policy variable is significant. Firm profitability would have increased on average by around 10 percent if the country had implemented all three crisis resolution measures considered.[15] Of course, these are simulated results for the average country, and actual results will differ widely across countries. In Sweden, many loans were removed from banks' balance sheets, and corporate-sector performance recovered relatively quickly. This also happened in Indonesia, but the gains in corporate-sector performance, if any, have been very limited so far, whereas the fiscal costs have been very large.

To assess the sustainability of the recovery, we investigate the factors influencing the difference in corporate performance after the crisis and before the crisis. We estimate the following model (equation [3]).

$$(3) \qquad \frac{\text{EBITDA}}{\text{Sales}} (\text{postcrisis}) - \frac{\text{EBITDA}}{\text{Sales}} (\text{precrisis}) =$$

$$f \frac{\text{EBITDA}}{\text{Sales}} (\text{precrisis}), (\text{Policy index, initial firm-specific variables [precrisis]},$$

industry dummies).

Equation (3) has the same explanatory variables as equation (1). The dependent variable tries to measure the lasting impact of the crisis on firm profitability. If the dependent variable is small, that is, the firm's profitabil-

---

15. The average increase of around 10 percent equals the regression coefficient of the policy index variable in equation (2) times three.

Table 6.8   **Sustainability: EBITDA/Sales**

Variable	OLS (1)	WLS (2)
Constant	0.095	−0.171
	(0.168)	(0.146)
EBITDA/sales precrisis	−0.840***	−0.565***
	(0.127)	(0.117)
Sales	0.006	0.019***
	(0.012)	(0.007)
Payables	−0.155	−0.233
	(0.151)	(0.159)
Leverage	−0.001	−0.007
	(0.076)	(0.063)
Short-term debt	−0.060*	−0.024
	(0.032)	(0.039)
Policy	0.040***	0.033***
	(0.013)	(0.012)
Adjusted R^2	0.306	0.202
Durbin-Watson stat	1.96	2.06
N	598	598

Notes: Dependent variable is the difference between the EBITDA-sales ratio in the postcrisis year and the EBITDA-sales ratio in the precrisis year. "EBITDA/sales precrisis" is the EBITDA-sales ratio in the precrisis year. "Policy" is an index of policy measures directed toward restoring financial stability. It is the sum of three dummy variables. The first dummy variable takes value 1 if the government has issued an unlimited guarantee on bank liabilities, and zero otherwise. The second dummy variable takes value 1 if the government has provided open-ended liquidity support to financial institutions, and zero otherwise. The third dummy variable takes value 1 if the government has established a publicly owned, centrally managed asset management company, and zero otherwise. "Sales" is the natural logarithm of net sales in thousands of U.S. dollars in the precrisis year. "Payables" is the ratio of payables to total assets in the precrisis year. "Leverage" is the ratio of total debt to assets in the precrisis year. "Short-term debt" is the ratio of short-term to total debt in the precrisis year. We include industry dummies, but these are not reported. We report heteroskedasticity-corrected standard errors between brackets. Equation (1) is estimated using ordinary least squares. Equation (2) is estimated using weighted least squares with weights related to the number of country observations.

***Significant at the 1 percent level.
*Significant at the 10 percent level.

ity has recovered to the level from before the crisis, then the recovery from the crisis can be thought to be sustainable. The regression results are presented in table 6.8.

We find that firms with high profitability at the onset of the crisis do not recover fully over the crisis period to precrisis levels of profitability. This suggests either that these firms had unsustainable levels of firm profitability, possibly associated with a precrisis credit boom, or that it takes more than one year for firms to recover fully from a systemic crisis. We also find some evidence that firms with relatively large amounts of short-term debt before the crisis have greater difficulties in recovering to their precrisis levels of firm profitability, which possibly reflects difficulties in resolving their financial distress. The other, firm-specific variables are not statistically significant.

We find that postcrisis levels of firm profitability are closer to their precrisis levels for firms in those countries that took (more) crisis resolution measures. According to the regression results, the simultaneous implementation of all three policy measures under consideration would increase firm profitability by some 12 percentage points of sales.

The policy index, being a composite index, does not allow us to disentangle the different effects of the three policy measures on changes in firm profitability.[16] Nevertheless, we speculate that our findings are the results of two types of actions. The provision of liquidity support and the extension of unlimited guarantees both restore confidence in the financial system and indirectly help improve the performance of corporations. The establishment of public asset management companies directly alleviates firms' financial conditions by removing nonperforming loans of corporations from banks and granting financial relief. Of course, these measures come at (substantial) fiscal costs.

The regression results may suffer from a potential endogeneity problem if the implementation of the crisis resolution measures is more likely in countries with a deeper financial crisis. In this case there would be reverse causality between the dependent variable, "drop in EBITDA-sales," and the Policy index variable. We performed some tests for the existence of this problem and did not find evidence that would suggest a major endogeneity problem in the regression results. Specifically, the policy index variable is not significantly correlated with the drop in EBITDA-sales between the precrisis period and the crisis period (the dependent variable in equation [1]), nor with the firms' initial debt structures (as measured by the ratio of debt to total assets or short-term debt to total debt in the precrisis period).[17] Also, an ordered probit or logit model with the policy index as dependent variable and the change in EBITDA-sales and debt structure indicators as explanatory variables does not produce any significant results. This suggests that reverse causality is not a major problem.

As robustness on our dating of crises, we ran the same regressions in equations (1) and (2) with a different crisis year, namely one year earlier than the crisis years reported in table 6.2. We found results that are very similar to those reported in tables 6.6 and 6.7. Again, we find that crisis resolution measures do not help to prevent the decline in firm profitability during the early stage of the crisis but are effective (although costly) in terms of the recovery from a crisis. For ease of presentation we do not include these results.

16. We noted earlier that such an exercise would produce highly unreliable results because of the high correlation among the three policy measures and the limited number of countries in the sample. We therefore do not make this effort.

17. The correlation between the policy index variable and the difference in EBITDA-sales in the precrisis period and the crisis period is only 3 percent; between the policy index variable and the initial debt-assets ratio 14 percent (but not significantly different from zero); and between the policy index variable and the initial ratio of short-term debt to total debt 11 percent (also not significantly different from zero).

6.5 Conclusions

The literature on systemic restructuring emphasizes the need for governments to actively intervene to overcome the many coordination problems in a systemic crisis and to relieve the shortage of financial capital, both of which impede progress with case-by-case restructuring. The core issue in dealing with a systemic crisis then becomes how to resolve coordination issues while preserving or enhancing incentives for normal, market-based restructuring and transactions. Achieving both goals requires consistent government policies, among both issues and sectors, and over time.

The literature also stresses that fiscal and monetary policies have to support the recovery process in a systemic crisis. Policies must strike the right balance between supporting the exchange rate and avoiding a serious credit crunch created by high interest rates. Supportive policies also cover other dimensions, such as the strictness of capital adequacy requirements and whether an allowance should be made for automatic rollover of payments by small and medium-sized enterprises during the early phases of a crisis. As extensively debated in the context of the East Asian crisis and earlier (for example, following Chile's 1982 crisis), these supportive policies have not always been in place during systemic crises.

Especially during the containment phase of a systemic crisis, but also afterward, governments have to balance achieving stability with aggravating moral hazard. One dimension is avoiding the extension of government guarantees of financial institutions' liabilities, which can create moral hazard and reduce freedom in future loss allocations. Another dimension is the closing or suspension of some financial institutions. Although it signals a certain supervisory stance and limits moral hazard, closing financial institutions can inhibit the restoration of depositors' confidence. In some systemic crises during which the institutional framework for bank resolution was weak and there was much uncertainty among depositors and investors on the intrinsic value of the banking system, closing banks without addressing the large problems in the financial system aggravated the crises.

Consistent financial reform involves, among other things, changes in prudential regulation affecting financial institutions' profitability and the availability of private capital. Capital adequacy requirements, for example, need to be made consistent with current and future bank profitability and the availability of new private capital. Raising capital adequacy requirements during a systemic crisis is often not useful because capital is negative, bank earnings are low or negative, and little or no new capital is available.

Consistent reform is also needed for public recapitalizations. Any public recapitalization of banks must take into account the availability of fiscal resources. In several crisis countries the recapitalization of financial institutions with government bonds did not restore public confidence because limited fiscal resources were available to back the bonds. A related intertemporal consistency issue in any crisis is government credibility. We did not address this issue directly in this chapter, but ex ante consistency is a precondition for credibility.

Finally, approaches to restructuring must be consistent with a country's institutional capacity. Institutional deficiencies can rule out approaches in some countries that may be best practices in other countries. These best practices can include heavy reliance on a market-based approach to corporate restructuring, in which banks are recapitalized and asked to work out debtors. Where corporate governance and financial regulation and supervision are weak, however, such an approach may be a recipe for asset stripping or looting rather than sustainable restructuring. Thus, emerging markets and industrial countries will need different approaches to systemic restructuring.

Although many of these lessons are often mentioned in the literature we reviewed, best practice policies are often not applied. Mistakes can be made in the middle of a crisis. Afterward, it is easy to point out these inconsistencies. Even before, however, there have been many clear cases of inconsistent financial restructuring programs. These inconsistencies usually develop because policy makers are trying to overcome political constraints, and it is hard to judge whether they do so in the most efficient manner. However, inconsistencies can also reflect genuine differences of opinion among policy makers and advisers on what constitutes best practice, as with the need to guarantee all liabilities during the early stages of a crisis. The end result is similar, in that consistency is often lacking.

Specific lessons from the empirical part of the paper reinforce some of the general lessons and add new evidence to some that may be more controversial. The analysis on data of corporate-sector performance suggests that a package of government guarantees on bank liabilities, the provision of liquidity support, and the setup of public asset management companies help both the recovery and sustainability, but that these policies do not mitigate the depth of the crisis. Although the empirical results suggest that measures such as asset management companies can help in the short run, they may not provide the right incentives for banks and firms to improve firm capital structures in the long run. Moreover, for all measures there will be a trade off: although they may speed up recovery, they have also been shown to increase fiscal cost.

More generally, government efforts to restructure need to take into account the political economy factors behind the causes of a crisis and its resolution. In this context there might be ways to change ownership structures in a systemic crisis so that recovery is expedited and a more sustainable outcome results. However, although we lack complete understanding of systemic crises, we know even less about the political economy of systemic crises.

References

Baer, Herbert, and Daniela Klingebiel. 1995. Systematic risk when depositors bear losses: Five case studies. In *Banking, financial markets, and systemic risk. Research in financial services: Private and public policy,* vol. 7. ed. George G. Kaufman, 195–302. Greenwich, Conn.: JAI Press.

Bank for International Settlements. 1999. Capital requirement and bank behaviour: The impact of the Basel accord. Basel Committee on Banking Supervision Working Paper no 1. Basel, Switzerland: Bank for International Settlements, April.

Bordo, Michael, Barry Eichengreen, Daniela Klingebiel, and Maria Soledad Martinez-Peria. 2001. Is the crisis problem growing more severe? *Economic Policy* 16 (32): 51–82.

Caprio, Gerard, and Daniela Klingebiel. 1996. Bank insolvencies: Cross-country experience. Policy Research Working Paper no. 1620. Washington, D.C.: World Bank.

———. 2002. Episodes of systemic and borderline financial crises. In *Managing the real and fiscal effects of banking crises,* ed. Daniela Klingebiel and Luc Laeven, 31–49. Washington, D.C.: World Bank.

Claessens, Stijn, Simeon Djankov, and Daniela Klingebiel. 2001. Financial restructuring in East Asia: Halfway there? In *Resolution of financial distress,* ed. Stijn Claessens, Simeon Djankov, and Ashoka Mody, 229–59. Washington, D.C.: World Bank.

Claessens, Stijn, Simeon Djankov, and Ashoka Mody, eds. 2001. *Resolution of financial distress.* Washington, D.C.: World Bank.

Claessens, Stijn, Simeon Djankov, and Lixin Colin Xu. 2000. Corporate performance in the East Asian financial crisis. *World Bank Research Observer* 15 (1): 23–46.

Claessens, Stijn, and Thomas Glaessner. 1997. *Are financial sector weaknesses undermining the East Asian miracle?* Directions in *Development.* Washington, D.C.: World Bank.

Colaco, Francis, Mary Hallward-Driemeier, and Dominique Dwor-Frecaut. 2000. Asian manufacturing recovery: A firm-level analysis. In *Asian corporate recovery: Findings from firm-level surveys in five countries,* ed. Dominique Dwor-Frecaut, Francis Colaco, and Mary Hallward-Driemeier, 1–19. Washington, D.C.: World Bank.

Dado, Marinela. 2000. Note on centralized asset management companies in Indonesia, Korea, and Thailand. Washington, D.C.: World Bank. Mimeograph.

Dado, Marinela, and Daniela Klingebiel. 2002. Decentralized, creditor-led corporate restructuring: Cross-country experience. Washington, D.C.: World Bank. Mimeograph, February.

Dollar, David, and Mary Hallward-Driemeier. 2000. Crisis, adjustment, and reform in Thailand's industrial firms. *World Bank Research Observer* 15 (1): 1–22.

Domac, Ilker, and Giovanni Ferri. 1999. The credit crunch in East Asia: Evidence from field findings on bank behavior. Washington, D.C.: World Bank. Mimeograph.

Edwards, Sebastian, and Jeffrey Frankel, eds. Forthcoming. *Preventing Currency Crises in Emerging Markets.* Chicago: University of Chicago Press.

Foley, Fritz. 2000. Going bust in Bangkok: Lessons from bankruptcy law reform in Thailand. Harvard Business School, Business Economic Department. Mimeograph, January.

Haggard, Stephen. 2001. The political economy of financial restructuring in East

Asia. In *Resolution of financial distress,* ed. Stijn Claessens, Simeon Djankov, and Ashoka Mody, 261–303. Washington, D.C.: World Bank.

Hart, Oliver, Rafael La Porta Drago, Florencio Lopez-de Silanes, and John Moore. 1997. A new bankruptcy procedure that uses multiple auctions. *European Economic Review* 41:461–73.

Honohan, Patrick, and Daniela Klingebiel. 2002. Controlling the fiscal costs of banking crises. In *Managing the real and fiscal effects of banking crises,* ed. Daniela Klingebiel and Luc Laeven, 15–29. Washington, D.C.: World Bank.

Klingebiel, Daniela. 2001. The role of asset management companies in the resolution of banking crises. In *Resolution of financial distress,* ed. Stijn Claessens, Simeon Djankov, and Ashoka Mody, 341–79. Washington, D.C.: World Bank.

Krueger, Anne, and Aaron Tornell. 1999. The role of bank restructuring in recovering from crises: Mexico 1995–98. NBER Working Paper no. 7042. Cambridge, Mass.: National Bureau of Economic Research.

Lane, Timothy, Atish Ghosh, Javier Hamann, Steven Phillips, Marianne Schultze-Ghattas, and Tsidi Tsikata. 1999. IMF-supported programs in Indonesia, Thailand, and Korea. IMF Occasional Paper no. 178. Washington, D.C.: International Monetary Fund, June.

Lindgren, Carl-Johan, Tomás J. T. Baliño, Charles Enoch, Anne-Marie Gulde, Marc Quintyn, and Leslie Teo. 2000. Financial sector crisis and restructuring: Lessons from Asia. IMF Occasional Paper no. 188. Washington, D.C.: International Monetary Fund, January.

Lindgren, Carl-Johan, Gillian Garcia, and Matthew I. Saal. 1996. *Bank soundness and macroeconomic policy.* Washington, D.C.: International Monetary Fund.

Ofek, E. 1993. Capital structure and firm response to poor performance: An empirical analysis. *Journal of Financial Economics* 34 (1): 3–30.

Sheng, Andrew, ed. 1996. *Bank restructuring: Lessons from the 1980s.* Washington, D.C.: World Bank.

Stiglitz, Joseph. 2001. Bankruptcy laws: Some basic economic principles. In *Resolution of financial distress,* ed. Stijn Claessens, Simeon Djankov, and Ashoka Mody, 1–23. Washington, D.C.: World Bank.

Stone, Mark, 2000a. The corporate sector dynamics of systemic financial crises. IMF Policy Discussion Paper no. 00/114. Washington, D.C.: International Monetary Fund.

———. 2000b. Large-scale post-crisis corporate sector restructuring. IMF Policy Discussion Paper no. 00/7. Washington, D.C.: International Monetary Fund.

Westbrook, Jay. 2001. Systemic corporate distress: A legal perspective. In *Resolution of Financial Distress,* ed. Stijn Claessens, Simeon Djankov, and Ashoka Mody, 47–64. Washington, D.C.: World Bank.

World Bank. 2000. *East Asia: Recovery and beyond.* Washington, D.C.: World Bank.

Comment   Peter B. Kenen

As I have been asked to discuss a paper on a subject to which I have not given a great deal of attention, my comments are those of an interested con-

Peter B. Kenen is the Walker Professor of Economics and International Finance at Princeton University.

sumer rather than an expert critic. I trust that the authors will treat them that way. Their paper has two parts; the first surveys the literature, and the second presents some new results. My comments, however, are in three parts. The first two track the authors' own; the third raises an additional question.

The Survey of the Literature

The compact survey in the first part of the paper left me somewhat puzzled. It sets out several desiderata that should govern financial and corporate restructuring and says that there may be trade-offs between them, but it does not tell us what to do when they come into conflict or cannot be satisfied. This is not the authors' fault; it resides in the nature of the problem at issue. Let me offer some illustrations that raise intriguing questions.

At several points, the authors emphasize the need for private-sector incentives to facilitate restructuring and minimize direct public-sector involvement. Here is one example:

> Successful corporate debt workouts require proper incentives for banks and borrowers to come to the negotiating table. . . . The incentive framework for banks includes accounting, classification, and provisioning rules . . . [It] also includes laws and prudential regulations. Regulators should ensure that undercapitalized financial institutions are properly disciplined and closed. The insolvency system should enable financial institutions to enforce their claims on corporations, . . . and provide for the efficient liquidation of enterprises that cannot be rehabilitated.

However, what if the various rules and systems are inadequate? It may be possible to design and introduce better systems rapidly, but the paper mentions recent cases in which it has taken too long—and in which the new systems have not worked well, partly because of the time required to recruit and train the people needed to make those systems work well. The authors assert that a crisis can be a good way to get difficult reforms accepted, but their own examples raise questions about that. Finally, it can take a great deal of time for banks and other creditors to enforce their claims against corporate debtors, and this raises another difficult issue.

The authors stress the need for quick and decisive action to rehabilitate the banking system, so as to avoid repeated, inadequate recapitalizations that prove in the end to be more expensive and less effective than a single comprehensive effort. The rapid rehabilitation of the banking system is indeed essential for the early and orderly rehabilitation of the corporate sector. Is that possible, however, if one must wait for the banks themselves to enforce their own claims on the corporate sector and discover through that process how large their own losses will be? Without knowing the true size of the banks' losses, it may be very hard to achieve a rapid, comprehensive recapitalization of the banking system.

The authors deftly distinguish between two ways of restructuring the corporate sector. An asset management corporation (AMC) puts the government in charge. The rapid capitalization of the banking system puts the private sector in charge. All other things being equal, most of us would presumably prefer to put the private sector in charge. In many cases, however, all other things are not equal. Or, to put it differently, they are equally unsatisfactory. There are incestuous relationships between the public and private sectors and within the private sector. Under these second-best conditions, the AMC approach has much to recommend it, especially if the AMC is also empowered to enforce expeditiously its own claims on the corporate sector by recourse to special arrangements that bypass unsatisfactory bankruptcy regimes. That may be the best way to clean up the banks' balance sheets quickly. There is merit, moreover, in the authors' suggestion that several AMCs be established under public ownership but under private management. Incentives built into the contracts with the private managers may be the most promising way to circumvent the incestuous relationships that could otherwise corrupt the AMCs' dealings with the banking and corporate sectors. Nevertheless, governments may be reluctant to give privately managed AMCs the special powers they may need to enforce their claims quickly.

Consider, finally, the authors' discussion of liquidity support and comprehensive guarantees of bank liabilities. Here again there is need to take account of the second-best situation in a particular country. It is, of course, better to have deposit insurance in place before the onset of a crisis. When there is no such system in place, however, ad hoc guarantees may be unavoidable. If the monetary authorities find it difficult to distinguish between illiquid and insolvent banks, they cannot expect depositors to do that. It is, I think, inappropriate to test the efficacy of guarantees by asking, as the paper does, whether they help to minimize distress in the corporate sector. The efficacy of such guarantees must be judged on a case-by-case basis, by asking what would have happened to the banking system if they had they not been used. How much more liquidity support would have been required? How much money would have crossed the foreign exchange market, causing a precipitous depreciation and worsening the plight of banks and firms with large foreign-currency debts?

The Regression Analysis

The point I have just made, about testing the efficacy of guarantees by looking for their impact on the corporate sector, leads me directly to the second part of the paper, which contains the authors' empirical work. For the reason already mentioned, I was not especially surprised to find that guarantees have no significant influence on the plight of the corporate sector. I was somewhat surprised, however, to find that liquidity support had a significantly positive effect on the sustainability of corporate recovery, measured by the change in the interest-coverage ratio. I was indeed surprised to find that liquidity support and the use of AMCs had statistically significant effects in several of the authors' regression equations.

Nevertheless, I have misgivings about those regression equations, because they depend so heavily on the use of dummy variables that vary across countries but not across firms. A single firm-specific variable, leverage, appears in tables 6.5 and 6.6 but is not statistically significant. The same variable appears in table 6.7 and is significant, but it is interacted there with two dummy variables, and there is no firm-specific variable in table 6.8. That last table, moreover, has *no* significant right-hand-side variable whatsoever—which leads me to make a suggestion. Because the use of the change in the debt-to-asset ratio did not yield any significant results in table 6.8, should the precrisis level of that same ratio be used as the only firm-specific explanatory variable in tables 6.5 and 6.6? It has no explanatory power in either table, save when interacted with a dummy variable, and its distribution in figure 6.4 is oddly different from those of the other firm-specific variables. Might it be better, then, to use the precrisis level of the interest-coverage ratio, not that of the debt-to-asset ratio, as the firm-specific proxy for leverage in tables 6.5 and 6.6?

Let me make one more suggestion, reflecting my misgivings about the use of country-specific dummy variables to explain firm-specific outcomes. It might be useful to ask whether the same dummy variables (or the policies for which they stand) help to explain the cross-country differences in the country means of the firm-specific data shown in table 6.3. There would appear to be big differences in the levels and changes of those means, but the authors have not sought to exploit them.

Going One Step Further

Let me conclude by raising a question that is not discussed in the paper. The authors may be right to say that crises help to foster the acceptance of far-reaching structural reforms. Acceptance, however, is not sufficient. Implementation is crucial, and that is a time consuming process—a point that the authors readily acknowledge. Thus far, however, the international community has failed to devise a menu of carrots and sticks designed to foster crisis-preventive financial reform in emerging-market countries. There are, by now, some sixty codes and standards aimed at describing best practice in the financial and corporate sectors, and several official bodies, including the Financial Stability Forum, have looked at ways of encouraging emerging-market countries to adopt those practices. Unfortunately, these bodies have come up empty-handed. There was talk of using the Core Principles for Banking Supervision to fine-tune the new version of the Basel capital-adequacy rules, but that was not done. The International Monetary Fund (IMF) has said that it will use adherence to a "critical mass" of codes and standards to judge a country's eligibility for a Contingent Credit Line, but that may prove to be a rather elastic test. In the end, the official sector seems to have decided that the private sector should apply the carrots and sticks—that it should reward compliance with key codes and standards by granting market access and should punish noncompliance by withholding market access.

That approach, however, runs up against a serious practical problem. I said before that the various codes and standards aim at defining best practice rather than minimally acceptable practice. Therefore, emerging-market countries insist on being judged and rewarded for the *progress* they have made, not by the *extent* to which they comply with the principal codes and standards. For their part, however, market participants have little interest in progress; they are concerned with observable compliance—and rightly so from their standpoint. We have therefore reached something of an impasse. The official community continues to insist that emerging-market countries undertake far-reaching structural reforms in the financial and corporate sectors but has done little to encourage reform. It has passed the buck to the private sector, which has neither the resources nor the incentives to oversee the long process of structural reform. As a result, the reform process has lagged badly in some countries and has barely begun in others. We may have to wait for the next crisis—not because it is a propitious time for reform but because it is the only feasible time. If that is so, however, the cost of delay will be paid inevitably as part of the cost of the next round of crises.

Discussion Summary

Joshua Aizenman pointed to the political economy considerations of guarantees and argued that structural reforms may not start at all in the absence of guarantees.

Martin Feldstein made a reference to the almost complete nationalization of Korean banks and, with respect to the issue of reprivatization, pointed to the problem of finding buyers while at the same time maintaining domestic ownership.

Vincent Reinhart remarked that the optimal choice of a restructuring vehicle depends on the pace of the ongoing "looting." He emphasized the importance of the separation of the banking and the corporate sector and the risk of a crisis spreading from the first sector to the latter. With respect to the empirical part of the paper, he asked whether the issue of survivor bias was accounted for.

Morris Goldstein remarked that it seems useful to have a task force (a "fire team") ready for immediate assistance with crisis assessment and management. This might prevent the blanket guarantees typically issued during the chaotic period immediately following the attack.

Jeffrey Frankel noted that the phrase *systemic crisis* is usually used to mean a crisis in a country that is sufficiently large and important to threaten the entire global financial system. This paper needs to be clear that it is using *systemic* in another sense.

Edwin M. Truman recommended that the authors take into account the large part of the economies being affected by crises. In particular, he added, if a large fraction of an economy is involved in a crisis, there are very few domestic investors capable of and willing to buy financial-sector assets. He also recommended that the authors include Japan in the sample.

Yung Chul Park remarked that Korea had made several contacts with the International Monetary Fund prior to the crisis.

Nouriel Roubini remarked that there are essentially only two possible solutions—either to offer a guarantee to depositors or to let the depositors bear the cost—and that, either way, the taxpayers will end up paying.

Martin Eichenbaum noted that part of the problem lies in smaller banking systems' being more likely to become subject to shocks.

Michael M. Hutchison made a reference to the Swedish banking crisis and noted how quickly a political consensus was reached for resolving the crisis. He argued that a prerequisite for the quick rescue in the case of Sweden is found in transparency and the separation of public and private sector. He asked if the regressions presented in the paper would be able to pick up such cross-country differences.

Michael P. Dooley remarked that an important implication of third-generation crisis models is that crises resolve nothing, an implication supported by the current paper, whereas policy changes are required in order to achieve lasting improvements.

Stijn Claessens argued that blanket guarantees are not always necessary and that it is possible to protect certain parts of the financial sector through more selective guarantees. He added that regardless of whether guarantees were used the same pattern of recoveries was observed in the data. He acknowledged the issue of limited demand for assets among foreign investors and the preference for selling assets to domestic buyers. He also agreed that the econometric analysis needs to control for survivor bias. In response to Truman, he remarked that Japan was not included in the data set due to uncertainty regarding the timing (start and end) of the Japanese crisis.

On the Fiscal Implications of Twin Crises

A. Craig Burnside, Martin Eichenbaum, and
Sergio Rebelo

7.1 Introduction

The classical view of currency crises is that they arise because governments print money to finance ongoing or prospective deficits. This view, embedded in so-called first-generation models and their modern variants, is especially appealing for explaining twin banking-currency crises (see, e.g., Krugman 1979; Flood and Garber 1984; Obstfeld 1986; Calvo 1987; Drazen and Helpman 1987; Wijnbergen 1991; Corsetti, Pesenti, and Roubini 1999; Dooley 2000; Lahiri and Végh 2000; and Burnside, Eichenbaum, and Rebelo 2001). These crises entail large fiscal costs, associated with restructuring and recapitalizing failing banking systems, that are not typically financed by large explicit fiscal reforms. Despite the appeal of these models, they suffer from an important empirical shortcoming: they generally predict that inflation rates should be high *after* a currency crisis. In reality, many large devaluations are followed by moderate rates of money growth and inflation. This raises three questions. First, how do governments actually pay for the fiscal costs of twin banking-currency crises? Second, what are the implications of different financing methods for postcrisis

A. Craig Burnside is lead economist in Poverty Reduction and Economic Management: Economic Policy at the World Bank. Martin Eichenbaum is professor of economics at Northwestern University and a research associate of the National Bureau of Economic Research. Sergio Rebelo is Tokai Bank Distinguished Professor of Finance at the Kellogg School of Management, Northwestern University, and a research associate of the National Bureau of Economic Research.

The authors thank Ariel Burstein, Kenneth Kletzer, and Rob Vigfusson for their comments and acknowledge the support of the World Bank Research Committee. The opinions expressed in this paper are those of the authors and not necessarily those of the Federal Reserve Bank of Chicago or the World Bank.

inflation rates? Finally, can the inflation predictions of first-generation-type models be reconciled with the data?

To pay for the fiscal costs of twin crises, a government must use a combination of the following strategies: (a) implementing an explicit fiscal reform by raising taxes or reducing spending; (b) explicitly defaulting on outstanding debt; (c) printing money to generate seigniorage revenues; (d) deflating the real value of outstanding nonindexed nominal debt; or (e) engaging in an implicit fiscal reform by deflating the real value of government outlays that are fixed, at least temporarily, in nominal terms (e.g., civil servant wages or social security payments).[1] In a world of forward-looking economic agents, different mixes of these strategies have different implications both for the severity of a currency crisis and for postcrisis inflation rates.

We analyze these implications using a version of the model in Burnside, Eichenbaum, and Rebelo (2001) in which a currency crisis is triggered by prospective government deficits. To simplify our exposition we reduce the model to its essential elements: a money demand specification, a government budget constraint, a rule for exiting the fixed exchange rate regime, and an assumption about the nature of monetary policy after the devaluation. We show that a government that pursues strategies (c)–(e) can pay for large fiscal costs associated with large devaluations while generating very moderate degrees of postcrisis inflation. Thus, models in which prospective deficits are the root cause of large currency crises can be reconciled with observed post–currency crisis inflation rates.

We begin our theoretical analysis with a version of the model in which purchasing power parity (PPP) holds and all government liabilities are perfectly indexed to inflation. This model predicts much lower devaluation rates and much higher inflation rates than those observed during currency crisis episodes.

We then consider two extensions to the basic model. First, we introduce two types of nonindexed government liabilities: domestic bonds issued before agents learned about prospective deficits, and public spending whose value is preset in units of domestic currency. With these elements, the model can generate more plausible implications for the behavior of inflation but can only produce moderate rates of devaluation.

Second, we eliminate the assumption of PPP. This breaks the link between domestic inflation and exchange rate depreciation. We introduce three departures from PPP: (a) nontradable goods (e.g., housing, education, and health); (b) costs associated with distributing tradable goods (e.g., transportation, wholesaling, and retailing); and (c) nominal rigidities in the

---

1. The fiscal costs could also be paid for with international aid, namely through subsidized loans granted by institutions such as the International Monetary Fund (IMF). Jeanne and Zettelmeyer (2001) argue that the subsidy element of IMF lending is small. For Korea and Mexico they estimate that this subsidy amounted to less than 1 percent of GDP.

prices of nontradable goods.These elements allow the model to account more closely for the high rates of devaluation and low rates of inflation that are often observed in the wake of currency crisis episodes.

We use our model to interpret two recent currency crises: Mexico in 1994 and Korea in 1997. Our analysis suggests that the Mexican government will likely pay for most of the fiscal cost of its crisis by printing money. In contrast, the Korean government is likely to do so via a mixture of future implicit and explicit fiscal reforms.

Estimates of the cost of the Mexican crisis vary widely, but, as a benchmark, we put it at roughly 15 percent of Mexico's 1994 gross domestic product (GDP). We estimate that the government has so far paid for about 30 percent of the fiscal cost of the crisis via a mix of debt deflation, fiscal reforms, and seigniorage. We show that the rest of the fiscal cost can be paid for by seigniorage revenues if the government prints money at historically typical rates. Consistent with what our model predicts for a crisis financed primarily by printing money, Mexico's twin crisis was associated with a relatively large rise in the rate of inflation.

The fiscal cost of the Korean crisis is thought to be roughly 24 percent of 1997 GDP.[2] Our calculations indicate that the government has so far paid for roughly 25 percent of this cost via a mix of debt deflation, fiscal reforms, and seigniorage revenue. Consistent with this estimate, the Korean government has accumulated a great deal of new debt—17.3 percent of GDP—to finance its crisis in the short run. Our model can account for the large devaluation and modest postcrisis inflation rates in Korea under the assumption that much of the remaining fiscal cost of the crisis will be financed through future explicit and implicit fiscal reforms.

The remainder of the paper is organized as follows. Section 7.2 uses the government's intertemporal budget constraint to discuss the different financing strategies available to the government. Section 7.3 presents our basic model. Section 7.4 discusses two extensions: incorporating nonindexed government liabilities and eliminating the PPP assumption. Section 7.5 contains our discussion of the Mexico 1994 and Korea 1997 crises. Section 7.6 contains concluding remarks.

7.2   The Government Budget Constraint

Explicit default aside, a government must satisfy its intertemporal budget constraint. In this section we display a version of this constraint that is useful for discussing the different strategies that a government can use to pay for the fiscal costs of a twin crisis. Later we adopt a particular model of

---

2. This estimate is from Standard and Poor's sovereign ratings services. See Goldstein (1998) for a discussion of various estimates of nonperforming bank loans that underlie the banking crisis in Korea.

speculative attacks to study how these strategies affect the severity of a currency crisis and postcrisis inflation rates.

We consider a continuous-time, perfect-foresight economy populated by an infinitely lived representative agent and a government. All agents, including the government, can borrow and lend in international capital markets at a constant real interest rate r.

For now we assume that there is a single consumption good in the economy and no barriers to trade, so that PPP holds:

$$(1) \qquad\qquad P_t = S_t P_t^*.$$

Here P_t and P_t^* denote the domestic and foreign price level respectively, while S_t denotes the exchange rate (defined as units of domestic currency per unit of foreign currency). For convenience, we assume that $P_t^* = 1$.

In each period the government purchases goods, levies lump sum taxes, and makes transfers to the representative agent. In addition, the government can print money and issue debt. Government spending, taxes, and transfers have an indexed component, with real values g_t, τ_t, and v_t, respectively. These variables also have nonindexed components with nominal values G_t, T_t, and V_t, respectively. It is convenient to define the variable X_t thus:

$$X_t = T_t - G_t - V_t$$

The government issues two types of debt. The first type is dollar denominated so that its real value is invariant to the domestic rate of inflation. We denote the dollar debt at the beginning of time t by b_t. The second type of debt is denominated in local currency and is not indexed to the domestic rate of inflation. To simplify matters, we assume that this debt takes the form of consols, issued before time zero. Each consol has a constant coupon denominated in local currency. Because expected inflation was zero when the bonds were issued, we assume, to simplify, that the coupon rate on the bonds is equal to the real interest rate, r. We denote the nominal value of the consols by B. To simplify notation, we assume that the stock of nominal debt remains constant and all new debt is dollar denominated.

We consider an economy that is initially operating under a fixed exchange rate so that $S_t = S$. At time zero, news arrives that the government's future liabilities will be higher than previously anticipated. We interpret the rise in liabilities as reflecting transfer payments associated with bank bailouts or with other fiscal liabilities of the government.

To be concrete, before time zero, private agents assumed that $v_t = v$ for all t. At time zero they learn that transfers will increase permanently after date T':

$$\begin{cases} v_t = v & \text{for } 0 \leq t < T', \\ v_t \geq v & \text{for } t \geq T', \end{cases}$$

where T' is a positive scalar. The precise value of T' is irrelevant for our results. We use ϕ to denote the present value of the increase in transfers:

(2)
$$\phi = \int_{T'}^{\infty} e^{-rt}(v_t - v)dt$$

The government's flow budget constraint is

(3)
$$\Delta b_t = -\Delta m_t \quad \text{if } t \in I,$$

$$\dot{b}_t = rb_t + \frac{rB}{S_t} - \tau_t + g_t + v_t - \frac{X_t}{S_t} - \dot{m}_t - \pi_t m_t \quad \text{if } t \notin I.$$

Throughout the paper, $\dot{x}_t$ denotes dx/dt. Here π_t is the inflation rate, $\dot{P}_t/P_t$. The variable m_t represents the dollar value of money balances, defined as $m_t = M_t/S_t$, where M_t denotes nominal money holdings. Note that $\dot{m}_t + \pi_t m_t$ is equal to the dollar value of seigniorage, $\dot{M}_t/S_t$. As in Drazen and Helpman (1987), equation (3) takes into account the possibility of discrete changes in m_t and b_t at a finite set of points in time, I. We will discuss the points at which these discrete changes occur.

According to equation (3), the change in b_t is equal to the primary deficit, $g_t + v_t - \tau_t - X_t/S_t$, plus the interest cost of servicing the indexed government debt (rb_t) plus the real cost of paying interest on the nonindexed consols, rB/S_t, minus seigniorage revenue, $\dot{m}_t + \pi_t m_t$.

The flow budget constraint, together with the condition $\lim_{t \to \infty} e^{-rt}b_t = 0$, implies the intertemporal budget constraint

(4)
$$b_0 = \int_0^{\infty} (\tau_t - g_t - v_t)e^{-rt}dt + \int_0^{\infty} \frac{X_t}{S_t}e^{-rt}dt$$
$$+ \int_0^{\infty} (\dot{m}_t + \pi_t m_t)e^{-rt}dt + \sum_{i \in I} e^{-ri}\Delta m_i$$
$$- \int_0^{\infty} \frac{rB}{S_t}e^{-rt}dt.$$

According to equation (4), the initial stock of real indexed government debt is equal to the real present value of current and future surpluses and seigniorage revenue minus the real present value of the consol payments.

It is useful to derive the conditions under which a fixed exchange rate is sustainable, so that $S_t = S$ for all t. For now we assume that there is no output growth and foreign inflation is zero (we relax these assumptions in section 7.5). Consequently, the government does not collect seigniorage under a fixed exchange rate regime, and its intertemporal budget constraint is given by

(5)
$$b_0 = \int_0^{\infty} (\tau_t - g_t - v_t)e^{-rt}dt + \int_0^{\infty} \frac{X_t}{S}e^{-rt}dt - \int_0^{\infty} \frac{rB}{S}e^{-rt}dt.$$

We assume that this sustainability condition holds before agents receive information at $t = 0$ about the new, higher, level of future deficits.

To see how prospective deficits can generate a currency crisis, recall our assumption that at $t = 0$ private agents learn that the present value of the deficit has increased by ϕ. Also suppose that private agents correctly believe that the government will not undertake an explicit fiscal reform that fully pays for ϕ. To simplify, suppose that $\int_0^\infty (\tau_t - g_t - v)e^{-rt}dt$ remains constant.[3] Then we can use equations (2) and (5) to rewrite equation (4) as

$$
(6) \qquad \phi = \int_0^\infty (\dot{m}_t + \pi_t m_t)e^{-rt}dt + \sum_{i \in I} e^{-ri}\Delta m_i
$$

$$
+ \left(\frac{B}{S} - \int_0^\infty \frac{rB}{S_t}e^{-rt}dt \right) - \left[\int_0^\infty \left(\frac{X_t}{S} - \frac{X_t}{S_t} \right) e^{-rt}dt \right].
$$

According to equation (6), the present value of the prospective deficits, ϕ, must be financed by a combination of (a) seigniorage revenues $[\int_0^\infty(\dot{m}_t + \pi_t m_t)e^{-rt}dt + \sum_{i \in I} e^{-ri}\Delta m_i]$; (b) a reduction in the real value of nonindexed debt $[B/S - \int_0^\infty(rB/S_t)e^{-rt}dt]$; and (c) an implicit fiscal reform that increases the real value of the nonindexed component of the fiscal surplus $[\int_0^\infty (X_t/S - X_t/S_t)e^{-rt}dt]$. It follows that the *only* way that the government can satisfy its intertemporal budget constraint is to use monetary policy to generate a present value of seigniorage revenues and implicit fiscal reform equal to ϕ.

To see this, suppose for a moment that the fixed exchange rate could be sustained after new information about higher deficits arrived. Then the money supply would never change and the government could not collect any seigniorage revenues. This, in conjunction with the fact that the price level would be fixed, implies that all of the terms on the right-hand side of equation (6) would equal zero. Then, however, the government's budget constraint would not hold. This would contradict the assumption that the fixed exchange rate regime was sustainable. We conclude that the government *must* at some point move to a floating exchange rate system.

The particular characteristics of a crisis depend on the financing mix chosen by the government. For example, the government could pay for most of the bank bailout by reducing the real value of outstanding nominal debt with a devaluation at time zero. Under these circumstances, the currency crisis would be associated with little future money growth or inflation. This scenario is closely related to the work of Cochrane (2001), Sims (1994), and Woodford (1995) on the fiscal theory of the price level.[4] In contrast, if the government does not have any nonindexed liabilities, then the bank bailout would have to be financed entirely via seigniorage revenues. This would have potentially very different implications for money growth and inflation. To analyze the implications of different financing strategies we must make

3. Our basic result would not be affected by a fiscal reform as long as the present value of the change in the primary surplus induced by the reform was less than ϕ.

4. See Corsetti and Mackowiak (1999), Daniel (2001), and Dupor (2000) for applications of the fiscal theory to open economies.

additional assumptions about government policy and the behavior of private agents. We discuss these assumptions in the following section.

7.3   The Basic Model

In this section we analyze a simple benchmark model in which PPP holds and the government does not have any nonindexed liabilities.

In addition to borrowing and lending in international capital markets, private agents can also borrow and lend domestic currency at the nominal interest rate, R_t. Under perfect foresight

(7) $$R_t = r + \pi_t,$$

where r and π denote the real rate of interest and inflation.

The demand for domestic money has the form suggested by Cagan (1956):

(8) $$\ln\left(\frac{M_t}{P_t}\right) = \ln(\theta) + \ln(Y) - \eta R_t$$

Here M_t denotes the beginning of period t domestic money supply, and θ is a positive constant. The parameter η represents the semielasticity of money demand with respect to the interest rate. To simplify, we assume that domestic agents' per period real income, Y, is constant over time.[5]

7.3.1   The Fixed Exchange Rate Regime

Suppose that the home country is initially in a fixed exchange rate regime so that $S_t = S$. Equation (1) implies that the domestic rate of inflation π_t is equal to the foreign rate of inflation, which we assumed to be zero. It follows from equation (7) that the nominal rate of interest is equal to the constant real interest rate: $R_t = r$ for all $t \geq 0$. Under a fixed exchange rate, the money supply must equal money demand:

(9) $$M = S\theta Y \exp(-\eta r).$$

Because the money supply is constant, the government cannot generate seigniorage revenues. Of course, if there were growth in either the foreign price level or domestic real income, the government would collect some seigniorage revenue in a fixed exchange rate regime. This possibility does not affect our basic argument. The present value of such seigniorage revenues would have already been incorporated into the government's precrisis intertemporal budget constraint.

7.3.2   A Currency Crisis

In the presence of prospective deficits, the government *must* at some point move to a floating exchange rate system. The precise time at which

5. See Lahiri and Végh (2000) for a discussion of the output effects of currency crises.

this occurs depends on (a) the government's rule for abandoning fixed exchange rates and (b) the government's new monetary policy.

With respect to (a) we follow a standard assumption in the literature that the government abandons the fixed exchange rate regime according to a threshold rule on government debt (see, e.g., Krugman 1979; Flood and Garber 1984). Specifically, we assume that the government floats the currency at the first point of time, t^*, when its net debt hits some finite upper bound. This is equivalent to abandoning the fixed exchange rate when the amount of domestic money sold by private agents in exchange for foreign reserves exceeds χ percent of the initial money supply. In addition to being a good description of what happens in actual crises, the threshold rule can be interpreted as a short-run borrowing constraint on the government: it limits how many reserves the government can borrow to defend the fixed exchange rate.[6] Rebelo and Végh (2001) discuss the circumstances in which it is optimal for a social planner to follow a threshold rule.[7] Although they use a general equilibrium model, their framework is similar in spirit to the model used here.

With respect to postcrisis monetary policy, we assume that at some point in the future ($t = T$) the government will engineer a discrete increase in the money supply equal to γ percent of M, defined in equation (9). Thereafter, the money supply will grow at rate μ. These assumptions imply that the money supply evolves according to[8]

$$(10) \qquad M_t = \begin{cases} e^{-\chi}M, & \text{for } t^* \leq t < T \\ e^{\gamma + \mu(t-T)}M, & \text{for } t \geq T. \end{cases}$$

This specification decouples the endogenous timing of the speculative attack from the time at which the government undertakes its new monetary policy. In equilibrium the parameters μ and γ must be such that the government's intertemporal budget constraint, equation (6), holds.

Note that the rate of inflation, the money supply, and the level of government debt can be discontinuous. However, the exchange rate path must be continuous. To see why, suppose to the contrary that there was a discontinuous increase in the exchange rate at time t^*. Because PPP implies that $P_t = S_t$, inflation would be infinity at t^*. This would imply that the nominal interest rate would also be infinity at t^* and that money demand would fall to

6. Drazen and Helpman (1987), as well as others, have proposed a different rule for the government's behavior: fix future monetary policy and allow the central bank to borrow as much as possible, provided the present value budget constraint of the government is not violated. This rule ends up being equivalent to a threshold rule. See Wijnbergen (1991) and Burnside, Eichenbaum, and Rebelo (2001) for a discussion.

7. This result emerges when there are significant real costs associated with a devaluation, such as loss of output.

8. Implicit in this description is the assumption that a solution for t^* such that $t^* < T$ exists. We will see that this assumption holds in our analysis.

zero. Because the government is only willing to buy χ percent of the money supply, this cannot be an equilibrium. We utilize the continuity of S_t extensively in the derivations below.

7.3.3   Solving for the Time of the Speculative Attack (t^*)

The key equation in determining the time of the speculative attack is the money demand function in equation (8) which implies[9]

$$(11) \qquad \ln P_t = \eta r - \ln(\theta Y) + \frac{1}{\eta} \int_t^{\infty} e^{-(s-t)/\eta} \ln(M_s) ds.$$

Because the exchange rate must be a continuous function of time, PPP implies that the price level too must be continuous. We now exploit this continuity requirement to solve for t^*.

By definition, the fixed exchange rate regime ends at time t^*. The price level an instant after t^* is given by

$$(12) \qquad \ln P_{t^*} = \eta r - \ln(\theta Y) + \frac{1}{\eta} \int_{t^*}^{\infty} \ln(M_s) e^{-(s-t^*)/\eta} ds.$$

An instant before the devaluation money demand implies that

$$(13) \qquad \ln M - \ln P = \ln(\theta Y) - \eta r.$$

Continuity of the price level at t^* requires that $\ln P_{t^*} = \ln P$. Using equations (12) and (13), we obtain

$$(14) \qquad \ln M = \frac{1}{\eta} \int_{t^*}^{\infty} \ln(M_s) e^{-(s-t^*)/\eta} ds.$$

Using equation (10) and the fact that the currency is devalued when the money demand falls by χ percent, we obtain

$$(15) \qquad \frac{1}{\eta} \int_{t^*}^{\infty} \ln M_s e^{-(s-t^*)/\eta} ds$$

$$= \ln M - \chi[1 - e^{-(T-t^*)/\eta}] + (\gamma + \mu\eta)e^{-(T-t^*)/\eta}.$$

Substituting equation (15) into equation (14), we can solve for the time of the speculative attack:[10]

$$(16) \qquad t^* = T - \eta \ln\left(\frac{\chi + \gamma + \mu\eta}{\chi}\right).$$

This formula implies that the speculative attack occurs before any money is printed: $t^* < T$.

9. See Sargent and Wallace (1973) for a derivation.
10. It can be shown that if the value of t^* implied by equation (16) is less than zero, the attack happens immediately; that is, $t^* = 0$. In this case the exchange rate is discontinuous at time zero.

Thus, other things equal, t^* is larger the longer the government delays implementing its new monetary policy (the larger is T) and the more willing the government is to accumulate debt (the higher is χ). In addition, the higher the interest rate elasticity of money demand (the larger is η) and the more money the government prints in the future (the higher are γ and μ), the smaller is t^*.[11] The intuition underlying these results is as follows. Once the fixed exchange rate regime is abandoned, inflation rises in anticipation of the increase in the money supply that occurs from time T on. A higher elasticity of money demand (η) makes it easier for the money supply to fall by χ percent. This means that the threshold rule is activated sooner, thus reducing the value of t^*. Higher values of μ and γ also reduce t^* because they lead to higher rates of inflation, making it possible for a drop of χ percent in the money supply to happen sooner.

7.3.4 Solving for the Equilibrium

Given fixed values for T and γ, the value of μ must be such that the government's intertemporal resource constraint, equation (6), holds. Since we initially abstract from nonindexed government liabilities ($B = 0$, $X_t = 0$), this constraint simplifies to

$$(17) \qquad \phi = \int_T^\infty (\dot{m}_t + \pi_t m_t)e^{-rt}dt + e^{-rt^*}\Delta m_{t^*} + e^{-rT}\Delta m_T.$$

Here we have used the fact that no seigniorage is collected between t^* and T because the money supply is constant during this time interval. We also used the fact that there are two jumps in real balances, the first at t^*, which triggers the devaluation, and the second at time T, when the government engineers a discrete jump in the money supply.

After time T the rate of inflation is constant and equal to the money growth rate, μ. This in turn implies that real balances are also constant and equal to $\theta Y \exp[-\eta(r + \mu)]$. Using this result, we can rewrite the constraint in equation (17) as

$$(18) \qquad \phi = e^{-rT}\frac{\mu}{r}\theta Y \exp[-\eta(r + \mu)] + e^{-rt^*}\Delta m_{t^*} + e^{-rT}\Delta m_T.$$

Solving for the equilibrium of the model amounts to solving equations (16) and (18) for the two unknowns (t^*, μ).

7.3.5 A Numerical Example

To discuss the properties of the model it is useful to present a numerical example. The parameter values that we use, summarized in table 7.1, are

11. Some caution is required in interpreting these results because we are not free to vary the parameters on the right-hand side of equation (16) independently of each other. When one parameter is varied, γ or μ must be adjusted to ensure that the government resource constraint is satisfied.

Table 7.1   Parameters for the Numerical Examples

Parameter	Description
A. Benchmark Case	
$\eta = 0.5$	interest elasticity of money demand
$\psi = 0.12$	threshold rule parameter
$S = 1$	initial exchange rate
$\theta = 0.06$	constant in the money demand function
$r = 0.04$	real interest rate
$Y = 1$	constant level of output
$\phi = 0.24$	present value of new transfers
$b_0 = -0.067$	initial debt level
$T = 1$	time of switch to new monetary policy
$\gamma = 0.12$	% increase in M at T relative to $t = 0$
$\delta = 0$	distribution cost of tradables
$\omega = 1$	share of tradables in CPI
$Z = 0$	nominal transfers
$B = 0$	nominal debt
B. Nominal Debt	
Same as A except	
$B = 0.05$	nominal debt
C. Implicit Fiscal Reform	
Same as B except	
$Z = 0.022$	nominal transfers
$T_2 = T + 2$	date until which transfers stay constant
D. Sticky Nontradables Prices	
Same as C except	
$\omega = 0.5$	share of tradables in CPI
$T_1 = T$	date until which nontradables prices are sticky
E. Distribution Costs for Tradables	
Same as D except	
$\delta = 1$	distribution cost of tradables

loosely based on Korean data. We normalized real income, Y, and the initial exchange rate, S, to 1. We set the semielasticity of money demand with respect to the interest rate, η, equal to 0.5. This is consistent with the range of estimates of money demand elasticities in developing countries provided by Easterly, Mauro, and Schmidt-Hebbel (1995). We set the constant $\theta = 0.06$ so that the model is consistent with the ratio of the monetary base to GDP in Korea before the crisis (6 percent). We set the real interest rate, r, to 4 percent.

Next we discuss the initial value of the debt, the fiscal cost of the currency crisis, and threshold rule parameters b_0, ϕ, and χ. Consistent with the assumptions of the basic model, we abstract, for now, from nonindexed debt and focus on the real consolidated foreign debt of the Korean government and the central bank. The Korea Institute for International Economic Policy estimated that the foreign debt of the public sector in June 1997 was

Table 7.2   **Results for Numerical Examples, No Explicit Fiscal Reform**

| | Inflation | | | Devaluation | | | Financing (% of Total) | | |
	Yr 1	Yr 2	Long Run	Yr 1	Yr 2	t^*	Seigniorage	Nominal Debt Deflation	Implicit Fiscal Reform
A. Benchmark	34.9	20.0	20.0	34.9	20.0	0.49	100.0	0.0	0.0
B. Nominal debt	30.9	16.1	16.1	30.9	16.1	0.52	83.4	16.6	0.0
C. Implicit fiscal reform	20.2	6.1	6.1	20.2	6.1	0.60	35.9	13.1	51.0
D. P^{NT} sticky	17.7	4.0	4.0	35.4	4.0	0.61	21.4	12.4	66.2
E. Distribution	14.0	1.0	1.0	57.8	1.0	0.64	7.2	9.8	83.0

equal to 2.0 trillion won.[12] According to the International Monetary Fund's *International Financial Statistics,* the value of the central bank's net foreign assets was approximately 28.0 trillion won. This suggests that the net foreign assets of the consolidated public sector were equal to roughly 26.0 trillion won or 6.7 percent of 1996 GDP. For now, we ignore the government's domestic debt and set b_0 to –0.067 (we incorporate domestic debt into the analysis in section 7.5). The parameter ϕ was set to 0.24, which is, in our view, a conservative estimate of the fiscal cost of Korea's banking crisis relative to its GDP.[13] The value of χ was set to 0.12 to match the fall in the monetary base between December 1996 and December 1997. We also set the value of γ to 0.12 to match the ratio of the average value of the monetary base in the second half of 1999 versus the first half of 1997. We set $T = 1$. Finally, we solved for the value of μ that satisfies the government's intertemporal budget constraint, which is $\mu = 0.18$. We emphasize that there is considerable uncertainty about the true values of all the aforementioned parameters. However, in practice we found that the qualitative characteristics of the results that we stress are robust to reasonable perturbations of the benchmark parameterization.

The first row of table 7.2 summarizes the implications of the benchmark model for inflation and the rate of devaluation. Figure 7.1 depicts the paths for the exchange rate, the price level, and the money supply in the benchmark model. Several features are worth noting. First, the attack happens after agents learn about prospective deficits (at $t = 0$) but before new monetary policy is implemented (at $T = 1$). As in Burnside, Eichenbaum, and Rebelo (2001), the model is consistent with the currency crisis not being predictable on the basis of classical fundamentals such as past inflation, deficits, and money growth. An observer of this economy might be tempted to attribute the crisis to self-fulfilling expectations. In fact, the collapse was caused by fundamentals—the need to finance prospective deficits with

12. The data are published on the web at [http://kipe.go.kr].
13. See Burnside, Eichenbaum, and Rebelo (2000) for a discussion.

A

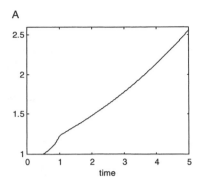

B

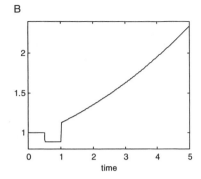

**Fig. 7.1   Solutions from the benchmark model: *A*, CPI and exchange rate;
B, money balances**

Notes: Time measured in years. Initial money balances are normalized to equal 1.

seigniorage revenues. Second, as in all first-generation models, there is a discrete drop in net foreign assets at the time of the attack. Third, the model reproduces the fact that inflation initially surges in the wake of the exchange rate collapse and then stabilizes at a lower level.

We conclude this section by discussing some obvious shortcomings of the model. First, the timing of the devaluation is deterministic: everybody knows the precise time at which the fixed exchange rate regime will collapse. This shortcoming can be remedied by introducing some element of uncertainty into the model, such as money demand shocks.[14] Second, the model predicts counterfactually large rates of inflation after a crisis. In our example inflation is 35 percent in the year of the crisis and 20 percent in steady state. This is inconsistent with the postcrisis inflation experience of countries like Mexico and Korea (see section 7.5). Finally, the model implies that the rate of inflation coincides with the rate of exchange rate depreciation. This, too, is inconsistent with the evidence. After a speculative attack, rates of devaluation are typically much larger than the corresponding rates of inflation.

7.4   Model Extensions

This section incorporates two extensions of our framework designed to address the second and third shortcomings of the benchmark model. First, we introduce nonindexed government liabilities. Second, we eliminate the assumption of PPP. With these modifications the model can account for two key features of the data: (a) the rate of devaluation in a currency crisis is typically much larger than CPI inflation, and (b) the rate of inflation can be quite moderate in the wake of a currency crisis.

14. See Flood and Garber (1984) and Drazen and Helpman (1988) for a discussion of speculative attack models with uncertainty.

7.4.1   Nonindexed Government Liabilities

We consider two types of nonindexed government liabilities: (a) domestic bonds (B) issued before agents learned about prospective deficits, and (b) public spending whose value is preset in units of domestic currency (X_t). In the presence of these liabilities the government budget constraint, equation (18), is replaced by

$$(19) \quad \phi = e^{-rT}\frac{\mu}{r}\theta Y \exp\left[-\eta(r + \mu)\right] + e^{-rt^*}\Delta m_{t^*}$$

$$+ e^{-rT}\Delta m_T + \left(\frac{B}{S} - \int_0^\infty \frac{rB}{S_t}e^{-rt}dt\right) - \left[\int_0^\infty\left(\frac{X_t}{S} - \frac{X_t}{S_t}\right)e^{-rt}dt\right].$$

Recall that the term $B/S - \int_0^\infty(rB/S_t)e^{-rt}dt$ is the revenue obtained from deflating nonindexed debt. The term $\int_0^\infty(X_t/S - X_t/S_t)e^{-rt}dt$ is the value of the implicit fiscal reform accomplished by deflating the nonindexed components of the fiscal surplus.

As in the basic model, t^* is given by equation (16), so the equilibrium values of t^* and μ can be computed using equations (16) and (19). Finally, equation (11) allows us to compute the equilibrium path for the price level and the exchange rate.

Nonindexed Debt

To see the impact of nonindexed debt on the model's implications for inflation and devaluation rates we now turn to a numerical example. We assume that nonindexed debt is equal to 5 percent of GDP ($B = 0.05$). As with our other parameter values, this number is loosely motivated by the Korean experience. Recall that nominal debt in the model is a perpetuity, so its duration is different from that of Korea's debt. For this reason it is not appropriate to use the measured stock of nonindexed debt on the eve of the crisis to calibrate B. We chose B so that the amount of revenue from debt deflation is roughly consistent with the evidence from Korea presented in section 7.5.

Table 7.2 shows that introducing nonindexed debt lowers the growth rate of money μ that is necessary to pay for ϕ. As a result, steady-state inflation declines from 20.0 percent in the base model to 16.1 percent. Obviously, with more initial nonindexed debt, the crisis could be financed with less recourse to inflation. For example, if B equaled 0.5, the rate of inflation would be 15.5 percent in the first year after the currency crisis and 2.1 percent thereafter. The government would only raise 14.6 percent of the fiscal cost of the crisis from seigniorage revenues. The balance would come from debt deflation. Thus, in principle, allowing for nonindexed debt can reconcile our basic model with the observation that inflation is often quite moderate after a currency crisis. However, for Mexico and the countries involved in the Asian crisis of 1997, there was not enough nonindexed debt for this to be a complete resolution of the problem.

Implicit Fiscal Reform

We now allow for an implicit fiscal reform as a source of revenue for the government. Specifically, we assume that $G = 0.02$; that is, nonindexed government spending is about 2 percent of GDP. In addition, we assume that G is fixed in nominal terms for roughly 2.5 years after the crisis and then starts growing at the rate of inflation. Thus, in this example the implicit fiscal reform amounts to a permanent reduction in the real value of government spending relative to GDP. In our case study of Korea we examine the sensitivity of our results to alternative mixes of implicit and explicit fiscal reforms.

Table 7.2 makes clear that allowing for an implicit fiscal reform has a significant impact on the model's predictions. Relative to the scenario in which the only nonindexed liability is nominal debt, year 1 inflation falls from 30.9 percent to 20.2 percent. Long-run inflation falls from 16.1 percent to 6.1 percent. The percentage of total fiscal costs raised by seigniorage falls from 83.4 percent to 35.9 percent, while the importance of debt deflation falls from 16.6 percent to 13.1 percent. Even though nonindexed government spending represents only 2 percent of GDP, the implicit fiscal reform pays for over 50 percent of the cost of the crisis.[15]

Allowing for debt deflation and implicit fiscal reform can render our model consistent with the observation that inflation rates are often moderate after a currency crisis. However, these extensions cannot explain the other shortcoming of the benchmark model: actual inflation is often much lower than the rate of devaluation associated with a currency crisis. We turn to this challenge next.

7.4.2   Deviations from Purchasing Power Parity

Up to this point, all of the models that we have considered assume that PPP holds. Consequently, by construction, the rate of inflation coincides with the rate of devaluation. To break the link between domestic inflation and exchange rate depreciation we introduce two departures from PPP into the model described in section 7.4.1: (a) nontradable goods and (b) costs of distributing tradable goods (e.g., transportation, wholesaling, and retailing).

Nontradable Goods

In the presence of nontradable goods the consumer price index (CPI), P_t is given by

---

15. To assess the robustness of our results we redid our calculations assuming that G is fixed in nominal terms for only five months. In this case, the implicit fiscal reform raises 33 percent of the total fiscal cost of the crisis. In this experiment the value of t^* is 0.57. The rate of inflation is 23.7 percent in the first year and 9.2 percent in the following years.

(20) $$P_t = (P_t^T)^\omega (P_t^{NT})^{1-\omega}.$$

Here P_t^{NT} denotes the price of nontradable goods and P_t^T the price of tradable goods. By assumption PPP holds for tradable goods, so $P_t^T = S_t$ for all t. Absent an explicit model of the nontradable goods sector, we assume that P_t^{NT} remains fixed for the first five months after the currency crisis. Thereafter P_t^{NT} moves one-to-one with the exchange rate. Consequently, a currency crisis is associated with a permanent decline in the relative price of nontradable goods. This assumption is motivated by the Korean experience. The price of nontradables in Korea increased by only 4.8 percent between October 1997 and April 1998, whereas it increased only by 5.6 percent between October 1997 and October 1998. Finally, we set $\omega = 0.5$, which corresponds to the share of tradables in Korea's CPI.[16]

Because we defined m_t as M_t/S_t, equation (19) remains unchanged. Equation (11) describes the evolution of the CPI. Equations (11) and (20), together with the path for P_t^{NT}, determine the behavior of the exchange rate. The equilibrium values of t^* and μ can be computed using equations (16) and (19).

Table 7.2 indicates that these modifications of the model have two effects. First, there is a relatively small decline in the amount of inflation induced by a currency crisis. Inflation is 17.7 percent in the first year after the crisis, while steady-state inflation is 4.0 percent. Second, and more importantly, the model now generates a large wedge between the initial rate of inflation and the rate of depreciation. Specifically, the currency crisis is now associated with a 35.4 percent rate of depreciation in the first year.

Distribution Costs

To induce an even larger wedge between inflation and depreciation we now allow for distribution costs in tradable goods. Proceeding as in Burstein, Neves, and Rebelo (2001) we assume that δ units of nontradables (transportation, wholesale, and retail) are required to distribute tradable goods. As in their paper, we assume that PPP holds for the import prices but not for the retail prices of tradable goods. The latter are given by $P_t^T + \delta P_t^{NT}$, so that the CPI is

$$P_t = (S_t + \delta P_t^{NT})^\omega (P_t^{NT})^{1-\omega}.$$

The last line of table 7.2 displays results for this version of the model under the assumption that $\delta = 1$.[17] Figure 7.2 depicts the paths for the ex-

16. This information was obtained from the *Annual Report on the Consumer Price Index,* National Statistical Office, Republic of Korea, 1998. Food; fuel; light and water; furniture and utensils; clothing and footwear; cigarettes; and toilet articles were classified as tradable goods. Medical care; education; culture and recreation; transportation and communication; and personal care services were classified as nontradables.

17. This value of δ is consistent with the evidence presented in Burstein, Neves, and Rebelo (2001).

A
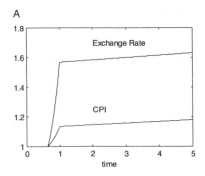

B
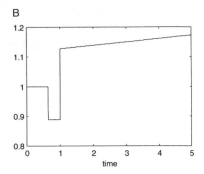

Fig. 7.2   Solutions from the model with sticky nontradables prices, distribution costs, and an implicit fiscal reform: *A*, CPI and exchange rate; *B*, money balances
Notes: Time measured in years. Initial money balances are normalized to equal 1.

change rate, the price level, and the money supply. Notice the stark difference between this model and the benchmark model discussed in section 7.3. In the benchmark model, inflation in the first year after the crisis is equal to 34.9 percent and declines to 20 percent in steady state. In addition, the rate of devaluation coincides with the rate of inflation. In contrast, the modified model implies first-year inflation roughly equal to 14 percent, while the currency devalues by over 50 percent. Moreover, steady-state inflation is only 1 percent. Clearly this version of the model can account for large devaluations without generating grossly counterfactual implications for inflation.

7.5   Two Case Studies

We now examine in some detail two recent crises, Mexico 1994 and Korea 1997, and discuss how the governments in these countries are paying for the fiscal costs associated with the crises. Our calculations suggest that Mexico will finance most of the fiscal costs associated with its crisis through seigniorage revenues. In contrast, our best guess for Korea is that it will pay for the bulk of the fiscal cost of its crisis through future explicit and implicit fiscal reforms.

7.5.1   The Government Budget Constraint Revisited

Up to now, we have abstracted from output growth and foreign inflation. To interpret the data we must amend the government budget constraint in equation (6) to incorporate these elements. To this end, suppose that domestic output and the U.S. price level grow at constant rates ζ and π^*, respectively. We normalize the U.S. price level at $t = 0$ to one. Consequently, P_t^* evolves according to

$$P_t^* = e^{\pi^* t}.$$

The presence of output growth and foreign inflation implies that, in a sustainable fixed exchange rate regime, real balances grow at rate ζ, and domestic inflation, π, is equal to π^*. It also implies that the government can collect seigniorage under a fixed exchange rate regime. To see this, it is convenient to focus on the benchmark model. Given PPP, the demand for real balances is given by

$$\frac{M_t}{P_t} = \frac{M_0}{P_0}e^{\zeta t},$$

$$\frac{M_0}{P_0} = \theta Y_0 \exp[-\eta(r + \pi^*)].$$

Here M_0/P_0 and Y_0 denotes real balances and output at time zero, respectively.

For S to remain constant, the money supply must grow at rate $\bar{\mu} = \zeta + \pi^*$. Under these circumstances, the dollar value of seigniorage flows at time t is

$$\frac{\dot{M}_t}{S_t} = (\zeta + \pi^*)\frac{M_0}{P_0}e^{(\zeta + \pi^*)t}.$$

The present value in dollars at time zero of seigniorage revenues collected under a sustainable fixed exchange rate regime is given by

$$\int_0^\infty \frac{\dot{M}_t}{S_t}e^{-(r+\pi^*)t}dt = (\zeta + \pi^*)\frac{M_0}{P_0}\frac{1}{r-\zeta}.$$

Finally, the new version of the government budget constraint in equation (6) is

$$(21) \quad \phi = \int_0^\infty \frac{\dot{M}_t}{S_t}e^{-(r+\pi^*)t}dt + \sum_{i\in I}\frac{\Delta M_i}{S_i}e^{-(r+\pi^*)i} - (\zeta + \pi^*)\frac{M_0}{P_0}\frac{1}{r-\zeta}$$

$$+ \left[\frac{B}{S} - \int_0^\infty \frac{(r+\pi^*)B}{S_t}e^{-(r+\pi^*)t}dt\right] - \left[\int_0^\infty \left(\frac{X_t}{S} - \frac{X_t}{S_t}\right)e^{-(r+\pi^*)t}dt\right].$$

The key implication of equation (21) is that not all of the seigniorage collected in the postcrisis period $[\int_0^\infty(\dot{M}_t/S_t)e^{-(r+\pi^*)t}dt + \Sigma_{i\in I}(\Delta M_i/S_i)e^{-(r+\pi^*)i}]$ contributes to financing the crisis. Part of those revenues $[(\zeta + \pi^*)(M_0/P_0)/(r - \zeta)]$ would have been collected under the fixed exchange rate regime. These revenues were required to fulfill the government's precrisis budget constraint. Only the difference between the seigniorage collected in the presence of the crisis and the hypothetical seigniorage that would have been collected in the absence of the crisis can be used to finance the new spending, ϕ. Inevitably, some assumptions are required to compute this hypothetical seigniorage.

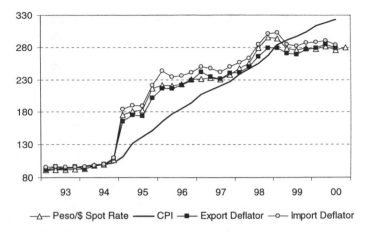

Fig. 7.3   Price indices in Mexico 1993–2000 (1994:3 = 100)

Source: The consumer price index is from Hacienda. The import and export deflators are from the Mexican national accounts (Hacienda).

Notes: All series are normalized so that their value in 1994:3 = 100 by creating a new series $Q_t = 100 P_t / P_{1994:3}$. The peso/\$ spot rate is the IFS period-average market rate (AF . . . ZF).

7.5.2   Mexico, 1994

Figure 7.3 displays four quarterly series for the period 1993 to 2000: the peso/dollar exchange rate, the CPI, and the export and import price deflators. Between 20 December and 31 December 1994 the peso-dollar exchange rate increased by 44 percent. By 2 January 1996 the cumulative increase in the peso-dollar exchange rate reached 121 percent. Although the export and import price indices moved closely with the exchange rate, the rate of CPI inflation was much lower than the rate of depreciation.

The currency crisis exacerbated an ongoing banking crisis.[18] The net result was a large rise in the Mexican government's prospective deficits associated with an impending bank bailout. Lindgren, Garcia, and Saal (1996) estimate the fiscal cost of the crisis to be 6.5 percent of GDP, which amounts to 27 billion dollars. On the other hand, Caprio and Klingebiel (1996) estimate the cost to be between 12 and 15 percent of GDP, with the upper bound translating into 63 billion dollars. More recently, Caprio and Klingebiel have revised their estimate to 20 percent of GDP. This corresponds to 84.3 billion dollars.[19]

In what follows we provide a rough estimate of what the Mexican gov-

18. Difficulties associated with rolling over short-run dollar-denominated debt no doubt played some role in the exact timing of the crisis. Here we are more concerned with understanding how the fiscal costs of the crisis were financed. See Krueger and Tornell (1999) and Sachs, Tornell, and Velasco (1996) for detailed discussions of the Mexico 1994 crisis.

19. We use 1994 GDP to compute the dollar amounts.

ernment has done to date to finance its fiscal costs. In addition, we discuss what the future growth rate of money would have to be to finance the remainder of the costs.

Seigniorage Revenues

We begin by discussing the seigniorage revenues raised by the Mexican government in the postcrisis period. Using monthly data on the monetary base we computed the present value of the seigniorage collected between November 1994 and December 2000.[20] The flows of seigniorage were discounted with a dollar interest rate $R^* = 0.065$.[21] Under our assumptions, the present value in 1994 of the seigniorage revenue collected between November 1994 and December 2000 was 20.2 billion dollars.

To calculate the part of this seigniorage that can be used to cover the fiscal costs of the crisis, we must compute the hypothetical seigniorage that Mexico would have collected during this period had the crisis not occurred. We compute the present value in 1994, measured in dollars, of this hypothetical seigniorage flow by making two assumptions. First, in the absence of the crisis, the growth rate of money from 1994 on would have been constant and equal to the average year-on-year growth rate of the monetary base in the period January 1989 to November 1994. This equals 18 percent per annum.[22] Second, the demand for real balances measured in dollars, M_t/S_t, would have grown at the average growth rate of output from 1980 to 2000 (roughly $\zeta = 0.027$). This implies that the present value of hypothetical seigniorage that would have been collected between November 1994 (time zero) and December 2000 is 13.9 billion dollars.[23] Thus, the net increase in seigniorage revenues collected up to December 2000 that can be used to finance the fiscal cost of the crisis is 6.3 billion dollars.

Debt Devaluation

At the end of September 1994 the government owed 138.7 billion pesos' worth of securitized debt and 10.1 billion pesos of nonsecuritized debt. Because we have no information on the indexation provisions of nonsecuri-

20. We used the IMF's *International Financial Statistics* database. The series we used for the monetary base is 14 . . . ZF, Reserve Money. This differs slightly from the Banco de Mexico's series for definitional reasons.

21. The average dollar return on twenty-eight day Mexican treasury peso-denominated securities was 6.5 percent from December 1994 to December 2000. This rate of return is similar to U.S. rates of interest. The average one-year U.S. Treasury bill yield from December 1994 to January 2000 was roughly 5.5 percent. So was the thirty-year zero-coupon yield estimated by J. Huston McCulloch for February 2001 and reported at [http://www.econ.ohiostate.edu/jhm/ts/ts.html].

22. This corresponds to a continuously compounded rate $\mu = 0.166$.

23. This was computed using the formula $\mu(M_0/S_0)[1 - e^{-(R^* - \zeta)h}]/(R^* - \zeta)$, where M_0 and S_0 are the November 1994 values of the monetary base and exchange rate and $h = 6.083$ (the number of years between November 1994 and December 2000).

tized debt, we adopted the conservative assumption that all of it was indexed. The securitized debt can be broken down into the following categories. *Cetes,* which are zero-coupon Mexican Treasury bills, represented 34 percent of securitized debt. *Tesobonos,* which are dollar-denominated zero-coupon bonds, represented 33 percent. *Ajustabonos,* which are inflation-indexed coupon bonds, represented 21 percent. *Bondes,* which are adjustable coupon bonds, represent 12 percent. To simplify, we treated both *bondes* and *tesobonos* as if they were perfectly indexed to the dollar. To compute the revenue in dollars generated by the debt deflation we considered only *cetes,* which are not indexed, and *ajustabonos,* which are indexed to the CPI, not to the dollar.

We consolidated the securitized debt of the government and the central bank. We only have information on the composition of securities held by the central bank for the end of 1994. At this time the Banco de Mexico held 2.5 billion pesos of *cetes* and held a negative position of 0.5 billion pesos in *ajustabonos.*

To compute the reduction in the dollar value of the outstanding Cetes in the aftermath of the crisis, we assumed that these bonds were distributed equally across four maturities: one, three, six, and twelve months. Within each maturity we assumed that the bonds were distributed equally across all possible expiration dates.[24] Consider a *cetes* of a given maturity and expiration date that was outstanding at date t. We compute its loss in dollar value between dates t and $t + 1$ as $F/S_t - F/S_{t+1}$, where F is the face value in pesos and S_t is the peso-dollar exchange rate at time t. We make similar assumptions with regard to *ajustabonos,* which come in maturities of three and five years. Specifically, we compute the loss in dollar value between dates t and $t + 1$ as $F_t/S_t - F_{t+1}/S_{t+1}$, where $F_t = F_{t-1}P_t/P_{t-1}$ and P_t is the CPI at date t.

These assumptions imply that the total revenue generated by debt deflation was 8.4 billion dollars. Most of this revenue (90 percent) was generated in the first month after the devaluation. This means that our calculations are not very sensitive to our timing assumptions about maturities and expiration dates.

Implicit and Explicit Fiscal Reform

Despite several changes in the tax code, it is difficult to find evidence of large explicit or implicit fiscal reforms.[25] According to Burnside (2000), the average cyclically adjusted primary surplus was 3.5 percent of GDP in the precrisis period 1991–94.[26] In the period 1995:1–1998:2 the average cycli-

---

24. In other words, for the three-month maturity we assumed that one third of the *cetes* would expire within one, two, and three months, respectively.

25. Fiscal reforms included an increase in the general value-added tax rate from 10 to 15 percent, as well as increases in the prices of public goods and services in 1995.

26. These estimates incorporate the impact of changes in the price of oil on Mexico's fiscal situation. See Kletzer (1997) for a discussion of the fiscal implications of external shocks.

cally adjusted primary surplus was 4.2 percent of GDP. These estimates suggest that overall the net effect of any fiscal reform was small.[27]

Here, using a simple methodology described in the appendix, we decompose the primary budget surplus, Δ_t, into three components,

$$(22) \qquad \Delta_t = \Delta_t + (\hat{\Delta}_t - \Delta_t) + (\Delta_t - \hat{\Delta}_t),$$

where Δ_t is the primary fiscal surplus that would have occurred in the absence of any crisis, and $\hat{\Delta}_t$ is the cyclically adjusted primary surplus. We describe the second term on the right-hand side of equation (22) as the fiscal reform component, and the third term is the cost-of-recession component.

We estimate that fiscal reforms $(\hat{\Delta}_t - \Delta_t)$ generated roughly 5.8 billion dollars in additional funds for the government. Because the nominal value of the Mexican government's nonindexed liabilities quickly began to rise after the crises, most of these reforms were explicit rather than implicit. We estimate the recession costs $(\Delta_t - \hat{\Delta}_t)$ to have been about 2.2 billion dollars.

Summary of What Has Been Done to Date

Adding up additional seigniorage (6.3 billion dollars), the revenue from debt devaluation (8.4 billion dollars), and the revenue from the fiscal reforms, net of recession costs (3.5 billion dollars), we estimate that, to date, the Mexican government has raised 18.2 billion dollars. This corresponds to 4.3 percent of 1994 Mexican GDP, which is close to Lindgren, Garcia, and Saal's (1996) estimate of the size of the crisis. If one accepts this estimate, the Mexican government has almost finished paying for the fiscal costs of the crisis. However, if one accepts Caprio and Klingebiel's (1996) estimates, much is left to be done.

Financing the Remaining Costs

Absent any indication of large impending fiscal reforms, it seems reasonable to suppose that the remainder of the fiscal costs will be paid for with seigniorage revenues. We estimate that the monetary base would have to grow at an annual rate of 21.2 percent, from 2001 on, to raise the additional 10.6 percent of GDP required to finance a crisis of the size estimated by Caprio and Klingebiel (1996).

We arrived at this number as follows. First, we estimated the seigniorage that would have been collected absent a crisis from January 2001 onward. We used the same assumptions that we employed to estimate hypothetical seigniorage for the period November 1994 to December 2000. These assumptions imply that the Mexican government would have raised seigniorage with a present value in 1994 equal to 55.9 billion dollars. Second, we estimated the present value (as of 1994) of the seigniorage revenues resulting

---

27. These calculations take into account the decline in the real value of taxes due to inflation, known as the Tanzi effect.

from a constant growth rate of the monetary base from January 2001 on-ward. Here we assumed that the growth rate of real balances measured in dollars would be equal to the historical average growth rate of real GDP from 1980 to 2000 (2.7 percent) and that the dollar interest rate would be 6.5 percent. Given these assumptions, a growth rate of the nominal base equal to 21.2 percent yields a present value of hypothetical seigniorage equal to 100.9 billion dollars. Thus, the extra seigniorage that can be used to pay for the crisis would equal 45.0 billion dollars (100.9–55.9). This is equivalent to 10.6 percent of 1994 GDP.

We emphasize that our estimate of the required growth rate of money is sensitive to the assumptions underlying our calculations. For example, if Mexico grows more quickly or the dollar interest rate is lower than we as-sumed, then the government will be able to cover the fiscal costs of the cri-sis with lower future money growth rates.

The key point is that, absent any sign of fiscal reforms, it seems quite likely that the bulk of the costs will be covered via explicit seigniorage rev-enues. This implies that the rate of inflation in Mexico is higher than it would have been had the implicit fiscal reform or the initial domestic debt been larger. We use our model to illustrate this point more concretely in the case of Korea, which we turn to next.

7.5.3 Korea, 1997

Figure 7.4 displays four quarterly series for the period 1996–2000: the won-dollar exchange rate, the CPI, and the export and import price indexes.

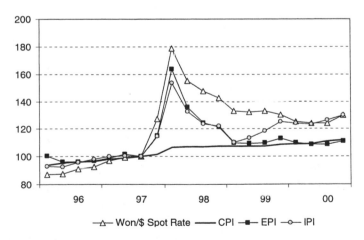

Fig. 7.4   Price indices in Korea 1996–2000 (1997:3 = 100)

Source: The consumer price index (CPI), export price index (EPI), and import price index (IPI) are all from the Bank of Korea website.

Notes: All series are normalized that their value in 1997:3 = 100 by creating a new series Q_t = $100 P_t / P_{1997:3}$. The won/\$ spot rate is the IFS period-average market rate (AF . . . ZF).

Between September 1997 and September 1998 the won-dollar exchange rate increased by 52.1 percent. Figure 7.4 shows that although the export and import price indexes moved closely with the exchange rate, CPI inflation was significantly lower than the rate of depreciation. Between September 1997 and September 1998 the CPI increased by just 6.9 percent.

As in Mexico, the currency crisis in Korea exacerbated existing problems in the banking system. As of December 1999, Standard and Poor's ratings service estimated that the fiscal cost of the banking crisis would be roughly 24 percent of GDP. In terms of 1997 GDP, this corresponds to 114.4 billion dollars.

In what follows we provide rough estimates of what the Korean government has done to date to finance the fiscal costs of the crisis. We then discuss the implications of alternative strategies for financing the remainder of the costs.

Seigniorage Revenues

Using monthly data on the monetary base and a dollar interest rate of 5.5 percent, we estimate that the present value of the seigniorage raised between October 1997 and October 2000 is equal to 5.6 billion dollars.

To compute the hypothetical seigniorage that the government would have raised absent a crisis we make several assumptions. First, in the absence of the crisis, the growth rate of money from late 1997 on would have been constant and equal to the average year-on-year growth rate of the monetary base in the period October 1993–October 1997. This equals 0.6 percent per annum ($\mu = 0.006$). Second, the demand for real balances in dollar terms would have grown at the average growth rate of output from 1980 to 1999. This equals 7.3 percent ($\zeta = 0.07$). These assumptions imply that the present value of hypothetical seigniorage that would have been collected between October 1997 and October 2000 is 0.4 billion dollars. Thus, the net increase in seigniorage revenues collected up to October 2000 that can be used to finance the fiscal cost of the crisis is 5.2 billion dollars.

Debt Devaluation

In Korea, as in Mexico, not all domestic public-sector debt is securitized. Because we know very little about the indexation of nonsecuritized debt we adopted the conservative assumption that all of it was indexed. We focus narrowly on the following securities: government bonds and monetary stabilization bonds issued by the central bank. The outstanding amounts of these two types of bonds at the end of December 1996 were, respectively, 25.7 and 25.0 trillion won.[28] In addition the central bank held government bonds worth 2.1 trillion won. Consequently, we assume that the securitized

---

28. For the figures on government bonds, see IMF (2000). For central bank debt and holdings of treasury securities, see the Bank of Korea website.

debt was equal to 48.6 trillion won (25.7 + 25.0 − 2.1). We use this December 1996 measure of the stock of debt to benchmark the stock of debt in October 1997.

We know much less about the maturity structure of Korean debt than we do about Mexican debt. Korean treasury bonds are issued in maturities of one, three, or five years.[29] Monetary stabilization bonds are issued with maturities between fourteen days and eighteen months. If we assume average expiration dates between six months and eighteen months across all types of bonds, we obtain estimates of the amount of debt devaluation ranging from 13.7 to 16.4 billion dollars. Over this range, the estimate is actually decreasing in the average maturity of the bonds due to the rebound in the value of the won after January 1998.

Implicit and Explicit Fiscal Reform

The Korean government appears to have implemented a combination of explicit and implicit fiscal reforms. On the explicit side, tax revenue has recently risen sharply relative to GDP. This suggests that either tax rates have been raised, the tax base has expanded, or that enforcement has been improved. On the implicit side, the won value of expenditures has risen very slowly since the crisis. For example, the public-sector wage bill actually declined slightly between 1997 and 1999 in won terms, representing a 6 billion dollar saving to the government over two years. Of course, we cannot be certain whether such savings were implicit—the result of contracts set in nominal terms—or explicit—via job losses or ex post wage freezes.

Using the same methodology as for Mexico, we put the present value of implicit and explicit fiscal reforms at roughly 34.4 billion dollars. Set against these gains are losses of 24.7 billion dollars in tax revenue due to the recession.

Summary of What Has Been Done to Date

Adding up additional seigniorage (5.2 billion dollars), the revenue from debt devaluation (13.7 billion dollars), and the revenue from fiscal reforms (34.4 billion dollars) net of recession costs (24.7 billion dollars), we obtain a total of 28.6 billion dollars. This corresponds to 6 percent of Korea's 1997 GDP. Because our estimate of the fiscal cost of the crisis is 24 percent of 1997 GDP, or 114.4 billion dollars, this leaves a shortfall of 85.8 billion dollars that must be raised in the future. This figure is close to the amount of new debt issued by the Korean government via the Korea Asset Management Corporation and the Korea Deposit Insurance Corporation and in other forms since 1997. In present value terms, this new debt is worth about 82 billion dollars.

---

29. The government has established the three-year bond as a benchmark in the postcrisis period.

Financing the Remainder of the Fiscal Cost

To finance the remainder of the fiscal cost, Korea could use a combination of further fiscal reforms and increased seigniorage. Suppose that the government raised all of the required revenue via seigniorage. What kind of monetary policy would they have to pursue in the future? To answer this question we make two assumptions. First, the growth rate of money from October 2000 equals 16.8 percent per annum. This is the average money growth rate between October 1998 and October 2000.[30] Second, from October 2000 on, real balances grow at 7.3 percent per annum. This is the average annual growth rate of real GDP between 1980 and October 2000. Under these assumptions Korea could raise the additional seigniorage it requires in roughly twenty-two years. From the standpoint of our model, this scenario seems unlikely because inflation would have been much higher than it actually is. Our model suggests that a more plausible scenario is that the government will raise the remainder of the revenue it needs through a combination of future implicit and explicit reforms and a very moderate amount of seigniorage.

To show this, we ask the question: how big does the future explicit reform have to be to rationalize Korea's postcrisis inflation experience? Various experiments with our model suggest that the answer is roughly 16 percent of GDP or 66.7 percent of the fiscal cost of the crisis.[31] Table 7.3 summarizes the key features of the equilibrium path of the model economy under this assumption. This example has a number of striking features. It is consistent with the observation that, one year after the crisis, inflation in Korea became extremely low. In the model the steady-state rate of inflation (attained after the first year) is 1.6 percent. Overall seigniorage only accounts for 10.6 percent of the cost of the crisis. Nevertheless, the model generates a realistically large depreciation of the won in the first year of the crisis (59.9 percent).

Understanding the Properties of the Extended Model

The ability of our model to rationalize large rates of devaluation along with moderate inflation is due to three features. First, even though seigniorage plays a small role in government finance, inflation-related revenue includes the value of the implicit fiscal reform and debt devaluation as well as seigniorage. Together these three sources of revenue account for roughly one third of the fiscal cost of the crisis. Eliminating the first two revenue sources and relying exclusively on seigniorage would result in substantially larger rates of inflation. In particular, inflation in the first year would jump to 20 percent and steady-state inflation would exceed 6 percent. Second,

30. At the end of October 2000, the value of Korea's stock of base money was about 24.3 billion dollars.
31. In these experiments we set $G = 0.003$ so that the fraction of the fiscal cost financed by the implicit reform is roughly 12 percent.

Table 7.3   Results for Numerical Example, Explicit Fiscal Reform (16% of GDP)

| Inflation | | | Devaluation | | | | Financing (% of Total) | | |
Yr 1	Yr 2	Long Run	Yr 1	Yr 2	t^*	Seigniorage	Nominal Debt Deflation	Implicit Fiscal Reform	Explicit Fiscal Reform
14.8	1.6	1.6	59.9	1.6	0.64	10.6	11.0	11.7	66.7

distribution costs play a key role in magnifying the rate of depreciation. To see this, suppose that we eliminate distribution costs ($\delta = 0$). Then the depreciation in the first year would only equal 32 percent instead of 59.9 percent. Inflation in the first year would rise to over 15 percent, and steady-state inflation would climb to 1.6 percent. If we also eliminate nontradables ($\omega = \delta = 0$), the model implies that the rate of depreciation in the first year is roughly 16 percent. Because PPP holds in this version of the model, the rate of inflation coincides with the depreciation rate. Finally, the model assumes that there is a period of very rapid money growth at some point after the crisis. This is captured by the assumption that there is a discrete increase in the money supply at $T = 1$.[32] If this money injection did not occur, then the rate of depreciation in the first year would be only 8.3 percent, a number far lower than observed in the data. We conclude that nonseigniorage inflation-related revenue, distribution costs, nontradable goods, and short-run monetization all play important roles in allowing the model to generate large rates of depreciation along with moderate inflation.

We conclude this section with a brief discussion of some of the model's empirical shortcomings. The most obvious is that it significantly overstates inflation in the first year after the crisis. The model predicts inflation on the order of 15 percent, whereas actual inflation in Korea was roughly 7 percent. This problem may reflect (a) the fact that we abstracted from the severe recession that occurred in Korea after the crisis, (b) the presence of measurement problems in the Korean CPI,[33] and (c) the fact that the prices of many nontradable services like medical care and education are controlled by the government.[34] In ongoing work Burstein, Eichenbaum, and

32. Recall that the value of γ used in our example was motivated by Korean data. Burnside, Eichenbaum, and Rebelo (2001) discuss the patterns of money growth across countries in the aftermath of the Asian currency crisis.

33. Devaluations may lead to a flight from quality as agents substitute away from imported items to lower-quality, locally produced substitutes. The methods used in Korea to choose the brands included in the CPI and the treatment of items that are no longer available may lead measured inflation to significantly understate actual inflation.

34. According to the 1998 *Annual Report on the Consumer Price Index* (National Statistical Office, Republic of Korea), the weight of government controlled prices in the Korean CPI is 20.8 percent. This includes goods and services in the following categories: medical care (5.1 percent), education (9.2 percent), culture and recreation services (3.4 percent), and public transportation (3.1 percent).

Rebelo (2001) use disaggregated CPI data to explore the quantitative importance of these factors.

A final shortcoming of the model is that it does not account for the different patterns of depreciation in Korea and Mexico. As is evident from figures 7.3 and 7.4, the Korean exchange rate displays a strong overshooting pattern that is completely absent in the Mexican case.[35] Understanding this difference strikes us as an important area for future research.

7.6   Conclusion

This paper explored the implications of different strategies for financing the fiscal costs of twin crises for inflation and depreciation rates. We do this using a first-generation-type model of speculative attacks that has four key features. First, the currency crisis is triggered by prospective deficits. Second, there exists outstanding nonindexed government debt whose real value can be reduced through a devaluation. Third, some governments' liabilities are not indexed to inflation, and their real value declines after a currency crises. Fourth, there are nontradable goods and costs of distributing tradable goods, so that PPP does not hold.

We use our model and the data to interpret the recent currency crises in Mexico and Korea. Our analysis suggests that the Mexican government is likely to pay for the bulk of the fiscal costs of its crisis through seigniorage revenues. As a consequence, rates of inflation have been relatively high. We anticipate that inflation will continue to be high in the future. In contrast, the Korean government is likely to rely more on a combination of implicit and explicit fiscal reforms. Under this assumption our model can account for both the large devaluation of the Korean won in 1997 and the fact that current rates of inflation in Korea are extremely low.

Appendix
Estimating the Size of Fiscal Reforms

Our procedure for computing the size of the fiscal adjustment after a crisis consists of two main ingredients:

1. Estimating the cyclically adjusted primary budget surplus.
2. Estimating what the budget surplus would have been in the absence of the crisis.

---

35. The Thai baht exhibited an overshooting pattern similar to that of the Korean won.

Estimating the Cyclically Adjusted Budget Surplus

Define the standard measure of the primary budget surplus as $\Delta_t \equiv R_t - E_t$, where R_t is revenue and E_t is primary expenditure. A cyclically adjusted measure of the primary surplus is $\hat{\Delta}_t \equiv \hat{R}_t - \hat{E}_t$, where $\hat{R}_t$ and $\hat{E}_t$ are cyclically adjusted measures of R_t and E_t.

Standard procedures for computing cyclically adjusted revenue and expenditure dictate that there are specific revenue and expenditure components that adjust automatically to the business cycle, whereas there are others that only move according to the government's discretion. To illustrate, suppose there are K revenue categories, of which K_1 adjust according to the business cycle and $K - K_1$ do not. Then revenue is given by

$$R_t = \sum_{i=1}^{K_1} R_{it} + \sum_{i=K_1+1}^{K} R_{it}.$$

Cyclically adjusted revenue is given by

$$\hat{R}_t = \sum_{i=1}^{K_1} \hat{R}_{it} + \sum_{i=K_1+1}^{K} R_{it},$$

where $\hat{R}_{it}$ is the ith cyclically adjusted revenue component. Note that some revenue categories are not adjusted because they are deemed to be purely discretionary or at least invariant to the business cycle. Typically, tax revenues and transfers to households are the types of categories that are cyclically adjusted. An adjusted revenue category would typically be estimated as

$$\hat{R}_{it} = R_{it} \exp[-\alpha_i(\ln Y_t - \ln \overline{Y}_t)],$$

where $\ln \overline{Y}_t$ is some measure of trend real GDP, and α_i is a measure of the elasticity of this category of revenue with respect to the output gap, $\ln Y_t - \ln \overline{Y}_t$.

In developing countries it is typical for tax revenue to move closely in proportion to GDP, whereas few if any of the expenditure categories exhibit a strong elasticity with respect to GDP. Motivated by this fact, and to simplify our analysis, we use a very simple procedure and compute $\hat{\Delta}_t = \hat{R}_t - E_t$, where $\hat{R}_t = [R_t/(P_t Y_t)]P_t \overline{Y}_t$, where P_t represents the GDP deflator. In other words, we assume that all changes in the ratio of revenue to GDP are discretionary. Thus, we have $\hat{\Delta}_t = R_t(\overline{Y}_t/Y_t) - E_t$. To obtain trend GDP we fit a linear trend to data on the logarithm of real GDP from 1980 to 2000.

The part of the budget surplus due to the business cycle is $\Delta_t - \hat{\Delta}_t$.

The Budget Surplus in the Absence of the Crisis

We denote the budget surplus in the absence of the crisis by $\overline{\Delta}_t$. We let $\overline{\Delta}_t = dP_t \overline{Y}_t$, where d is the average primary surplus (as a fraction of GDP) in an

N-year window prior to the crisis. We set $N = 4$ so that for Mexico the window is 1991–94, and for Korea it is 1994–97.

The Size of the Fiscal Reform

Suppose we have observed government finance data for H years after the crisis. We compute the size of the fiscal reform, in dollars, as

$$\text{FR} = \sum_{t=1}^{H}(1 + R)^{-t}\frac{\hat{\Delta}_t - \overline{\Delta}_t}{S_t}$$

where S_t is the local currency–dollar exchange rate and R is the assumed dollar interest rate.

Recession Costs

We estimate recession costs as

$$\text{RC} = \sum_{t=1}^{H}(1 + R)^{-t}\frac{\Delta_t - \hat{\Delta}_t}{S_t}.$$

Decomposition of the Budget Surplus

Our decomposition of the budget data means that

$$\Delta_t = \overline{\Delta}_t + (\hat{\Delta}_t - \overline{\Delta}_t) + (\Delta_t - \hat{\Delta}_t),$$

where the first component is the trend, the second is the fiscal reform, and the last is the cyclical.

References

Burnside, Craig. 2000. Fiscal policy, business cycles, and growth in Mexico. World Bank.

Burnside, Craig, Martin Eichenbaum, and Sergio Rebelo. 2000. Understanding the Korean and Thai currency crises. *Economic Perspectives* 24 (September): 45–60.

———. 2001. Prospective deficits and the Asian currency crisis. *Journal of Political Economy* 109:1155–97.

Burstein, Ariel, Martin Eichenbaum, and Sergio Rebelo. 2001. Why are rates of inflation so low after large devaluations? Northwestern University Department of Economics. Mimeograph.

Burstein, Ariel, João Neves, and Sergio Rebelo. 2001. Distribution costs and real exchange rate dynamics during exchange-rate-based stabilizations. *Journal of Monetary Economics.*

Cagan, Phillip. 1956. Monetary dynamics of hyperinflation. In *Studies in the Quantity Theory of Money,* ed. Milton Friedman, 25–117. Chicago: University of Chicago Press.

Calvo, Guillermo. 1987. Balance of payments crises in a cash-in-advance economy. *Journal of Money, Credit and Banking* 19:19–32.

Caprio, Gerard Jr., and Daniela Klingebiel. 1996. Bank insolvencies: Cross country experience. Policy Research Working Paper no. 1620. Washington, D.C.: World Bank.

Cochrane, John. 2001. Long-term debt and optimal policy in the fiscal theory of the price level. *Econometrica* 69:69–116.

Corsetti, Giancarlo, and Bartosz Mackowiak. 1999. Nominal debt and the dynamics of currency crises. Growth Center Discussion Paper no. 820. New Haven, Conn.: Yale University, Department of Economics.

Corsetti, Giancarlo, Paolo Pesenti, and Nouriel Roubini. 1999. Paper tigers? A model of the Asian crisis. *European Economic Review* 43:1211–36.

Daniel, Betty. 2001. A fiscal theory of currency crises. *International Economic Review* 42 (November): 969–88.

Dooley, Michael. 2000. A model of crises in emerging markets. *The Economic Journal* 110:256–72.

Drazen, Allan, and Elhanan Helpman. 1987. Stabilization with exchange rate management. *Quarterly Journal of Economics* 102:835–55.

———. 1988. Stabilization with exchange rate management under uncertainty. In *Economic Effects of the Government Budget,* ed. Elhanan Helpman, Assaf Razin and Efraim Sadka, 310–27. Cambridge: MIT Press.

Dupor, William. 2000. Exchange rates and the fiscal theory of the price level. *Journal of Monetary Economics* 45:613–30.

Easterly, William, Paolo Mauro, and Klaus Schmidt-Hebbel. 1995. Money demand and seigniorage-maximizing inflation. *Journal of Money Credit and Banking* 27:583–603.

Flood, Robert, and Peter Garber. 1984. Collapsing exchange rate regimes: Some linear examples. *Journal of International Economics* 17:1–13.

Goldstein, Morris. 1998. *The Asian financial crisis: Causes, cures, and systemic implications.* Washington, D.C.: Institute for International Economics.

International Monetary Fund (IMF). 2000. Republic of Korea: Statistical appendix. IMF Staff Country Reports no. 00/10. Washington, D.C.: International Monetary Fund.

Jeanne, Olivier, and Jeromin Zettelmeyer. 2001. International bailouts, moral hazard, and conditionality. *Economic Policy* 16 (33): 407–32.

Kletzer, Kenneth M. 1997. Volatility, external debt, and fiscal risk: Simulations of the impact of shocks on fiscal adjustment for thirteen Latin American countries. University of California at Santa Cruz, Department of Economics. Manuscript, September.

Krueger, Anne, and Aaron Tornell. 1999. The role of bank restructuring in recovering from crises: Mexico 1995–98. NBER Working Paper no. 7042. Cambridge, Mass.: National Bureau of Economic Research.

Krugman, Paul. 1979. A model of balance-of-payments crises. *Journal of Money, Credit, and Banking* 11:311–25.

Lahiri, Amartya, and Carlos Végh. 2000. Output costs, BOP crises, and optimal interest rate policy. University of California, Los Angeles, Department of Economics. Mimeograph.

Lindgren, Carl-Johan, Gillian Garcia, and Matthew I. Saal. 1996. *Bank soundness and macroeconomic policy.* Washington, D.C.: International Monetary Fund.

Obstfeld, Maurice. 1986. Speculative attack and the external constraint in a maximizing model of the balance of payments. *Canadian Journal of Economics* 29: 1–20.

Rebelo, Sergio, and Carlos Végh. 2001. When is it optimal to abandon a fixed exchange rate? Northwestern University, Kellogg School of Management, Department of Finance. Mimeograph.

Sachs, Jeffrey, Aaron Tornell, and Andres Velasco. 1996. The collapse of the Mexican peso: What have we learned? *Economic Policy* 22:13–56.

Sargent, Thomas J., and Neil Wallace. 1973. The stability of models of money and growth with perfect foresight. *Econometrica* 41:1043–48.

Sims, Christopher. 1994. A simple model for the determination of the price level and the interaction of monetary and fiscal policy. *Economic Theory* 4:381–99.

Wijnbergen, Sweder Van. 1991. Fiscal deficits, exchange rate crises, and inflation. *Review of Economic Studies* 58:81–92.

Woodford, Michael. 1995. Price level determinacy without control of a monetary aggregate. *Carnegie-Rochester Conference Series on Public Policy* 43:1–46.

Comment   Kenneth Kletzer

This is a very well-done paper that leaves little for a discussant to criticize. The authors set out a useful task, address it in an appropriate and interesting manner, and present the analysis in a very readable way. I will first summarize the paper as I interpret the problem and the analysis. I will then place it in the context of the literature on financial crises and finally turn my attention to some possible modifications that may help relate the model better to its motivation.

The object of the paper is to set up a model of the fiscal costs of a currency and domestic banking crisis that can be calibrated and compared to the fiscal responses of the governments of some crisis countries. The fiscal costs include contingent deposit guarantee liabilities of the government, whether explicit or implicit, that are realized as the result of a banking crisis. These liabilities can include cumulative losses of the banking system before the collapse of an exchange rate peg as well as the balance sheet costs for the banks of the devaluation itself. The primary point made by the authors is that governments have a number of fiscal instruments available for meeting the increase in public-sector liabilities consequent to a twin crisis and do not need to resort only to conventional seigniorage revenues in the aftermath of a collapsing exchange rate regime. To motivate their analysis of the mix of fiscal measures that might be used by the government, the authors argue that postcrisis inflation rates in several countries suffering currency and banking crisis in recent years have been inconsistent with the rates of domestic credit growth that would be needed to fill the budgetary gap alone. They further argue that sizes of crisis devaluations have exceeded those that would be predicted by simple currency crisis models given subsequent rates of monetization and inflation.

The centerpiece of the model is the intertemporal budget constraint of the consolidated government. Prior to a currency crisis, the exchange rate is

Kenneth Kletzer is professor of economics at the University of California, Santa Cruz.

fixed, but private agents suddenly learn that future government liabilities are higher than anticipated. The implication that the rate of domestic credit creation will rise in the future leads to the eventual collapse of the exchange rate peg. This is essentially the first-generation model of a currency crisis as in Krugman (1979) with the modification that the rate of domestic credit growth rises at some predetermined date. The shadow exchange rises as the date of eventual monetization approaches until it reaches the fixed rate and the speculative attack occurs. The timing of the attack and the postcrisis rate of depreciation vary with the extent to which future increases in public-sector liabilities are monetized (after the sudden news that deficits will rise in the future, agents have perfect foresight in the model). The public-sector budget constraint highlights the alternative means available to the government for financing a sudden rise in transfer payments. These include monetization, deflation of nominally indexed public debt, default on public debt, and increases in the real primary surplus of the government.

The model of a currency crisis used here is the prospective deficits version by the authors (Burnside, Eichenbaum, and Rebelo 2001). The idea that anticipated future monetization of public-sector budget deficits can bring about the collapse of an exchange rate peg has been used in other applications of the first-generation currency crisis models. For example, it appears in the analysis of borrowed reserves in Buiter (1987), of the quasi-fiscal costs of sterilization in Calvo (1991) and of reserve accumulation as self-protection against crises in Kletzer and Mody (2000). In the basic first-generation models, the assumption that domestic credit grows at a constant rate before and after the speculative attack is inessential. However, the prospective deficits version of this model may help to explain the empirics of recent financial crises without resorting to a multiplicity of equilibria, just as intended by the authors. I find this a compelling reason to add fiscal policy detail to the model and compare the calibrated model to the data.

One potential criticism of the model is that a portion of the prospective deficits is created by the currency collapse itself. For example, the fiscal costs of a banking sector bailout can be exacerbated by the balance sheet effects of a devaluation when banks have borrowed in foreign currency and lent in domestic currency. The realization of public-sector liabilities contingent on the collapse of the exchange rate regime can lead to multiple equilibria, just as in the second generation of currency crisis models.[1] However, contingent liabilities associated with the deterioration of a fragile domestic financial system can lead to a progressive rise in government liabilities following capital account liberalization, resulting in the eventual collapse of

1. Public-sector liabilities that are contingent on devaluation underlie the logic of a third generation of currency crisis models. The role of contingent liabilities for generating crises has been emphasized recently by Calvo (1998), Dooley (2000), and others, following up the observations and ideas of Diaz-Alejandro (1985).

an exchange rate peg with certainty. This process was identified and its importance so well emphasized by Carlos Diaz-Alejandro (1985).[2]

In the model, prospective deficits are assumed to be nonconditional in the analysis, even though the postcrisis increase in government liabilities has been contingent on the regime collapse in recent episodes. The paper uses estimates of the cost of domestic financial bailouts that account for the impact of devaluation on the net liabilities of the government associated with banking crises. There are two effects of devaluation—a rise in nominal deposit insurance and other liabilities due to exacerbation of an ongoing banking crisis, and the decrease in the real value of the cost of public bailouts of the financial sector. The estimates of the impact of devaluation in the case of Mexico and Korea in the paper give net increases in government liabilities, so that the possibility of multiple equilibria cannot be dismissed.

Turning to the argument that ex post inflation was inconsistent with the rate of depreciation following crises, the authors introduce nontraded goods to allow relative price changes to explain part of the nominal depreciation of the currency. They also add distribution costs to the domestic price of tradable goods. The retail sale of tradable goods requires an input of nontradable goods. These two assumptions are realistic and put a wedge between the domestic rate of inflation and the nominal rate of depreciation. In the theoretical model, this acts in the correct direction, allowing a depreciation that exceeds inflation. As we look at figure 7.3, however, we see that the rate of inflation for Mexico adjusts to the rate of depreciation of the peso over a three-year horizon. Indeed, from the crisis in December 1994 to the middle of 1997 and thereafter, we see that the CPI and the peso-dollar spot rate converge. I believe that the data portrayed in the figure suggests sluggish nominal price adjustment in Mexico with only a temporary real depreciation following the crisis.

We see a different time series relationship between the nominal exchange rate and the rate of domestic inflation following the Korean crisis in figure 7.4. Data for Thailand generate an analogous picture. The rise and fall in the won price of the dollar are not explained by the dynamics of relative prices in the model, but perhaps an interpretation (within the confines of the paper) is that private actors were uncertain about the eventual policy response of fiscal and monetary authorities in the wake of the crisis. It is also interesting to note that the CPI does not rise to the medium-term level of the won. In the context of the model, this seems to be represented by a permanent real depreciation sustained by ex post fiscal policies. The data, however, may reflect an exchange rate policy other than a pure float.

2. Velasco (1987) first modeled this process in an essay in memory of Diaz-Alejandro. Chinn and Kletzer (2000) and Dekle and Kletzer (forthcoming) provide somewhat different models with microeconomic detail of an increasingly fragile domestic banking system under a fixed exchange rate.

On the basis of figures 7.3 and 7.4 and the modelling of departures from purchasing power parity, I think that it would be useful to add nominal rigidities to the calibrated model. Sluggish nominal price adjustment could be used to match the rate of convergence of the price level to the exchange rate for Mexico and might allow the authors to simulate the exchange rate path for Korea. Indeed, it is sluggish nominal price adjustment that allows overshooting of the exchange rate in the standard monetary model of the exchange rate. A natural model of nominal price adjustment to adopt here would be the staggered price setting model of Calvo (1983).

The main contribution of this paper is its approach for calculating the fiscal adjustment to a financial crisis and how this adjustment can be reconciled with the ex post rates of nominal depreciation and domestic inflation. The authors have taken care in estimating unanticipated inflation tax revenues from the devaluation of various public-sector obligations. These include nominally indexed public debt of different maturities and public-sector wages, transfer payments, and similar obligations. The method used for distinguishing the impact of fiscal reforms, both explicit and implicit (reduction in the real value of public sector wages, and so forth), on the primary budget surplus is notably sensible. The authors do raise some appropriate ways to improve their estimates of the fiscal adjustment to crises, but the paper is already thorough and careful.

Some of the most interesting conclusions of this paper are the authors' estimates of how much fiscal adjustment remains for both Mexico and Korea. I think the comparison of historical rates of seigniorage revenue generation by each government to the remaining costs of the crisis is particularly useful. The conclusions that Mexico may have already or can be expected to meet the costs of the crisis through the printing press is consistent with the model, postcrisis rates of inflation and depreciation, and historical experience. Similarly, the conclusion that Korea has not yet paid the full fiscal costs of the crisis and is unlikely to do so by generating higher rates of seigniorage revenues is both an interesting and a useful conclusion of the calibration exercise. The calculation of fiscal adjustment in this paper is taken seriously, and the paper makes a very useful contribution to the literature on currency crisis management. I realize that calculating the fiscal response for each country is time-consuming, but I encourage the authors to extend their calculations of fiscal adjustment (and of how much adjustment remains) to Thailand, Indonesia, and Malaysia.

References

Buiter, Willem. 1987. Borrowing to defend the exchange rate and the timing and magnitude of speculative attacks. *Journal of International Economics* 23:221–39.
Burnside, Craig, Martin Eichenbaum, and Sergio Rebelo. 2001. Prospective deficits and the Asian currency crisis. *Journal of Political Economy* 109 (6): 1155–97.

Calvo, Guillermo A. 1983. Staggered prices in a utility-maximizing framework. *Journal of Monetary Economics* 12 (September): 383–98.

———. 1991. The perils of sterilization. *IMF Staff Papers* 38:921–26.

———. 1998. Varieties of capital account crises. In *The debt burden and its consequences for monetary policy,* ed. G. Calvo and M. King, 181–202. Basingstoke, England: Macmillan.

Chinn, Menzie D., and Kenneth M. Kletzer. 2000. International capital inflows, domestic financial intermediation, and financial crises under imperfect information. In *Financial crises in emerging markets,* ed. Rueven Glick, 196–237. New York: Cambridge University Press.

Dekle, Robert, and Kenneth M. Kletzer. Forthcoming. Domestic bank regulation and financial crises: Theory and empirical evidence from East Asia. In *Preventing currency crises in emerging markets,* ed. J. Frankel and S. Edwards. Chicago: University of Chicago Press.

Diaz-Alejandro, Carlos. 1985. Goodbye financial repression, hello financial crash. *Journal of Development Economics* 19:1–24.

Dooley, Michael P. 2000. A model of crises in emerging markets. *The Economic Journal* 110:256–72.

Kletzer, Kenneth M., and Ashoka Mody. 2000. Will self-protection policies safeguard emerging markets from crises? In *Managing financial and corporate distress: Lessons from Asia,* ed. C. Adams, R. Litan, and M. Pomerleano, 413–45. Washington, D.C.: Brookings Institution.

Krugman, Paul R. 1979. A model of balance-of-payments crises. *Journal of Money, Credit, and Banking* 11:311–25.

Velasco, Andrés. 1987. Financial crises and balance of payments crises: A simple model of the Southern Cone experience. *Journal of Development Economics* 27: 263–83.

Discussion Summary

Allan Drazen remarked that the model could be seen as too rich; in particular, it encompasses several types of uncertainty regarding the choice of future policy, suggesting that certain dynamics of the model can be explained by several different paths of expectations. He also recommended that the paper elaborate on the political considerations regarding the choice of crisis management policies.

Andrew K. Rose asked whether the model could be applied to different types of crises, such as the California energy crisis. In response, *Martin Eichenbaum* noted that the currency of California is pegged to the U.S. dollar and that the model explicitly rules out the possibility of default.

Nouriel Roubini noted that the pass-through of inflation has been very small. He added that exchange rates tend to overshoot and, as a plausible explanation, suggested that the possibility of financing of fiscal costs through seigniorage revenues would initially incur a large depreciation. He argued that once the financial markets realized that no additional money was printed, the exchange rate would revert.

Jong-Wha Lee asked whether it was possible to match permanent shifts in real exchange rates within the framework of the model.

Joshua Aizenman made a reference to the substantial current account adjustment of the Korean economy and wondered whether the model was able to replicate such magnitudes. He suggested that the model was missing the element of capital flight.

Olivier Jeanne remarked that the dynamics of the exchange rate in this model were quite reminiscent of the Dornbusch overshooting model. He also noted a discrepancy between the model and the facts: market participants did not seem to worry very much about the fiscal consequences of banking bailouts at the time of the Asian crisis. For example, in the months that followed the outburst of the crisis, the *Financial Times* Currency Forecaster referred to fiscal deficits only one time in its analysis of currency developments in Asia, and this was to worry that excessively tight fiscal policies would delay the recovery. This seems difficult to reconcile with the model. However, Martin Wolf recently presented in the *Financial Times* an analysis of the Turkish crisis that is very close to Burnside, Eichenbaum, and Rebelo's model. Maybe, he jokingly wondered, this is a case of reality coming closer to theory.

Andrew Berg commented on the calibration of the model and expressed concern with the choice of base period for the case of Mexico.

John McHale noted that it is very difficult for a crisis-hit economy to issue long-term nonindexed debt and politically hard to maintain nonindexed expenditures.

Sergio Rebelo noted that the main focus of the paper is the analysis of the role for seigniorage in the context of large depreciations absent of substantial inflation. He pointed out that the paper is concerned with crisis management rather than with the possible causes of the crisis. He agreed that a useful extension of the paper would be to build a stochastic model. With respect to the issue of overshooting, he pointed out that the paper discusses cases of economies other than Korea and Mexico. On the issue of the data set, he noted that prices are hard to measure because a large fraction of prices in emerging market economies are controlled by governments. As an example, he noted that this is the case for 20 percent of Mexican prices. As a further example, he pointed to the case of Korea, where the price of a good no longer in stock is set to the price of the good when it was in stock, thereby tending to understate inflation. In response to Roubini, he noted that prices and exchange rates display a large degree of comovement.

8

An Evaluation of Proposals to Reform the International Financial Architecture

Morris Goldstein

8.1 Introduction

The 1960s were the heyday of would-be reformers of the international monetary system, as widening cracks in the dollar exchange standard brought forth a host of reform proposals, eventually culminating in the early 1970s in the floating of major-currency exchange rates and in the first allocation of the new international reserve asset, the Special Drawing Rights (SDR). After a long lull, phase two of that reform effort has taken place over the past six or seven years under the banner of strengthening the international financial architecture (IFA).[1] In this latter case, the motivation for reform was supplied by the Mexican peso crisis of 1994–95 and, even more so, by the Asian financial crisis of 1997–98. As in the 1960s, the list of reform proposals has been long and varied.

In this paper, I provide a preliminary assessment of some of the leading reform proposals. Because the IFA covers such a wide subject area, it is necessary to be selective in a short paper.[2] Here, I have used the lending poli-

Morris Goldstein is the Dennis Weatherstone Senior Fellow at the Institute for International Economics.

The author is indebted to Andrew Berg, C. Fred Bergsten, Stanley Fischer, and John Williamson for helpful comments on an earlier draft. He is also grateful to Trond Augdal for superb research assistance.

"An Evaluation of Proposals to Reform the International Financial Architecture" by Morris Goldstein is (c) 2001, Institute for International Economics.

1. By the IFA, I mean the institutions, policies, and practices associated with the prevention and resolution of banking, currency, and debt crises, primarily (but not exclusively) in emerging economies.

2. For a detailed list of ongoing reform activities in the IFA, see IMF (2000c). An integrated analysis of IFA reform issues can be found in Eichengreen (1999) and Council on Foreign Relations Task Force (1999). Williamson (2000) presents an analysis of reform proposals, including several made by groups not covered in this paper.

cies and practices of the International Monetary Fund (IMF) as a convenient organizing device to discuss selected key issues in the reform debate.[3] More specifically, section 8.2 looks at proposals to increase the interest rate or reduce the maturity of IMF loans. Section 8.3 focuses on proposals to restrict the size of IMF rescue packages. Section 8.4, which covers the most ground, examines various dimensions of IMF conditionality, including proposals to replace ex post macroeconomic policy conditionality with prequalification based on structural policies, proposals to reduce the scope and detail of IMF conditionality, proposals to narrow currency regime choices or increase private-creditor burden sharing, and proposals to condition IMF assistance on the implementation of international financial standards. Finally, in section 8.5, I offer some concluding remarks on priorities for IFA reform over the next year or two.

Instead of attempting to review comprehensively the burgeoning literature on the IFA, I have selected a subset of leading reform proposals by drawing on a group of recent appraisals of the IFA, including the "Report of an Independent Task Force Sponsored by the Council on Foreign Relations" (hereafter, the CFR Report [1999] and CFR Task Force); the "Report of the International Financial Institution Advisory Commission" (hereafter, the Meltzer Report 2000 and Meltzer Commission); the "U.S. [Clinton Administration] Treasury Department Response to the International Financial Institution Advisory Commission" (hereafter, U.S. Treasury 2000); the "Report from Group of Seven Finance Ministers to the Heads of State and Government" at Fukuoka, Japan on 8 July 2000 (hereafter, G7 Finance Ministers 2000); the "Statement of G7 Finance Ministers and Central Bank Governors" at Palermo, Italy on 17 February 2001 (hereafter, G7 Communiqué 2001); speeches on the IMF by former U.S. Treasury Secretary Lawrence Summers at the London Business School in December 1999 (Summers 1999) and before the Congress International Monetary and Finance Committee in April 2000 (Summers 2000); and speeches on the need for an international lender of last resort, on the IMF, and on the IMF's Contingency Credit Line (CCL) by IMF First Deputy Managing Director Stanley Fischer in New York in January 1999 (Fischer 1999); in Washington, D.C. in February 2000 (Fischer 2000a); and in Mexico City in November 2000 (Fischer 2000b), respectively.

8.2   Interest Rates and Maturity of International Monetary Fund Loans

The proposition that an official lender of last resort should lend at a penalty rate dates at least as far back as Bagehot (1873). If the interest rate is too low, borrowers that are in trouble may not face a sufficient incentive

---

3. I have also used this format in Goldstein (2000). The present paper updates and expands upon the analysis in the earlier one.

to be more careful next time; they will also see the official lender as their first, not last, resort. In addition, borrowers that are not currently in trouble may take excessive risks because they know that there is a cheap source of credit available if things turn out badly.

Taking heed of Bagehot's famous counsel, it has often been suggested that the IMF increase the interest rate it charges borrowers. Countries that enter into standby and Extended Financing Facility (EFF) arrangements with the IMF pay an interest rate (called the *rate of charge*) that is a weighted average of short-term interest rates in the Group of Five countries (the United States, France, Germany, Japan, and the United Kingdom) plus a small surcharge. The rate of charge averaged 4.7 percent in 1997, 4.4 percent in 1998, 3.9 percent in 1999, and 5.1 percent in 2000. Developing countries have to pay much more than that to access private international capital markets, especially when they are encountering crisis conditions. For example, emerging-market bond spreads (relative to U.S. Treasuries) have fluctuated from 375 to 1,700 basis points since the outbreak of the Thai crisis in mid-1997. This large difference between IMF and private borrowing costs is sometimes characterized as an unwarranted subsidy that promotes both excessive borrowing from the IMF and borrower "moral hazard."

In late 1997, the IMF seemingly took some account of this criticism by endowing its newly created Supplemental Reserve Facility (SRF) with an interest rate of 300–500 basis points above the rate of charge on regular IMF loans (with the rate higher for longer repayments than for shorter ones). This higher interest rate, however, need not apply to the whole loan. For example, in the recent (December 2000) program with Argentina, only one fifth of the IMF's $13.7 billion commitment was made available under the SRF; the other 80 percent was provided under normal standby terms.

Former U.S. Treasury Secretary Summers (2000) concluded in April 2000 that "a strong case could be made for an overall increase in the basic rate of charge" (p. 5). It has been reported that in late summer 2000 the Group of Seven (G7) countries pushed the IMF's executive board for a modest increase in the rate of charge but that opposition from developing countries and some others blocked that proposal; in the end, the compromise was to impose an interest rate premium only for "large" IMF loans; see section 8.3.

The Meltzer Commission (2000) concluded that IMF interest rates were much too low; specifically, they proposed that IMF borrowing cost be set at a premium over the sovereign yield paid by the borrowing country one week prior to applying for an IMF loan. The U.S. Treasury (2000) argued that such a penalty rate would be too high—so high as to worsen the underlying financial position of the borrowing country. Stanley Fischer (1999), the IMF's former first deputy managing director, has maintained that the penalty rate charged by the lender of last resort should be defined relative to the interest rate during normal times (not one week prior to the crisis), because the objective of the rescue is to achieve the good, nonpanic, equilibrium. This would imply penalty rates closer to SRF terms than to "Meltzer" terms.

If SRF interest rate terms were extended to all nonconcessional IMF lending, I suspect that the impact would be greater on the speed with which countries repay their IMF borrowings than on the frequency of IMF borrowing.

When countries finally decide to ask the IMF for emergency financial assistance, it is usually in dire circumstances when financing from the private capital markets is unavailable in large amounts. Politicians who are fighting for survival are not likely to be deterred from going to the IMF by a higher interest rate (see Eichengreen 2000). In this connection, it is relevant to note that neither Turkey nor Argentina—both of which recently secured IMF financing packages in excess of 500 percent of their IMF quotas—were apparently dissuaded by either SRF interest rate terms or the new interest rate premium for large loans. All of this suggests that the decision to go to the IMF is apt to be less price elastic than the decision of how rapidly to repay the IMF loan—especially if the interest rate rises (as with the SRF) the longer the loan is outstanding. Crisis countries have more room for maneuvering at the time of repayment than they do at the outbreak of the crisis.

We should also not forget that a big difference between (upper credit tranche) IMF loans and loans from the private sector is that the former come with strong policy conditionality. When comparing IMF loans to private-sector loans, we have to look at the "conditionality-equivalent" interest rate, not just the nominal interest rate. A strong hint that conditionality matters is that, despite the large difference in nominal borrowing costs between the IMF and private markets, we do not observe emerging economies tripping over themselves in a rush to come to the IMF at the first sign of balance-of-payments trouble. Instead, countries come to the IMF late in the game. Conditionality (along with the IMF's senior creditor status) also gives IMF loans a higher probability of repayment than loans made by private creditors, implying that the market-clearing nominal interest rate for IMF loans is lower than that for private-sector ones. Again, the implication is that an increase in the rate of charge may not have a huge impact on the frequency of IMF borrowing (as long as IMF conditionality remains intrusive in both scope and detail).

What about the maturity of IMF loans? Standby arrangements cover a one- to three-year period, and drawings are phased on a quarterly basis. Repayments on standby arrangements used to be mandated within 3.25 to 5 years of each drawing; under the so-called facilities initiative agreed upon in September, 2000, repayment maturities were shortened to 2.25 to 4 years. Extended Financing Facility arrangements, which are meant to address adjustment problems that require bold structural transformation of the economy, normally run for three years (and can be extended for a fourth) and have phasing comparable to standby arrangements. The same facilities initiative also shorted repayment maturities for EFFs—from 4.5 to 10 years of the drawing to 4.5 to 7 years. Because the SRF was meant to deal with "exceptional balance of payments difficulties due to a large, short-term financing need resulting from the sudden disruptive loss of market confidence," it was created with shorter than normal repayment terms, namely 1 to 1.5 years after each disbursement.

The Meltzer Commission (2000) favored a more drastic cutback in the maturity of IMF loans—to a maximum of 120 days with only one allowable rollover (leading to a maximum maturity of 240 days). They argue that the IMF ought to be lending solely to counter liquidity crises (not insolvency crises) and that liquidity crises are typically very short-lived. The Meltzer Commission noted that prolonged use of IMF resources has been a serious shortcoming of IMF lending, with twenty four of the IMF's member countries in debt to the IMF in thirty or more of the past fifty years, and forty six more countries in debt for at least twenty of those years.

The U.S. Treasury (2000) called the Meltzer repayment period "unrealistically short." It noted that even in recent success cases, countries needed much longer than four months to be in a position to repay IMF loans. Fischer (1999) rejected the notion that it is straightforward to distinguish cases of illiquidity from insolvency. He argued that this distinction is often indeterminate in a crisis because it depends on how well the crisis is managed.

The G7 finance ministers (2000), along with former U.S. Treasury Secretary Summers (2000), have acknowledged that prolonged use of IMF resources needs to be more strongly discouraged, although they do not suggest a specific maturity cap. They would rely on an SRF-like price incentive to encourage prompt repayment. The G7 finance ministers' report (2000) argued that for all nonconcessional IMF facilities "the interest rate should increase on a graduated basis the longer countries have IMF resources outstanding." They appeared to be aiming for something closer to SRF maturities (one to two years) than to Meltzer maturities (four to eight months). In addition, there was a definite suggestion to make more selective and less frequent resort to the longer-maturity EFF window (in favor of shorter-maturity standby arrangements). Summers (2000) argued that the countries that are likely to fit the EFF's (new) requirements are lower-income transition countries that are undertaking far-reaching structural reforms to secure stabilization, and countries with incomes just above the threshold for concessional IMF financing under the Poverty Reduction and Growth Facility.

The IMF's Articles of Agreement (Article I) speak of making the IMF's general resources "temporarily available" to members dealing with balance-of-payments problems. This is in sharp contrast to the track record of frequent prolonged use of IMF resources. Consequently, moving to reduce the maturity and repayment periods for IMF loans makes sense. Charging higher interest rates for longer repayment periods ought to help promote that objective. Likewise, making resort to the EFF less frequent should keep the IMF from getting too involved in those longer-term structural aspects of development that are best handled by the World Bank (see discussion in section 8.4 on the scope of IMF conditionality). It seems neither necessary nor desirable, however, to insist on repayment within a few months' time, as do the Meltzer Commission recommendations. Drawing on a sample of fifty industrial and developing countries over the 1975–97 period, an IMF (1998) study found that it typically takes over one and one-half years for GDP growth to return to trend after a currency crisis, and more than three years for output growth to recover from a banking crisis; the recovery times for severe currency crises and for twin crises (that is, for currency crises that were accompanied by banking crises) were even longer.[4] The (output) recoveries from both the Asian crisis and the Mexican crisis have been unusually rapid. Policy should not be set solely in terms of the best performers. Moreover, in many cases, the relatively rapid resumption of market access was accelerated by large-scale bailouts and "blanket guarantees" (including large, uninsured creditors of banks)—bailouts that we should seek to avoid or reduce in the future. Additionally, in cases in which the illiquidity/insolvency distinction is more blurred (e.g., a crisis in which the holes in the balance sheets of banks or corporations are hard to gauge quickly), it will be helpful to have longer than eight months for countries to repay.

The current mood on repayment maturities can be contrasted with that prevailing at the time the longer-maturity IMF lending windows (the EFF, the Structural Adjustment Facility, and the Enhanced Structural Adjustment Facility) were created. At that time, the maturity of IMF loans was also under attack, but from the opposite direction (see, e.g., Helleiner 1987; Camdessus 1987; and Conable 1987). Then, the criticism was that IMF lending programs were too short-sighted, too focused on correcting balance-of-payments disequilibria, and not focused enough on promoting sustainable economic growth. Demand management alone could not do the job; supply measures were needed, and these would take time. The recommended prescription was greater financial support for structural reforms, along with longer program periods and repayment maturities to allow those structural reforms to take root and bear fruit. Now that many more developing countries have access to private capital markets, that private capital flows have become extremely large relative to official finance, and that prolonged use of IMF resources has become a widespread problem, the pendulum is swinging back the other way.

8.3   Size of International Monetary Fund Loans

Size is another important dimension of IMF lending. The IMF's normal access limits for its loans are expressed in terms of a country's quota in the

4. Goldstein, Kaminsky, and Reinhart (2000) also find longer recovery periods after crises (particularly after banking and twin crises) than implied by "Meltzer" repayment maturities.

IMF. The normal access limits are 100 percent of quota annually and 300 percent on a cumulative basis. By this metric, the amounts committed under rescue packages for Mexico (1995), Thailand (1997), Indonesia (1997), Brazil (1998), Argentina (2000), and Turkey (2000) were exceptionally large, because they were in the range of 500–830 percent of quota. The rescue package for South Korea (1997) was much larger still—1,900 percent of quota.[5]

Amounts actually disbursed under the Asian rescue packages were, however, considerably smaller than amounts committed. More fundamentally, the IMF has maintained that metrics other than quotas (or absolute dollar figures) should be used to evaluate the size of packages. Fischer (1999) and Mussa (1999) have noted that IMF quotas have not kept pace with the growth of GDP, trade, or capital mobility, and therefore that quotas constitute a poor benchmark for evaluating the size of IMF loans. Fischer noted that if the IMF quotas were today the same size relative to output of IMF member countries as they were in 1945, quotas would be three times larger; adjusting quotas for the growth of world trade over the same period would leave them nine times larger. Mussa argued that official financing in the Asian crisis was not large relative to the decline in gross private capital flows during that period, or to the crisis countries' current-account adjustments, or to the huge output losses borne by the crisis countries.

Much of the recent concern has been that large rescue packages may contribute to moral hazard on the part of private creditors to emerging economies. If private creditors come to expect that IMF loans to emerging-economy governments will make these governments more capable and more likely to bail them out in cases of adverse circumstances, then private creditors will act less prudently in monitoring the performance of borrowers. Put in other words, if private creditors are shielded unduly from the consequences of poor lending and investment decisions, market discipline will suffer and future crises will become more likely.

It is widely acknowledged that moral hazard is a problem with all insurance arrangements. The solution is not to have no insurance but rather to limit the amount of payment (e.g., coinsurance or deductibles) or to price the insurance appropriately (i.e., with higher insurance rates for more risky policy holders). Critics of large rescue packages also concede that a lender of last resort, by providing emergency assistance to an illiquid (but not insolvent) borrower and thereby preventing a costly default and its spillover to other borrowers, serves a useful function for the economy as a whole. Moreover, it is recognized that equity holders and bond holders suffered large losses in the Asian crisis and that banks took a sizable hit during the Russian crisis. Still, most of the critics conclude that smaller IMF rescue packages would reduce lender moral hazard, improve market discipline and

---

5. One of the reasons the rescue package for Korea was so large relative to its quota is that Korea's quota is so small for its economic size.

crisis prevention, and prevent IMF money from financing sustained capital flight. In addition, smaller packages would provide a practical mechanism for introducing private-sector involvement (because any shortfall between debt payments and liquid assets inclusive of IMF loans would need to be covered, one way or another, by the private sector).

At the same time, even those who regard the (lender) moral hazard criticism as greatly exaggerated acknowledge that IMF rescue packages in the run-up to the Russian crisis of 1998 were too large and were a key reason that investors continued to pour money into Russian government securities (GKOs) despite weak economic fundamentals. They argue, however, that there is no empirical evidence suggesting that moral hazard was driving private capital flows to Mexico or to Asia in the run-up to their crises, or that the composition of capital flows has since then switched in favor of the lenders (banks) usually singled out as the main beneficiaries of lender moral hazard (see Zhang 1999; Eichengreen and Hausman 2000). They also emphasize that IMF rescue packages are loans, not grants, with reasonable interest rates and a history of very low default; because there are no losses on these loans, IMF lending cannot be considered a "direct" source of moral hazard.[6] Moreover, they maintain that moral hazard is small relative to the real hazards facing developing countries in today's capital markets.

Even though the Meltzer Report (2000) concluded that IMF loans generated serious moral hazard problems ("the importance of the moral hazard problem cannot be overstated," 33), the Commission did not recommend smaller IMF rescue packages as an antidote for that problem. Echoing the Bagehot (1873) guideline that a lender of last resort should "lend freely" (albeit at a penalty rate and on good collateral), they proposed that the IMF lend on a substantial scale—indeed, up to one year's tax revenue—to countries that have met certain prequalification criteria. This could produce massive rescue packages, far larger than any loans the IMF has extended heretofore. As noted by the U.S. Treasury (2000), such a lending guideline applied to, say, Brazil in 1997 would have resulted in a $139 billion rescue package—3,088 percent of Brazil's quota in the IMF and almost ten times as large as the IMF rescue package extended to Brazil in early 1999. The Meltzer Commission proposed instead that moral hazard problems be tackled by encouraging financial institutions in the borrowing countries to adopt higher standards of safety and soundness and by discouraging reliance on short-term borrowing.

The CFR Task Force issued the strongest call for a return to smaller IMF

---

6. See Mussa (1999). He refers to "indirect" moral hazard as a situation in which international financial support facilitates moral hazard by national governments. The Meltzer Report (2000) has this in mind when it charges that the IMF "did little [in Asia] to end the use of the banking and financial systems to finance government-favored projects, eliminate so-called 'crony capitalism' and corruption, or promote safer and sounder banking and financial systems" (33).

loans. The CFR Report (1999) argued that the IMF should distinguish "country crises" (crises that do not threaten the functioning of the international financial system) from "systemic crises" and should treat the two differently. For country crises, the IMF should return to normal access limits (100–300 percent of quota). For systemic crises, the IMF should turn to systemic lending windows—the existing New Arrangement to Borrow (NAB) if the crisis is mainly the result of the borrowing country's policy inadequacies and an IMF program is needed to correct those policy shortcomings, and a newly created "contagion facility" if the country is mainly a victim of contagion. To activate either the NAB or the contagion facility, a supermajority of creditor countries would have to reach the judgment that the crisis was systemic. Once activated, however, the systemic facilities could provide large access, and the contagion facility would be funded by a special allocation of IMF Special Drawing Rights (SDRs).

According to the CFR Report (1999), smaller IMF loans for country crises would still permit some cushioning of the recession, some smoothing operations in foreign exchange markets, and a modest contribution toward the cost of bank restructuring and recapitalization. These loans would not, however, be large enough to support the defense of overvalued fixed exchange rates or to bail out large uninsured private creditors. It is often suggested that there is a certain unique size of an IMF rescue package that is needed to restore confidence in the crisis country. The CFR Report rejected that view. It notes that some empirical studies have found that asset prices typically fail to stabilize right after the signing of an IMF program (see Brealey and Kaplanis 1999); instead, stability comes later, when there is stronger evidence of political leadership and when there are concrete policy actions to deal with policy shortcomings. Yes, the CFR Task Force acknowledged that smaller IMF rescue packages would probably increase the cost of market borrowing for developing countries and perhaps reduce somewhat the flow of private capital to them. However, it argues that because net private capital flows to emerging economies in the 1990–96 period were too large and the interest rate spread on that borrowing too low, some moderate move in the opposite direction would be no bad thing.

By going to smaller IMF loans for country crises, by making IMF loans to countries with unsustainable debt profiles conditional on greater private-creditor burden sharing, by encouraging all countries to include "collective action clauses" in their sovereign bond contracts, and by allowing the IMF to approve standstills declared by the debtors with unsustainable debt profiles, it would be possible, the CFR Report (1999) believes, to reduce significantly indirect (lender) moral hazard stemming from IMF rescue packages.[7]

---

7. On the importance of collection action clauses and creditor steering committees, see Eichengreen (1999).

The U.S. Treasury (2000) has rejected the very large IMF loans implicit in the Meltzer Commission recommendations as "unrealistic and undesirable" and as surpassing the financial capacity of the IMF and increasing moral hazard.

It was only relatively recently that the U.S. Treasury and G7 finance ministers came out in favor of an incentive to reduce the scale of IMF loans. In September 2000, as part of the facilities initiative, the IMF executive board agreed to impose an interest rate surcharge for large IMF loans: 100 basis points for IMF loans equal to 200 percent of quota, rising to 300 basis points for loans above 300 percent of quota.

The CFR view and the U.S. Treasury view on the scale of IMF financing differ on at least three grounds.

First, as regards constraints or disincentives on large rescue packages, the Clinton Treasury preferred a price (interest rate) mechanism, whereas the CFR Task Force preferred a quantity-cum-governance constraint (i.e., loans above 300 percent of quota would have to be deemed systemic by a super-majority of creditors, and those official creditors—not the IMF—would bear the credit risk). A disadvantage of the interest rate approach (and of leaving the decision to be made by the borrower) is that countries in crisis may be willing to pay a large premium to get enough IMF resources to defend overvalued exchange rates or to bail out uninsured private creditors, even if there is no systemic risk involved. If such a demand for large rescue packages is relatively price-inelastic—as I believe it is—then lender moral hazard will not be much deterred by such a (moderate) size-related premium.

One aim of requiring super-majorities for large packages is to counteract the bias for creditor countries to regard crises in their own neighborhood as systemic (even if they are not). Another aim is to counteract the bias toward discounting unduly the effect of a bail-out today on the probability of future crises. The disadvantage of the quantity-cum-governance approach is the risk of ineffectiveness or inaction in the face of a genuine systemic threat: that is, a super-majority of official creditors may allow the crisis to spread by refusing to extend the larger loan.

Difference number two is that the Treasury's approach gives more discretion to IMF management and to U.S. authorities in deciding when to activate very large rescue packages. The definition of *exceptional circumstances*, which activates abnormally large access under standby and EFF arrangements, and the definition of *systemic*, which activates very large access under the SRF and CCL, are in the eye of the beholder and do not require super-majority consent. In contrast, the CFR approach makes the decision to activate very large access one is that is shared more equally among a wider group of creditor countries.

The financing of very large rescue packages constitutes yet a third difference. Under existing IMF policy, the large access afforded under the SRF and CCL are financed out of the IMF's existing quota pool of resources. This runs the risk that if there are many serious financial crises occurring simultaneously and if it has been some time since the IMF has had a quota increase (as in 1998), then the IMF may not have enough resources to put out such a large and contagious fire. In contrast, the CFR approach provides new money for systemic contagion cases by financing large access with a special SDR allocation.

Those favoring large IMF rescue packages sometimes argue that they are the financial analogue to the "[Colin] Powell doctrine" on military intervention: be selective in choosing where to intervene, but once the decision is made to go in, employ "overwhelming force" to guarantee a successful outcome. In my view, that analogy is flawed in at least three respects.

To begin with, the IMF's de facto capacity to mobilize overwhelming financial force (along the lines recommended in the Meltzer Report) is limited. Unlike national central banks, the IMF cannot create money. Even in periods when the IMF's liquidity situation is relatively comfortable, I doubt that the IMF's main shareholders would be comfortable approving loans that run potentially to thousands of percent of the borrowing country's quota (in the absence of an extraordinary systemic threat). Where sovereign entities are involved, willingness to pay needs to be assessed along with ability to repay, and actual and perceived inequities in burden sharing linked to the repayment of IMF loans—both across groups within the borrowing country (e.g., taxpayers versus large domestic creditors of banks) and across countries (e.g., workers in the borrowing country versus private creditors in the lending countries)—means that willingness to pay is not a sure thing. Unlike national central banks, the IMF does ask for collateral on its loans. Although arrears to the IMF have been relatively infrequent in the past, they are hardly unknown. In fact, the way the IMF currently calculates its rate of charge has been influenced by a brief but unhappy upsurge in arrears in the 1980s. This does not deny that the essence of a good official crisis lender is that it is willing to supply loans in a crisis to solvent borrowers in amounts not available from private lenders. However, it does underline that there are nontrivial repayment risks associated with very large IMF loans. My reading is that large IMF rescue packages are already unpopular in the legislatures of some large creditor countries. They would surely be much more so if there were a large default to the IMF and to creditor governments. The reality is that the IMF will not be given the same lender-of-last-resort capability as a national central bank even if the penalties for defaulting on an IMF loan were much larger than they are today.

Second, the effectiveness of large financial force in restoring stability to countries is less assured than in the military example. With country rescues, winning the confidence game requires good crisis management and, in particular, good macroeconomic and supporting policies. If crisis management is poor, then the financing gap will get much larger (via capital flight) than originally assumed and even a very large IMF loan is likely to be inadequate to the task at hand. The spat between Prime Minister Ecevit and President Sezer (just before two important Turkish Treasury Bill auctions) is illustrative of how quickly a large IMF program can lose market confidence when prospects for policy implementation deteriorate unexpectedly. In contrast, if the accompanying policies are good, it may be possible to restore stability and confidence with IMF loans within normal access limits. The fact that asset prices do not seem to stabilize immediately after the announcement of an IMF program supports the view that the amount of IMF money is not all that matters, and maybe not even the main thing that matters (see, e.g., Haldane 1999).

Third, even large IMF loans that are repaid on time and that are effective in restoring stability carry a moral hazard risk that private lenders will be even less careful in the future in assessing the creditworthiness of borrowers. Such moral hazard seems more important in the financial sphere than in the military one. Some observers have dismissed the practical significance of lender moral hazard by noting that several empirical studies have failed to find a link between earlier large rescue packages (e.g., Mexico in 1994–95 or Asian crisis countries in 1997) and the postcrisis behavior of interest rate spreads for emerging-market borrowers.

A new study by Dell'Ariccia, Gödde, and Zettelmeyer (2000) suggests that most of the previous work on the empirical significance of lender moral hazard–cum–IMF rescue packages is methodologically flawed.[8] They argue persuasively that a good event study has to satisfy three conditions: (a) it has to change the public perception of the extent or the character of future international crisis lending; (b) it has to be unexpected (otherwise the reaction to the event could show up before the event rather than after it); and (c) it must not lead to a reassessment of risks other than through the expectations of future international rescues.[9] The events following the Russian default in August 1998 come closest to meeting these requirements for a valid experiment. They also show that it is inappropriate to look only at impact of the event on the average level of spreads for a single country; instead, the test should look to changes in the level of spreads in a wide range of countries, to changes in the sensitivity with which spreads react to fundamentals, and to changes in the cross-country variance of spreads (also controlling for fundamentals). In the end, their results find strong evidence consistent with the existence of (lender) moral hazard. At the very least, the findings of Dell'Ariccia, Godde, and Zettelmeyer should give pause to those who dismiss lender moral hazard in the 1990s as peanuts.

If large IMF rescue packages are to be discouraged, there remains the

8. This criticism would apply, for example, to Zhang (1999) and Lane and Phillips (2000).

9. Because rescue funds are fungible, there is also the complication that the indirect, moral-hazard impact of international rescues may extend to a variety of domestic institutions and domestic creditors, and some of these may not issue publicly traded debt.

question of how best to do so. Not surprisingly (given my role as project director and author of the CFR Report), I regard the CFR approach to discouraging large rescues as preferable to the interest rate–premium approach recently adopted by the IMF's Executive Board.

8.4   International Monetary Fund Policy Conditionality

Yet another element of Bagehot's (1873) guideline for a (national) lender of last resort is that lending should be done on "good collateral." Good collateral serves several purposes. It provides a test of whether the borrower is just illiquid rather than insolvent (i.e., a solvent borrower has good collateral to pledge; an insolvent one does not). Because the good collateral has market value, it safeguards the solvency of the lender. It also avoids the potentially time-consuming process of negotiating and monitoring conditions on the borrower that would maximize the likelihood of repayment. Additionally, it reduces (borrower) moral hazard by discouraging the borrower from holding risky assets that would not be accepted as good collateral.

The IMF does not lend to countries against collateral. Instead, it lends to countries that have a balance-of-payment need under "adequate safeguards." What are these safeguards? The main one is the policy action(s)—so-called conditionality—that the borrowing country agrees to undertake to qualify for the loans. These policy conditions are meant to correct the underlying balance-of-payments problem and to restore the borrower's ability to repay the IMF. Policy conditions are negotiated and agreed between the borrowing country and the IMF. These conditions typically cover macroeconomic policies (i.e., monetary and fiscal policies), exchange rate policy, and a range of structural policies (e.g., financial-sector policies, trade policy, reform of public enterprises, etc). As a further safeguard, IMF disbursements are made in phases or "tranches" (rather than all at once), with the ability to draw that tranche dependent on the borrower's meeting certain predetermined performance criteria.[10] Because some other lenders (both official and private) condition their lending to the borrowing country on either the existence or the successful implementation of an IMF program, the amount of funding that the borrowing country can lose by not meeting the performance criteria is usually larger than the loss of IMF support. If the borrower does not repay the IMF on time, it faces loss of access to future IMF lending and ultimately even expulsion. Moreover, because member countries regard their creditor position in the IMF as part of their international reserves, the IMF has consistently maintained the view that it cannot reschedule its loans to countries with debt-servicing difficulties.

---

10. These performance criteria are meant to be within the control of the borrower. If unexpected developments intrude that prevent the borrower from meeting the performance criteria, the borrower may be granted a waiver to draw anyway.

Some observers submit that the explicit and implicit costs that would be associated with not repaying IMF loans give the IMF a de facto if not de jure status as a preferred (senior) creditor.

Supporters of the IMF would concede that the above description of IMF conditionality does not do justice to the problems often encountered in its implementation. In some cases, negotiations over policy conditions can be long and contentious, and the borrowing country may never take "ownership" of the program. Nonobservance of performance criteria can lead to interruptions in IMF drawings. Sometimes funding may continue despite nonobservance of performance criteria because of political pressures from a variety of sources (including the IMF's major shareholder countries). In still other cases, the economic analysis and advice embodied in the policy conditions may be inappropriate for the unfolding economic conditions on the ground (e.g., the recession may be deeper than anticipated when the program was formulated) and revisions to program design may be too slow in coming. Borrowing countries that do not repay on time may either get de facto rescheduling (extension of new IMF loans to repay earlier ones) or may get many chances to repay before their eligibility for new loans is cut off or before they get expelled. Still, supporters argue that the existing system of conditionality works reasonably well most of the time and that, just as importantly, it works better than the alternatives.

Here, I take up four dimensions of policy conditionality that have been much debated in the discussion of the need for IMF reform, namely, (a) ex post policy conditionality versus ex ante conditionality (i.e., prequalification based on structural-policy preconditions); (b) the scope of conditionality; (c) currency regime and private-sector burden-sharing aspects of conditionality; and (d) implementation of international financial standards.[11]

8.4.1   Ex Post Policy Conditionality versus Preconditions (Ex Ante Conditionality)

The Meltzer Report (2000) was extremely critical of the existing (ex post) approach to IMF conditionality. The majority in the Meltzer Commission (2000) concluded that detailed IMF policy conditionality has "burdened IMF programs in recent years and made such programs unwieldy, highly conflictive, time consuming to negotiate, and often ineffectual" (7). They went on to argue that there was no evidence of systematic, predictable effects from most of the IMF's policy conditionality. Later on, they maintained (not entirely consistently) both that if the IMF did not exist, the market would force a country in crisis to follow similar policies and that IMF policy conditionality in the Asian crisis actually made the crisis coun-

11. There is also an issue of whether IMF conditionality should supercede any conditionality that would be linked to crisis lending from "regional" official crisis lenders (such as an Asian Monetary Fund).

tries worse off than they would have been without IMF assistance. Put in other words, when the bottom-line results in IMF program countries look good, the outcome would have happened anyway (without the IMF); and when the results look bad, they reflect the negative influence of IMF policy conditionality and advice.

The Meltzer Report (2000) did not recommend that the IMF insist on "good collateral" as a substitute for its policy conditionality (despite the fact that the Commission's chairman favored this prescription in his recent writings on how to redesign the Fund; see, e.g., Meltzer 1999). Some have argued that if countries in crises were able to satisfy a stringent collateral requirement, then they wouldn't need the IMF (i.e., they would be able to use this collateral to borrow from private creditors); hence, little "additional" financial stability would be obtained by such a reform. Although one can point to episodes in which even borrowers with good collateral could not get credit in a panic, perhaps the Commission gave this "additionality" argument some weight. Or perhaps the Commission became convinced that giving the IMF a more established de jure status as a preferred creditor—lending only to countries that met certain prequalification requirements (see discussion below)—would provide sufficient protection for the IMF against credit risk. Or perhaps the collateral idea simply was not deemed attractive enough to elicit majority support either within the Commission or outside more generally.

The Meltzer Report (2000) did recommend that the IMF eliminate most of the macroeconomic and structural policy conditions that have characterized (upper credit tranche) IMF programs in the past. It proposed instead that countries qualifying for short-term IMF liquidity assistance would need to meet the following preconditions: (a) freedom of entry and operation for foreign financial institutions; (b) regular and timely publication of the maturity structure of outstanding sovereign and guaranteed debt and off–balance sheet liabilities; (c) adequate capitalization of commercial banks, either by a significant equity position à la international standards or by subordinated debt held by nongovernmental and unaffiliated entities; and (d) a proper fiscal requirement. These new rules would be phased in over a period of five years.

Those developing countries that met these preconditions would be eligible immediately for short-term liquidity assistance; those that did not meet these preconditions would not be eligible (unless there is an unusual situation in which the "crisis poses a threat the global economy"). Larger industrial countries would not be eligible for IMF liquidity assistance; their central banks would assume this task.

In order to establish the seniority of IMF claims on borrowing countries, members would exempt the IMF from negative pledge clauses and would give the IMF specific legal priority with respect to all other creditors (secured and unsecured). Countries that defaulted on IMF debts would not be eligible for loans or grants from other multilateral agencies or other member countries.

The Meltzer Commission plan would not prohibit the IMF from continuing to offer advice on a wider range of economic policies (including the currency regime) in its Article IV consultations with developing countries; moreover, these reports would be published promptly. Industrial countries could opt out of these IMF consultations if they wished. However, the IMF could NOT make its advice on economic policy a condition for its loans. Nor could the IMF make other types of loans for whatever purpose. Longer-term institutional assistance to foster economic development would be the responsibility of a reconstructed World Bank or regional development banks. The IMF's Poverty Reduction and Growth Facility (PRGF) would be closed.

The structural policy preconditions in the Meltzer Report have been criticized on four counts.

First, there is the charge that the (majority in the) Meltzer Commission misread history. This criticism is evident within the Meltzer Commission itself from the dissent penned by four commission members appointed by the Congressional Democrats (namely, C. Fred Bergsten, Richard Huber, Jerome Levinson, and Esteban Torres).[12] In looking at the fifty-year tenure of the IMF and the World Bank (hereafter, the IFIs), the dissenters concluded that "the bottom line of the 'era of the IFIs,' despite obvious shortcomings, has been an unambiguous success of historic proportions in both economic and social terms" (119). They note, in addition, that almost all the crisis countries of the past few years, ranging from Mexico to the countries of East Asia to Brazil, have experienced rapid "V-shaped" recoveries; that never in human history have so many people advanced so rapidly out of abject poverty; and that more than half of the world's population now lives under democratic governments. In short, "the allegations of the report simply fail to square with history" (121).

The CFR Report (1999), while stressing the need for IMF reform, painted a more favorable picture of IMF involvement. For example, in evaluating the IMF's role during the Asian crisis, the report concluded: "As costly as the Asian crisis has been, no doubt we would have seen even deeper recessions, more competitive devaluations, more defaults, and more resort to trade restrictions if no financial support had been provided by the IMF to the crisis countries. . . . [T]here can be legitimate differences of view

---

12. The Meltzer Commission had eleven members. Six of those (Allan Meltzer, chairman; Charles Calomiris, Tom Campbell, Edwin Feulner, Lee Hoskins, and Manuel Johnson) were appointed by the Congressional Republicans; the other five members (Fred Bergsten, Richard Huber, Jerome Levinson, Jeffrey Sachs, and Esteban Torres) were appointed by the Congressional Democrats. In the end, eight members (all six Republican appointees, Jeff Sachs, and Richard Huber) voted for the report, and four members were opposed (including Richard Huber, who supported both the majority and minority reports).

about IMF advice on fiscal and monetary policy in the crisis countries. . . . But we had a look in the 1930s at how serious global instability is handled without an IMF, and few would want to return to that world" (88).

The IMF interprets the existing empirical studies on the effects of IMF programs differently than did the Meltzer Commission. Fischer (2000a), for example, summed up the recent studies as follows: "The consensus view now seems to be that in a typical [IMF] program, economic activity will be depressed in the short term as macroeconomic policies are tightened, but that growth subsequently revives as structural reforms take root. Meanwhile, the balance of payments improves, removing the need for further Fund financing. The impact on inflation is usually favorable . . . although in general not large enough to be statistically significant" (8).

A second line of criticism is that the Meltzer preconditions would suffice neither to prevent financial crises nor to achieve the balance-of-payments adjustment necessary to restore countries' ability to repay the IMF; some critics would go farther and argue that reliance of these preconditions alone would promote financial instability.

Again, the dissenting group within the Meltzer Commission reached conclusions at odds with those of the majority group. Specifically, the former argued that the majority would have the IMF totally ignore the macroeconomic policy stance of the crisis country, thereby sanctioning IMF support for countries with runaway budget deficits and profligate monetary policies. They go on to conclude that "this would virtually eliminate any prospect of overcoming the crisis; it would instead enable the country to perpetuate the very policies that triggered the crisis in the first place and thus greatly increase the risk of global instability" (121). They also note that the "proper fiscal requirement" included in the preconditions is left undefined in the report and, if left open to content, would require IMF conditionality of the same type that the majority rejects.[13]

The U.S. Treasury (2000) agreed with the Meltzer Commission dissenters on the effectiveness of the proposed Meltzer preconditions: "the proposed eligibility criteria are too narrow. Even where they are met, they would be unlikely to protect economies from the broad range of potential causes of crises. The criteria focus on the financial sector, and yet even problems that surface in the financial sector often have their roots in deeper economic and structural weaknesses" (17). The treasury worries further that combining large IMF disbursements with ineffective eligibility requirements could actually increase the amount of moral hazard in the system.

Criticism number three is that it would prove neither feasible nor desir-

---

13. My IIE colleague, C. Fred Bergsten, who was a member of both the Meltzer Commission and the CFR Task Force, maintains that both the undefined "proper fiscal requirement" and the systemic override (that allows assistance to countries that do not meet the prequalification criteria if there is a threat to the global economy) were added to the Meltzer Report at the last minute in an attempt to reduce the impact of the joint dissent.

able to exclude completely from IMF financing countries that did not meet the structural preconditions. Fischer (1999) offers the following assessment on that point: "It is doubtful that the international community would be indifferent to the fate of countries that do not meet the pre-qualification requirements, or to the instability that might be generated when they get into trouble and are denied help. In practice, in such circumstances the large industrial countries would probably find another, less transparent, way to help the country in crisis" (10). I suppose the retort of the Meltzer Commission would be that other ways of assisting countries that don't meet the prequalification requirement are to be preferred to IMF assistance because they would be more (not less) transparent and would not risk turning the IMF into a political slush fund.

The all-or-nothing approach to eligibility for IMF assistance was rejected by the CFR Task Force. In its recommendations, countries that follow a set of "good housekeeping" crisis prevention policies qualify for a lower interest rate from the IMF than do countries that do not follow these policies. However, the latter group is not excluded from IMF assistance.

In its evaluation of the Meltzer Commission's prequalification criteria, the U.S. Treasury (2000) argued: "this recommendation would preclude the IMF from being able to respond to financial emergencies and support recovery in the vast majority of its members, possibly including all of the emerging market countries affected by the financial crises of 1997 and 1998.[14] The exclusive focus on relatively strong emerging economies would leave out most of the Fund's membership, notably all low income countries and many transition economics" (17).

Yet a fourth set of criticisms of the Meltzer preconditions is that their implementation would involve more serious operational problems and raise more questions than the authors imply. For one thing, as argued in the CFR Report (1999), it is far from clear that prequalification would deter speculative attacks. Hong Kong, for example, had $60–100 billion of reserves in 1997–98 and pledges of financial support from Beijing; yet it faced strong attacks on its currency during that period. For another, it is probably naive to assume that the decision to declare countries that originally met the preconditions as ineligible (because of subsequent backtracking on compliance) would not be subject to strong political pressures. Also, the report does not discuss who would monitor compliance with the preconditions; if the answer is that national regulatory authorities would do it (see the later discussion on international financial standards), then there is a serious question of whether those judgments would be objective. Last but not least, there are questions about whether some of the preconditions would have their intended effects. For example, Garber (2000) has argued that a subor-

---

14. Bergsten (2000) made essentially the same point in earlier testimony on the Meltzer Report before the Senate Committee on Banking, Housing, and Urban Affairs.

dinated debt requirement for banks (similar to the proposal advanced by the Meltzer Commission) could likely be manipulated and evaded, thereby weakening its attraction as a mechanism for stronger market discipline.

The notion of prequalifying for IMF liquidity assistance applies presently only to drawings under the IMF's recently established (April 1999) CCL. Countries can qualify for the CCL if they have good macro policies, are complying with international financial standards, and have constructive relations with their private creditors. So far, no country has applied for the CCL. According to the IMF (Fischer 2000b), the unpopularity of the CCL probably owed to its (earlier) pricing structure: because the interest rate on the CCL was the same as that on the SRF, there was no incentive to prequalify; in addition, access to the credit line was not seen as automatic enough (if a crisis broke out). An alternative hypothesis is that the unpopularity derives from the ambiguous signal that applying for the CCL sends (i.e., it could be interpreted as suggesting the country is expecting trouble); in addition, because the IMF has recently speeded up its decision-making for disbursement from other IMF facilities in a crisis, prequalification may not confer as much of an advantage as previously supposed.

In September 2000, as part of the "facilities initiative," the IMF's executive board agreed to make the CCL more attractive by reducing the interest rate surcharge (from the previous 300 basis points to 150 basis points), by reducing slightly the commitment fee, and by making monitoring arrangements less intensive and the activation review less demanding. We will see if those sweeteners attract any more bees.

I do not find the Meltzer structural-policy preconditions attractive as an alternative way of qualifying countries for IMF financial assistance. Although meeting those criteria would, ceteris paribus, reduce the risk of getting into a crisis, they are not sufficient by themselves to deter a crisis; just as important, they are not very useful for getting out of a crisis once it hits.

Recent cross-country empirical research on financial development and on vulnerability to a banking crisis does indeed suggest that easing restrictions on foreign bank entry positively affects the efficiency of the domestic banking system and reduces banking fragility, particularly in emerging economies with small financial systems (see Barth, Caprio, and Levine 2000; Caprio and Honohan 2000). Also, many of the concerns about foreign-bank entry—for example, that foreign banks will destabilize the flow of credit during a crisis, or that foreign banks will drive domestic banks out of business, or that foreign banks will lower the effectiveness of banking supervision—have not found empirical support (see Goldberg, Dages, and Kinney 2000; Claessens and Jansen 2000). Likewise, I believe that better public disclosure and more timely publication of data on the currency and maturity composition of debt would be helpful in discouraging the buildup of large currency and maturity mismatches (see section 8.5).

However, helpful is not the same thing as adequate to the task at hand. The same empirical research that shows that vulnerability to emerging-market banking crises is reduced by easier entry of foreign banks also shows that it would be reduced by lower state ownership of banking systems, by less generous deposit insurance and official safety nets, and by other factors (including wider banking powers)—and the Meltzer preconditions say nothing about those determinants of fragility. More generally, freedom of entry in banking plus a subordinated debt requirement are not likely to be adequate substitutes for the wider range of factors outlined (e.g., "fit and proper" requirements for getting a banking license) in the Basel Core Principles of Banking Supervision and in the recent empirical literature. In addition, although empirical research suggests that many currency crises are preceded by banking crises, many others are not (see Goldstein, Kaminsky, and Reinhart 2000). Giving huge credit lines to countries without any monetary policy conditionality seems counter-intuitive. The fiscal policy precondition is not discussed in a serious way in the Meltzer Report; it reads like an afterthought.

Freedom of entry for foreign banks and timely reporting of debt maturities will not get a country out of a balance-of-payments crisis. Without measures to reduce absorption and to switch expenditure from foreign to domestic goods, the crisis country's ability to repay is not likely to improve. Although I share the Meltzer Commission's desire to reduce the scope and intrusiveness of present IMF structural policy conditionality, this does not look like the best way to do it.

I am not a big fan of the CCL. I believe the design flaws there extend beyond pricing and that it is possible to create a superior lending window to deal with the systemic cases of cross-country contagion along the lines outlined in the CFR Report (1999).

8.4.2   Scope and Detail of Conditionality

None of the charges leveled at the IMF during the Asian crisis was probably more widespread than the criticism that the IMF has allowed the scope and detail of its conditionality to become overextended, particularly in the area of structural policies (see Feldstein 1998). The most visible manifestation of the reach of IMF programs was the vast array of structural conditions (more than 100) in the IMF's 1997 program with Indonesia (see Goldstein 2003). These included, inter alia, measures dealing with reforestation programs; phasing-out of local content programs for motor vehicles; discontinuation of support for a particular aircraft project and for special privileges granted to the National Car; abolition of the compulsory 2 percent after-tax contribution to charity foundations; development of rules for the Jakarta Clearinghouse; the end of restrictive marketing agreements for cement, paper, and plywood; the elimination of the Clove Marketing Board; the termination of requirements on farmers for the forced planting of sugar cane; the introduction of a micro credit scheme to assist small businesses; and eighteen specific follow-up actions to the findings of the audit of Bank Indonesia.

A recent comprehensive review of IMF structural policy conditionality is contained in Goldstein (2003). Among the main findings were the following: (a) structural policy conditionality is a now a common and important element of IMF conditionality; (b) combining prior actions, performance criteria, structural benchmarks, and program reviews, it has been typical over the past three or four years for a one-year standby arrangement to have about a dozen structural conditions and for a three-year EFF program to have on the order of fifty such conditions; (c) about two-thirds of those conditions fell in the areas of fiscal policy, financial-sector reform, and privatization, with the rest scattered across a fairly wide field; (d) structural conditions in the IMF's recent programs with Indonesia, South Korea, and Thailand were more numerous and detailed than is usually the case; (e) there has been a pronounced upward trend in structural policy conditionality over the past fifteen years, and this trend has become steeper in the 1990s; (f) there has been a shift over time in the instruments used by the IMF to monitor structural conditionality, with resort to structural benchmarks, conditions for program reviews, and prior actions having risen faster than formal performance criteria; (g) obtaining compliance with IMF conditionality has been a serious problem (including the IMF's structural policy conditionality), with the compliance rate hovering at about 50 percent and falling over time; (h) for the most part, the IMF's structural policy recommendations reflect the economics profession's consensus of what constitutes sensible policy reform, although some serious mistakes on sequencing have sometimes taken place; and (i) the IMF's recent experience with structural conditionality as a whole indicates that the IMF has bitten off more—in both scope and detail—than either it or its member countries can chew. There are limits, no matter how numerous and detailed the IMF's monitoring techniques, to how far the IMF can push a country to undertake structural reforms that it is not committed to.

This upward trend in IMF structural policy conditionality reflects many influences. The following seven factors (discussed more fully in Goldstein 2003) merit mention.

1. In the 1970s and early 1980s, IMF programs came under sharp criticism from many developing countries as being too demand-oriented and too short-run, and as not paying enough attention to economic growth, to supply-side reforms, and to income distribution. Because it was developing countries that increasingly constituted the demand for IMF resources, neither the IMF nor creditor governments could easily dismiss that criticism. New lending windows with higher structural policy content and with lending terms more favorable to low-income countries were created, and moni-

toring techniques for gauging compliance with structural policy conditions evolved.

2. The huge transformation task faced by the transition economies—especially in the first half of the 1990s—made structural policies and the building of a market infrastructure the name of the game in that region. The IMF (along with the European Bank for Reconstruction and Development) was at the center of the technical assistance and policy lending to those transition economies. Again, structural benchmarks came to be relied upon as a way of monitoring structural policy conditionality across a wide front. When structural problems arose in later crises (Asia), the same monitoring techniques were applied.

3. All the while, the IMF was more and more interpreting its mandate as being broader than just promoting macroeconomic and financial stability and helping countries to manage financial crises. From the mid-1980s on, economic growth and, later, high-quality growth were given increased prominence. Additionally, after the Mexican peso crisis of 1994–95, crisis prevention—with particular attention to strengthening financial systems at the national level and developing international standards and codes of good practice—moved up on the agenda as well.

4. Crises that involve severe balance sheet problems of banks and private corporations lead to more structural policy–intensive IMF programs than do those that stem from traditional monetary and fiscal policy excesses, and the Asian crises of 1997–98 had those balance sheet problems in spades.

5. The long-standing and growing problem of obtaining good compliance with IMF programs led over time to greater reliance on prior actions and to more wide-ranging and detailed structural policy conditions, presumably in an effort to penalize poor earlier track records, to thwart evasion, and to detect slippage at an earlier stage. The IMF's 1979 Guidelines for Conditionality in standby arrangements—which might have reined in excessive structural policy conditionality—came to be viewed by the IMF's executive board as broad principles of intention, not as something to be monitored carefully and enforced.[15]

6. In the meantime, a wide array of legislative groups, nongovernmental organizations, and even other international financial organizations came to the see an IMF letter of intent as the preferred instrument of leverage for their own agendas in emerging economies. Yes, the International Labor Organization might be the logical place to push core labor standards, but it does not have the teeth of an IMF program. Simultaneously, various G7

15. Guideline 9 of the 1979 Guidelines states: "Performance criteria will be limited to those that are necessary to evaluate implementation of the program with a view to ensuring the achievement of its objectives. Performance criteria will normally be confined to (i) macroeconomic variables, and (ii) those necessary to implement specific provisions of the Articles. . . . Performance criteria may relate to other variables only in exceptional cases when they are essential for the effectiveness of the member's program because of their macroeconomic impact."

governments—and particularly the IMF's largest shareholder—were finding it increasingly difficult to get congressional support for "clean" IMF funding bills. Reflecting this congressional pressure from both major parties, the U.S. executive director at the IMF has been obliged to support with voice and vote a long list of structural policies (ranging from protection of the environment to promotion of economic deregulation and privatization of industry), and the U.S. Treasury is required to report annually to the Congress on its compliance with relevant sections of the Foreign Operations, Export Financing, and Related Programs Appropriation Act of 1999. Likewise, in countries where there was prolonged use of IMF resources, IMF letters of intent sometimes became an instrument of leverage that the finance ministry could use to push structural reforms on other departments in the government that were opposed. In short, everybody has gotten in on the act.

7. Unlike other IFIs, the IMF and the World Bank have sufficient "ground troops" to perform on-site visits to all countries. In addition, at least in official circles, the IMF has developed a reputation for being able to act quickly and efficiently. When new structural challenges have arisen, there has therefore been a tendency to say, "give it to the IMF; they go there anyway; just have them add a few specialists on problem X to the mission." The management of the IMF has apparently not said "no" very often to those demands.

In Feldstein's (1998) view, when the IMF contemplates including a particular policy reform in its programs with emerging economies, it should ask itself two questions: is this reform necessary to restore the country's access to international capital markets, and would the IMF ask the same measures of a major industrial country if it were the subject of a IMF program? If the answer to either question is "no," then that policy should not be part of the IMF program.

According to the CFR Report (1999), the traditional separation of responsibilities between the IMF and the World Bank had become blurred in recent years, to the disadvantage of both institutions and their clients. It recommended that the IMF confine the scope of its conditionality to monetary, fiscal, exchange rate, and financial-sector policies. A recent external review of IMF surveillance by a group of outside experts led by former Bank of Canada Governor John Crow (see Crow, Arriazu, and Thygesen 1999) outlined the same boundaries for the IMF's core competence. Financial-sector policies (and surveillance) were included in the IMF's mandate under the rationale that banking and financial-sector problems were much more connected than other structural policy areas to the prevention, management, and resolution of financial crises. The CFR Task Force also recommended that the World Bank should concentrate on the longer-term structural and social aspects of economic development and should expand its work on social safety nets. The World Bank should not be involved in crisis management, emergency lending, or macroeconomic policy advice.

The Meltzer Report (2000) recommended that the IMF cease lending to countries for long-term structural transformation (as in the transition economies) and for long-term development assistance (as in sub-Saharian Africa). It would eliminate the IMF's concessional lending window for poor countries, the PRGF. Long-term structural assistance to support institutional reform and sound economic policies would be the responsibility of the World Bank and the regional development banks (i.e., the Asian Development Bank, the African Development Bank, and the Inter-American Development Bank).

The U.S. Treasury (2000) opposed the Meltzer Commission's recommendations that the PRGF be closed and that long-term assistance to foster development and sound economic policies be handled exclusively by the World Bank and the regional development banks. It emphasized that poverty reduction in poor developing countries will not occur without economic growth and that good growth performance in these countries will not take place without sound macroeconomic policies. Because the treasury saw the IMF's particular expertise in helping countries to set up appropriate macroeconomic frameworks as not being shared by the multilateral development banks (MDBs), it was opposed to transferring this responsibility from the IMF to the MDBs. Moreover, it did not feel that the IMF's advice on macroeconomic policy would be influential in poor countries unless it was supported by some IMF lending arrangement. It also hinted that bilateral contributions funding the IMF's concessional lending activities might be cut back to some extent if the IMF were no longer involved in lending to poor countries. All this having been said, the U.S. Treasury (2000) did acknowledge that the IMF's role in concessional lending "needs to change significantly" (22). Specifically, it called within the PRGF for a clearer division of labor between the IMF and the World Bank, with the IMF focusing on macroeconomic policy and structural reform in related areas (tax policy and fiscal management) and with the World Bank taking the lead on national poverty-reduction strategies and other structural reforms.

The IMF has defended strenuously its lending activities to poor countries. Fischer (2000a) argued that poor countries also have macroeconomic problems and that they have a right like every other member to access the facilities of the IMF. He also maintained that the new PRGF will improve lending to the poor countries because it forces the IMF, in cooperation with the World Bank, "to make sure that the macroeconomic framework is fully consistent with what needs to be done for social reasons" (4).

In their report of July 2000, G7 finance ministers (2000) expressed support for the IMF's role in the PRGF. The report also noted that the issues dealt with by the IMF and the World Bank are increasingly interrelated. It acknowledged that a "clearer definition of their respective responsibilities and activities" would be desirable but did not provide any specific suggestions on what this definition should be. Indeed, it pretty much ducked the issue. At their meeting in February 2001 (the first one to include new U.S. Treasury Secretary O'Neill), G7 finance ministers and central bank governors issued a short communiqué (G7 2001); under the heading of strengthening the international financial architecture, they looked forward to "further progress on prioritization of IMF conditionality" (2).

Given the long-standing pressures emanating from both industrial and developing economies to use the IMF to pursue wide-ranging goals, the practical difficulties of getting the IMF to focus on a leaner agenda should not be underestimated. Still, there are signs from both new IMF Managing Director Horst Kohler (2000) and from new U.S. Treasury Secretary Paul O'Neill that they want to get the IMF "back to basics" and to streamline IMF conditionality. If they can sustain that shift in direction, they will deserve our applause.[16] For reasons laid out in both the CFR Report (1999) and the Crow Report (1999), I think the most sensible definition of IMF core competence is monetary, fiscal, exchange rate, and financial-sector policies; the rest should be the comparative advantage and primary responsibility of other IFIs.

I question the argument that if the PRGF were transferred to the World Bank, the IMF would be unable to have a significant influence on the macroeconomic framework in its poorer member countries. If the focus of the PRGF is really on long-term poverty reduction strategies, the World Bank should take the lead role (which would include supplying the financing). To ensure that the IMF's voice on macroeconomic policies is heard loud and clear, the IMF should have a strong "sign off" mechanism. Giving the World Bank its own PRGF-type lending window hardly seems a good solution; why does the world need two windows to do nearly the same thing? The institutional specifics of IFI lending facilities need to give way to a sensible and consistent division of labor—not the other way around.

8.4.3   Currency-Regime and Burden-Sharing Aspects of IMF Conditionality

No discussion of IMF conditionality would be complete without addressing currency regime and private-creditor burden-sharing issues.

The list of larger emerging economies with relatively open capital markets that have been able to maintain a fixed exchange rate for five years or longer is now very short: Argentina and Hong Kong. During the past six years, Mexico, most of the Asian crisis countries, Russia, Brazil, and Turkey (among others) have all been forced to abandon publicly declared exchange

---

16. Also commendable was the decision of the IMF last year to eliminate several lending facilities that were no longer needed (namely, the Buffer Stock Financing Facility, the Currency Stabilization Fund, and the Debt and Debt Service Reduction Facility).

rate targets of one kind or another. The main lesson of this experience is that emerging economies should choose either a regime of managed floating or a hard peg (i.e., a currency board or dollarization). Adjustable peg regimes (so-called soft pegs) are too fragile for a world of high capital mobility—both because they offer no workable exit mechanism once the fixed rate becomes overvalued, and because there are strict limits to how long emerging economies can keep interest sky-high in a currency defense (especially when the country has a weak banking system or the corporate sector has a high debt-equity ratio, or the economy is in recession, or the government has a large fiscal deficit with a great deal of floating rate debt). Despite these vulnerabilities, history suggests that some emerging economies will be tempted to try to maintain overvalued soft pegs if they think they can get large-scale IMF or G7 financial support in a crisis; the Brazilian crisis in early 1999 was a leading case in point.

The Meltzer Commission (2000) argued that countries should avoid pegged or adjustable exchange rates and suggested that the IMF use its Article IV consultations to make countries aware of the costs and risks associated with pegged or adjustable rates. The report states that fluctuating exchange rates or hard pegs would be a better regime choice. However, the Meltzer Report did *not* recommend that the IMF include the currency regime as one of the structural preconditions for IMF liquidity assistance, arguing that stabilizing budget and credit policies is far more important than the choice of exchange rate regime.

The CFR Report (1999) went further than the Meltzer Commission on the choice of currency regime. The report concluded that managed floating should be the IMF's main-line currency regime recommendation for emerging economies, with hard pegs also advocated in particular circumstances.[17] More noteworthy, the CFR Task Force recommended that the IMF NOT provide large-scale financial assistance to countries that are intent on defending arguably overvalued fixed exchange rates.[18] In this sense, the CFR Task Force would make exchange rate policy an integral part of IMF conditionality.

This consensus on currency regime choices for emerging economies also seems to be shared by the IMF. Fischer (2000a) noted that all the countries that recently had major international crises had relied on a pegged or fixed exchange rate system before the crisis. He also projected that "we are likely

17. Under the IMF's existing Articles of Agreement, countries can choose any currency regime (with the exception of linking the currency to gold). However, this does not mean that the IMF cannot ask countries to follow a particular exchange rate policy as a condition for IMF financial assistance.

18. A sizeable minority (eleven of twenty-nine members) of the CFR Task Force also took the view that there could no stability for emerging-economy currency regimes and no international financial stability more broadly until there was greater stability in G3 currency relationships. Toward that end, they proposed a "target zone" plan for the G3 currencies. The majority of the task force, however, rejected this approach.

to see emerging market countries moving towards the two extremes, of either a flexible rate or a very hard peg—and in the long run, the trend is most likely to be towards fewer currencies" (10).

The "corners" view of currency regimes for emerging economies was likewise endorsed by the Clinton Treasury. Summers (1999) has stated that countries maintaining a fixed rate should be expected to make explicit the extent to which monetary policy is being subordinated to the exchange rate objective, and (if using fixed rates as a tool of disinflation) to disclose the nature of their exit strategy. He concluded that "countries that are involved with the world capital market should increasingly avoid the 'middle ground' of pegged rates with discretionary monetary policies, in favor of either more firmly institutionalized fixed rate regimes or floating" (4).

In my view, the "corners school" consensus on currency regimes for emerging economies is soundly based on the lessons of experience. The key question is whether the G7 and the IMF are prepared to act on that recommendation when push comes to shove by not providing large-scale support for defense of overvalued fixed rates. I don't think merely advising emerging economies on choice of regime in Article IV consultations (as recommended by the Meltzer Commission) will get the job done.

We also need to understand better why so many emerging economies exhibit a serious "fear of floating," as documented in several recent empirical papers (see, e.g., Calvo and Reinhart 2000). One explanation is history, that is, a long memory by domestic and foreign creditors of earlier periods of high inflation (and also, sometimes, negative or very low real interest rates). This memory can lead private creditors to think that any temporary easing of monetary policy means the authorities are again "off to the races." Brazil's recent postcrisis experience, however, with managed floating–cum–inflation targeting and an independent central bank, suggests that history need not be insurmountable. A second and more weighty explanation is that many of these economies have large, unhedged, foreign currency–denominated liability positions on the part of banks or corporations; given that mismatch, a large depreciation would make many banks and firms insolvent, with large adverse effects on the real economy à la the Asian crisis.[19] Here, dollarization is seen as a sensible second best policy choice, given the difficulty of reaching the first best policy, namely, reducing or eliminating the mismatch itself. To me, however, the usual arguments put forward as to why the first best policy option is not available (e.g., private capital markets will not lend to emerging economies in their own currency) are not convincing. Thus, I still regard managed floating—probably with inflation targeting as a nominal anchor—as the preferred choice in most circumstances.

I suspect that the choice between the two corners over the next few years

19. Turkey's banks are also reported having suffered large losses in the recent (February 2001) depreciation of the lira due to unhedged currency positions.

will depend heavily on the real-life experiment now going on in Latin America. If Argentina's currency board eventually disappears because the cost of not having (domestic) monetary policy available to help emerge from anemic economic growth proves too great to bear, then the momentum for currency boards and dollarization will fade in favor of managed floating. On the other hand, if Brazil is unable to sustain its recent progress on inflation or the exchange rate runs out of control, then managed floating could well become a relic for most emerging economies. We will see who wins the race; right now, I would bet on the managed-floating horse.

Turning to private-sector involvement (PSI), the aim is to see that private creditors do not escape from paying their fair share of the burden of crisis resolution. As outlined earlier, the worry is that if private creditors do not "take a hit" when they make poor lending and investment decisions, there will not be sufficient incentive to undertake more careful risk assessment in the future.

Judging from a recent report of G7 Finance Ministers (2000), congressional testimony by former U.S. Treasury Secretary Summers, and a recent progress report on IFA reform by the IMF (2000a), the official sector (at least in the major industrial countries) felt it had made real progress on PSI. In this connection, the G7 finance ministers (2000) have noted that "private sector investors and lenders have been more involved in the financing of recent IMF-led programs" (2). Similarly, in listing recent important achievements on the reform of the IFA (in testimony before the House Banking Committee in March of this year), Secretary Summers stated that "we have found new ways to involve the private sector in the resolution of crises—most notably in the cases of Korea and Brazil" (2–3). Additionally, an IMF (2000c) progress report observed that "two recent cases of efforts to secure private sector involvement with members that had lost spontaneous access to capital markets through the restructuring of international bonds had been encouraging" (14); later on, however, that IMF report also acknowledged that "only limited progress has been made in lifting institutional constraints to debt restructuring" (17). The references above are to the less-than-voluntary rollover (albeit with a government guarantee and interest rates 150–200 basis points higher than precrisis rates) of interbank credits by G7 commercial banks in South Korea in early 1998, to the voluntary rollover of interbank and trade lines in Brazil in March 1999, to a tougher initial negotiating stance by the IMF or the Paris Club in several recent (1999 and 2000) emerging-market bond restructurings (Ecuador, Nigeria, Pakistan, Romania, and the Ukraine), and to rather limited success in encouraging creditor committees and inclusion of "collective-action clauses" (CACs) in sovereign bond contracts (at least among the G7 countries).

Some private analysts do not share this (rosy) assessment. Eichengreen (2000), for example, in a recent comprehensive review of PSI over the past few years, concluded that efforts to enhance significantly the participation of the private sector in crisis management and resolution have so far been a "failure" (1). Moreover, a recent IMF *International Capital Markets Report* (2000b) acknowledged that all the recent successful bond exchanges have involved some form of "substantial sweetener" for existing bond holders.

The Meltzer Report (2000) basically ducked on the PSI issue, notwithstanding its concern about lender moral hazard. It concluded that "the development of new ways of resolving sovereign borrower and lender conflicts in default situations should be encouraged but left to participants until there is better understanding by debtors, creditors, and outside observers of how, if at all, public-sector intervention can improve negotiations" (50).

In contrast, the CFR Report (1999) took a more activist position on PSI. More specifically, the report recommended (a) that all countries, including the G7 countries, commit to including CACs in their sovereign bond contracts and require that such clauses be present in all new sovereign bonds issued and traded in their markets; (b) that the IMF advise all emerging economies to adopt a "structured early intervention and resolution" approach to deposit insurance reform in their banking systems and reward countries that do so; (c) that the IMF make it known that it will provide emergency financial assistance only when there is a good prospect of the recipient country's achieving balance-of-payments (BOP) "viability" in the medium term (including a sustainable debt and debt-servicing profile); (d) that, in extreme cases of unsustainable debt profiles, the IMF expect as a condition for its support that debtors engage in good-faith discussions with their private creditors with the aim of reaching a more sustainable debt profile; and (e) that the IMF recognize that orderly debt rescheduling may be facilitated by having the debtor declare a temporary payments standstill (with the final decision to impose the standstill resting with the debtor country, not the IMF).[20] The aim of the CFR approach was to reduce lender moral hazard at the national and international level and to promote timeliness and orderliness in private debt rescheduling, but without going so far as to promote borrower moral hazard.

The IMF, U.S. Treasury, and G7 finance ministers all seem to have favored a differentiated case-by-case approach to PSI, guided by a few principles. They also favor some institutional changes but are not very specific about what they are willing to do to make these changes come about. A recent G7 finance ministers report (2000) illustrates the point. They say that the IMF should "encourage" use of CACs to facilitate more orderly crisis resolution, but they do not indicate what form this encouragement should take. Similarly, they say that use of CACs in international bonds issued by emerging economies in G7 financial markets should be "facilitated" but do not say how. They recommend different approaches to PSI depending on

20. Only one of the twenty-nine members of the CFR Task Force (namely, William Rhodes of Citigroup) dissented from the private-sector burden-sharing and CAC recommendations.

the borrowing country's medium-term debt and balance-of-payments profile. Where that profile is sustainable, they prescribe catalytic official financing and policy adjustment or voluntary approaches to overcome creditor coordination problems. Where the debt and BOP profiles are not sustainable, a broader spectrum of actions by private creditors—including comprehensive debt restructuring—is regarded as appropriate.

Contrary to the authors of the Meltzer Report, I do not believe that the PSI problem will solve itself in the marketplace. What the official sector does on PSI inevitably influences the balance of power between official debtors and private creditors in debt negotiations (as the IMF implicitly acknowledged in the late 1980s when it finally endorsed selective use of IMF "lending into arrears" to private creditors).

Like the authors of the CFR Report, I think the G7 countries will need to be more activist in facilitating wider use of CACs in sovereign bond contracts, as well as in endorsing selective use of temporary standstills. Eichengreen (2000) estimates that at present slightly more than half of all international bonds and about two thirds of all emerging-market issues do not contain CACs. In recent empirical work (Eichengreen and Mody 2000 and Eichengreen 2000), Eichengreen also demonstrates that (counter to the claims made by some private-creditor groups, like the Institute for International Finance) neither CACS nor internationally sanctioned standstills are likely to raise borrowing costs for emerging economies: CACs seem to lower borrowing costs for more creditworthy emerging economies and raise them for less creditworthy ones, and results for cross-country differences in creditor rights suggest that a well-designed IMF-sanctioned standstill would reduce borrowing costs (that is, the prevention of a creditor grab race has a more powerful effect on borrowing cost than the weakening of creditor rights). The decisions by the United Kingdom and Canada to include CACs in some of their sovereign bond contracts is welcome; other G7 countries should now follow their lead. Standstills could be given some legal force by following the recent proposal of Canadian Finance Minister Paul Martin (Martin 1999) to require all cross-border financial contracts to include (ex ante) a provision recognizing the IMF's authority to declare a standstill. Although it is true (as emphasized by Frankel and Roubini 2000) that some recent international bond exchanges for small emerging economies have permitted de facto rescheduling without recourse to CACs (or even in their absence), those exchanges were accompanied by substantial sweeteners to creditors; in addition, in those cases in which CACS were present, the implicit threat of invoking them may have facilitated the (voluntary) exchange.

I also continue to believe that PSI will not be successful until there is an agreement to limit the size of IMF rescue packages (for nonsystemic cases), until the official sector insists (in cases of unsustainable debt profiles) on appropriate debt restructuring with private creditors as a condition for IMF financial support, and until most emerging economies have in place good deposit insurance systems. Although it is true that small(er) rescue packages may not quell an investor panic, neither is it assured that large rescue packages (in the politically feasible range) will do so, and smaller packages at least introduce PSI in a direct way. Although initial IMF efforts in Romania and the Ukraine to condition its support on PSI were unsuccessful, this tells us relatively little about prospects for success in larger emerging-market economies where the stakes for private creditors would be bigger. Finally, most lender moral hazard occurs at the national level, not at the international level, and this will continue until good deposit insurance systems and other elements of an incentive-compatible financial safety net are in place.[21]

8.4.4 Implementation of International Financial Standards

The elements of IFA reform discussed thus far in this paper are not likely to have much of an impact on crisis prevention in emerging economies unless those economies also undertake a broad and determined effort to strengthen their domestic banking and financial systems. After all, over the past fifteen years, there have been more than sixty five episodes in which banking problems in emerging economies got so bad that the entire banking system was rendered insolvent. In the Asian crisis countries, we are now looking at fiscal costs of bank recapitalization that range from 10 to 60 percent of GDP (see World Bank 2000).

One of the key mechanisms being used to guide this upgrading of financial systems in emerging economies is international financial standards. Each of these standards is drawn by an international group of experts and represents agreement on minimum requirements for good practice. The Financial Stability Forum (FSF) has now decided that twelve of these standards are crucial for sound financial systems and deserve priority implementation. The twelve key standards (known as the "compendium of standards") cover data dissemination, banking supervision, insurance supervision, securities regulation, insolvency regimes, corporate governance, accounting, auditing, payment and settlement, market integrity, fiscal policy transparency, and monetary and financial policy transparency.

Establishing standards is one thing. Getting countries to implement and enforce these "voluntary" standards is another. In seeking to identify incentives that would speed the implementation of international financial standards, the official sector has relied on two channels.[22]

---

21. By a "good" deposit insurance system, I mean one that puts large uninsured creditors of banks at the back of the queue when failed banks are resolved, that places stringent accountability conditions on senior economic officials when they invoke "too large to fail," and that gives banking supervisors better protection against strong political pressures for regulatory forbearance.

22. Originally, there was also to be a third incentive channel, which would link implementation of international financial standards to preferred risk weights in the revised Basel Capital Accord. I understand, however, that this idea has recently been shelved.

First, there is the expected market payoff. If market participants can tell who is and who is not implementing the standards and if complying countries are regarded as more creditworthy, then the latter should be the beneficiaries of a lower market cost of borrowing. Early on, there was some hope that the private credit rating agencies might take up the task of evaluating compliance with standards and publish the results. That has not happened. Instead, it is the official sector—and, primarily, the IMF—that has taken the lead in this process. A few examples illustrate the process. The IMF now posts on the internet the list of countries that have signed on to the data dissemination standard. Similarly, for the banking supervision standard, the IMF prepares Reports on the Observance of Standards and Codes (ROSCs); so far, ROSCs for about fifteen countries have been completed and another twenty or so are under preparation. The decisions to have a ROSC and to have the report published are at the discretion of countries; the majority of completed ROSCs have been published. The IMF and the World Bank jointly produce Financial Sector Assessment Programs (FSAPs) that evaluate financial-sector vulnerabilities as well as assessing compliance with those financial-sector standards that affect stability. World Bank staff expect to have about six corporate governance and six accounting reports available soon (see IMF 2000c).

Two factors have constrained the market payoff channel. One is the concern that naming publicly the noncomplying countries could precipitate runs or crises. Recently, however, that concern appears to be waning. Within the past few months, the FSF published the list of offshore financial centers whose regulatory and supervisory practices are regarded as lax; the Organization for Economic Cooperation and Development named jurisdictions that promote harmful tax competition; and the Financial Action Task Force identified fifteen jurisdictions that were judged to be uncooperative in the fight against money laundering. This recent public naming of names could be ushering in a more aggressive stance by the official sector. The other constraint is that evaluation of compliance in areas outside the competence of the IMF and the World Bank presupposes a good deal of interagency cooperation and coordination. This still remains a bottleneck.

The second incentive channel for implementation of financial standards is the Bretton Woods channel. More specifically, the IMF and the World Bank could give those countries implementing the standards a better insurance deal (larger access or lower interest rates) when they needed financial assistance. This still appears to be on the drawing board. Implementation of financial standards is supposed to be one of the eligibility factors for accessing the CCL, but, as mentioned earlier, no country has yet applied for CCL assistance.

The U.S. Treasury and the G7 finance ministers appeared be on the same page as far as where they wanted to go with the standards. In brief, they were encouraging countries to sign up for assessments of compliance with the standards and to allow the results to be published; in addition, they were encouraging the IMF to identify which standards should have the highest priority for which countries. They were also asking the FSF to see if there are farther supervisory and regulatory incentives that would promote observance of the standards.

The Meltzer Report (2000) took a different tack. It recommended that financial standards should be set by the Bank for International Settlements (BIS) and that implementation of standards, and decisions to adopt them, should be left to domestic regulators and legislators. Perhaps they were relying on regulatory competition to eventually induce reform.

In contrast, the CFR Report (1999) called on the IMF to monitor countries' compliance with standards (at least the ones that fall into its core competence) and to charge lower interest rates to countries that make better crisis prevention efforts, where implementation of standards would be one of the key elements in "crisis prevention efforts." Furthermore, the report urged that this risk-based insurance premium apply to all the IMF's nonconcessional lending, not just to the CCL. In addition, the CFR Task Force recommended that the IMF publish its evaluations of compliance with standards so that the markets could take note.

Implementation of international financial standards is one of the areas in IFA reform that has shown the most progress over the past few years.

Any recommendation to have domestic regulators act as the sole evaluator of compliance with standards is a bad idea. It is very unlikely that such self-evaluations will be objective rather than self-serving. In this connection, a survey sent to 129 countries in 1996 by the Basel Committee on Banking Supervision is instructive; on element after element of banking supervision (from government-directed lending to loan classification procedures to independence of the supervisory agency . . . on and on), a very high proportion of respondents ranked themselves as doing a very good job— and this despite the sorry record of banking crises over the preceding twenty years, to say nothing of the banking crises to come (just a year or so after the survey) in Asia;[23] I understand that a more recent Basel Committee survey again demonstrated the strong bias in self-evaluation. Assessment of compliance with international financial standards should continue to be done by (more objective) international agencies with the relevant expertise, at least until the private sector is prepared to take up that task in a serious way. The recent decisions by the FSF and other official agencies to publicly name names of non-complying economies suggests that they have crossed the Rubicon on this issue. This should increase the market payoff to implementing the standards.

The next bottlenecks that need to be tackled are better coordination among the evaluating agencies, and making the private sector—and partic-

---

23. See Goldstein (1997) for a discussion of the survey results.

ularly the major rating agencies—more familiar with the official evaluations. It would be very helpful to have assessments on key standards collected and published in one place—say, in the IMF's Article IV consultation report. In addition, the IMF, the World Bank, and the FSF should increase efforts to publicize their evaluations; until the rating agencies and other market participants become convinced that such (official) evaluations of compliance are useful in evaluating creditworthiness, their impact on market borrowing costs will be minimal.

8.5   Concluding Remarks

More has been happening on reform of the IFA over the past five years than many people think. However, progress has been quite uneven. Progress has been considerable in the setting and implementation of international financial standards. Currency regimes for emerging economies have likewise improved, although that has been forced by the market, not by the official sector. The redesign of IMF lending facilities is also moving in the right direction. Much less progress has been made, however, on discouraging currency mismatching, on PSI, and on refocusing the mandates of the IMF and the World Bank. That is where the priority needs to be over the next year or two.

One of the key lessons that we should take away from the emerging-market financial crises of the past seven or eight years is that a 30 percent-plus devaluation is a very different animal when banks and corporations have large currency mismatches than when they do not. One only has to compare the widespread insolvencies and deep output losses in the Asian and Mexican crises on the one side (in which currency mismatches were large prior to devaluation) with the more moderate effects during the Brazilian crisis on the other side (in which mismatches were much smaller) to see what difference it makes to the bottom line. Moreover, wherever large currency mismatches exist, there will be understandably be great reluctance to accept a large devaluation even when the real exchange rate is significantly overvalued, thereby often making the final exchange rate adjustment even larger.

Discouraging currency mismatching is particularly challenging for private-sector borrowing. Whereas an enlightened government debt manager may be able to internalize the externalities associated with unhedged foreign currency borrowing, private-sector actors often see it differently. If others are availing themselves of lower interest rates on foreign currency–denominated debt, competitive pressures may tempt them to do so as well; in addition, there is always the possibility that losses on foreign currency borrowing induced by a devaluation may be bailed out by the authorities (especially if the borrower is a bank).

Most of the antidotes for the currency mismatching problem proposed so far (that is, dollarization, prohibiting foreign currency–denominated loans, and making such obligations unenforceable in domestic courts of developing countries) seem to me to be either too costly or too drastic.[24] I would rather see more emerging economies follow Mexico's recent lead by combining a managed floating rate with active development of hedging mechanisms. In addition, every request for an IMF program should contain data on existing currency mismatching by the banking and corporate sectors, analysis of the sustainability of these mismatches (including scenarios of what the consequences of a devaluation would be), and explicit conditions for reducing the mismatch (if the existing or prospective mismatch is judged to be too large). Furthermore, in either its *International Capital Markets Report* or its *World Economic Outlook*, the IMF should be drawing attention (on a regular basis) to currency mismatch figures for all countries that have significant involvement with private international capital markets; some of that kind of analysis has appeared in recent issues of the Bank of England's *Financial Stability Review*, and it could be extended by the IMF. The more that private market participants are aware of the magnitude of currency mismatching, the better the chances that market pressures would be brought to bear to reduce it before a crisis takes place.

Turning to PSI, the analysis in section 8.4 suggests that there could be large dividends to putting in place an incentive-compatible system of deposit insurance for banks in emerging economies, to cutting back on the size of IMF rescue packages for non-systemic crises, and to encouraging greater use of CACs and (in extreme cases) internationally sanctioned standstills as well.

The former managing director of the IMF, Michel Camdessus, was fond of saying, "The fund should do more and do it better." I would argue that the fund should do less so that it can do it better. Comparative advantage should apply to the IFIs as well as to their member countries.

A way needs to be found to resist the constant calls on the IMF to become a "general-purpose organization." Its core competence in monetary, fiscal, exchange rate, and financial-sector policies should be protected; this will require the cooperation of the membership, and particularly of the largest shareholders. It will also require firmness from the IMF's new managing director. If IMF structural conditionality is to be streamlined, IMF management will have to say "no" more than in the past—to requests for IMF assistance when the expectation is low that the country will implement IMF policy conditions, to G7 governments when they propose new tasks for the IMF that go beyond the IMF's core competence, to nongovernmental organizations that seek to use a country's letter of intent with the IMF to advance agendas that (even if desirable) lie outside the IMF's mandate, and to

24. For analysis of the currency mismatching problem and what to do about it, see Dooley (1999) and Krueger (2000).

developing-country finance ministers who want to use micro conditions in IMF programs to impose spending discipline on other government ministries that could not be agreed upon in their national legislatures. None of this means that the IMF should not take account of social needs in its programs or that it cannot provide good service to its poorer member countries (any more than making price stability the key objective of central banks means that they should ignore the real economy or financial stability). However, it does mean that both the IMF and the World Bank have to allow their 19th Street partner to lead in the areas of its comparative advantage, as well as rationalizing their lending windows.

References

Bagehot, Walter. 1873. *Lombard street: A description of the money market.* London: William Clowes and Sons.

Barth, James, Gerard Caprio, and Ross Levine. 2001. Bank regulation and supervision: What works best. Policy Research Working Paper no. WPS2725. Washington, D.C.: World Bank, November.

Bergsten, C. Fred. 2000. Reforming the international financial institutions: A dissenting view. Testimony before the Senate Committee on Banking, Housing, and Urban Affairs. 9 March.

Brealey, R., and E. Kaplanis. 1999. The impact of IMF assistance on asset values. London: Bank of England. Working Paper.

Calvo, Guillermo, and Carmen Reinhart. 2000. Fear of floating. NBER Working Paper no. w7993. Cambridge, Mass.: National Bureau of Economic Research, November.

Camdessus, Michel. 1987. Opening remarks. In *Growth-oriented adjustment programs*, ed. Vittorio Corbo, Morris Goldstein, and Mohsin Khan, 7–11. Washington, D.C.: International Monetary Fund and World Bank.

Caprio, Gerard, and Patrick Honohan. 2000. *Finance for growth: Policy choices in a volatile world.* Washington, D.C.: World Bank, December.

Claessens, Stijn, and Marion Jansen. 2000. Overview. In *The internationalization of financial services: Issues and lessons for developing countries*, ed. Stijn Claessens and Marion Jansen. Washington, D.C.: World Bank.

Conable, Barber. 1987. Opening remarks. In *Growth-oriented adjustment programs*, ed. Vittorio Corbo, Morris Goldstein, and Mohsin Khan, 3–6. Washington, D.C.: International Monetary Fund and World Bank.

Council on Foreign Relations Independent Task Force (CFR Task Force). 1999. *Safeguarding prosperity in a global financial system: The future international financial architecture*, Carla Hills and Peter Peterson, co-chairs, Morris Goldstein, project director (CFR Report). Washington, D.C.: Institute for International Economics.

Crow, John, Ricardo Arriazu, and Niels Thygesen. 1999. *External evaluation of IMF surveillance* (Crow Report). Washington, D.C.: International Monetary Fund, August.

De Gregorio, Jose, Barry Eichengreen, Takatoshi Ito, and Charles Wyplosz. 1999.

An Independent and Accountable IMF. Geneva: International Center for Monetary and Banking Studies and Centre for Economic Policy Research.

Dell'Ariccia, Giovanni, Isabel Gödde, and Jeromin Zettelmeyer. 2000. Moral hazard and international crisis lending: A test. Washington, D.C.: International Monetary Fund, November.

Dooley, Michael. 1999. Debt management in developing countries. University of California at Santa Cruz, Department of Economics Mimeograph.

Eichengreen, Barry. 1999. *Toward a new international financial architecture: a practical post-Asia agenda.* Washington, D.C.: Institute for International Economics.

———. 2000. *Can the moral hazard caused by IMF loans be reduced?* Geneva Report on the World Economy no. 1. London: Centre for Economic Policy Research.

Eichengreen, Barry, and Ricardo Hausman.1999. Exchange rates and financial fragility. In Federal Reserve Bank of Kansas City, 329–68. *New challenges for monetary policy,* Kansas City: Federal Reserve Bank of Kansas City.

Eichengreen, Barry, and Ashoka Mody. 2000. Would collective action clauses raise borrowing costs? World Bank Working Paper no. 2363. Washington, D.C.: World Bank, June.

Feldstein, Martin. 1998. Refocusing the IMF. *Foreign Affairs* 78 (2): 93–109.

Financial Times, "IMF Agrees Need to End Mission Creep," Stephen Fidler, July 19.

Fischer, Stanley. 1999. On the need for an international lender of last resort. Journal of Economics Perspectives 13 (4): 85–104.

———. 2000a. Presentation to the International Financial Institution Advisory Commission (Meltzer Commission). Washington, D.C.: International Monetary Fund, February.

———. 2000b. Strengthening crisis prevention: The role of contingent credit lines. Speech to Banco de Mexico. Mexico City, Mexico. 15 November.

Frankel, Jeffrey, and Nouriel Roubini. 2003. Industrial country policies. In *Economic and financial crises in emerging-market economies*, ed. Martin Feldstein. Chicago: University of Chicago Press.

Garber, Peter. 2000. Notes on market-based bank regulation. Ed. Joseph Bisignano, William Hunter, and George Kaufman, 255–60. In *Global Financial Crises: Lessons from Recent Events,* Boston: Kluwer Academic.

Goldberg, Linda, Gerard Dages, and Daniel Kinney. 2000. Foreign and domestic bank participation in emerging markets: Lessons from Mexico and Argentina. Federal Reserve Bank of New York. Mimeograph, March.

Goldstein, Morris. 1997. *The case for an international banking standard.* Policy Analyses in International Economics, no. 47. Washington, D.C.: Institute for International Economics.

———. 1998. *The Asian financial crisis: Causes, cures, and systemic implications.* Policy Analyses in International Economics, no. 55. Washington, D.C.: Institute for International Economics.

———. 2000. Strengthening the international financial architecture: Where do we stand? IIE Working Paper no. 00-8. Washington, D.C.: Institute for International Economics, October.

———. 2003. IMF structural programs. In *Economic and financial crises in emerging-market economies*, ed. Martin Feldstein, Chicago: University of Chicago Press.

Goldstein, Morris, Graciela Kaminsky, and Carmen Reinhart. 2000. *Assessing financial vulnerability: An early warning system for emerging economies.* Washington, D.C.: Institute for International Economics.

Group of Seven Finance Ministers. 2000. Strengthening the international financial architecture. Report to the Heads of State and Government. Fukuoka, Japan. 8 July.

Group of Seven Finance Ministers and Central Bank Governors. 2001. Statement. Palermo, Italy, 17 February.

Haldane, Andy. 1999. Private sector involvement in financial crises: Analytics and public policy approaches. Bank of England, *Financial Stability Review*, 7: 184–202.

Helleiner, Gerald. 1987. Comment on adjustment and economic growth. In *Growth-oriented adjustment programs*, ed. Vittorio Corbo, Morris Goldstein, and Mohsin Khan, 107–14. Washington, D.C.: International Monetary Fund and World Bank.

International Financial Institution Advisory Commission (Meltzer Commission). 2000. *Report of the International Financial Institution Advisory Commission*, Allan H. Meltzer, chairman (Meltzer report). Washington, D.C.:

International Monetary Fund. 1998. *World Economic Outlook*. Washington, D.C.: International Monetary Fund.

———. 2000a. IMF board agrees on changes to Fund financial facilities. Public Information Notice no. 00/79. Washington, D.C.: International Monetary Fund.

———. 2000b. *International capital markets report*. Washington, D.C.: International Monetary Fund.

———. 2000c. Report of the acting managing director to the International Monetary and Financial Committee on Progress in Reforming the IMF and Strengthening the Architecture of the International Financial System. Washington, D.C.: International Monetary Fund, April.

Kohler, Horst. 2000. Address to the board of governors of the Fund. Annual Meeting of the IMF and World Bank Group. Prague, Czechoslovakia. 26 September.

Krueger, Anne. 2000. Conflicting demands on the International Monetary Fund. *American Economic Review*, 90 (2):38–42.

Lane, Timothy, and Steven Phillips. 2000. Does IMF financing result in moral hazard? International Monetary Fund Working paper no. 00/168. Washington DC, International Monetary Fund, October.

Martin, Paul. 1999. The international financial architecture: The rule of law. 12 July. Available at [http://www.fin.gc.ca/newsse99/99-063_2e.html].

Meltzer, Allan. 1999. What's wrong with the IMF? What would be better? In *The Asian financial crisis*, ed. William Hunter, George Kaufman, and Thomas Krueger, 241–60. Boston: Kluwer Academic.

Mussa, Michael. 1999. Reforming the international financial architecture: Limiting moral hazard and containing real hazard. In *Capital flows and the international financial system*, Sydney: Reserve Bank of Australia.

Summers, Lawrence. 1999. The right kind of IMF for a stable global financial system. Speech to the London School of Business. London, England. 14 December.

———. 2000. Testimony before the International Monetary and Finance Committee. Washington, D.C.: 16 April.

U.S. Treasury. 2000. Response to the report of the International Financial Institution Advisory Commission. Washington, D.C.: U. S. Treasury. 8 June.

Williamson, John. 2000. The role of the IMF: A guide to the reports. International Economics Policy Briefs, no. 00-5. Washington, D.C.: Institute for International Economics, May.

World Bank. 2000. *Global economic prospects and the developing countries*. Washington, D.C.: World Bank.

Zhang, Allan. 1999. Testing for moral hazard in emerging market lending. IIF Discussion Paper no. 99-1. Washington, D.C.: Institute for International Finance.

Comment   Andrew Berg

Morris Goldstein's paper is a comprehensive, authoritative, sensible, and well-written insider's guide to the architecture debate as it stood at the end of the Summers-Rubin-Camdessus administration. It is organized around a daunting array of proposed reforms, from exchange rate policy to package size to deposit insurance and the relative role of the World Bank and the International Monetary Fund (IMF). For purposes of discussion, I want to divide them into three categories:

1. Those whose advisability is controversial and depends on the diagnosis of the problem. Here I would place the question of the size of IMF packages and the appropriate role of private-sector burden sharing.

2. Those that are controversial because of feasibility concerns. Here, the most important proposal is a greater reliance on ex ante conditionality, as many of the radical proposals for reform hinge on this. Ex ante conditionality that worked—for example, conditioning support on prior measures to maintain a strong banking system—would hold the promise of avoiding moral hazard while allowing large bailouts that can solve at least the liquidity-related market failures. The doubts are about whether it can work in practice, for example whether appropriate ex ante conditions can be defined and whether the IMF can behave in a time-consistent manner.

3. Those that have been more or less agreed upon and whose implementation has begun. Here the main question is how much they will help. Examples include changing the interest rates and tenor of IMF lending and developing international codes and standards in a variety of areas.

Rather than organizing my comments around various proposals, I want to organize thinking around a few key analytic questions. I will focus on category-1 issues, which implies trying to link proposed solutions to diagnoses of the problems to be solved.

An analysis of the international architecture problem depends on two main considerations. The first is the importance of market failure in international capital markets. For liquidity crises, this failure may be associated with multiple equilibria in exchange rates and capital markets or "irrational" contagion. For solvency or debt crises, the problem may be the absence of sovereign bankruptcy procedures. This, in turn, may imply an inability to efficiently resolve debt overhang, a rush for the exit by creditors, an inefficient lack of new money in the absence of mechanisms for collective action, and so on.

Andrew Berg is deputy division chief in the financial studies division of the research department of the International Monetary Fund.

The second key consideration is the significance of the moral hazard associated with bailouts by official creditors.

I will now try to place views on a key category-1 issue, the appropriate size of rescue packages, in this framework. The Meltzer Commission (MC) report places substantial emphasis on potential market failures in terms of liquidity crises resulting from the lack of an international lender of last resort. They (more or less implicitly) give little weight to problems associated with the absence of an international bankruptcy procedure, in that there seems to be little concern about developing mechanisms to resolve bankruptcies beyond letting the market take care of them. The MC report also clearly considers that moral hazard associated with the action of the IMF is substantial.

Figure 8C.1 illustrates the MC views in moral hazard–market failure space. Recommended rescue package size rises as opinions move toward the northeast in this figure. As befits the complexity of their analysis, the MC gets three areas. The spot on the upper right reflects the MC view of liquidity crises, which is that there is great risk of moral hazard associated with bailouts but that market failures are potentially large. Recommended package is modest (or zero). The dark spot in the upper left represents the MC belief that ex ante conditionality solves the moral hazard problems, so that recommended package size is enormous (much greater than has been observed) as long as ex ante conditionality is enforced. The larger area in the lower right represents the MC views on solvency crises, as much as they can

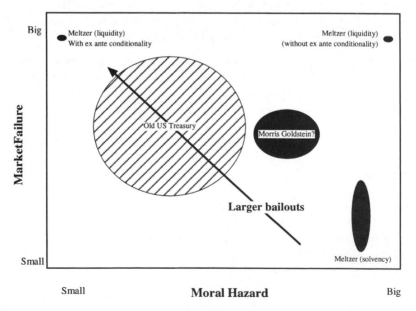

Fig. 8C.1   Market failure and moral hazard

be ascertained. Moral hazard is key, whereas it is unclear that market failure is significant.

The Rubin-Summers Treasury and the Camdessus-Fischer IMF (US-TIMF) believed that market failures were potentially large, large enough to justify rescue packages of unprecedented size. The failures include contagion as well as liquidity crises, as in Korea in 1997, when creditors could be coordinated to stay in, but only with substantial official support. There was also recognition of market failure in the context of debt workouts, although less was done about it. As befits the case-by-case approach, views are relatively indistinct, resulting in the large oval in the figure. Preferred package sizes are similarly varied, depending on the degree of moral hazard in the particular case (which depends in part on how far the country is toward the insolvency end of the spectrum) and how unnecessarily bad the situation would be absent support.

Goldstein argues for somewhat smaller rescue packages than under the USTIMF regime. I confess I do not find his arguments convincing here. He argues that the IMF (and others) should not try to back the defense of overvalued pegs, although they can still help in the aftermath. Most of the large IMF-led packages we have in mind, though, did not involve the defense of pegs (the Mexico, Thailand, Korea, and Indonesia programs, for example, all *followed* devaluations). He also argues that packages alone are never enough and that they can never be large enough. None of this speaks to the (admittedly quite difficult) question of how large they should be.

As I noted above, the importance of moral hazard plays a determinative role in recommendations for the size and nature of rescue packages. Goldstein clearly thinks it is very important but does not explain why or how much. The logic for the potential of moral hazard is clear; the harder question is how much there is in practice. For some, fear of moral hazard should deter large rescue packages no more than it argues for banning fire departments. For others, it is the dominant feature of international capital markets.

My own view is that cases vary but that it is rarely a major factor. As pointed out by Jeanne and Zettelmeyer (2001), the size of the direct subsidy associated with the rescue packages would seem too small for them to generate major moral hazard. Evidence presented by Dell'Ariccia, Gödde, and Zettelmeyer (2000) suggests strongly that there is some moral hazard, as suggested by the increase in spreads and their tighter relationship to fundamentals after the Russian default of 1998. As those authors argue, the Mexico bailout of 1994–95 was not a good "natural experiment" to test the implications of the bailout itself as distinct from other things that went on at the same time. Nonetheless, the evidence about the Mexican bailout of 1994–95 argues strongly that the combined effects of the Mexican crisis itself and the associated bailout were negative for emerging-market spreads, even in Asia. At a minimum, the insurance was not perceived to be complete. My impression, based on more anecdotal evidence, is also that there was very little thought that the IMF might actually have to bail out the Asian tigers prior to the crisis of 1997. Financial booms can precede financial busts without moral hazard.[1]

I do not want to give the impression that the USTIMF had a fully articulated rationale for package sizes. On the contrary, the process has been entirely ad hoc. Politics have played an important role, of course, but there have also been efforts to conduct gap-filling exercises to determine how much is needed. The traditional IMF financing gap analysis assumes some feasible but broadly "good" scenario with an amount of adjustment deemed appropriate. The resulting balance-of-payments financing gap must be closed with IMF (or other "exceptional") official lending. An alternative approach that has emerged in the major crises of the 1990s has been to examine the vulnerability of the country to a shortage of liquidity. In practice, specific categories of liabilities have been the focus of the liquidity crisis, and calculations of required package size have typically involved assuming that these categories will flee the country, whereas others may be rolled over. The at-risk categories have varied across episodes. It is not clear, in general, what claims should be the focus of the liquidity crisis; presumably expectations may coordinate around many equilibria.

These sorts of calculations, especially (but not only) the traditional analysis, would seem to assume some type of imperfect capital mobility. Put alternatively, the assumption is that sterilized intervention can work, in that it can keep incipient gaps from resulting in sharp interest rate increases or depreciations. My own view, although this is taking us far afield of Goldstein's paper, is that a complete view of appropriate package size will probably need to consider seriously imperfect capital mobility. Models of package size that assume perfect capital mobility have a hard time rationalizing the sort of interior solutions observed in practice (as shown by Jeanne and Wyplosz, chap. 4 in this volume). It may be that the practice is indefensible; alternatively, it may be that, especially in times of crisis, demands for the assets of a country are sloped, or certain types or categories of investments are more likely to flee.

The debate on private-sector involvement (PSI) or burden sharing is in many ways the dual of the discussion of package size. I would characterize the USTIMF view as having been one that found the liquidity/solvency distinction useful for describing the role of PSI. In cases that are toward the pure liquidity end of the spectrum, most notably Korea in 1997, PSI can be

---

1. DeRosa (2001) strongly asserts that moral hazard from the Mexico bailout led to the Asian crisis. He tells a number of stories about how market participants behaved in the run-up to the Asian crisis; however, that suggest a much different picture. They emphasize the role of shortsighted speculators' placing undue confidence in pegs, without a thought of the IMF. Indeed, he argues for a close analogy between the European exchange rate mechanism crisis in which surely confidence in IMF bailouts played no role) and the Asian crises.

helpful, although it may well be counterproductive to push for too much. Of course, the corollary is that a serious liquidity crisis might call for a large package. A demand for a standstill or other comprehensive PSI, as called for in recent years by some non-U.S. Group of Seven (G7) officials, requires an implausible leap of faith that such a standstill will coordinate expectations around a good equilibrium rather than leading to a rush for the exits.

For cases in which a major rescue package and policy adjustment are unlikely to solve the problem—that is, for crises that are closer to being solvency crises, the approach has been different. Indeed, since 1998 Pakistan, Ukraine, Ecuador, and Russia have defaulted on international debt. Although the IMF thus did not fully bail out creditors and avert default in these cases, it was often involved in the postdefault workouts. These sorts of cases have received much less attention in the public architecture debate, and in Goldstein's paper, than the Mexico-style bailouts without PSI. Recent events in Argentina have suggested that such solvency crises may return to a prominence they enjoyed in the 1980s, rather than the liquidity crises that have received so much attention of late.

More issues are raised by these sorts of cases than I can fully discuss here. It may be useful, though, to touch on the role of the IMF and other official creditors. In practice, the IMF has generally provided a seal of approval of the eventual workout, which was nonetheless negotiated between the countries and their creditors. The IMF was to some extent the agent of official bilateral creditors, who required, through the Paris Club process, that an inforce IMF program accompany their own rescheduling efforts. The IMF thus has found itself in the role of certifying that the debt write-down was sufficient to restore solvency and also that the country was making a reasonable effort to repay what it could.

Key unresolved questions are many:

- Have the potential coordination problems associated with the debt workouts been satisfactorily resolved? In some cases it may be that fears of legal action and insufficient debtor protection have led to minimal write-downs, such that debt overhang remains a serious problem.
- What is the potential role of collective action clauses in overcoming free-rider problems? In practice, debtors have not exploited these clauses even when available. In the case of Ecuador, they proved unnecessary. The debt contracts in Ecuador's external bond debt, as with most Eurobonds, permitted all but key financial terms of the arrangements to be modified with a 50 percent majority (through so-called exit amendments). Ecuador achieved its debt write-down by offering to exchange outstanding bonds for new ones of a smaller face value. Creditors accepting the exchange of their bonds had to first agree to exit amendments that substantially weakened the legal claims of holdouts. Thus, in the end, most bondholders tendered their bonds. Peru's recent

experience in which the sovereign settled with holdout claimants after the creditors had won some court cases, on the other hand, suggests that holdouts may remain an important obstacle to debt workouts. It is still unclear at this point whether Ecuador will provide a model for more complicated debt workout situations such as may occur in the future.

- The question of how the burden of write-downs is to be shared between private creditors and official bilateral creditors has been the source of great friction. In a typical Paris Club arrangement, amortizations over the IMF program period are rescheduled at low contractual interest rates. It can usually be safely assumed that subsequent amortizations will also be rescheduled on the same terms, although the Paris Club will make no commitment. Legal and political constraints also make it difficult for Paris Club to accept face-value reductions for all but the poorest debtors. Private-sector creditors, on the other hand, want a restructuring of the entire stock of debt, but they may willing to accept large face-value reductions, particularly in return for cash payments up front.

- Both private and public creditors are suspicious that the other set of creditors is getting a better deal, in part because they have sharply different views about how to compare these two types of reschedulings. The core of the difficulty lies in how to value the net present value (NPV) of future Paris Club amortizations (or, as it is sometimes said, whether to think about stocks or flows). The private sector tends to want to calculate the NPV of the stock of Paris Club debt, both rescheduled and not (yet) rescheduled. This may be substantial, because no face-value reductions take place and no further reschedulings can be assumed. Paris Club creditors, on the other hand, know they will likely never actually see a cent, due to future reschedulings, so they have a tendency to look at cash flows over the IMF program period. They thus look askance at large cash payments to the private-sector creditors, although these are often highly valued by these creditors and can be a condition for a successful exchange.

I have spent most of my time so far today on type-1 solutions as I categorized them above, that is, on those that are controversial mostly because of differing views of the nature of the problem. Let me touch a bit on some of the other parts of the paper. Section 8.2 discusses various changes in the terms of IMF lending. On the whole, the conclusion is that these may be useful changes but that they will not make much difference. I agree, largely for the reasons Goldstein lays out in the paper. Section 8.4 covers a wide variety of elements of IMF conditionality.

By far the most important question is whether the IMF can usefully condition assistance ex ante on structural policies or the implementation of international financial standards. This would hold the promise of allowing the easing of some of the market failures while mitigating the related costs of moral hazard. As Goldstein outlines in the paper, the obstacles to movement in this direction are enormous, however, I see at least a couple of problem areas.

First, a switch to ex ante conditionality may not be time-consistent. We may not know what conditions to put down. In this case, many crises may happen anyway, and we will be faced with the possibility that a supplemental reserve facility (SRF)–type response would be, at that point, optimal. Similarly, authorities may not accept that they will only be helped if they satisfy ex ante conditions. That is, they may still count on the bailouts. The cost of the IMF's failing to satisfy these expectations could be high (under the assumption that SRF packages do in fact help, ignoring strategic considerations). One lesson is that merely adding ex ante conditionality to the current facilities (along the lines of the contingency credit line) is not likely to make much difference, because it will tend to be weak in terms of conditions and countries will not want it anyway, counting on the SRF if they really get in trouble. A more dramatic switch to purely ex ante conditionality would be risky: If no one noticed or believed the regime change, there would be no reason for crisis incidence to go down, and the worst of both worlds might prevail, at least for a time: high crisis incidence because of moral hazard but no mitigating support packages. (Jeanne and Zettelmeyer 2001 contains a useful discussion of this issue.)

Second, the resistance from developing country countries to any sort of dramatic move to ex ante conditionality would be extremely fierce. Moreover, such a move would, according to some, require amendments to the IMF articles. Of course, a unified and motivated G7 could presumably still make it happen.

In his discussion of the question of currency regimes, Goldstein suggests that the trend to the corners (i.e., to hard pegs or floats) is real and welcome. I would only add that the jury is still out on this question. Even though floating regimes do, I think, offer a real degree of freedom to many emerging markets, it is always possible that a sufficient degree of pressure on an exchange rate may lead the authorities to move from leaning against the wind to defending a parity, from which a crisis may ensure. In this case, managed floats are no panacea. Evidence in Berg, Borensztein, and Pattillo (2001) shows that currency crises have been no more likely to occur in fixed than flexible exchange rates over the 1973–99 period in a sample of twenty five emerging-market economies, consistent with a view that this sort of occurrence is common. As for the other corner, Argentina's recent experience may remind us that Panama has had more IMF programs than any other country over the last couple of decades.

I found it hard to see how to make operational the recommendation to streamline structural conditionality and the need to streamline. Almost everyone is in favor of simplified and focused conditionality in theory, but they typically disagree about what should be focused on. Goldstein wants the IMF to go back to basics, but at various points he advocates the following: the publishing of detailed assessments of how countries are observing various codes and standards; publication of in-depth analyses of financial systems; the collection and reporting of data on maturity mismatches; a central role for the IMF in calling for payments standstills; and the enforcement by the IMF of good deposit insurance schemes. Collectively, this represents an extremely ambitious set of initiatives. The World Bank can perhaps carry some of the load, but it is worth emphasizing that for some time there has been widespread agreement that the division of labor between the World Bank and the IMF should move in this direction. The problem has been that the World Bank has not been able, in practice, to step up to the plate.

To conclude, the movement to reform the international architecture has been in some disarray for several years, because little progress was made on some key fronts after the Asia crisis. According to a common view, what began as architecture has ended up as interior decorating. Most disappointing to some observers has been the continuing practice in the later Clinton-Camdessus administration of providing large bailouts to emerging-market debtors such as Turkey and Argentina in 2000.

For a time, it seemed that the change of administration in 2001 could provide an opportunity to take a dramatically different tack. According to the view that market failures are fairly limited in importance and moral hazard a dominant problem in international capital markets, a reduction in the role of the IMF could be a useful tonic. Emerging markets would be encouraged to build institutions that would encourage stable capital flows. Moreover, ex ante conditionality seems to promise a way to buffer some of the most extreme vagaries of international capital markets while avoiding the alleged dangers of severe moral hazard created by the current system. Moreover, only in a context of a regime change might a credible switch to a new regime be achieved. If policy makers around the world could be convinced that bailouts were in fact no more, some of the potential costs of that switch might be mitigated.

However, as of this writing, the opportunity to make a clear and hence credible break with the past may have been lost. The response to crises in Argentina and Turkey has so far been broadly similar. Meanwhile, there is little to suggest that effective ex ante conditionality is in serious prospect of being in place in the foreseeable future.

Events may be moving much faster, though, than the architecture debate itself. Let me emphasize two dimensions. First, there would seem to be more differentiation among emerging-market countries than has been observed for much of the 1990s. Whereas countries such as Argentina and Turkey are mired in major crises, others, such as Mexico, Chile, and Poland, may have graduated. This latter group may be able to benefit from floating exchange rates to buffer shocks, have debt stocks that appear readily manageable, and are gradually developing domestic capital markets in a way that may reduce dependence on volatile external capital flows over time.

The other major change that is occurring, and this one is more clear-cut, is that the crises that loom now are quite different from most of the major ones of the mid- to late 1990s, in that they seem to be mainly debt/solvency crises. Indeed, we see a disconcerting return to many of the problems associated with the debt crises of the 1980s. Much of the impetus for the first major bailout of the 1990s, the Mexico program in 1995, was a desire to avoid another "lost decade." By that measure, the Mexico rescue package must be judged a major success, at least for Mexico. I fear we will shortly see whether a (different) dramatic new policy response is needed to the new debt crises. Major debt workouts in international capital markets may turn out to be terribly painful, and it may become clear that more laissez-faire approaches to the role of the IMF will also turn out to be very costly. In any case, we can be fairly confident that the architectural debate will look very different in their wake.

References

Berg, Andrew, Eduardo Borensztein, and Catherine Pattillo. 2001. Assessing early warning systems: How have they worked in practice? IMF Working Paper draft. Washington, D.C.: International Monetary Fund, November.

Dell'Ariccia, Giovanni, Isabel Gödde, and Jeromin Zettelmeyer. 2000. Moral hazard and international crisis lending: A test. Paper presented at the IMF First Annual Research Conference, November. Available at [http://www.imf.org].

DeRosa, David. 2001. *In defense of free capital markets*. Princeton, N.J.: Bloomberg Press.

Jeanne, Olivier, and Jeromin Zettelmeyer. 2001. International bailouts, moral hazard, and conditionality. *Economic Policy* 33 (October): 409–24.

Discussion Summary

Jeffrey Shafer remarked that it makes little sense to adopt a smaller rescue package than what is needed for the crisis economy. He pointed to the distinction between liquidity and solvency issues and emphasized the importance of sustaining voluntary private-sector involvement. He noted that on the one hand it will be politically difficult for international financial institutions to be selective, whereas on the other hand these institutions will risk becoming increasingly discredited if they do not develop the capacity for being selective.

Richard Portes remarked that the paper would benefit from a more elaborate discussion of the controversy over whether rules or discretion should guide IMF policies. He observed that the extensive debate following the

Mexican and Asian crises on the international financial architecture seems to have had little effect on recent policies toward countries such as Turkey and Argentina.

Vincent Reinhart remarked that borrowing from the IMF is an adverse signal and noted that countries doing so still get subsidized.

Nouriel Roubini remarked that there is a trade-off between large-scale and small-scale private-sector involvement. He noted that the Meltzer proposal entails changing the current five-pillar structure of the IMF into a one-pillar system.

Peter B. Kenen wondered how the Meltzer proposal could be implemented and argued that it essentially implies closing down the IMF and re-opening a new IMF consisting only of the qualifying countries. With respect to the size of packages, he noted that the pre-Mexico level of funds seems inadequate for the more recent crises. He added that the announced size of a package may be somewhat misleading because programs are tranched and parts are conditional on policies adopted.

Morris Goldstein remarked that more needs to be said with respect to the division between the IMF and the World Bank. In terms of the appropriate size of rescue packages, he favored conditioning package sizes on whether a crisis is systemic or non-systemic, although, admittedly, such a distinction is not clear-cut, because a crisis is always systemic for the neighbors and trading partners of the crisis country. He questioned whether it is possible to replicate the bailout of the Mexican crisis and argued that it seems impossible to achieve improved credit assessment unless investors perceive that there is a substantial amount of risk involved.

III

The Impact

9

Recovery and Sustainability in East Asia

Yung Chul Park and Jong-Wha Lee

9.1 Introduction

Over the three years since the crisis broke out in 1997, the five Asian countries—Indonesia, Korea, Thailand, Malaysia, and the Philippines—managed impressive recoveries. The recoveries were faster than expected by anyone. The economies started to bottom out in the second half of 1998. The rebounding of the growth rate in 1999 was no less drastic than its free-fall. In Korea, for example, the growth rates showed a turnaround from –6.7 percent in 1998 to 10.7 percent in 1999.

The purpose of this paper is to make an assessment of this speedy adjustment from the crisis in East Asia. In particular, we analyze the macroeconomic adjustment process of the East Asian currency crisis in a broad international perspective. First, we assess the impacts of the crisis on gross domestic product (GDP) growth using a cross-country data set, which compiled all currency crisis episodes over the period from 1970 to 1995. From these cross-country data, we draw some stylized facts about the adjustment of key macroeconomic variables during the crisis. Then we investigate the critical factors that determine the adjustment process.

Our analysis of cross-country patterns shows that GDP growth rates drop with the eruption of a crisis but then recover quickly to the precrisis level in two or three years, showing a V-pattern of adjustment. Thereafter, the GDP growth rates tend to rise slightly above the precrisis levels, but then

Yung Chul Park is a professor of economics at Korea University. Jong-Wha Lee is a professor of economics at Korea University.

The authors thank Robert Barro, Richard Portes, and conference participants for their helpful comments on an earlier draft. Si-Yeon Lee and Do-Won Kwak provided able research assistance.

they subside to a more sustainable level. We also compare the adjustment patterns of GDP growth rates between two subgroups of the currency crisis episodes, one with conditional financial assistance from the International Monetary Fund (IMF) and the other without. We find that the adjustment process was much sharper in the group of the crisis episodes with the IMF program compared to those without. That is, in the IMF-program countries, GDP growth rates start to fall precipitously even before the eruption of a crisis but then recover to their precrisis level more quickly in two years.

The macroeconomic adjustment process in East Asia is in general consistent with these stylized patterns. However, the degree of initial contraction and following recovery has been far greater in East Asia than what the cross-country evidence predicts. This paper tries to make an evaluation of what factors contributed to the sharper contraction and the quicker recovery in East Asia compared with the cross-country patterns.

As we will discuss in section 9.3, we believe that a large number of internal and external factors are responsible for the deeper crisis and the quicker recovery in East Asia. The origin and the nature of the shock, the initial conditions, the development of external environments, and the stabilization and structural adjustment policies taken must have a significant consequence on the adjustment path, as they did in the eruption of the crisis. From cross-country regressions based on the sample of previous crisis episodes, we find that depreciation of exchange rate, expansionary macroeconomic policies, and favorable global environments are the critical determinants of the postcrisis recovery. In the regression, the financial assistance from the IMF is found to have no independent impact on the recovery process.

We find that the quick recoveries in East Asia have been driven largely by the accommodating macroeconomic policies, favorable external environments, and more export-oriented structure. Korea, Malaysia, and Thailand shifted to a relaxation of monetary and fiscal policies by the second half of 1998, and then their economy took off. The sharp real depreciation of currency must have a bigger impact on more open Asian economies. Favorable external development also helped the quick improvement in East Asian exports. In this sense, the East Asian process of adjustment is not much different from the stylized pattern from the previous currency crisis episodes over the period from 1970 to 1995. However, the stylized pattern of adjustment cannot explain why the crisis was more severe and the recovery much faster than what was expected from the previous experiences of crisis. This paper argues that the sharper adjustment pattern in East Asia is due to the severe liquidity crisis that was triggered by investors' panic and then amplified by the weak corporate and bank balance sheet.

The stylized pattern of real GDP growth from the cross-country episodes displays that the crisis-hit countries can recover their precrisis or noncrisis average growth rate in three years after the crisis. Hence, it raises a question of whether the East Asian economies will be able to return to the precrisis trend rate of growth.

Although the financial crisis of 1997 abruptly brought a halt to Asia's period of robust growth, there was little in Asia's fundamentals that inevitably led to the crisis. This paper discusses the long-term prospects for growth in East Asia. From the cross-country regressions, we find that there is no evidence of a direct impact of a currency crisis on long-run growth. This suggests that, with a return to the core policies that resulted in rapid growth, the East Asian economies can again return to sustained growth.

The paper is organized as follows. Section 9.2 discusses the methodology for our cross-country analysis and presents central features in the macroeconomic adjustments of the crisis-hit countries. Then, using regression analysis based on the cross-country data, we assess the factors that can explain the behaviors of GDP growth rates during the crisis. Section 9.3 reviews the recent recoveries in East Asia and compares them with the stylized patterns from the cross-country analysis. We analyze the driving forces of the faster recovery in East Asia. Section 9.4 discusses the issue of the sustainability of the current recovery. Concluding remarks are found in the final section.

9.2   Cross-Country Patterns of Adjustment to Currency Crisis

9.2.1   Data

In order to assess the postcrisis adjustment of the crisis-hit countries, one needs first to define a currency crisis. Several alternative indicators and methods have been used in the literature to identify the year when a crisis erupted in each country. Frankel and Rose (1996) and Milesi-Ferreti and Razin (1998) used the nominal depreciation rate of the currency. Sachs, Tornell, and Velasco (1996), Radelet and Sachs (1998), and Kaminsky and Reinhart (1999) combined the depreciation rate with additional indicators such as losses in foreign reserves, increase in the interest rate, and reversal in capital accounts to identify the crisis.

Each definition still has its own limitations. A large-scale depreciation can occur in an orderly manner without a speculative attack. Identifying unsuccessful speculative attacks is a difficult task. Reliable data on reserves and interest rates in developing countries are often unavailable. Reserves or interest rates can change irrespective of an attack. Lee and Rhee (2002) suggested an alternative measure based on the initiation of an IMF stabilization program. However, countries often receive the IMF program after a crisis breaks out or without a currency crisis. Governments may sign an IMF agreement not necessarily because they need foreign exchange, but because they want austerity conditions to be imposed (Przeworski and Vreeland 2000).

Because the purpose of this paper is not to improve the measure of a currency crisis, we use the conventional nominal depreciation rate of the currency as a benchmark measure. However, in contrast to Frankel and Rose (1996), we use quarterly data, instead of annual data, to define a currency crisis. That is, based on quarterly data, a country is judged to have a currency crisis in the specific year when it has a nominal depreciation of currency of at least 25 percent in any quarter of the year and the depreciation rate exceeds the previous quarter's change in the exchange rate by a margin of at least 10 percent. Thus, our definition captures the incidences of currency crises that were severe but short-lived, perhaps due to successful interventions in the foreign exchange market. During the period from 1970 to 1997, the total number of currency crises was 260. We use a window of plus/minus two years to identify an independent crisis. That is, if there was a precedent crisis within two years before a crisis, we count the latter as a consecutive crisis, not an independent one. This procedure yields a total of 192 currency crisis episodes.[1]

Then, we divide all crisis episodes into two groups based on whether the crisis-hit countries entered into an IMF program or not. We have compiled data on all types of IMF programs that include standby arrangements, Extended Fund Facility (EFF) arrangements, Structural Adjustment Facility (SAF), and Enhanced Structural Adjustment Facility (ESAF) over the period from 1970 to 1997.[2] The program is identified by the year when the loans are approved. Thus, if a country received financial assistance from the IMF during the year of, or one year after, the currency crisis, we consider it a case of a currency crisis with the IMF program. Note that the decision on participation in the IMF program following a currency crisis can be determined endogenously by various factors. A country may enter into agreements with the IMF when it faces a more severe foreign reserve crisis or a worse macroeconomic situation (Conway 1994). However, relying on the IMF conditionality may be just a way to impose domestically unpopular austerity policies (Przeworski and Vreeland 2000).

Table 9.1 shows a summary of data on currency crises based on our definition during the period from 1970 to 1997. There were 192 currency crisis episodes during this period. The number of crises was increasing over time, from forty in the 1970s, to sixty nine in the 1980s, to eighty three in the 1990s (1990–97). According to this data set, the number of countries that experienced at least one crisis was ninety nine.[3] Thus, on average each country had

---

1. Lee, Hong, and Rhee (2001) describe the data in more detail. The authors are grateful to Kiseok Hong and Changyong Rhee for sharing their cross-country data set.
2. The data come from Lee and Rhee (2000), who compiled the information from the IMF *Annual Report* for each year.
3. The sample does not include the former Soviet Union countries that experienced currency crises and subsequently received financial assistance from the IMF in the early 1990s.

Table 9.1   **Incidence of Currency Crises and IMF Program Participation Over the Period 1970–97**

		IMF Program Participation	
Period	Total Currency Crises	Yes	No
1970–97	192	71	121
1970–79	40	12	28
1980–89	69	24	45
1990–97	83	35	48

Notes: A currency crisis is defined as occurring in the year when a country has a nominal depreciation of currency of at least 25 percent in any quarter of a year and the depreciation rate exceeds the previous quarter's change in the exchange rate by a margin of at least 10 percent. If the country under a currency crisis received financial assistance from the IMF during the year of or one year after the currency crisis, it is classified as a case of a currency crisis with IMF program participation. Our sample does not include the former Soviet Union countries and counts only independent crises by imposing a plus/minus two years window.

1.86 crises over the period. Out of the 192 crisis episodes, 72 of them featured participation in an IMF program.

9.2.2   Macroeconomic Adjustment During the Currency Crisis

On the basis of the currency crisis index, we investigate how the crisis-hit economies, on average, behave during the five years prior to and following the crisis. We first look at the movement of growth rates of real GDP and then investigate the sources of output changes by looking at the movements of GDP expenditure components and major macroeconomic policy variables in the typical crisis-hit country during the period before and after the crisis. We also construct a control group of tranquil observations. If a country was not subject to any crisis within a window of plus/minus two years surrounding a specific year, it is counted as a noncrisis country in that specific year.

The behavior of the macroeconomic variables between the two subgroups—one with conditional financial assistance from the IMF and the other without—is also compared.

We use the data for the period from 1970 to 1995. Thus, we attempt to draw the stylized pattern of macroeconomic adjustment from the crisis episodes that had occurred prior to the Asian crisis. There are 176 independent currency crises during this period, and in 64 episodes of them the countries participated in an IMF program.

Real Gross Domestic Product Growth

Figure 9.1 shows the movements of the average GDP growth rates during the five years prior to and following the crisis; that is, from $t - 5$ to $t + 5$,

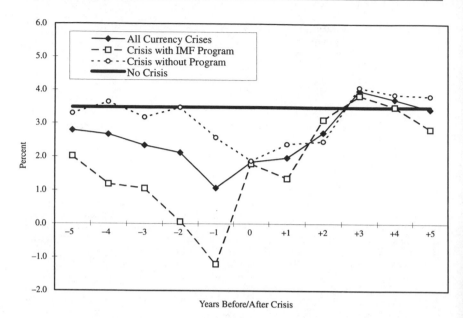

Fig. 9.1   Changes in GDP growth rates during the currency crises

where t is the year of a currency crisis. For comparison, we include a straight line, which indicates the average GDP growth rate during the tranquil period, which did not experience a currency crisis or enter into an IMF program within a window of plus or minus two years.

In general, we find that the growth rates, on average, exhibit a V-type pattern of adjustment over the period before and following the crisis. The growth rates during the period three to five years prior to the crisis are slightly lower than the average during the tranquil period of 3.5 percent. The growth rate continues to decline over time, from 2.7 percent in $t - 4$ to 1.1 percent in $t - 1$, implying that economic conditions are aggravated prior to the eruption of a crisis.

The growth rate increases slightly in the crisis year, which confirms that most currency crises have indeed been expansionary. As in Gupta, Mishra, and Sahay (2000), we also find that about 70 percent of the currency crises in our sample led to an output increase in the crisis year. The average GDP growth rate of the crisis-hit countries remains at about 1.9 percent over the crisis year and one year after. However, the GDP growth rate recovers its noncrisis level quickly, in three years after the crisis, reaching 4.0 percent in $t + 3$—that is, about 0.5 percentage points higher than the average of the noncrisis economies. Thus, the growth rate tends to exceed its precrisis or tranquil period average, indicating that after a crisis the country's level of GDP returns to the level of its precrisis growth path. Eventually, the growth rate tapers off and returns to the level of the tranquil period in four and five years after the crisis. This V-type pattern and the speed of recovery are broadly consistent with the findings in Hong and Tornell (1999) and Gupta, Mishra, and Sahay (2000).

Figure 9.1 compares the behavior of the GDP growth rates between the two subgroups, one with conditional financial assistance from the IMF and the other without. We find that the adjustment process shows a much sharper V-type pattern in the program countries than in the nonprogram countries. The program countries start with lower growth rates of around 1.2 percent in $t-4$ and continue to slow down. They reach the trough, where the growth rate is -1.2 percent, in one year prior to the initiation of the currency crisis.

This magnitude of decline in growth rates is much larger than that of the nonprogram countries. At the trough, the growth rate of the crisis-hit program countries is about 4.7 percentage points lower than that of the noncrisis economies. Thereafter, rebounding from the deeper trough, the program countries show a quicker recovery. The GDP growth rate begins to recover from the crisis year and reaches its precrisis level quickly, within two years after the onset of a crisis. The nonprogram countries also begin to recover a year after the crisis, and then their growth rates stabilize at the noncrisis level from $t+3$.

The fact that the program countries have much lower growth rates than the nonprogram countries confirms that only a very serious macroeconomic situation forces a country to enter into agreements with the IMF. Nevertheless, it is intriguing that the crisis-hit countries show a quicker recovery from a deeper recession with participation in the IMF program.

Gross Domestic Product Expenditure Components

Panels A to F of figure 9.2 show the movements of the components of GDP expenditure during the five years prior to and following the crisis.

Panel A shows that the share of private-consumption expenditure in GDP remains stable over the period. In other words, consumption moves closely with GDP. The adjustment pattern is similar in both program and nonprogram countries. For the overall period, the ratio of consumption to GDP in the crisis-hit economies exceeds the noncrisis tranquil period average, indicating that private consumption is high in the crisis-hit countries, and even after a crisis these countries' level of private saving does not increase to the level of the noncrisis countries.

Panel B of figure 9.2 shows that, in contrast to consumption, the investment (private plus public investment) ratio shows more fluctuations. The level is no higher in the crisis-hit economies than in the noncrisis countries. For four to five years prior to the crisis, the investment ratio remains at an average level of tranquil observations of 22.8 percent. Thus, a stylized fact is that the crisis-hit countries have had "overconsumption," but not necessarily "overinvestment," compared to the level of the noncrisis countries. In

A

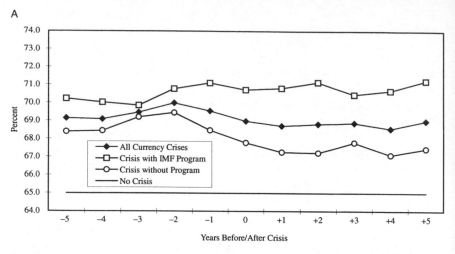

B

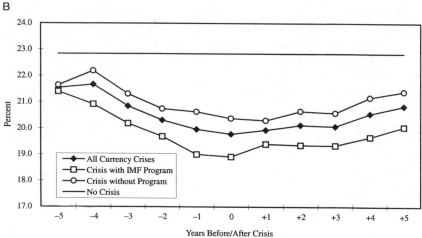

C

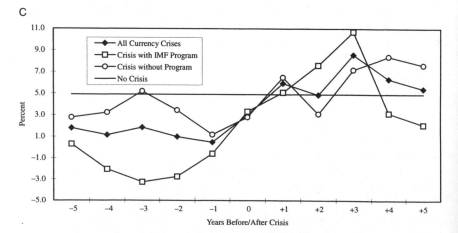

Fig. 9.2   Changes in GDP expenditure components during the currency crises: *A,*
private consumption in GDP; *B,* **investment rate;** *C,* **real export growth rate;** *D,* **export
share in GDP;** *E,* **real import growth rate;** *F,* **import share in GDP.**

D

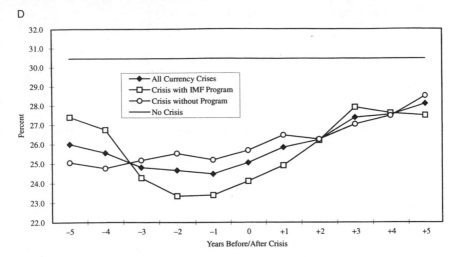

E

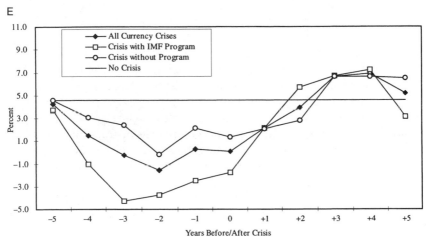

F

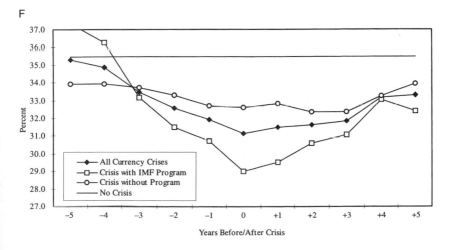

Fig. 9.2   (cont.)

the crisis-hit countries, the investment rate tends to decline during the precrisis period, reaching 19.8 percent in the crisis year. After the crisis, the investment rate increases gradually but does not return to the level of the precrisis or tranquil period, remaining at 20.9 percent for five years following the crisis. A popular claim regarding the role of the IMF conditionality is that the austerity program has an adverse effect on investment. Panel B of figure 9.2 seems to support this claim. The IMF-program countries have experienced a more severe investment contraction than the other group in the precrisis period, as the investment ratio declines continuously from 21.4 percent in $t-5$ to 18.9 percent in t. In the postcrisis period of the crisis-hit countries in which an IMF program is introduced, the investment rate does not recover to the precrisis level, remaining at 19.7 percent in $t+4$ and 20.1 percent in $t+5$. In contrast, the investment rate returns to the precrisis level in the nonprogram crisis-hit countries in five years after the crisis.

In the crisis-hit countries, domestic expenditure or demand either slowly recovers or remains permanently below the precrisis level. In contrast, export demand shows a quick recovery during the postcrisis period. Panel C shows that in the crisis-hit countries, real export growth rates jump from less than 1 percent in $t-1$ to 3.0 percent in the crisis year and to 5.9 percent in $t+1$, and then they remain at over 5 percent over the postcrisis period. For both program and nonprogram countries, export growth during the postcrisis period is faster than that of the precrisis or tranquil period and, thus, leads a strong recovery. Consequently, as shown in panel D of figure 9.2, after the currency crisis the export share increases permanently above the precrisis level. However, note that on average the export share in all crisis-hit countries is still lower than that of the noncrisis average.

During the early postcrisis period the quick recovery of export growth is accompanied by a contraction of import demand. The pattern of import reduction is more conspicuous in the program countries where import growth rates are negative in the precrisis period as well as the crisis year. Panels E and F of figure 9.2 show that although the growth rate of imports recovers to the precrisis and noncrisis average in two years following the crisis, its share in GDP remains below the noncrisis average of 35.5 percent. The growth of exports and imports shows that the ratio of current account to GDP improves quickly after the crisis. Thus, net exports tend to lead the recovery in the crisis-hit countries.

Macroeconomic Policy Indicators

Public consumption is an indicator of fiscal policy. Panels A and B of figure 9.3 show that public consumption growth rates tend to slow down slightly in the crisis year and then recover to the precrisis as well as noncrisis average. However, in the first year following the crisis, there is contrasting behavior between the program countries and nonprogram countries. Whereas the public consumption growth rate is over 5.0 percent for the

A

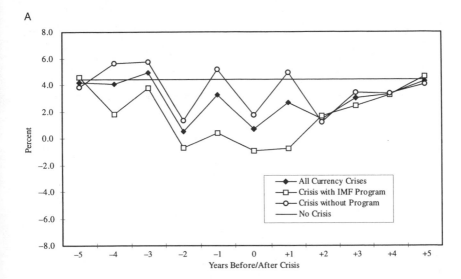

B

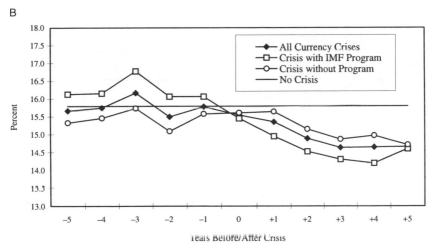

Fig. 9.3   Macroeconomic policy indicators during the currency crises: *A,* **real public consumption growth rate;** *B,* **public consumption in GDP;** *C,* **real money supply (M2) growth rate;** *D,* **real bank credit growth rate.**

nonprogram countries, it is –0.8 percent for the program countries in the year of $t + 1$. This confirms that an agreement with the IMF introduces a contractionary fiscal policy in the program country. Reflecting this sharp contraction in public consumption expenditure, the ratio of public consumption to GDP declines quickly in $t + 1$ with the IMF program. The ratio remains at the level lower than the precrisis or noncrisis average in both program and nonprogram countries even five years after a crisis.

Like fiscal policy, monetary policy of the program countries contrasts

C

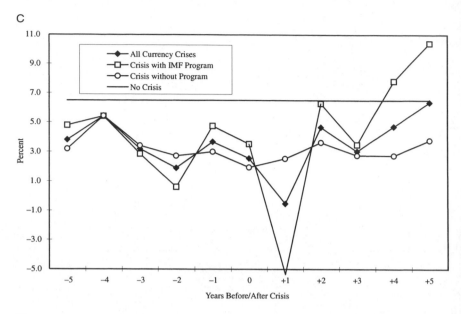

D

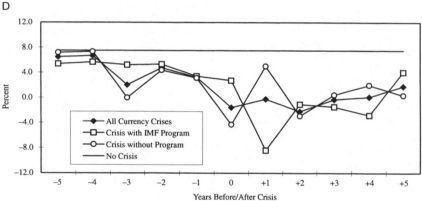

Fig. 9.3   **(cont.)**

sharply with that of the nonprogram countries. Panel C of figure 9.3 shows that the real money supply growth rate remains positive throughout the years following the crisis and increases over time to return to the precrisis level in five years after the crisis in the nonprogram countries. In contrast, in the sample of the crisis-hit countries with IMF program participation, money supply growth is negative. Thereafter, it returns to the precrisis average growth rate. The sharp reduction in money supply in the program countries implies that, as in fiscal policy, participation in an IMF program brings in tight monetary policy in the crisis-hit economy.

It is claimed that a currency crisis often develops into a banking crisis. As

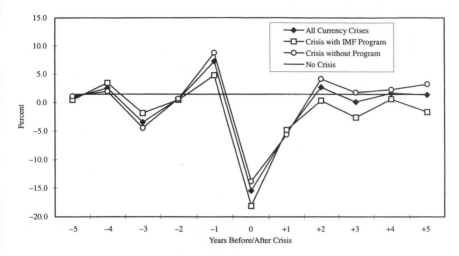

Fig. 9.4   Change in real exchange rate during the currency crises

international lending declines suddenly, a weak banking sector is unable to play a proper intermediation role. Banks reduce the supply of credit to the private sector. Panel D shows that credit supply growth indeed slows down in the crisis-hit countries. For four to five years prior to the crisis, the real credit growth rate is 7.4 percent. Thereafter, credit growth rates decline over time, reaching –1.6 percent in the crisis year. Even five years after the crisis, credit growth does not return to the level of the precrisis or tranquil period. The slowdown of real credit growth is more pronounced in the IMF-program countries. The supply of real credit declines by more than 8 percent in the year following the crisis and thereafter continues to slow down throughout the postcrisis period.

The robust growth of net exports during the postcrisis period is likely to be related to the real exchange depreciation associated with (or caused by) the currency crisis. Figure 9.4 shows that a currency crisis causes a sharp real depreciation of the exchange rate by about 15 percent in the crisis year. The real exchange rate also depreciates by 5.3 percent in the year following the crisis. Thereafter, it appreciates about 2 percent per year. Hence, the real exchange remains depreciated after the crisis. The pattern of adjustment in the real exchange rate is similar in the program and nonprogram countries.

9.2.3   Determinants of the Postcrisis Recovery

We believe there are a large number of factors that determine the stylized pattern of adjustment in real output growth in the crisis-hit countries. Broadly speaking, there are four major factors that influence the adjustment pattern: (a) the origin and nature of the shock; (b) initial conditions; (c) domestic policies; and (d) external environments.

Origin and Nature of the Shock

The origin and nature of the shock that has provoked a crisis can influence the evolution of the crisis. Many currency crises can be attributed to macroeconomic mismanagement—large budget deficits and consequent monetary expansion in a fixed exchange rate regime—as was the Latin America debt crisis in the early 1980s. In this case, real depreciation of the currency and contraction of domestic absorption help to restore internal and external balance, leading to improvement in the economy.

Investors' panic can intensify the effects of speculative attacks on currency. In particular, when the capital account is liberalized, a bad expectation by foreign investors can easily lead to a sudden reversal of foreign lending, thereby causing a significant contraction of the domestic economy. In particular, the adverse impact will be magnified if domestic corporations and financial institutions are heavily leveraged by large, unhedged, and short-term foreign currency debts. When a sharp and unexpected depreciation wreaks havoc with highly leveraged corporate and bank balance sheets, a sudden reversal of capital flows exacerbates the downturn in investment and the economy (Krugman 1999; Aghion, Bacchetta, and Banerjee 2000). However, once the investors' panic calms down and foreign capital resumes its inward flow, the economy can rebound quickly to its long-term trend.

Initial Conditions

Differences in initial conditions could result in different patterns of adjustment. For example, structural variables such as per capita output and openness could be important in determining the pattern of postcrisis recovery.

The level of initial per capita GDP can influence the growth rate in the postcrisis period. In growth theory, a country with a lower initial per capita GDP is in a more favorable position for future growth. The fundamental idea is that the gap in existing capital and technology between the current and steady-state levels offers a chance for rapid catching up, via high rates of capital accumulation as well as the diffusion of technology from more technically advanced economies. In addition, when a currency crisis leads an economy to a lower level of per capita income relative to that of its own trend, the subsequent growth rate of the economy that rebounds to its potential growth would be higher.

Openness can also influence the speed and extent of the postcrisis recovery. When the economy is more export-oriented, a quicker improvement in the current account follows a currency devaluation. Lee and Rhee (2000) argue that the quick recovery of the Korean economy may have been possible because of its openness and export orientation. An export-oriented economy benefits more from devaluation after the crisis, and a subsequent improvement in the current account could in turn help restore foreign investors' confidence and hence stability in the foreign exchange market.

Several studies also point out that the behavior of macroeconomic variables prior to the crisis can influence the degree of real output contraction. For example, a rapid expansion of bank credit or lending boom during the precrisis period is critical to the postcrisis recovery (Sachs, Tornell, and Velasco 1996; Hong and Tornell 1999). Gupta, Mishra, and Sahay (2000) find that the higher the size of short-term external debt and the amount of private capital flows in the years prior to the crisis, the more severe the contraction of output during the crisis period.

Policy Factors

Macroeconomic and structural reform policies implemented by the government for crisis management can play a key role in the postcrisis adjustment of real output. Fiscal policy has a direct impact on domestic demand. Monetary policy plays a critical role in determining domestic consumption and investment.

In addition to the macroeconomic stabilization policies, structural reform programs can have significant effects on the adjustment path. It is often argued that structural reforms introduced by the IMF play a catalytic role in resuming foreign trade and private capital inflows to a crisis-hit economy and thus contribute to its fast recovery, because the commitment to the reform program improves foreign investors' confidence in the economy. The critics of the IMF program, however, argue that the implementation of financial restructuring in conjunction with contractionary macroeconomic policies can make a credit crunch more severe than otherwise after the crisis.

For external demand, a larger depreciation of the exchange rate is expected to increase export earnings while cutting down import demand to improve the current account.

External Environments

A global economic environment is also critical to the postcrisis adjustment of crisis-hit countries. Business fluctuations of the world economy can influence postcrisis growth, because they have a substantial impact on the terms of trade and export earnings of the crisis-hit country.

To the extent that the relevant data are available, we carry out an empirical assessment of the factors determining the pattern of postcrisis recovery. The explanatory variables that we consider to explain the speed and the extent of postcrisis recovery include per capita real GDP in the crisis year; world economic growth, which is an average of per capita GDP growth rates of a crisis-hit country's trading partners weighted by its trade share; an interactive term of the real exchange depreciation rate with openness (trade-GDP ratio); real public consumption growth; and real money supply growth. We also include an investment rate.[4]

The regression also includes a dummy variable for the IMF-program countries to see if participation in an IMF program had any impact on the recovery process. Upon entering an agreement with the IMF, a member government subscribes to the IMF conditionality, which typically entails fiscal austerity, tight monetary policy, and currency devaluation. Because we include macroeconomic policies variables separately in the regression, the dummy variable may be able to capture the effect of the IMF program participation in postcrisis recovery.

We also control the differences in country-specific factors that may influence the potential growth path, by including the average growth rate for three to five years prior to the crisis. However, we do not include the precrisis macroeconomic policy variables in the regressions, because the impact of these variables on the postcrisis recovery is extensively discussed in Hong and Tornell (1999) and Gupta, Mishra, and Satay (2000). Also, we cannot incorporate any variables that measure structural vulnerabilities of the corporate and financial sectors due to the lack of broad cross-country data.

The dependent variable in the regression is the average growth rate of real GDP during the postcrisis period over k years.[5]

$$(1) \qquad y_{i,t+k} = \frac{1}{k} \sum_{j=1}^{k} (\ln \text{GDP}_{i,t+j} - \ln \text{GDP}_{i,t+j-1}), \quad I = 1, \dots, N,$$

where $\text{GDP}_{i,t+j}$ is real GDP for country i in the j years after the crisis year (t) and N is the number of crisis episodes in our sample. Then, $y_{i,t+k}$ represents the real GDP growth rate, averaged over the postcrisis period of k years. Because we are mostly interested in short-term recovery, we choose k from 1 to 5. In the previous literature, k was often chosen arbitrarily, and thus cross-section data in which each country had only one observation were used for empirical investigation. Our framework differs significantly in that we use panel data. Thus, we utilize both cross-section and time-dimension information. Our regression specification is as follows.

$$(2) \qquad y_{i,t+k} = \beta' X_{i,t+k} + \varepsilon_{i,t+k}, \quad i = 1, \dots, N, \quad k = 1, \dots, 5.$$

where X denotes the vector of the explanatory variables. Note that some independent variables, such as real GDP in the crisis year, precrisis average

---

4. Investment ratio can be considered an endogenous variable. The regression results do not change qualitatively when we have excluded investment ratio from the regressions. Note that investment includes public investment in addition to private investment. The regressions for investment rate are presented in table 9.4.

5. We have also estimated another specification by using the reversal of GDP growth rate between the crisis-hit (that is, $t - 1$ and t) and the postcrisis period, instead of postcrisis GDP growth, for the dependent variable in the regressions. We find the results do not change much.

growth rate, and an IMF program dummy, are identical across all five equations. Fiscal policy variable is included as an average over the period from the crisis year t to the postcrisis year $t + k$, while monetary growth and real exchange depreciation variables are included as an average over the period from the crisis year t to the postcrisis $t + k - 1$.

We estimate this system of the five equations by a seemingly unrelated regression (SUR) technique that corrects for heteroskedasticity in each equation and correlation of the errors across the equations.

Table 9.2 displays our estimates of the basic regression for postcrisis recovery at various horizons that was applied to a total of 101 previous crisis episodes during the period from 1970 to 1995.

We find a strong and statistically significant negative relation between the initial real per capita GDP and the postcrisis growth rate at all horizons, implying that countries with lower per capita income tend to have larger in-

Table 9.2   **Determinants of the Pace of Recovery from the Currency Crises (A sample of 101 crisis episodes between 1970 and 1995)**

	Dependent Variable: Average GDP Growth Rate from $t + 1$ to $t + k$				
$t + k =)$	$t + 1$	$t + 2$	$t + 3$	$t + 4$	$t + 5$
Real GDP per capita at t	−2.037*	−1.240*	−1.028*	−0.817*	−0.816*
PPP-adjusted, log	(0.532)	(0.380)	(0.324)	(0.283)	(0.257)
Precrisis GDP growth average,	−0.137	−0.030	0.060	0.057	0.090
$t - 3$ to $t - 5$	(0.135)	(0.097)	(0.083)	(0.072)	(0.066)
World per capita GDP growth	0.445*	0.261	0.469*	0.580*	0.541*
average, $t + 1$ to $t + k$	(0.225)	(0.175)	(0.155)	(0.166)	(0.198)
Investment ratio average,	0.133*	0.136*	0.123*	0.125*	0.104*
$t + 1$ to $t + k$	(0.031)	(0.037)	(0.032)	(0.028)	(0.026)
Real exchange rate change × trade	0.032	0.004	−0.034**	−0.062*	−0.086*
share average, t to $t + k - 1$	(0.023)	(0.020)	(0.019)	(0.023)	(0.029)
Public consumption growth	0.035	0.057*	0.072*	0.078*	0.086*
average, t to $t + k$	(0.032)	(0.025)	(0.021)	(0.019)	(0.024)
Real money supply growth	0.006	0.012	0.011	0.003	−0.0001
average, t to $t + k - 1$	(0.015)	(0.011)	(0.010)	(0.009)	(0.010)
IMF program participation	−1.042	0.194	0.179	−0.215	−0.040
dummy	(0.968)	(0.699)	(0.589)	(0.515)	(0.468)
No. of crisis episodes	101	101	101	101	101
	0.14	0.17	0.24	0.30	0.33

Notes: Standard errors reported in parentheses. The system has five equations, in which the dependent variables are the average real GDP growth rates over k years from the crisis year, t. The system is estimated the seemingly unrelated regression (SUR) technique, which allows for different error variances in each equation and for correlation of these errors across equations. Each equation has a different constant term, which is not reported. An increase in real exchange rate indicates a real appreciation.

*Significant at the 90 percent level.

**Significant at the 95 percent level.

creases in GDP growth over the period after the crisis. The impact of initial GDP on the postcrisis recovery is much larger in the year following the crisis, but then it become smaller in the later years of the postcrisis period. The estimated coefficients imply that a 10 percentage point drop in per capita GDP in the crisis year is associated with a 0.2 percentage point [2.04 ∗ ln(0.9)] increase in GDP growth in the first year after a crisis erupted, but with a 0.1 percentage point increase on average over five years after the crisis.

The world growth variable also has a significantly positive coefficient in most of the regressions. The estimated coefficient implies that a 1 percentage point increase in world per capita GDP growth is associated with about a 0.5 percentage point increase in GDP growth of the crisis-hit country in the postcrisis period.

The result also confirms the strong association between investment and GDP growth over the period of adjustment in the crisis-hit economies. The coefficients show that an increase of 10 percentage points in the ratio of investment to GDP is typically associated with an increase in the growth rate of about 1.3 percentage points per year.

Among the macroeconomic policy variables, the fiscal variable (measured by public consumption growth) turns out to be most significant for the recovery in all postcrisis periods except for the year of $t + 1$. The estimated coefficients imply that an increase of the public consumption growth rate by 10 percentage points leads to an increase in GDP growth rate by 0.5–0.9 percent.

In contrast to the positive and significant contribution of fiscal policy, monetary policy turns out to be less important for postcrisis recovery. The average growth rates of real money supply are insignificant in all equations. One might argue that the weak effect of monetary policy on real output even in the short run is not credible. However, in our view, the real impact of monetary policy is ambiguous in the crisis-hit economies. Contractionary monetary policy, which is part of the IMF programs, can contribute to postcrisis growth as it helps stabilize prices and improve the current account.[6]

The test shows that the interactive term between trade share and exchange rate depreciation variables has a significant impact on the postcrisis GDP growth in only a few years following a crisis. The estimated coefficient shows that for the country with the average openness ratio of 0.6, a real exchange depreciation of 10 percent raises real GDP growth rate by about 0.4 percent per year over the four years after the crisis.

We also examined whether the agreements with the IMF had any impact on the postcrisis recovery. The estimated coefficient turns out to be statistically insignificant. Hence, there is no evidence that IMF programs had any

---

6. Goldfajn and Gupta (1999) find that the use of tight monetary policy is accompanied by a sharper recovery of output during the currency crises.

Table 9.3   **Regressions for Investment Rate in the Postcrisis Period**

$(t + k =)$	Dependent Variable: Average Investment Ratio from $t + 1$ to $t + k$		
	$t + 1$	$t + 2$	$t + 3$
GDP growth in the precrisis	0.281**	0.410*	0.349*
period average, $t - 3$ to $t - 5$	(0.152)	(0.141)	(0.156)
Real exchange rate change	0.007	−0.012	0.011
average, t to $t + k - 1$	(0.040)	(0.036)	(0.040)
Public investment–GDP ratio	1.460*	1.319*	1.256*
average, t to $t + k$	(0.231)	(0.131)	(0.111)
Real money supply growth	0.010	0.085*	0.133*
average, t to $t + k - 1$	(0.036)	(0.040)	(0.046)
IMF program participation	1.002	1.748	1.798
dummy	(1.296)	(1.222)	(1.158)
No. of crisis episodes	81	81	81
R^2	0.60	0.65	0.68

Notes: Each equation is estimated by the least squares method. Robust standard errors reported in parentheses. Constant term is included, but not reported.
**Significant at the 90 percent level.
*Significant at the 95 percent level.

significant impact on the recovery process after a currency crisis when other factors were controlled.[7]

Macroeconomic policies may have an additional impact on growth by influencing the level of investment. Table 9.3 shows the results of regressions for the investment rate. We find that both public investment and real money supply growth play a quite significant role in promoting investment from the beginning of the postcrisis period, whereas exchange rate depreciation is insignificant. The estimated coefficient for public investment suggests that an increase of 1 percentage point in the ratio of public investment to GDP contributes to an increase in the total investment ratio by more than 1 percentage point, between 1.3 and 1.5. Hence, public investment increases total investment more than one for one, implying that public investment does not crowd out an equal amount of private investment from domestic sources by competing in product markets or financial markets. Thus, public investment, perhaps by improving the condition of social infrastructure, stimulates private investment and thus contributes to the postcrisis recovery by augmenting capital accumulation. An increase in real money supply growth by about 10 percentage points leads to an increase in investment-

7. A problem can occur in this regression when participation in the IMF program is endogenously determined. To avoid this simultaneous problem, we need to use an instrumental-variable technique. We do not implement this approach yet due to the lack of an ideal instrument.

GDP ratio by about 0.9–1.3 percentage points per year over the two years following the crisis.

9.3   Assessments of the Recovery Process in East Asia

9.3.1   Macroeconomic Adjustments in East Asia

The economic turmoil that broke out in Thailand in July 1997 swept through East Asia, and its devastating impacts were much more severe than anyone had expected. The countries that fell victim to the crisis suffered a sharp reduction in real income. In 1998, the growth rate plunged from the precrisis average of 7.0 percent to –13.2 percent in Indonesia, –10.4 percent in Thailand, –7.5 percent in Malaysia, –6.7 percent in Korea, and –0.6 percent in the Philippines. However, since 1999 the five crisis-hit Asian countries have managed impressive recoveries, which have been faster than the similar previous episodes of recovery in other parts of the world. The rebounding of the growth rate in 1999 was no less drastic than its free-fall. Korea stood out as the best performer in that year by growing at 10.7 percent. For the other countries, the growth rate ranged from 5.4 percent in Malaysia to 0.2 percent in Indonesia.

With the passage of time, the recovery process has gained momentum. The growth outturn in 2000 is estimated to be higher than that of 1999 in four of the affected economies—Indonesia, Thailand, Malaysia, and the Philippines. In Korea, the growth rate slowed down from 10.7 percent to 8.3 percent.

Figure 9.5 shows the GDP growth rates of the five affected economies. The adjustment process in East Asia that can be inferred from changes in

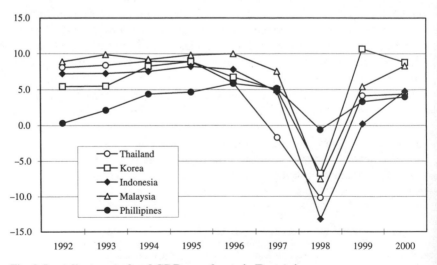

Fig. 9.5   Adjustment of real GDP growth rate in East Asia

Table 9.4   **Macroeconomic Adjustment in East Asia, 1993–2000**

	1993	1994	1995	1996	1997	1998	1999	2000
		A. Indonesia						
GDP growth rate (%)	7.25	7.54	8.22	7.82	4.70	–13.20	0.23	4.8
Expenditure on GDP								
Private consumption growth rate	11.77	7.83	12.58	9.72	7.82	–3.32	1.48	3.6
Share in GDP, %	58.5	58.7	61.0	62.1	64.0	71.2	72.1	67.3
Government consumption								
growth rate	0.19	2.31	1.34	2.69	0.06	–15.37	0.69	6.5
Share in GDP, %	9.0	8.6	8.0	7.7	7.3	7.1	7.2	7.0
Gross domestic investment								
growth rate	4.88	10.83	11.01	11.97	6.89	–31.81	–15.85	8.9
Share in GDP, %	29.5	32.0	33.4	32.5	33.0	21.0	17.2	17.9
Exports of goods and services								
growth rate	6.81	9.94	7.72	7.56	7.80	11.18	–32.06	27.1
Share in GDP, %	26.8	27.4	27.2	27.2	28.0	35.8	24.3	26.9
Imports of goods and services								
growth rate	4.65	20.30	20.94	6.86	14.72	–5.29	–40.90	21.1
Share in GDP, %	23.8	26.6	29.7	29.5	32.3	35.2	20.8	23.3
Policy indicators								
Government capital expenditure								
as % of inv.	27.0	23.3	19.7	17.8	14.8	24.1	n.a.	n.a.
Growth rate of real M2	10.5	11.5	17.8	19.2	19.0	5.0	–8.0	12.2
Annual real bank credit growth								
rate	13.9	12.2	12.5	14.5	17.2	–25.0	–56.5	9.8
Real effective exchange rate	n.a.	n.a.	100	109.5	104.5	52.7	74.5	59.1
		B. Korea						
GDP growth rate (%)	5.49	8.25	8.92	6.75	5.01	–6.69	10.66	8.8
Expenditure on GDP								
Private consumption growth rate	5.60	8.19	9.60	7.07	3.50	–11.43	10.32	7.1
Share in GDP, %	54.4	54.4	54.7	54.9	54.1	51.3	51.2	57.3
Public consumption growth rate	4.58	1.90	0.81	8.17	1.45	–0.41	–0.60	1.3
Share in GDP, %	11.1	10.4	9.7	9.8	9.5	10.1	9.1	10.2
Gross domestic investment								
growth rate	5.87	8.55	9.37	7.50	–1.44	–16.68	2.90	8.0
Share in GDP, %	34.4	36.4	37.2	37.9	33.4	22.0	26.0	28.7
Exports of goods and services								
growth rate	11.30	16.08	24.59	11.21	21.44	13.25	16.35	19.9
Share in GDP, %	24.6	26.4	30.2	31.5	36.4	44.2	46.4	51.9
Imports of goods and services								
growth rate	6.21	21.58	22.36	14.25	3.18	–22.40	28.94	20.0
Share in GDP, %	25.1	28.2	31.7	33.9	33.3	27.7	32.3	35.7
Policy indicators								
Government capital expenditure								
as % of inv.	6.0	6.7	8.6	10.0	11.0	21.6	18.8	17.3
Growth rate of real M2	11.8	12.4	11.2	10.9	9.7	19.5	26.6	23.1
Annual real bank credit growth								
rate	6.8	13.7	10.3	14.4	14.4	4.3	18.8	15.4
Real effective exchange rate	n.a.	n.a.	100	104.5	100.3	83.1	90.8	92.5

(continued)

Table 9.4 (continued)

	1993	1994	1995	1996	1997	1998	1999	2000
C. Malaysia								
GDP growth rate (%)	9.89	9.21	9.83	10.00	7.54	−7.50	5.42	8.
Expenditure on GDP								
Private consumption growth rate	6.25	9.39	11.66	6.87	4.31	−10.80	2.53	12.
Share in GDP, %	48.3	48.4	49.2	47.8	46.4	44.7	43.5	42.
Government consumption								
growth rate	8.43	7.87	6.06	0.73	7.63	−7.84	20.08	1.
Share in GDP, %	13.0	12.9	12.4	11.4	11.4	11.3	12.9	10.
Gross domestic investment								
growth rate	15.41	14.14	19.04	6.71	8.87	−36.29	0.54	27.
Share in GDP, %	41.7	44.9	49.2	47.3	48.9	30.2	26.9	26.
Exports of goods and services								
growth rate	11.54	21.91	18.96	9.23	5.42	−0.21	13.76	16.
Share in GDP, %	80.3	89.7	97.1	96.5	94.6	102.0	110.1	117.
Imports of goods and services								
growth rate	15.04	25.64	223.7	4.89	5.74	−19.37	11.58	25.
Share in GDP, %	83.3	95.9	108.0	102.9	101.2	88.2	93.4	106.
Policy indicators								
Government capital expenditure								
as % of inv.	13.5	12.4	12.9	12.0	11.9	23.8	n.a.	n.
Growth rate of real M2	23.0	7.9	16.8	20.8	14.7	−6.7	14.2	8.
Annual real bank credit growth								
rate	7.1	10.2	26.5	16.9	19.9	−2.2	0.5	4
Real effective exchange rate	n.a.	n.a.	100.0	106.5	105.5	86.8	87.6	72
D. The Philippines								
GDP growth rate (%)	2.13	4.39	4.67	5.85	5.19	−0.59	3.32	4
Expenditure on GDP								
Private consumption growth rate	3.05	3.72	3.82	4.62	4.99	3.45	2.64	3
Share in GDP, %	78.8	78.3	77.7	76.8	76.6	79.7	79.2	70
Government consumption								
growth rate	6.15	6.13	5.62	4.10	4.67	−1.95	5.41	−1
Share in GDP, %	8.0	8.1	8.2	8.1	8.0	7.9	8.1	12
Gross domestic investment								
growth rate	8.00	7.14	4.94	9.94	9.77	−9.00	−0.11	2
Share in GDP, %	22.7	23.6	23.3	24.8	26.3	22.2	21.1	17
Exports of goods and services								
growth rate	6.26	19.77	12.04	15.40	17.15	−21.04	3.65	17
Share in GDP, %	34.9	40.1	42.9	46.8	52.1	41.4	41.5	46
Imports of goods and services								
growth rate	11.48	14.51	16.03	16.73	13.49	−14.71	−2.79	2
Share in GDP, %	43.9	48.2	53.4	58.9	63.6	54.5	51.3	5
Policy indicators								
Government capital expenditure								
as % of inv.	15.0	13.7	13.4	8.1	8.0	8.0	11.0	n
Growth rate of real M2	20.2	16.0	16.2	14.2	20.2	−1.2	9.4	0.
Annual real bank credit growth								
rate	30.7	19.2	31.8	38.8	20.2	−15.4	−6.3	−
Real effective exchange rate	n.a.	n.a.	100.0	110.4	111.0	94.0	100.8	6

Table 9.4   (continued)

	1993	1994	1995	1996	1997	1998	1999	2000
			E. Thailand					
GDP growth rate (%)	8.38	8.95	8.90	5.93	−1.68	−10.17	4.16	4.4
Expenditure on GDP								
Private consumption growth rate	8.43	7.87	7.55	6.83	−1.05	−12.33	3.49	4.6
Share in GDP, %	55.8	55.2	54.6	55.0	55.4	54.0	53.7	56.4
Government consumption								
growth rate	5.11	8.19	5.37	11.91	−3.03	1.94	2.82	6.5
Share in GDP, %	8.3	8.2	7.9	8.4	8.3	9.4	9.3	11.5
Gross domestic investment								
growth rate	8.55	10.83	10.04	8.08	−18.59	−35.17	−1.72	11.8
Share in GDP, %	40.9	41.6	42.7	43.0	33.7	19.0	20.5	22.7
Exports of goods and services								
growth rate	12.74	14.25	15.50	−5.53	8.41	6.72	8.86	19.5
Share in GDP, %	42.4	44.4	47.1	42.0	46.3	55.1	57.5	64.2
Imports of goods and services								
growth rate	11.78	15.75	19.87	−0.52	−11.38	−22.28	20.24	24.6
Share in GDP, %	44.9	47.7	52.5	49.3	44.4	38.4	44.4	47.5
Policy indicators								
Government capital expenditure								
as % of inv.	12.9	13.4	12.0	16.6	23.4	29.3	23.1	17.7
Growth rate of real M2	15.1	7.7	11.3	6.8	10.9	1.6	5.1	−0.9
Annual real bank credit growth								
rate	18.6	24.6	15.1	9.4	13.6	−11.3	−6.0	−17.3
Real effective exchange rate	n.a.	n.a.	100.0	109.2	102.4	90.0	93.5	73.6

Source: Asian Development Bank online country data, available at [http://www.adb.org/Statistics/country.asp].

Notes: The share of expenditure components in GDP is constructed based on data in constant prices. n.a. = not available.

the growth rates seems to be in general consistent with the stylized V-pattern we observe from the previous crisis episodes. However, the East Asian experience is in marked contrast to the stylized pattern of adjustment in GDP growth in that the degree of initial contraction and subsequent recovery has been far greater than what can be predicted from the previous cross-country evidence.

The initial GDP contraction in 1998 was largely caused by the collapse of investment: the level of domestic capital formation plummeted in all five countries in 1998. The contraction amounted to more than 30 percent in Indonesia, Malaysia, and Thailand, 17 percent in Korea, and 9 percent in the Philippines (table 9.4).

Compared to investment demand, private consumption fell to a lesser degree. The consumption-GDP ratio remained mostly stable in the crisis period, which is consistent with the cross-country stylized pattern. In contrast, the investment-GDP ratio dropped sharply. In Korea, for example, it fell from 33.4 percent in 1997 to 22.0 percent in 1998. Investment demand

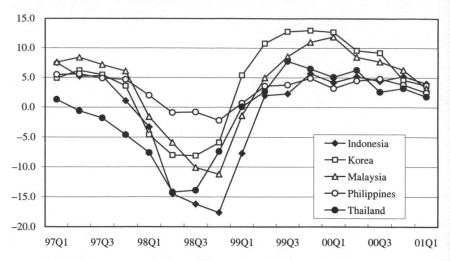

Fig. 9.6 Quarterly changes of real GDP growth in East Asia (y-o-y, %)

A

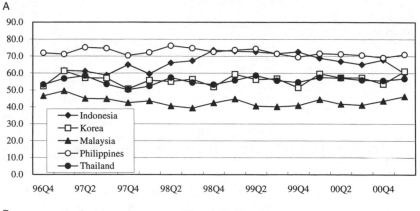

B

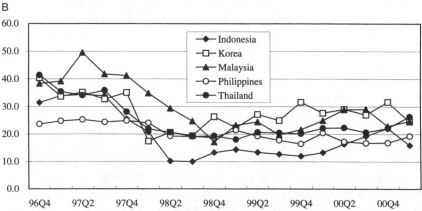

Fig. 9.7 Quarterly movements of GDP components in East Asia: *A,* **private consumption in GDP;** *B,* **investment rate;** *C,* **real export growth rate;** *D,* **real import growth rate**

C

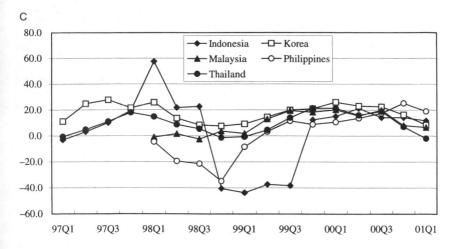

D

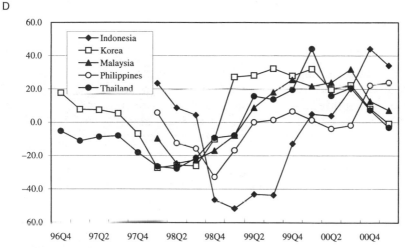

Fig. 9.7   (cont.)

started to recover somewhat in 1999 in Korea and Malaysia, but it has continued to decline in the other countries.

While domestic demand was sluggish, a large increase in net export paved way for the initial recovery of the Asian economies. Import demand declined in all of the crisis-hit countries in 1998 by a substantial amount, ranging from 22 percent in Korea and Thailand to 5.3 percent in Indonesia, whereas exports continued to grow or remained unchanged in all countries except the Philippines.

It is therefore clear that net exports led the recovery in East Asia. Figures 9.6 and 9.7, based on quarterly data, demonstrate the pattern of adjustment in more detail. A close examination of the quarterly rates of GDP growth

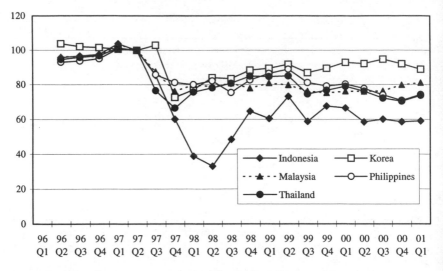

Fig. 9.8   Real effective exchange rate in East Asia (1997:2 = 100)

shows that both Korea and Thailand reached the trough as early as in the second quarter of 1998, and Indonesia, Malaysia, and the Philippines two quarters later (see figure 9.6). Overall, the recession in East Asia bottomed out in the second half of 1998, less than a year after the crisis had broken out. As shown in figure 9.7, the subsequent recovery in 1999 was led mostly by a surge in net exports. Over the postcrisis period, the ratio of private consumption to GDP has remained stable in all countries except for Indonesia. In Indonesia, private consumption expenditure rose in 1998. In Korea and Malaysia, the investment rate started to increase from the latter half of 1998, whereas in the other countries the investment ratio has declined.

An increase in public investment appears to have contributed to the resurgence of total investment expenditure in Korea and Malaysia. Table 9.4 shows that in both countries the fraction of government capital expenditure in total investment jumped from 11 percent in 1997 to over 21 percent in 1998.

The large depreciation of currency has backed up the quick surge of net exports since 1998. Table 9.4 and figure 9.8 show that the level of real effective exchange rates in the five crisis-hit East Asian countries depreciated by 22 percent on average, ranging from 12 percent in Thailand to 50 percent in Indonesia in 1998.

9.3.2   Factors Behind the Speedy Adjustment in East Asia

A large number of internal and external factors are likely to have contributed to the pattern of macroeconomic adjustment to the crisis in East Asia. On the basis of the cross-country evidence and available information on the pattern of macroeconomic adjustment in East Asia, we attempt to identify some of the factors that have engineered the postcrisis recovery.

Macroeconomic Factors

According to the empirical examination of the stylized pattern of adjustments from the previous 160 currency crisis episodes over the period from 1970 to 1995, which show a V-type adjustment of real GDP growth, a large real depreciation, expansionary monetary and fiscal policy, and an improvement in the global economic environment have been responsible for the upturn of the crisis-hit countries. In this sense, the East Asian process of adjustment is not much different from the stylized pattern. The same factors contributed to the quick postcrisis recovery of the East Asian economies.

Exchange Rate Depreciation and Openness. An important structural factor driving the speedy adjustment in East Asia may have been the region's higher level of openness. With a relatively large trade sector and export orientation, these economies benefited from a large depreciation of the real exchange rate. The level of openness in terms of the share of export and import in GDP ranges from 200 percent in Malaysia to 60 percent in Indonesia. Thus, compared to other crisis-hit economies before them, the depreciation is likely to have had a bigger impact on the more open East Asian economies. Note that the size of real exchange depreciation in the East Asian countries was comparable to the average depreciation rate in the previous crisis episodes.

One special feature of the East Asia crisis is that, compared to the cross-country evidence, the impact of depreciation on real depreciation on real output showed up as early as one year after the crisis. The large real exchange depreciation therefore restored external balance without much delay in East Asia. The flexibility in the labor market may have facilitated this swift adjustment, because the shift of resources from the nontradables to the tradables sector elicited by the massive real exchange rate depreciation requires flexible factor market.

Favorable External Environment. The quick improvement in East Asian exports has been supported by favorable external developments. The global economy was strong in 1999. The U.S. economy has been able to absorb a large amount of exports of the East Asian economies. The U.S. per capita GDP growth rates were 3.3–3.4 percent in 1998 and 1999 and jumped to 4.4 percent in 2000, which by far exceeded the average growth rate of 2.0 percent over the period from 1970 to 1995. As we saw from the cross-country regressions in section 9.2, global economic growth has a strong impact on the postcrisis recovery, in particular in the early years following the crisis. The deterioration in terms of trade that precipitated the crisis reversed in

1999. In particular, the increase in the prices of semiconductors helped to boost Korean, Malaysian, and Thai exports.

Macroeconomic Policy Adjustment. Concerning macroeconomic policy management, the swift change in policy stance toward expansion has supported a quick recovery of the crisis-hit economies. In Korea, relaxation of monetary and fiscal policy began around in April of 1998. A comparison of the turning points in the adjustment process measured by growth rates of the quarterly GDP with the timing of policy changes, broadly speaking, confirms that easing of monetary and fiscal policy has quickened the pace of recovery in both Thailand and Malaysia (figure 9.9). Thailand shifted to a modest relaxation of macroeconomic policy in June 1998, and its economy took off in the fourth quarter of the same year after zero growth in the preceding quarter. In particular, public consumption expenditure increased significantly in the latter half of 1998. It was not until the third quarter of 1998—the end of August—that a relaxation of monetary and fiscal policy was announced in Malaysia, and its economy moved out of the trough one quarter later. In Indonesia, on the contrary, because of the continuing weakness of the rupiah, monetary policy remained contractionary until the second quarter of 1999. However, public consumption increased sharply in the third quarter of 1999. This expansion boosted output growth in 1999. In the Philippines, monetary policy was slightly contractionary over the postcrisis period, whereas public consumption expenditure has been growing since the first quarter of 1999.

The positive role of expansionary macroeconomic policies in postcrisis recovery raises the question of whether the initial tightening of monetary and fiscal policy was too harsh and maintained for too long and as a consequence deepened the crisis. In order to deal with the crisis itself—stopping bank runs, protecting the payment system, and stemming capital outflows—the IMF prescribed tight monetary policy together with fiscal austerity, which initially led to a sharp increase in interest rates. The contractionary monetary and fiscal policy has been criticized by many, including Radelet and Sachs (1998) and Feldstein (1998), as having been unnecessary because these countries were suffering from a liquidity problem. They imply that the traditional IMF prescriptions may have done more harm than good because they drove many highly leveraged but viable firms out of business, thereby deepening the downturn of the economy. The contribution of initial austerity from IMF programs remains controversial. On the other hand, it is quite clear that the swift change of macroeconomic policy stance toward an expansionary one helped these economies recover quickly. Fiscal policy had become contractionary immediately after the crisis, but it was reversed quickly to be expansionary. Change in monetary policy stance then followed. Once the depreciation of the currency was arrested and stability returned to the foreign exchange market, the authorities of the crisis

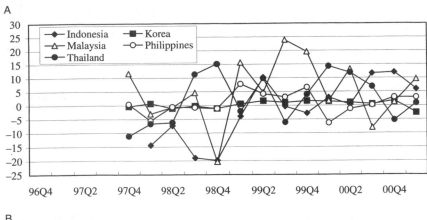

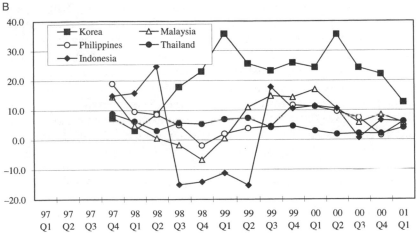

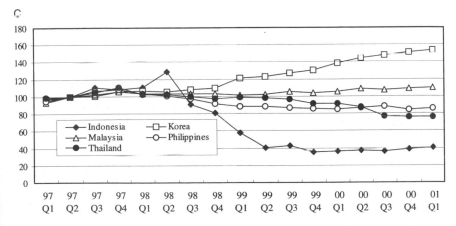

Fig. 9.9 Policy indicators in East Asia: *A*, real public consumption growth; *B*, real money supply growth; *C*, real credit (1997:2 = 100)

countries were able to adjust gradually the interest rates downward and expand money supply.

Panic and Balance Sheet Effects

The contraction of real income in the East Asian countries that suffered the crisis was much larger, and the subsequent recovery of these countries has been much faster, than what can be predicted from the previous episodes of crisis elsewhere. There must be additional factors that have contributed to the deeper contraction and the quicker recovery in East Asia. We consider that the East Asian crisis has an aspect of a severe liquidity crisis caused by investors' panic. This nature of the crisis must have an important role in the macroeconomic adjustment during the crisis.

Panic and Spread of the Crisis. There is general agreement that a fixed peg to a currency basket dominated by the U.S. dollar when the current account was piling up deficits was one aspect of policy mismanagement that triggered the crisis in Thailand. In a recent paper, Williamson (2000) shows that had it been implementing a basket, band, and crawl (BBC) rule, Thailand might have staved off its crisis, because the country was suffering from a balance-of-payments crisis. However, the Thai crisis was contagious, as shown by Park and Song (2001a, b), and even a good exchange rate management using the BBC rule could not have saved other crisis victims like Indonesia and Korea from the contagion.

Although macroeconomic policies and economic fundamentals of Korea and Indonesia were regarded as being sound and credible, many foreign investors simply moved out of East Asian financial markets when they realized that most East Asian countries would suffer from macroeconomic and structural problems similar to those that were driving Thailand to the brink of debt default. With the withdrawal of foreign lenders and investors from the region, other East Asian countries experienced a sharp liquidity crisis and balance sheet problems associated with a large currency depreciation, causing a regionwide crisis explicable by a second- and third-generation model of the crisis. That is, the contagion of the Thai crisis set in motion a crisis characterized by self-fulfilling prophecy and balance sheet deterioration in other East Asian countries, which did not have a serious balance-of-payment problem. Once hit by contagion, the BBC system was simply unable to stave off the crisis because the band could not be maintained.

Why did foreign portfolio investors panick so much and exhibit herd behavior? They initially moved into East Asia with large sums of money to be invested in all types of local securities and real assets with the mistaken notion that rapid growth in the region would be sustained or that their investments would be protected by government guarantees. Most of the foreign investors paid little attention to the structural problems of the financial and corporate sections that began to haunt East Asia before moving in. When these problems came to light in the midst of currency depreciation and interest rate increases, they were startled. The ensuing fear of losing their investments then drove them to a state of panic, and every investor was scrambling to reach the exit.

Thus, one critical factor that could explain both the initial sharper contraction and the faster recovery is related to changes in the expectations of foreign investors and both domestic households and firms on economic prospects of the crisis countries. When foreign investors began to lose confidence in East Asian economies, capital flows abruptly reversed. As shown in table 9.5, in 1997 private net capital flows reversed by $115 billion (from a $120 billion inflow in 1996 to a $5 billion outflow). It is no wonder that this large-scale shift in financial inflows provoked deep contractions, huge depreciation, and financial embarrassment. The argument goes that once investors' panic calms down and foreign capital resumes inflow, the economy rebounds to its long-term trend.

Immediately after the crisis, there was rampant speculation that the crisis countries might not be able to avoid foreign debt default and hence might have to declare a debt moratorium. The international financial community, including international financial institutions, also did not hesitate to lay the blame on the East Asian countries for the crisis. With the emerging consensus that the crisis countries had profound problems that were more serious than had been realized before, the prospect for recovery in East Asia turned from bad to worse. Many were skeptical that these countries had the institutional capacity and political will to carry out the necessary structural reforms. Even if they had, the skeptics pointed out that these

Table 9.5   **Capital Flows to the Five Asian Economies (in US $billions)**

	1996	1997	1998	1999	2000[a]
External financing, net (A + B)	118.6	39.5	−15.2	−4.9	−1.2
A. Private flows, net	119.5	4.9	−38.7	−5.2	−3.8
Equity investment	16.8	5.2	16.8	30.1	15.6
Direct equity	4.8	6.8	12.3	14.6	9.5
Portfolio equity	12.0	−1.7	4.5	15.4	6.1
Private creditors	102.7	−0.3	−55.5	−35.3	−19.3
Commercial banks	69.6	−17.4	−48.8	−29.3	−15.3
Nonbank private creditors	33.2	17.2	−6.7	−6.0	−4.1
B. Official flows, net	−0.9	34.6	23.5	0.2	2.6
International financial inst.	−1.9	22.7	19.7	−4.6	2.5
Bilateral creditors	1.0	11.9	3.8	4.9	0.1

Source: Institute for International Finance, January 2001.

Note: The five countries include South Korea, Indonesia, Thailand, Malaysia, and the Philippines.

[a]Estimated.

crisis countries would take many years to put their houses in order. Under these circumstances, it is quite possible that the households and firms as well as foreign investors came to believe that the crisis was a permanent shock that would lead to a new equilibrium lower in terms of output and employment than when the crisis was seen as a temporary shock. This perception of permanency may have induced domestic consumers and investors to cut down their spending much more than they otherwise would have during the first six months of the crisis. However, the extensive criticism of East Asia diminished and gradually gave way to a more optimistic outlook for the crisis economies, and the realization that the crisis might be a temporary phenomenon started sinking into the minds of consumers and investors, thereby encouraging their spending.

In restoring the confidence of foreign investors, large support packages from the IMF made some contribution. The funding helped to reduce the short-term liquidity constraints of the economies and provide resources to stem the exchange rate depreciation. There were other turning points. Korea, for example, reached an agreement with its creditor in February 1998 to lengthen the maturities of the short-term foreign currency loans (Radelet and Sachs 1998).[8] After the agreement was reached, at least some of foreign credit facilities, including trade credit, were restored. With this restoration of the credit linkage, the fear of the debt default abated considerably.

Balance Sheet Effects. A large decrease in aggregate investment demand during the crisis period suggests that corporate distress was one of the main factors responsible for the sharper contraction in output in East Asia. Structural weaknesses in the corporate and bank balance sheets were often pointed out as the main channel through which the effect of foreign disturbances was magnified in the East Asian crisis (Krugman 1999; Stone 2000).

The reversal of capital inflows combined with a sudden downward shift in expectation could lead to a sharp depreciation of the exchange rate. The large unexpected depreciation was much more disastrous in East Asia because most firms were highly leveraged. When the bulk of corporate debts is denominated in the U.S. dollar while revenues and assets are in local currency, the depreciation deteriorates the balance sheets of firms and inflicts large losses. Table 9.6 shows that foreign exchange losses of the Korean firms amounted to more than 17 trillion won, which was about 3.8 percent of GDP, in 1997.[9] These losses, together with the increase in foreign debt financing costs, result in a decline in the present value of the equity of the corporate sector. Gray (1999) estimates that a 50 percent depreciation reduces

---

8. They did not do so voluntarily, but at the urging of the Group of Seven governments and the IMF, and only when they were convinced that they would be repaid with handsome returns.

9. According to Hahm and Mishkin (2000), the foreign liabilities accounted for about 16 percent in total corporate debt in 1997 in Korea.

Table 9.6   **Foreign Exchange Losses of the Korean Corporate Sector (in billion won %)**

	1997	1998	1999
Gains on foreign exchange transactions (A)	−2,692	−784	203
Gains on foreign exchange valuation (B)	−14,571	−1,026	2,533
Total gains (A + B)	−17,263	−1,810	2,736
% of total assets	−2.4	−0.2	0.3
% of GDP	−3.8	−0.4	0.6

Source: Authors' estimates based on the Bank of Korea *Financial Statement Analysis.*

Table 9.7   **The Ratio of Foreign Liabilities to Foreign Assets of the Banking Sector (%)**

	Dec. 1996	Mar. 1997	June 1997	Sept. 1997	Dec. 1997	Mar. 1998	June 1998	Sept. 1998	Dec. 1998
Indonesia	1.4	1.7	1.8	1.8	1.5	1.2	1.0	0.8	0.8
Korea	1.3	1.3	1.3	1.3	0.9	0.8	0.8	0.8	0.9
Malaysia	2.6	2.5	2.8	2.3	2.1	1.6	1.4	1.3	1.7
The Philippines	1.8	1.7	1.9	2.0	1.7	1.8	1.7	1.6	1.4
Thailand	6.9	7.3	6.8	5.5	4.7	4.2	3.2	2.5	2.3

Source: Asian Development Bank, based on data from IMF, *International Financial Statistics.*
Note: Ratios calculated with gross foreign liabilities and assets of deposit money banks.

the equity value of Korean corporations by 9 percent and that of Indonesian corporations by 21 percent. The lower equity value leads to lower investment.

The balance sheets of the financial institutions were also very vulnerable to the currency depreciation. Because in East Asia banks had a large amount of foreign liabilities in their balance sheets, they suffered losses emanating from the currency mismatch.[10] In June 1997 the ratio of foreign liabilities to foreign assets of the banking sector ranged from 1.3 in Korea to 6.8 in Thailand (table 9.7). Maturity mismatches also created another vulnerability. Korean data show that short-term foreign liabilities were more than two times larger than short-term foreign assets (table 9.8).

After banks and other nonbank financial institutions suffer a sharp decline in their profits and hence a substantial erosion of their capital base, they are downgraded by the rating agencies and often denied access to international financial markets. As experienced by many money-losing financial institutions in East Asia, foreign banks and other institutional investors simply cut the lines of credit they had offered through the interbank loan

10. In 1997 the foreign liabilities accounted for about 55 percent of banks' total liabilities in Korea, 27 percent in Thailand, and 15 percent in Indonesia (Asia Development Bank [ADB] 2000).

Table 9.8   Foreign Assets and Liabilities Outstanding at Financial Institutions in Korea (in US $billions)

	Dec. 1996	Mar. 1997	June 1997	Sept. 1997	Dec. 1997	Mar. 1998	June 1998	Sept. 1998	Dec. 1998
Assets									
Total	67.2	70.4	72.1	72.0	72.0	70.5	71.2	68.1	63.9
Long-term	30.6	33.2	33.2	32.5	27.3	25.9	27.1	26.0	24.7
(% of total)	(46)	(47)	(46)	(45)	(38)	(37)	(38)	(38)	(39)
Short-term	36.6	37.2	38.9	39.5	44.7	44.6	44.1	42.1	39.2
(% of total)	(54)	(53)	(54)	(55)	(62)	(63)	(62)	(62)	(61)
Liabilities									
Total	116.5	126.2	129.4	127.1	89.9	83.8	79.8	74.0	70.9
Long-term	43.5	46.0	48.1	51.7	47.5	45.0	58.6	55.6	52.0
(% of total)	(37)	(36)	(37)	(41)	(53)	(54)	(73)	(75)	(73)
Short-term	73.0	80.2	81.3	75.4	42.4	38.8	21.2	18.4	18.9
(% of total)	(63)	(64)	(63)	(59)	(47)	(46)	(27)	(25)	(27)
Net liabilities									
Total	49.3	55.8	57.3	55.1	17.9	13.3	8.6	5.9	7.0
Long-term	12.9	12.8	14.9	19.2	20.2	19.1	31.5	29.6	27.3
Short-term	36.4	43.0	42.4	35.9	−2.3	−5.8	−22.9	−23.7	−20.3
Long-term asset/ liabilities (%)	70.3	72.1	69	62.8	57.4	57.5	46.2	46.7	47.5
Short-term asset/ liabilities (%)	50.1	46.3	47.8	52.3	105.4	114.9	208	228.8	207.4

Source: Bank of Korea.

market and refused the rollover of short-term loans when their client institutions were in trouble. This refusal created a serious liquidity problem as well as balance sheet loss problems at the East Asian financial institutions. Faced with the liquidity problem, many banks and nonbank financial institutions had to reduce their supply of loans in both local and foreign currencies drastically even to their viable loan customers.

The mounting losses caused by the bank balance sheet deterioration is bound to increase the country risk premium of the crisis-hit countries. A rise in the country risk premium, in turn, pushes up the cost of capital and lowers the present value of the equity of the corporate sector. Gray (1999) estimates that an 8 percent temporary rise in the country risk premium for a year leads to a drop of 7 percent in the present value of corporate equity in Korea and 2 percent in Indonesia.[11]

An increase in the interest rate and currency depreciation together with other shocks can reduce the equity value of the corporate sector below a threshold that triggers widespread default. The risk of default was higher in

11. The high domestic interest rate, which aims at stemming rapid depreciation, has the same devastating effect on the value of corporate-sector equity and thus investment.

East Asia, where firms were highly leveraged with a large amount of short-term liabilities. The firms with a larger share of short-term debt faced more difficulties in financing and were unable to service their debts: bankruptcies soared, thereby magnifying the crisis.

In the recovery process, macroeconomic stability plays a crucial role for the normal operation of viable firms. Stabilization of the exchange rate and interest rate improves the equity value of the corporate sector and thus promotes investment. Improved confidence leads to an increase in spending. The restructuring of the corporate sector is necessary in order to reduce the vulnerability of the corporate sector and thus prevent the future crisis. However, in the short run, a quick recovery cannot be engineered unless there is resurgence of domestic demand.

9.3.3   Structural Reform and Recovery[12]

At the beginning of the crisis, there was widespread belief that the crisis countries' commitment to structural reforms would be critical to the recovery in East Asia. The reforms were expected to help East Asia emerge from the crisis with more stable, transparent, and efficient financial and corporate sectors. This expectation of reform espousing a market-oriented system would then improve long-term growth prospects and, at the same time, restore market confidence, thereby inducing the return of foreign lenders and investors to the region.

Three years into the reform process, the crisis countries have accomplished a great deal in improving the soundness and profitability of financial institutions and alleviating corporate distress. The World Bank (2000) argues that "assertive structural adjustment helped restore credit flows and boosted consumer and investor confidence" (7). However, it is not clear whether and to what extent financial and corporate restructuring has contributed to the ongoing recovery. Most of the serious structural problems that were identified as the major causes of the crisis in Indonesia, Korea, Malaysia, and Thailand could not have been resolved over a span of two years. In fact, banks are still holding in their balance sheets a large volume of nonperforming loans and remain undercapitalized in all four countries. Many corporations in the region are still unable to service their debts. As for institutional reform, new banking and accounting standards, disclosure requirements, and rules for corporate governance have been introduced, but they are not rigorously enforced. It will take many years for the new system to take root.

Because the crisis countries are not even halfway to restructuring their financial institutions and corporations, it would be presumptuous to argue that the reform efforts have established a foundation for sustainable growth in East Asia. Nor would it be correct to assert that the gain in efficiency

---

12. See Park (2001a,b) for more details.

through the restructuring, which is difficult to measure at this stage, has been one of the principal factors driving the recovery. The improvement in efficiency is likely to be realized and translated into high growth over a longer period of time, certainly longer than two years.

The available pieces of evidence also do not support the contention that the market-oriented reform has contributed to restoring market confidence in the East Asian crisis countries; it certainly did not appear to have done so during the first two years of the crisis. International credit rating agencies report that the reforms in the banking sector in the crisis countries have not gone through enough to ensure that these economies would be able to forestall another financial crisis. Only toward the end of 1999 did Moody's and Standard & Poor's upgrade the sovereign credit ratings of Korea and Malaysia to the lowest investment grade from the speculation grade. By that time, the recovery was in full swing in East Asia. Journalistic accounts have abounded with similar concerns and continued to raise doubts regarding the effectiveness of the reform in the crisis countries. Under these circumstances, most foreign investors would find it risky to return to the crisis countries, but they have. Many of the foreign investors appear to have been lured back by the rapid recovery and substantial improvements in external liquidity resulting from large surpluses on the current account.

Reflecting recovery rather than ratings improvement, capital inflows in East Asia have been rising. Because policy changes and structural reforms are subject to many uncertainties and require a long period of time to take effect, international banks and global institutional lenders do not seem to have either the patience or ability to monitor and assess the effects of structural reforms. This is particularly true when they are preoccupied with the short-term performance of their portfolios.

9.3.4   Differences in Postcrisis Performance among the Asian Countries

The five Asian countries most affected by the Asian financial crisis showed the speedy recovery that was faster than anyone had expected. However, the extent of the recovery from the crisis differed among the five countries. By the end of 1999 only Korea had surpassed its precrisis peak level of GDP. Malaysia and the Philippines did it later in 2000, whereas Thailand and Indonesia still need another year or so to recover to their precrisis output level.

Table 9.4 indicates that the difference in the postcrisis recovery in 1999 reflects mainly the difference in the performance of investment and export growth among the Asian countries. Although the annual growth rate of export in 1999 amounted to 16.4 percent in Korea, 13.8 percent in Malaysia, and 8.9 percent in Thailand, it was –32.1 percent in Indonesia. After investment ratios had dropped sharply in the five Asian countries in 1998 due to the crisis, they showed slow recovery in 1999 in both Korea and

Malaysia. By contrast, in the other three Asian countries investment ratios contracted further in 1999.

The investment contractions reflect the significant distress in both the corporate and financial sectors. The financial crisis caused deterioration of the firms' balance sheets. Then the deterioration of the balance sheets of firms caused a massive accumulation of nonperforming loans at banks and other nonbank financial institutions. The accumulation of bad loans cut into profits and consequently decreased the equity value of the financial institutions. Decapitalized financial institutions, as a result of the mounting losses, were forced to curtail their lending to both viable and nonviable firms, thereby exacerbating the downturn of investment.

In the bank-oriented financial system that characterizes the financial structure of the crisis-hit countries in East Asia, the repercussion of the bank failure is much more pervasive and felt throughout the economy. Because of their dominance, therefore, banks are likely to bring down many viable firms when they are not able to function as intermediary.

Data show that the investment and output contractions in the Asian countries are closely associated with the sluggish bank lending. Although monetary supply began to expand in 1999 for the five Asian economies, the supply of bank credit in real terms continued to slow down in three of them—Indonesia, Thailand, and the Philippines (panels B and C of figure 9.9). In fact, more than three years after the crisis, real credit supply remains below the precrisis level yet in those three countries. The investment ratio recovered most quickly in Korea, where real credit increased at the highest rate over the postcrisis period.

9.4   Prospects for Long-Term Growth in East Asia

As the recovery continues in East Asia, there is a growing hope that these economies will be able to return to the precrisis level of robust growth. In this section, we make an assessment of the long-term growth prospects for East Asia.

9.4.1   Impacts of a Currency Crisis on Long-Term Growth

In this section we investigate the impact of a currency crisis on long-run growth based on a cross-country regression framework. We control all important growth determinants and then examine whether a currency crisis has had any independent impact on GDP growth in the long run.

A wide variety of external environment and policy variables will affect growth prospects by changing the long-run potential income and the rate of productivity growth. Basing our calculations on the results from previous empirical research, we consider the following variables as the important determinants of long-run per capita income growth: (a) initial income; (b) hu-

Table 9.9   **Long-Run Impact of Currency Crisis on Per Capita Growth Rate**

Estimation Method	Seemingly Unrelated Regression	
	Equation (1)	Equation (2)
Initial GDP per capita, log	−1.965	−1.975
	(0.360)	(0.365)
Years of schooling	0.350	0.357
	(0.246)	(0.247)
Investment rate	0.084	0.085
	(0.033)	(0.032)
Terms of trade change, % per annum	0.084	0.086
	(0.036)	(0.037)
Government consumption, % in GDP	−0.139	−0.140
	(0.032)	(0.032)
Rule-of-law index	1.212	1.195
	(0.830)	(0.829)
Openness, 1 = most open	2.726	2.708
	(0.482)	(0.485)
Currency crises, no. in previous decade	0.043	0.211
	(0.033)	(0.436)
Currency crises with IMF program, no. in previous decade		−0.386
		(0.670)
R^2	0.54, 0.37	0.54, 0.37
N	84, 82	84, 82

Notes: The system has two equations, where the dependent variables are the growth rate of real per capita GDP for each of the two periods: 1975–85 and 1985–95. The estimations use the SUR (seemingly unrelated) estimation technique, which allows the error term to be correlated across the two periods and to have a different variance in each period. Each equation is allowed to have a different constant term (not reported). Standard errors are shown in parentheses. The R values and the number of observations apply to each period separately.

man resources, (c) investment rate; (d) exogenous shock (terms of trade changes), and (d) institutions and policy variables (government consumption, rule of law, and openness).[13] For the measure of human capital stock, we use the average years of secondary and higher school education for the population aged 15 and over, available from Barro and Lee (2001). The rule-of-law index is a measure for the quality of institutions, which is based on the evaluation by international consulting firms that give advice to international investors. The openness measure is based on Sachs and Warner (1995). This index is calculated as the fraction of years during the period in which the country was considered to be open to trade and thus sufficiently integrated with the global economy. The evaluation of the country's openness is made on the basis of four dimensions of trade policy: average tariff rates, quotas and licensing, export taxes, and black market exchange rate premium.

Table 9.9 presents the results of regression for per capita real GDP

13. Our specification closely follows Barro (1997) in selecting the explanatory variables.

growth rate using the explanatory variables just described. The data are a panel set of cross-country data over the two decades 1975–85 and 1985–95. The system of two equations is estimated by a SUR technique, which allows for the correlation of the errors across the equations.

The regressions show that most of the controlling variables are the significant determinants of long-term growth. For instance, the coefficient on the log value of initial GDP is highly significant. Thus, it provides strong evidence for conditional convergence: That is, a poor country with a lower initial income level grows faster when the variables influencing the steady-state level of income are controlled. Specifically, the coefficient in column (1) of table 9.9 implies that a country at half the income level of another country grows by 1.4 percentage points [= 2.04% * ln(2)] faster than the richer country.

We add to the regression a variable that measures the occurrence of currency crises. The variable is constructed with the number of currency crises that each country experienced during the past decade. We have used the number of crises over the period 1970–75 for the first equation and the period 1975–85 for the second equation. Thus, we test whether an experience of a currency crisis can have an impact on growth in the next decade. The estimated coefficient turns out to be statistically insignificant, implying that there is no direct impact of currency crises on growth in the long run. In column (2) of the regression, we add another variable that represents the number of currency crises with the IMF program participation. We also found no significance for this variable.

Although there is no direct impact of a currency crisis on long-run growth, it would be possible that a currency crisis or IMF program can have an indirect impact on long-run growth by influencing the controlling variables. For instance, if the investment ratio becomes permanently lowered by the post-crisis stabilization program in the crisis-hit countries, it would have a negative impact on growth in the long run. On the contrary, if the IMF structural reform improves the quality of institutions, then a currency crisis with IMF program participation can have a positive impact on growth.

9.4.2 Sustainability of East Asian Growth

The quick turnaround of the Asian economy from the 1997 crisis has brightened the region's economic prospects. Despite the impressive record of the recovery, however, not everyone is sanguine about East Asia's future prospects. The World Bank and the IMF, for example, are not optimistic about the prospects of these countries' sustaining the ongoing recovery, largely because weaknesses of financial institutions and balance sheet problems of corporations still remain unresolved in the region.

The macroeconomic performance of the crisis countries in the next few years will provide important clues to the question of whether these countries will be able to return to the pre-crisis trend rate of growth. Up to the present, the pattern of recovery in East Asia has been quite similar to that of Mexico after its crisis in 1994.

Although the financial crisis of 1997 abruptly brought a halt to Asia's period of robust growth, there was little in Asia's fundamentals that inevitably led to the crisis. The key to the Asian crisis was too much short-term capital flowing into weak and undersupervised financial systems. This suggests that, with better financial management and a return to the core policies that resulted in rapid growth, the East Asian economies can again return to sustained growth (Radelet, Sachs, and Lee 2001). The major factors that brought the relatively high growth in East Asia were high rates of saving, good human resources, trade openness, and maintenance of good institutions. In terms of these fundamentals, East Asia still keeps strong potential for a sustained growth.

However, in the long term, the growth rate will be lower than the previous precrisis average of 7 percent. The convergence factor, which was found to be quite strong in the cross-country growth regression in the last section, implies that the faster growth in the last decades in itself will force the East Asian economies to grow at a slower pace in the next decade. That is, the East Asian countries now have a much smaller gap in reproducible (physical and human) capital and technical efficiency from their long-run potential levels than they had in the last decades. Hence, the East Asian economies will face a smaller chance for rapid catching up, via high rates of capital accumulation as well as the diffusion of technology from more technically advanced economies in the next decade, and will inevitably become adjusted to a lower growth path.

The coefficient in the cross-country growth regressions implies that the convergence factor alone makes the Asian economies grow by about 1.5 percentage points slower over the next decade, compared to the last decades, in which they had started with less than one half of the current income. Hence, unless the economies could achieve substantial improvements in other fundamental factors, such as quality of institutions, they would grow at the range of 5 percent per year in GDP.

9.5   Concluding Remarks

The contraction of real income in the East Asian countries that suffered the crisis that erupted in 1997 was much larger, and the subsequent recovery of these countries has been much faster, than what can be predicted from the previous episodes of crisis elsewhere. The purpose of this paper has been to identify some of the factors that may explain the severity of and rapid recovery from the crisis. According to our empirical examination of macroeconomic developments following the crisis in East Asia, including a V-type adjustment of real GDP growth, a large real depreciation, expansionary monetary and fiscal policy, and an improvement in the global economic environment have been responsible for the upturn of the crisis-hit countries. In this sense, the East Asian process of adjustment is not much different from the stylized pattern observed from the previous 176 currency crisis episodes over the period from 1970 to 1995. However, the stylized pattern of adjustment cannot explain why the crisis was more severe, and the recovery has been much faster, than what was expected from the previous experiences of crisis. This study argues that the East Asian financial upheaval was in large measure a liquidity crisis caused by investors' panic. Once the liquidity constraint was eased, as it was during the first half of 1998, domestic demand has since surged again, and the crisis countries have been able to move toward the precrisis path of growth.

References

Aghion, Philippe, Philippe Bacchetta, and Abhijit Banerjee. 2000. Currency crises and monetary policy in an economy with credit constraints. Harvard University, Department of Economics. Working Paper.

Asia Development Bank. (ADB). 2000. *Asian recovery report 2000.* Manila, the Philippines: Asia Development Bank.

Barro, Robert. 1997. *Determinants of economic growth: A cross-country empirical study.* Cambridge: MIT Press.

Barro, Robert, and Jong-Wha Lee. 2001. International data on educational attainment: Updates and implications. *Oxford Economic Papers* 53 (3): 241–63.

Conway, Patrick. 1994. IMF lending programs: Participation and impact. *Journal of Development Economics* 45:365–91

Feldstein, Martin. 1998. Refocusing the IMF. *Foreign Affairs* 77:20–33.

Frankel, Jeffrey A., and Andrew K. Rose. 1996. Currency crashes in emerging markets: An empirical treatment. *Journal of International Economics* 41:351–66.

Goldfajn, Ilan, and Poonam Gupta. 1999. Does monetary policy stabilize the exchange rate following currency crisis? IMF Working Paper no. WP/99/42. Washington, D.C.: International Monetary Fund.

Gray, Dale. 1999. Assessment of corporate sector value and vulnerability: Links to exchange rate and financial crises. World Bank Technical Paper no. 455. Washington, D.C.: World Bank.

Gupta, Poonam, Deepak Mishra, and Ratna Sahay. 2000. Output response during currency crises. Washington, D.C.: International Monetary Fund and World Bank. Mimeograph.

Hahm, Joon-Ho, and Frederic Mishkin. 2000. Causes of the Korean financial crisis: Lessons for policy. NBER Working Paper no. 7483. Cambridge, Mass.: National Bureau of Economic Research.

Haque, Nadeem Ul, and Mohsin S. Kahn. 1998. Do IMF-supported programs work? A survey of the cross-country empirical evidence. IMF Working Paper no. WP/98/169. Washington, D.C.: International Monetary Fund.

Hong, Kiseok, and Aaron Tornell. 1999. Post-crisis development of Asia. Korea Development Institute. Mimeograph.

Kaminsky, Gracicla, and Carmen M. Reinhart. 1999. The twin crises: The causes of banking and balance-of-payments problems. *American Economic Review* 89 (3): 473–500.

Krugman, Paul. 1999. Balance sheets, the transfer problem, and financial crises. In

International finance and financial crises: Essays in honor of Robert P. Flood, Jr., ed. Robert P. Flood, Andrew Rose, Assaf Razin, and Peter Isard, 31–56. Norwell, Mass.: Kluwer Academic.

Lee, Jong-Wha, Kiseok Hong, and Changyong Rhee. 2001. The macroeconomic adjustment during the currency crises. *Kyung Je Hak Yon Ku* 49 (2): 227–53.

Lee, Jong-Wha, and Changyong Rhee. 2002. Macroeconomic impacts of the Korean financial crisis: Comparison with the cross-country patterns. *World Economy* 25(4): 539–62.

Milesi-Ferreti, Gian Maria, and Assaf Razin. 1998. Current account reversal and currency crises: Empirical regularities. IMF Working Paper no. WP/98/89. Washington, D.C.: International Monetary Fund.

Park, Yung Chul. 2001a. East Asian dilemma: Restructuring out or growing out? *Essay in International Economics* no. 223. Princeton, N.J.: Princeton University.

———. 2001b. A post crisis paradigm of development for East Asia: Governance, markets, and institutions. Korea University, Department of Economics. Mimeograph.

Park, Yung Chul, and Chi-Young Song. 2001a. Financial contagion in the East Asian crisis: With special reference to the Republic of Korea. In *International financial contagion*, ed. Stijn Classens and Kristin Forbes, 241–65. Norwell, Mass.: Kluwer Academic.

———. 2001b. Institutional investors, trade linkage, macroeconomic similarities, and the contagious Thai crisis. *The Journal of Japanese and International Economies* 15:199–224.

Przeworski, Adam, and James R. Vreeland. 2000. The effect of IMF programs on economic growth. *Journal of Development Economics* 62:385–421.

Radelet, Steven, and Jeffrey Sachs. 1998. The East Asian financial crisis: Diagnosis, remedies, prospects. *Brookings Papers on Economic Activity*, Issue no. 1:1–74. Washington, D.C.: Brookings Institution.

Radelet, Steven, Jeffrey Sachs, and Jong-Wha Lee. 2001. Determinants and prospects of economic growth in Asia. *International Economic Journal* 15 (3): 1–30.

Sachs, Jeffrey, Aron Tornell, and Andrei Velasco. 1996. The collapse of the Mexican peso: What have we learned? *Economic Policy* 22:13–56.

Sachs, Jeffrey, and Andrew Warner. 1995. Economic Reform and the process of global integration. *Brookings Papers on Economic Activity*, Issue no. 1:1–118. Washington, D.C.: Brookings Institution.

Stone, Mark. 2000. The corporate sector dynamics of systemic financial crises. IMF Working Paper no. WP/00/114. Washington, D.C.: International Monetary Fund.

Williamson, John. 2000. *Exchange-rate regimes for East Asia: Reviving the intermediate option.* Policy Analysis in International Economics, no. 60. Washington, D.C.: Institute for International Economics.

Comment   Richard Portes

This paper examines two main issues: First, there is an analysis of cross-country patterns of adjustment in currency crises. This is a "cross-

Richard Portes is professor of economics at London Business School and a research associate of the National Bureau of Economic Research.

sectional event study," as in Eichengreen and Rose (chap. 3 in this volume). Second, the authors discuss the pattern of recovery in East Asia during 1999–2000. At times, the reader may feel that these are two separate papers. The graphs look the same, although the first set use annual data, whereas those on the recovery use quarterly figures; but the style and method of analysis differ considerably. There is not much connection between the two; the main link originally seemed to be the role of International Monetary Fund (IMF) programs, but they do not in fact appear in the discussion of East Asia.

In looking at the cross-country patterns, the authors identify 160 crisis episodes. They define a crisis only in terms of exchange rate depreciation (ignoring, for example, loss of reserves in cases in which the currency is attacked and successfully defended, as well as banking or debt crises). They distinguish between countries that adopt IMF programs to deal with the crisis and those that do not.

This distinction makes no difference to the behavior of output in the period leading up to the crisis and thereafter. The crisis countries' growth rates fall from $t - 4$ to $t - 1$, then *rise* in t—both for countries that adopt IMF programs and for the full sample. Here we may draw a contrast with Eichengreen and Rose: their output loss effect occurs in t and $t + 1$. The reason for this quite significant difference between the two papers is not clear.

The authors do find differences between IMF-program countries and others: the V-shaped behavior of output is stronger for the former, which make a quicker recovery from a deeper recession. They also exhibit a stronger fall in the share of investment (an effect that lasts through $t + 5$), a sharper V-shape for the share of imports, and a substantially sharper fall of public consumption, real M2 and bank credit.

What does all this mean? The puzzle is accentuated by the finding that the IMF program dummy is insignificant in the postcrisis recovery regressions! There are some similarities in postcrisis behavior between those countries with programs and the rest: the real exchange rate behaves similarly; the import share is identical in $t + 5$; and so is the export share (a striking statistical artifact). That, however, is all. The puzzle is not resolved, and equations of the type used in the paper to describe the recovery period are unlikely ever to get us very far. They use a few endogenous variables (investment, real M2, the real exchange rate, public consumption) on the right-hand side, and there is no underlying structure.

The finding that poorer countries recover more strongly from crises is interesting. It is consistent with the conjecture that crises in general have much more limited effects on rich countries—in particular, the conjecture that if Eichengreen and Rose were to look at Organization for Economic Cooperation and Development (OECD) countries (say) separately, they would not exhibit the output loss effect from crisis that is the key finding of their paper.

When we turn to the specific episode of East Asia—the crisis of 1997–98 and the recovery of 1999–2000—the volatility of external financing is the first striking phenomenon. Moreover, annual data very much understate the violence of the shock: for example, Korea experienced an outflow of $27 billion in 1997:3–1997:4, including $19 billion in 1997:4 alone. The commercial banks have been withdrawing funds continuously from the region since mid-1997, including 2000. In the crisis period itself, 1997–98, the international financial institutions put in $42 billion, while the banks withdrew $66 billion. Of course, if the international financial institutions had not injected so much, the banks might not have been able to take it out.

The authors' characterization of the postcrisis period might be summarized as "V for victory": a combination of policies and underlying positive fundamentals permitted a quick and strong recovery. The initial contraction is attributed mainly to a fall in investment, with fairly stable private consumption. The recovery appears to have come mainly from net exports, due to a big real depreciation in very open economies, with some stimulus from public investment in Korea and Malaysia and fairly early relaxation of monetary and fiscal policies. The argument is essentially that the stress on structural reforms is misplaced—or, at least, that such reforms could not have been the source of recovery, because they could not have had such rapid effects. The authors maintain that the underlying fundamentals of the crisis economies were in fact stronger than critics believed, so that with better financial management and a macro stimulus, they were able fairly easily to return to the precrisis growth path.

In this view, restructuring and reform was much less essential than the IMF and many observers contended. The supply side was flexible enough to respond despite the unfavorable balance sheet effects of exchange rate depreciation. If the underlying supply side is strong, then it's all a question of demand, and depreciation in the context of the generally favorable external environment of 1998–2000, together with an early switch to expansionary policies, gave the necessary demand-side stimulus. This view is consistent with the absence of identifiable effects from IMF programs. I find it attractive, although I do not think the paper gives very convincing support for it.

Discussion Summary

James Levinsohn suggested that selection bias might be an explanation for the insignificant IMF coefficients the authors found. Just as higher mortality rates for patients undergoing treatment in the Mayo clinic are found, the authors' regression understates the positive effect of the IMF because only the "sickest" cases receive a program.

Gian Maria Milesi-Ferretti referred to a paper coauthored with Assaf Razin in which they studied the evolution of output growth following crises but attempted to control for precrisis economic conditions, rather than postcrisis outcomes, so as to limit endogeneity problems. He also observed that the authors' definition of crises identifies many hyperinflation episodes, such as those in Argentina and Brazil, during which the nominal exchange rate depreciates very rapidly. These events are not meaningful currency crises, he argued. *Peter B. Kenen* said that the role of net exports seems central to the argument, but in most cases the effect came from a contraction of imports rather than an expansion of exports. Thus, it could not have been a stimulus to recovery. Second, the work does not account for the fact that the IMF program might affect some of the right-hand-side dummy variables.

Edwin M. Truman stated that there were warnings about the coming crisis, although they were not as dire as the crisis turned out to be. German banks were, for example, not allowed to treat Korea as an OECD country under the Basel capital requirements, as was also the case for Mexico. Also, he argued, one should try to match countries with their initial conditions in order to compare growth rates productively.

Nouriel Roubini argued that there is too much emphasis on illiquidity in the authors' description of Korea. He supported his argument with details such as the fact that seven out of the thirty biggest *chaebol* went into bankruptcy in 1997 before the crisis. So, he concluded, there were substantial problems in the Korean economy besides illiquidity and besides the oftencited problems, such as crony capitalism. He explained the recovery by the amount of reform undertaken. Thus, the rapid Korean recovery is explained by the deeper corporate restructuring undertaken and not by the expansionary monetary and fiscal policy adopted by all of the crisis countries. Korea reformed more than Thailand, which reformed more than Indonesia; Japan did not reform at all, and these observations explain their respective rates of recovery.

Martin Feldstein remarked that the regressions pool all data from 1975 but both crises and IMF programs changed a lot over that period. He also observed that aside from a description of the recovery of growth rates there is no discussion of levels. It therefore remains unclear whether there was overshooting so the loss in output was permanent. Besides that, he observed that many banks and corporations were taken over by the government and that this is not reform: these institutions now got their financing from the government. These institutions received liquidity by being taken over, but this is not restructuring. The crucial stage, and possibly the big surprise, will be when the government divests itself of these institutions.

William Easterly argued that any conclusions with regard to the IMF dummy in the regressions are flawed, because some of the right-hand-side variables are the policy variables, which the IMF tries to affect. Thus, when these are controlled for, the IMF's effect is not evaluated fairly.

Michael P. Dooley noted that the reversal in the current account is a solution to the external problem because it pays off the foreign creditors, but it still does not generate the internal transfer to cover the loss in the banking system, and that is where there are potential output effects. There still has to be a big redistribution from taxpayers to the government to privatize the banks. Without that, he doubted whether there will be recovery of output growth.

Morris Goldstein observed that even when self-selection bias is accounted for, as in the paper by Michael Hutchison, there still does not seem to be any significant effect of the IMF on growth, or maybe only a small temporary negative one. It still does not generate wonderful positive effects for the IMF.

Yung Chul Park responded that Kenen's point is right: the paper should differentiate between contraction of imports and expansion of exports.

It is not fair to say, he argued, that the international community knew about these structural problems—crony capitalism, moral hazard, and the like. Moreover, he noted that he has a record of many international investors who were willing to extend credit lines at the time. The bankruptcies were partly a result of the restructuring implemented at the time. He emphasized that these structural problems did not trigger the crisis, and this supports the liquidity argument.

In response to Dooley's comment, he observed that Korea now has the resources for domestic restructuring. The problem remains the political will to undertake them. It is very hard to restructure and reallocate resources without creating serious social dissention in a democratic society.

Jong-Wha Lee agreed that it is hard to isolate the net effect of IMF program. The regressions controlled only for precrisis GDP level and growth rate, he said, but these are assumed to proxy for many other variables. In response to Feldstein, he also observed that recovery was indeed fast and growth rates were overshooting for some countries, including Korea, and that GDP levels did recover.

A Cure Worse Than the Disease?
Currency Crises and the Output Costs of IMF-Supported Stabilization Programs

Michael M. Hutchison

10.1 Introduction

There is considerable debate over the output and employments effects of IMF-supported stabilization programs. This controversy seems especially heated for countries facing acute balance-of-payments problems and currency crises, as witnessed in 1997 in Korea, Indonesia, Thailand, and elsewhere. Stiglitz (2000), for example, supports critics of the International Monetary Fund (IMF) who argue that "the IMF's economic 'remedies' often make things worse—turning slowdowns into recessions and recessions into depressions." Some academic work also reaches this conclusion. Bordo and Schwartz (2000), for example, conclude, "the recent spate of [IMF] rescues may be the case of the medicine doing more harm than good" (60).[1] Similar statements by other leading economists are commonplace.

Despite these strong statements about the value of recent IMF programs, no consensus has emerged about the impact of these programs on the real

Michael M. Hutchison is professor of economics at the University of California, Santa Cruz.

Research assistance from Ilan Neuberger is gratefully acknowledged. Hiro Ito, Kimberly Peterson, and Sum-Yu Chiu helped with data collection. Timothy Lane and Patricia Gillett graciously helped in obtaining data on IMF programs. Comments from NBER conference participants, and especially the discussant, Gian Maria Milesi-Ferretti, are appreciated. Thanks also to brownbag workshop participants at the University of California, Santa Cruz, especially Michael P. Dooley, Rob Fairlie, and Donald Wittman.

1. Part of the criticism against the IMF is that it contributes to moral hazard by creating the expectation of bailouts (implicit debt guarantees) whenever countries face balance-of-payments problems. Empirical evidence on this point is mixed. For example, Dreher and Vaubel (2001) find support for moral hazard associated with IMF programs, whereas Lane and Phillips (2000) do not. See Willett (2001) for a recent review and evaluation of the literature on the debate surrounding the role of the IMF.

side of the economy.[2] Most empirical studies using panel data sets and regression techniques find that IMF-supported programs improve the balance of payments and current account (e.g., Khan 1990; Conway 1994; Bordo and Schwartz 2000). This is not surprising, because a key purpose of the IMF is "to give confidence to members by making the Fund's resources temporarily available to them under adequate safeguards, thus providing them with the opportunity to correct maladjustments in their balance of payments without resorting to measures destructive of national or international prosperity" (IMF *Articles of Agreement,* Article I [v]).

Views on the ultimate output and employment effects of IMF programs, however, appear much more divergent than on the balance-of-payments effects. On the surface, it may seem odd that countries would choose to participate in an IMF stabilization program if it were not in their best interests to do so. That is, participation in a program would presumably be unlikely if the output costs were perceived to be particularly large, outweighing the benefits arising from improvement in the balance of payments, continued access to credit markets, and so on. Stiglitz (2000) and others argue, however, that although officially the IMF does not force countries to participate in programs and negotiate conditions, "[i]n practice, it undermines the democratic process by imposing policies."

A number of previous studies have attempted to measure the output costs of IMF-program participation. However, these studies have reached radically different conclusions, with results suggesting sizable declines in output growth arising from participation in IMF programs (e.g., Przeworski and Vreeland 2000) or quite strong positive output effects (e.g., Dicks-Mireaux, Mecagni, and Schadler 2000). These conflicting results arise from several sources, including differences in the types of IMF programs that are investigated; differences in the groups of countries that are investigated (e.g., poor developing vs. emerging-market economies); differences in the methodologies that are employed; and, perhaps most important, how other factors influencing output growth are taken into account.

One area that has not been sufficiently addressed in previous work is the role of severe currency or balance-of-payments crises on output growth and how these events interact with subsequent participation in IMF programs. We argue that Heckman's (1979) inverse Mills ratio (IMR) approach does not adequately control for selection bias in this case, because "participation equations" in this literature (predicting whether a country participates in an

---

2. There is a large literature reviewing the effects of IMF-supported stabilization programs. See, for example, Beveridge and Kelly (1980), Bird (1996), Bordo and James (2000), Connors (1979), Conway (2000), Edwards (1989), Gylafson (1987), Killick, Malik, and Manuel (1992), McQuillan and Montgomery (1999), Mussa and Savastano (2000), Pastor (1987), and Santaella (1996). Bird, Hussain, and Joyce (2000) investigate the factors that cause countries to enter repeatedly into IMF programs, and Joyce (2001) investigates the factors that determine the duration of IMF programs.

IMF program) generally have low explanatory power. This is partly because two-thirds of IMF programs are not associated with severe balance-of-payments or currency crises (discussed in section 10.4). Our approach, by contrast, is to measure the output cost of participation in an IMF program and investigate whether there are feedback effects that make implementation of programs especially problematic in the immediate aftermath of or concurrent with an ongoing balance-of-payments or currency crisis. Our study focuses on three related questions: First, given that a country is already facing a severe currency crisis, does participation in an IMF-supported stabilization program tend to make real gross domestic product (GDP) growth weaker? Second, can one identify the channels (policy instruments) through which participation in IMF-supported programs affect real GDP? Third, how much of the downturn in East Asia following the 1997 currency crisis may be attributed to participation in IMF programs?

To address the first question, we control for the effect of a currency crisis on real GDP and consider whether there is an additional effect arising from IMF-program participation at this time. We want to be sure that the effect of a currency crisis on GDP is not inadvertently attributed to participation in an IMF program. The second question asks whether we can identify the policy channel or policy mechanism through which IMF-program participation affects real GDP growth. Beyond providing countries with access to substantial lines of credit, IMF programs are generally associated with conditions on the future conduct of fiscal, credit, and other policies. Identifying the way IMF conditionality affects the formulation of policy in practice (ex post)—as opposed to the agreements themselves (ex ante)—is an important step in determining how participation in programs might affect GDP. If the critics of the IMF are right and conditionality leads to overly restrictive macroeconomic policies and poor output performance, then it should show up in the data. Finally, the answer to the third question should shed light on the macroeconomic performance of East Asian countries that faced currency crises in 1997, distinguishing those that entered into IMF programs (Korea, Thailand, the Philippines, and Indonesia) from the country that did not participate (Malaysia).

To investigate these issues we focus on short-run IMF stabilization programs (Stand-By Agreements and Extended Fund Facilities) that are explicitly focused on balance-of-payments adjustment, rather than programs directed primarily toward structural reform and poverty reduction. The broadest spectrum of developing and emerging-market countries possible is considered, where the key limitation on the number of countries is the availability of macroeconomic data. The estimation methodology employed to investigate real growth effects of IMF programs is the General Evaluation Estimator (GEE). In this context, we control for the occurrence of recent currency or balance-of-payments crises and also test for interaction effects between the two events. This allows us to answer the question:

Is the adverse output effect of a currency crisis made worse when the IMF steps in with a stabilization package? We test the basic model using a panel data set with country-specific fixed effects. Simple reaction functions are also estimated to characterize the influence of IMF programs on the formulation of macroeconomic policy. We take into account the effect of recent currency crises on policy as well as the effects of self-selection bias.

Section 10.2 discusses the GEE methodology and how we control for recent occurrences of currency crises. Section 10.3 discusses the data employed in the study and our selection of IMF programs to investigate. Section 10.4 provides a statistical background and summary statistics on the size, frequency over time, and regional distribution of IMF programs. We also consider the probability of a country's adopting an IMF program conditional upon its having had a recent currency crisis. Section 10.5 presents the primary empirical results of the study. This section presents estimation results of the "reduced-form" output equation with explanatory variables that include balance-of-payments or currency crises and IMF program participation. It also applies the model to an explanation of the recessions faced by East Asian countries following the 1997 currency crisis. Section 10.6 presents results from estimating policy reaction functions and the effect of IMF programs on credit policy. Section 10.7 concludes the paper.

10.2   GEE Methodology: Controlling for Currency and Balance-of-Payments Crises

The basic GEE methodology employed in our study was first applied to the evaluation of IMF programs by Goldstein and Montiel (1986). It is based on the idea that one can derive a counterfactual—what would have happened to an IMF-participating country if it had not adopted a program—by investigating the policy responses of nonparticipating countries. The key element in this approach is that it must be possible to characterize macroeconomic policy choices by a simple and stable (over time and across countries) reaction function that holds for both participating and nonparticipating countries. We extend this standard model by introducing currency or balance-of-payments crisis as an additional factor influencing the evolution of output. We also introduce an interactive term that measures any additional adverse effect on output that is associated with IMF programs directly following a currency crisis.

The growth of real GDP for the ith country at time $t (y_{it})$ is explained by policies that would have been observed *in the absence* of an IMF-supported program ($\mathbf{X}_{it}$); exogenous external factors ($\mathbf{W}_{it}$); the recent occurrence of a currency or balance-of-payments crisis ($D_{i(t-1)}^{CC}$); the existence of an IMF-supported program (D_{it}^{IMF}); and unobservable random disturbances (ε_{it}).

$$(1) \qquad y_{it} = \beta_0 + \beta_k X_{it} + \alpha_h W_{it} + \beta^{CC} D^{CC}_{i(t-1)} + \beta^{IMF} D^{IMF}_{it}$$
$$+ \beta^{int}(D^{CC}_{i(t-1)} * D^{IMF}_{it}) + \varepsilon_{it}$$

where X is a k-element vector of policy variables for country i at time t that would be observed in the absence of IMF support, W is an h-element vector of exogenous variables for country i at time t, $D^{CC}_{i(t-1)}$ is a dummy variable equal to unity if the country has recently experienced a currency crisis (and zero otherwise), D^{IMF}_{it} is a dummy variable equal to unity if a short-run IMF program is in effect (and zero otherwise), $D^{IMF}_{it} * D^{CC}_{i(t-1)}$ is an interaction term measuring additional effects on output growth arising from a currency crisis that is immediately followed by an IMF program, and ε_{it} is a zero mean, fixed variance, serially uncorrelated disturbance term.[3] β_0 is a vector of country fixed effects (allowing average growth rates to vary across countries in the sample), β_k is a k-element vector measuring the impact of policy changes on output, α_h is an h-element vector measuring the impact of exogenous factors on output, β^{CC} measures the effect of currency or balance-of-payments crises on output growth, β^{IMF} measures the affect on output from participation in an IMF-supported stabilization program, and β^{int} measures the effect of the interaction term.

After postulating a rule for the k-element vector of policies that would have taken place in the absence of an IMF-supported program (X_{it}), the model is estimated (with fixed effects) using panel data drawn from countries and periods in which IMF support was in place and those in which IMF support was absent. The aim is to get consistent estimates for β^{IMF} and β^{int}—the effects of IMF support on output.

Policies adopted in the absence of an IMF-supported program (X_{it}) are directly observable only for nonprogram periods, and a key part of the GEE estimation approach is therefore to construct a counterfactual for policies during programs. This counterfactual is based upon a policy reaction function that links changes in the policy instrument to the deviation of the observed lagged value for output growth from its desired value (y^d_{it}). The policy reaction function is described by

$$(2) \qquad \Delta x_{it} = \gamma[y^d_{it} - y_{i(t-1)}] + \eta_{it}$$

where η_{it} is a zero mean, fixed variance, serially uncorrelated error term assumed to be uncorrelated with ε_{it}, and Δ is the difference operator. The parameter γ indicates the extent to which the policy instrument is adjusted in response to disequilibria in the target variable. Substituting equation (2) into equation (1) and subsuming desired output growth into the vector of fixed-effect constant terms for each country (β_0) gives

---

3. See Dooley (2000) and Gupta, Mishra, and Sahay (2000) for discussions of the factors that cause output to fall following a currency crisis.

(3) $\Delta y_{it} = \beta_0' - (\beta_k \gamma_k + 1) y_{i(t-1)} + \beta_k X_{i(t-1)} + \alpha_h W_{it} + \beta^{CC} D^{CC}_{i(t-1)}$
         $+ \beta^{IMF} D^{IMF}_{it} + \beta^{int}(D^{CC}_{i(t-1)} * D^{IMF}_{it}) + \varepsilon_{it} + \beta_k \eta_{it})$

Equation (3) is the basic GEE reduced-form model as applied in earlier studies (Dicks-Mireaux, Mecagni, and Schadler 2000; Goldstein and Montiel 1986; and others). The usefulness of the model, as discussed in detail in Dicks-Mireaux, Mecagni, and Schadler (2000), depends on (a) whether individual country behavior may be aggregated in a stable (across countries and time) uniform model; (b) whether it may be assumed that the policy reaction function of a program country, had it not received IMF support, is identical to that of nonprogram countries that did not seek support; and (c) whether the additive term $\beta^{IMF} D^{IMF}_{it}$ and the interactive term $\beta^{INT}(D^{IMF}_{it} * D^{CC}_{it})$ can fully capture all the channels (static and dynamic) through which participation in IMF programs may affect output growth.

Unlike previous studies, we control for the (lagged) occurrence of currency and balance-of-payments crises as a predetermined variable in the output growth equation. We also take into account the possibility that an interactive effect (operating between currency crises and the adoption of IMF programs) may have an additional impact on output growth. Leaving out these terms could leave the output growth equation misspecified and lead to biased estimates.

10.3   Selection of International Monetary Fund Programs and Data Description

10.3.1   Selection of International Monetary Fund Programs

The main IMF facilities designed to meet short-run balance-of-payments stabilization are Stand-By Arrangements (SBA) and the Extended Fund Facility (EFF).[4] In general, IMF members can access credit tranches from the General Resources Account (GRA) either by means of IMF program arrangements or by means of "outright purchases." Outright purchases are limited, typically, to the first 25 percent of the member's quota and do not involve any phasing or conditionality. Stand-By Arrangements have been the main instrument through which members gain access to further credit tranches.[5] Stand-By Arrangements typically last for twelve to eighteen months (the legal maximum is three years), and first tranche drawings do not require strict conditionality. Any drawings beyond the first tranche require both phasing out and stricter conditionality and are limited

4. This discussion is based on International Monetary Fund (2000).
5. As the Articles of Agreement state, they were defined as "a decision by the Fund by which a member is assured that it will be able to make purchases from the General Resources Account in accordance with the terms of the decision during a specified period and up to a specified amount" (Article XXX [b]).

to 100 percent of quota annually (300 percent cumulatively together with the EFF, as discussed below). Repurchase obligations last about three and one-quarter to five years from the date of purchase.

The EFF, established in 1974, provides somewhat longer-term financing to countries in need of structural economic reforms. Extended Fund Facility arrangements typically last for three years; phasing and conditionality are similar to the SBAs, with an emphasis on longer-term structural reforms. Quota limits are identical to the SBAs, whereas repurchases last much longer (four and one-half to ten years). Both facilities are subject to the same rate of interest for repayments.[6] The supplemental reserve facility (SRF), introduced in 1997 in the Korean stabilization program, aims to supplement resources made available under SBAs and the EFF in order to provide financial assistance for exceptional balance-of-payments difficulties. Penalty interest rates (increasing over time) and short repayment periods (one to one and one-half years) insure that these are taken only in exceptional circumstances.[7]

We use the SBA and EFF programs (and, for Korea in 1997, the new SRF program) as our definition of IMF-supported stabilization programs. These are the only programs clearly linked to short-term balance-of-payments adjustment. (There are no cases of SBA and EFF programs' being approved in the same year in this data sample.) By contrast with these programs, some IMF facilities are designed with other objectives in mind. We do not include these programs, because their primary objective is not short-run balance-of-payments stabilization and adjustment.

For example, separate from the GRA, the IMF established the structural adjustment facility (SAF) in 1986 for "all low-income countries . . . that are in need of such resources and face *protracted* balance of payments problems" (italics mine),[8] and its successor, the Enhanced Structural Adjustment Facility (ESAF), in 1987. In 1999, the ESAF was replaced by the Poverty Reduction and Growth Facility (PRGF). These are managed separately by the IMF and are financed from the sale of IMF-owned gold together with resources provided by members in the form of loans or grants to the IMF, as trustee, for the purpose of helping low-income member countries. These resources are used to finance highly concessional low-interest loans. Eligible countries can withdraw up to 185 percent of their quota conditional on their balance-of-payment needs and the strength of their adjustment program. The interest rate charged is 0.5 percent, and repayments are over a ten-year period.

---

6. Starting in 1989, the rate of charge was linked directly to the SDR interest rate, and adjusted weekly.

7. In our sample, the only such case is the agreement with Korea in 1997.

8. As determined by the International Development Association (IDA), the World Bank's concessional window (the current cutoff point for IDA eligibility is a 1999 per capita GDP level of $885).

By contrast with our study, Dicks-Mireaux, Mecagni, and Schadler (2000) focus on the structural adjustment programs in their research (SAF and ESAF) and measure the effects of these IMF-supported programs on poor developing economies. Bordo and Schwartz (2000), on the other hand, consider both IMF stabilization and structural adjustment programs and use a mixed sample of twenty emerging-market and developed countries (including Australia and New Zealand). Similarly, Przeworski and Vreeland (2000) do not differentiate between programs, including both stabilization and structural adjustment IMF programs. However, similar to us (and unlike Bordo and Schwartz 2000 or Dicks-Mireaux, Mecagni, and Schadler 2000), they consider a broad set of developing countries. Our basic results, however, are robust to broadening the definition of IMF programs to include the SAF and ESAF.

10.3.2   Defining Currency and Balance-of-Payments Crises

Our indicator of currency and balance-of-payments crises is constructed from "large" changes in an index of currency pressure, defined as a weighted average of monthly real exchange rate changes and monthly (percent) reserve losses.[9] Following convention (e.g., Kaminsky and Reinhart, 1999) the weights are inversely related to the variance of changes of each component over the sample for each country. Our measure, taken from Glick and Hutchison (2000, 2001), presumes that any nominal currency changes associated with exchange rate pressure should affect the purchasing power of the domestic currency, that is, result in a change in the real exchange rate (at least in the short run). This condition excludes some large depreciations that occur during high-inflation episodes, but it avoids screening out sizable depreciation events in more moderate inflation periods for countries that have occasionally experienced periods of hyperinflation and extreme devaluation.[10] An episode of severe exchange rate pressure is defined as a value in the index—a threshold point—that exceeds the mean plus two times the country-specific standard deviation, provided that it also exceeds 5 percent.[11] The first condition insures that any large (real)

9. Our currency pressure measure of crises does not include episodes of defense involving sharp rises in interest rates. Data for market-determined interest rates are not available for much of the sample period in many of the developing countries in our dataset.

10. This approach differs from that of Kaminsky and Reinhart (1999), for example, who deal with episodes of hyperinflation by separating the nominal exchange rate depreciation observations for each country according to whether inflation in the previous six months was greater than 150 percent, and they calculate for each subsample separate standard deviation and mean estimates with which to define exchange rate crisis episodes.

11. Other studies defining the threshold of large changes in terms of country-specific moments include Kaminsky and Reinhart (1999); Kaminsky, Lizondo, and Reinhart (1998); and Esquivel and Larrain (1998). Kaminsky and Reinhart (1999) use a 3–standard deviation cutoff. Although the choice of cutoff point is somewhat arbitrary, Frankel and Rose (1996) suggest that the results are not very sensitive to the precise cutoff chosen in selecting crisis episodes.

depreciation is counted as a currency crisis, and the second condition attempts to screen out changes that are insufficiently large in an economic sense relative to the country-specific monthly change of the exchange rate.

For each country-year in our sample, we construct binary measures of currency crises, as defined above (1 = crisis, 0 = no crisis). A currency crisis is deemed to have occurred for a given year if the currency pressure index for any month of that year satisfies our criteria (i.e., two standard deviations above the mean as well as greater than 5 percent in magnitude). To reduce the chances of capturing the continuation of the same currency crisis episode, we impose windows on our data. In particular, after identifying each "large" indication of currency pressure, we treat any similar threshold point reached in the following twenty-four-month window as a part of the same currency episode and skip the years of that change before continuing the identification of new crises. With this methodology, we identify 160 currency crises over the 1975–97 period.

10.3.3   Other Variables in the Output Growth Equation and Policy Function

Estimation of the reduced-form output growth equation (3) for the output growth equation necessitates that the external exogenous variables influencing output growth (vector ω_{it}) and the (lagged) policy instruments (vector $x_{i(t-1)}$) be identified. The external exogenous factors included are (trade-weighted) external growth rates of major trading partners and the lagged rate of real exchange rate overvaluation.[12] The (lagged) policy factors considered are the change in the budget surplus to GDP ratio, inflation, and credit growth.

In the policy reaction function estimates of equation (2), we also consider regional dummy variables and a measure of policy "autocracy."[13] In controlling for sample selection bias, a probit equation explaining the likelihood of IMF-program participation is estimated. Other variables employed in this estimation, not noted above, are the (lagged) ratio of foreign exchange reserves to imports, the change in the ratio of current account to GDP, and real per capita GDP growth. These macroeconomic data series are taken from the IMF's *International Financial Statistics* CD-ROM.

The minimum data requirements to be included in our study are that GDP data are available for a minimum of ten consecutive years over the period 1975–97. This requirement results in a sample of sixty-seven developing

---

12. Real exchange rate overvaluation is defined as deviations from a fitted trend in the real trade-weighted exchange rate. The real trade-weighted exchange rate is the trade-weighted sum of the bilateral real exchange rates (defined in terms of CPI indices) against the U.S. dollar, the German mark, and the Japanese yen. The trade weights are based on the average bilateral trade with the United States, the European Union, and Japan in 1980 and 1990.

13. Autocracy is an index ranging from 1 to 10, with 10 indicating the most "closed" political system. The source of this variable is the "polity" database.

Table 10.1   **IMF Programs in Developing Countries: Approvals by Time (1970–99)**

	Short-Term Programs (SBA, ESBA, EFF)	Long-Term Programs (SAF, ESAF, PRGF)	All IMF programs
1970–74	85 (37.12) [0.9]		85
1975–79	113 (82.66) [2.0]		113
1980–84	169 (298.42) [3.9]		169
1985–89	115 (265.78) [2.2]	58 (87.44) [4.2]	173
1990–94	109 (275.34) [2.0]	46 (110.62) [5.8]	155
1995–99	87 (1168.48) [2.2]	63 (148.30) [7.0]	150
Totals	678	167	845

Notes: Figures are number of programs approved. Figures in parentheses are average size of program in million SDRs. Figures in brackets are average size of program relative to GDP (%). The size relative to GDP statistic is limited by data availability.

countries.[14] We use annual observations in our analysis. Although we employ monthly data for our (real) exchange rate pressure index to identify currency crises and date each by the year in which it occurs, using annual data enables inclusion of a relatively large number of countries. The appendix table provides details on the countries included in the sample, the currency crisis dates, and the periods when countries participated in IMF programs.

10.4   Summary Statistics: International Monetary Fund Programs, Currency Crises, and the Economy

10.4.1   International Monetary Fund Programs: Size, Growth, and Regional Distribution

The frequencies of the IMF programs are shown in table 10.1 (for all countries) over the 1970–99 period. (Descriptive statistics on IMF programs reported in tables 10.1 and 10.2 cover the 1970–99 period, whereas the other tables involving statistical analysis cover the 1975–97 period.) The total number of programs, the average size in terms of SDRs (in paren-

14. The developing country sample excludes major oil-exporting countries.

Table 10.2   **IMF Programs: Approvals by Region (1970–99)**

	SBA	EFF	ESAF	PRGF
Totals	493	69	113	11
Latin America	146	26	13	1
	(29.6)	(37.7)	(11.5)	(9.0)
Middle East	14	6	1	0
	(2.80)	(8.70)	(0.88)	(0.00)
East and South Asia	62	12	12	1
	(12.6)	(17.4)	(10.6)	(9.0)
Africa	177	16	77	9
	(35.9)	(23.2)	(68.1)	(82.0)
Eastern Europe and the former USSR	68	8	9	
	(13.8)	(11.6)	(8.0)	
Other	26	1	1	0
	(5.30)	(1.40)	(0.88)	(0.00)

Notes: Figures are number of programs approved. Figures in parentheses are percent of IMF program by region.

theses), and the size of the average program as a percentage of the recipient country's GDP (in brackets) are given in the table. The table is divided into short-term stabilization (the focus of our study) and longer-term structural adjustment programs, and it is also separated into five-year intervals.

Over the thirty-year period, 845 IMF programs were approved, of which 678 were short-run stabilization programs—SBAs or the EFF. Only 167 were longer-term structural adjustment programs—SAF, ESAF, or the PRGF.

The number of programs reached a peak in the early 1980s (with the Mexican debt crisis and debt problems in other Latin American countries), both in terms of number of programs (169) and size relative to the economies involved (average program size over 4 percent of GDP). The number of IMF programs is not growing, nor is the size relative to the economies involved (about 2 percent of GDP in 1995–99). The size of the average program in terms of SDRs jumped in the late 1990s, however, due to the large economic size of the countries going to the IMF for assistance (e.g., Brazil, Indonesia, Mexico, the Russian Federation, and South Korea).[15]

The regional breakdown of program approvals is given in table 10.2. The short-term stabilization programs (SBA and EFF) are primarily directed to Latin America and Africa, with about 30 and 35 percent respectively of program approvals. Africa dominates the long-term structural programs (SAF or ESAF and PRGF) with 70 percent of the programs over the period.

15. This includes the disbursement to Korea under the SRF.

10.4.2   Currency Crises and International Monetary Fund
         Program Participation

An important part of our study is to investigate the link between currency
crises, real output developments, and IMF stabilization programs. Table
10.3 shows the relative frequencies of currency crises and IMF stabilization
program participation for the sixty-seven countries in our sample over the
1975–1997 period. Panel A shows the contemporaneous frequencies (and
associated chi-squared independence tests), that is, contemporaneous currency crises and contemporaneous IMF program participation. Statistical
independence of these observations is rejected at the 99 percent level of confidence, but only 18 percent of IMF-program participation observations
are associated with currency crises. However, a substantially higher percentage (28 percent) of the currency crisis observations coincide with IMF-
program observations.

Panel B shows the link between IMF programs and contemporaneous
and lagged currency crises. This shows a stronger link than the contemporaneous relationship. Statistical independence is again rejected (at
greater than 1 percent significance). Thirty-three percent of contemporaneous IMF-program participation observations are associated with either
a contemporaneous or previous (one-year lag) currency crisis. Similarly,
28 percent of contemporaneous or lagged currency crises are associated
with a contemporaneous IMF program. Hence, almost one-third of currency crisis observations are linked to an IMF program within the current
year or the next year. Of course, this implies that about two-thirds of the

Table 10.3   **Relative Frequency of Crises and IMF-Program Participation**

	Frequency (%) and Significance Levels
A. Contemporaneous Frequencies	
Short-term IMF programs associated with a contemporaneous currency crisis	18%
Currency crisis associated with a contemporaneous short-term IMF program	28%
Chi independence test for contemporaneous IMF and currency crisis series	0.0004
B. Contemporaneous and Lagged Frequencies	
Short-term IMF programs associated with a contemporaneous or lagged $(t-1)$ currency crisis	33%
Contemporaneous or lagged $(t-1)$ currency crisis associated with a short-term IMF program	28%
Chi independence test for contemporaneous IMF and currency crisis series	0.0000

currency crisis observations are not linked with IMF-program participation.

10.4.3   Macro Developments: Participation or Nonparticipation and Before and After Statistics

Tables 10.4–10.6 present summary statistics on the timing of IMF-programs (SBA and EFF) participation and key macroeconomic developments. Table 10.4 shows sample mean values for macroeconomic developments during program years and nonprogram years. The first two columns report the statistics for all countries (both for those countries that at some point participated in IMF programs and for those that did not), focusing on nonprogram observations and IMF-program observations. Real GDP growth was about 4 percent (1,082 observations) during the nonprogram years and 2.9 percent during the program years (585 observations). This difference is significantly different at the 99 percent level of confidence (t-

Table 10.4   **Summary Statistics: Short-Term IMF Programs: Means**

Variable	All Countries (67 Countries)		IMF-Participating Countries (60 Countries)		Non-IMF Countries[a]:
	Nonprogram Years	Program Years	Nonprogram Years	All Years	All Years
Real GDP growth	4.18	2.94	3.62	3.36	6.83
		(4.83***)	(-2.62***)	(1.28)	(-9.10***)
	[1,082]	[585]	[895]	[1,480]	[187]
Inflation	18.43	25.01	20.29	22.08	8.26
		(-3.09***)	(2.05*)	(-0.99)	(4.16***)
	[1,061]	[549]	[897]	[1,446]	[164]
Current account– GDP ratio (%)	-5.09	-5.01	-5.81	-5.49	-0.01
		(-0.14)	(1.28)	(-0.60)	(-4.33***)
	[858]	[473]	[719]	[1,192]	[139]
Credit growth	25.11	26.71	26.19	26.39	18.75
		(-0.77)	(0.24)	(-0.11)	(2.28**)
	[1,074]	[567]	[917]	[1,484]	[157]
Budget surplus– GDP ratio (%)	-3.36	-4.44	-4.04	-4.20	0.00
		(3.22***)	(-1.19)	(0.59)	(-8.52***)
	[952]	[507]	[796]	[1,303]	[156]

Notes: Figures in parentheses are statistics for difference in means with the column to the left. Figures in brackets are number of observations.

The countries that have never participated in a short-term IMF program (either SBA or EFF), and that are included in our data set, are Botswana, Hong Kong, Malta, Malaysia, Paraguay, Singapore, and Swaziland.

***Significant at the 1 percent level.
**Significant at the 5 percent level.
*Significant at the 10 percent level.

Table 10.5   **Before and After Summary Statistics: IMF Short-Term Programs (four-year window: Means)**

Variable	Average of 2 Years Before IMF Program	During IMF Program Years	Average of 2 Years After IMF Program
Real GDP growth	3.20	2.94	4.23
		(0.53)	(−2.68***)
			[−1.46]
	{114}	{585}	{132}
Inflation	32.18	25.01	21.00
		(1.42)	(1.01)
			[0.57]
	{116}	{549}	{133}
Current account–GDP ratio	−5.97	−5.01	−5.20
		(−1.15)	(0.24)
			[0.53]
	{90}	{473}	{110}
Credit growth	37.39	26.71	27.11
		(2.46**)	(−0.12)
			[0.64*]
	{121}	{567}	{140}
Budget surplus–GDP ratio	−5.76	−4.44	−4.71
		(−2.09**)	(0.44)
			[1.17]
	{109}	{507}	{132}

Notes: Figures in parentheses are *t*-statistic for difference in means with the column to the left. Figures i brackets are *t*-statistic for difference in means with the first column. Figures in braces are number of ot servations.
***Significant at the 1 percent level.
**Significant at the 5 percent level.
*Significant at the 10 percent level.

statistic equal to 4.83). Inflation and budget deficits are significantly higher during the program years, but no substantive difference between program and non-program years is detected in the growth rate of credit or the current account balance.

There may be systematic differences in the types of countries that approach the IMF for assistance, however. Focusing only on countries participating in IMF programs (second, third, and fourth columns) avoids this selection bias. For countries involved in IMF programs (at some point during the sample), average GDP growth was 3.6 percent during nonprogram years and 2.9 percent during program years. This difference is statistically significant. Inflation was also significantly lower during the nonprogram years. No difference is discernible in credit growth or the budget and current account balances.

If one simply compares IMF-program countries (both during program and nonprogram years) with those not having a program during the sample

Table 10.6   **Before and After Summary Statistics: IMF Short-Term Programs**
                       (two-year window: Mean values)

Variable	1 Year Before IMF Program	During IMF Program Years	1 Year After IMF Program
Real GDP growth	2.62	2.94	4.34
		(−0.56)	(−2.47**)
			[−1.98**]
	{76}	{585}	{84}
Inflation	32.28	25.01	21.71
		(1.24)	(0.68)
			[1.15]
	{76}	{549}	{85}
Current account–GDP ratio	−5.23	−5.01	−4.18
		(−0.24)	(−0.84)
			[−0.63]
	{59}	{473}	{68}
Credit growth	39.39	26.71	28.98
		(2.48**)	(−0.54)
			[1.22]
	{79}	{567}	{88}
Budget surplus–GDP ratio	−5.98	−4.44	−4.46
		(−2.07**)	(0.02)
			[−1.44]
	{70}	{507}	{75}

Notes: Figures in parentheses are t-statistic for difference in means with the column to the left. Figures in brackets are t-statistic for difference in means with the first column. Figures in braces are number of observations.
***Significant at the 1 percent level.
**Significant at the 5 percent level.
*Significant at the 10 percent level.

period, the differences are substantial—but not surprising. Countries that have never participated in an IMF program during our sample period—presumably not having had a need to participate—exhibit much stronger economic fundamentals: much higher GDP growth rates (6.8 percent versus 3.4 percent), lower inflation, lower credit growth, and balanced positions in the current account and budget.

Table 10.5 focuses on the before and after time series of countries participating in IMF programs. Four-year windows are imposed. The table shows that output growth does *not* decline substantially when a country enters an IMF program, but it does increase significantly during the two-year period following the program. Credit growth, by contrast, falls significantly during the IMF program and stays at the lower rate of growth following the program. No statistically significant shifts are noted in the time pattern of inflation, the current account balance, or the budget surplus.

Table 10.6 undertakes the same decomposition as table 10.5 but instead imposes only a two-year window, together with a one-year interval before and after IMF program participation. Real GDP growth is not much different one year before and during an IMF program, but it rebounds substantially the year following a program. Inflation drops before, during, and after programs, but the variation in the sample is so great that the differences are not statistically significant. Credit growth drops sharply following an IMF program and stays lower one year following a program. The budget balance improves during an IMF program and stays at a lower level following the program.

Tables 10.5 and 10.6 clearly demonstrate that economies typically experience slow growth prior to entering into an IMF program, and sluggish growth continues until the program is concluded. It does not appear that participation in the IMF program directly contributed to slower growth. Inflation and credit growth both declined during the IMF-program period and stayed lower than in the preprogram period. In short, these summary statistics paint a classic recession-rebound pattern, but it is not clear if IMF program participation played a role.

10.5   Real Output Effects of International Monetary Fund Programs

10.5.1   General Evaluation Estimator Estimates

The reduced-form GEE estimates (equation [3]) are reported in table 10.7. White's consistent standard errors are reported. The first column reports the model without controlling for country fixed effects or currency crises. The lagged control variables are the change in the budget surplus ratio, inflation, credit growth, external (world) output growth, and real exchange rate overvaluation. A lagged dependent variable, as suggested in the theoretical formulation of the model, is also included. The focus is the coefficient on the IMF-program dummy. The coefficient estimate is statistically significant (99 percent level of confidence) and indicates that real GDP growth is lowered by about 1 percent during each year of IMF-program participation.

The estimated coefficients on lagged external growth (positive) and lagged real exchange rate overvaluation (negative) have the predicted signs and are statistically significant. In terms of the policy variables, the estimated coefficient on the lagged change in the budget surplus is positive, and the estimated coefficient on lagged credit growth is negative. Both are statistically significant. Interpreting these coefficients in terms of reaction functions, the rise in the lagged budget surplus (rise in credit growth) could lead to a more expansionary (restrictive) *contemporaneous* fiscal policy (credit policy) and hence a rise (fall) in output growth. Other interpretations are possible. For example, countries with more sustainable fiscal policies and lower credit growth may have systemically higher real output growth

Table 10.7   **Output Growth Equation Estimates (Dependent variable: real GDP growth rate)**

Variable	Coefficient				
	(1)	(2)	(3)	(4)	(5)
Constant	3.787***	4.169***	4.164***	4.444***	4.147***
	(8.02)	(7.52)	(7.37)	(7.70)	(7.43)
Change in budget surplus–GDP	13.607***	7.412*	7.213*	7.266*	7.254*
ratio $(t-1)$	(3.31)	(1.89)	(1.81)	(1.82)	(1.81)
Inflation $(t-1)$	-0.005	0.003	0.003	0.002	0.003
	(-0.82)	(0.56)	(0.55)	(0.46)	(0.61)
Credit growth $(t-1)$	-0.009	-0.009**	-0.009**	-0.009**	-0.010**
	(-1.55)	(-2.14)	(-2.08)	(-2.03)	(-2.13)
Real GDP growth $(t-1)$	0.094	0.139**	0.146**	0.150**	0.148**
	(1.34)	(2.25)	(2.31)	(2.39)	(2.32)
External growth rates (t)	0.275***	0.253***	0.255***	0.268***	0.259***
(weighted average)	(3.17)	(2.69)	(2.71)	(2.82)	(2.75)
Real exchange rate	-0.030***	-0.033***	-0.030***	-0.030***	-0.030***
overvaluation $(t-1)$	(-4.37)	(-4.19)	(-3.66)	(-3.61)	(-3.49)
IMF participation dummy	-1.010***	-0.740*	-0.781**	-0.659	-0.749*
for short-term programs (t)	(-3.37)	(-1.87)	(-2.02)	(-1.44)	(-1.82)
Currency crises dummy $(t-1)$		-1.496***	-1.161***	-1.107**	-1.089**
		(-3.32)	(-2.80)	(-2.39)	(-2.34)
Currency crises dummy (t)			-0.805**	0.765*	-0.761*
			(-1.89)	(-1.65)	(-1.64)
Lagged-contemporary				-0.195	-0.202
interactive term $D_{it}^{IMF} * D_{i;\,t,\,or\,(t-1)}^{CC}$				(-0.30)	(-0.32)
Dynamics for IMF participation					
dummy for Short-term					-0.457
programs[a] $(t-1, t-2, t-3)$					(0.10)
Adjusted R^2	0.12	0.22	0.23	0.22	0.22
	1,128	966	958	958	958
Durbin-Watson statistic	1.61	2.00	1.99	1.98	1.98

Note: All regressions, except the first, include country dummies. Numbers in parentheses are *t*-statistics.
Sum of the coefficients of the IMF dummy lagged for $t-1$, $t-2$, and $t-3$ (*t*-statistic on sum of lags reported). *F*-statistic (joint significance of three lagged values) is 0.86.
***Significant at the 1 percent level.
**Significant at the 5 percent level.
*Significant at the 10 percent level.

rates. Inclusion of fiscal and credit variables may be picking up important cross-country differences in economic performance.

Column (2) reports results for the model with country fixed effects (dummy variables for each country to capture the significant differences in growth rates over the full sample period) and the currency crisis variable. These variables are highly statistically significant, increasing the overall explanatory power of the model (*R*-squared) from 12 percent to 21 percent. A currency crisis in year $t-1$ is associated with a decline in output growth in year t of about 1.5 percentage points. The coefficient estimate on the IMF-participation variable decreases substantially when the currency crisis variable is taken into account, indicating that output growth is about 0.74 percentage points less annually for each year of IMF-program participation. This coefficient estimate, however, is only significant at the 90 percent level of confidence.

Column (3) reports the results of the model when both contemporaneous and lagged currency crisis variables are included in the regression. Both of the currency crisis variables are negative and statistically significant. The coefficient estimate on the IMF-program participation is similar (0.78) to the result reported in column (2).

Column (4) reports the results where the model includes an interactive term measuring the occurrence of an IMF program that takes place around the time of a recent occurrence of a currency crisis (i.e., contemporaneous or in the previous year). The model estimates again suggest that a currency crisis leads to an output loss, but the coefficient estimate (−0.66) on the IMF-program dummy variable is not statistically significant. Is the output loss associated with a currency crisis magnified if an IMF program is approved in the same year or immediately following a severe balance-of-payments or currency crisis? The interaction term in column (4) is not statistically significant, indicating that the output loss associated with a crisis does not appear to be affected by a country's participation in an IMF program.

Column (5) reports results from estimating a more dynamic specification of the model. The objective is to investigate whether the adverse effects from participating in an IMF program dissipate, or perhaps intensify, over time. This is accomplished by including three lags of the IMF-participation variable. It appears that the adverse output effects are felt during the years of IMF program participation (generally one to three years), but no significant additional effects are observed in subsequent years. That is, neither the sum of the coefficients on the three lagged values of program participation nor the joint test is statistically different from zero (see footnote a to table 10.7).

In sum, the results are robust and indicate that participating in an IMF program, regardless of whether a currency or balance-of-payments crisis has recently occurred, "costs" about 0.6–0.8 percentage points of real GDP growth annually. Our estimates are about half the size of the negative impact reported by Przeworski and Vreeland (2000)[16] or Bordo and Schwartz

16. Przeworski and Vreeland (2000) estimate a long-run growth model (using capital and labor growth as independent variables), dividing the sample into (IMF) program observations and nonprogram observations. They also include the IMR in the regression. Their conclusions regarding the growth effects of IMF-program participation are based on the difference between the estimated constant terms in the two regressions.

(2000),[17] and similar in magnitude to Conway (1994). Unlike Conway (1994), however, we do not find that the reduction in growth is followed by higher future output growth.[18]

It is noteworthy that we also tested for sample selection bias in the estimation procedure, and the results were unaffected. The estimates on the IMF and currency-crisis variables did not change, and the coefficient on IMF was not statistically significant. (The probit equation estimated to measure self-selection bias is presented in table 10A.3.) Of course, insignificance of the IMR variable may be either because selection bias is not an important issue or because the participation equation is misspecified. These results are not reported for brevity but are available from the author upon request. This finding is similar to Dicks-Mireaux, Mecagni, and Schadler (2000). (We do find IMR significant in the policy reaction functions, however.)

10.5.2 Extensions: IMF Program Dating and Downturns Prior to IMF Program Approvals

Table 10.8 presents several extensions of the basic output growth model. The first two columns use the conventional dating scheme employed in table 10.7, dating the IMF program in the calendar year in which it was approved. The first column adds a one-year leading indicator of IMF program participation ("lead IMF program participation dummy, $t + 1$") and the second column adds a one-year leading indicator of IMF program *approval* (only the year of approval; subsequent program years are coded as zero). The descriptive evidence presented in table 10.6 suggests that a downturn in output tends to lead (by one year) participation in an IMF program. A lagged dependent variable included in the basic output growth equation helps to account for this dynamic. If cycles are irregular, however, inclusion of the IMF leading variable might be able to better capture downward shifts in output growth occurring with some regularity prior to IMF program participation. The leading IMF dummy variable is not significant in either column (1) or (2), however, and the contemporaneous effects are quite similar to those reported in table 10.7.

The second two columns use an alternative-dating scheme for the imple-

17. Bordo and Schwartz (2000) report a contemporaneous effect of IMF programs of -1.61 ($t = 0.97$) and a one-year lagged effect of 2.24 ($t = 2.67$). The contemporaneous effect is insignificantly different from zero, and the one-year lagged effect is significant at the 99 percent level of confidence. On balance, their results indicate that IMF-program participation has a net positive effect on growth. Surprisingly, they conclude that "The main detriment [of IMF-program participation] is a temporary reduction in real growth" (57) and "the impression given by the annual data . . . that turning to the IMF may be harmful to a country's real economic performance" (60). Our results are not directly comparable, however, because they have a limited sample of emerging-market and developed countries and include short-run stabilization programs, structural adjustment, and poverty reduction programs in their study.

18. Similar to us, Conway (1994) uses only SBA and EFF programs in his study.

Table 10.8   Output Growth Equation: Extensions (Dependent variable: real GDP growth rate)

	Coefficient			
Variable	Standard Dating		Alternative Dating	
Constant	4.171***	4.068***	4.159***	4.032***
	(7.36)	(7.29)	(7.48)	(7.26)
Change in budget surplus–GDP ratio ($t-1$)	7.080*	6.912*	7.042*	6.635*
	(1.77)	(1.71)	(1.78)	(1.64)
Inflation ($t-1$)	0.003	0.003	0.003	0.003
	(0.56)	(0.54)	(0.57)	(0.56)
Credit growth ($t-1$)	−0.009**	−0.009**	−0.009**	−0.009**
	(−2.11)	(−2.12)	(−2.10)	(−2.12)
Real GDP growth ($t-1$)	0.146**	0.150**	0.147**	0.152**
	(2.33)	(2.41)	(2.36)	(2.42)
External growth rates (t) (weighted average)	0.253***	0.264***	0.252***	0.267**
	(2.69)	(2.81)	(2.72)	(2.85)
Real exchange rate overvaluation ($t-1$)	−0.030***	−0.029***	−0.030***	−0.029**
	(−3.62)	(−3.42)	(−3.53)	(−3.44)
IMF program participation dummy (t)	−0.647*		−1.217**	
	(−1.77)		(−2.71)	
Lead IMF program participation dummy ($t+1$)	−0.266		0.303	
	(−0.69)		(0.73)	
IMF program approval dummy (t)		−0.878*		−0.583
		(−1.93)		(−1.51)
Lead IMF program approval dummy ($t+1$)		−0.550		0.305
		(−1.42)		(0.74)
Currency crises dummy ($t-1$)	−1.137***	−1.178***	−1.110***	−1.228**
	(−2.72)	(−2.86)	(−2.67)	(−2.98)
Currency crises dummy (t)	−0.778*	−0.643	−0.772*	−0.783*
	(−1.84)	(−1.52)	(−1.83)	(−1.83)
Adjusted R^2	0.23	0.23	0.23	0.22
N	958	958	958	958
Durbin-Watson statistic	1.99	2.00	1.99	2.00

Note: All regressions include country dummies. Numbers in parentheses are t-statistics.
***Significant at the 1 percent level.
**Significant at the 5 percent level.
*Significant at the 10 percent level.

mentation of IMF programs that has been used by Dicks-Mireaux, Mecagni, and Schadler (2000) and others. This dating scheme dates the IMF program to be in effect in year t if it was approved in the first half of year t or in the second half of year $t-1$. Again the leading IMF-program dummy variable is not statistically significant. However, the estimated contemporaneous effects of IMF programs on output growth using the alternative dating scheme do change somewhat. In particular, the estimated negative effect of an IMF program in column (3) (IMF program participation) rises to −1.22 and is significant at the 95 percent level of confidence. By contrast, the estimated output effect in the year of an IMF program *approval* is insignificant. These results indicate that changes in the dating scheme of IMF program implementation and program definition (whether defined as all years of participation or only the first year of approval) affect the results to some extent but do not change the basic findings.

We also estimated the basic model over the 1990–97 period, because the evolving nature of IMF programs and conditionality may have changed their effect on output. In particular, the number of conditions attached to IMF programs have increased in the 1990s. The coefficient on the IMF dummy drops to only –0.36 in this regression and is not significant at conventional levels.

10.5.3   The East Asian Financial Crisis and Output Contraction

Figure 10.1 presents the predicted values for output growth for the five East Asian countries that experienced a severe currency and balance-of-payments crisis in 1997. These predictions are for 1998 and based on 1997

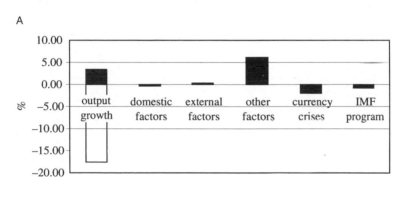

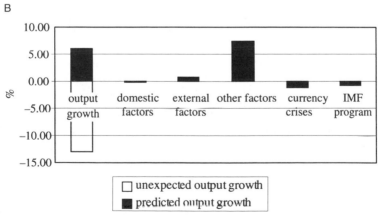

Fig. 10.1   Real GDP growth in East Asia 1998 (predicted values and forecast error):
A, **Indonesia;** *B,* **Korea;** *C,* **Malaysia;** *D,* **The Philippines;** *E,* **Thailand**

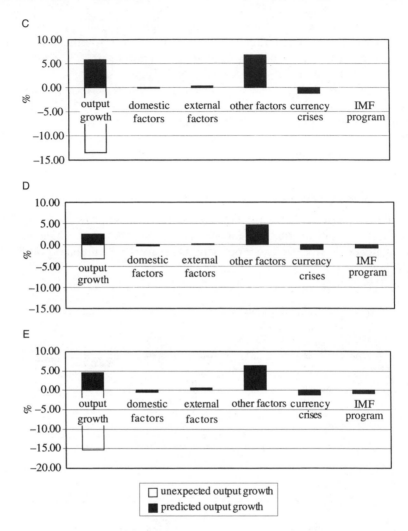

Fig. 10.1   **(cont.) Real GDP growth in East Asia 1998 (predicted values and forecast error): *A,* Indonesia; *B,* Korea; *C,* Malaysia; *D,* The Philippines; *E,* Thailand**

values of the explanatory variables, and the coefficient estimates—including country-specific fixed effects—are based on the model presented in column (3) of table 10.7 (estimates are based on 1975–97 data). The explanatory factors leading to the 1998 predicted value are decomposed into (a) domestic factors (change in budget surplus, inflation, and credit growth); (b) external factors (external growth and real exchange rate overvaluation); (c) other factors (previous year's output growth and country-specific fixed effect); (d) the currency crisis effect; and (e) the IMF-participation effect.

Predicted output growth for all five countries is positive in 1998, and the forecast error (unexpected declines in output) is therefore very large. The negative effect exerted by the currency crisis and subsequent participation in an IMF program is entirely dominated by positive "other factors"— mainly a history of very strong growth in the region and the consequently large country-specific fixed effect growth factor—and a modestly support-ive external growth environment. The effect of the currency crisis was ex-pected to slow output growth by 1–2 percentage points, and IMF-program participation (for Indonesia, Thailand, Korea, and the Philippines) lowers predicted growth by about 0.8 percentage points.

The largest unexpected fall in real GDP was Indonesia (17.6 percentage points) and the least in the Philippines (3 percentage points). The average of the four negative forecast errors for the four countries participating in IMF programs was 12.3 percentage points, not much different from the 13.5 point unexpected fall in Malaysia's GDP. Not participating in the IMF program did not appear to help Malaysia avoid a huge fall in output, and this decline was similar to others in the region.[19] The 0.8 predicted negative effect of participating in an IMF program pales by comparison with the ac-tual declines in output observed.

There appears to have been a common shock or common vulnerability in these countries—not related to the IMF and unobserved in this model— causing the unexpectedly large collapse in output.[20] All of these countries had serious banking problems that were associated with currency crises, a characteristic likely to cause substantially greater output effects, working through the disruption of credit and other channels (Glick and Hutchison 2001). Taiwan, Hong Kong, and Singapore avoided the worst of the cur-rency and banking problems because they did not have significant external (foreign-currency-denominated) short-term debt positions. Other factors, such as an abrupt loss of confidence after two decades of rapid growth and unrealistically high expectations for the region, may also have played a role.

10.6   Is Policy Changed by International Monetary Fund– Program Participation?

An important assumption underlying the GEE strategy is that it is pos-sible to characterize policy actions in the form of stable and systematic re-

---

19. Kaplan and Rodrik (2001) argue that, following the crisis, the imposition of capital con-trols in Malaysia, as opposed to adoption of an IMF program, led to a faster recovery and lower unemployment compared to Thailand and South Korea. They compare the aftermath of the imposition of controls in 1998 with the adoption of IMF programs in 1997 by Korea and Thailand (using the time-shifted difference-in-difference specification). However, this ap-proach does not take into account a counterfactual that the Malaysian currency crisis prob-ably would not have extended to September 1998 if it had adopted an IMF program in 1997.

20. It is possible that the "common shock" was indeed especially severe austerity programs associated with the IMF programs and perhaps mimicked by Malaysia to gain international acceptance of its policies. However, the evidence reported by Kaplan and Rodrik (2001) and others, and the imposition of capital controls by Malaysia, does not support this view.

action functions (equation [2]). This may prove extremely difficult because we are attempting to identify common responses from a broad spectrum of developing and emerging-market countries over a thirty-year period. The work of Dicks-Mireaux, Mecagni, and Schadler (2000) highlights the problems in identifying a consistent policy reaction function even among low-income developing economies. For example, they do not find any significant determinants of the fiscal balance or net domestic credit. They conclude that "these estimates provide a weak basis for deriving estimates of the unobservable counterfactuals" (508).

Table 10.9 presents our estimates of policy reaction functions for domestic credit growth—a primary policy instrument for many developing economies. Domestic credit growth is also a key indicator of monetary policy used by the IMF in conditionality and surveillance. Equations for narrow money growth, broad money growth, and government budget policy-reaction functions were also estimated, but the results are much weaker and not reported for brevity.

Column (1) reports the results of the basic policy-reaction-function model for all observations in the sample (program and nonprogram years), and columns (2) and (3) report the estimates over the program and nonprogram observations, respectively. Consistent with the theoretical formulation of the model, the macroeconomic determinants consist of lagged values of the current account surplus (relative to GDP), inflation, real GDP growth, and whether the country experienced a currency crisis. Also included are regional dummy variables and a dummy variable for the form of government ("autocracy"). Further, in the equations for nonprogram years and program years we have included the IMR to control for sample selection bias. (The probit model estimated with IMF-program approvals as the dependent variable is reported in table 10A.3. The IMR is calculated from the predicted values of this model.)

The only significant macroeconomic predictors of credit growth, shown in columns (1)–(3), are lagged inflation and the occurrence of a currency crisis in the previous year. The coefficient estimates of lagged inflation range between 0.6 and 0.7, indicating that a 1 percentage point rise in inflation is associated with a rise (fall) in nominal credit growth (real credit growth) of about 0.7 (0.3) percentage points. Interpreting this equation as a reaction function suggests that, in response to a rise in inflation, the authorities respond by reducing real credit growth. The coefficient on the (lagged) currency crisis variable is positive and significant in columns (1) and (3), indicating that countries generally respond to currency crises by expanding credit growth.

The constant term is much lower during IMF programs (6.9) relative to the nonprogram observations (28.8), suggesting more restrictive policy on average during the IMF-program years. The IMR is significant in the IMF-program-years regression (column [3]), indicating that sample selection

Table 10.9   **Policy Reaction Function Estimates (Dependent variable: credit growth)**

	Coefficient				
	All Years	Program Years	Nonprogram Years	All Years	
Explanatory Variable	(1)	(2)	(3)	(4)	(5)
Constant	10.252***	6.892	28.769***	40.045***	39.857***
	(4.23)	(1.39)	(4.46)	(4.55)	(4.67)
Change in current account– GDP ratio $(t-1)$	–11.720	48.131	–67.246**	–19.938	–18.511
	(–0.49)	(0.87)	(–2.05)	(–0.89)	(–0.83)
Inflation $(t-1)$	0.615***	0.641***	0.661***	0.390***	0.394***
	(4.97)	(3.06)	(4.24)	(2.86)	(2.95)
Real GDP growth $(t-1)$	0.063	0.024	–0.385	–0.267	–0.277
	(0.22)	(0.09)	(–0.78)	(–1.08)	(–1.13)
Autocracy	–0.337	–0.022	–0.511	0.409	0.509*
	(–1.17)	(–0.06)	(–1.11)	(1.32)	(1.64)
Africa dummy	–0.520	–0.544	–6.897	–33.074***	–35.168***
	(–0.19)	(–0.15)	(–1.47)	(–4.03)	(–4.33)
Asia dummy	3.328**	4.411	0.163	–23.709***	–24.277***
	(2.00)	(1.51)	(0.08)	(–2.82)	(–2.97)
Latin America dummy	4.558**	6.738*	5.228*	–25.626***	–25.463***
	(2.24)	(1.73)	(1.77)	(–3.30)	(–3.36)
Inverse Mills ratio (sample selection correction)		1.373	49.661***		
		(0.75)	(3.40)		
IMF participation dummy (t)				–3.942*	–1.285
				(–1.84)	(–0.67)
Currency crises dummy $(t-1)$	3.737	–3.315	19.210***	3.798	11.326**
	(1.06)	(0.64)	(3.01)	(1.16)	(2.19)
Interactive term $(D_{it}^{IMF} * D_{i(t-1)}^{CC})$					–15.645**
					(–2.44)
Adjusted R^2	0.38	0.47	0.41	0.44	0.44
	987	322	505	987	987
Durbin-Watson statistic	1.73	1.27	1.92	1.81	1.83

Note: Column (4) and (5) regressions also include country dummies. Numbers in parentheses are t-statistics.

***Significant at the 1 percent level.
**Significant at the 5 percent level.
*Significant at the 10 percent level.

bias is an issue: countries do not randomly enter into IMF programs, and their decision to participate is systematically linked to domestic credit growth.

The regressions reported in columns (4) and (5) cover all years and control for IMF-program participation by including a dummy variable in the regression. Country-specific dummy variables are included in these regressions—a fixed-effects model formulation—in order to control for the wide variation in average credit growth across countries. These results indicate the importance of controlling for country fixed effects in attempting to explain credit growth over such a wide diversity of countries. The impact of inflation is substantially reduced (to 0.4), indicating that inflation reduces real credit growth. The dummy variable on autocracy is also significant in one formulation of the model, as are the regional dummy variables.

We find that, in column (4), IMF programs reduce domestic credit growth by about 4 percentage points during the period they are in effect. Inclusion of the interactive term, in column (5), indicates that currency crises tend to induce greater credit expansion (by 11 percentage points), and the joint coincidence of a recent currency crisis and current IMF program is associated with a contraction of credit by about 15 percent annually. The joint effect of a currency crisis (lagged) followed by an IMF program is estimated to reduce credit growth by about 5.6 percentage points (11.2–1.3–15.6).

These results suggest that IMF-program participation is associated with restrictive credit growth. Investigations of budget policy and money growth, however, did not indicate any link between IMF-program participation and policy. Even the credit reaction function is fairly weak, however, likely reflecting shifts in policy over time and the fact that the types of countries going to the IMF for assistance have very different characteristics from countries not going to the IMF.

10.6.1   The East Asian Financial Crisis and Credit Growth

The empirical credit growth equation (column [4] of table 10.9) is employed to predict credit growth for the five East Asian countries that experienced currency crises in 1997. Predicted credit growth was divided into component parts and the "unexpected" (forecast error) calculated. In every case, credit growth in 1998 is predicted to be quite strong, ranging from 15.5 (the Philippines) to 24.4 (Indonesia). Participation in IMF programs lowered predicted credit growth by about 4 percentage points, and the predicted response to the currency crises increased predicted credit growth by about 4 percentage points.[21]

A sharp and unanticipated contraction (negative forecast error) was experienced in every country except for Indonesia following the East Asian currency crisis. The countries that participated in IMF programs experienced smaller unexpected declines (Korea, –8.4 percent; the Philippines, –17.5 percent; Thailand, –18.2 percent) than did Malaysia (–23.2), and Indonesia experienced a sharp, unpredicted jump in credit. The observed decline, as opposed to the negative forecast error, in credit growth was also largest in Malaysia at –2.7 percent. Indonesia, by contrast, experienced an 18.6 percent unpredicted rise in credit and an observed rise of 43 percent. Similar to the output growth prediction results, Malaysia was hurt at least as much by the Asian currency crisis as the IMF-program countries.

---

21. These results are not reported for brevity but are available from the author upon request.

10.7 Conclusion

The estimated cost of an IMF stabilization program, in terms of forgone output growth, is about 0.6–0.8 percentage points during each year of program participation. Currency crises also reduce output growth over a two-year period by about 2 percentage points. Participation in an IMF-supported program following a balance-of-payments or currency crisis, however, does not appear to mitigate or exacerbate the output loss. This is despite the fact that countries participating in IMF programs seem to follow much tighter credit policy when facing a severe balance-of-payments crisis. Moreover, there is some evidence that the decline in GDP growth generally precedes the approval of an IMF program and may not be attributable to program participation per se. These results are robust to estimation technique, model specification, types of IMF programs included, and corrections for sample selection bias.

The huge declines in output and credit growth in the wake of the 1997 Asian currency crisis were much larger than predicted by historical patterns linking GDP developments to currency crises, IMF program participation, external conditions, and policy developments. Indeed, the models predicted fairly robust output growth and credit growth in 1998 despite the currency crises and, in most cases, participation in IMF-supported programs. The unexpected falls in output and credit were also very large in Malaysia, even though it chose not to participate in an IMF stabilization program at the time. Whether a country decided to participate in an IMF-supported program at the time of the Asian currency crisis seems to have had little affect on the ultimate output cost.

The effect of IMF-supported stabilization programs on output growth—judging by the experiences of sixty-seven countries with over 450 programs—does not appear large in comparison with the average growth rates of developing and emerging-market economies over the 1975–97 period. Nonetheless, whether the cost of participating in an IMF-supported stabilization program exceeds the benefit measured in terms of balance-of-payments adjustment and continued access to credit markets is an open question to be answered by policy makers in the countries involved.

Appendix

Participation in IMF-Supported Stabilization Programs

Table 10A.3 presents a probit equation attempting to explain participation in short-term IMF programs by a variety of economic determinants. Our selection of economic determinants is guided by previous literature in this area, especially Knight and Santaella (1997), who test a number of supply-side (e.g., willingness of the IMF to approve programs) and demand-side (e.g., demand of a particular country for IMF credits) determinants. This literature demonstrates that entering into an IMF agreement is not random, but guided by "a clear set of observable economic factors that are strongly correlated with the event of approval of a financial arrangement" (431). They find that a low level of international reserves, low per capita GDP, high ratio of external debt service (to export earnings), movements in the real exchange rate, weak GDP growth, and a low rate of domestic investment induce countries to seek an IMF-supported program. Policy measures to enhance fiscal revenues, reduce government expenditures, tighten domestic credit, and adjust the exchange rate are significant factors likely to win IMF approval of programs.

We report similar results in table 10A.3. We find that an improvement in the budget surplus helps win IMF approval of programs, whereas lower foreign exchange reserves (relative to imports) and a currency crisis induce countries to seek an IMF program. Countries in Africa and Asia are less likely to have short-term IMF programs approved. There is no discernible shift in the probability of having an IMF program approved in the 1980s and 1990s compared to earlier periods and, surprisingly, we find no connection between program approval and inflation, real exchange rates, real per capita GDP growth, or the level of real GDP per capita. Other lagged values were investigated but did not add explanatory power to the model.

There are 862 observations in sample, and the model (at the 25 percent predicted probability cutoff point) predicts 71 percent of the observations correctly. However, although 80 percent of the "no program participation" observations are correctly predicted, only 34 percent of the "program approval" observations are correctly predicted. At the 10 percent probability cutoff point, however, 96 percent of the "program participation" observations are correctly predicted, but only 32 percent of the "no participation" observations.

Table 10A.1   **Countries Included in Data Set**

Emerging Markets (25 Countries)	Other Developing Countries (42 Countries)	
Argentina	Bangladesh	Mali
Brazil	Belize	Morocco
Chile	Bolivia	Mozambique
Colombia	Botswana	Myanmar
Costa Rica	Burundi	Nepal
Cyprus	Cameroon	Nicaragua
Dominican Republic	Ecuador	Nigeria
Hong Kong	Egypt	Pakistan
Indonesia	El Salvador	Paraguay
Jordan	Equatorial Guinea	Peru
Korea	Ethiopia	Sierra Leone
Malaysia	Fiji	Sri Lanka
Malta	Ghana	Swaziland
Mauritius	Grenada	Syria
Mexico	Guatemala	Uganda
Panama	Guinea-Bissau	Zambia
The Philippines	Guyana	Zimbabwe
Singapore	Haiti	
South Africa	Honduras	
Thailand	India	
Trinidad and Tobago	Jamaica	
Tunisia	Kenya	
Turkey	Laos	
Uruguay	Madagascar	
Venezuela	Malawi	

Table 10A.2   **Occurrences of Currency Crises and IMF Program Participation**

	Currency Crises	IMF Programs
Argentina	1975, 1982, 1989	1972[f], 1973[f], 1975[f], 1976[a], 1976[f], 1977[a], 1983[a], 1984[a], 1987[a], 1989[a], 1991[a], 1992[b], 1996[a]
Bolivia	1981, 1983, 1988, 1991	1973[a], 1980[a], 1986[a], 1986[c], 1988[c], 1994[c]
Brazil	1982, 1987, 1990, 1995	1970[a], 1971[a], 1972[a], 1983[b], 1988[a], 1992[a]
Chile	1985	1970[a], 1972[f], 1973[f], 1974[a], 1975[a], 1985[b], 1989[a]
Colombia	1985	1970[a], 1971[a], 1972[a], 1973[a]
Costa Rica	1981	1976[a], 1980[a], 1981[b], 1982[a], 1985[a], 1987[a], 1989[a], 1991[a], 1993[a], 1995[a]
Dominican Republic	1985, 1987, 1990	1983[b], 1985[a], 1991[a], 1993[a]
Ecuador	1982, 1985, 1988	1970[a], 1972[a], 1983[a], 1985[a], 1986[a], 1988[a], 1989[a], 1991[a], 1994[a]
El Salvador	1986, 1990	1970[a], 1972[a], 1980[a], 1982[a], 1990[a], 1992[a], 1993[a], 1995[a], 1997[a]
Guatemala	1986, 1989	1970[a], 1972[a], 1981[a], 1983[a], 1988[a], 1992[a]
Haiti	1977, 1991	1970[a], 1971[a], 1972[a], 1973[a], 1974[a], 1975[a], 1976[a], 1977[a], 1978[b], 1982[a], 1983[a], 1986[c], 1989[a], 1995[a], 1996[d]

(*continued*)

Table 10A.2 (continued)

	Currency Crises	IMF Programs
Honduras	1990	1971[a], 1972[a], 1979[b], 1982[a], 1990[a], 1992[c]
Mexico	1976, 1982, 1985, 1994	1977[b], 1983[b], 1986[a], 1989[b], 1995[a]
Nicaragua	1993	1970[a], 1972[a], 1979[a], 1991[a], 1994[c]
Panama		1970[a], 1971[a], 1972[a], 1973[a], 1974[a], 1975[a], 1977[a], 1978[a], 1979[a], 1980[a], 1982[a], 1983[a], 1985[a], 1992[a], 1995[a], 1997[b]
Paraguay	1984, 1986, 1988, 1992	
Peru	1976, 1979, 1987	1970[a], 1977[a], 1978[a], 1979[a], 1982[b], 1984[a], 1993[b], 1996[b]
Uruguay	1982	1970[a], 1972[a], 1972[f], 1975[a], 1976[a], 1976[f], 1977[a], 1979[a], 1980[a], 1981[a], 1983[a], 1985[a], 1990[a], 1992[a], 1996[a], 1997[a]
Venezuela	1984, 1986, 1989, 1994	1989[b], 1996[a]
Grenada	1978	1975[a], 1979[a], 1981[a], 1983[b]
Guyana	1987, 1989	1970[a], 1971[a], 1972[a], 1973[a], 1974[a], 1974[f], 1975[a], 1976[a], 1978[a], 1979[b], 1980[b], 1990[a], 1990[c], 1994[c]
Belize		1984[a]
Jamaica	1978, 1983, 1990	1973[a], 1974[f], 1977[a], 1978[b], 1979[b], 1981[b], 1984[a], 1987[a], 1988[a], 1990[a], 1991[a], 1992[b]
Trinidad & Tobago	1985, 1988, 1993	1989[a], 1990[a]
Cyprus		1980[a]
Jordan	1983, 1987, 1989, 1992	1972[f], 1973[f], 1989[a], 1992[a], 1994[b], 1996[b]
Syria	1977, 1982, 1988	1972[f]
Egypt	1979, 1989	1973[f], 1977[a], 1978[b], 1987[a], 1991[a], 1993[b], 1996[a]
Bangladesh	1975	1972[f], 1974[a], 1975[a], 1979[a], 1980[b], 1983[a], 1987[c], 1990[c]
Myanmar	1975, 1977	1973[a], 1974[af], 1977[a], 1978[a], 1981[a]
Sri Lanka	1977	1971[a], 1972[f], 1973[f], 1974[af], 1977[a], 1979[b], 1983[a], 1991[c]
Hong Kong		
India	1976, 1991, 1995	1974[f], 1981[b], 1991[a]
Indonesia	1978, 1983, 1986, 1997	1970[a], 1971[a], 1972[a], 1973[a], 1997[a]
Korea	1980, 1997	1970[a], 1971[a], 1972[a], 1973[a], 1974[a], 1975[a], 1977, 1980[a], 1981[a], 1983[a], 1985[a], 1997[a], 1997[e]
Laos	1995	1975[f], 1980[a], 1989[c], 1993[c]
Malaysia	1986, 1997	
Nepal	1975, 1981, 1984, 1991, 1995	1975[a], 1985[a], 1987[c], 1992[c]
Pakistan		1972[a], 1973[a], 1974[a], 1980[b], 1981[b], 1988[ac], 1993[a], 1994[bc], 1995[a], 1997[bd]
The Philippines	1983, 1986, 1997	1970[a], 1971[a], 1972[a], 1973[af], 1974[a], 1975[a], 1976[f], 1979[a], 1980[a], 1983[a], 1984[a], 1986[a], 1989[b], 1991[a], 1994[b]
Singapore	1975	
Thailand	1981, 1984, 1997	1978[a], 1981[a], 1982[a], 1995[a]
Botswana	1984, 1996	
Burundi	1976, 1983, 1986, 1989, 1997	1970[a], 1972[f], 1976[a], 1986[c], 1991[c]

Table 10A.2 (continued)

	Currency Crises	IMF Programs
Cameroon	1982, 1984, 1994	1980[a], 1988[a], 1991[a], 1994[a], 1995[a], 1997[d]
Equatorial Guinea	1991, 1994	1980[a], 1985[a], 1988[c], 1993[c]
Ethiopia	1992	1981[a], 1992[c], 1996[d]
Ghana	1978, 1983, 1986	1979[a], 1983[a], 1984[a], 1986[a], 1987[bc], 1988[c], 1995[d]
Guinea-Bissau	1991, 1996	1974[f], 1982[a], 1986[a], 1987[a], 1987[c], 1991[c], 1995[c], 1997[d]
Kenya	1975, 1981, 1985, 1993, 1995, 1997	1975[b], 1978[a], 1979[a], 1980[a], 1982[a], 1985[a], 1988[ac], 1989[c], 1993[c], 1996[c]
Madagascar	1984, 1986, 1991, 1994	1977[a], 1980[a], 1981[a], 1982[a], 1984[a], 1985[a], 1986[a], 1987[c], 1988[a], 1989[c], 1996[d]
Malawi	1982, 1985, 1992, 1994	1979[a], 1980[a], 1982[a], 1983[b], 1988[ac], 1994[a], 1995[cd]
Mali	1993	1971[a], 1982[a], 1985[a], 1988[ac], 1992[c], 1996[d]
Mauritius	1979	1978[a], 1979[a], 1980[a], 1981[a], 1983[a]
Morocco	1983, 1990	1971[a], 1976[f], 1980[b], 1981[b], 1982[a], 1983[a], 1985[a], 1988[a], 1990[a], 1992[a]
Mozambique	1993, 1995	1987[c], 1990[c], 1996[d]
Nigeria	1986, 1989, 1992	1987[a], 1989[a], 1991[a]
Zimbabwe	1982, 1991, 1994, 1997	1981[a], 1983[a], 1992[bc]
Sierra Leone	1988, 1990, 1997	1976[f], 1977[a], 1979[a], 1981[b], 1984[a], 1986[c], 1994[c]
Swaziland	1975, 1979, 1982, 1984	
Tunisia	1993	1970[a], 1986[a], 1988[b]
Uganda	1981, 1987, 1989	1970[a], 1976[f], 1980[a], 1981[a], 1982[a], 1983[a], 1987[c], 1989[c], 1994[c], 1997[d]
Zambia	1985, 1994	1972[f], 1973[a], 1975[f], 1976[a], 1978[a], 1981[b], 1983[a], 1984[a], 1986[a], 1995[c]
Fiji	1986	1974[a]

Notes: Currency crises defined by criteria described in text, with twenty-four-month exclusion windows imposed. IMF programs specified below.

[a] Stand By and Extended Stand By Agreements (SBA).

[b] Extended Fund Facility (EFF).

[c] Structural Adjustment Facility (SAF) and Enhanced Structural Adjustment Facility (ESAF).

[d] Poverty Reduction and Growth Facility (PRGF).

[e] Supplemental Reserve Facility (SRF).

[f] Contingency and Compensatory Fund Facility (CCFF).

Table 10A.3 **Participation Equation in Short-Term IMF Programs: Probit Estimation Results**

Variable	Partial Derivative
Constant	−0.165**
	(−2.21)
Post-1979 dummy	0.031
	(0.54)
Change in current account–GDP ratio	−0.258
	(−0.94)
Change in budget surplus–real GDP ratio $(t-2)$	−0.678*
	(−1.86)
Change in budget surplus–real GDP ratio $(t-1)$	0.747**
	(2.22)
Inflation $(t-1)$	0.000
	(0.96)
Real per capita GDP growth $(t-1)$	0.001
	(0.79)
Foreign exchange reserves to imports ratio $(t-1)$	−0.215***
	(−3.97)
Real per capita GDP – level $(t-1)$	0.000
	(−0.35)
Real exchange rate overvaluation $(t-1)$	0.000
	(0.72)
Currency crises dummy $(t-1)$	0.083**
	(2.49)
Africa dummy	−0.154***
	(−2.99)
Asia dummy	−0.120**
	(−2.34)
Latin America dummy	0.005
	(0.10)
Autocracy	0.001
	(0.25)
Goodness-of-fit (10% cutoff)	
% of observations correctly called	32
% of IMF programs correctly called	96
% of no program correctly called	17
Goodness-of-fit (25% cutoff)	
% of observations correctly called	71
% of IMF programs correctly called	34
% of no program correctly called	80
N	862
Log likelihood function	−388.90
Significance level	0.000

Note: Dependent variable: approval of short-term IMF programs.
***Significant at the 1 percent level.
**Significant at the 5 percent level.
*Significant at the 10 percent level.

References

Beveridge, W., and M. Kelly. 1980. Fiscal content of financial programs supported by stand-by arrangements in the upper credit tranches, 1969–78. IMF Staff Papers 27 (June): 205–49. Washington, D.C.: International Monetary Fund.

Bird, G. 1996. The International Monetary Fund and developing countries: A review of the evidence and policy options. *International Organization* 50 (3): 477–511.

Bird, G., M. Hussain, and J. Joyce. 2000. Many happy returns? Recidivism and the IMF. Wellesley College Department of Economics Working Paper no. 2000-04. Wellesley, Mass.

Bordo, M. D., and H. James. 2000. The International Monetary Fund: Its present role in historical perspective. NBER Working Paper no. 7724. Cambridge, Mass.: National Bureau of Economic Research, June.

Bordo, M. D., and A. Schwartz. 2000. Measuring real economic effects of bailouts: Historical perspectives on how countries in financial distress have fared with and without bailouts. NBER Working Paper no. 7701. Cambridge, Mass.: National Bureau of Economic Research, May.

Connors, T. 1979. The apparent effects of recent IMF stabilization programs. International Finance Discussion Paper no. 135. Washington, D.C.: Board of Governors of the Federal Reserve System, April.

Conway, P. 1994. IMF lending programs: Participation and impact. *Journal of Development Economics* 45:365–91.

———. 2000. IMF programs and economic crisis: An empirical study of transition. University of North Carolina, Chapel Hill, Department of Economics. Manuscript, January.

Dicks-Mireaux, L., M. Mecagni, and S. Schadler. 2000. Evaluating the effect of IMF lending to low-income countries. *Journal of Development Economics* 61:495–526.

Dooley, M. 2000. International financial architecture and strategic default: Can financial crises be less painful? *Carnegie-Rochester Conference Series on Public Policy* 53:361–77.

Dreher, A., and R. Vaubel. 2001. Does the IMF cause moral hazard and political business cycles? Evidence from panel data. University of Mannheim, Department of Economics. Manuscript, February.

Edwards, S. 1989. The International Monetary Fund and the developing countries. A critical evaluation. *Carnegie-Rochester Conference Series on Public Policy* 31:7–68.

Esquivel, G., and F. Larrain. 1998. Explaining currency crises. Harvard Institute for International Development. Mimeograph.

Frankel, J., and A. Rose. 1996. Currency crashes in emerging markets. An empirical treatment. *Journal of International Economics* 41 (November): 351–66.

Glick, R., and M. Hutchison. 2000. Capital controls and exchange rate instability in developing economies. Federal Reserve Bank of San Francisco Center for Pacific Basin Studies Working Paper no. PB00-05. San Francisco: Federal Reserve Bank of San Francisco, December.

———. 2001. Banking and currency crises: How common are twins? In *Financial crises in emerging markets,* ed. R. Glick, R. Moreno, and M. Spiegel, 35–69. Cambridge: Cambridge University Press.

Goldstein, M., and P. Montiel. 1986. Evaluating fund stabilization programs with multicountry data: Some methodological pitfalls. *IMF Staff Papers* 33 (June): 304–44. Washington, D.C.: International Monetary Fund.

Gupta, P., D. Mishra, and R. Sahay. 2000. Output response during currency crises. International Monetary Fund. Manuscript, May.

Gylafson, T. 1987. Credit policy and economic activity in developing countries with

IMF stabilization programs. Princeton Essays in International Finance 60 (August): 81–96.

Heckman, J. 1979. Sample selection bias as a specification error. *Econometrica* 47 (January): 153–61.

International Monetary Fund. 2000. Review of fund facilities: Preliminary considerations. Washington, D.C.: International Monetary Fund.

Joyce, J. 2001. Time present and time past: A duration analysis of IMF programs spells. Federal Reserve Bank of Boston Working Paper no. 01-02. Boston: Federal Reserve Bank of Boston, March.

Kaminsky, G., S. Lizondo, and C. Reinhart. 1998. Leading indicators of currency crises. *IMF Staff Papers* 45 (March): 1–48.

Kaminsky, G., and C. Reinhart. 1999. The twin crises. The causes of banking and balance-of-payments problems. *American Economic Review* 89 (June): 473–500.

Kaplan, E., and D. Rodrik. 2001. Did the Malaysian capital controls work? NBER Working Paper no. W8142. Cambridge, Mass.: National Bureau of Economic Research, February.

Khan, M. 1990. The macroeconomic effects of fund-supported adjustment programs. *IMF Staff Papers* 37 (June): 195–231.

Killick, T., M. Malik, and M. Manuel. 1992. What can we know about the effects of IMF programs? *The World Economy* 15:575–97.

Knight, M., and J. Santaella. 1997. Economic determinants of IMF financial arrangements. *Journal of Development Economics* 54:405–36.

Lane, T., and S. Phillips. 2000. Does IMF financing result in moral hazard? IMF Working Paper no. WP/00/168. Washington, D.C.: International Monetary Fund, October.

McQuillan, L., and P. Montgomery, ed. 1999. *The International Monetary Fund: Financial medic to the world.* Stanford, Calif.: Hoover Institution Press.

Mussa, M., and M. Savastano. 2000. The IMF approach to economic stabilization. *NBER macroeconomics annual 1999,* ed. Ben S. Bernanke and Julio Rotemberg, 79–122. Cambridge: MIT Press.

Pastor, M. 1987. The effects of IMF programs in the third world: Debate and evidence from Latin America. *World Development* 15 (February): 249–62.

Przeworski, A., and J. Vreeland. 2000. The effect of IMF programs on economic growth. *Journal of Development Economics* 62:385–421.

Santaella, J. 1996. Stylized facts before IMF-supported macroeconomic adjustment. *IMF Staff Papers* 43:502–44. Washington, D.C.: International Monetary Fund.

Stiglitz, J. 2000. What I learned at the world economic crisis. *The New Republic,* 17 April, 56–61.

Willett, T. 2001. Understanding the IMF debate. *The Independent Review* 5 (4): 593–610.

Comment   Gian Maria Milesi-Ferretti

Identifying the effects of International Monetary Fund (IMF) programs on economic growth and on other macroeconomic variables is a difficult task. In this paper, the author follows the methodology first laid out by Goldstein and Montiel (1986) to examine whether IMF programs for stabilization

Gian Maria Milesi-Ferretti is in the European I department of the International Monetary Fund.

purposes have measurable effects on economic performance. The novelty in this study consists in the use of data on currency crises: the author asks whether currency crises provide additional explanatory power to the basic growth regressions used to identify the effects of IMF programs, and whether the presence of an IMF program during a currency crisis has a significant effect on growth. The study focuses on emerging economies and excludes those less-developed countries that borrowed at concessional rates under the structural adjustment facilities.

The paper is well written, and the basic inputs to the empirical analysis are clearly presented to the reader. An appendix lists both the IMF programs the paper considers and the dates of the currency crises, and the formal panel regression analysis is preceded by a careful examination of the data. For example, the author documents the path of economic growth and other variables such as inflation and the current account before and after IMF programs. The crucial difficulty in identifying the effects of IMF programs on economic variables is the standard selection bias problem: Countries that borrow from the IMF typically do so because they face balance-of-payments difficulties, and it is therefore likely that their overall macroeconomic situation will be worse than the one faced by countries that do not borrow from the IMF. Indeed, considering the list of countries in the author's sample that never borrowed from the IMF, we find several of the fastest-growing developing and emerging economies of the past three decades: Botswana, Hong Kong, Malaysia, and Singapore.

My comments will mostly focus on the specification of the model used by the author and the policy implications that are drawn in section 10.6 and in the conclusions.

What Eff ects of Fund Programs Can the Model Identify?

As mentioned above, the model used by the author is standard in the literature. The Generalized Evaluation Estimator (GEE) addresses the selection bias problem by attempting to construct a counterfactual—that is, determine how economic policy would have been conducted in the absence of an IMF program—and to use this counterfactual to identify the actual impact of IMF programs on economic growth. The basic equation is

(1) $$y_{it} = \beta_i + \beta_k X_{it} + \alpha_h W_{it} + \beta^{IMF} D_{it}^{IMF} + \varepsilon_{it}$$

where X_{it} is a vector of economic policy variables in the absence of IMF programs. The counterfactual is constructed assuming that policies in the absence of an IMF program are set according to the policy reaction function

(2) $$\Delta X_{it} = \gamma(y_i^d - y_{i,t-1}) + \eta_{it}.$$

Estimation is conducted substituting equation (2) into equation (1) without actually proceeding to the estimation of the policy reaction function in equation (2).

We also know from the literature that this approach has serious weaknesses, the primary one being the extremely poor explanatory power exhibited by the postulated policy reaction functions when these are separately estimated. In addition to this, the reader should also keep in mind what type of effects of IMF programs the above specification can identify. As highlighted by Dicks-Mireaux, Mecagni, and Schadler (2000), this specification can capture "direct" effects of IMF programs on performance, related to the availability of external funds to weather the balance-of-payments difficulties, or the effects of programs on confidence (say, through their impact on the risk premium). However, this specification is not appropriate for capturing the effects of IMF programs on economic policy conduct (for example, on monetary and fiscal policy) and through this channel on growth. This can easily be seen by considering the following, more general specification of equation (1):

$$(3) \qquad y_{it} = \beta_i + \beta_k \tilde{\mathbf{X}}_{it} + \alpha_h \mathbf{W}_{it} + \beta^{\mathrm{IMF}} D_{it}^{\mathrm{IMF}} + \varepsilon_{it}$$

where the vector $\tilde{\mathbf{X}}_{it} = \mathbf{X}_{it} + \mathbf{X}_{it}^{\mathrm{IMF}} D_{it}^{\mathrm{IMF}}$ so that economic growth depends on actual economic policy conduct $\hat{\mathbf{X}}_{it}$ and allowance is made for a systematic difference in the conduct of economic policy in the presence of IMF programs. The estimation of the effects of IMF programs in this case also requires the use of the policy reaction function in equation (2) (which determines the value of policies in the absence of IMF programs when these are not directly observable). However, in general the two formulations will not be equivalent, unless it is assumed that the effects of IMF programs on policy are constant across policy variables. This must be kept in mind when one examines whether economic policy is systematically different during IMF programs, as the author does in section 10.5.

Policy Reaction Functions

In section 10.5, the author proceeds to the actual estimation of policy reaction functions for the policy variables included in the regression in equation (1). Only the results of the credit growth regressions are reported, because the explanatory power of the other policy reaction function is very limited.

In these regressions, the author shows that policy under IMF programs appears to be systematically different from policy in the absence of programs, with credit growth being lower. This finding seems reasonable, considering the typical design of IMF programs. However, inferring from this finding that the negative effects of IMF programs on growth identified using the GEE could work through a negative impact on growth of tight credit policy is problematic for two reasons. First, as mentioned above, the formulation used by the author in the GEE regressions is not appropriate for capturing the effects on growth of different policies under IMF programs. Second, and most important, the regressions show a systematic *negative* effect of credit growth on output growth, and therefore they do not seem to identify any negative effect of "tight credit" on economic performance.

Interestingly, in the estimation of the credit policy reaction function for nonprogram years there appears to be a significant effect of selection bias: the inverse Mills ratio (IMR) is statistically very significant. This suggests that selection bias may indeed be a problem also in the estimation of the growth regressions, but the author does not find there any significant impact of the IMR.

The Choice of Variables

In general the author uses a fairly standard specification for growth regressions. I am only unclear about the use of the *change* in the budget balance in the growth regressions and the use of the lagged *change* in the current account as an explanatory variable for credit growth. In both cases the level of the underlying variable would seem to be a much more logical choice.

Other Issues

I am also concerned that some of the author's results concerning the impact of inflation on growth as well as differences in inflation between program and nonprogram years may be contaminated by the presence of a few countries that suffered bouts of hyperinflation: Argentina, Bolivia, Brazil, Nicaragua, and Peru. Also, while in the regressions it is perfectly reasonable to use a log-difference specification for inflation, this is less appropriate for the comparison of program and nonprogram years, given that for relatively high rates of inflation the log difference is a poor approximation of the actual inflation rate.

Although I concur with the construction of the currency crises index, which takes into account variations in the real rather than the nominal exchange rate (thus correcting for the presence of high inflation, high depreciation episodes) I am surprised that the methodology does not detect a currency crisis in Chile in 1982, a year of high real depreciation and substantial reserve losses.

In summary, the author has made a valuable effort in his attempt to identify the degree to which IMF programs and currency crises affect economic performance. The shortcomings of the paper are those of the overall methodology being used.

References

Dicks-Mireaux, Louis, Mauro Mecagni, and Susan Schadler. 2000. Evaluating the effect of IMF lending to low-income countries. *Journal of Development Economics* 61 (April): 495–526.
Goldstein, Morris, and Peter Montiel. 1986. Evaluating fund stabilization programs

with multi-country data: Some methodological pitfalls. *IMF Staff Papers* 33:304–44. Washington, D.C.: International Monetary Fund.

Discussion Summary

Martin Feldstein questioned the treatment of the endogeneity problem for IMF programs. He remarked that it is not clear whether the insignificance of the IMR coefficient means there is no selection bias (participation is random) or the process does not account for it and estimation is still biased. Also, he questioned whether the fact that the IMF provides a "good housekeeping" seal of approval is accounted for in the empirical work.

Morris Goldstein mentioned an interdependence problem. Even if Malaysia does not want an IMF program, it might still adopt IMF policy recommendations in order to get acceptance by international markets. Thus, the IMF had an effect on Malaysia even though it did not implement a program there.

Kenneth D. West noted that the insignificance of the IMR term is also pervasive in labor studies.

William Easterly remarked that there is a very high rate of repetition in IMF programs. Some countries go to the IMF repeatedly for many years, which suggests the IMF is not successful in whatever it is trying to do.

Nouriel Roubini suggested using a variable that proxies for the currency mismatch in the balance sheet (net foreign debt times the amount of devaluation).

Michael P. Dooley remarked that domestic credit is a variable that is very closely watched by the IMF staff and that the IMF always negotiates for contractionary credit policy. This could be the only thing that differentiates program countries. This, he noted, corresponds to the paper's findings.

Martin Eichenbaum asked what the IMF is trying to do. If it is trying to build reserves, then it is successful. As for structural change, he doubted that the IMF actually manages to achieve much, considering the institutional and cultural character of these reforms.

Michael Hutchison responded that dealing with self-selection bias appeared to be very difficult. It hinges on developing a stable policy reaction function over time and space. Handling currency crises up front was an attempt to control better for policy responses. In response to Feldstein's comment, he commented that an attempt to split the sample to examine whether the 1975–90 period was different from what followed was made but that no significant structural break was detected. In response to Goldstein's comment, Hutchison stated that if Malaysia took the same policy measures then the question remains whether the contribution of the IMF loan facility for the other East Asian countries helped with a faster recovery. Also, he noted that his participation equation, as is shown in the appendix, is not very good. Therefore, it is difficult to know whether the insignificance of the IMR is because a stable participation equation was not identified or that it does not exist and participation is random.

11

IMF and World Bank Structural Adjustment Programs and Poverty

William Easterly

Poverty reduction is in the news for both the International Monetary Fund (IMF) and the World Bank. The IMF website says:

> In September 1999, the objectives of the IMF's concessional lending were broadened to include an explicit focus on poverty reduction in the context of a growth oriented strategy. The IMF will support, along with the World Bank, strategies elaborated by the borrowing country in a Poverty Reduction Strategy Paper (PRSP).

For its part, the World Bank headquarters has built into its lobby wall the slogan "our dream is a world free of poverty." In a joint statement issued by the President of the World Bank and the Managing Director of the International Monetary Fund in April 2001, they declared poverty "the greatest challenge facing the international community" and an issue concerning which "the Bank and Fund have an important role to play" (World Bank and International Monetary Fund 2001, 2).

The recent East Asian currency crisis and its aftershocks in other countries generated intense concern about how the poor were faring under structural adjustment programs supported by the Bank and the IMF. The poverty issue is so red-hot that IMF and World Bank staff began to feel that

William Easterly is senior advisor of the Development Research Group at the World Bank.

Views expressed here are not necessarily those of the World Bank. The author is grateful to Martin Ravallion and Shaohua Chen for making their poverty spells database available. He is also grateful for discussions with Paul Collier, David Dollar, Peter Lanjouw, and Martin Ravallion, for several rounds of discussion with discussant Ted Truman, and for comments by Anders Aslund, Ricardo Hausmann, Nora Lustig, Aart Kraay, Michael Kremer, Sergio Schmukler, and John Williamson and by participants in the NBER pre-conference, the first annual IMF research conference, and the NBER conference. Any remaining errors are the responsibility of the author alone.

every action inside these organizations, from reviewing public expenditure to vacuuming the office carpet, should be justified by its effect on poverty reduction.

At the same time, there has been a long-standing criticism from the left of World Bank and IMF structural adjustment programs as disproportionately hurting the poor:

> When the International Monetary Fund (IMF) and World Bank arrive in southern countries, corporate profits go up, but so do poverty and suffering. Decades of promises that just a little more "short-term" pain will bring long-term gain have exposed the IMF and World Bank as false prophets whose mission is to protect those who already control too much wealth and power.

> A report published today by the World Development Movement (WDM) shows that the International Monetary Fund's (IMF) new Poverty Reduction Strategies are acting as barriers to policies benefiting the world's poorest people.

> Many developing countries suffered . . . sustained increases in prosperity, accompanied by dramatic increases in inequality and child poverty . . . under the auspices of IMF and World Bank adjustment programmes.

> In country after country, structural adjustment programs (SAPs) have reversed the development successes of the 1960s and 1970s, with . . . millions sliding into poverty every year. Even the World Bank has had to accept that SAPs have failed the poor, with a special burden falling on women and children. Yet together with the IMF it still demands that developing countries persist with SAPs.

This paper examines the effect of IMF and World Bank adjustment lending on poverty reduction.[1] I briefly examine the effect of IMF and World Bank adjustment lending on growth and find no effect (suitably instrumenting for adjustment lending), which is in line with the previous long and inconclusive literature. My main result is that IMF and World Bank adjustment lending lowers the growth elasticity of poverty, that is, the amount of change in poverty rates for a given amount of growth. This means that economic expansions benefit the poor less under structural adjustment, but at the same time economic contractions hurt the poor less. What could be the mechanisms for such a result?

There could be several possible explanations. I first speculate that IMF and World Bank conditionality may be less austere when lending occurs during an economic contraction, whereas conditionality may require more macro adjustment during an expansion. If macro adjustment dispropor-

---

1. I follow the convention of using *adjustment lending, structural adjustment, structural adjustment lending,* and *structural adjustment programs* as interchangeable terms. Later I distinguish between *structural adjustment lending* and *structural adjustment policies.*

tionately hurts the poor—say, because fiscal adjustment, for example, is implemented through increasing regressive taxes like sales taxes or decreasing progressive spending like transfers—then we get the result that IMF and World Bank adjustment lending lowers the growth elasticity of poverty. Adjustment lending could even include an explicit fiscal insurance mechanism, such as an increase in subsidies, that cushions the effect of contractions on the poor but is accompanied by a reduction in subsidies in times of expansion. We can test this hypothesis explicitly by evaluating the behavior of fiscal policy and macro policy variables during expansions and contractions, with or without adjustment lending.

A nearly opposite hypothesis is that IMF and World Bank conditionality may itself cause an expansion or contraction in aggregate output—depending on the composition of the structural adjustment package—but not affect the poor very much. This view would see the poor as mainly deriving their income from informal sector and subsistence activities, which are not affected much by fiscal policy changes or adjustments in macro policies. Structural adjustment packages usually imply that some previously favored formal-sector activities must contract while other formal-sector activities newly favored can expand. The net effect may be overall contraction or expansion, depending on the initial sizes of the declining and expanding sectors and the specific policy measures in the structural adjustment package. However, if the poor are not tightly linked to either the expanding or the contracting formal sector, then the amount of poverty change for a given amount of output change may not be very high under structural adjustment. An expansion or contraction in the absence of adjustment lending, on the other hand, may reflect economy-wide factors that lift or sink all boats.

IMF and World Bank adjustment programs typically force the government to make adjustments in a few highly visible macroeconomic indicators, which again affect mainly the formal sector. On the other hand, a home-grown reform program (for example, that of China over the last two decades, with only three adjustment loans in the 1980s and none in the 1990s) would generally include a more sweeping transformation of incentives that affect the formal and informal sectors alike.

11.1   Data and Concepts for Paper

I have data for 1980–98 on all types of IMF lending and on World Bank adjustment lending. International Monetary Fund lending includes standbys, extended arrangements, Structural Adjustment Facilities, and Enhanced Structural Adjustment Facilities (recently renamed Poverty Reduction and Growth Facilities). The latter two kinds of operations are concessional for low-income countries. World Bank adjustment lending includes structural adjustment loans, sectoral structural adjustment loans, and structural adjustment credits (the latter is concessional for low-income countries). The data are reported in the year that the loans are approved. Hence, my data take the form of a number of new World Bank and IMF adjustment loans approved each year. For any time period I consider in this paper, I consider the average number of new World Bank and IMF adjustment loans per year.

Conditionality associated with these loans is well known: macroeconomic conditions like reduced budget deficits, devaluation, and reduced domestic credit expansion, and structural conditions like freeing controlled prices and interest rates, reducing trade barriers, and privatizing state enterprises. Although the IMF is associated more with the former and the World Bank with the latter, in practice neither will proceed with an adjustment loan unless the other is satisfied with progress on its area of responsibility. Of course, there will be variation across adjustment loans in exactly what policy conditions are imposed, but it is still an interesting question to ask what the impact of adjustment lending is on average—just as innumerable IMF and World Bank internal studies have done.

For data on poverty, I use an updated version of Ravallion and Chen's (1997) database on poverty spells. These authors were careful to choose spells and countries for which the definition of poverty was constant and comparable over time and across countries. The source of the data is household surveys. They report the proportion of the population that is poor at the poverty line of $2 per day at the beginning of and the end of the spell (they also report the poverty rates for a poverty line of $1 per day, but I choose to use the former because many countries have a zero initial value at $1 per day). They also report the Gini coefficients at the beginning and the end and the mean income in the household survey at the beginning and the end. They report data on 155 spells for sixty-five developing countries (table 11.1 gives the countries and numbers of spells for each). The spells are quite short (median length three years), so I interpret them more as cyclical fluctuations in mean consumption and poverty rather than as long-run tendencies in growth and poverty reduction. Table 11.1 gives the descriptive statistics for all the data.

Table 11.1   Descriptive Statistics on Variables Used

	Change in Poverty	Mean Consumption Growth	Initial Gini	Initial Poverty Rate	Adjustment Loans Year
Mean	6.0%	−1.1%	39.5	41.2	0.62
Median	−0.1%	0.0%	39.5	36.3	0.50
Std. dev.	31.5%	11.1%	11.1	29.6	0.60
N	149	155	155	154	150

11.2   Results on Adjustment Lending and Poverty Reduction

Following Ravallion (1997), I regress the change in poverty rate on growth of mean income and the interaction of growth of mean income with the Gini coefficient. The idea of this specification is that if the poor have a low share in existing income (high Gini), they will likely have a low share in newly created income (low growth elasticity of poverty reduction). I also include the level of the initial Gini for completeness. To test the effect of IMF and World Bank adjustment lending, I include the variable measuring number of adjustment loans per year during the poverty spell and also interact this variable with growth.

There is the well-known selection bias problem with World Bank and IMF lending. This lending goes to countries that are in trouble, and this trouble could include initial high poverty rates. We could even imagine that World Bank and IMF programs go to countries that are more likely to reduce poverty rapidly. With these concerns in mind, I instrument for World Bank and IMF lending. I follow the practice of the foreign aid literature in using dummies that measure friends of influential donors, including a dummy for Central America, one for Egypt, and one for Franc Zone countries. I also include continent dummies as instruments for lending, because both the World Bank and IMF have a different department for each continent, and these different departments may have different propensities to make loans. I also include initial income as an instrument of adjustment loan frequency.

With the same set of instruments, I also tested the direct effect of adjustment lending on growth, not controlling for any other factors. In line with a long and inconclusive literature, I found no systematic effect of adjustment lending on growth. (A recent paper by Przeworski and Vreeland [2000] reviews the long inconclusive literature on the IMF, whereas they themselves find a negative effect controlling for selection bias. Some internal World Bank and IMF studies have found positive effects of their programs on growth. I do not intend to make the effect of structural adjustment on growth a major focus of the paper, because structural adjustment would of course alleviate poverty if it raised growth and worsen it if it lowered growth.) Of course, behind this zero average result is concealed a set of expansions and contractions that depended in part on the particulars of the adjustment program in each country and time period. In general, we would expect that an adjustment program would disfavor some sectors that were previously artificially protected or subsidized and favor other sectors that benefit from a change in relative prices in their favor. Whether expansion or decline dominates depends in part on the relative sizes of the expanding and declining sectors (as pointed out by Rauch [1997]).

Table 11.2   **Regression Results on Change in Poverty, Growth, and Adjustment Programs**

Variable	Ordinary Least Squares: Regression 1		Ordinary Least Squares: Regression 2		Two-Stage Least Squares: Regression 3	
	Coefficient	t-statistic	Coefficient	t-statistic	Coefficient	t-statistic
C	0.039	1.82	0.319	4.68	0.381	4.23
GROWTH	−1.892	−8.24	−5.481	−8.27	−5.452	−4.67
GINI1			−0.006	−3.83	−0.006	−3.65
PROGRAM			−0.019	−0.62	−0.114	−1.31
GROWTH*GINI1			0.058	3.27	0.057	2.68
GROWTH*PROGRAM			1.790	7.37	2.027	3.49
N	149		144		126	

Variable definitions
GROWTH   Log rate of growth per annum in mean of household survey
GINI1   Initial Gini coefficient
PROGRAM   Number of IMF/World Bank adjustment loans initiated per annum
CENTAM   Dummy for Central America
FRZ   Dummy for Franc Zone
EGYPT   Dummy for Egypt and Israel
SSA   Dummy for Sub-Saharan Africa
LAC   Dummy for Latin America
ECA   Dummy for Eastern Europe and Central Asia
EASIA   Dummy for East Asia
LGDPPC   Log of initial per capita income (Summers-Heston)

Notes: Dependent variable: Log rate of change per annum in percent of population below $2 per day. Instruments for PROGRAM: CENTAM EASIA EGYPT FRZ SSA LAC ECA GROWTH, CENTAM × GROWTH, EASIA × GROWTH, FRZ × GROWTH, EGYPT × GROWTH, SSA × GROWTH, GINI1 × GROWTH, LAC × GROWTH, ECA × LGDPPC.

The result on expansions strongly reducing the rate of poverty—or output crises raising the rate of poverty—is familiar from other studies (Ravallion and Chen 1997; Dollar and Kraay 2000; Bruno, Ravallion, and Squire 2000; Lustig 2000; Ravallion 2000). Without controlling for other variables, the mean growth elasticity of poverty is about 1.9 (table 11.2).

The significant coefficient on the interaction term between the Gini coefficient and the growth rate also confirms the Ravallion (1997) and Bruno, Ravallion, and Squire (2000) result (table 11.2). Ten percentage points higher Gini will lower the growth elasticity of poverty by 0.6 percentage points. A not-often-noticed implication of this result is that the poor will be hurt less by output contraction in a highly unequal economy than in a relatively equal one, simply because the poor have a low share of output to begin with. The initial Gini also has a direct negative effect on the change in poverty, suggesting a reversion to greater equality if a country begins highly unequal.

The new result in this paper is that, although adjustment lending has no direct effect on poverty reduction, it has a strong interaction effect with eco-

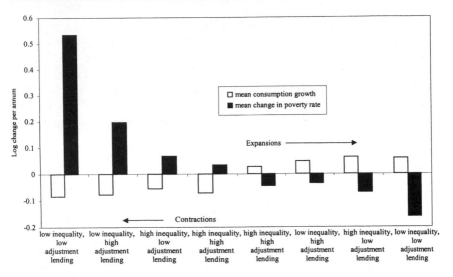

Fig. 11.1   Contractions and expansions, with varying levels of inequality and adjustment lending

nomic growth (table 11.2).[2] The absolute value of the growth elasticity of poverty declines by about two points for every additional IMF or World Bank adjustment loan per year. The results are strong either in ordinary least squares (OLS) or instrumenting for World Bank and IMF programs with the instruments shown. The instruments for selection bias are plausibly exogenous, and they do a sufficiently good job explaining World Bank and IMF programs that I still obtain a significant result when using these instruments.

This means that the poor benefit less from expansions during a structural adjustment program than in expansions without an adjustment program, while they are at the same time hurt less by contractions. Expansion under adjustment lending is less pro-poor, whereas contraction under adjustment lending is less anti-poor. The welfare of the poor may have increased from the income-smoothing effect of adjustment lending.

On the other hand, it is disappointing that the poor do not share fully in growth in those cases in which there are recoveries that accompany adjustment lending. Because the World Bank and the IMF ultimately wish to restore growth in the economies to which they make adjustment loans, it is worrisome that positive growth has less of a poverty-reducing impact with high World Bank IMF involvement.

Figure 11.1 illustrates the results. Countries with a low level of adjust-

2. IMF (1999) found that "In seven SAF/ESAF countries for which data are available, poverty rates declined by an average of 20 percent under IMF-supported adjustment programs, implying an average annual reduction of 5.3 percent." This study did not control for mean growth.

ment lending (AL) as measured by PROGRAM and low inequality have both greater increases in poverty during contraction and greater falls in poverty during expansions than do countries with a high level of IMF and World Bank lending and high inequality. (The terms *high* and *low* AL here simply mean the upper and lower 50 percent of the sample as measured by the number of programs per year; expansion is the average of all increases in mean income, and contraction is the average of all decreases in mean income).

Another way of illustrating the weakened link between growth and poverty reduction with high inequality and high adjustment lending is to calculate the number of perverse outcomes in quartiles of the sample defined by high and low inequality and high and low adjustment lending. A perverse outcome is defined as either a mean expansion with an increase in poverty or a mean contraction with a decrease in poverty. Such perverse outcomes are rare except in the case in which both inequality and adjustment lending are high, when they account for 27 percent of the sample (figure 11.2).

What is the marginal impact on poverty of IMF and World Bank adjustment loans? If we specify a counterfactual of zero adjustment lending to all countries in the sample, we find that the effect of the actual adjustment loans on the number of poor was a net increase of 14 million. This represents an increase of 0.4 percentage points in the population-weighted average poverty rate in the sample. The outcome reflects the net effect of an increase in the number of poor compared to the counterfactual of no

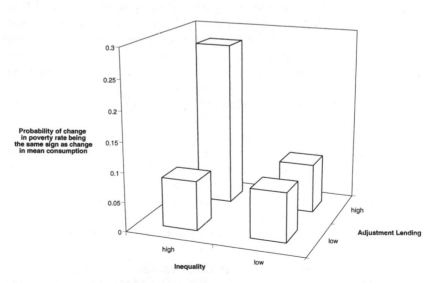

Fig. 11.2   Probability of perverse poverty-growth outcomes depending on level of inequality and adjustment lending

Table 11.3   **Poverty Elasticities with Respect to Growth for Different Gini Coefficients and Adjustment Loan Intensity**

	Number of Adjustment Loans		
Gini coefficient	0	0.5	1
30	-3.8	-2.7	-1.7
45	-2.9	-1.9	-0.9
60	-2.1	-1.0	0.0

Note: Number of adjustment loans is average per year during survey period.

adjustment loans in growing countries like India,[3] whereas there was a decrease in poverty compared to the counterfactual in contracting countries like Russia and Ukraine. The unweighted median change in the poverty rate associated with adjustment loans is 0.0.

Table 11.3 uses the coefficients from regression (2) to calculate the poverty elasticity with respect to growth at different levels of the Gini coefficient and adjustment loans per year (AL). The middle cell is close to using the average value for Gini and AL, and we reproduce the familiar elasticity of 2. However, there is great fluctuation around this average for different measures of the Gini and AL. If there are no adjustment loans and inequality is very low, then poverty is extremely elastic with respect to growth (3.8). China in 1990–92 is an example of an observation that would approximately fall in this cell. At the other extreme, a highly unequal country receiving adjustment loans sees no effect of growth or contraction on poverty. Colombia in 1995–96 is an example of a country that would roughly fit in this cell.

I performed several robustness checks on these results. First, I looked for asymmetries between expansion and contraction in both growth effects and the interaction term with adjustment lending. I found no evidence for any asymmetries—the interaction term between adjustment lending and growth remains statistically significant in the separate samples of expansions and contractions.

Second, I added the initial poverty rate both in levels and as an interaction term. The initial poverty rate enters with a negative sign in levels—indicating some tendency of poverty to revert to the mean—but it leaves the significance of the interaction term between adjustment lending and growth unchanged.

Third, I entered the mean household consumption from the household survey, both in levels and as an interaction term with growth. It left the coefficient on the growth and adjustment program interaction unchanged in

3. Even though India and China received only a small number of adjustment loans (in China's case, all in the 1980s), removal of even this small number of loans still has a large effect because of their large populations.

magnitude and significance, whereas the mean household consumption was not significant either in levels or as an interaction term with growth.

Fourth, one might think that what matters is the total size of the adjustment loan. I try controlling for the flow of resources under IMF and World Bank loans in addition to the number of loans. The interaction of this resource flow with growth is insignificant, whereas the significance of the interaction between number of adjustment loans and growth remains significant.

Fifth, there is a common conception that the content of IMF and World Bank conditions has changed over time, away from straight macroeconomic adjustment and toward more structural reform that may have helped the poor more. A priori, this is unlikely to be an important factor, because the bulk of the poverty spells in my sample start after the mid-1980s (only 13.5 percent of the sample has a start date before 1986). This was after the IMF had moved from pure standby operations to longer-term adjustment lending, and the World Bank always stressed structural measures. In any case, I find that if I split the sample into the period before and after 1989, which is the median start date of the poverty spells in the sample, there is no difference in results between the two subperiods.

Sixth, I try omitting transition countries from Eastern Europe and the former Soviet Union. I find no change in the pattern of results.

Given all the interest in currency crises, I examine the four currency crisis cases that are in the present sample: Mexico (1989–95), Indonesia (1996–99), Russia (1996–98), and Thailand (1996–98). All of them had at least one adjustment loan per year during the period before and during the crisis (table 11.4). Growth was negative in all cases, but the increases in poverty were fairly modest except for Indonesia. We should not make much out of four data points in a sample of 126 observations (and certainly there are too few data to dummy them out as a group), but it is still interesting to see if we can explain the differential poverty response to currency-output crises with the regression. We can understand Mexico's low poverty-growth elasticity as reflecting its high inequality and its receipt of adjustment loans. Thailand's near-zero poverty-growth elasticity could be rationalized as a consequence of its high adjustment intensity and its relatively average rate of inequality. Indonesia fits the story with a slightly below average elasticity associated with low inequality but relatively intense adjustment lending. Russia is an outlier, with a high elasticity despite an extraordinarily high number of adjustment loans per year.

11.3 Testing the Countercyclicality of Adjustment Lending

One possible explanation for the poverty-smoothing effect of adjustment lending may be that conditionality on macro adjustment is tougher during expansions than contractions, because the IMF and World Bank may fear

Table 11.4   Growth, Poverty, and Adjustment Lending in Currency Crises

	Spell	Mean Growth (%)	Rate of of Poverty (%)	Poverty with Respect to Growth Elasticity	% of Population Below $2/Day, Beginning	% of Population Below $2/Day, End	Gini Coefficient, Beginning	Average No. of Adjustment Loans per Year
Indonesia	1996–1999	-4.3	7.5	-1.73	50.51	63.21	36.45	1.0
Mexico	1989–1995	-1.9	1.5	-0.81	38.80	42.47	55.14	1.0
Russia	1996–1998	-0.6	1.3	-2.16	24.43	25.08	48.03	2.5
Thailand	1996–1998	-1.8	-0.2	0.10	28.25	28.15	43.39	1.5

deepening a contraction with excessive austerity. If the poor disproportionately suffer from austerity, then in contractions they will suffer less for a
given rate of mean income decline, while, conversely, they will do less well
for a given rate of growth in expansions. Second, the principal means of fiscal adjustment under adjustment programs during expansions may be
through regressive taxation measures like sales taxes, which lower the benefits to the poor of mean income growth. Third, World Bank and IMF lending programs may explicitly include "social safety nets" that cushion the
effect of a contraction on the poor, whereas these transfers may be reduced
during expansions. I will first test for countercyclicality of these variables
and then test their effect on the poverty rate.

Table 11.5 tests the countercyclicality of adjustment lending by presenting means of macro and fiscal policy variables for quartiles of the sample
divided between expansions and contractions and between high and low
adjustment lending. We find some evidence for countercyclicality of adjustment lending. Inflation is above average during contractions under high
adjustment lending, suggesting that conditions on monetary growth and
domestic credit expansion may be less tough if the economy is otherwise experiencing a contraction. (There could also be reverse causation from
above-average inflation to economic contraction, but then why does this not
show up under low adjustment lending?) Most interesting of all, transfers
are significantly above average during contractions under adjustment lend-

Table 11.5   **Deviations of Policy Variables from Long-Run Averages under Expansions and Contractions with Different Levels of Adjustment Lending (*t*-statistics in italics)**

Variable	Expansion and High-Adjustment Lending	Expansion and Low-Adjustment Lending	Contraction and High-Adjustment Lending	Contraction and Low-Adjustment Lending
Macro Policies (Log Deviations)				
Black market	−6.7%	−7.3%	−6.2%	5.4%
premium	*−1.61*	*−2.45*	*−1.09*	*0.94*
Inflation	−0.7%	0.4%	6.9%	6.3%
	−0.72	*0.21*	*2.63*	*0.61*
Real exchange rate[a]	−13.7%	−4.1%	−14.5%	−0.3%
	−4.90	*−1.36*	*−3.68*	*−0.06*
Real interest rate	0.0%	2.9%	2.5%	−3.1%
	0.02	*0.94*	*0.64*	*−0.46*
Fiscal Policies (% of GDP)				
Budget surplus	0.28	0.67	0.63	0.18
	0.39	*2.10*	*1.40*	*0.26*
Transfers	−0.57	0.00	0.86	−0.18
	−1.94	*0.01*	*2.44*	*−0.45*
Taxes on domestic	−0.12	0.32	−0.48	0.31
goods and services	*−0.63*	*1.84*	*−1.53*	*1.21*

[a]Negative indicates depreciation.

ing, whereas they are significantly below average during high-AL expansions; there is no such countercyclical behavior of transfers under low adjustment lending. Other macro and fiscal policy variables do not show significant deviations from the means in the quartile subsamples.

Table 11.6 does various tests of the equality of means across the quartiles displayed in table 11.5. Under high adjustment lending, I confirm that inflation and transfers are significantly higher under contractions than under expansions, again reinforcing the possibility of countercyclicality of monetary and fiscal policy under adjustment lending.

There are some other interesting differences in means. The black market premium moves countercyclically under low adjustment lending—low during expansions and high during contractions. Causation here could run in both directions, but what is important for the poor is the pattern of cyclical covariation. Adjustment lending eliminates this countercylicality, which would tend to smooth consumption of the poor if they suffer disproportionately from high black market premiums.

The other strong pattern that emerges is that adjustment lending is associated with a more depreciated real exchange rate, regardless of whether mean consumption is expanding or contracting. This is no doubt because devaluation is often a condition of IMF programs. There may also be reverse causation from currency collapses to the initiation of World Bank and IMF adjustment loans. Devaluation itself may be expansionary or contractionary (Gupta, Mishra, and Sahay 2000), perhaps depending on the size of the initial current account imbalance and the currency denomination of public and private debt relative to the tradables intensity of those who owe the debts.

So there is some evidence that adjustment lending has countercyclical effects in ways that may smooth the consumption of the poor. However, is there direct evidence that these effects account for the lower growth elasticity of poverty under adjustment lending? Unfortunately, it is difficult to find evidence that these policy variables are responsible for smoothing poverty under adjustment lending. The three examples of variables for which adjustment lending altered the cycle—inflation, the black market premium, and fiscal transfers—do not show any direct effect on poverty, either directly or interacted with growth (table 11.7). Entering these variables leaves the interaction effect of growth and adjustment lending on poverty unchanged.

Easterly and Fischer (2001) find some evidence that inflation increases poverty, when inflation is measured in absolute terms rather than relative to country averages. They also find that the poor are more likely than the rich to mention inflation as a top national problem in opinion surveys. Because of the difference in methodology, I do not think the results of table 11.7 contradict the Easterly-Fischer results on the effects of inflation on poverty. I interpret the inflation deviation as a measure of the cyclical component of

Table 11.6   Testing for Countercyclical Effects of IMF and World Bank Adjustment Lending (AL; *t*-statistics in italics)

Variable	High AL Different from Low AL during Expansions		High AL Different from Low AL during Contractions		Expansions Different from Contractions during High AL		Expansions Different from Contractions during Low AL	
	Coefficient on High AL Dummy	Observations	Coefficient on High AL Dummy	Observations	Coefficient on Expansion Dummy	Observations	Coefficient on Expansion Dummy	Observations
	Macro Policies (Log Differences)							
Black market premium	0.01	58	−0.12	49	0.00	60	−0.13	47
	0.11		*−1.36*		*−0.06*		*−2.13*	
Inflation	−0.01	67	0.01	54	−0.08	62	−0.06	59
	−0.49		*0.06*		*−2.79*		*−0.67*	
Real exchange rate[a]	−0.10	57	−0.14	47	0.01	56	−0.04	48
	−2.31		*−2.31*		*0.17*		*−0.70*	
Real interest rate	−0.03	69	0.06	59	−0.02	64	0.06	64
	−0.75		*0.75*		*−0.56*		*0.89*	
	Fiscal Policies (% of GDP)							
Budget surplus	−0.40	43	0.44	43	−0.35	41	0.49	45
	−0.55		*0.53*		*−0.43*		*0.64*	
Transfers	−0.57	42	1.05	42	−1.43	39	0.19	45
	−1.46		*1.94*		*−3.05*		*0.39*	
Taxes on domestic goods or services	−0.44	43	−0.79	42	0.36	40	0.01	45
	−1.69		*−1.95*		*0.95*		*0.04*	

[a]Negative indicates depreciation.

Table 11.7   **Regression of Poverty Rate on Possible Mechanisms for Poverty Smoothing through Adjustment Lending**

Variable	Regression 1		Regression 2		Regression 3	
	Coefficient	t-statistic	Coefficient	t-statistic	Coefficient	t-statistic
C	0.010	1.00	0.006	0.64	0.020	1.46
GROWTH	−5.086	−6.36	−4.252	−5.72	−7.654	−5.57
GINI1*GROWTH	0.076	4.35	0.055	3.20	0.127	4.21
GROWTH*PROGRAM	0.713	2.13	0.752	2.13	1.180	2.57
GROWTH*PIDEV	−0.930	−1.17				
PIDEV	−0.028	−0.62				
GROWTH*BMPDEV			−1.200	−1.50		
GROWTH*TRANSFERS					−0.088	−0.57
TRANSFERS					−0.004	−0.35
N	99		91		65	

New variables
  PIDEV   Deviation of log inflation from average 1980–98
  BMPDEV   Deviation of log black market premium from average 1980–98
  TRANSFERS Deviation of transfers/GDP from average 1980–98

Notes: Dependent variable: log change in poverty rate. Method: two-stage least squares. Instrument list: C GROWTH GINI1 CENTAM EASIA EGYPT SSA GROWTH, CENTAM × GROWTH, EASIA × GROWTH, EGYPT × GROWTH, SSA × GROWTH, LAC × GROWTH, FRZ × GROWTH, ECA LGDPPC LAC ECA FRZ LPOP GROWTH, LPOP × GROWTH.

inflation that may be altered by IMF and World Bank adjustment lending. This cyclical component of inflation doesn't seem to have an effect on the log change in the poverty rate, in contrast to the negative effect of very high absolute inflation on the poor.

The message of table 11.7 is consistent with the alternative hypothesis mentioned at the beginning of the paper. The kind of macroeconomic and fiscal policy measures that the World Bank and IMF usually support may themselves cause an expansion or contraction in the aggregate economy, depending on the composition of adjustment packages. However, these policies may not affect the poor very much because the poor derive much of their income from the informal sector or subsistence production. I do not test this hypothesis directly, but I adduce a few illustrative bits of information. First, I show that there is a strong cross-section association between measures of the size of the informal sector (taken from Enste and Schneider 1998) and the poverty rate (using the same poverty data on percent below $2 per day).[4] The scatter diagram is presented in figure 11.3.

The statistical association is very strong, as shown in table 11.8. One per-

4. I include Enste and Schneider's informal sector size for the ten richest economies in the world and assume their poverty rate is zero. The association is just as strong leaving out the rich economies, however. I am grateful to Arup Banerjee for pointing out this data source and the association between poverty rates and the size of the informal sector.

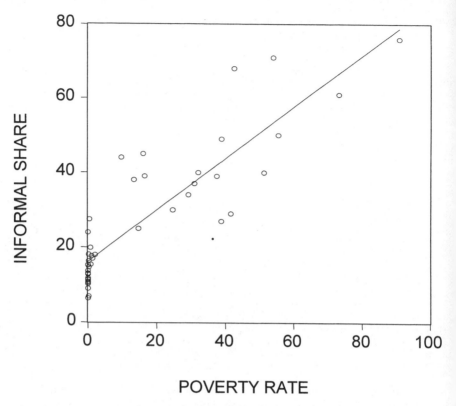

Fig. 11.3   Association between poverty rate and share of informal sector

centage point more of the population below $2 a day is associated with 0.7 more percentage points of the population in the informal sector. This evidence suggests that the poor are indeed in the informal sector.

This cross-section evidence is confirmed with fragmentary data from household surveys that show that the poor derive much of their income from informal and subsistence income. I offer a suggestive example from Zambia and Burkina Faso in table 11.9. Self-employment income is extremely important for the poorest deciles in Zambia. The bias is less extreme in Burkina Faso, but the poorest still have their earnings skewed toward self-employment income. These surveys are suggestive of the importance of the informal sector for the poorest households, lending credence to the relative insulation of the poor from structural adjustment measures.

Lipton and Ravallion (1995, 2601) stress that there is considerable heterogeneity within the urban informal sector, with an individual's poverty depending more on individual attributes like human capital than on any economywide labor market distortion leading to the creation of an infor-

Table 11.8   Regression of Informal Sector Share on Poverty Rate

Variable	Coefficient	Standard Error	t-statistic	Prob.
C	16.10031	1.679363	9.587155	0.0000
POVERTY_RATE	0.690322	0.059128	11.67513	0.0000
R^2	0.768765			
Adjusted R^2	0.763125			
S.E. of regression	8.900320			
Sum squared resid.	3247.843			
Log likelihood	−153.9921			
Mean dependent var.	27.64651			
S.D. dependent var.	18.28715			
Akaike info criterion	7.255447			
Schwarz criterion	7.337363			
F-statistic	136.3087			
Prob. (F-statistic)	0.000000			

Notes: Dependent variable: INFORMAL_SHARE. Method: least squares. Included observations: 43.

Table 11.9   Sources of Income: Percent Share by Income Decile, from Poorest to Richest

Income Decile	Zambia Household Survey — Profits and Self-Employment Income	Wages	Burkina Faso Household Survey — Profits and Self-Employment Income	Wages
1	100	0	42	58
2	99	1	32	68
3	94	6	21	79
4	67	33	19	81
5	45	55	17	83
6	17	83	15	85
7	12	88	18	82
8	11	89	21	79
9	10	90	27	74
10	36	64	46	54

Sources: Devarajan (2000).

mal sector. Other distortions may exclude the poor from taking advantage of reforms under structural adjustment, like lack of access to credit. Van de Walle (2000) shows evidence of lower return to formal-sector investments (irrigation in her specific example) for the less educated. Lundberg and Squire (2000) find that the bottom quintile is the only quintile not to benefit from trade openness. The poor may be geographically isolated from the formal-sector economy, which may be exacerbated by poor infrastructure. Whatever the distortion or initial endowment at work, the individuals who are poor may be ill placed to take advantage of new opportunities created by structural adjustment programs, just as they may suffer less from the destruction of old opportunities enjoyed by protected sectors prior to structural adjustment.

The effect of IMF and World Bank structural adjustment programs on policies, as mandated from the top, is usually limited to a few highly visible macroeconomic indicators—like the fiscal balance and devaluation (expenditure-reducing and expenditure-switching policies). Again, these seem more likely to affect the formal than the informal sector. In economies growing under home-grown reform programs, where government ownership of the program creates stronger motivation for genuine change, the transformation of incentives is likely to be economywide—stimulating both the informal and formal sectors. China in the 1990s is a good example of home-grown reform without adjustment lending, although it was open to advice from international financial institutions (IFIs). China reduced the percent living on less than $2 a day from 71 percent in 1990 to 50 percent in 1998. Chile 1987–1994 is another example of rapid reduction in poverty with an indigenous reform program and very little adjustment lending. Despite high inequality, the percent living on less than $2 a day in Chile fell from 31 in 1987 to 20 in 1994. El Salvador is an example of an economy going in the other direction, with economic expansion and intensive adjustment lending, but seeing poverty actually increase over this period.

11.4   Conclusions

The results in this paper are suggestive that IMF and World Bank adjustment lending provides a smoothing of consumption for the poor, lowering the rise in poverty for a given contraction, but also lowering the fall in poverty for a given expansion. Adjustment lending seems to play a similar role to inequality in lowering the sensitivity of poverty to the aggregate growth rate of the economy.

The lower sensitivity of poverty to growth under adjustment lending is bad news during expansions and good news during contractions. If we think of the normal steady state of the economy as being one of positive growth, then adjustment lending is bad news for the growing economy; it means the poor share less in the expansion of the economy. One might think that adjustment lending happens only during non-steady-state output crises. It could also be that adjustment lending hurts the poor in the short run but helps them in the long run by raising growth. Unfortunately, there is little evidence of adjustment lending's raising growth in the long run. This is a question that has been intensively studied, with few convincing results. The bare facts are not supportive. There were thirty-six countries that the IMF and World Bank gave ten or more adjustment loans over 1980–98. The median growth rate of income per person in this group over the past two decades was zero (which is also the median growth rate of the entire developing-country sample, and of the sample of poverty spells in this paper).

Adjustment lending has been so continuous for some economies that it is hard to speak of it as purely a transitional phenomenon. This continual dependence on the IFIs, requiring in some cases relief from past IFI loans, is itself cause for concern. If adjustment loans had to be repeated ten times or more, this clearly does not speak well of the effectiveness of the treatment.

From a political economy point of view, lowering the sensitivity of poverty to the aggregate growth rate could be dangerous because it gives the poor less of a stake in overall good economic performance. This might increase the support of the poor for populist experiments at redistributing income.

These results could be interpreted to give support to either the critics or the supporters of structural adjustment programs. To support the critics, growth under structural programs is less pro-poor than in economies not under structural adjustment programs. To back the supporters, contractions under structural adjustment hurt the poor less than contractions not under structural adjustment programs.

The question that further research should pursue is why structural adjustment lending reduces the sensitivity of poverty to growth. Although there is evidence that adjustment lending alters the cycle for some policy variables, there is no evidence that these alterations affect poverty.

I speculate that the poor depend more on the informal sector, which is not directly affected as much as the formal sector by economic reforms under adjustment loans. More generally, the poor may be ill placed to take advantage of new opportunities created by structural adjustment reforms, just as they may suffer less from the loss of old opportunities in sectors that were artificially protected prior to reforms. The poor may also benefit more from sweeping home-grown reform programs than those in which the government reforms are limited to a few highly visible indicators constrained by IMF and World Bank adjustment loans. A recent World Bank report on aid and reform in Africa found no relationship between adjustment lending (or aid more generally) and the development of such a broad consensus (Devarajan, Dollar, and Holmgren 2001). As this report puts it, "successful reformers have consultative processes that result in a broad consensus for reform."

One distinction that should be made is between "structural adjustment lending" and "structural adjustment policies." This paper has tested the effect of the former but not the latter. There is considerable international evidence that structural adjustment *policies,* like macroeconomic stabilization, financial development, openness to trade, and removal of price distortions, improve growth potential—and thus strengthen poverty reduction.[5] However, the success of adjustment loans at changing policies is very mixed. The tests for this paper found a strong effect only for the real

---

5. The literature on this subject is vast. See Easterly and Levine (2001) for a demonstration that good policies matter for growth.

exchange rate. The IMF noted in 1995 that the "record of achieving . . . low inflation" under its programs in low-income economies "was at best mixed." Half of those with IMF programs had inflation go down and half had it go up (Schadler 1995, 39). For example, Zambia had eleven adjustment loans from 1985 to 1996, but it had inflation above 40 percent for every one of those years except two. This pattern is part of the more general historical record that foreign aid and adjustment lending have not discriminated much between good and bad policies. As the World Bank (1998, 48) notes, "there is a long legacy of failed adjustment lending where there was no strong domestic constituency for reform." It may be that structural adjustment measures succeeded in changing only a few token indicators, like the real exchange rate, that affected mainly the formal sector, but left the economywide pattern of incentives otherwise untouched.

The results may not be so surprising in view of the recent vintage of the concern for poverty in IMF and World Bank adjustment packages, well after the poverty spells that make up most of my sample. In other words, for most of the period, IMF and World Bank adjustment lending was not designed to reduce poverty directly, and so it is not surprising that they were not unusually effective at doing so. The results of adjustment lending may change as the IFIs emphasize more poverty reduction under adjustment lending. Alternatively, the results may suggest that adjustment loans are not a very effective vehicle for reducing poverty, and the IFIs and the government would do better by directing resources toward programs that directly target poverty. These could include income subsidies for the poor, infrastructure targeted toward poor areas, improved access to credit (possibly through microcredit schemes), subsidies for inputs to subsistence production, and improved access to market information (such as through information technology) for the poor.

An aggregate result like this is a useful guide for further research. Further research should probably take the form of more detailed case studies like those in Devarajan, Dollar, and Holmgren (2001). If we think of a matrix that has on one dimension good or bad policies, and on the other dimension adjustment lending or not, we could examine cases from each of the four cells. These cases could examine the interrelationship among adjustment lending, country ownership, policy reform, targeted poverty measures, growth, and poverty reduction.

Appendix

Table 11A.1   **Countries with Poverty Spells, 1980–99**

Country	# Spells	Country	# Spells
Algeria	1	Mali	1
Bangladesh	4	Mauritania	2
Belarus	3	Mexico	2
Brazil	5	Moldova	1
Bulgaria	3	Morocco	1
Chile	3	Nepal	1
China	8	Niger	1
Colombia	3	Nigeria	2
Costa Rica	3	Pakistan	3
Czech Republic	1	Panama	4
Dominican Republic	1	Paraguay	1
Ecuador	2	Peru	2
Egypt	1	The Philippines	4
El Salvador	2	Poland	4
Estonia	2	Romania	2
Ethiopia	1	Russia	3
Ghana	2	Senegal	1
Guatemala	1	Slovakia	1
Honduras	4	Slovenia	1
Hungary	1	Sri Lanka	2
India	10	Thailand	4
Indonesia	5	Trinidad and Tobago	1
Ivory Coast	5	Tunisia	1
Jamaica	4	Turkey	1
Jordan	2	Turkmenistan	1
Kazakhstan	2	Uganda	1
Kenya	1	Ukraine	3
Korea	1	Uzbekistan	1
Kyrgyzstan	2	Venezuela	5
Latvia	3	Yemen	1
Lesotho	1	Zambia	2
Lithuania	3	Grand total	155
Madagascar	1		
Malaysia	4		

Source: Ravallion and Chen 1997 (updated by the authors).

References

Bruno, Michael, Martin Ravallion, and Lyn Squire. 2000. Equity and growth in developing countries: old and new perspectives on the policy issues. In *Distributive justice and economic development: The case of Chile and developing countries,* ed. Andres Solimano, Eduardo Aninat, and Nancy Birdsall, 37–65. Ann Arbor: University of Michigan.

Devarajan, Shanta. 2000. A macroeconomic framework for poverty reduction strategies. World Bank. Mimeograph.

Devarajan, Shanta, David Dollar, and Torgny Holmgren. 2001. *Aid and reform in Africa: Lessons from 10 case studies.* Washington, D.C.: World Bank.

Dollar, David, and Aart Kraay. 2000. Growth is good for the poor. World Bank. Mimeograph.

Easterly, William, and Stanley Fischer. 2001. Inflation and the poor. *Journal of Money, Credit, and Banking* 33 (2, part 1): 160–78.

Easterly, William, and Ross Levine. 2001. It's not factor accumulation: Stylized facts and growth models. *World Bank Economic Review* 15:177–219.

Enste, Dominik, and Friedrich Schneider. 1998. Increasing shadow economies all over the world: Fiction or reality? IZA Discussion Paper no. 26. December. Munich, Germany.

Gupta, Poonam, Deepak Mishra, and Ratna Sahay. 2000. Output response during currency crises. International Monetary Fund and World Bank. Mimeograph.

International Monetary Fund (IMF). 1999. The IMF and the poor. Pamphlet Series no. 52. Washington, D.C.: International Monetary Fund.

Lipton, Michael, and Martin Ravallion. 1995. Poverty and policy. In *Handbook of Development Economics,* vol. 3B, ed. Jere Behrman and T. N. Srinivasan, 2551–658. Amsterdam: Elsevier.

Lundberg, Mattias, and Lyn Squire. 2000. The simultaneous evolution of growth and inequality. World Bank. Mimeograph.

Lustig, Nora. 2000. Crises and the poor: Socially responsible macroeconomics. *Economia* 1 (1): Washington, D.C.: Brookings Institution.

Przeworski, Adam, and James Vreeland. 2000. The effect of IMF programs on economic growth. *Journal of Development Economics* 62:385–421.

Rauch, James. 1997. Balanced and unbalanced growth. *Journal of Development Economics* 53 (June): 41–66.

Ravallion, Martin. 1997. Can high-inequality developing countries escape absolute poverty? *Economics Letters* 56 (1): 51–57.

———. 2000. Growth, inequality, and poverty: Looking beyond averages. World Bank. Mimeograph.

Ravallion, Martin, and Shaohua Chen. 1997. What can new survey data tell us about recent changes in distribution and poverty? *World Bank Economic Review* 11 (2).

Schadler, Susan. 1995. *IMF conditionality: Experience under stand-by and extended arrangements.* IMF Occasional Paper no. 128. Washington, D.C.: International Monetary Fund, September.

Van de Walle, Dominique. 2000. Are returns to investment lower for the poor? Human and physical capital interactions in rural Vietnam. World Bank Policy Research Working Paper no. 2425. Washington, D.C.: World Bank.

World Bank and International Monetary Fund. 2001. Fighting poverty and strengthening growth in low-income countries. Joint memorandum of the president of the World Bank and the managing director of the International Monetary Fund. Development Committee no. DC 2001-011. 18 April.

Comment   Edwin M. Truman

Introduction

William Easterly's paper on the impact of International Monetary Fund (IMF) and World Bank structural adjustment programs on poverty should be troubling to most readers because he believes he has found evidence of an adverse effect of adjustment lending on the link between growth and poverty. However, serious questions can be raised about his methodology and the interpretation of his results.

This paper is about *adjustment* lending by the international financial institutions (IFIs); it is not about *structural* adjustment lending by those institutions. The author inappropriately, in my view, uses results about the former to criticize the latter. Easterly states that critics may conclude "growth under structural adjustment programs is less pro-poor than in economies not under structural adjustment programs." On the other hand, supporters of such programs may conclude that "contractions under structural adjustment hurt the poor less than contractions not under structural adjustment programs."

It is important to understand what he finds: (a) growth reduces poverty, (b) adjustment lending has "no direct effect on poverty reduction," and (c) adjustment lending "has a strong interaction effect with economic growth," which means, in his words, that "the poor benefit less from expansions during a structural adjustment program than in expansions without an adjustment program, while they are at the same time hurt less by contractions." It is the third statement that is the focus of the paper.

It is more surprising that Easterly finds a positive statistical association between adjustment lending and dampening the effect of growth on poverty during downturns than that he finds a positive statistical association between adjustment lending and dampening of the effect of growth on poverty during an expansion. My prior would have been that adjustment lending was associated with relatively bad times, and the lower the growth rate in those bad times, the larger the impact on poverty.

The issue of the impact of adjustment lending on poverty is important. For that reason we should hold research on this topic to a high standard. The basic problem with this paper is that Easterly does not succeed in establishing the reason that an absence of adjustment lending should produce a larger impact of growth on poverty. The reader is left with two alternative explanations: First, adjustment lending does not affect the very poor because they are more often part of the informal economy. This is interesting,

Edwin M. Truman is a senior fellow at the Institute for International Economics.

Comment by Edwin M. Truman on chapter 11, "IMF and World Bank Structural Adjustment Programs and Poverty" by William Easterly is © 2001, Institute for International Economics.

but not very useful. Second, a distinction is made between home-grown re-form programs and programs mandated from outside the country. This distinction is not well supported by the facts. International financial institutions do not require members to borrow from them. Members come to them precisely when their policies have failed or continue to fail. It is Easterly's apparent lack of appreciation of this distinction that contributes to his misunderstanding of the nature of the selection bias that undermines his statistical results.

What is a Structural Adjustment Lending Program?

A major problem with Easterly's paper is that it adopts a broad and misleading definition of structural adjustment lending by the IFIs. It is wrong to lump essentially all types of IMF lending together with various types of World Bank structural adjustment lending for purposes examining the impact of IFI structural adjustment lending programs. International Monetary Fund and World Bank lending to support structural adjustment in member economies differs from lending to support macroeconomic stabilization. The former involves an attempt to attack some of the deeper problems that have affected the performance of these economies. Easterly is careful to distinguish in his conclusions between structural adjustment lending and structural adjustment policies, but he is not careful in his statistical analysis to distinguish between adjustment lending and structural adjustment lending, and he uses the two terms interchangeably in the main body of his paper. This is unfortunate when much of the current debate is about the structural content of IFI lending.

Easterly's lending data go back to 1980, when the conditionality in most IMF programs was aimed simply at macroeconomic stabilization and had little to do with structural considerations. As is reported in the recent IMF review of structural conditionality in programs (International Monetary Fund 2001), less than one-fifth of the upper credit tranche standby and extended arrangements approved in 1985 and 1986 had any performance criteria related to structural measures. As a consequence, in its recent review the IMF's data on its structural conditionality do not start until 1987; the big surge in such lending was after 1994. Goldstein (2001) also documents this point.

It is true that by 1980 the IMF had its Extended Fund Facility (which dates from 1974), but the Structural Adjustment Facility was not established until 1986. It is also true that the World Bank has made structural adjustment loans for many years, but most of the loans for a good part of the 1980s were merely disguised balance-of-payments loans. In other words, Easterly should have sorted out the true from the ersatz structural adjustment loans from the Bretton Woods institutions before he started his statistical analysis. It is not enough, in my view, just to split the sample at 1989.

Second, even in the case of lending by the IFIs that all would agree was focused primarily on achieving structural objectives, those objectives come in various shapes and sizes. For example, what would we expect to be the impact on poverty of a program directed at restructuring the financial system of a member country? We would expect very little impact one way or another, but other factors (omitted variables) meanwhile may produce Easterly's statistical correlations. What about loans directed at reducing pricing distortions or rationalizing tariff structures? We would expect more of an impact, and we should be interested in the sign, but we should question whether the impact would be statistically similar across countries.

Third, structural adjustment lending has many different objectives, depending in large part on the circumstances of the members. Structural adjustment lending for a country in transition (Russia and Ukraine) differs from structural adjustment lending for an emerging-market economy (Korea or Thailand). Structural adjustment lending in Africa today also differs from such lending (primarily) to Latin American countries in the late 1980s and early 1990s. It is misleading to expect that lending to countries in substantially different amounts and circumstances will be associated with similar effects in a broad statistical analysis. Moreover, structural adjustment programs differ in size and in their degree of emphasis on structural adjustment; a better variable to try to capture the impact of such programs would be the size of the program in special drawing rights (SDR) or dollars per capita rather than just the number of programs approved by the IMF and World Bank executive boards. Easterly reports that he tried to control for any interaction effect with the absolute size of loans, but it was insignificant, whereas the interaction effect with the number of loans remained significant. This is puzzling, as is the fact that there was no multicollinearity problem in the estimation. One is left wondering whether the statistical results are dominated by a large number of small loans to a large number of small countries.

Fourth, it is important to worry about the contemporaneous impact of adjustment lending on poverty and to try to design programs that at a minimum cushion those impacts, but any significant positive payoffs from this type of program, one would expect, would be felt with a considerable lag after the lending occurs. Adjustment lending programs are not known as sources of instant gratification. Structural adjustment, in particular, is a complex process that even at its most effective normally has effects over time. Easterly compounds this problem by his use of "poverty spells" (pairs of substantially similar poverty surveys) of different lengths and treating them as identical dependent variables. Moreover, as Easterly notes, in many instances adjustment programs are of different lengths, efforts may not be sustained, and the lending programs may be suspended or cancelled. One might expect these differences to affect the results. It is disturbing that a researcher as serious and respected as Easterly did not take the time to refine his data.

In summary, my major criticism of this paper is that it combines apples, oranges, grapes, tomatoes, pasta, potatoes, red meat, and raw fish. It is not too surprising that the result is not particularly appetizing. We should be surprised that there are any "statistically significant" results at all.

Counterfactual and Other Methodological Issues

In addition to Easterly's misleading categorization of IFI adjustment lending programs, his paper raises serious methodological issues, some familiar to students of this literature and some less so. The familiar issue is the potential bias in the selection of the countries that have and have not had any or much lending from the IFIs. What we have is a problem of the counterfactual or control group. It is unfortunate in this connection that the reader is not provided with a full cross-classification of so-called adjustment lending with the "poverty spells." We are told in passing that India and China are countries that have had few or no such loans and Russia and Ukraine had a large number.

I commented above about the inappropriate inclusion of lending to the latter two countries in the sample, but how are we to think about China and India? Calling China's economic reform program "home-grown" is a distortion of the facts. Over the past twenty years, China has undergone a great deal of structural adjustment, often under the close tutelage of the IFIs. Moreover, China received three adjustment loans from the IFIs during the 1980s. China had two standby arrangements with the IMF in which the Chinese authorities laid out in considerable detail their reform plans.[1] India, on the other hand, has undergone very little structural adjustment, and many observers wring their hands about the Indian situation. India had a substantial IMF program in the early 1990s, and it is generally regarded as a success.

My basic point is that Easterly does not seriously address the statistical problem of selection bias; his use of instruments drawn from the foreign aid literature does not do the trick. The issue is not which countries may have had a political leg up to help to obtain IFI financial assistance, but the nature of their economic and financial circumstances that drove them to seek assistance from the IFIs. Building a convincing statistical counterfactual is a complex issue, but researchers must try harder to come to grips with it in studies of this nature.

Second, researchers know a lot about IFI programs, and it is troubling, for example, when Easterly lists a number of speculations about what the IMF or World Bank may "fear" about contractions, or what "may be" the nature of a change in taxation that was part of a program, or what "may"

---

1. Chile (1987–94) is another poor example of a home-grown adjustment program unsupported by IFI lending. Chile economic programs during this period were drawn up in close cooperation with the IMF and World Bank, and the only reason that they did not receive financial support from those institutions through most of that period was political.

have been included with respect to social safety nets when these are facts that are known or knowable.

Third, macroeconomic conditions have a lot to do with what is going on in the background with adjustment programs, but the amount of macroeconomic analysis in this paper is limited to a look at the countercyclicality of IFI lending. No attempt is made there to control for economic circumstances (for example, external financial difficulties) in the actual statistical tests; no attempt is made to differentiate trend from cycle. On the other hand, Easterly was careful to split his sample between periods with contractions and periods with expansions to see if there is a statistical difference in his interaction term.

Fourth, it would be useful to know more about the 150 (more or less) data points. Although Easterly summarizes the data, the reader would like to know more in order to evaluate his results. He makes much of the distinction between "poverty spells" during which there are expansions and those in which there are contractions in income or consumption. (Disconcertingly, the two concepts are used interchangeably.) We are told that median consumption growth is zero, the mean is –1.1 percent, and the standard deviation is 11.1 percent, but that is not a lot of information. Figure 11.2 provides summary information on perverse poverty-growth outcomes (expansions associated with increases in poverty, or contractions associated with a decline in poverty) sorted on the basis of the level of inequality and adjustment lending. In the cell with high inequality and high adjustment lending, 27 percent of the observations are perverse. This strikes one as rather significant, but we are not told whether the perversity is evenly distributed between expansions and contractions.

Finally, Easterly tries to tease out of his data set information on four instances of currency crisis: Indonesia, Mexico, Russia, and Thailand. He does not "make much" (his words) of the data points. Each case involved a contraction (negative growth) and an above-average amount of adjustment lending according to Easterly's crude definition. He notes, almost in passing, that "the increases in poverty were fairly modest except for Indonesia." In fact, the ex post elasticities for the four cases range from –2.16 to 0.1, compared with the estimated average of –1.9. Moreover, the mean of these four observations is –1.1, three standard deviations below the mean in the total sample. It would appear that on average in these four cases that involved heavy doses of *structural* adjustment lending, the so-called damping effect of such lending, through whatever mechanism, was unusually pronounced.

This type of gross cross-section analysis has provided policy makers with valuable insights in the past, when the work is carefully done. One can appreciate the challenge involved in enriching the data used for this type analysis, but in this case, too much useful and relevant information has been discarded or ignored.

Results and Policy Implications

What implications for policy should we draw from this paper?

First, Easterly generates a statistical result that adjustment lending appears to dampen the effect of growth (expansion or contraction) on poverty without, in my view, establishing a convincing story or mechanism that might produce this effect. He acknowledges that doing so is crucial to his analysis, but the issue is not fully resolved by his paper. He finds that adjustment lending alters the cycle for some policy variables, but he also finds no evidence that these alterations affect poverty. Without a convincing mechanism, one worries about correlation without causation.

Second, the author's concluding remarks on the issue of a mechanism focus on the informal sector and suggests that adjustment lending is irrelevant to poverty alleviation because the poor are largely found in the informal sector. This is a rather narrow view of both poverty and adjustment lending. It is one thing to think that adjustment in an economy, no matter how defined or supported, has a minimal direct and immediate impact on the informal sector and, therefore, on poverty, but that is not the same as being irrelevant. In the longer run, the overall efficiency of the economy does matter because we expect that as a consequence of growth the poorest will move from the informal sector to the formal sector.

Third, it is useful to be reminded that, even in cases of classical stabilization programs that are supported by IFI lending, attention should be paid to the impact on poverty. However, in some cases, a country has been living beyond its means, and the growth of and, sometimes, even the level of aggregate expenditure needs to be curbed or reduced to restore overall balance to the economy. If this occurs evenly across income classes, poverty will increase. The question for the policy maker is whether the distribution of expenditure *can* be twisted even as the overall level or growth is adjusted. It is a reasonable goal, and one that deserves attention, but the near-term objective in programs undertaken in the context of overall economic stabilization efforts is to try to avoid expenditure cuts that have a disproportionate impact on the poorest, even though, as Easterly concedes, these are "recent vintage" concerns, and maybe not the best grounds for criticizing IFI lending over the past twenty years.

Fourth, in *structural* adjustment programs, appropriately defined, attention to details is even more important. It should not be difficult to improve the efficiency of existing programs ostensibly intended to assist the poorest while reducing their overall cost, because too many of such programs are not really directed at reducing poverty but rather at subsidizing the middle class, if not the upper class. The challenge to do better is not always easy to meet, in particular at a time of crisis, when the design phase of structural programs is compressed. Nevertheless, we know what has to be done. Take, for example, the matter of subsidized petroleum product prices in oil-producing countries. From an overall efficiency standpoint, the cost of the subsidy involved is often outrageous. Nevertheless, political leaders are reluctant to reduce the subsidy substantially and appeal to resistance by the poor to justify their reluctance when the true political resistance comes from a broader and more politically active segment of the population. The objective should be to design programs to rationalize petroleum product prices *and* use some of the fiscal savings to address more directly and effectively the needs of the poor, at the extreme, for example, via direct income transfers.

Finally, do we conclude from Easterly's paper that there should be more or less *structural* adjustment lending by the IFIs? There is an active debate on this issue, especially within the IMF, as we know from Goldstein (chap. 8 in this volume), although that debate focuses not so much on support for structural adjustment as on which IFI should take the lead. On the basis of this paper, we are justified in concluding that (a) the issue of the impact on poverty and the poor needs to be further researched and (b) the overall effectiveness of such lending needs to receive greater scrutiny.

The author states that for many of the countries in his sample "adjustment lending has been so continuous . . . it is hard to speak of it as purely a transitional phenomenon." Whether one is talking about macroeconomic adjustment or structural adjustment properly defined, prolonged access to the IFIs is a problem for the countries because they are falling further behind, for the IFIs themselves because they are failing in their missions, and for the system as a whole because support for rational policies and instruments is being undermined. This paper does not help to advance that worthy agenda. It certainly does not add much to the debate when Easterly rests part of his criticism of prolonged use on the fact that the median growth rate of income per person in a group of thirty-six heavy IFI borrowers over the period 1980–98 was zero because the median consumption growth per household in his overall sample of sixty-four countries was also zero.

Easterly argues that "structural adjustment policies" promote poverty reduction but implies that "structural adjustment lending" by the IFIs in support of those policies is counterproductive. This is a rather curious distinction to make. To make it on the basis of a contrast between so-called home-grown programs and programs mandated from the top (of the IFIs or the borrowing governments) just does not hold water. It displays an incomplete understanding of IFI lending programs over the past twenty years; countries face external financial or other deep-seated economic difficulties and turn, with varying degrees of success, to the IFIs for financial and policy assistance. Researchers will have to come to grips better with those realities in their statistical analyses if they are to deal adequately with the problem of selection bias in studies of this type.

Easterly is right that more careful and detailed research needs to be done on these important matters, but I do not believe that his aggregate results yet provide much of a useful guide for further research.

References

Goldstein, Morris. 2001. IMF structural conditionality: How much is too much? IIE Working Paper no. 01-4. Washington, D.C.: Institute for International Economics, April.
International Monetary Fund. 2001. Structural conditionality in IMF-supported programs. Washington, D.C.: International Monetary Fund. 16 February.

Discussion Summary

Morris Goldstein suggested that the World Bank's mandate was poverty reduction but that the IMF did not share this mandate. He therefore concluded that it is not clear why IMF loans were included and why they should be relevant to the poor.

Olivier Blanchard noted that there is a need to consider the elasticity of poverty with respect to the trend and the cyclical component of growth separately. These might be different, so this differentiation suggests a different explanation for the paper's findings—possibly that cyclical growth has less effect on poverty rates.

Jeffrey Shafer questioned why the paper assumed that the programs should affect poverty relative to economic growth. It is not within the IMF's mandate, after all. One needs, he noted, to examine whether there actually is an effect on poverty that is separate from the effect on growth. In any case, he concluded, there is a role for IFIs that is independent of their poverty reduction rhetoric.

Martin Feldstein pointed to the fact that the official line of both institutions is poverty reduction; therefore, it is essential to examine whether they actually do what they say they do.

Jeffrey A. Frankel suggested that the IMF most likely mitigates downturns and increases long-run growth and only thus decreases poverty. While one hopes all this is true, it remains unclear whether there is an effect on income distribution that is separate from the growth channel.

Lant Prichett, using the analogy of a sheriff's role in maintaining order, argued that the IMF's role should not be measured by its effect on program countries only but rather by its effect on the international system of payments as a whole.

William Easterly responded that much of the criticism of the IMF and World Bank claims that structural adjustment increases poverty, and so it is relevant to consider the effect of adjustment loans on poverty both through the growth channel and through other channels. He also stated that the results probably do not reflect the effect of adjustment loans (ALs) on long-run growth and poverty because the poverty spells measure used is mostly for short-term data. He noted, as well, that opponents of the World Bank and IMF might misuse these results but that this possibility should not affect research conducted even within those institutions.

Martin Eichenbaum and *Edwin M. Truman* suggested that instead of using program dummies it might prove fruitful to include the size of programs (in absolute levels or per capita), because bigger programs should have stronger effects than very small ones. *Michael Dooley* concluded that if cycles are symmetric and ALs are indeed cutting down volatility, then the effect is beneficial for the poor.

12

Impacts of the Indonesian Economic Crisis
Price Changes and the Poor

James Levinsohn, Steven Berry, and Jed Friedman

12.1 Introduction

In July 1997, following the decline of the Thai bhat, the Indonesian rupiah fell dramatically (or so it seemed at the time). Since that initial decline of the rupiah, the Indonesian economy has undergone tremendous change. The rupiah has been subject to large swings, prices of some goods have risen substantially, and billions of dollars have been loaned by international lending organizations. These are not subtle changes. In this paper, we make a first-pass attempt at providing early estimates of the impact of the Indonesian economic crisis on Indonesia's poor.

Although some might argue that the very poor are so impoverished that they are essentially insulated from swings in the international economy, it is more frequently argued that the very poor are among the most vulnerable to such swings. This is especially probable for the urban poor. Furthermore, in countries with little or no social insurance, any impacts of price changes on the very poor are unlikely to be muted by government policies in the way that they might be in richer countries.

These issues matter. From a broad humanitarian view, the magnitude of

James Levinsohn is professor of economics and public policy at the University of Michigan and a research associate of the National Bureau of Economic Research. Steven Berry is the James Burrows Moffatt Professor of Economics at Yale University and a research associate of the National Bureau of Economic Research. Jed Friedman is an associate economist at RAND and a research fellow with the William Davidson Institute.

The authors are grateful to Anderson Ichwan and Edwin Pranadjaja for invaluable assistance in translating from Indonesian to English. They are also grateful to Alan Winters for helpful suggestions and encouragement. The paper has benefited from suggestions from Mark Gersovitz and Gene Grossman. Thanks to the World Bank and the Swedish Ministry for Foreign Affairs for research support. The views expressed in this paper are those of the authors and do not necessarily represent those of the World Bank.

the price changes and the size of the affected population argue that there is value simply to understanding what has happened. From a more narrow political view, the political economy of price changes may well depend in crucial ways on who bears the brunt of price increases. From the viewpoint of organizations such as the International Monetary Fund (IMF) that offer policy advice and (sometimes) loan conditionality, understanding how that advice might affect the poor is important. Finally, from a ridiculously narrow academic perspective, there is not an abundance of research on possible links between the international economy and the very poor.

In this paper, we use pre-crisis household-level data from approximately 60,000 households throughout Indonesia. These data provide a detailed view of expenditure patterns prior to the onset of the crisis. We match these expenditure data to detailed postcrisis data on prices. By combining these sources of data, we analyze how the inflation that followed the financial crisis affected households. Special attention is paid to how the crisis affected the very poor.

We find that prices for most commodities did indeed jump dramatically and that these price increases tended to hit the cost of living of poor households disproportionately hard. The impact, though, varies with where the household lives, because it turns out that the price increases were not uniform throughout the country. Further, it matters whether the household was in an urban or rural area. Rural households were better able to alleviate some of the disadvantageous price increases through limited self-production of food. The poor urban households, on the other hand, were the most adversely impacted.

The paper proceeds by including some background on the crisis in the next section. Section 12.3 presents the data, and section 12.4 describes our methodology. Section 12.5 presents results on the importance of heterogeneity in prices, products, and consumers. Section 12.6 investigates the impacts of the crisis on the poor, while section 12.7 concludes.

12.2   Some Background

We begin by setting the stage. The changes the Indonesian economy has undergone are dramatic. The purpose of this section is to very briefly review some of those changes. As background, table 12.1 provides some information on recent changes in prices and exchange rates. From December 1996 until July 1997, the rupiah traded in a narrow range of around 2,400 to the U.S. dollar. The consumer price index (CPI) provided by the Bank of Indonesia shows stable prices for each of four aggregates—food, housing, clothing, and health. In July 1997, the Thai bhat nose-dived and the rupiah followed suit. In table 12.1, this appears in the August 1997 entry, where the rupiah is reported at 3,035 to the dollar. Although this was a sudden depreciation on the order of 20 percent, prices rose only with a lag. Throughout the remainder of 1997, the rupiah continued to depreciate against the dollar and (except in November) against the yen. The food CPI rose from 105

Table 12.1   Some Background

	Rupiah Exchange Rates		CPI for			
	US$	100 Yen	Food	Housing	Clothing	Health
1996 Dec.	2,383.00	2,058.39	100.52	101.98	100.99	102.08
1997 Jan.	2,396.00	1,965.56	103.33	102.67	101.91	104.46
Feb.	2,406.00	2,000.63	105.99	102.90	102.43	105.32
Mar.	2,419.00	1,955.92	105.28	103.29	102.64	105.59
Apr.	2,433.00	1,921.19	105.24	103.99	102.62	107.56
May	2,440.00	2,095.15	105.30	104.82	102.71	107.69
Jun.	2,450.00	2,148.49	104.45	105.18	102.88	108.15
Jul.	2,599.00	2,210.83	105.93	105.82	102.80	108.41
Aug.	3,035.00	2,546.48	107.60	106.34	103.48	108.77
Sep.	3,275.00	2,715.56	109.59	107.58	104.56	109.21
Oct.	3,670.00	3,061.33	113.50	108.35	107.14	110.67
Nov.	3,648.00	2,867.48	117.25	106.82	107.01	112.27
Dec.	4,650.00	3,578.31	120.54	107.84	110.58	114.18
1998 Jan.	10,375.00	8,304.99	133.26	113.79	127.30	124.22
Feb.	8,750.00	6,895.21	157.79	123.28	145.14	148.98
Mar.	8,325.00	6,316.16	166.71	128.61	161.39	155.88
Apr.	7,970.00	6,034.46	176.56	131.56	168.39	164.12
May	10,525.00	7,580.14	183.42	136.99	176.01	168.06
Jun.	14,900.00	10,583.91	196.39	139.17	195.29	171.97
Jul.	13,000.00	9,048.21	220.27	146.93	219.23	186.41
Aug.	11,075.00	7,824.11	240.31	153.51	225.73	197.99
Sep.	10,700.00	7,921.25	261.00	155.92	225.22	204.49
Oct.	7,550.00	6,546.72	256.16	157.35	220.97	208.58
Nov.	7,300.00	5,903.77	255.70	158.11	215.99	210.71
Dec.	8,025.00	7,000.49	263.22	159.03	219.71	212.54
1999 Jan.	8,950.00	7,697.62	281.09	160.62	232.11	214.07

Source: Bank of Indonesia data available online [http://www.bi.go.id/ind/datastatistik/index.htm].

to 120—a noticeable increase but not an overwhelming one. The CPI for housing, clothing, and health care rose yet more modestly. On the economic policy front, the IMF approved a $10 billion loan, while the World Bank pledged $4.5 billion for a three-year program.

It was not until 1998 that matters became considerably more problematic. On 8 January, sometimes referred to as "Black Thursday," the rupiah began a free fall, and news accounts reported panic-like food purchasing. The exchange rate fell at one point in January to above 16,000 rupiah per dollar, and the CPI for food jumped almost as much in January as it had the previous six months combined. The CPI for clothing jumped even more. As international pressure to drop a proposed currency board increased and aid was deferred, uncertainty mounted. For the first four months of 1998, prices continued to rise, as documented in the last four columns of table 12.1. In May 1998, riots spread, and over one thousand people were reported killed. The World Bank postponed two loans totaling over one billion dollars, and the World Bank and IMF as well as many embassies evacuated nonessential staff. On 21 May, President Suharto resigned. The rupiah traded at around 11,000 immediately after the resignation. The Bank of Indonesia reported the largest monthly rupiah-to-dollar rate in June 1998—14,900. Thereafter the rupiah began a gradual appreciation (albeit from an astoundingly low level.) The CPI reported rising prices through September 1998. The CPI for food reached 261 (relative to a level of about 100 in January 1997), while the CPIs for housing, clothing, and health hit 156,225, and 204, respectively. (Throughout this period the CPI for housing was relatively more stable—perhaps reflecting the somewhat nontraded nature of housing.) Although peaceful protests turned violent in Jakarta in mid-November 1998, order was quickly restored.

It would of course be a tremendous oversimplification to attribute these changes to the international economy, or to any other single cause. Price levels and exchange rates are endogenously determined. Our goal is to analyze the impact of the changes surveyed in table 12.1, but we do not attempt to analyze the root cause(s) of the macroeconomic changes. We realize, for example, that it is (barely) conceivable that purely domestic inflation suddenly ran rampant, leading to the rupiah's depreciation, and in this (unlikely) scenario, the price changes in table 12.1 would have little to do with the international economy. Given most accounts of the East Asian crisis and the contagious behavior of other East Asian exchange rates and price levels, it seems plausible that there was indeed an international element to the changes surveyed in table 12.1.

Our goals include a more disaggregated analysis of the impacts of the price changes. The aggregated nature of the figures in table 12.1 hides potentially important heterogeneity. The first type of heterogeneity concerns heterogeneity within commodity groups. For example, "Food" contains hundreds of items, and it is possible that the price behavior of those items consumed by the nonpoor is quite different from the price behavior of food items consumed principally by the poor. The second type of heterogeneity is geographical. Indonesia is a geographically dispersed country where simple arbitrage may be costly due to transport costs. This suggests that there may be significant price variation within a narrowly defined product class across geographic areas. What happens to prices in especially poor areas may be quite different from what happens to prices in the wealthier areas. The third type of heterogeneity is across consumers. Our focus is *not* on the representative consumer; rather, we care about the consumption patterns of the very poor. Examining aggregate consumption patterns may be quite misleading in this context.

12.3   Data Concerns and Constraints

There are many ways one could estimate how the large changes in prices in Indonesia over the last one and a half years have affected the poor. In the end, the methods used will depend quite crucially on the available data. With this in mind, we briefly outline the data that are, and are not, available. We begin with the unattainable ideal. In the best case, one would have detailed consumption data that spanned the period before and after the financial crises of 1997–98 for thousands (or tens of thousands) of households. The time series variation would allow the researcher to examine how consumption patterns changed when faced with the large price changes. The large household survey would give the researcher enough households so that a focus on the very poor would still allow a sufficient number of observations. It would also be important to have detailed price data on a disaggregated set of commodities. These data would need to cover the most recent two years. Even these data, ideal and unattainable as they are, would pose significant econometric issues due to the nature of the questions posed. This is because what we want to know is how households in a particular part of the income distribution behaved in response to price changes, and even the most sophisticated demand systems typically estimate a utility-consistent demand structure for a *representative* consumer. Although with infinite data one could estimate a demand structure for just a particular decile of the income or wealth distribution, this would be massively inefficient. (A topic of future research is the estimation of a utility-consistent demand system that explicitly accommodates the heterogeneity inherent in studying how the poor respond to price changes.)

In fact, the data described above simply do not exist.[1] The good news, though, is that reality is less removed from this ideal than is usually the case. Indonesian data sources are in fact quite good. Indonesia conducts an extensive household consumption survey (SUSENAS) covering on the order of 50,000 households. Most recently, these surveys have been conducted in 1981, 1984, 1987, 1990, and 1993.[2] Although the surveys are large, they are not panels. That is, there is no systematic effort to track the same households over time. These surveys cover a wide geographic range of the country and contain very detailed consumption data.[3] The data do not contain prices, however. Rather, the data contain unit values that are defined as expenditure divided by quantity. These unit values may differ across households that in fact face identical prices due to differences in the quality of the households'

---

1. A special wave of the Indonesia Family Life Survey was conducted in late 1998 to investigate the immediate effects of the crisis. This data set, a true panel of households, can compare household consumption in late 1998 to a corresponding period one year earlier. Frankenberg, Thomas, and Beegle (1999) summarize the initial findings. The study surveys 1,900 households in seven provinces and thus does not provide the geographic coverage or sample size suitable for our purposes.

2. A survey was also conducted in 1996, but we have not been provided with those data yet.

3. For 203 individual food items, the survey recorded the quantity and value consumed by the household in the last week. For 89 individual and aggregate nonfood items, the survey recorded annual expenditures as well as expenditures in the month preceding the survey. For those households that consumed their own self-produced food, the survey imputed the value of that food. For those households that owned housing, SUSENAS imputed a monthly rental payment.

consumption. (I.e., although all households in a village may face the same prices for high-quality and low-quality rice, the unit values recorded for a household that bought mostly high-quality rice will be higher than the unit values recorded for the household that bought mostly low-quality rice.) This type of data can be (and in fact has been) used to estimate demand elasticities exploiting the spatial variation in the data using methods developed by Deaton (1988). We base our analysis on consumption data from the 1993 SUSENAS, the most recent wave available to us. The 1993 SUSENAS surveyed 65,600 households throughout the entire country. We have reduced our sample to the 58,100 households that have sufficient consumption and household information for the analysis that follows. To the extent that consumption patterns change over time, we are concerned about the accuracy of using 1993 consumption data to measure behavior in 1997. We investigate this by examining expenditure patterns as they evolved over the course of prior waves of the SUSENAS. We found some definite trends. In particular, the proportion of expenditure on food decreases slightly but steadily across each SUSENAS. This is probably due to rising real incomes. These trends may have persisted until 1997. To the extent that our consumption baskets are calculated with 1993 and not 1997 data, our measured impacts of the crisis will diverge from the actual impacts. However, one of our primary concerns is to highlight the heterogeneous effects of the crisis among households. The relative consumption baskets (among rich and poor households, or rural and urban households) did not change as much as the absolute consumption baskets over the 1993–97 period, and, consequently, the bias along this dimension is likely to be slight.

We also have very recent price data that have been supplied by the Badan Pusat Statistik (BPS). The price data contain monthly price observations for forty-four cities throughout the country over the period January 1997 to October 1998. This time period, which begins before the advent of the crisis, spans the steep devaluation of the rupiah and subsequent stabilization at the new higher rate. We employ a single price change measure: the percent change in prices from January 1997 to October 1998. By adopting such a long time period, from before the onset of rapid inflation until after the inflation had largely abated, we hope to capture a robust measure of the price changes brought on by the crisis.

The price data supply price information for both aggregate goods, such as food or housing, and individual goods, such as cassava or petrol. There are approximately 700 goods with observed prices in the data. However, the type of goods observed varies by city, perhaps reflecting taste and consumption heterogeneity throughout the country. On average, a particular city has price information on about 350 goods. Jakarta has as many as 440 goods listed, whereas some small cities only have price information for 300 goods.

Each of the twenty-seven Indonesian provinces is represented by at least one city in the price data. In order to match households from the SUSE-NAS data to as local a price change as possible, we calculate province-specific price changes from the city-level data. For those provinces that have only one provincial city in the price data, we take those price changes as representative of the whole province. For those provinces with more than one city in the price data, we calculate an average provincial price change using city-specific 1996 population weights.

The accuracy of this extrapolation of city price data to an entire province will surely vary with the size and characteristics of the province considered. For example, Jakarta, the national capital, is also its own province, and the observed price changes may fairly accurately represent the price changes faced by residents throughout the province. On the other hand, the price changes for Irian Jaya, a vast mountainous province, are based on price changes observed in the provincial capital, Jayapura. Price changes in the provincial capital may not be a completely accurate proxy for price changes in remote rural areas. Indeed, a recent study suggests that overall inflation in rural areas is approximately 5 percent higher than in urban areas (Frankenberg, Thomas, and Beegle 1999).[4] We frequently report separate results for the urban and rural poor, and the fact that the price data were collected in the cities should be kept in mind as those results are reviewed.

For certain groups of goods the price data are more disaggregated than the consumption data reported in the SUSENAS. In order to link the new price data with the existing consumption data, we use the prices for those commodities that appear in both the price data set and the SUSENAS. In some cases, we also aggregate commodities in the price data to match a product category in the SUSENAS data.[5] The match between the price data and the consumption data is good, but not perfect. We find that we have detailed price data for most, but not all, of the goods that comprise a household's total expenditure. On average, expenditures on matched goods account for 75 percent of a household's total expenditure. We return to this point later.

12.4 Methodologies

Given our data sources, the usual approach to investigating how the Indonesian poor were affected by the recent crisis would be to do the following. First, one would estimate a demand system, ideally one based on an underlying utility-consistent framework. The SUSENAS surveys would

4. The same study also presents some evidence that the BPS price data may understate inflation by as much as 15 percent. To the extent that this is true, the impact of the crisis is even greater than measured here.

5. In these cases, we take simple averages of the products that comprise a single product in the SUSENAS data.

provide the data for such a demand system. Based on the estimated elasticities from that demand system, one would then estimate the welfare impact of the price changes that occurred recently in Indonesia. Special emphasis would be placed on how the poor were impacted by the crisis. It turns out that there are some very severe problems with this approach, given the data and the policy goals. In order to better motivate what we *do* do, we first highlight the problems with the approach outlined above.

Estimating demand elasticities from the SUSENAS is not an especially satisfying endeavor. The SUSENAS is a cross-sectional survey of households. Although we do have multiple waves, there is no panel, or time series, nature to the data. As noted above, the SUSENAS contains data on expenditures and on quantities consumed, but not on prices. Expenditures divided by quantities give unit values, and, as outlined in Deaton (1988), there is a misguided temptation to use these unit values as prices. As noted earlier, a naive swap between unit values and prices is wrong because unit values reflect the quality of the product as well as the market price. Deaton shows that under the appropriate separability conditions, one can exploit the spatial nature of the data to back out the true price elasticities. The idea is that within a geographic unit—say, a village—the prices will be the same, although they are unobserved by the econometrician. Unit values, however, will differ across households within the village. This within variation allows the econometrician to identify the quality effect: incomes vary and the observed unit values vary, but, by assumption, underlying prices are the same. The variation across villages, controlling for village fixed effects, allows one to then back out the true price elasticities, because the real price variation occurs only through the spatial dimension. All of this leads to a multistep estimation algorithm developed by Deaton (1988). The estimator employed deals quite carefully with the errors-in-variables issues that the use of unit values raises.

So what's the problem? This methodology is probably the best available, but it has some real drawbacks. From an economic perspective, it is troubling that the resulting demand elasticities are not consistent with an underlying utility framework. If at the end of the day one wants to compute a welfare measure such as compensating or equivalent variation, one needs to work with a framework that allows one to identify the primitives of the underlying utility function. From an econometric perspective, it is problematic that the methodology does not deal with the endogeneity of product quality. Consumers choose the quality as well as quantity of the products bought, and this induces the usual simultaneity concerns. These issues, though, are perhaps just academic quibbles. The bigger problems arise due to the policy application at hand. Recall that we are concerned with better understanding how the price changes affected the poor. There are at least three reasons that the methodology is ill suited to adequately addressing this concern. First, the estimated elasticities are essentially local approximations based on consumer behavior at the observed prices. Hence, the

SUSENAS might give pretty good estimates of how households respond to a price change on the order of 5 percent. When the price changes under consideration are instead on the order of 100 to 300 percent, the answer is essentially dictated by the choice of functional forms. This is troubling for most any parametric approach to the estimation of demand elasticities. Second, the underlying framework is one of a representative consumer. Our concern, though, is with anything but the representative consumer. Rather, we are especially focused on the very poor. F. Scott Fitzgerald wrote that the rich are different. So, we suspect, are the poor. A demand system that explicitly considers consumer heterogeneity is called for, but this is not currently available. Finally, it is not feasible to estimate a complete demand system at a highly disaggregated product level. There are simply too many products. The obvious solution is to aggregate products, but this aggregation hides very important variation in consumption patterns and price changes. Alternatively, one can estimate own-price elasticities (but not cross-price elasticities) for many disaggregated products.

We have done such an exercise with the SUSENAS data. Employing a simple ordinary least squares (OLS) framework, and controlling for some observed household characteristics, we have estimated own-price elasticities for individual food items. We do not attempt to correct for the quality effects discussed above. The elasticities, identified by the cross-sectional variation in unit values and quantities, yield the expected negative coefficients and are quite precisely estimated. For example, we estimated the own-price elasticity for rice to be –0.43 with a standard error of 0.02, and the same estimate for ground coffee yields a coefficient of –0.84 with a standard error of 0.01. Most of the point estimates for the 193 food items fall between –0.3 and –0.8. Only a handful of estimates exceed –1, perhaps indicating relatively inelastic demand even at the most disaggregate level. When the analysis includes fixed effects for each district (kabupaten), the point estimates, still precisely estimated, tend to be a bit larger in absolute value, but still very few exceed an estimate of –1.[6] Of course, these estimated own-price elasticities, like most parametric approaches, are subject to some of the problems mentioned above.

Our principal approach in this paper is nonparametric. As with the econometric approach outlined above, we will need to assume that the 1993 SUSENAS survey provides a reasonably accurate picture of consumption patterns before the crisis. We then use the price changes that actually occurred to predict who the price changes would have affected. This approach has both advantages and disadvantages. On the up side, it does not rely on functional forms, and we can more easily explore the three types of heterogeneity listed above. On the down side, it essentially ignores the possibility

---

6. A positive correlation between unobserved quality and price might also bias our estimates toward zero.

of substituting away from relatively more expensive goods. Consequently, our method will provide an upper bound on the predicted impacts of the price changes on the poor. The best approach is to combine the heterogeneity highlighted with the nonparametric approach with the structural economic relationships estimated by the econometric approach. We will do this, and this exercise has convinced us of the need to do this, but it is a longer-term project.

12.5   Heterogeneity

Our methods are motivated by our desire to capture the heterogeneity in prices, products, and consumers. We begin our analysis by simply documenting the extent of this heterogeneity. This serves two functions. First, it illustrates the importance of using methods that do not aggregate across the dimensions of heterogeneity. Second, it highlights exactly which sorts of heterogeneity are most important, and this will inform our analysis of the price changes.

12.5.1   Price Heterogeneity across Regions

We begin by analyzing how prices for narrowly defined products vary across Indonesia over the course of the financial crisis. The raw data that are used for this exercise are monthly prices for about 700 products that are collected on a city basis by the BPS. These data are then used to create the official CPIs for the entire country. Monthly prices for so many products in very many cities constitute a rather unwieldly data set. We have aggregated the data in three dimensions. In terms of the time series dimension, we simply computed the price change for each product for the period spanning January 1997 to October 1998. Hence, the twenty-two monthly price changes were reduced to one price change that spanned from before the crisis to the most recent data. This simplification is not without costs, for the reduced data set is no longer able to address questions about the timing of price changes across provinces. It may have taken more time for price increases to have occurred in the more distant provinces, and this sort of information is no longer retrievable with the reduced data set. In the geographic dimension, we have aggregated to create price series for each of twenty-seven provinces, as explained above. In the product dimension, for some analysis we have collapsed the 700 or so products into approximately 180 products or aggregates that we are able to match with goods in the consumption data (SUSENAS).

The price data are reported in *levels,* but we focus our analysis in this paper on *changes.* There is little doubt that some places are more expensive to live in than others. Our interest, however, is whether the financial crisis had a differential impact on different regions of Indonesia. Hence, price changes seem the appropriate focus.

The notion that the overall impact of the financial crisis may have had geographically differential impacts finds some empirical support in ongoing work by Poppele, Sumarto, and Pritchett at the World Bank in their working paper "Social Impacts of the Indonesian Crisis: New Data and Policy Implications" (1999). Relying on data sources different from those used in this paper, Poppele, Sumarto, and Pritchett found that the geographic impact of the crisis on poverty was quite uneven. We return to these results in section 12.6 where we evaluate the impact of the crisis on the poor.

The geographic pattern of price increases differs according to the specificity of the products considered. At the most general level, the price index encompassing all goods does not show much regional variation. An unweighted average of the general price index for each province shows that prices increased an average of 92.5 percent from January 1997 to October 1998. The general price index on a province-by-province basis ranged from an increase of 70 percent in Nusa Tenggara Timor (NTT) to an increase of 119 percent in East Java. As a baseline, the standard error of the series of provincial general price indexes is about 11 percent. Figure 12.1 shows the empirical distribution of the provincial general price index increases. As noted above, it varies from 70 percent to 120 percent, and most provinces are in the 80–100 percent range. Given the different consumption patterns across provinces across provinces and the geographic separation of many provinces, this does not seem like very much heterogeneity. However, this is deceiving.

There are 184 products and product aggregates that appear in both the SUSENAS and our price data. We have computed the change in the price index for all of them. The standard error of the change in the price index, as

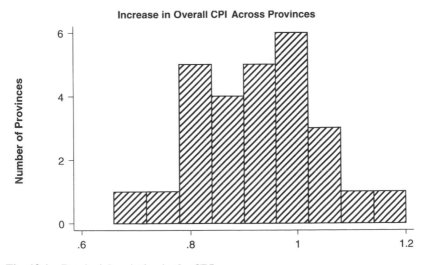

Increase in Overall CPI Across Provinces

Fig. 12.1   **Provincial variation in the CPI**

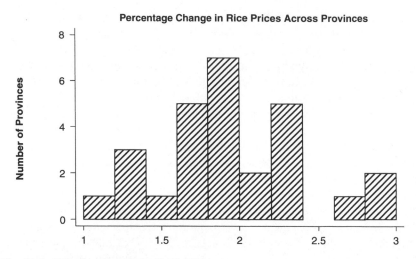

Fig. 12.2   Provincial variation in rice prices

one looks across provinces, is greater than 11 percent (that of the general price index) in over 170 of them. There are some extreme examples, but one that is more representative and is especially important is the geographic dispersion of the price increase for rice. Figure 12.2 shows the empirical distribution of the percentage changes in the price of rice. It varies from around 110 percent (in South Sumatra) to around 280 percent (in South and Central Kalimantan.) The fact that the price increases of individual products show much more geographic variation than that of the overall price index means that the price increases of products covary negatively across provinces. Loosely speaking, when the price of one product goes up a lot in a province, the price of another product goes up by less, so that the increase in the general price index is not that different across provinces.[7]

The substantial geographic variation of price increases following the financial crisis has economic implications. Suppose the poor consume a similar basket of goods regardless of where they live. In such a case, the economic impact of the crisis on the poor may vary substantially across regions. For example, if the poor always devote a substantial share of their budget to rice, the poor would have been much more adversely affected in

7. An alternative explanation, which we have investigated and rejected, is somewhat more complicated. There are about 700 products that comprise the overall price index. Not all of these appear in the SUSENAS consumption data. It could have been the case that the products that contribute to the general price index but do not appear in our consumption data contribute to the dampening of the variance of the general price index. This would happen if the excluded products had price increases that negatively covaried with the included products. We have gone back and investigated this possibility using all 700 prices, and, although there is some negative covariance between the price increases of included and excluded products, it is modest and does not explain the dampened variance of the province-level general price index.

South and Central Kalimantan than in Sumatra. Alternatively, if the poor consume very different baskets of goods in different regions, spatial price variation may in fact be coupled with a fairly uniform impact of the crisis on the poor. Further, if the poor are not evenly distributed across the provinces (and they are not), the geographic variation in prices has an additional impact that can serve to either alleviate or exacerbate the impact of the crisis on the poor.[8]

12.5.2   Product Heterogeneity across Product Aggregates

The previous subsection documented the spatial variation of prices. The general price index did not vary that much across provinces, but the prices of individual goods did. This finding has implications for product aggregation. If one wishes to estimate a demand system, some product aggregation is necessary. It is simply too hard to estimate a demand system for 184 (much less the original 700!) products complete with the all-important cross-price elasticities. One common practice is to aggregate products into groups such as food, housing, clothing, and the like. One can then estimate a demand system using the aggregated products. This is a relatively attractive option when the products that underlie the aggregate have price changes that are somewhat uniform. That is simply not the case in the Indonesian data. In this section, we document this finding and explain some economic implications of product heterogeneity across product aggregates. Like the spatial heterogeneity documented in the previous section, this type of heterogeneity also informs the methodology we use to investigate the impact of the crisis on the poor.

The price data have seven aggregate commodities, which in turn sum to the general price index. These aggregates are foodstuffs, prepared food, housing, clothing, health services, transportation, and education and recreation. Each of these is comprised of many individual products. The degree of disaggregation varies. There are 262 individual items under "foodstuffs," whereas there only about 40 or 50 for "health services" and for "transportation."

In order to abstract from heterogeneity across provinces and focus on the heterogeneity at the product level, we first collapse the data set and consider only the average price increase for each product when the average is taken across provinces. Hence, we compute the average increase in the price of the aggregate "foodstuff" as well as the average price increase in each of the 262 goods that comprise that aggregate. This removes the spatial dimension of the data. Figure 12.3 graphically illustrates the heterogeneity of the price increases of the products that comprise the aggregate for foodstuffs. In figure 12.3, one notes that although one or two products had either price decreases

---

8. The spatial variation in price changes might in principle help to econometrically identify demand elasticities, but this would require concurrent (and unavailable) data on household expenditures.

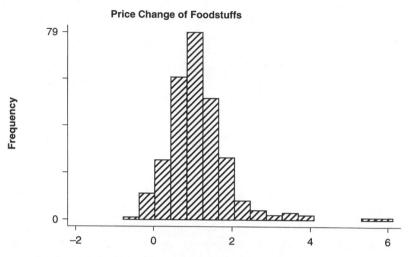

Fig. 12.3   Variation in food prices across products

Table 12.2   Product Heterogeneity

Product Aggregate	Number of Individual Products	Average Price Increase (%)	Standard Deviation of Price Increases (%)	Minimum Price Increase (%)	Maximum Price Increase (%)
Foodstuffs	262	112.8	80.5	−68.3	612
Prepared foods	72	78.4	41.6	0.04	169
Housing	105	107.7	76.4	0.4	499
Clothing	94	80.3	46.4	−0.04	214
Health services	38	85.8	51.2	0.0	263
Transportation	48	77.3	84.1	−0.13	482
Education & recreation	43	73.1	71.5	−9.70	310

Notes: Price increases are from January 1997 through October 1998. Average price increases are computed as the average across all provinces reporting price data for a given good.

greater than 50 percent or price increases greater than 400 percent, most products had price increases in the zero to 200 percent range. The results of this aggregation across provinces for all product categories are provided in table 12.2.

Table 12.2 lists, for each of the seven aggregates, the number of individual products, the average price increase when the average is taken across all the products that comprise the aggregate, the standard deviation of the price increases, and the minimum and maximum price increase. (One should keep in mind that these standard deviations do not account for the regional variation in price increases, only the variation of the average price increases.) For example, there are 262 products that comprise the aggregate "foodstuffs." Of these 262 products, one had an average price decrease of about 68 percent (a leafy vegetable that defies English translation), whereas one had an average increase of over 600 percent (red onions). Of all foodstuffs, the average price increase was 114 percent, and the standard deviation of the price increase was about 80 percent. There was, in sum, tremendous variation in the average price changes of individual food items. This pattern holds for all of the aggregate commodities.

Once we have abstracted from spatial price variation, we have seen that how much prices increase depends on the degree of aggregation with which we define a product. This too has economic implications. Consider foodstuffs as an example. If poor households consume a different basket of specific food items than do the nonpoor, the poor may be quite differentially affected by the crisis. Perhaps the food items whose prices skyrocketed most were imported luxury items, whereas the price rise for basic stables was more modest. Using an aggregate for foods will hide this important source of heterogeneity. This reasoning suggests that one should examine the impact of the crisis at the most disaggregated level. There is, however, a line of reasoning that works in the opposite direction. The methodology we use to investigate the impact of the crisis on the poor essentially assumes that there is no substitutability among goods (this is discussed in some detail below). Although the assumption of perfectly inelastic demands is clearly not correct, it is less incorrect as goods are more broadly defined. For these competing reasons, we analyze the impact of the crisis at different levels of product aggregation.

12.5.3 Heterogeneity across Households

The above two subsections have documented the heterogeneity of prices across provinces and within product aggregates. The purpose of this subsection is to illustrate the heterogeneity of households in the sample. One can either do this correctly, and write the ensuing book, or be too brief, while giving a glimpse into relevant dimensions of household heterogeneity. Our choice will be obvious.

Table 12.3 quantifies how a handful of household characteristics vary across the population, both overall and by income groups. The first column gives the (weighted)[9] means of per capita household income, expenditure, whether the head of the household had completed secondary school, the size of the household, the budget share of food in total expenditure, whether the household was rural, and the age of the household head. Means are reported for three separate deciles in the income distribution, as well as the overall sample. The sample is made up of the 58,100 households (from SUSENAS) included in the subsequent analysis.

Table 12.3 indicates that income is quite unequally distributed, as the aver-

---

9. When computing means, we use the sampling weights reported by SUSENAS.

Table 12.3   **Household Heterogeneity**

	Bottom Decile	Middle Decile	Top Decile	Overall
Per capita income	19,241	51,959	229,097	61,596
	(3,916)	(2,411)	(74,424)	(218,335)
Per capita expenditure	21,687	46,028	136,271	49,726
	(11,342)	(10,985)	(91,594)	(41,859)
Schooling	0.2526	0.5097	0.7628	0.4734
	(0.4345)	(0.4999)	(0.4253)	(0.4993)
Household size	4.3958	3.7722	3.6142	3.8911
	(1.6940)	(1.6500)	(1.7225)	(1.6911)
Food share of income	0.83483	0.5569	0.3233	0.5824
	(1.3818)	(0.1375)	(0.1462)	(0.5182)
Rural	0.9222	0.6767	0.3042	0.6959
	(0.2678)	(0.4677)	(0.4601)	(0.4600)
Age of household head	47.877	43.828	43.147	45.000
	(13.714)	(13.980)	(13.467)	(13.910)
Number of households	5,811	5,811	5,811	58,100

Source: 1993 SUSENAS.

Notes: Deciles are by per capita household income. The middle decile includes households with per capita incomes between the 50th and 60th percentile. All means are weighted by population sampling weights. Household size is defined as number of adults plus one-half the number of children under ten. Income and expenditure values are in current (1993) rupiahs.

age income at the top decile is almost twelve times that of the bottom decile. Expenditure is less unequally distributed. Only about 25 percent of the very poor household heads have graduated secondary school, whereas almost 75 percent of those in the top decile have done so. Richer households are smaller. (We have defined household size as the number of adults plus one-half times the number of children.) About 90 percent of the households in the bottom decile are rural, whereas about 70 percent of those in the top decile are urban. Households in the bottom decile devote about 85 percent of their income to food, whereas those in the top devote only a bit more than one-third of that share. As noted in table 12.1, the CPI for food rose by more than the CPI for other categories, and this alone suggests that at this very aggregated level, the poor may have been more adversely affected by the financial crisis.

As important as the averages across deciles reported in table 12.3 are the standard errors of these averages. Even within households in the poorest decile, there is tremendous variation in the income share devoted to food consumption, the household size, the age of the head of the household, and whether the head of the household has completed secondary school. The very poor are themselves a quite heterogeneous group.

The poorest households do not just spend a larger share of their budget on food than middle- and high-income households, but, as mentioned earlier, they also purchase a very different basket of products. Even within the category of food, poor households typically buy different items from those

Table 12.4   **Expenditure Shares (%)**

Product	Bottom Decile	Mean	Top Decile
Food	68.1	62.2	46.9
Cereals	27.6	17.8	6.9
Rice	24.8	16.7	6.4
Tubers	2.2	1.1	0.4
Cassava	0.7	0.4	0.1
Fish	4.6	5.4	4.4
Meat	0.7	2.2	4.0
Eggs and milk	1.2	2.5	3.5
Chicken eggs	0.8	1.3	1.3
Vegetables	7.3	5.9	3.7
Legumes and soy products	2.8	2.6	1.6
Fruit	1.9	2.5	3.0
Oil and animal fat	3.8	3.1	1.8
Beverages	4.2	3.7	2.4
Sugar	2.7	2.4	1.5
Seasonings	2.6	2.3	1.4
Salt	0.3	0.2	0.1
Ready-made food and beverages	4.2	6.9	8.7
Tobacco and beetle leaf	4.5	5.3	3.9
Filter clove cigarettes	1.1	2.6	2.7
Nonfood	31.9	37.8	53.1
Housing, fuel, lighting, and water	15.8	17.5	22.2
Estimated monthly rent if owned	5.7	7.5	11.8
Electricity	0.7	1.4	2.4
Kerosene	2.7	2.8	1.9
Firewood	5.3	3.0	0.5
Health care	0.9	1.2	1.7
Education	1.4	1.9	3.2
Gasoline (for transport)	0.0	0.6	2.1
Clothing, shores, and hats	6.4	6.2	5.5
Durable goods	1.7	2.7	4.9
Taxes and insurance	0.6	1.0	2.1

Source: 1993 SUSENAS.

Notes: Durable goods include items such as furniture, household utensils, jewelry, and vehicles. Expenditure shares are given as a percentage of total household expenditures. Deciles are ranked by per capita household income.

wealthier households buy. This is apparent in table 12.4, which presents the mean expenditure shares for the overall sample as well as for those households in the top and bottom per capita household income deciles. As expected, poor households spend a greater share of total expenditures on food than rich households (68 percent for those in the bottom decile compared with 47 percent in the top decile).[10] Even within food items, spending

10. Because we are now looking at food outlays as a share of total expenditures, and not income, the figures here will differ from those in table 12.3.

patterns vary by income level. The poor spend a far greater share on basic foodstuffs such as cereals and tubers (30 percent of all expenditures) than the wealthy (7 percent). Indeed, expenditures on rice alone comprise one-quarter of all expenditures for poor households, compared with 6 percent for the wealthy. In contrast, the wealthy devote more than twice the expenditure share as the poor to meat, eggs and milk, and prepared food and beverages. Among nonfood expenditures, the wealthy devote proportionately more resources to housing and education and are more reliant on electricity and gasoline (for transport), whereas the poor spend significantly higher proportions on kerosene and firewood. Because the prices of individual products do not all move together, the fact that richer and poorer households buy different products suggests that the financial crisis may have differentially affected richer and poorer households in a complicated way. If one could simply multiply the poor's consumption basket by some scalar to get the rich's consumption basket, untangling the impact of the financial crisis on the poor would be simpler. However, that is not the case.

12.6   Changes in the Cost of Living and the Impact of the Crisis on the Poor

The purpose of the previous section has been to establish that (a) price changes varied a great deal across Indonesian provinces so that *where* a household lived may matter when evaluating the impact of the financial crisis; (b) price changes varied a great deal depending on how one aggregates products, so that the degree of disaggregation of product definition matters when evaluating the impact of the financial crisis; and (c) households themselves are very heterogeneous, so a methodology investigating the impact of the financial crisis should accommodate this heterogeneity. With these concerns in mind, we now turn to measuring the impact of the crisis on the poor.

We measure the impact of the crisis on households (rich and poor) by computing household-level cost-of-living indexes. Because we only have data on consumption patterns well before the crisis, we use these precrisis consumption baskets to compute what is essentially a Lespeyres cost-of-living index for each household. This index provides a *maximum* bound on the impact of the crisis, because the index does not take into account the substitution toward relatively less costly products that surely takes place (to some extent) after price increases. Denoting the price of good i faced by household j in time t by p_{ijt} and expenditure shares by q_{ijt}, the household cost-of-living index for household j is given by

$$C_j = \frac{\sum_{i=1} p_{ij1} q_{ij0}}{\sum_{i=1} p_{ij0} q_{ij0}}.$$

We compute 58,100 cost-of-living indices, or as many indices as there are households in our sample.

We actually compute three such household-level indices. The first index that we compute matches the price changes of goods in the price data with the monthly expenditures of the same goods in the 1993 SUSENAS. For the monthly expenditure of food items, we simply convert the recorded weekly expenditures to monthly equivalents. For nonfood items, we use the monthly average of annual expenditures, and not the expenditures in the month preceding the survey, in order to more accurately measure monthly expenditures for durables that are infrequently purchased. We attempt to match goods across the two data sets at the lowest level of aggregation possible. For the case of food (both raw and prepared), we were able to match 132 different individual goods between the two data sets. In the case of nonfood items, we matched 52 different goods, both individual goods, such as firewood and kerosene, and aggregate goods, such as toiletries or men's clothing. Hence, the i subscript in the Lespeyres formula above runs from 1 to 184. Through this matching, we were able to account for 75 percent of total household expenditures on average—a little greater for poor households and a little less for rich ones. This index is, then, an average of the observed price changes, with each price change weighted by the household-specific expenditure share for that good.

The second index is computed for the case in which we use 19 aggregate commodities instead of the original 184 that we matched between SUSENAS and the BPS price data. These aggregates include fifteen food categories, such as cereals and meat, and four nonfood categories, such as housing and clothing. The motivation for this is twofold. First, recall that the Lespeyres index, by construction, ignores substitutability across products. By defining products more broadly, as in the second index, we reduce the likely overstatement of the impact of the crisis. Put another way, when products are broadly defined, those aggregates are going to be less elastically demanded than the disaggregated products. The second motivation for this index stems from the fact that the disaggregated index only accounted for about 75 percent of households' expenditures. It is possible that for many households, the goods excluded in the first index may either exacerbate or mitigate the measured welfare effects, depending on the relative price changes of those goods. The expenditures for these aggregates (e.g., meat, cereals, housing, etc.) are also supplied by the 1993 SUSENAS, and the price changes for these aggregates are found in the price data. A benefit of this index is that it covers nearly 100 percent of the individual household's expenditures. Of course, by attempting to compensate for the above potential biases, we may be introducing another bias, aggregation bias, which we have also previously discussed.

The third index that we compute accounts for the services provided by owner-occupied housing and for self-produced agriculture. Many households, especially in rural areas, own their home. Although the price of housing has increased, these households are, in an absolute sense, perhaps not better off (they are still living in the same house). However, these households are better off relative to those that do not own their home. We account for the services provided by owner-occupied housing by treating the imputed rental value for these homes as a negative expenditure. Many households produce some of their own food. Over 90 percent of these households are classified as rural. Households that consume self-produced foodstuffs also tend to be net exporters of agricultural products.[11] As the price of food rose, the value of their production also increased. Clearly, if the household was a net exporter of food, the household would benefit from the price increase. To the extent that a household produced some of its own food, such production would mute the impact of price increases relative to a household that purchased food in the market. We modify the first index to account for self-produced agricultural products by treating the imputed value of self-produced food as a negative expenditure.[12] Note that this modified index will understate the effects of the price increases to the extent that we do not observe or adjust for price increases of intermediate inputs used in agricultural production. On the other hand, this index does not allow supply responses to the increased food prices, and one would expect more self-production in the goods whose relative prices increased the most.

12.6.1   Nonparametric Evidence

Figure 12.4 provides kernel density estimates of the first and third indexes. The biggest difference between the two densities is the existence of households that are *better* off after the crisis due to the consumption of self-produced (and now more expensive) agricultural goods. Although there are not very many of these households (less than 10 percent of the sample), they are nonnegligible. More generally, including household production muted the cost-of-living increases, and this was especially true in the rural areas.

Table 12.5 summarizes how the cost-of-living index varied across per capita household income deciles. This table begins to address the impact of the crisis on the very poor.[13] Because the rapid price change resulting from the crisis may have differentially affected rural and urban areas, we report

11. Fifty-four percent (weighted) of households in the sample report operating an agricultural business. 69 percent (weighted) of those households report income from the sale of agricultural goods.

12. There is a long-standing debate over whether shadow prices in rural households engaged in agricultural production equate market prices for agricultural inputs such as labor or land. To the extent that these shadow prices may diverge from market prices, the "valuation" for self-produced food, based on market prices, will not be entirely accurate. Benjamin (1992) presents evidence from rural Java that household shadow prices for agricultural inputs such as labor are not significantly different from market prices.

13. We use income to measure "poor" and "nonpoor" although we are well aware of the controversy around this definition. Our results were substantively the same when we looked at expenditure or food-related expenditure instead of income. See Chaudhuri and Ravallion (1994) for an investigation of the relative merits of these various poverty indicators.

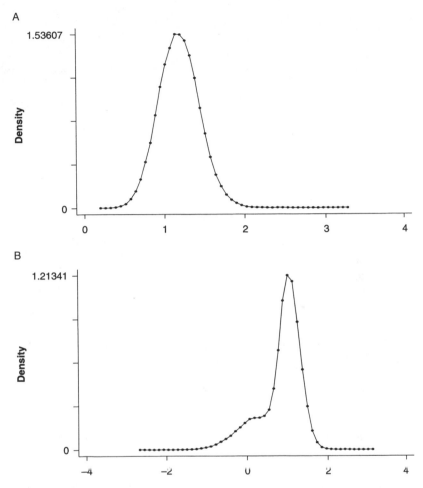

Fig. 12.4   Distribution of the cost of living: *A,* **Index without self-production;** *B,* **Index with self-production**

separate results for rural and urban households. When we do not take into account self-production and use disaggregated product definitions (index 1), we find that the cost of living for the poorest urban households increased an average of 128 percent over the January 1997 through October 1998 period. The increase for urban households in the top income decile was 89 percent. Among rural households, where the overall cost-of-living increases were greater, the parallel figures are 136 percent for the poorest and 107 percent for the wealthiest households. For both rural and urban households, we find that the increase in the cost of living declines monotonically by income decile. Hence, in both areas, the poorer a household was, the greater was the increase in its cost of living.

Table 12.5   Cost-of-Living Indexes and Income Levels

	Index 1		Index 2		Index 3	
Income Decile	Urban	Rural	Urban	Rural	Urban	Rural
1	1.28	1.36	1.25	1.32	1.11	0.73
2	1.26	1.34	1.24	1.30	1.07	0.74
3	1.21	1.32	1.21	1.28	1.06	0.74
4	1.19	1.30	1.19	1.27	1.04	0.75
5	1.14	1.28	1.16	1.25	1.03	0.75
6	1.11	1.26	1.14	1.24	1.01	0.79
7	1.07	1.22	1.12	1.21	0.98	0.81
8	1.03	1.19	1.09	1.19	0.95	0.80
9	0.98	1.14	1.05	1.16	0.91	0.84
10	0.89	1.07	0.99	1.12	0.80	0.83
Overall average	1.19		1.20		0.84	

Notes: Price index 1 is computed across all disaggregated commodities and does not take into account either self-produced agriculture or owner-occupied housing. Price index 2 is computed across about twenty aggregated commodities and does not take into account either self-produced agriculture or owner-occupied housing. Price index 3 is computed across all disaggregated commodities and accounts for both owner-occupied housing and self-produced goods. Deciles are by per capita household income.

The middle columns of table 12.5 (index 2) use the more aggregated product definitions. The results are very similar to those using the disaggregated product definitions, although the differences across income deciles are mitigated, mostly because wealthier households in both areas now have somewhat higher cost-of-living increases. The overall similarities between the two indexes are striking, given that index 2 employs broadly aggregate goods demanded less elastically than the individual goods of index 1. Thus, while the Lespeyres index is, by construction, an overestimate of the true change in the cost of living, the bias may not be huge. Indeed, the averages of the first and second indexes are almost identical. It remains the case that the poorer households saw their cost of living increase by more than did wealthier households.

The final two columns of table 12.5 now account for housing services and self-produced food. As suggested by the kernel density estimates in figure 12.4, the increases in the cost of living are substantially muted relative to the figures for index 1 in both areas, although this is especially true for rural households due to the tendency of rural households to engage in agricultural production. The average increase falls from 120 percent in index 1 to 84 percent. (In results not reported here, we find that it is indeed self-produced agriculture and not owner-occupied housing that accounts for most of the difference between the indexes.) Interestingly, for rural households there is no longer a differential impact across the income spectrum. Indeed, the cost-of-living increase is now slightly *greater* for the wealthier rural households, suggesting that self-production has equalized the impact of the financial crisis across the income deciles in rural areas. The story is quite different for urban households, however, where there is still a clear monotonic decrease in the changes in cost of living. The cost of living for the poorest urban households increased 111 percent, whereas the wealthiest households faced an increase of only 80 percent. It is important to note that the cost of living increases for the wealthy *urban* households are greater than those measured for the poor or median *rural* households. Thus, this index suggests the impacts of the crisis have been greater for urban areas than for rural, and greatest overall for the urban poor.

We turn now from variation across household income to the regional variation in the cost-of-living indices. Table 12.6 gives the change in the cost-of-living index for urban and rural households in each province. As an example, using index 1 (disaggregated products and no correction for housing services or self-production), the cost of living for urban households in Aceh increased 102 percent, while for rural households it increased 125 percent. For most provinces, index 1 and index 2 (with aggregated products) give similar results. As in table 12.5, we find that when we do not account for housing services and self-production, rural households consistently faced greater increases in their cost of living than did their provincial urban counterparts. Our index 1 results suggest that there was substantial regional variation in the cost of living. In Irian Jaya, to the far east, the increase in urban cost of living measured 75 percent, whereas in southeast Sulawesi, the increase was 138 percent. The regional variation for rural households is equally dramatic. In southeast Sulawesi, rural households faced a 161 percent cost-of-living increase, whereas in Irian Jaya the increase was only 91 percent.

When we focus on an index that accounts for housing services and self-produced agriculture (index 3), the regional variation remains, but the urban-rural comparison is changed. The depreciation of the rupiah helped export-oriented provinces, and the increased cost of food was offset by household production in rural areas. In every province, rural households faced a smaller increase in their cost-of-living index than did their urban counterparts. In some provinces, the differences are especially large. In East Timor and Irian Jaya, the cost of living for rural households only increased about 39 percent. The pattern of regional variation remains, because other provinces had increases (for rural households) more than double that.

We view the particular results for some provinces with some caution because our results do not always coincide with the results reported by Poppele, Sumarto, and Pritchett (1999). For example, they report that on Sulawesi, 70 percent of rural Kecamatans reported that things were better in August 1998 than they were one year prior. Although these measures are subjective, this figure is hard to reconcile with our cost-of-living changes. Overall, the Poppele, Sumarto, and Pritchett results suggest substantial regional variation (as do we) and that rural households fared relatively better

Table 12.6   **Regional Variation of Cost-of-Living Indexes**

Province	Region Type	Index 1	Index 2	Index 3
Aceh	Urban	1.02	1.10	0.98
	Rural	1.25	1.25	0.63
North Sumatra	Urban	1.13	1.18	1.05
	Rural	1.39	1.36	0.87
West Sumatra	Urban	1.02	1.12	0.85
	Rural	1.26	1.26	0.64
Riau	Urban	0.94	1.04	0.90
	Rural	1.14	1.14	0.85
Jambi	Urban	1.00	0.99	0.95
	Rural	1.24	1.16	0.78
Bengkulu	Urban	1.18	1.29	1.10
	Rural	1.52	1.51	1.09
South Sumatra	Urban	1.06	1.16	0.96
	Rural	1.31	1.31	0.63
Lampung	Urban	0.98	1.11	0.85
	Rural	1.17	1.18	0.69
Jakarta	Urban	0.93	1.01	0.87
	Rural	n.a.	n.a.	n.a.
West Java	Urban	1.06	1.12	0.93
	Rural	1.21	1.23	0.67
Central Java	Urban	1.05	1.06	0.96
	Rural	1.18	1.16	0.78
Yogyakarta	Urban	1.15	1.14	0.92
	Rural	1.36	1.23	0.80
East Java	Urban	1.13	1.17	0.97
	Rural	1.33	1.29	0.98
Bali	Urban	1.08	1.10	0.97
	Rural	1.29	1.27	0.95
NTB	Urban	1.25	1.22	1.14
	Rural	1.50	1.41	1.01
NTT	Urban	0.84	0.85	0.74
	Rural	0.98	1.02	0.09
East Timor	Urban	0.92	1.06	0.83
	Rural	1.02	1.07	0.39
West Kalimantan	Urban	1.10	1.26	0.98
	Rural	1.49	1.53	0.76
Central Kalimantan	Urban	1.09	1.14	1.03
	Rural	1.43	1.37	0.71
South Kalimantan	Urban	1.13	1.12	1.07
	Rural	1.45	1.28	0.85
East Kalimantan	Urban	0.90	1.02	0.83
	Rural	1.14	1.18	0.80
North Sulawesi	Urban	1.05	1.04	0.98
	Rural	1.23	1.14	0.88
Central Sulawesi	Urban	1.21	1.23	1.10
	Rural	1.52	1.40	0.70
South Sulawesi	Urban	0.93	1.00	0.84
	Rural	1.09	1.13	0.42

Table 12.6   (continued)

Province	Region Type	Index 1	Index 2	Index 3
Southeast Sulawesi	Urban	1.38	1.37	1.3
	Rural	1.61	1.54	0.98
Maluku	Urban	0.95	1.06	0.90
	Rural	1.19	1.22	0.61
Irian Jaya	Urban	0.75	0.81	0.67
	Rural	0.91	0.89	0.38

Notes: Price index 1 is computed across all disaggregated commodities and does not take into account either self-produced agriculture or owner-occupied housing. Price index 2 is computed across about twenty aggregated commodities and does not take into account either self-produced agriculture or owner-occupied housing. Price index 3 is computed across all disaggregated commodities and accounts for both owner-occupied housing and self-produced goods. n.a. = not applicable.

(as do we once we account for household production). These general findings are also echoed in Frankenberg, Thomas, and Beegle (1999).

It might be interesting to investigate how the provincial and regional changes in the cost of living reported here vary with other provincial characteristics such as mean income or expenditure levels. Have wealthier or poorer regions of the country experienced higher cost-of-living increases? For rural areas, there is little correlation between mean per capita household income or expenditures and increases in mean cost of living. However, for urban areas the cost-of-living changes are negatively and significantly correlated with provincial mean household income (and, to a lesser extent, expenditures). Thus, urban areas with lower average household income experienced greater price changes than the more wealthy cities. These findings hold true for any of the three indexes. Another provincial characteristic more sensitive to the distribution of income within the province is the provincial population share categorized as poor. What might be the relation between regional variation in price changes and regional variation in poverty? We take as our poverty measure the population share deemed poor by Bidani and Ravallion (1993) from calculations based on the 1990 SUSE-NAS. Although these poverty indicators pertain to a period seven years before the currency crisis, it is unlikely that the relative variation in regional poverty profiles would be much changed in the intervening years. We find no relation between the provincial cost-of-living increases and the provincial poverty indicators for urban areas. We also find no relation between cost-of-living changes and poverty indicators in rural areas when our cost of living is measured by index 1 or index 2.[14] However, the cost-of-living changes as determined by index 3 are negatively and significantly correlated

14. Poppele, Sumarto, and Pritchett (1999), using different poverty measures, also find no association across regions between the impacts of the crisis and precrisis levels of poverty.

Table 12.7   Cost-of-Living Regressions

Independent Variable	OLS	Fixed Effects	OLS	Fixed Effects	OLS	Fixed Effects
Dependant Variable: Index 1 (Index without Housing or Self-Production)						
ln(Income)	−0.100	−0.098	−0.151	−0.154	−0.146	−0.150
	(0.001)	(0.001)	(0.001)	(0.001)	(0.001)	(0.001)
Rural	0.163	0.158	0.141	0.138	0.138	0.135
	(0.002)	(0.001)	(0.002)	(0.001)	(0.002)	(0.001)
ln(Size)		0.143	0.147	0.142	0.146	
		(0.002)	(0.001)	(0.002)	(0.001)	
Degree			−0.023	−0.019		
			(0.001)	(0.001)		
Dependent Variable: Index 3 (Index with Housing and Self-Production)						
ln(Income)	−0.046	−0.028	−0.046	−0.029	−0.049	−0.031
	(0.003)	(0.003)	(0.003)	(0.003)	(0.003)	(0.003)
Rural	−0.214	−0.201	−0.214	−0.201	−0.212	−0.199
	(0.004)	(0.004)	(0.004)	(0.004)	(0.004)	(0.004)
ln(Size)		−0.000	0.001	0.000		0.001
		(0.005)	(0.005)	(0.005)		
Degree			0.014	0.012		
			(0.004)	(0.004)		

Note: Regressions had approximately 58,000 observations.

with the share of rural provincial population deemed poor. Hence, provinces with a greater proportion of poor experienced lower cost-of-living increases than the more well-off rural areas once adjustments for agricultural self-production were made.

12.6.2   Parametric Evidence

The results in tables 12.5 and 12.6 suggest that the crisis affected the cost of living of the poor more than that of the rich, at least for indexes 1 and 2, and urban households more than rural ones, after we account for owned housing and self-produced food. In order to investigate how the cost of living varies conditional on more than one household attribute, regression analysis is helpful. Our approach is simple and descriptive. It is without structural interpretation.

Regression results are summarized in table 12.7.[15] The top half of table 12.7 includes results using the cost-of-living index that does *not* account for housing services or self-produced food. We include three specifications and two estimation methods. All specifications are linear, with the index being regressed on two to four explanatory variables. In each specification, we include the log of income and a dummy variable that takes a value of 1 if the

15. The regressions reported in table 12.7 are not weighted by sampling weights, but we find that doing so makes little to no substantive difference in the results.

household is rural. (We use the actual index instead of its log because the index when accounting for self-production may be negative.) In the most parsimonious specification, OLS yields a coefficient of –0.100 on log income and 0.163 on the rural dummy variable. Each is quite precisely estimated. The coefficient on log income has a natural interpretation. The negative sign on the coefficient indicates that the cost of living rises with declines in income. The poor are harmed most. A value of –0.100 indicates that as income doubles (a 100 percent increase), the cost-of-living index falls by 10 points (0.10). The coefficient of –0.10 is large when considered in conjunction with the range of incomes. At the 10th percentile, household income is 75,802, whereas it is only 101,667 at the 20th percentile. At the 80th and 90th percentiles, income is 324,167 and 460,656. These large absolute differences translate into large differences in the cost of living. Because income is easily five times larger at the high end of the distribution than at the low end, the –0.100 coefficient corresponds to a cost-of-living index that is 50 points higher for poor households. This strikes us as a large disparity in the cost of living. The coefficient on "rural," still in the simplest OLS specification, is 0.163, indicating that rural households have a cost-of-living increase 16 points higher than their urban counterparts. Recall, though, that this result is for the index that does not account for self-production.

Our main focus is on how robust these results are to other specifications. Because we are not being guided by theory, the decision of which other regressors might be included in the regression is essentially arbitrary. Insofar as included regressors might covary with income or rural location, the coefficients on log income and the rural dummy might change. We include two additional regressors. One is the log of household size, where children under ten are counted as one-half and adults as one. The other included variable ("degree") is a dummy variable set to 1 if the head of the household is a secondary school graduate. We find that the inclusion of household size increases (in absolute value) the coefficient on log income to –0.151. The coefficient on the rural dummy remains relatively stable. Household size itself conditionally covaries positively with the price index. Larger households face larger cost-of-living increases. Controlling also for the education of the head of the household has virtually no impact on the other coefficients.

There is good reason to believe that the residuals of the regression may be correlated by province. This would be consistent with the substantial regional variation that we found in earlier cuts of the data. Provinces seem to matter. For this reason, we estimated all specifications with a province fixed effects estimator. This effectively sweeps out any cross-province variation, so the estimates instead capture only within-province variation. We find that the inclusion of province fixed effects makes remarkably little difference to the estimates. All coefficients are about the same as with OLS. Put another way, the variation in the data that gave rise to the OLS estimates also exists at the province level.

In the bottom half of table 12.7, we use the cost-of-living index that accounts for housing services and self-produced agriculture (index 3). The results are broadly consistent with those in tables 12.5 and 12.6. We focus first on the OLS estimates. In our most parsimonious specification, we find that the coefficient on log income is –0.046, and the coefficient on the rural dummy variable is –0.214. Hence, if household income doubles, the cost of living decreases 4 points. Because income at the 10th percentile is about one-sixth of that at the 90th percentile, these results indicate that the cost of living is about 25 points (0.25) higher for the very poor. This is a large difference, because the mean of the cost-of-living index is only 0.83. The OLS coefficient on log income is stable across specifications and is always precisely estimated. The coefficients on log income are always smaller with the index that includes self-production, and this is consistent with the notion that self-production mutes the impact of the crisis on the poor. It remains the case, though, that the poor are more adversely affected than the wealthy.

When we include housing services and self-production, the coefficient on the rural dummy variable becomes negative. Hence, when we account for these influences, urban households faced a higher cost of living. The difference is on the order of 20 points, which, again, is large given the mean of the index (0.83). This coefficient is also stable across specifications. That the crisis affected urban households more than rural ones is consistent with the preliminary results of Poppele, Sumarto, and Pritchett (1999) as well as with Frankenberg, Thomas, and Beegle (1999). We find that household size no longer seems to matter and that the coefficient on the education of the head of household becomes negative. The former effect is consistent with larger households' having more housing services and self-produced agriculture. The later effect is consistent with higher-education households' engaging in less self-production. Finally, including provincial fixed effects mutes the impact of log income, but it remains the case that the coefficient is precisely estimated and negative. Little else changes with the fixed effects.[16]

12.7   Conclusions and Caveats

12.7.1   Conclusions

The recent financial crisis in Indonesia has resulted in dramatic price increases. When we ask if these price increases have hit the cost of living of poor households disproportionately hard, the answer is usually "yes." Just how hard the poor have been hit, though, depends crucially on where the house-

---

16. We also experimented with an interaction term between log income and the rural dummy. In those (unreported) results, we find that Priceindex = $2.22 - 0.10 \times \ln(y) - 1.46 \times$ Rural $+ 0.10 \times (\ln(y) \times$ Rural$)$. All coefficients were precisely estimated. Hence, the negative relationship between income and the price index (index 3) is present only for households in urban areas (as we might expect, given the findings in table 12.5).

hold lives, whether the household is in a rural or urban area, and just how the cost of living is computed. What is clear is that the notion that the very poor are so poor as to be insulated from international shocks is simply wrong. Rather, in the Indonesian case, the very poor appear the most vulnerable.

Our results emphasize the importance of heterogeneity when measuring the impact of the Indonesian economic crisis on households. We find that prices vary substantially across the disparate regions of Indonesia. Prices also vary across the types of goods considered. Households are also quite heterogeneous, even within income deciles, with respect to observable characteristics. On top of this variation, consumption patterns vary both by region and by income class. For these reasons, we find it most helpful to think about *distributions* of responses, and we have employed methods that, in most cases, do not rely on particular parametric assumptions.

By matching data on price changes with data on household consumption from a nationally representative Indonesian data source, we have calculated household-specific cost-of-living increases. Because our measure—a Lespeyres-type index—does not account for potential substitution among products, our figures provide an upward bound on the likely increase in the cost of living. We find a substantial increase in the mean cost of living, on the order of 130 percent, if we disregard the relative benefits of self-produced agriculture and owned housing. The measured increase is greater for poorer households and households in rural areas. There is a great deal of provincial variation in the measured cost-of-living increases, although, as evidenced by the fixed effects estimation results, there is as much variation within provinces as between them.

Our results also illustrate the role that agricultural self-production and owned housing played in dampening the impact of the crisis. When we account for these benefits, the estimated mean cost of living falls to 84 percent, and this cost is now lower for rural households. Of all households, the urban poor appear the most adversely impacted by the crisis. Their cost of living tended to rise the most, and, being poor, these households are presumably among the least able to absorb these increases.

12.7.2 . . . And Caveats

There are several reasons to view our results with caution. These include the absence of information about wages and incomes, potential problems with the price data that underlie our indexes, the fact that we used 1993 consumption data to proxy 1997 consumption patterns, the biases inherent in a Lespeyres index approach, and the confounding influences of shocks other than that of the economic crisis. Each is discussed in turn.

Wages

This paper has analyzed variations in the changes in nominal prices during the Indonesian economic crisis. Of course we would also like to know what has happened with wages and income to better measure the real effects of the crisis. Unfortunately, our data contain no information on the changes in household income over the course of the crisis. However, two alternative sources of data do have some information on wage changes. Data from the BPS (obtained from their web site at [http://www.bps.go.id]) reveal that nominal wages for many broad occupational classifications have increased throughout 1998. For example, the reported increase in the mean wage from September 1997 through September 1998 for industrial workers stands at 26 percent. The median wage has also increased an almost identical 25 percent. Workers in the basic metal and metal working industries witnessed the highest wage increases, of about 40 percent, while wages in the paper and chemical industries increased less than 20 percent. There is also extensive regional variation in nominal wage increases. The largest wage gains reported were for workers in Sulawesi, who experienced increases of 87 percent, whereas wages in Jakarta increased only 12 percent. It is apparent, however, that the nominal increase in wages was not nearly enough to offset the detrimental effects of the rapid price changes. Frankenberg, Thomas, and Beegle (1999) find significant erosion in the real wage, especially for workers in urban areas, where the real wage has fallen 30 percent for men and 37 percent for women. The real wage has declined less in rural areas (18 percent for men and 19 percent for women), although overall wages are still significantly lower for rural workers.

Although rising nominal wages will dampen the impact of rising prices, that helps only workers who actually earn the wages. Workers who instead become unemployed are hit doubly hard. Badan Pusat Statistik statistics indicate that unemployment rose from about four million workers in 1997 to over five million in 1998. On the other hand, the crisis has led to a slightly higher proportion of men, and a considerably higher proportion of women, currently working. The increased proportion working is largely due to unpaid family workers entering the labor force and somewhat mitigates the detrimental effects of the decline in real wages and the rise in unemployment. This is apparent in the reported changes in household per capita expenditures, where the declines, although still significant, are not as large as the declines in wages. According to Frankenberg, Thomas, and Beegle (1999), mean per capita household expenditures have fallen 34 percent in urban areas and 13 percent in rural areas (although the median per capita expenditures have declined only 5 percent and 2 percent for urban and rural households, respectively).

Inaccurate Price Data

Our price data come from observations in urban areas. Due to the lack of information on rural prices, we extend these measured price changes to rural areas. However, prices in rural areas, especially remote areas, may behave quite differently. Frankenberg, Thomas, and Beegle (1999) determine that overall inflation may be slightly higher (5 percent higher) in rural areas than in urban. As well, at least for the seven provinces for which they have some limited independent price data, Frankenberg, Thomas, and Beegle suggest that actual inflation may be as much as 15 percent higher than the BPS-derived inflation estimates. This is another reason to view our results with caution.

1993 Consumption Data

We base our household expenditure shares on consumption data from the 1993 SUSENAS. As incomes rise, consumption patterns change. This is apparent if we review expenditure shares over the 1987–93 period, where a smaller proportion of total expenditures is devoted to basic foodstuffs, such as rice, for all households throughout the period-specific income distribution. Up until the economic crisis, this trend was likely to continue. To the extent that our consumption baskets are calculated with 1993 and not 1997 data, our measured impacts of the crisis will diverge from the actual impacts. However, we are also concerned with the heterogeneous effects of the crisis among households, and the relative consumption baskets (among rich and poor households, or rural and urban households) are not likely to have changed as much as the absolute consumption baskets over the 1993–97 period.

The Lespeyres Index

We have examined the impact of the crisis with price data that both pre- and postdate the crisis, but we do not observe quantities corresponding the higher prices. For households that do not engage in any self-production (which would include virtually all urban households), this means that our cost-of-living index is an upper bound on the true change in the cost of living. For households that do engage in agricultural self-production, the bias is lessened.

Not a Controlled Experiment

It is easy to forget that the Indonesian economic crisis was not the only change in the economic environment over this period. Concurrent with the crisis, some areas of Indonesia were hard hit by forest fires and others by drought. These and other disasters affect prices, so not all the price changes we observe in the data are due solely to the economic crisis. Put another way, prices would have changed some even absent the crisis.

For all of these reasons (and surely more), one should view our results with some caution. On the other hand, the severity of the crisis and the sheer magnitude of the affected population argue for presenting some evidence given the currently available data. That has been one aim of this paper. Another was to document the high degree of heterogeneity in the effects of the crisis across such dimensions as region, household location, and income.

References

Benjamin, Dwayne. 1992. Household composition, labor markets, and labor demand: Testing for separation in agricultural household models. *Econometrica* 60 (2): 287–322.
Bidani, Benu, and Martin Ravallion. 1993. A regional poverty profile for Indonesia. *Bulletin of Indonesian Economic Studies* 29 (3): 37–68.
Chaudhuri, Shubham, and Martin Ravallion. 1994. How well do static indicators identify the chronically poor? *Journal of Public Economics* 53 (3): 367–94.
Deaton, Angus. 1988. Quality, quantity, and the spatial variation of price. *American Economic Review* 78 (3): 418–30.
Frankenberg, Elizabeth, Duncan Thomas, and Kathleen Beegle. 1999. The real costs of Indonesia's economic crisis: Preliminary findings from the Indonesia family life surveys. RAND Labor and Population Program, Working Paper Series no. 99-04. Santa Monica, Calif.: RAND.
Poppele, Jessica, Sudarno Sumarto, and Lant Pritchett. 1999. Social impacts of the Indonesian crisis: New data and policy implications. Background note for the Consultative Group for Indonesia update. Washington, D.C.: World Bank, January.

Comment   Lant Pritchett

This paper is a valuable contribution to a study of the impacts of the Indonesian crisis. I'd like to make comments in three areas: the time series evolution of the impact, and estimates of the impact, of the crisis; the regional distribution of impacts; and the household. My comments are in part academic but principally draw on my experience of living in Indonesia from August 1998 to August 2000, during which time I switched the academic hat for the role of helping the World Bank and government of Indonesia finance, design, and implement safety net programs aimed at mitigating the impacts of the financial crisis.

First, on the *time evolution* of the impact of the crisis this paper was actually a crucial part of unraveling a puzzle that confronted us in trying to determine the impact on poverty of the crisis. In September 1998 there were two estimates of the poverty impact of the crisis. One, from the government's statistics agency, was that absolute poverty had increased from 11 percent precrisis to over 40 percent. This estimate was badly methodologically flawed in that it scaled up the poverty line by the inflation rate while assuming that nominal incomes were fixed (the basic point that every buyer has a seller and vice versa got lost in the heat of the moment).

On the other hand, there were overly sanguine estimates coming from the

Lant Pritchett is a lecturer in public policy at the Kennedy School of Government, Harvard University.

World Bank and others. These estimates pointed out that, although gross domestic product (GDP) had fallen 15 percent, it was mainly driven by a dramatic collapse in investment, and personal consumption expenditures (the closest aggregate analogue to the expenditures used in calculating poverty) had fallen by only about 3 percent. If the usual elasticities between consumption expenditures and poverty held, this meant that poverty had increased very, very little. This view had some logic to it, but the sanguinity it implied was belied by the enormous sense of crisis in the country—and not just in the financial circles.

As it happens, that view too was wrong (as we came to realize, at least, by December 1998) precisely because it overlooked the heterogeneous impact of relative price shifts across households emphasized in this paper. The main action, and the simplest way to think about the issue, was just to think about rice. Rice is a tradable commodity (even though it is bulky and hence actual trade is not large as a fraction of the total market) and hence the rapid devaluations, especially during January 1998 and then again following the political crisis in May 1998, had created an enormous gap between world prices and domestic prices. The logistics agency was able to stabilize domestic prices only until August, and during three weeks in August alone the price of rice rose over 50 percent. Because rice was a much larger component of the consumption bundle of the poor than of the nonpoor, this meant that the poverty line—the level of consumption expenditures necessary—increased by much more than measured CPI inflation.

Therefore, the increase in poverty caused by the crisis came on very suddenly and was much larger than anyone had expected—an increase of at least 15 percentage points (not the mistaken 30 of the statistics agency, but not the puny 3 of the first-round World Bank estimates either).

The second point on the time series of impact was the evolution of nominal wages, which is of course a weakness of pure price-based measures of impact. Because Indonesia has been a low-inflation country (less than 20 percent since the inflations of the late 1960s) there was little short-run indexation of wages. Therefore the impact effect was almost perfectly measured by price changes, because nominal wages responded very slowly. However, as inflation accelerated it was clear that real wages had clearly overshot, as they had fallen by 40 percent or more (and more for the poor than nonpoor, given the relative price effects). By 1999, one year after the crisis increase in rice prices (which followed the financial crisis of 1997 by one year), inflation had been contained, there were favorable developments in the price of rice (partly occasioned by reductions in the international dollar price), and real wages had recovered substantially.

Second, the *regional* dimension of the crisis was an important dimension, especially in trying to design programs to mitigate impact, because we needed to know where to focus. Here there are three points.

On the urban/rural difference in impact, I think of the impact of the crisis as an earthquake, which means we got the impact of the crisis right, then wrong. That is, there is no question that the epicenter of the crisis was urban areas: this was principally a crisis of the collapse of the modern sector tied into international finance. However, although that was the epicenter, the shock waves rolled out to affect everyone in two ways. The price effects of the devaluation passed into prices, so that even the peasant farthest removed from the financial centers saw his or her real wages fall. Also, however, the labor markets in Indonesia are very integrated between rural and urban areas (especially on Java), so that what began as a loss of work for urban construction workers, bus drivers, and informal service providers quickly spilled into a loss of remittances to their rural families and then an impact on the rural labor market as they returned from the cities.

On the distribution of the impact across provinces, there were clearly areas in which at least some benefited from the crisis—the areas that grew agriculture exports, especially. In some areas the phrase was *hidup krismon* ("long live the monetary crisis"), and one often heard reports that local Suzuki dealerships were short of stock and were shipping from Jakarta to the outer islands to meet demand.

The third point, and this is more closely related to the paper methodologically, is the inability of price changes to distinguish between demand and supply shocks. That is, it is impossible to tell a priori whether prices are rising more in an area exogenously and hence represent a negative shock or whether prices are increasing in that area because there is a positive shock and hence demand is driving up prices more in that region than others. As I look at the distribution of price changes reported in the paper, I am not sure whether I am seeing negative welfare effects, positive "demand pull" effects, or measurement error. Certainly from a program design point of view we would have had a very difficult time convincing the authorities to allocate the fiscal resources being devoted to the crisis on the basis of price changes alone.

Third, although this method does give a good look at some heterogeneity across households at an aggregate level (e.g., rural versus urban poor), one thing we learned was that the churning in household welfare was huge, even relative to the large changes in averages. We were lucky to have several panel data sets collected that spanned the crisis. In those we could see that more than one-quarter of those who were "in poverty" in the postcrisis period were more than 50 percent above the poverty line in the precrisis data. Not surprisingly, the increase in poverty was not a uniform downward shift in the income distribution but a downward shift accompanied by enormous churning.

One thing this points to was the heterogeneity even within income and regional groups. For instance, the paper makes the good point that whether you grew your own rice made a huge difference, because the negative price impact was at least partially offset by a positive gain in income (conceptually) from own-produced rice consumed. However, even if groups like the "poorest 10 percent of rural households" produced on average 50 percent of the rice they consumed, obviously not all households produced 50 percent; rather, some produced zero, others 100 percent, and everything in between.

This is also true within regions. As we got more data, we realized that even within areas that were booming it was not the case that everyone was benefiting, and even in booming export crops the gains were slow to pass into real wage gains. Thus, even within "winner" regions there were huge differences between "winner" and "loser" households.

This meant in targeting programs we either had to go universal or devise a mechanism that did better than aggregate groupings, or else the risk of missing some badly shocked households within aggregates was very large. In the event, there was a mix of programs, some universal (or nearly so), some targeted at the community level, and some (such as labor creation) that targeted "self-selection."

In conclusion, this paper is an excellent illustration of beginning to trace through the impacts of the crisis, which are fundamentally complex, as relative price and employment shifts produce reallocations across regions and households. In the end, the programs that were implemented benefited from the conceptual clarity this type of exercise brings, but unfortunately program design was often more determined and constrained by politics and administrative pragmatics than by good estimates of the impacts.

Discussion Summary

Olivier Blanchard inquired why food prices increased more than the prices of other goods—as a lot of these are nontradable. *Lant Pritchett* replied that rice, the major component of food expenditures in Indonesia, is a tradable because there was a lot of export of rice and even re exporting of subsidized imported rice. *Jeffrey A. Frankel* added that rice is a textbook example of a traded good subject to world market prices.

John McHale related this paper to the causes of the output loss following a crisis. He noted that participants have been attributing the loss to balance sheet effects, but this paper finds declines in real wages. In industrial countries such declines are typically long run, but this, it seems, was not the case in Indonesia.

Martin Feldstein noted that following these price increases it is likely that households reduced, first of all, their consumption of durables, such as clothing. He then suggested ways to account for that in the data and thus measure more accurately the immediate loss, in terms of current consumption of nondurables (food), that was caused by the crisis.

Allan Drazen commented that this paper stresses the heterogeneity of the effects of crises on different groups, which is a topic that is typically ignored. This heterogeneity, he noted, has political economy implications for getting support for adjustment programs, because there were even, as Pritchett made clear, gainers from the real exchange rate depreciation. Also, he noted that many times the adjustment is not undertaken not because domestic policy makers don't know what should be done, as *Martin Eichenbaum* implied in a previous comment, but because they don't have the political support to implement it.

Jong-Wha Lee suggested better characterization of the ones who were hardest hit in terms of education levels, age, and the like. In terms of unemployment, for example, he asked who were the ones who lost their jobs and whether that loss was permanent. This information has significance for social expenditure decisions.

Lastly, *Jeffrey Shafer* remarked that identifying the reasons for heterogeneity, such as the distinction between urban and rural, is very important. This heterogeneity is important both for mitigating policy questions and because it is a result of policy decisions.

James Levinsohn noted that differentiating between demand and supply shocks should, as Pritchett noted, be accounted for, provided better data are available. The exact way in which households adjusted is not entirely clear. He mentioned a survey that found that there was a huge disinvestment in jewelry—households sold the jewelry they owned. In response to Feldstein's comment, Levinsohn noted that it is worthwhile trying to account for this change in consumption patterns, but better time series data might be needed.

Peter B. Kenen also noted that it would not change the results much, because expenditures on clothing and on the durable component of housing are relatively small in poor or rural communities.

Pritchett remarked, in response to Drazen, that although there certainly is a political economy of adjustment, it doesn't focus on objections to adjustment because it hurts the rural poor. Typically, as was the case in Indonesia with fuel and rice subsidies, the poor have no political power, and objections to adjustment come from the middle class. He noted that the Indonesian government chose to continue subsidizing fuel massively, and not rice, because of such considerations.

Contributors

Andrew Berg
International Monetary Fund
700 19th Street NW
Washington, DC 20431

Steven Berry
Department of Economics
Yale University
Box 208264
37 Hillhouse Avenue
New Haven, CT 06520-8264

Olivier Blanchard
Department of Economics,
    E52-373
Massachusetts Institute of
    Technology
50 Memorial Drive
Cambridge, MA 02138

A. Craig Burnside
The World Bank
1818 H Street NW
Washington, DC 20433

Dongchul Cho
Korea Development Institute
PO Box 113, Cheongryang
Seoul 113, Korea

Stijn Claessens
Finance Group
University of Amsterdam
Roetersstraat 11
1018 WB Amsterdam
The Netherlands

Robert Dekle
Department of Economics
University of Southern California
Los Angeles, CA 90089

Michael P. Dooley
Deutsche Bank
31 West 52nd Street
NYC01-1204
New York, NY 10019

Allan Drazen
The Eitan Berglas School of
    Economics
Tel Aviv University
Ramat Aviv, Tel Aviv 69978
Israel

William Easterly
MC3-337
The World Bank
1818 H Street NW
Washington, DC 20433

Martin Eichenbaum
Department of Economics
Northwestern University
2003 Sheridan Road
Evanston, IL 60208

Barry Eichengreen
Department of Economics
University of California, Berkeley
549 Evans Hall, #3880
Berkeley, CA 94720-3880

Robert P. Flood
International Monetary Fund
700 19th Street NW
Washington, DC 20431

Jeffrey A. Frankel
Kennedy School of Government
Harvard University
79 JFK Street
Cambridge, MA 02138

Jed Friedman
RAND
1700 Main Street
PO Box 2138
Santa Monica, CA 90407-2138

Morris Goldstein
Institute for International Economics
1750 Massachusetts Avenue
Washington, DC 20036

Michael M. Hutchison
Department of Economics
Social Sciences I
University of California, Santa Cruz
Santa Cruz, CA 95064

Olivier Jeanne
Research Department
Room 10-548L
International Monetary Fund
700 19th Street NW
Washington, DC 20431

Peter B. Kenen
Department of Economics
Fisher Hall
Princeton University
Princeton, NJ 08544

Kenneth Kletzer
Department of Economics
Social Sciences I
University of California,
    Santa Cruz
Santa Cruz, CA 95064

Daniela Klingebiel
The World Bank
1818 H Street NW
Washington, DC 20433

Luc Laeven
The World Bank
1818 H Street NW
Washington, DC 20433

Jong-Wha Lee
Department of Economics
Korea University
Anam-dong, Sungbuk-ku
Seoul 130-701, Korea

James Levinsohn
Department of Economics
University of Michigan
Ann Arbor, MI 48109-1220

Gian Maria Milesi-Ferretti
European I Department
Room 9-212D
International Monetary Fund
700 19th Street NW
Washington, DC 20431

Yung Chul Park
Department of Economics
Korea University
1, 5-Ka, Anam-dong, Sungbuk-ku
Seoul 136-701, Korea

Richard Portes
London Business School
Regents Park
London NW1 4SA
England

Andrew Powell
Universidad Torcuato di Tella
Miñones, 2177-C1428ATG
Buenos Aires
Argentina

Lant Pritchett
Kennedy School of Government
Harvard University
79 JFK Street
Cambridge, MA 02138

Sergio Rebelo
Kellogg Graduate School of
    Management
Leverone Hall
Northwestern University
Evanston, IL 60208-2001

Andrew K. Rose
Haas School of Business
    Administration
University of California, Berkeley
Berkeley, CA 94720-1900

Edwin M. Truman
Institute for International Economics
1750 Massachusetts Avenue
Washington, DC 20036

Sujata Verma
Department of Economics
Kenna Hall
Santa Clara University
Santa Clara, CA 95053

Kenneth D. West
Department of Economics
University of Wisconsin
7458 Social Science Building
1180 Observatory Drive
Madison, WI 53706

Charles Wyplosz
The Graduate Institute of
    International Studies
PO Box 36
1211 Geneva 21
Switzerland

Author Index

Subject Index